Introductory Statistics for Business and Economics

Thomas H. Wonnacott

Associate Professor of Mathematics
University of Western Ontario

Ronald J. Wonnacott

Professor of Economics
University of Western Ontario

JOHN WILEY & SONS, INC.
New York · London · Sydney · Toronto

*To Wassily Leontief
and John Tukey*

Library of Congress Catalogue Card Number: 74-37785

ISBN 0-471-95972-3

Printed in the United States of America.

10 9 8 7 6 5 4

introductory statistics
for business
and economics

pREfACE

This textbook is specifically designed for students in economics and business, at a level slightly above the elementary texts by Hoel and Jessen or by Freund and Williams. Our objective is to introduce students to most of the underlying logic normally available in much more advanced mathematical statistics texts; for example, how sampling and inference are based on the theory of probability and random variables. But we use the simplest possible mathematics consistent with a sound presentation. Fortunately, this is only slightly more difficult than the mathematics in most elementary books. Calculus appears only in sections where the argument is difficult to develop without it; although this puts the calculus student at an advantage, we have made a special effort to design these sections so that a student without calculus can also understand the material. Problems and examples, rather than abstract theory, are used to introduce new material; the necessary theory is presented only after the student has a clear intuitive idea of what is happening.

Another major objective is to show the logical relation between topics that have often appeared in texts as separate and isolated chapters; for example, the equivalence of interval estimation and hypothesis testing, of the t test and F test, and of analysis of variance and regression using dummy variables. In every case our motivation has been twofold: to help the student to appreciate the underlying logic, and to help him arrive at answers to practical problems.

We have placed high priority on the regression model, not only because regression is widely regarded as the most powerful tool of the practicing statistician but also because it provides a good focal point for understanding such related techniques as correlation, analysis of variance, and chi square. We have also placed considerable emphasis on extending simple regression in several directions including multiple regression and nonlinear regression.

This textbook has grown directly out of our first edition of *Introductory Statistics,* which was aimed at two broad audiences: (1) students in service courses in statistics provided by mathematics departments; and (2) students in business and economics. In revising that book it became increasingly clear that there would be major advantages in satisfying each of these markets separately with two volumes. Accordingly the second edition of *Introductory Statistics* (concurrently appearing) is directed to students in service courses; it involves a complete revision of *Introductory Statistics* plus new chapters on chi-square and nonparametric tests. At the same time we have written this present text for the business and economics audience; it contains the same material plus a set of special-interest topics.

Standard chapters (like "Time Series" and "Index Numbers") are all included—but more completely than in most texts. Our objective is to provide the concise and simple treatment that will keep this material within the range of beginning students. However, working within this restraint, we provide more modern material than has appeared in many other elementary texts: for example, the economists' theory of revealed preference is very simply introduced with index numbers, and provides a much more profound understanding of what indexing is all about; similarly the time series chapter includes not only the standard topics (seasonal, trend adjustment, and the like) but also a simplified discussion of autocorrelated error and what to do about it, and an introduction to spectral analysis. There is also a chapter on estimating simultaneous equations—a very important topic for both business and economics, and like spectral analysis, a topic that previously has been available only in much more advanced books and articles. Our original reaction was that these topics could not possibly be introduced at this elementary level; however, by teaching them in an increasingly simplified way over several years, we hope we have been able to remove much of the academic mystery that has kept them beyond the reach of under-graduates in the past.

This book is designed for maximum flexibility. Basic classical statistics is presented in the 14 chapters of Part I, while Part II includes 10 optional self-contained chapters, including those referred to in the paragraph above, plus chapters on Bayesian decisions (of increasing importance for business students), game theory, sample design, and so on. Thus an instructor can choose any combination of the chapters in Part II to round out his course. While the text is kept simple, the more sophisticated interpretations and developments are reserved for footnotes and starred sections. In all instances these are optional; a special effort has been made to allow the more elementary student to skip these completely without losing continuity. Moreover, some of the finer points are deferred to the instructor's manual. Thus the instructor is allowed, at least to some degree, to tailor the level as well as the content of the course to his students' background.

Problems are starred (*) if they are more difficult. They are set with an arrow ($\Rightarrow$) if they introduce important ideas taken up later in the text. They are in parentheses ( ) if they duplicate previous problems and thus provide optional exercise only.

An outline of how various statistical procedures are related is provided inside the front cover; in our experience this overview is very useful for the student both for review and for future reference. A glossary of symbols is given following the Table of Contents.

Our experience has been that Part I and a selection of chapters in Part II provide about the right amount of material for a two-semester course. A single semester introduction is easily designed to include the first 8 to 12 chapters.

So many people have contributed to this book that it is impossible to thank all of them. However, special thanks go, without implication, to the following for their generous help: Harvey J. Arnold, David A. Belsley, Ralph A. Bradley, Edward Greenberg, Leonard Kent, Mike Lovell, R. W. Pfouts, Paul Wonnacott and, especially, Franklin M. Fisher. Finally we thank the instructors and students in business and economics courses who have used the first edition of *Introductory Statistics* in the past three years; their comments have proved very valuable in tailoring this book for their audience.

London, Ontario, Canada, 1972   *Thomas H. Wonnacott*
                                                   Ronald J. Wonnacott

CONTENTS

CHAPTER 5   Two Random Variables

CHAPTER 6   Sampling

CHAPTER 7   Estimation I

CHAPTER 8   Estimation II

CHAPTER 9   Hypothesis Testing

CHAPTER 10   Analysis of Variance

CHAPTER 11 Introduction to Regression

CHAPTER 12 Regression Theory

CHAPTER 13 Multiple Regression

CHAPTER 14 Correlation

PART II SELECTED TOPICS

glossary of symbols

SYMBOL	MEANING	DEFINITION OR OTHER IMPORTANT REFERENCE
(a) ENGLISH LETTERS		
a ($\hat{\alpha}$)	estimated regression intercept	Figure 11-7, (11-13)
ANOCOVA	analysis of covariance	Figure 13-11
ANOVA	analysis of variance	Table 10-6
b ($\hat{\beta}$)	estimated regression slope	Figure 11-7, (11-16)
BES	best easy systematic estimator	(7-26)
BLUE	best linear unbiased estimator	Figure 12-3
c	number of columns in two-way table. Or center of a unimodal, symmetric distribution	(10-36), (17-22). (7-25), Figure 16-4
C	constant coefficient in a contrast	(10-25), (10-29)
C^2	modified chi-square variable	(8-27)
d	statistic used to test randomness	(16-49)
d.f.	degrees of freedom	(8-11)
D	difference in two matched observations. Or Durbin-Watson statistic for testing serial correlation	(8-19), (16-28). (19-38)
e	regression error	(12-3), (12-4)
E	(also F, G, etc.) = event	(3-6)
$\overline{E}$	not E	(3-17)
$E(X)$	expected value of X, $= \mu_X$	(4-17b)
E_i	expected value in ith category	Table 17-1
F	variance ratio	(10-7), (10-17), Table 10-6, (10-37), (14-22)
H_0	null hypothesis	(9-12)
H_1	alternate hypothesis	(9-13)
iff	if and only if	(3-24)
IV	instrumental variable(s)	(20-17)

SYMBOL	MEANING	DEFINITION OR OTHER IMPORTANT REFERENCE
lim	the limit of ... , as n approaches infinity	(3-1)
$L(\ )$	likelihood function	(18-2), (18-17)
MAD	mean absolute deviation	(2-4)
MLE	maximum likelihood estimate(tion)	Table 18-1
MSD	mean squared deviation	(2-5a), (7-13)
MSS	mean sum of squares	Table 10-6
MSSD	mean square successive difference	(16-46)
n	sample size	(6-34)
N	population size	(6-34)
$N(\ ,\ )$	normal distribution, with specified mean and variance	(6-28)
O_i	observed value in ith category	Table 17-1
OLS	ordinary least squares (or least squares)	(11-8), (20-14)
P	sample proportion	(1-2), (6-26)
$Pr(E)$	probability of event E	(3-7)
$Pr(E/F)$	conditional probability of E, given F	(3-22)
$p(x)$	probability function of X	(5-5)
$p(x,y)$	joint probability function of X and Y	(5-2b)
$p(x/y)$	conditioned probability function of X, given $Y = y$	(5-10)
r_0, r_1	regrets in Bayesian hypothesis testing	(15-58), (15-59)
r	simple correlation. Or number of rows in two-way table	(14-4), (14-14). (10-36), (17-22)
r^2	coefficient of determination	(14-30)
$r_{XY/Z}$	partial correlation of X and Y, if Z were held constant	(14-37)
R	multiple correlation. Or statistic in runs test	(14-39), (14-40). (16-40)
s^2	variance of sample. Or residual variance in regression	(2-6a). (12-24)
s_{XY}	sample covariance of X and Y	(14-5), (20-5)

SYMBOL	MEANING	DEFINITION OR OTHER IMPORTANT REFERENCE
s_p^2	pooled variance of samples	(8-16), (10-29)
S	sum, or number of binomial successes	(5-32a), (6-3) Table 4-3
SS	sum of squares, (i.e., variation)	Table (10-6)
t	student's t variable	(8-10), (12-27), (14-23)
var	variance, $= \sigma^2$	(4-4), (4-10)
V	variance spectrum. Or value of game	(19-16). (24-7)
W	weighted sum. Or Wilcoxon-Mann-Whitney test statistic	(5-32b). (16-31)
X	(also Y, V, W, etc.) = random variable. Or regressor in original form	(4-1), Figure 4-1. (11-4)
x	(also y, v, etc.) = (realized) value of X. Or regressor in terms of deviations from the mean	Figure 4-1. (11-5)
$\bar{X}$	sample mean of X (note this is a different usage than $\bar{E}$)	(2-1a), (6-9)
$\bar{x}$	(realized) value of $\bar{X}$. After Chapter 8 this distinction between capital and little letters is forgotten	(7-9)
$\hat{Y}$	fitted value of Y	Figure 11-4, (12-25)
Z	standard normal variable. Or a second regressor	(4-13), (8-9). Table 13-1

(b) GREEK LETTERS are generally reserved for population parameters as follows:

α	probability of type I error. Or population regression intercept	Table 9-1. (12-1)
β	probability of type II error. Or population regression slope	Table 9-1. (12-1)
γ	population regression coefficient	(13-1)
Δ	population mean difference	(16-60)

SYMBOL	MEANING	DEFINITION OR OTHER IMPORTANT REFERENCE
θ	any population parameter	(7-11)
$\hat{\theta}$	sample estimator of θ	(7-11)
μ	population mean	(4-3), (4-9), (4-17a)
μ_0	regression mean at X_0. Or population mean, assuming null hypothesis (H_0) is true	Figure 12-6, (12-40). (9-9)
μ_1	population mean, assuming alternate hypothesis (H_1) is true	(9-20)
ν	population median	(16-7)
π	population proportion	(1-2), (4-7), (6-26)
Π	product of	(18-11)
Φ	population variance spectrum	(19-16)
ρ	population correlation coefficient, or serial correlation of time series error	(14-2), (19-3)
ρ_{XY}	population correlation of X and Y	(5-28), (5-31), (14-2)
σ	population standard deviation	(4-4)
σ^2	population variance	(4-4), (4-5), (4-19)
σ_{XY}	population covariance of X and Y	(5-23), (5-24), (5-25)
Σ	sum of	Table 2-2
χ^2	chi-square variable	(8-28), (17-3), (17-20)

(c) OTHER MATHEMATICAL SYMBOLS

$E \cup F$	E or F, or both	(3-10)
$E \cap F$	E and F	(3-11)
$\underset{=}{\triangle}$	equals, by definition	(2-1a)
$\simeq$	approximately equals	(2-1b)
$\sim$	is distributed as	(6-28)

PART 1

basic STATISTICS

CHAPTER 1

iNTROduCTiON

*He uses statistics as a drunken man uses lampposts—
for support rather than for illumination.*

Andrew Lang

The word "statistics" originally meant the collection of population and economic information vital to the state. From that modest beginning, statistics has grown into a scientific method of analysis now applied to all the social and natural sciences, and one of the major branches of mathematics. The present aims and methods of statistics are best illustrated with a familiar example.

1-1   EXAMPLE

Before every presidential election, the pollsters try to pick the winner; specifically, they try to guess the proportion of the population that will vote for each candidate. Clearly, canvassing all voters would be a hopeless task. As the only alternative, they survey a sample of a few thousand in the hope that the sample proportion will be a good estimate of the total population proportion. This is a typical example of *statistical inference* or *statistical induction:* the (voting) characteristics of an unknown population are inferred from the (voting) characteristics of an observed sample.

As any pollster will admit, it is an uncertain business. To be *sure* of the population, one has to wait until election day when all votes are counted. Yet if the sampling is done fairly and adequately, we can have high hopes that the sample proportion will be close to the population proportion. This will allow us to estimate the unknown population proportion π from the observed sample proportion P, as follows:

$$\pi = P \pm \text{a small error} \qquad (1\text{-}1)$$

with crucial questions being, "How small is this error?" and "How sure are we that we are right?"

Since this typifies the very core of the book, we state it more precisely, in the language of Chapter 7 where you will also find the proof and a fuller understanding.

If the sampling is random and large enough, we can state with 95% confidence that

$$\pi = P \pm 1.96 \sqrt{\frac{P(1 - P)}{n}} \qquad (1\text{-}2)$$

where π and P are the population and sample proportion, and n is the sample size.

As an illustration of how this formula works, suppose we have sampled 1,000 voters, with 610 choosing the Democratic candidate. With this sample proportion of .61, equation (1-2) becomes

$$\pi = .61 \pm 1.96 \sqrt{\frac{.61(1 - .61)}{1000}}$$

or approximately

$$\pi = .61 \pm .03 \qquad (1\text{-}3)$$

Thus, with 95% confidence, we estimate the population proportion voting Democrat to be between .58 and .64.

This is referred to as a *confidence interval,* and making estimates of this kind will be one of our major objectives in this book. The other objective is to *test hypotheses.* For example, suppose an ardent Republican friend claims that the Republican candidate will win the election. In mathematical terms, this hypothesis may be written: $\pi < .50$. On the basis of the information in equation (1-3) we would reject this hypothesis, of course. In general, there is a very close association of this kind between confidence intervals and hypothesis tests; indeed, we will show that in many instances they are equivalent procedures.

We can make several other crucial observations about equation (1-2).

1. The estimate is *not* made *with certainty;* we are only 95% confident. We must concede the possibility that we are wrong—and wrong because we were unlucky enough to draw a misleading sample. For example, even if less than half the population is in fact Democratic, it is still possible, although unlikely, for us to run into a string of Democrats in our sample. In such circumstances, our conclusion (1-3) would be dead wrong. Since this sort of bad luck is possible, but not likely, we can be 95% confident of our conclusion.

2. As sample size n increases, we note that the error allowance in (1-2) decreases. For example, if we increased our sample to 10,000 voters, and continued to observe a Democratic proportion of .61, the 95% confidence interval would become more precise:

$$.61 \pm .01 \qquad\qquad (1\text{-}4)$$

This is also intuitively correct: a larger sample contains more information, and hence allows a more precise conclusion.

3. Suppose we feel that 95% confidence is not good enough, and instead want to be 99% sure of our conclusion. If the additional resources for further sampling are not available, then we can increase our confidence only by making a less precise statement.

   As will be shown in Chapter 7, for 99% confidence the formula (1-2) must have the coefficient 1.96 enlarged to 2.58; this yields the 99% confidence interval,

$$.61 \pm .04$$

which is broader and less precise than the 95% confidence interval (1-3). The more certain we wish to be right, the more vague we must be; but in any case, we note that any statistical statement will be prefaced by *some* degree of uncertainty.

1-2   **INDUCTION AND DEDUCTION**

Figure 1-1 illustrates the difference between inductive and deductive reasoning. Induction involves arguing from the specific to the general, i.e., from the sample to the population. Deduction is the reverse—arguing from the general to the specific, i.e., from the population to the

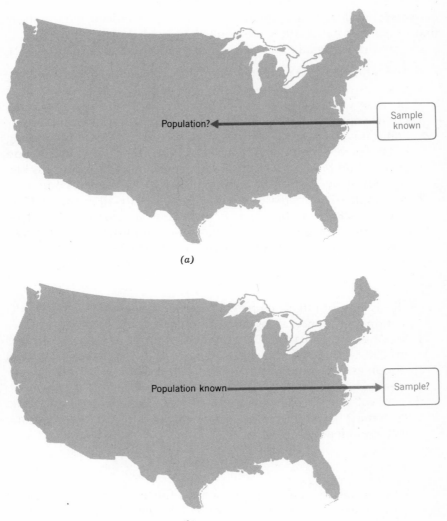

FIGURE 1-1 Induction and deduction contrasted. (a) Induction (statistical inference). (b) Deduction (probability).

sample.[1] Equation (1-1) represents inductive reasoning; we are arguing from a sample proportion to a population proportion. But this is only

---

[1]You can easily keep these straight with the help of a little Latin, and recognition that the population is the point of reference. The prefix *in* means "into" or "towards." Thus *in*duction is arguing towards the population. The prefix *de* means "away from." Thus *de*duction is arguing away from the population. Finally, statistical *in*ference is based on *in*duction.

possible if we study the simpler problem of deduction first. Specifically, in equation (1-1) the *inductive* statement (that the population proportion can be inferred from the sample proportion) is based on a prior *deduction* (that the sample proportion is likely to be close to the population proportion).

Chapters 2 through 6 are devoted to deduction. This involves probability theory, leading up to such questions as, "With a given population, how will a sample behave? Will the sample be 'on target'?" Only when this deductive issue is resolved can we move to questions of statistical inference in later chapters. There we turn the argument around and ask "From a given observed sample, what can we conclude about the unknown population?"

1-3   WHY SAMPLE?

We sample, rather than study the whole population, for any one of three reasons.

(1) Limited resources.
(2) Limited data available.
(3) Destructive testing.

1. Limited resources almost always play some part. In our example of preelection polls, funds were not available to observe the whole population.

2. Sometimes there is only a small sample available, no matter what cost may be incurred. For example, an anthropologist may wish to test the theory that the two civilizations on islands *A* and *B* have developed independently, with their own distinctive characteristics of weight, height, etc. But there is no way in which he can compare the two civilizations *in toto*. Instead he must make an inference from the small sample of the 50 surviving inhabitants of island *A* and the 100 surviving inhabitants of island *B*. The sample size is fixed by nature, rather than by the researcher's budget.

   There are many examples in business. An allegedly more efficient machine may be introduced for testing, with a view to the purchase of additional similar units. The manager of quality control simply cannot wait around to observe the entire population this machine will produce. Instead a sample run must be observed, with the decision on efficiency based on an inference from this sample.

3. Sampling may involve destructive testing. For example, suppose we wish to know the average life of light bulbs produced by a certain factory. It would be folly to insist on observing the whole population of bulbs until they burn out.

HOW TO SAMPLE

In statistics, as in business or any other profession, it is essential to distinguish between bad luck and bad management. For example, suppose a man bets you $100 at even odds that you will get an ace (i.e., 1 dot) in rolling a die. You accept the challenge, roll an ace, and he wins. He's a bad manager and you're a good one; he has merely overcome his bad management with extremely good luck. Your only defense against this combination is to get him to keep playing the game—with your dice.

If we now return to our original example of preelection polls, we note that the sample proportion of Democrats may badly misrepresent the population proportion for either (or both) of these reasons. No matter how well managed and designed our sampling procedure may be, we may be unlucky enough to turn up a Democratic sample from a Republican population. Equation (1-2) relates to this case; it is assumed that the only complication is the luck of the draw, and not mismanagement. From that equation we confirm that the best defense against bad luck is to "keep playing"; by increasing our sample size, we improve the reliability of our estimate.

The other problem is that sampling can be badly mismanaged or biased. For example, in sampling a population of voters, it is a mistake to take their names from a phone book, since poor voters who often cannot afford telephones are badly underrepresented.

Other examples of biased samples are easy to find and often amusing. "Straw polls" of people on the street are often biased because the interviewer tends to select people that seem civil and well dressed; a surly worker or harassed mother is overlooked. A congressman cannot rely on his mail as an unbiased sample of his constituency, for this is a sample of people with strong opinions, and includes an inordinate number of cranks and members of pressure groups.

The simplest way to ensure an unbiased sample is to give each member of the population an equal chance of being included in the sample. This, in fact, is essentially the definition of a "random" sample.[2] For a sample to be random, it cannot be chosen in a sloppy or haphazard way; it must be carefully designed. Only if a sample is random, will it be free of bias and, equally important, only then will it satisfy the assumptions of probability theory, and allow us to make scientific inferences of the form (1-2).

In some circumstances, the only available sample will be a nonrandom

_____

[2]Strictly speaking, this is called "simple random sampling," to distinguish it from more complex types of random sampling. A more complete and mathematical definition is given in Section 6-1.

one. While probability theory often cannot be strictly applied to such a sample, it still may provide the basis for a good educated guess—or what we might term the *art* of inference. Although this art is very important, it cannot be taught in an elementary text; we therefore consider only scientific inference based on the assumption that samples are random. The techniques for ensuring this are discussed further in Chapter 6.

dEScRipTivE STATisTiCS foR sAMplES

Figures won't lie, but liars will figure.

General Charles H. Grosvenor

2-1 INTRODUCTION

We have already discussed the primary purpose of statistics—to make an inference to the whole population from a sample. As a preliminary step, the sample must be simplified, and reduced to a few descriptive numbers; each is called a sample *statistic*.

In the very simple example of Chapter 1, the pollster would record the answers of the 1000 people in his sample, obtaining a sequence such as D D R D R. . . . where D and R represent Democrat and Republican. The best way of describing this sample by a single number is the statistic *P*, the sample proportion of Democrats; this will be used to make an inference about π, the population proportion. Admittedly, this statistic is trivial to compute. In the sample of the previous chapter, computing the sample proportion (.61) required only a count of the number voting Democrat (610), followed by a division by sample size, ($n = 1,000$).

We next consider the more substantial computations of statistics for summarizing two other samples:

(a) The number of children in a sample of 50 American families.
(b) The average height of a sample of 200 American men.

2-2   **FREQUENCY TABLES AND GRAPHS**

(a) Discrete Example

In a sample of U.S. families, suppose we record the number of children X, which takes on the values 0, 1, 2, 3, ... We call X a "discrete" random variable because it assumes only a finite (or countably infinite) number of values. The results are shown in Table 2-1. Our ultimate aim will be an inference about average family size in the U.S. population; but first we must efficiently describe and summarize our sample.

Table 2-1   Number of Children in a Sample of
U.S. Families

0, 2, 2, 3, 5, 1, 2, 0, ... 4, 2.

To simplify, we keep a running tally of each of the possible outcomes in Table 2-2. In column 3 we record for example that 13 is the frequency (f) that we observed for a two-child family. That is, we obtained this outcome on 13/50 of our sample observations; this proportion (.26) is called relative frequency (f/n), and is recorded in the last column.

The information in column 3 is called a "frequency distribution," and is graphed in Figure 2-1. The "relative frequency distribution" in the last column could be similarly graphed; note that the two graphs are identical except for the vertical scale. Hence, a simple change of vertical scale transforms Figure 2-1 into a relative frequency distribution.

Table 2-2   Calculation of the Frequency, and Relative Frequency of the
Number of Children in a Sample of 50 American Families

(1)	(2)	(3)	(4) Relative Frequency $\left(\dfrac{f}{n}\right)$
Number of Children	Tally	Frequency (f)	
0	⊥⊥⊥ ⊥⊥⊥ ⊥⊥⊥	15	.30
1	⊥⊥⊥ ⊥⊥⊥	10	.20
2	⊥⊥⊥ ⊥⊥⊥ |||	13	.26
3	⊥⊥⊥		6	.12
4	|||	3	.06
5	|||	3	.06

$$\sum f = 50 = n \qquad \sum\left(\frac{f}{n}\right) = 1.00$$

where $\sum f$ is "the sum of all f"

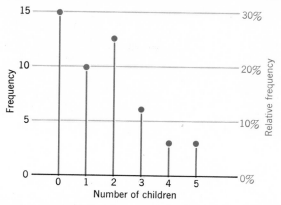

FIGURE 2-1   Frequency and relative frequency distribution of the number of children in a sample of 50 American families.

(b) Continuous Example

Suppose we take a sample of 200 men, with the height of each recorded in inches. We call height X a "continuous" random variable, since an individual's height might be any value, such as 64.328 inches.[1] It no longer makes sense to talk about the frequency of this specific value of X; chances are we will never again observe anyone exactly 64.328 inches tall. Instead we can tally the frequency of heights within a class or cell, (e.g., 58.5" to 61.5") as in Table 2-3. Then the frequency and relative frequency are tabulated as before.

The cells have been chosen somewhat arbitrarily, but with the following conveniences in mind:

1. The number of cells is a reasonable compromise between too much detail and too little. Usually 5 to 15 cells is appropriate.
2. Each cell midpoint, which hereafter will represent all observations in the cell, is a convenient whole number.

The grouping of the 200 observations into cells is illustrated in Figure 2-2, where each observation is represented by a dot. The grouped data

---

[1] We shall overlook the fact that although height is conceptually continuous, in practice the measured height is rounded to a few decimal places at most, and is therefore discrete. In this case we sometimes find observations occurring right at the cell boundary. Where should they be placed—in the cell above or the cell below?

One of the best solutions is to systematically move the first such borderline observation up into the cell above, move the second such observation into the cell below, the third up, the fourth down, etc. This is an arbitrary procedure, but it does keep $\overline{X}$ pretty well unbiased.

Table 2-3   Frequency, and Relative Frequency of the Heights of 200 Men

Cell No.	(1) Cell Boundaries	(2) Cell Midpoint	(3) Tally	(4) Frequency, f	(5) Relative Frequency $\dfrac{f}{n}$
1	58.5–61.5	60	||	2	.01
2	61.5–64.5	63	┼┼┼┼ ┼┼┼┼	10	.05
.	.	66	.	48	.24
.	.	69	.	64	.32
.	.	72	.	56	.28
.	.	75	.	16	.08
7	76.5–79.5	78	||||	4	.02

$$\sum f = 200 = n \qquad \sum \frac{f}{n} = 1.00$$

is then graphed in Figure 2-3. This frequency distribution, or so-called histogram, uses bars to represent frequencies as a reminder that the observations occurred throughout the cell, and not just at the midpoint.

We next turn to the question of how we may characterize a sample frequency distribution with a single descriptive number (statistic). In fact, there are two very useful concepts: the first is the center of the distribution and the second is the spread. These concepts will be illustrated with the continuous distribution of men's heights; but their application to discrete distributions (such as family size) is even more straightforward, and is left as an exercise.

2-3   CENTER OF A DISTRIBUTION

There are many different ways to measure the center of distribution. Three of these—the mode, the median, and the mean—are discussed below, starting with the simplest.

(a) The Mode

Since mode is the French word for fashion, the mode of a distribution is defined as the most frequent (fashionable) value. In the example of men's heights, the mode is 69 inches, since this cell has the greatest frequency, or highest bar in Figure 2-3. Generally, the mode is *not* a good measure of central tendency, since it often depends on the arbitrary grouping of the data. (In Problem 2-5, we note that by redefining cell boundaries, the mode can be shifted up or down considerably.) It is also possible to draw a sample where the largest frequency (highest bar

FIGURE 2-2 The grouping of observations into cells, illustrating the first two columns of Table 2-3.

FIGURE 2-3

in the group) occurs twice; this unfortunate ambiguity is left unresolved, and the distribution is called "bimodal."

(b) The Median

This is the 50th percentile; i.e., the value below which half the values in the sample fall. Since it splits the observations into two halves, it is sometimes called the middle value. In the sample of 200 detailed heights shown in Figure 2-2, the median (say, 69.41) is easily found by reading off the 100th value[2] from the left; but if the only information available is the grouped frequency distribution in Figure 2-3, the median can only be approximated by choosing an appropriate value within the median cell.[3]

---

[2] Or 101st value. This ambiguity is best resolved by defining the median as the average of the 100th and 101st values. In a sample with an odd number of observations, this ambiguity does not arise.

[3] The median cell is clearly the 4th, since this leaves 30% of the sample values below and 38% above. The median value can be closely approximated by moving through this

(cont'd)

(c) The Mean ($\bar{X}$)

This is sometimes called the arithmetic mean, or simply the average, and is the most common central measure. The original observations (X_1, $X_2, \ldots, X_n$) are simply summed, then divided by n. Thus we define

$$\bar{X} \triangleq \frac{1}{n} (X_1 + X_2 + \cdots + X_n)$$

$$\bar{X} \triangleq \frac{1}{n} \sum_{i=1}^{n} X_i \tag{2-1a}$$

where $\triangleq$ means "equals, by definition."

The average for the sample of heights could be computed by summing all 200 observations and dividing by 200. However, this tedious calculation can be greatly simplified by using the grouped data in Table 2-3. Let f_1 represent the number of observations in cell 1, where each observation may be approximated[4] by the cell midpoint, x_1. Similar approximations hold for all the other cells too, so that

$$\bar{X} \simeq \frac{1}{n} \left[\underbrace{(x_1 + x_1 + \cdots + x_1)}_{f_1 \text{ times}} + \underbrace{(x_2 + x_2 + \cdots x_2)}_{f_2 \text{ times}} + \cdots + \underbrace{(x_7 + \cdots x_7)}_{f_7 \text{ times}} \right]$$

where $\simeq$ represents approximate equality; it follows that

$$\bar{X} \simeq \frac{1}{n} \{ f_1 x_1 + f_2 x_2 + \cdots f_7 x_7 \}$$

$$\simeq \frac{f_1}{n} x_1 + \frac{f_2}{n} x_2 + \cdots \frac{f_7}{n} x_7$$

$$\simeq \sum_{i=1}^{7} \left(\frac{f_i}{n} \right) x_i$$

---

median cell from left to right to pick up another 20% of the observations. Since this cell includes 32% of the observations, we move 20/32 of the way through this cell. Thus our median approximation is $67.5 + (20/32)3 = 69.4$.

[4] In approximating each observed value by the midpoint of its cell, we sometimes err positively, sometimes negatively; but unless we are very unlucky, these errors will tend to cancel. Even in the unluckiest case, however, the overall error in the sample mean will be less than half the cell width. Note that cell midpoints are designated by the small x_i, to distinguish them from the observed values X_i.

For a discrete distribution such as family size, however, there is no approximation necessary; then (2-1b) will be exactly true.

In general, for grouped data

$$\overline{X} \simeq \sum_{i=1}^{m} x_i \left(\frac{f_i}{n}\right) \tag{2-1b}$$

where (f_i/n) = relative frequency in the ith cell, and m = number of cells. We number this equation (2-1b) to emphasize that it is the equivalent of (2-1a), appropriate for grouped data. Formula (2-1b) is used to calculate the mean height in column 3 of Table 2-4. We can think of this as a "weighted" average, with each x value weighted appropriately by its relative frequency.

Table 2-4 Calculation of Mean and Variance of a Sample of 200 Men's Heights. (An easier coded method is shown later in Table 2-5)

Given		Calculation of $\overline{X}$ using (2-1b)	Calculation of MSD using (2-5b) ($\overline{X}$ rounded to 69)		
(1)	(2)	(3)	(4)	(5)	(6)
x_i	$\dfrac{f_i}{n}$	$x_i\left(\dfrac{f_i}{n}\right)$	$(x_i - \overline{X})$	$(x_i - \overline{X})^2$	$(x_i - \overline{X})^2\left(\dfrac{f_i}{n}\right)$
60	.01	.60	−9	81	.81
63	.05	3.15	−6	36	1.80
66	.24	15.84	−3	9	2.16
69	.32	22.08	0	0	0
72	.28	20.16	3	9	2.52
75	.08	6.00	6	36	2.88
78	.02	1.56	9	81	1.62

$$\overline{X} \simeq \sum x_i\left(\frac{f_i}{n}\right)$$

$$= 69.39$$

$$\text{MSD} \simeq \sum (x_i - \overline{X})^2 \left(\frac{f_i}{n}\right)$$

$$= 11.79$$

Comparing (2-5b) and (2-6b):

$$s^2 = \text{MSD}\left(\frac{n}{n-1}\right)$$

$$= 11.79\left(\frac{200}{199}\right) = 11.85$$

$$s = \sqrt{11.85} = 3.44$$

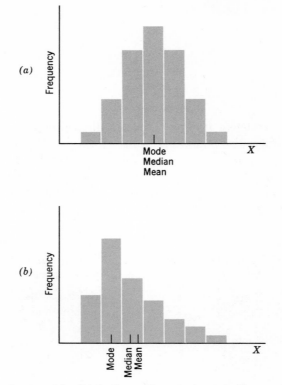

FIGURE 2-4(a) A symmetric distribution with a single peak. The mode, median, and mean coincide at the point of symmetry. (b) A right-skewed distribution, showing mode < median < mean.

(d) Comparison of Mean, Median, and Mode

These three measures of center are compared in Figure 2-4. In panel (a) we show a distribution which has a single peak and is symmetric (i.e., one half is the mirror image of the other); in this case all three central measures coincide. But when the distribution is skewed to the right as in (b), the median falls to the right of the mode; with the long scatter of observations strung out in the right-hand tail, we have to move from the mode to the right to pick up half the observations. Moreover, the mean will generally lie even further to the right, as explained below.

(e) Interpreting the Mean by an Analogy from Physics.

The 200 heights appear in Figure 2-2 as points along the X-axis. If we think of these observations as equal masses (each observation a one pound mass, for example), and the X-axis as a weightless supporting rod, we might ask where this rod balances. Our intuition suggests "the center."

The precise balancing point, also called the center of gravity, is given by the formula

$$\frac{1}{n} \sum X_i$$

which is exactly the formula for the mean. Thus we are quite justified in thinking of the sample mean as the "balancing point" of the data, and representing it in graphs as a fulcrum ▲.

Now it can easily be seen why the mean lies to the right of the median in a right-skewed distribution, as shown in Figure 2-4b. Experiment by trying to balance at the median. Fifty percent of the observed values then lie on either side, but the observations to the right tend to be further distant, tilting the distribution down on the right. Balance can be achieved only by placing the fulcrum (mean) to the right of the median.

PROBLEMS

2-1 The daily output (in thousands) of an international corporation in six different countries is

$$9, 8, 2, 2, 6, 3$$

(a) What is the mean daily output per country? The median? The mode?

(b) Calculate the deviations from the mean $(X_i - \bar{X})$. What is the average deviation?

(c) For another international corporation operating in 9 countries, the daily output had a mean of 7.8, a median of 6.1 and a mode of 9.0. What was the total daily output?

2-2 Find the mean, median, and mode of the following sample of the daily sales of 20 retail outlets. Graph the frequency distribution.

$$
\begin{array}{ccccccc}
7 & 4 & 10 & 9 & 6 & 9 & 7 \\
8 & 11 & 6 & 8 & 10 & 11 & 6 \\
10 & 10 & 8 & 11 & 6 & 5 &
\end{array}
$$

2-3 Sort the following daily profit figures of 25 newsstands into 8 cells, whose midpoints are 55, 60, . . . , 90.

55.31	81.47	64.90	70.88	86.02	77.25	76.73	84.21	56.02
84.92	90.23	78.01	88.05	73.37	87.09	57.41	85.43	
74.76	86.51	86.37	76.15	88.64	84.71	66.05	83.91	

(a) Approximately what are the mean, median, and mode?

(b) Graph the relative frequency distribution.

2-4 Sort the data of Problem 2-3 into 4 cells, whose midpoints are 60, 70, 80, 90. Then answer the same questions as in Problem 2-3.

2-5 Summarize the answers to the previous two problems by completing the following table.

	Mean	Median	Mode
Original data (exact values)	77.78	81.47	Not defined
—Fine grouping (Problem 2-3)			
—Coarse grouping (Problem 2-4)			

(a) Why is the mode not a good measure?

(b) Which gives a closer approximation to the true ungrouped median (or mean): the coarse or the fine grouping?

2-6 Explain in your own words the relative advantages of the mean, the median, and the mode.

2-7 In selling a house, a real estate agent stated that average income in the subdivision was $20,000; yet at a protest meeting of taxpayers from the subdivision (where he is also a resident), he states that the typical income is only $12,000. Can this apparent contradiction be explained? Is he necessarily being dishonest?

2-8 (a) The exports of a random sample of 5 countries were found to increase in one year by:

$$10\%, 8\%, 2\%, 15\%, 12\%$$

Would the average of these figures give you a good indication of "the increase in world trade"? Explain.

(b) Define a better measure of the increase in world trade if the initial export levels of the above countries were 19, 2, 5, 14, 10, respectively (in billions of dollars).

2-4   SPREAD OF A DISTRIBUTION

Although average height may be the most important characteristic (statistic) of the sample, it is also important to know how spread out or varied are the sample observations. As with measures of center, we find that there are several measures of spread; we start with the simplest.

(a) The range

The range is simply the distance between the largest and smallest value.

$$\text{Range} \triangleq \text{largest} - \text{smallest observation}$$

For men's heights, in Figure 2-3, the range is 21 (i.e., 79.5 − 58.5). It may be fairly criticized on the grounds that it tells us nothing about the distribution except where it ends. And these two extreme values may be very unreliable. We therefore turn to measures of spread which take account of all observations.

(b) Mean Absolute Deviation (MAD)

The average deviation, as its name implies, is found by calculating the deviation of each observed value from the mean; these deviations $(X_i - \bar{X})$ are then averaged by summing and dividing by n. Although this sounds like a promising measure, in fact it is worthless; positive deviations always cancel negative deviations, leaving an average of zero.[5] This sign problem can be avoided by ignoring all negative signs and taking the average of the *absolute* values of the deviations, as follows.

$$\text{The Mean Absolute Deviation, MAD} \triangleq \frac{1}{n} \sum_{i=1}^{n} |X_i - \bar{X}| \qquad (2\text{-}4)$$

---

[5]This was illustrated in Problem 2-1b. It may be generally proved as follows, (here and wherever else it will cause no ambiguity, we shall abbreviate the Σ sign by dropping its subscript and superscript):

$$\text{Average deviation} \triangleq \frac{1}{n} \sum_{i=1}^{n} (X_i - \bar{X}) \qquad (2\text{-}2)$$

$$= \frac{1}{n} \left(\sum X_i - n\bar{X} \right)$$

$$= \frac{1}{n} \sum X_i - \bar{X}$$

$$= 0 \qquad (2\text{-}3)$$

(c) Mean Squared Deviation (MSD)

Although MAD intuitively is a good measure of spread, it is mathematically intractable.[6] We therefore turn to an alternative means of avoiding the sign problem—namely, squaring each deviation.

$$\text{Mean Squared Deviation, MSD} \triangleq \frac{1}{n} \sum_{i=1}^{n} (X_i - \bar{X})^2 \qquad (2\text{-}5a)$$

For grouped data,

$$\text{MSD} \simeq \sum_{i=1}^{m} (x_i - \bar{X})^2 \left(\frac{f_i}{n}\right) \qquad (2\text{-}5b)$$

(d) Variance and Standard Deviation

MSD is a good measure, provided we wish only to describe the sample. But typically we shall want to go one step further, and use this to make a statistical inference about the population. For this purpose it is better to use the divisor $n - 1$ rather than[7] n. The resulting sample statistic is referred to as the variance.

$$\text{Variance, } s^2 \triangleq \frac{1}{n-1} \sum_{i=1}^{n} (X_i - \bar{X})^2 \qquad (2\text{-}6a)$$

For grouped data,

$$s^2 \simeq \frac{1}{n-1} \sum_{i=1}^{m} (x_i - \bar{X})^2 f_i \qquad (2\text{-}6b)$$

The values of MSD and s^2 are calculated in Table 2-4, where $\bar{X}$ has been rounded[8] in order to avoid fractions. Finally we define

$$\text{Standard Deviation, } s \triangleq \sqrt{\text{variance}} \qquad (2\text{-}7)$$

---

[6] One difficulty is the problem of differentiating the absolute value function.

[7] Technically, this makes the sample variance an unbiased estimator of the population variance, as shown in Chapter 7.

[8] This rounding makes very good sense for hand calculations. If we denote the

(cont'd)

Note that by taking the square root, we compensate for having squared terms in defining the variance in (2-6a), so that s is reduced to the same units as the X observations.

In conclusion, the sample mean $\overline{X}$ is the most common measure of center, and the sample standard deviation s the most common measure of spread. Borrowing the language of physics, we refer to $\overline{X}$ and s^2 as the first and second moments of the sample.

PROBLEMS

2-9 Compute the variance of the data of Problem 2-1.

2-10 For the grouped data of Problem 2-3, compute the range, mean absolute deviation, and standard deviation.

(2-11)[9] For the grouped data of Problem 2-4, compute the standard deviation.

2-5   LINEAR TRANSFORMATIONS (CODING)

(a) Change of Origin

Suppose that the men's heights in our example are measured relative to a norm of 69 inches. Since X_i denotes the old height in inches (e.g., 75), let X_i' denote the new measure (e.g., 6). The two measures are related by the equation

$$X_i' = X_i - 69 \tag{2-11}$$

In nonmathematical terms, this new measurement is simply "the number of inches an individual is taller $(+)$ or shorter $(-)$ than the norm of 69 inches." It is easy to guess that the mean using this new measure is just 69 less than the mean using the old measure:

$$\overline{X}' = \overline{X} - 69 \tag{2-12}$$

---

rounding error by e, we shall prove in (4-23) that this causes

the variance to be overestimated by the amount e^2 approximately   (2-8)

which is usually negligible. But if full accuracy is required, the rounding error can be easily compensated for by subtracting e^2 from the rounded s^2. For example, in Table 2-4, since $e = 69.39 - 69 = .39$, if we subtract $e^2 = .15$ from the rounded $s^2 = 11.85$, we obtain the true $s^2 = 11.70$. Since this rounding error is generally not worth considering, we shall usually ignore it.

[9] Problems with parentheses closely resemble previous problems, and so are recommended only if further drill is desired.

FIGURE 2-5 Change of origin (shift).

On the other hand, the *spread* of our observations will be exactly the same, regardless of which measurement is used:

$$s_{X'} = s_X \qquad (2\text{-}13)$$

These two points are illustrated in Figure 2-5, and generalized in the following theorem.[10]

$$
\left.
\begin{array}{l}
\text{If} \quad X_i' = X_i - a \\
\text{then} \quad \overline{X}' = \overline{X} - a \qquad (2\text{-}15) \\
\text{and} \quad s_{X'} = s_X \qquad (2\text{-}16)
\end{array}
\right\} \quad (2\text{-}14)
$$

----

[10]**proof** To prove (2-15) consider

$$\overline{X}' \triangleq \frac{1}{n} \sum X_i'$$

By (2-14)

$$= \frac{1}{n} \sum (X_i - a)$$

$$= \frac{1}{n} \left[\sum X_i - na \right]$$

$$= \overline{X} - a$$

To prove (2-16) it will be enough to prove the equality of variances.

$$s_{X'}^2 \triangleq \frac{1}{n-1} \sum (X_i' - \overline{X}')^2$$

$$= \frac{1}{n-1} \sum [(X_i - a) - (\overline{X} - a)]^2$$

$$= \frac{1}{n-1} \sum (X_i - \overline{X})^2 = s_X^2$$

FIGURE 2-6   Change of scale (shrink).

(b) Change of Scale

Suppose that the men's heights are measured in quarter-feet (units of 3 inches). Denoting this new measure by X_i^*, we see for example that $X_i = 72$ inches would be converted to $X_i^* = 24$ quarter-feet, and generally

$$X_i^* = \tfrac{1}{3}X_i \tag{2-17}$$

Once more it is easy to guess that the mean using this new measure is just 1/3 the mean using the old:

$$\bar{X}^* = \tfrac{1}{3}\bar{X} \tag{2-18}$$

The standard deviation will also be 1/3 as much as before:

$$s_{X*} = \tfrac{1}{3}s_X \tag{2-19}$$

These two points are illustrated in Figure 2-6, and generalized in the following theorem:[11]

$$
\left.
\begin{array}{lll}
\text{If} & X_i^* = bX_i & \\
\text{then} & \bar{X}^* = b\bar{X} & (2\text{-}21) \\
\text{and} & s_{X*} = |b|\, s_X & (2\text{-}22)
\end{array}
\right\} (2\text{-}20)
$$

(c) General Linear Transformations

It is now appropriate to combine the above two theorems into one. For the general linear[12] transformation, we have the following theorem:

---

[11] The proof resembles that of (2-14) and is left as an exercise.

[12] Transformation (2-23) is called linear because, for fixed values of a and b, the graph of $Y = a + bX$ is a straight line (with slope b and Y-intercept a).

The proof of (2-23) resembles that of (2-14), and is left as an exercise. Of course, proving all of theorems (2-23), (2-20) and (2-14) would be redundant. Only theorem (2-23) needs proof; then (2-20) and (2-14) follow as special cases.

$$\left.\begin{array}{ll} \text{If} & Y_i = a + bX_i \\ \text{then} & \bar{Y} = a + b\bar{X} \qquad (2\text{-}24) \\ \text{and} & s_Y = |b|\, s_X \qquad (2\text{-}25) \end{array}\right\} (2\text{-}23)$$

This theorem may be interpreted very simply: if the *individual* observations (X_i) are linearly transformed (into corresponding Y_i values), then the *mean* observation is transformed in exactly the same way, and the *standard deviation* is changed by the factor $|b|$, with no effect from a.

(d) Application to Coding

In future chapters we shall draw upon the theory of linear transformations in various contexts. However, it does have one immediate use; it can be applied to find a simpler computation of $\bar{X}$ and s_X than that shown in Table 2-4. This involves three steps:

1. Code all the X_i values into a new set of Y_i values. Our computations will be most simplified if we use the formula

Table 2-5   Coded Computation of Mean and Standard Deviation of a Sample of 200 Men's Heights (Compare with Table 2-4)

(1)	(2)	(3)	(4)	For s_Y^2, using $\bar{Y}$ rounded to 0	
	Coding		For $\bar{Y}$	(5)	(6)
x_i	$y_i = \dfrac{x_i - 69}{3}$	f_i	$f_i y_i$	$(y_i - \bar{Y})^2$	$(y_i - \bar{Y})^2 f_i$
60	-3	2	-6	9	18
63	-2	10	-20	4	40
66	-1	48	-48	1	48
69	0	64	0	0	0
72	1	56	56	1	56
75	2	16	32	4	64
78	3	4	12	9	36

$$\sum f_i y_i = 26 \qquad\qquad \sum (y_i - \bar{Y})^2 f_i = 262$$

$$\bar{Y} = \frac{\sum f_i y_i}{n} = \frac{26}{200} \qquad\qquad s_Y^2 = \frac{262}{199}$$

$$= .13 \qquad\qquad\qquad = 1.316$$

$$\bar{X} = 3\bar{Y} + 69 \qquad\qquad s_X = 3 s_Y$$

$$\bar{X} = \underline{\underline{69.39}} \qquad\qquad = 3\sqrt{1.316}$$

$$s_X = \underline{\underline{3.44}}$$

$$Y_i = \frac{X_i - \text{one of the cell midpoints}}{\text{cell width}} \tag{2-26}$$

In the example of heights, let us somewhat arbitrarily use the cell midpoint 69, so that

$$Y_i = \frac{X_i - 69}{3} \tag{2-27}$$

This is clearly a linear transformation of the form of (2-23), with $a = -69/3$ and $b = 1/3$. Moreover, it is evident that when $X_i = 69$, $Y_i = 0$. Furthermore, as X_i progresses by steps of 3, Y_i progresses in unit steps. With these guidelines we can fill in the appropriate Y values in column 2 of Table 2-5; this coding is illustrated in Figure 2-7.

2. Compute the mean and standard deviation of the Y values. We note in the successive columns of Table 2-5 how easily this is now done.
3. With $\bar{Y}$ and s_Y now in hand, we are in a position to translate this mean and standard deviation back into X values. The theory of linear transformations (2-23) applied to (2-27) yields:

$$\bar{Y} = \frac{\bar{X} - 69}{3} \tag{2-28}$$

and

$$s_Y = \tfrac{1}{3}s_X \tag{2-29}$$

From (2-28)

$$\bar{X} = 3\,\bar{Y} + 69 \tag{2-30}$$
$$= 69.39$$

FIGURE 2-7   The coding of Table 2-5, from inches (X) into quarter-feet (Y). A change of origin as well as scale.

From (2-29)

$$s_X = 3s_Y \tag{2-31}$$
$$= 3.44$$

Thus the simple coded computation of $\overline{X}$ and s_X is complete.

PROBLEMS

2-12 By coding the heights shown in Table 2-5 from inches (X) into feet (Y), carry out a line or two of the computation of $\overline{X}$ and s_X. Show your linear transformation with a diagram similar to Figure 2-7. Why is the coding used in the text preferred?

2-13 Use coding to find the mean and standard deviation of the data in Problem 2-3.

2-14 Find the mean of the following 11 measurements:

239510 239250 239860 239360
239480 239430 239230 239680
239370 239290 239850

(*Hint*. It is natural to simply drop the first 3 digits of every number, and just work with the numbers 510, 250, ... This is mathematically justified—it is just the linear transformation $Y = X - 239,000$.)

2-15 To find out whether *nonlinear* transformations are trickier, suppose $Y_i = X_i^2$, where $X_i = 1,3,5$. Then is $\overline{Y} = (\overline{X})^2$?

(2-16) Using coding, find the mean and standard deviation of the data of Problem 2-4.

(2-17) Find the mean and standard deviation of the following sample of 50 executive ages. Graph the relative frequency distribution.

35	46	63	69	54	50	62	68	38	40
55	43	42	59	45	44	57	47	48	46
43	64	49	36	59	60	42	60	42	38
51	50	66	63	57	56	51	38	61	54
50	44	48	69	64	37	56	53	62	52

Review Problems

2-18 The weekly wage rates for 5 major industrial groupings are listed below. Find the average weekly wage.

Industry	A	B	C	D	E
% of employment	30%	25	20	20	5
Weekly wage ($)	$120	150	120	100	80

2-19 Suppose the number of children was recorded for each of 25 families, obtaining the following data:

2, 4, 1, 0, 1, 3, 0, 4, 2, 6, 0, 0, 2, 3, 1, 5, 4,
0, 3, 1, 2, 5, 3, 4, 1.

(a) Construct a frequency table and graph.
(b) Find the sample mean and standard deviation.

2-20 The following table gives the actual percent of farmland that was harvested (as opposed to pasture, woodlot, etc.) in the U.S.A. in 1959, according to region. Compute the percentage harvested in the U.S.A. as a whole.

Region	Amount of Farmland (millions of acres)	Percent Harvested
North	421	46.7%
South	357	21.0%
Mountain	264	8.7%
Pacific	80	18.8%
U.S.A.	1,122	?

2-21 A certain species of beetle was sampled, yielding the following 10 lengths, in centimeters: 1.5, 1.0, 1.2, 1.0, 1.1, 1.0, 1.6, 1.2, 1.4, 2.0. Find the median, mean, range, variance, and standard deviation
(a) For the original lengths.
(b) If the lengths are expressed in mm (1 cm = 10 mm).
(c) If the lengths are expressed as "centimeters above a standard beetle length of 1.1," (i.e., the sample values become $+.4$, $-.1$, .1, $-.1$, $\cdots$).

2-22 Suppose the disposable annual incomes of the 5 million residents of a certain country had a mean of $4800 and a median of $3400.
(a) What is the total national disposable income?
(b) What would you say is the disposable income of the "typical resident?"
(c) Is disposable income distributed fairly equally, i.e., what is the shape of the distribution?

⟹ 2-23[13] Throw a die 50 times (or else simulate this by consulting the random numbers[14] in Appendix Table IIa). Graph the relative frequency distribution, and calculate the sample mean

    (a) After 10 throws;

    (b) After 20 throws;

    (c) After 50 throws;

    (d) After millions of throws (guess).

[13]Problems with arrows are especially important, because they introduce later sections of the text.

[14]In simulation, disregard the digits 0, 7, 8, and 9. The remaining 6 digits will of course still be equally likely, and hence provide an accurate simulation of a die.

CHAPTER 3
probability

The urge to gamble is so universal and its practice so pleasurable that I assume it must be evil.

Heywood Broun

3-1   **INTRODUCTION**

In the next four chapters we make deductions about a sample from a known population; this will then be turned around in Chapter 7 and later chapters, where we shall make inferences about an unknown population from an observed sample.

If the population of American voters is 55% Democrat, we cannot be certain that exactly the same percentage of Democrats will occur in a random sample. Nevertheless, it is "likely" that "close to" this percentage will turn up in our sample. Our objective is to define "likely" and "close to" more precisely; in this way we shall be able to make useful predictions. First, however, we must lay a good deal of ground work. Prediction in the face of uncertainty or chance requires a knowledge of the laws of *probability,* and this chapter is devoted exclusively to their development. We start with the simplest examples—tossing coins and rolling dice.

(a) Definition

Consider again our example in Chapter 1, in which the reader gambled against rolling an ace on a die. This gamble was based on the judgement that this outcome was unlikely. Now let's be more specific, and try to define its probability precisely. Intuitively, since this is but one of six equally probable outcomes, we might (correctly) guess its probability to be one in six, or one-sixth—provided it is an honest die. Alternatively we might say that if the die were thrown a large number of times, the relative frequency (of rolling an ace) would approach one-sixth (as in Problem 2-23). This is a useful operational approach; thus, if we suspect that this die is not, in fact, a fair one, we could test by tossing it many times, and observing whether or not the relative frequency of this outcome approached one sixth.

This definition of probability as "the limit of relative frequency," is formally stated as:

$$\Pr\,(e_1) \triangleq \lim \frac{n_1}{n} \qquad (3\text{-}1)$$

where e_1 is the outcome ("ace")
  n is the total number of times that the trial is repeated (die is thrown)
  n_1 is the number of times that the outcome e_1 occurs, [also called $n(e_1)$ or the frequency f]

$\dfrac{n_1}{n}$ is therefore the relative frequency of e_1

$\lim$ is "the limit of . . . , as n approaches infinity."

We shall use this definition of probability because it provides the clearest intuitive idea. However, you will find in Section 3-6 that it involves conceptual difficulties; thus, if you choose to study probability further you will soon be forced to turn to an axiomatic approach.

(b) Elementary Properties of Probability

We generalize by considering an experiment with N elementary outcomes $(e_1, e_2, \ldots, e_i, \ldots, e_N)$. The relative frequency n_i/n of any outcome e_i must be positive, since both the numerator and denominator are positive; moreover, since the numerator cannot exceed the denominator, relative frequency cannot exceed 1. Thus

$$0 \le \frac{n_i}{n} \le 1$$

The same relations are true in the limit, so that from (3-1)

$$0 \le Pr(e_i) \tag{3-2}$$

and

$$Pr(e_i) \le 1 \tag{3-3}$$

Next we note that the frequencies of all possible outcomes sum to n.

$$n_1 + n_2 + \cdots n_N = n$$

Dividing this equation by n, we find that all the *relative* frequencies sum[1] to 1.

$$\frac{n_1}{n} + \frac{n_2}{n} + \cdots + \frac{n_N}{n} = 1$$

This same relation is true in the limit, so that

$$Pr(e_1) + Pr(e_2) + \cdots Pr(e_N) = 1 \tag{3-4}$$

PROBLEMS

3-1 (a) Throw a thumbtack 50 times. Define tossing the point up as e_1. Record your results as in the following table:

Trial Number (n)	Point Up?	Frequency of "Ups" (n_1) Accumulated	Relative Frequency (n_1/n)
1	No	0	.00
2	Yes	1	.50
3	Yes	2	.67
4	No	2	.50
5	Yes	3	.60
.	.	.	.
.	.	.	.
.	.	.	.
10			
20			
30			
40			
50			

[1]This was first noted in the last column of Table 2-2.

(b) Show your results on the following graph:

(c) What is your best guess of the probability of tossing the point up?

3-2 Toss a coin 25 times. Define a head as e_1, and proceed as in Problem 3-1.

3-3 Roll a pair of dice, and define "a total of 7 or 11" as the event E. (You may simulate this by drawing a pair of random numbers—properly restricted to the digits 1 through 6, of course.) Repeat 50 times and proceed as in Problem 3-1.

3-2   OUTCOMES AND THEIR PROBABILITIES

(a) The Outcome Set—An Example

In the previous section, the die example was an experiment where the outcomes $e_1, e_2, \ldots, e_6$ were numerical, and involved no complications. Usually, an experiment will have a more complex set of outcomes.

For example, suppose the experiment consists of planning a family of 3 children, boys (B) or girls (G). A typical outcome occurs when a boy is followed by two girls, denoted by the sequence (B, G, G). The list of all possible outcomes, or outcome set, is shown in Figure 3-1a. Since most experiments of interest to the practical statistician are sampling experiments, the outcome set is also often known as the *sample space S.*

We note several features. The order in which the set of eight outcomes $\{e_1, e_2, \ldots, e_8\}$ is listed doesn't matter. Whenever this is the case, it is a mathematical convention to use curly brackets. Thus the two outcome sets $\{e_1, e_2, \ldots, e_8\}$ and $\{e_2, e_8, \ldots, e_1\}$ are the *same* set.

However, (B, B, G) and (B, G, B) are separate and distinct outcomes; in this case, when the order in which B and G appear is an essential feature, we use *round* brackets and call the result an *ordered* triple. Each such experimental outcome may be represented by a point.

$$\begin{aligned}
\cdot (B, B, B) &= e_1 \\
\cdot (B, B, G) &= e_2 \\
\cdot (B, G, B) &= e_3 \\
\cdot (B, G, G) &= e_4 \\
\cdot (G, B, B) &= e_5 \\
\cdot (G, B, G) &= e_6 \\
\cdot (G, G, B) &= e_7 \\
\cdot (G, G, G) &= e_8
\end{aligned}$$

FIGURE 3-1(a)   Outcome set in planning a family of 3 children.

To simplify calculations without restricting our concepts in any way, let us suppose that boys and girls are equally likely, and that births are independent[2] (i.e., having a boy on the first birth does not change the probability of having a boy on the second); then all 8 outcomes are equally probable. Since all 8 probabilities must sum to 1 according to (3-4), we have

$$\Pr(e_1) = \Pr(e_2) = \cdots = \Pr(e_8) = \frac{1}{8} \qquad (3\text{-}5)$$

(b) Outcome Trees

Often the probability of an outcome is much more difficult to calculate. As a concrete example, suppose a biased coin (which will turn up heads 2/3 of the time, tails 1/3), is flipped three times. The possibilities, H and T, are listed in Figure 3-1b toss by toss:

Consider a typical outcome—for example, the third one listed, (HTH). Its probability can be calculated using the concept of relative frequency: imagine millions of people gathered together, each performing this experiment of flipping a biased coin 3 times. If we summarize the result after the first toss, 2/3 of the people would report H, and 1/3 T. This is the very definition of probability, and is indicated by the first branching of the tree in Figure 3-1b. Of these people who initially had H, only 1/3 would report T on the second toss, and of these, only 2/3 would finally report H on the third toss. Thus

$$\frac{2}{3} \text{ of } \frac{1}{3} \text{ of } \frac{2}{3} = \frac{4}{27}$$

_____

[2] Actually, in the U.S., the probability of a boy is .51 rather than 1/2, and there is also some evidence that births are not quite independent. However, these differences between reality and our simplifying assumptions are small enough to be ignored in this problem.

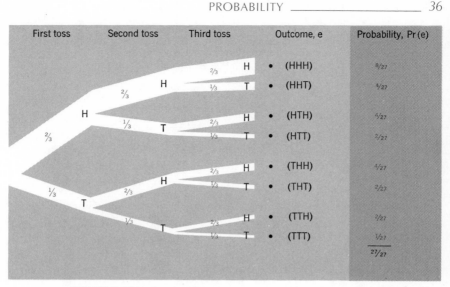

First toss	Second toss	Third toss	Outcome, e	Probability, Pr(e)
		H $\frac{2}{3}$	• (HHH)	$8/27$
	H $\frac{2}{3}$	T $\frac{1}{3}$	• (HHT)	$4/27$
H		H $\frac{2}{3}$	• (HTH)	$4/27$
$\frac{2}{3}$	T $\frac{1}{3}$	T $\frac{1}{3}$	• (HTT)	$2/27$
		H $\frac{2}{3}$	• (THH)	$4/27$
	H $\frac{2}{3}$	T $\frac{1}{3}$	• (THT)	$2/27$
T $\frac{1}{3}$		H $\frac{2}{3}$	• (TTH)	$2/27$
	T $\frac{1}{3}$	T $\frac{1}{3}$	• (TTT)	$1/27$
				$\overline{27/27}$

FIGURE 3-1(b)   An outcome tree for 3 tosses of a biased coin.

of the people would report the outcome (HTH). This relative frequency, or probability, is shown in the last column.

As another example, consider a fair coin being flipped 3 times. Then the outcome tree in Figure 3-1b remains exactly the same; only the probabilities change. The probabilities on each branching are now 1/2, so that every outcome has probability

$$\frac{1}{2} \text{ of } \frac{1}{2} \text{ of } \frac{1}{2} = \frac{1}{8}$$

You can confirm that flipping a fair coin 3 times is a simulation of the experiment of having 3 children—just replacing H and T with B and G; thus the above calculation confirms (3-5).

3-3   **EVENTS AND THEIR PROBABILITIES**

(a) Example of an Event

In planning their 3 children, the couple may hope for the event

E: at least 2 boys

This event includes outcomes e_1, e_2, e_3, and e_5 in Figure 3-1a. We might say the event E is the collection of points $\{e_1, e_2, e_3, e_5\}$ as in Figure 3-2. In fact, this is a convenient way to generally define an event:

An event E is a subset of the outcome set S	(3-6)

(b) Probability of an Event

We now ask "What is the probability of E?" Using the definition of limiting relative frequency, we may write

$$\Pr(E) = \lim \frac{n_E}{n} \tag{3-7}$$

where n_E = frequency of E. But of course E occurs whenever the outcomes e_1, e_2, e_3, or e_5 occur. Thus

$$n_E = n_1 + n_2 + n_3 + n_5$$

and from (3-7)

$$\Pr(E) = \lim \frac{n_1 + n_2 + n_3 + n_5}{n} \tag{3-8}$$

$$= \lim \left(\frac{n_1}{n} + \frac{n_2}{n} + \frac{n_3}{n} + \frac{n_5}{n} \right)$$

$$= \Pr(e_1) + \Pr(e_2) + \Pr(e_3) + \Pr(e_5)$$

$$= \tfrac{1}{8} + \tfrac{1}{8} + \tfrac{1}{8} + \tfrac{1}{8} = \tfrac{1}{2}$$

The obvious generalization of (3-8) is that the probability of an event is the sum of the probabilities of all the points (or outcomes) included in that event, that is

$$\Pr(E) = \sum \Pr(e_i) \tag{3-9}$$

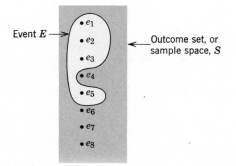

FIGURE 3-2   An event as a subset of points within an outcome set (the same as in Figure 3-1(a)).

Table 3-1   Several Events in the Experiment of Figure 3-1a
(Planning 3 Children)

Three alternative ways of naming an event			
(1) Arbitrary Symbol for Event	(2) Verbal Description	(3) Outcome List	(4) Probability
E	At least 2 boys	$\{e_1, e_2, e_3, e_5\}$	4/8
F	Second child a boy followed by a girl	$\{e_2, e_6\}$	2/8
G	Fewer than 2 boys	$\{e_4, e_6, e_7, e_8\}$	4/8
H	All the same sex	$\{e_1, e_8\}$	2/8
I	No boys	$\{e_8\}$	1/8
I_1	Exactly 1 boy	$\{e_4, e_6, e_7\}$	3/8
I_2	Exactly 2 boys	$\{e_2, e_3, e_5\}$	3/8
I_3	Exactly 3 boys	$\{e_1\}$	1/8
J	Less than 2 girls	$\{e_1, e_2, e_3, e_5\}$	4/8

summing over just those outcomes e_i which are in E. We again note an analogy between mass and probability: the mass of an object is the sum of the masses of all the atoms in that object; the probability of an event is the sum of the probabilities of all the outcomes included in that event.

Various events are considered in Table 3-1; all the outcomes included in each event are listed in column 3. Since the probability of each outcome is 1/8, the calculation of the probability of each event in column 4 is very simple. The value of specifying an event by its outcome list is further evident when we consider the first and last events in this table. In fact, they are the same event; although this may not have been clear immediately from the description, the list makes it obvious.

(c) Combining Events

In planning their 3 children, the couple may be disappointed if there are fewer than 2 boys, or if all are of the same sex; referring to Table 3-1, this is the event "G or H," also denoted by $G \cup H$, and read "G union H." From the lists of Table 3-1 it can be seen that

$$G \cup H = \{e_4, e_6, e_7, e_8, e_1\}.$$

In general, for any two events G, H, we define

$G \cup H \overset{\Delta}{=}$ set of points which are in G, or in H, or in both.   (3-10)

A little abstract art in Figure 3-3a, called a Venn diagram, illustrates this definition. Since five of the eight equiprobable outcomes are included in $G \cup H$, its probability is 5/8.

The couple would be doubly disappointed in the event "G and H," that is, if there were fewer than 2 boys, *and* all children were the same sex. This is clearly a much more restricted combined event, consisting only of those outcomes that satisfy *both* G and H. Using a Venn diagram as in Figure 3-3b, we see that there is only one outcome [$e_8 = (GGG)$] that qualifies. This combined event is denoted by $G \cap H$, and is read[3] "G intersect H" as well as "G and H." The lists in Table 3-1 confirm that

$$G \cap H = \{e_8\}$$

since the only outcome appearing in both G and H is e_8. Hence the probability of $G \cap H$ is 1/8. In general, for any 2 events G, H, we define

$$G \cap H \overset{\Delta}{=} \text{set of points which are in both } G \text{ and } H. \qquad (3\text{-}11)$$

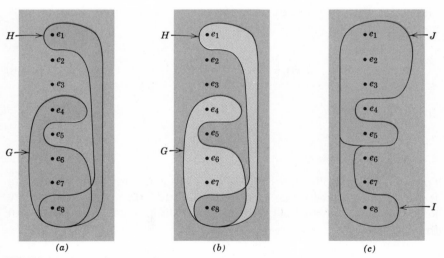

(*a*)	(*b*)	(*c*)

FIGURE 3-3   Venn diagrams, illustrating probability of combined events. (The rectangle in each case represents the whole sample space; hence the probability of all points (or outcomes) within a rectangle sum to 1.) (a) $G \cup H$ shaded, "G or H"; (b) $G \cap H$ shaded, "G and H"; (c) $I \cup J$ shaded.

---

[3] To remember when $\cup$ or $\cap$ is used, it may help to recall that $\cup$ stands for "Union," and that $\cap$ resembles the letter "A" in the word "And." These technical symbols are used to avoid the ambiguity that might occur if we used ordinary English. For example, the sentence "$E \cup F$ has 5 points" has a precise meaning, but the informal "E or F has 5 points" is ambiguous.

(d) Probabilities of Combined Events

We have already shown how Pr $(G \cup H)$ may be found from the Venn diagram in Figure 3-3. Now we should like to develop a formula. First consider a pair of events that do not have any points in common, such as I and J from Table 3-1. (We also say that they are mutually exclusive, or do not overlap). From Figure 3-3c it is obvious that

$$\text{Pr } (I \cup J) = \text{Pr } (I) + \text{Pr } (J) \qquad (3\text{-}12)$$
$$\tfrac{5}{8} = \tfrac{1}{8} + \tfrac{4}{8}$$

But this simple addition does not always work. For example

$$\text{Pr } (G \cup H) \neq \text{Pr } (G) + \text{Pr } (H) \qquad (3\text{-}13)$$
$$\tfrac{5}{8} \neq \tfrac{2}{8} + \tfrac{4}{8}$$

What has gone wrong in this case? Since G and H overlap, in summing Pr (G) and Pr (H) we count the intersection $G \cap H$ *twice*; this is why (3-13) overestimates. This is easily corrected; subtracting $\text{Pr}(G \cap H)$ eliminates this double counting. Thus for any events G and H, it is generally true that

$$\text{Pr } (G \cup H) = \text{Pr } (G) + \text{Pr } (H) - \text{Pr } (G \cap H) \qquad (3\text{-}14)$$

In our example

$$\tfrac{5}{8} = \tfrac{4}{8} + \tfrac{2}{8} - \tfrac{1}{8}$$

Formula (3-14) applies not only to those cases where G and H overlap. It also applies in cases like (3-12) where I and J do not overlap, where Pr $(I \cap J) = 0$, and this last term in (3-14) disappears. Then we obtain the special case

$$\text{Pr } (I \cup J) = \text{Pr } (I) + \text{Pr } (J)$$
if I and J are mutually exclusive. $\qquad (3\text{-}15)$

A collection of several events is defined as mutually exclusive if there is no overlap whatsoever, i.e., if no outcome belongs to more than one event. For example, in Table 3-1, events I, I_1, and I_2 are mutually exclusive; but E, F, and I are not, because E and F overlap at e_2.

(e) Partitions and Complements

The collection of events $\{I, I_1, I_2, I_3\}$ is mutually exclusive, and also "covers" the whole sample space S. We therefore call it a partition of S. In general, we define:

> A partition of a sample space S is a collec-
> tion of mutually exclusive events $\{I, \ldots I_n\}$ (3-16)
> whose union is the whole sample space S.

$$I \cup I_1 \cup I_2 \cdots \cup I_n = S$$

Thus a partition completely divides the sample space into nonoverlapping events, as illustrated in Figure 3-4b.

In Table 3-1 note that G consists of exactly those points that are not in E. We therefore call G the "*complement* of E," or "not E," and denote it by $\overline{E}$. In general, for any event E

$$\overline{E} \triangleq \text{set of points in sample space not in } E.   \quad (3\text{-}17)$$

An event and its complement $\{E, \overline{E}\}$ form a very simple partition. Because these events are mutually exclusive, by (3-15)

$$\text{Pr}\,(E \cup \overline{E}) = \text{Pr}\,(E) + \text{Pr}\,(\overline{E}) \quad\quad (3\text{-}18)$$

and since $E \cup \overline{E}$ constitutes all of S,

$$\text{Pr}\,(E \cup \overline{E}) = 1 \quad\quad (3\text{-}19)$$

Substituting (3-19) into (3-18)

$$1 = \text{Pr}\,(E) + \text{Pr}\,(\overline{E})$$

$$\overline{\overline{\text{Pr}\,(\overline{E}) = 1 - \text{Pr}\,(E)}} \quad\quad (3\text{-}20)$$

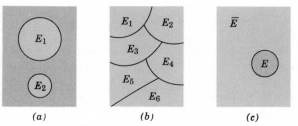

(a)   (b)   (c)

FIGURE 3-4   Venn diagrams to illustrate definitions. (a) E_1 and E_2 are mutually exclusive; (b) $E_1, E_2, \ldots, E_6$ form a partition; (c) Complement, $\overline{E}$.

As an example, consider the probability of getting at least one boy in a family of 3 children. The complement is "no boys" and is very simple to calculate. Thus

$$Pr \text{ (at least one boy)} = 1 - Pr \text{ (no boys)}$$
$$= 1 - \tfrac{1}{8}$$
$$= \tfrac{7}{8}$$

This is not the only way to answer this question, but it is by far the simplest since Pr (no boys) is so easy to evaluate. You should be on the alert for similar problems: the key words to watch for are "at least," "more than," "less then," "no more than," etc.

PROBLEMS

3-4 (a) Use a tree diagram to derive the outcome list if a blindfolded man is to draw two chips from an urn containing 5 red chips, 4 white, and 1 black. Assume he replaces the first chip before drawing the second? What is the probability that both chips will be the same color?
(b) Repeat (a), except that the first chip, once drawn, is not replaced.

3-5 Use Venn diagrams to determine which of the following statements are true:
(a) $\overline{E \cup F} = \overline{E} \cup \overline{F}$
(b) $\overline{E \cup F} = \overline{E} \cap \overline{F}$
(c) $\overline{E \cap F} = \overline{E} \cap \overline{F}$
(d) $\overline{E \cap F} = \overline{E} \cup \overline{F}$
(The true statements are known as De Morgan's laws.)

3-6 When a penny and a nickel are tossed, the outcome set could be written as a tree or as a rectangular array:

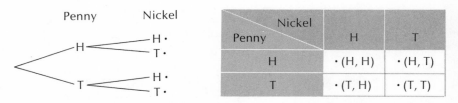

In the same two ways, list the outcome set when a pair of dice are thrown—one red, one white. Then calculate the probability of
(a) A total of 4 dots.
(b) A total of 7 dots.
(c) A total of 7 or 11 dots (as in Problem 3-3).
(d) A double.

(e) A total of at least 8 dots.

(f) A double 3.

(g) A 1 on one die, 5 on the other.

(h) Would you get the same answers if the dice were both painted white? In particular, compare the chance of a {3, 3} combination to the chance of a {1, 5} combination.

3-7 Suppose a coin was unfairly tossed 3 times in such a way that over the long run, the following relative frequencies were observed

e	Pr(e)
· (H H H)	.15
· (H H T)	.10
· (H T H)	.10
· (H T T)	.15
· (T H H)	.15
· (T H T)	.10
· (T T H)	.10
· (T T T)	.15

Suppose we are interested in the following events:

G: fewer than 2 heads

H: all coins the same

K: fewer than 2 tails

L: some coins different

Find the following probabilities.

(a) $\Pr(G)$; $\Pr(H)$; $\Pr(G \cup H)$; $\Pr(G \cap H)$

(b) Verify that (3-14) holds true.

(c) $\Pr(K)$; $\Pr(L)$; $\Pr(K \cup L)$; $\Pr(K \cap L)$

(d) Verify that (3-14) holds true.

3-8 In planning a family of 4 children, a couple is interested in the following events:

A: all the same sex

B: precisely 1 boy

C: at least 2 boys

(a) Evaluate $\Pr(A) + \Pr(B) + \Pr(C)$. Do these events form a partition?

(b) Redefine A as "all girls." Do A, B, C now form a partition? What is $\Pr(A) + \Pr(B) + \Pr(C)$?

3-9 Continuing Problem 3-8, let Y denote the number of changes in

sex sequence. For example, the outcome (BGBB) may be written (B/G/BB), where the two changes are indicated by slashes; similarly, the outcome (B/GGG) has only 1 change. What is
(a) $\Pr(Y = 1)$
(b) $\Pr(Y = 2)$

3-10 (a) What is the probability of at least one boy in 4 children?

(b) What is the probability of at least one boy in 10 children?

⇒3-11 Suppose a class of 100 students consists of several groups, in the following proportions:

	Men	Women
Taking math	17%	38%
Not taking math	23%	22%

If a student is chosen by lot to be class president, what is the chance the student will be:
(a) A man?
(b) A woman?
(c) Taking math?
(d) A man, or taking math?
(e) A man, and taking math?
(f) If the class president in fact turned out to be a man, what is the chance that he is taking math? Not taking math?

⇒3-12 The men of a certain college engage in various sports in the following proportions:

Football, 30% of all men.

Basketball, 20%.

Baseball, 20%.

Both football and basketball, 5%.

Both football and baseball, 10%.

Both basketball and baseball, 5%.

All three sports, 2%.

If a man is chosen by lot for an interview, use a Venn diagram to calculate the chance that he will be:
(a) An athlete (playing at least one sport)?
(b) A football player only?
(c) A football player or a baseball player?

If an *athlete* is chosen by lot, what is the chance that he will be:

(d) A football player only?

(e) A football player or a baseball player?

(f) Use your result in (a) to extend (3-14) to an expression for Pr $(G \cup H \cup I)$.

3-4   CONDITIONAL PROBABILITY

Continuing with the example of planning 3 children, suppose that the family is completed, and we are informed that there were fewer than 2 boys, i.e., that event G had occurred. Given this condition, what is the probability that event I (no boys) occurred? This is an example of "conditional probability," and is denoted as Pr (I/G), or "the probability of I, given G." By keeping in mind that our relevant outcome set in Figure 3-5a is reduced to G, it is evident that Pr $(I/G) = 1/4$.

The second illustration in Figure 3-5b shows the conditional probability of H (all the same sex), given G (less than 2 boys). Our knowledge of G means that the only relevant part of H is $H \cap G$ (no boys) and thus Pr $(H/G) = 1/4$. This example is equivalent to the preceding one; we are just asking the same question in two different ways.

Suppose Pr (G), Pr (H), and Pr $(G \cap H)$ have already been computed for the original sample space S. It will be convenient to have a formula for Pr (H/G) in terms of these that holds for any events H and G. We

FIGURE 3-5   Venn diagrams to illustrate conditional probability. (a) Pr(I/G). (b) Pr(H/G). Note Pr(H/G) is identical to Pr(I/G).

therefore turn to the definition (3-1) of probability as relative frequency. We imagine repeating the experiment n times, with G occurring $n(G)$ times, of which H also occurs $n(H \cap G)$ times. The ratio[4] is the conditional relative frequency, and in the limit

$$\Pr(H/G) \triangleq \lim \frac{n(H \cap G)}{n(G)} \qquad (3\text{-}21)$$

On dividing numerator and denominator by n, we obtain

$$\Pr(H/G) = \lim \frac{n(H \cap G)/n}{n(G)/n}$$

$$\Pr(H/G) = \frac{\Pr(H \cap G)}{\Pr(G)} \qquad (3\text{-}22)$$

This formula is often used in a slightly different form, obtained by cross multiplying by $\Pr(G)$ and noting of course that $\Pr(H \cap G) = \Pr(G \cap H)$

$$\Pr(G \cap H) = \Pr(G)\Pr(H/G) \qquad (3\text{-}23)$$

PROBLEMS

3-13 In this problem, we shall again simulate the family planning problem. Flip three coins over and over again (or use the random digits three at a time, letting an even number be H, and an odd number be T). Record your results in the following table:

Trial Number n	Does G (less than 2 heads) occur?	Accumulated Frequency $n(G)$	If G occurs, does H (all coins the same) also occur?	Accumulated Frequency $n(H \cap G)$	Conditional Relative Frequency $n(H \cap G)/n(G)$
1	No				
2	Yes	1	Yes	1	1.00
3	No				
4	Yes	2	No	1	.50
5	Yes	3	Yes	2	.67
.					
.					
.					

---

[4]We shall always assume that any probability used as a divisor is nonzero, of course. Thus $\Pr(G)$ in (3-22), and $n(G)$ in (3-21) are assumed to be nonzero, as is $\Pr(F)$ in (3-25).

After 50 trials, is the relative frequency $n(H \cap G)/n(G)$ close to the probability calculated theoretically in the previous section? (If not, it is because of insufficient trials, so pool the data from the whole class.)

3-14 Using the unfair coins and definitions of Problem 3-7, calculate
   (a) $\Pr(H/G)$ (c) $\Pr(K/L)$
   (b) $\Pr(\overline{H}/G)$ (d) $\Pr(L/K)$

3-15 (a) A consumer may buy brand X or brand Y but not both. The probability of buying brand X is .06, and brand Y is .15. Given that the consumer bought either X or Y, what is the probability that he bought brand X?
   (b) If events A and B are mutually exclusive, is it always true that

$$\Pr(A/A \cup B) = \frac{\Pr(A)}{\Pr(A) + \Pr(B)}$$

3-16 A bowl contains 3 defective light bulbs (D) and 2 good bulbs (G). A sample of 2 bulbs is drawn. List a convenient sample space. For each of the following events, diagram the subset of outcomes included and find its probability.
   (a) Second bulb is D.
   (b) First bulb is D.
   (c) Second bulb is D, if the first bulb is D.
   (d) First bulb is D, if the second bulb is D.
   (e) Both bulbs are D.
   Then note the following features, which are perhaps intuitively obvious also:
   (f) The answers to (a) and (b) agree, as do the answers to (c) and (d).
   (g) Show that the answer to (e) can be found alternatively by applying (3-23) to parts (b) and (c).
   (h) Extend (g): if 3 bulbs are drawn what is the probability that all 3 are D?

3-17 Two cards are drawn from an ordinary deck. What is the probability that:
   (a) They are both aces?
   (b) They are the two black aces?
   (c) They are both honor cards (ace, king, queen, jack or ten)?

3-18 A poker hand (5 cards) is drawn from an ordinary deck of cards. What is the chance of drawing, in order,
   (a) 2 aces, then 3 kings?
   (b) 2 aces, then 2 kings, finally a queen?
   (c) 4 aces, then a king?

What is the chance of drawing, in any order whatsoever,

(d) 4 aces and a king?

(e) 4 aces?

(f) "Four of a kind" (i.e., 4 aces, or 4 kings, or 4 jacks, etc.)?

If the 5 cards are drawn with replacement (i.e., each card is replaced in the deck before drawing the next card, so that it is no longer a real poker deal), what is the probability of drawing, in any order,

(g) Exactly 4 aces?

3-19 A supply of 10 light bulbs contains 2 defective bulbs. If the bulbs are picked up in random order, what is the chance that

(a) The first two bulbs are good?

(b) The first defective bulb was picked 6th?

(c) The first defective bulb was not picked until the 9th?

⟹3-20 Two dice are thrown, and we are interested in the following events:

E: first die is 5

F: total is 7

G: total is 10

By calculating the probabilities using Venn diagrams, show that:

(a) $\Pr(F/E) = \Pr(F)$.

(b) $\Pr(G/E) \neq \Pr(G)$.

(c) $\Pr(E/F) = \Pr(E)$.

(d) Would you guess that (c) is logically related to (a), or just an accident?

3-21 A company employs 100 persons—75 men and 25 women. The accounting department provides jobs for 12% of the men and 20% of the women. If a name is chosen at random from the accounting department, what is the probability that it is a man? That it is a woman?

⟹3-22 (Bayes' Theorem). In a population of workers, suppose 40% are grade school graduates, 50% are high school graduates, and 10% are college graduates. Among the grade school graduates, 10% are unemployed, among the high school graduates, 5% are unemployed, and among the college graduates 2% are unemployed.

If a worker is chosen at random and found to be unemployed, what is the probability that he is a college graduate?

Since this problem is important as an introduction to Chapter 15, its answer is given in full for you to read after attempting your own solution.

Answer. Think of probability as proportion of the population, if you like, in the following Venn diagram:

In the new (red) sample space, (3-22) gives

$$Pr\,(C_3/E) = \frac{.002}{.067} = .03$$

Alternatively, you could have solved this problem using a tree diagram.

Notes on Bayes' Theorem. This is an example of Bayes' theorem, which may be generally stated as follows:

Certain *"causes"* (class of education) $C_1, C_2, \ldots C_m$, have *prior probabilities* Pr (C_i). In a sense the causes produce an *"effect"* E (unemployment) not with certainty, but with conditional probabilities Pr (E/C_i). Using conditional probability manipulations to turn this around, we calculate eventually the probability of a cause given the effect, i.e., the posterior probability Pr (C_i/E):

Given	*Deduced*
Pr (C_i)	
	→ Pr (C_i/E)
Pr (E/C_i)	

$\Rightarrow$3-23 In a certain country, it rains 40% of the days and shines 60% of the days. A barometer manufacturer, in testing his instrument in the lab, has found that it sometimes errs: on rainy days it erroneously predicts "shine" 10% of the time, and on shiny days it erroneously predicts "rain" 30% of the time.

(a) In predicting tomorrow's weather before looking at the barometer, the (prior) chance of rain is 40%. *After* looking at the barometer and seeing it predict "rain," what is the (posterior) chance of rain?

(b) What is the posterior chance of rain if an improved barometer (error rates of 10% and 20% respectively) predicts "rain"?

(c) What is the posterior chance of shine if the improved barometer predicts "rain"?

3-5 INDEPENDENCE

In Problem 3-20 we noticed that $\Pr(F/E) = \Pr(F)$. This means that the chance of F, knowing E, is exactly the same as the chance of F, without knowing E. That is, knowledge of E does not change the probability of F at all. It seems reasonable, therefore, to call F statistically independent of E. In fact, this is the basis for the general definition:

An event F is called *statistically independent*

of an event E iff[5] $\Pr(F/E) = \Pr(F)$ (3-24)

Of course, in the case of events G and E in Problem 3-20, where $\Pr(G/E) \neq \Pr(G)$, we would say that G was statistically *dependent* on E. In this case, knowledge of E changes the probability of G.

We now develop the consequences of F being independent of E. According to (3-23),

$$\Pr(E \cap F) = \Pr(E) \Pr(F/E)$$

When we substitute (3-24) we obtain

For independent events,

$$\Pr(E \cap F) = \Pr(E) \Pr(F)$$ (3-25)

---

    [5]iff is an abbreviation for "if, and only if." Although the "only if" part should be understood implicitly in definitions, it helps to write it out explicitly this way.

In other words, for independent events, we may apply the intuitively appealing multiplication rule, just as we did, say, in calculating probabilities in a tree diagram (the first occurrence of independence that we met).

Furthermore, (3-25) implies that

$$\frac{Pr\ (E \cap F)}{Pr\ (F)} = Pr\ (E)$$

i.e.,

$$Pr\ (E/F) = Pr\ (E) \qquad (3-26)$$

That is, E is independent of F. In other words, the result in Problem 3-20(c) was no accident: whenever F is independent of E, then E must be independent of F. In view of this symmetry, we may henceforth simply state that E and F are statistically independent of each other, whenever any of the three logically equivalent statements (3-24), (3-25), or (3-26) is true. Usually, statement (3-25) is the preferred form, in view of its symmetry. Sometimes, in fact, this "multiplication formula" is taken as the definition of statistical independence. But this is just a matter of taste.

Notice that so far we have insisted on the phrase "*statistical* independence," in order to distinguish it from other forms of independence—philosophical, logical, or whatever. For example, we might be tempted to say that in our dice problem, F was "somehow" dependent on E because the total of the two tosses depends on the first die. This vague notion of dependence is of no use to the statistician, and will be considered no further. But let it serve as a warning that *statistical* independence is a very precise concept, defined by (3-24), (3-25), or (3-26) above.

Now that we clearly understand statistical independence, and agree that this is the only kind of independence we shall consider, we shall run no risk of confusion if we are lazy and drop the word "statistical." Our results so far are summarized as follows:

	$Pr\ (E \cup F)$	$Pr\ (E \cap F)$
general theorem	$= Pr\ (E) + Pr\ (F) - Pr\ (E \cap F)$	$= Pr\ (E)\ Pr\ (F/E)$
special case	$= Pr\ (E) + Pr\ (F)$ if E and F are mutually exclusive; i.e., if $Pr\ (E \cap F) = 0$	$= Pr\ (E)\ Pr\ (F)$ if E and F are independent; i.e., if $Pr\ (F/E) = Pr\ (F)$

PROBLEMS

3-24 Three coins are fairly tossed, and we define:

E_1: first two coins are heads;

E_2: last coin is a head;

E_3: all three coins are heads.

Try to answer the following questions intuitively (does knowledge of the condition affect your betting odds?). Then verify by drawing the sample space and calculating the relevant probabilities for (3-24).

(a) Are E_1 and E_2 independent?

(b) Are E_1 and E_3 independent?

3-25 Repeat Problem 3-24 using the three unfair coins whose sample space is as follows (as in Problem 3-7).

e	Pr (e)
· (H H H)	.15
· (H H T)	.10
· (H T H)	.10
· (H T T)	.15
· (T H H)	.15
· (T H T)	.10
· (T T H)	.10
· (T T T)	.15

3-26 If E and F are any 2 mutually exclusive events, what can be said about their independence?

3-27 A certain electronic mechanism has 2 lights which have been observed on or off with the following long-run relative frequencies:

Light 1 \ Light 2	On	Off
On	.15	.45
Off	.10	.30

This table means, for example, that both lights were simultaneously off 30 percent of the time.

(a) Is "light 1 on" independent of "light 2 on"?

(b) Is "light 1 off" independent of "light 2 on"?

*(c)[6] Are the answers to (a) and (b) logically related, or just a fluke? (Try changing the probabilities in the table so as to keep (a) true; then is (b) true also? If not, you have found the "counterexample" that shows it was a fluke. If (b) does turn out to be true in several cases, can you prove it will *always* be true, by establishing the logical relation—as we did in (3-26) for example?)

3-28 A single card is drawn from a deck of cards, and we define:

$$E: \text{it is an ace}$$

$$F: \text{it is a heart.}$$

Are E and F independent, when we use
(a) An ordinary 52-card deck?
(b) An ordinary deck, with all the spades deleted?
(c) An ordinary deck, with all the spades from 2 to 9 deleted?

3-6   OTHER VIEWS OF PROBABILITY

In Section 3-1 we defined probability as the limit of relative frequency. There are several other approaches, including *symmetric* probability, *axiomatic* probability, and *subjective* probability.

(a) Symmetric Probability

The physical symmetry of a fair die assures us that all six of its outcomes are equally probable. Thus

$$\Pr(e_1) = \Pr(e_2) = \cdots = \Pr(e_6)$$

In order that these six probabilities sum to one, each must be 1/6. In general, for an experiment having N equally likely outcomes or points, for each point e_j

$$\Pr(e_j) = \frac{1}{N}$$

Then, for an event E consisting of N_E points, the probability is given by (3-9) as

$$\Pr(E) = \sum \Pr(e_j) = N_E\left(\frac{1}{N}\right)$$

---

[6]Starred problems are optional, since they are more difficult and/or theoretical.

where the summation Σ extends only over points e_j in E (N_E in number). Thus, for equally probable outcomes

$$Pr\,(E) = \frac{N_E}{N} \tag{3-27}$$

For example, in rolling a fair die what is the probability that the number of dots is an even number? Since this event consists of three of the six equiprobable elementary outcomes (2, 4, or 6 dots), its probability is 3/6.

Symmetric probability theory begins with (3-27) as the definition of probability, and gives a simpler development than our earlier relative frequency approach. However, our earlier analysis was more general; although the examples we cited often involved equiprobable outcomes, the theory we developed was in no way limited to such cases. In reviewing it, you should confirm that it may be applied whether or not outcomes are equiprobable; special attention should be given to those cases (e.g., Problem 3-26) where outcomes were not equiprobable.

Not only is symmetric probability limited because it lacks generality; it also has a major philosophical weakness. Note how the definition of probability in (3-27) involves the phrase "equally probable"; we are guilty of circular reasoning.

Our own relative frequency approach to probability suffers from the same philosophical weakness. We might ask what sort of limit is meant in equation (3-1)? It is logically possible that the relative frequency n_1/n behaves badly, even in the limit; for example, no matter how often we toss a die, it is just conceivable that the ace will keep turning up every time, making $\lim n_1/n = 1$. Therefore, we should qualify equation (3-1) by stating that the limit occurs with high *probability*, not logical certainty. In using the concept of probability in the definition of probability, we are again guilty of circular reasoning.

(b) Axiomatic Objective Probability

The only philosophically sound approach, in fact, is an abstract axiomatic approach. In a simplified version, the following properties are taken as axioms:

axioms

$$
\begin{aligned}
&Pr\,(e_i) \geq 0 &&\text{(3-2) repeated} \\
&Pr\,(e_1) + Pr\,(e_2) \cdots + Pr\,(e_N) = 1 &&\text{(3-4) repeated} \\
&Pr\,(E) = \sum Pr\,(e_i) &&\text{(3-9) repeated}
\end{aligned}
$$

Then the other properties, such as (3-1), (3-3), and (3-20) are theorems derived from these axioms—with axioms and theorems together comprising a mathematical model that allows us to analyze and predict physical situations such as tossing dice, etc.

Equation (3-1) is a particularly important theorem, and is known as the *law of large numbers*. While its proof is too complicated for this elementary text, (3-3) and (3-20) may be proved very easily, and will illustrate how nicely this axiomatic theory can be developed: for any event E,

$$
\begin{array}{ll}
0 \leq \text{Pr}(E) & \text{(3-28), like (3-2)} \\
\text{Pr}(E) \leq 1 & \text{(3-29), like (3-3)} \\
\text{Pr}(\overline{E}) = 1 - \text{Pr}(E) & \text{(3-30), repeating (3-20)}
\end{array}
$$

proof   According to axioms (3-9) and (3-2), $\text{Pr}(E)$ is the sum of positive terms, and is therefore positive; thus (3-28) is proved.

To prove (3-30), we write out axiom (3-4):

$$
\underbrace{\text{Pr}(e_1) + \text{Pr}(e_2) +}_{\text{Terms for } E} \underbrace{\cdots + \text{Pr}(e_N)}_{\text{Terms for } \overline{E}} = 1
$$

According to (3-9), this is just

$$
\text{Pr}(E) + \text{Pr}(\overline{E}) = 1 \tag{3-31}
$$

from which (3-30) follows.

In (3-28) we proved that every probability is positive or zero. In particular $\text{Pr}(\overline{E})$ is positive or zero; substituting this into (3-31) finally ensures that

$$
\text{Pr}(E) \leq 1 \qquad \text{(3-29) proved.}
$$

(c) Subjective Probability

Sometimes called personal probability, this is an attempt to deal with unique historical events that cannot be repeated, even conceptually, and hence cannot be given any frequency interpretation. For example, consider events such as a doubling in the stock market average within the next decade, or the overthrow of a certain government within the next month. These events are described by the layman as "likely" or "unlikely," even though there is no hope of estimating this by observing their relative frequency. Nevertheless, their likelihood vitally influences policy decisions, and as a consequence must be estimated in some rough-and-ready way. It is only then that decisions can be made on what risks are worth taking.

To answer this practical need, an axiomatic theory of personal probability has been developed. Roughly speaking, personal probability may be interpreted as the odds one would give in betting on an event; we shall find this a useful concept later in decision theory.

Review Problems

3-29 A tetrahedral (four-sided) die has been loaded. Find $Pr(e_4)$ if possible, given the following conditions. (If the problem is impossible, state so.)
(a) $Pr(e_1) = .2$; $Pr(e_2) = .4$; $Pr(e_3) = .1$
(b) $Pr(e_1) = .4$; $Pr(e_2) = .4$; $Pr(e_3) = .3$
(c) $Pr(e_1) = .6$; $Pr(e_3) = .2$
(d) $Pr(e_1) = .7$; $Pr(e_2) = .5$

3-30 In a family of 3 children, what is the chance of
(a) At least one girl?
(b) At least 2 girls?
(c) At least 2 girls, given at least one girl?
(d) At least 2 girls, given that the eldest child is a girl?

3-31 Suppose that the last 3 customers out of a restaurant all lose their hat-checks, so that the girl has to hand back their 3 hats in random order. What is the probability
(a) That no man will get the right hat?
(b) That exactly 1 man will?
(c) That exactly 2 men will?
(d) That all 3 men will?

3-32 Find (without bothering to multiply out the final answer) the probability that
(a) A group of 3 people (picked at random) all have different birthdays?
(b) A group of 30 people all have different birthdays?
(c) In a group of 30 people there are at least two people with the same birthday?
(d) What assumptions did you make above?

3-33 A bag contains a thousand coins, one of which has heads on both sides. A coin is drawn at random. What is the probability that it is the loaded coin, if it is flipped and turns up heads without fail
(a) 3 times in a row?
(b) 10 times in a row?
(c) 20 times in a row?

3-34 Repeat Problem 3-33 when the loaded coin in the bag has both H and T faces, but is biased so that the probability of H is 3/4.

3-35 The long experience of a clinic in diagnosing patients referred to them is that 1/10 have disease A, 2/10 have disease B, and 7/10 are essentially in good health. Of those with disease A, 9/10 have headaches; of those with disease B, 1/2 have headaches; and of those in good health, 1/20 have headaches. If you are diagnosing a patient in this clinic, and he has a headache, what is the probability that he has

(a) Disease A
(b) Disease B
(c) Good health.

3-36 (a) If you had your choice today between the following two bets, which would you take?

Bet 1 (Election Bet)
If the Democratic candidate wins the next presidential election, you will then win a $10,000 prize (and win nothing otherwise).
Bet 2 (Jar Bet)
A chip will be drawn at random from a jar containing 1 black chip and 999 white chips. If the chip turns out black, you will then win the $10,000 prize (and win nothing otherwise).

(b) Repeat choice (a), with a slight change—make the composition of the urn the opposite extreme: 999 black chips and 1 white chip.

(c) Obviously your answers in parts (a) and (b) depended upon your subjective estimate of American politics; there were no objective "right answers." However, the odds in the urn were so lopsided that there undoubtedly is widespread agreement in part (a) to prefer the election bet, and in part (b) to prefer the jar bet. The question is: as you gradually increase the black chips from 1 to 999, at what point do you become indifferent between the two bets? Is it reasonable to call this your subjective probability of a Democrat winning?

(d) What is your subjective probability that
  (1) the Dow-Jones average (of certain stock market prices) will advance at least 10% by the end of a year (365 days);
  (2) the world's population will double or more by the end of this century;
  (3) the air pollution in Manhattan will be worse at the end of 10 years than it is now;
  (3) the Mets will win another World Series before 1980.

Chapter 4

RANDOM VARIABLES AND THEIR DISTRIBUTIONS

We must believe in luck. For how else can we explain the success of those we don't like?

Jean Cocteau

DISCRETE RANDOM VARIABLES

In the planning of 3 children in Figure 3-1a, suppose the couple is primarily interested in the number of boys. This is an example of a *random variable* and is customarily denoted by a capital letter:

$$X = \text{the number of boys}$$

The possible values of X are 0, 1, 2, 3; however, they are not equally likely. To find what the probabilities are, it is necessary to examine the original sample space, repeated in Figure 4-1. Thus, for example, the event "one boy" ($X = 1$) consists of 3 of the 8 equiprobable outcomes; hence its probability is 3/8. Similarly, the probability of each of the other events is computed. Thus in Figure 4-1 we obtain the probability distribution of X, shown in color.

The mathematical definition of a random variable is "a numerical-valued function defined over a sample space." But for our purposes we can be less abstract; it is sufficient to observe that

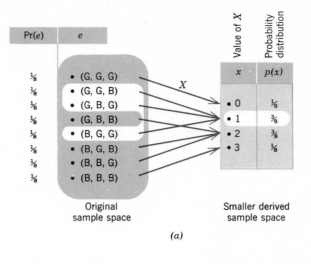

Original sample space   Smaller derived sample space

(a)

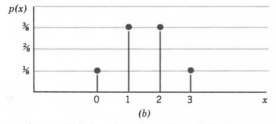

(b)

FIGURE 4-1   (a) The random variable X = "number of boys." (b) Graph of its probability distribution.

> A discrete random variable takes on various values with probabilities specified by its probability distribution.[1]   (4-1)

In the general case of defining a probability distribution, as shown in Figure 4-2, we begin in the original sample space by considering events such as $(X = 0)$, $(X = 1)$, . . . , in general $(X = x)$; note that capital X represents the random variable while small x represents a specific value

---

[1]Although the intuitive definition (4-1) will serve our purposes well enough, it is not always as satisfactory as the more rigorous mathematical definition which stresses the random variable's relation to the original sample space. Thus, for example, the random variable Y = the number of girls, is seen to be a different random variable from X = the number of boys. Yet X and Y have the *same probability distribution,* and anyone who used the loose definition (4-1) might be deceived into thinking that they were the *same random variable.* In conclusion, there is more to a random variable than its probability function.

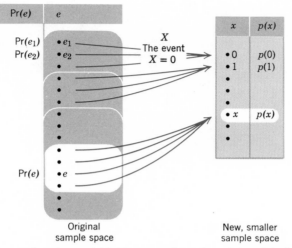

FIGURE 4-2   A general random variable X as a transformation of the original sample space to a new, condensed sample space shown as $0, 1, 2, \ldots$, the set of positive integers. (To be more general, however, we should allow negative, fractional, and even irrational values as well. Thus our notation should be $x_1, x_2, \ldots, x_i, \ldots$ rather than $0, 1, 2, \ldots, x, \ldots$.)

it may take. For these events we calculate the probabilities and denote[2] them $p(0), p(1), \ldots p(x) \ldots$. This probability distribution $p(x)$ may be presented equally well in any of the 3 customary forms for a function:

1. Table form, as in Figure 4-1a.
2. Graph form, as in Figure 4-1b.
3. By formula, as in Equation (4-7) given later on.

The usefulness of a random variable is clear from Figures 4-1 and 4-2: the original sample space (outcome set) is reduced to a much smaller and more convenient numerical sample space. The original sample space is introduced to enable us to calculate the probability distribution $p(x)$ for the new space; having served its purpose, the old unwieldy space is then forgotten. The interesting questions can be answered very easily in the new space. For example, referring to Figure 4-3, what is the probability of 1 boy or fewer? We simply add up the relevant probabilities in the new sample space

$$\Pr (X \leq 1) = p(0) + p(1) = \tfrac{1}{8} + \tfrac{3}{8} = \tfrac{1}{2} \tag{4-2}$$

---

[2]This notation, like any other, may be regarded simply as an abbreviation for convenience. Thus, for example, $p(1)$ is short for $\Pr (X = 1)$, which in turn is short for "the probability that the number of boys is one."

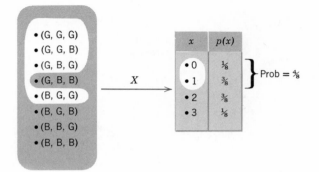

FIGURE 4-3   The event $X \leq 1$ in both sample spaces, illustrating the easier calculation in the new sample space.

The answer could have been found, but with more trouble, in the original sample space.

PROBLEMS

4-1   (Note how similar this problem is to Problems 3-8 and 3-9.)
In planning a family of 4 children, find the probability distribution of
(a) $X =$ the number of boys
(b) $Y =$ the number of changes in sex sequence.

4-2   When 2 fair dice are thrown, find the probability distribution of
(a)   the total number of dots, $S = X_1 + X_2$
(b)   the difference (absolute value) between the numbers, $D = |X_1 - X_2|$.

⟹4-3   To review Chapter 2, consider the planning of 3 children, and again let $X =$ the number of boys (0, 1, 2, 3). Simulate this "experiment" either by tossing 3 coins, or by using the random numbers in Appendix Table IIa.
Repeat this experiment 50 times, recording the frequency table of X. Then calculate
(a)   the relative frequency distribution
(b)   the mean $\bar{X}$, using (2-1b)
(c)   the mean squared deviation MSD, using (2-5b)
(d)   the variance s^2.

⟹4-4   If the experiment in Problem 4-3 were repeated millions of times (rather than 50 times), to what value would the calculated quantities tend?

4-2   MEAN AND VARIANCE

In Chapter 3 we defined probability as limiting relative frequency. Now we notice the close relation between the relative frequency distribution observed in Problems 4-3 and 4-4, and the probability distribution calculated in Figure 4-1, for planning 3 children: if the sample size were increased without limit, the relative frequency distribution would settle down to the probability distribution.

From the relative frequency distribution we calculated the mean $\overline{X}$ and variance s^2 of the *sample*[3]. It is natural to calculate analogous values from the probability distribution, and call them the mean μ and variance σ^2 of the probability distribution $p(x)$, or of the random variable X itself (or even call them μ and σ^2 of the conceptual *population* of all possible repetitions of this experiment, of which we chose a sample of 50). Thus, we define

$$\text{Population mean, } \mu \triangleq \sum_{x} x \, p(x) \qquad \begin{array}{l} (4\text{-}3) \\ \text{like } (2\text{-}1b) \end{array}$$

$$\text{variance, } \sigma^2 \triangleq \sum_{x} (x - \mu)^2 \, p(x) \qquad \begin{array}{l} (4\text{-}4) \\ \text{like } (2\text{-}5b) \end{array}$$

Here we are following the usual custom of reserving *Greek* letters[4] for *population* values. The computation of σ^2 can be often simplified by using the formula[5]

$$\sigma^2 = \sum x^2 p(x) - \mu^2 \qquad (4\text{-}5)$$

———————

[3] Strictly speaking, we calculated MSD as well as s^2. However, as $n \to \infty$, they become indistinguishable.

[4] μ is the Greek equivalent of m for mean, and σ the Greek equivalent of s for standard deviation.

[5] *Proof that (4-5) is equivalent to (4-4).* Reexpress (4-4) as:

$$\sigma^2 = \sum (x^2 - 2\mu x + \mu^2) p(x)$$

and noting that μ is a constant,

$$\sigma^2 = \sum x^2 \, p(x) - 2\mu \sum x \, p(x) + \mu^2 \sum p(x)$$

Since $\sum x \, p(x) = \mu$ and $\sum p(x) = 1$,

$$\sigma^2 = \sum x^2 \, p(x) - 2\mu(\mu) + \mu^2(1)$$

$$= \sum x^2 \, p(x) - \mu^2 \qquad (4\text{-}5) \text{ proved}$$

Table 4-1 Calculation of the Mean and Variance of X = number of boys

Given Probability Distribution		Calculation of μ using (4-3)	Calculation of σ^2 using (4-4)			Easier calculation of σ^2 using (4-5); multiply columns (1) and (3)
(1) x	(2) $p(x)$	(3) $x\,p(x)$	(4) $(x - \mu)$	(5) $(x - \mu)^2$	(6) $(x - \mu)^2\,p(x)$	(7) $x^2\,p(x)$
0	1/8	0	$-3/2$	9/4	9/32	0
1	3/8	3/8	$-1/2$	1/4	3/32	3/8
2	3/8	6/8	$+1/2$	1/4	3/32	12/8
3	1/8	3/8	$+3/2$	9/4	9/32	9/8
		$\mu = 12/8$ $= 1.5$			$\sigma^2 = 24/32$ $= .75$	$\sum x^2\,p(x) = 24/8$ $\mu^2 = 18/8$ difference $\sigma^2 = 6/8$ ✓

For the number of boys X in a family of 3 children, we compute μ and σ^2 in Table 4-1, which is analogous to Table 2-4.

Since a clear distinction must be made between sample and population values (especially for the argument in Chapters 6 and 7), we emphasize: μ is called the population mean since it is based on the conceptual population of all possible repetitions of the experiment; on the other hand, we call $\overline{X}$ the sample mean since it is based on a mere sample drawn from the parent population. Similarly σ^2 and s^2 represent population and sample variance, respectively.

Since the definitions of μ and σ parallel those of $\overline{X}$ and s, we find parallel interpretations. We continue to think of the mean μ as a weighted average, using probability weights rather than relative frequency weights. The mean is also a fulcrum and center. The standard deviation is a measure of spread.

When a random variable is linearly transformed, the new mean and variance behave in exactly the same way as when sample observations were transformed in Section 2-5 (the proof is quite analogous and is left to Problem 4-24). For future reference, we state these results in Table 4-2. We could write out verbally all the information in this table, working across the rows, as follows: consider any random variable X, with mean

Table 4-2 Linear Transformation (Y) of a Random Variable (X)

Random Variable	Mean	Variance	Standard Deviation
X	μ_X	σ_X^2	σ_X
$Y \triangleq a + bX$	$\mu_Y = a + b\mu_X$	$\sigma_Y^2 = b^2\sigma_X^2$	$\sigma_Y = |b|\,\sigma_X$

μ_X and variance σ_X^2; if we define a new random variable Y as a linear function of X (specifically $Y = a + bX$), then the mean of Y will be $a + b\mu_X$, and its variance will be $b^2\sigma_X^2$.

PROBLEMS

4-5 Compute μ and σ^2 for the probability distributions in Problem 4-1. As a check, compute σ^2 in 2 ways—from the definition (4-4), and from the easy formula (4-5).

(4-6) Compute μ and σ^2 for the random variables of Problem 4-2.

4-7 Letting $X =$ the number of dots rolled on a fair die, find μ_X and σ_X. If $Y = 2X + 4$, calculate μ_Y and σ_Y in 2 ways:
(a) By tabulating the probability distribution of Y, then using (4-3) and (4-4).
(b) By Table 4-2.

(4-8) A bowl contains chips numbered from 1 to 5. There are five 5's, four 4's, etc. Let X denote the number on a chip drawn at random.
(a) Make a table of the probability function.
(b) Find μ_X and σ_X.

4-9 An exam consists of 4 multiple-choice questions, each with a choice of 3 answers. Let X be the number of correct answers when the student has to resort to pure guessing for each answer. Find the distribution, and the mean and variance of X.

⟹4-10 Let X be a random variable with mean μ and standard deviation σ. What are the mean and standard deviation of Z, where
$$Z = \frac{X - \mu}{\sigma}$$

4-11 Suppose that the whole population of American families in 1963 yielded the following table for family size. (This includes young, incomplete families. For simplicity, the actual data was slightly altered by truncating at 6.)

Children	0	1	2	3	4	5	6
Proportion of families	.43	.18	.17	.11	.06	.03	.02

(a) Let X be the number of children in a family selected at random. (This selection may be done by lots: imagine each family being recorded on a chip, the chips well mixed, and then one drawn.) Find μ_X and σ_X.
(b) Now let a child be selected at random (rather than a family),

and let Y be the number of children in his family. (This selection may be done by a teacher, for example, who picks a child by lot from the register of children.) What are the possible values of Y? Find the probability distribution, and compute μ_Y and σ_Y.

(c) Is μ_X or μ_Y more properly called the "average family size"?

4-3   THE BINOMIAL DISTRIBUTION

There are many types of discrete random variables. We shall study one—the binomial—as an example of how a general formula can be developed for a probability distribution.

The classical example of a binomial variable is

$$S = \text{number of heads in } n \text{ tosses of a coin}$$

In order to generalize, we shall speak of n independent "trials," each resulting in either "success" or "failure," with respective probabilities π and $(1 - \pi)$. Then the total number of successes S is called a binomial random variable.

There are many practical random variables of this type, some of which are listed in Table 4-3. We shall now derive a simple formula for the probability distribution $p(s)$. As an example, consider the special case in which we compute the probability of getting 3 heads in tossing a

Table 4-3   Examples of Binomial Variables

Trial	Success	Failure	π	n	S
Tossing a fair coin	Head	Tail	1/2	n tosses	Number of heads
Birth of a child	Boy	Girl	Practically 1/2	Family size	Number of boys in family
Throwing 2 dice	7 dots	Anything else	6/36	n throws	Number of sevens
Drawing a voter in a poll	Democrat	Republican	Proportion of Democrats in the population	Sample size	Number of Democrats in the sample
The history of one atom which may radioactively decay during a certain time period	Decay	No change	Very small	Very large, the number of atoms in the sample	Number of radioactive decays

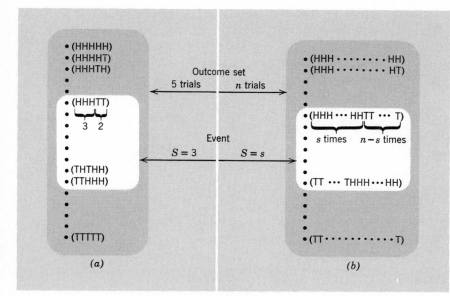

FIGURE 4-4   Computing binomial probability. (a) Special case: 3 heads in 5 tosses of a coin. (b) General case: s successes in n trials.

biased coin 5 times, as shown in Figure 4-4a. Each point in our outcome set is represented as a sequence of five of the letters H (success) or T (failure). We concentrate for example on the event "three heads" ($S = 3$), and show all outcomes that comprise this event. In each of these outcomes, H appears three times, and T twice. Since the probability of H is π and T is $(1 - \pi)$,

Then for example, the sequence	Then in general, the sequence

$$\underset{3}{\underbrace{HHH}}\ \underset{2}{\underbrace{TT}}$$

$$\underset{s \text{ times}}{\underbrace{HH \cdots H}}\ \underset{(n-s) \text{ times}}{\underbrace{TT \cdots T}}$$

has probability

$$\pi \cdot \pi \cdot \pi \cdot (1 - \pi) \cdot (1 - \pi)$$
$$= \pi^3(1 - \pi)^2$$

has probability

$$\pi \cdot \pi \cdots (1 - \pi) \cdot (1 - \pi) \cdots$$
$$= \pi^s(1 - \pi)^{n-s}$$

this simple multiplication being justified by the independence of the trials. We further note that all other outcomes in this event have the same probability. For example, the probability of HTHHT is

$$\pi \cdot (1 - \pi) \cdot \pi \cdot \pi \cdot (1 - \pi) = \pi^3(1 - \pi)^2$$

The same factors appear; they are only ordered differently.

Now we only have to determine how many such sequences (outcomes) are included in this event. This is precisely the number of ways in which the three H's and two T's can be arranged. This number of ways is denoted by $\binom{5}{3}$ or C_3^5,

and is[6]	or, in general
$$\binom{5}{3} = \frac{5!}{3!(5-3)!} = 10$$	$$\binom{n}{s} = \frac{n!}{s!(n-s)!}$$

To summarize:

The event	In general, the event
$$(S = 3)$$	$$(S = s)$$
includes	includes
$$\binom{5}{3} = 10$$	$$\binom{n}{s}$$
outcomes, each with probability	outcomes, each with probability
$$\pi^3(1-\pi)^2 = (\tfrac{1}{2})^3(\tfrac{1}{2})^2 = \tfrac{1}{32}$$	$$\pi^s(1-\pi)^{n-s}$$
Hence its probability is	Hence its probability is
$$p(3) = \Pr(X = 3)$$ $$= \binom{5}{3}\pi^3(1-\pi)^2$$ $$= \frac{5!}{3!2!}(\tfrac{1}{2})^3(\tfrac{1}{2})^2 = \tfrac{10}{32}$$	$$p(s) = \binom{n}{s}\pi^s(1-\pi)^{n-s} \qquad (4\text{-}7)$$ This derivation is illustrated in Figure 4-5.

---

[6]This formula is developed as follows. In how many ways can we fill five spots with five distinct objects, designated H_1, H_2, H_3, T_1, T_2? We have a choice of 5 objects to fill the first spot, 4 the second, and so on; thus the number of options we have is:

$$5 \cdot 4 \cdot 3 \cdot 2 \cdot 1 = 5! \qquad (4\text{-}6)$$

But this is not quite the problem at hand; in fact we cannot distinguish between H_1, H_2 and H_3—all of which appear as H. Thus many of our separate and distinct arrange-

(cont'd)

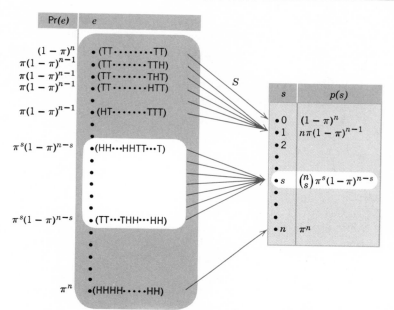

FIGURE 4-5   Computing binomial probability of s successes in n trials.

As a final example, we return to our previous illustration of planning three children. What is the probability of exactly 2 boys? Assuming each birth is an independent trial in which $\pi = 1/2$, and noting that $n = 3$ and $s = 2$ in (4-7), we have

$$p(2) = \binom{3}{2} (\tfrac{1}{2})^2 (\tfrac{1}{2})^{3-2} = \frac{3!}{2!1!} (\tfrac{1}{2})^3 = \tfrac{3}{8}$$

which confirms the previous result in Figure 4-1.

From (4-7) a table of the binomial distribution has been computed for

---

ments in (4-6), (e.g., $H_1H_2H_3T_1T_2$ and $H_2H_1H_3T_1T_2$) cannot be distinguished, and appear as the single arrangement HHHTT. Thus (4-6) involves serious overcounting. How much?

We overcounted $3.2.1 = 3!$ times because we assumed in (4-6) that we could distinguish between H_1, H_2, and H_3 when in fact we cannot. (3! is simply the number of distinct ways of arranging H_1, H_2, and H_3.) Similarly, we overcounted $2.1 = 2!$ times because we assumed in (4-6) that we could distinguish between T_1 and T_2, when in fact we cannot. When (4-6) is deflated for overcounting in both these ways, we have

$$\frac{5!}{3!2!} = \frac{5!}{3!(5-3)!}$$

selected n and π, and appears in Appendix Table IIIb. It should be used whenever possible, to avoid repeating the tedious calculations in (4-7). For example, when $n = 3$ and $\pi = .50$, we find in Table IIIb that $p(2) = .375$, which confirms the value $3/8$ above.

Some problems require the accumulated probability in the right-hand tail which is computed in Appendix Table IIIc.

PROBLEMS

Note that $\binom{n}{s}$ as well as the complete binomial distribution $p(s)$ are tabulated in Table III of the Appendix, for your optional use.

4-12 (a) Construct a diagram similar to Figure 4-5 to obtain the proba-
     bility distribution for the number of heads S when 4 coins are
     tossed; use general π. Check that your answer agrees with (4-7).
     (b) Then set $\pi = \frac{1}{2}$, to obtain the distribution for a fair coin.
     (c) From (b), calculate μ and σ^2.
     (d) Graph the distribution of (b), showing μ.

4-13 A chip is drawn from a bowl containing 2 red, 1 blue, and 7 black
     chips. The chip is replaced, and a second chip is drawn, and so
     on until 5 chips have been drawn (sampling with replacement).
     (a) Let S = the total number of red chips drawn. Tabulate and
     graph its probability distribution. Find μ and σ^2.
     (b) Repeat (a), for Y = the total number of blue chips.

4-14 Check the probability distribution of Problem 4-9 using the bi-
     nomial formula or tables.

(4-15) In rolling 3 dice, let S be the number of aces that occur. Tabulate
     and graph the probability distribution of S. Find μ and σ^2.

4-16 On a blind toss of a dart, suppose the probability of hitting the
     target is 1/5. What is the probability that in 6 tosses you will hit
     the target
     (a) Exactly 2 times?
     (b) At least 3 times? (Table IIIc helps)
     (c) At most 2 times?
     (d) What crucial assumption are you implicitly making? Why may
     it be questionable?

⇒4-17 On the basis of the above questions, can you guess the mean
     of a general binomial variable, in terms of n and π? Can you guess
     the variance? (These will be derived in Chapter 6).

*4-18 (Requires calculus). Graph the function $f(z) = e^{-(1/2)z^2}$, showing
     its
     (a) Symmetry
     (b) Asymptotes

(c) Maximum

(d) Points of inflection.

4-4   **CONTINUOUS DISTRIBUTIONS**

In Chapter 2 we saw how a continuous quantity such as height was best graphed with a relative frequency histogram. The histogram of heights of Figure 2-3 is reproduced in Figure 4-6a below. (For purposes of illustration, we measure height in feet, rather than inches. Furthermore, the y-axis has been shrunk to the same scale as the x-axis.) The sum of all the relative frequencies in Figure 4-6a is of course 1, as first noted in Table 2-2. We shall now find it convenient to change the vertical scale to relative frequency *density* as in Figure 4-6b, with this rescaling designed specifically to make the total *area* equal to 1. We accomplish this by defining

$$\text{relative frequency density} \triangleq \frac{\text{relative frequency}}{\text{cell width}} \qquad (4\text{-}8)$$

$$= \frac{\text{relative frequency}}{1/4}$$

$$= 4 \ (\text{relative frequency}).$$

FIGURE 4-6 (a) Relative frequency histogram with Σ heights = 1; (b) Rescaled into relative frequency density, making total area = 1.

Thus in Figure 4-6, panel (*b*) is 4 times as high as panel (*a*); we also confirm that panel (*b*) has area equal[7] to 1.

In Figure 4-7 we show what happens to the relative frequency density of a continuous random variable as

1. Sample size increases.
2. Cell size decreases.

With a small sample, chance fluctuations influence the picture. But as sample size increases, chance is averaged out, and relative frequencies settle down to probabilities. At the same time, the increase in sample size allows a finer definition of cells. While the area remains fixed at 1, the relative frequency density becomes approximately a curve, the so-called probability density function, which we shall refer to simply as the probability distribution, denoted by $p(x)$.

If we wish to compute the mean and variance from Figure 4-7c, the discrete formulas (4-3) and (4-4) can be applied. But if we are working with the probability density function in Figure 4-7d, then integration (which calculus students will recognize is the limiting case of summation) must be used; if a and b are the limits of X, then (4-3) and (4-4) become

$$\text{Mean, } \mu = \int_a^b x\, p(x)\, dx \tag{4-9}$$

$$\text{Variance, } \sigma^2 = \int_a^b (x - \mu)^2\, p(x)\, dx \tag{4-10}$$

---

[7] To prove in general that the total area of the relative frequency density is always 1, we first obtain from (4-8) the following statement for each cell:

relative frequency = (relative frequency density) × (cell width)

$$= \left(\begin{array}{c} \text{length of relative frequency} \\ \text{density cell} \end{array} \right) \times \text{(cell width)}$$

= area of relative frequency density bar.

Summing over all cells,

$$\Sigma \text{ relative frequency} = \text{total area of relative frequency density}$$

Since the relative frequencies sum to 1, we have proved:

total area of relative frequency density = 1

FIGURE 4-7   How relative frequency density may be approximated by a probability density as sample size increases, and cell size decreases. (a) Small n, as in Fig. 4-7b. (b) Large enough n to stabilize relative frequencies. (c) Even larger n, to permit finer cells while keeping relative frequencies stable. (d) For very large n, this becomes (approximately) a smooth probability density curve.

All the theorems that we state about discrete random variables are equally valid for continuous random variables, with summations replaced by integrals. Proofs are also very similar. Therefore, to avoid tedious duplication, we give theorems for discrete random variables only, leaving it to you to supply the continuous case yourself if you ever need it.

4-5   THE NORMAL DISTRIBUTION

For many random variables, the probability distribution is a specific bell-shaped curve, called the *normal* curve, or Gaussian curve, as shown in Figures 4-8 to 4-11. It is the single most useful probability distribution in statistics; for example, errors that are made in measuring physical and economic phenomena often are normally distributed. In addition, there are other useful probability distributions (such as the binomial) which often can be approximated by the normal curve.

(a) Standard Normal Distribution

The probability distribution of the standard normal variable Z is defined to be

$$p(z) = \frac{1}{\sqrt{2\pi}}\, e^{-(1/2)z^2} \qquad\qquad (4\text{-}11)$$

The constant $1/\sqrt{2\pi}$ is a scale factor required to make the total area 1. The symbols π and e denote important mathematical constants, ap-

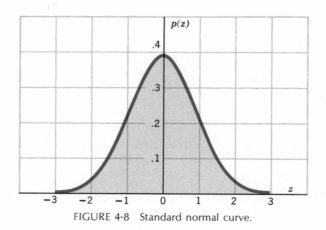

FIGURE 4-8   Standard normal curve.

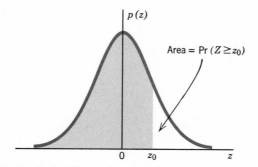

FIGURE 4-9   Probability enclosed by the normal curve above z_0.

proximately 3.14 and 2.718 respectively. We draw the normal curve[8] in Figure 4-8 reaching a maximum at $z = 0$. We confirm in (4-11) that this is so: as we move to the left or right of 0, z^2 increases in the negative exponent; therefore $p(z)$ decreases, approaching zero in both tails. This curve is also symmetric: since z appears only in squared form, $-z$ generates the same probability in (4-11) as $+z$. This confirms the shape of this standard normal curve as we have drawn it in Figure 4-8. The mean and variance of Z can be calculated by integration using (4-9) and (4-10); since this requires calculus, we quote the results without proof:

$$\mu_Z = 0$$
$$\sigma_Z = 1$$

It is for this very reason, in fact, that Z is called a *standard* normal variable. Later when we speak of "standardizing" any variable, this is precisely what we mean: shifting it so that its mean is 0 and rescaling it so that its standard deviation (or variance) is one.

The probability (area) enclosed by the normal curve above any specified value (say z_0) also requires calculus to evaluate precisely, but may be easily pictured, as in Figure 4-9. This evaluation of probability, done once and for all, has been recorded in Table IV of the Appendix. Students without calculus can think of this as accumulating the area of the approximating rectangles, as in Figure 4-7c.

---

[8] In Problem 4-18 you may have confirmed that the graph of (4-11) is that shown in Figure 4-8.

The mathematical constant $\pi = 3.14$ is not to be confused with the π used in Section 4-3 to designate probability of success.

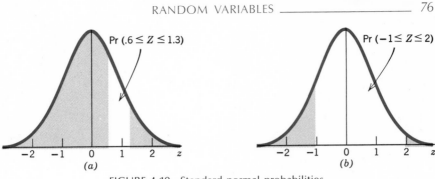

FIGURE 4-10 Standard normal probabilities.

To illustrate Table IV we find

$$Pr(Z \geq .6) = .2743$$

As a second example, suppose we want to find

$$Pr(.6 \leq Z \leq 1.3) = ?$$

which is shown in Figure 4-10a. This can be expressed as

$$Pr(Z \geq .6) - Pr(Z \geq 1.3)$$

which is found in Table IV to be

$$.2743 - .0968 = .1775.$$

As a third example, suppose we want to find

$$Pr(-1 \leq Z \leq 2) = ?$$

which is shown in Figure 4-10b. This can be expressed as the complement

$$1 - [Pr(Z \geq 2) + Pr(Z \leq -1)]$$

Because of the symmetry of the normal curve, the last term can be read from the table by noting that

$$Pr(Z \leq -1) = Pr(Z \geq 1) = .1587$$

Thus the complete answer is

$$1 - [.0228 + .1587] = .8185$$

As a final example, you may confirm that the probability enclosed between 2 standard deviations above and below the mean is over 95%:

$$Pr(-2 \leq Z \leq 2) = .9544$$

PROBLEMS

4-19 If Z is a standard normal variable, use Appendix Table IV to evaluate:
(a) $Pr(-1 \leq Z \leq +1)$.
(b) $Pr(-\infty \leq Z \leq 1.64)$.
(c) $Pr(-2.33 \leq Z \leq \infty)$.
(d) $Pr(-2 \leq Z)$.
(e) $Pr(Z \leq 2)$.

4-20 (a) If $Pr(-z_0 \leq Z \leq z_0) = .95$, what is z_0?
(b) If $Pr(-z_0 \leq Z \leq z_0) = .99$, what is z_0?

(b) General Normal Distribution

If a random variable X is normally distributed, with mean μ and standard deviation σ, its probability distribution has the formula[9]

$$p(x) = \frac{1}{\sqrt{2\pi}\,\sigma} e^{-\left(\frac{1}{2}\right)\left(\frac{x-\mu}{\sigma}\right)^2} \tag{4-12}$$

We notice that in the very special case in which $\mu = 0$ and $\sigma = 1$, (4-12) reduces to the standard normal distribution (4-11). But more important, regardless of what μ and σ may be, we can transform *any* normal variable X in (4-12) into the standard form (4-11) by defining,

$$Z = \frac{X - \mu}{\sigma} \tag{4-13}$$

Z is recognized as just a linear transformation of X, as shown in Figure 4-11. Whereas the mean and standard deviation of a general normal variable X can take on any values, the standard normal variable Z is unique—with mean 0 and standard deviation 1, as proved in Problem 4-10.

To evaluate any normal variable X, we therefore transform X into Z, and then evaluate Z in the standard normal table (Appendix Table IV).

---

[9] To prove that (4-12) is centered at μ, we note that the peak of the curve occurs when the negative exponent attains its smallest value 0, i.e., when $x = \mu$. It may also be shown that (4-12) is scaled by the factor σ. Finally, it is bell shaped for the same reasons given in part (a).

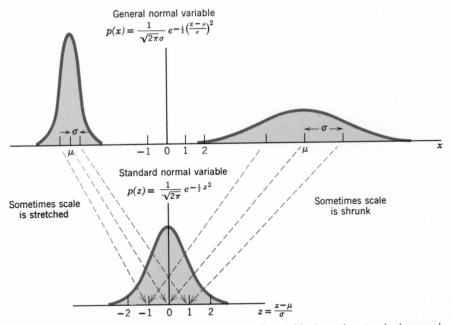

FIGURE 4-11   Linear transformation of any normal variable into the standard normal variable.

For example, suppose that X is normal, with $\mu = 100$ and $\sigma = 5$. What is the probability of getting an X value of 110 or more? That is, we wish to evaluate

$$\Pr(X \geq 110) \tag{4-14}$$

First (4-14) can be written equivalently[10] as

$$\Pr\left(\frac{X - \mu}{\sigma} \geq \frac{110 - 100}{5}\right) \tag{4-15}$$

which, noting (4-13), is

$$\Pr(Z \geq 2) \tag{4-16}$$

We see that (4-16) is the standardized form of (4-14), and from Table IV we evaluate this probability to be .0228. Moreover, the standardized

---

[10] Any inequality is preserved if both sides are diminished by the same amount ($\mu = 100$) and divided by the same positive amount ($\sigma = 5$).

form (4-16) allows a clearer interpretation of our original question; in fact, we were asking "What is the probability of getting a normal value at least two standard deviations above the mean?" The answer is: very small—about one in fifty.

As a final example, suppose a bolt picked at random from a production line has a length X which is a normal random variable with mean 10 cm and standard deviation 0.2 cm. What is the probability that its length will be between 9.9 and 10.1 cm? That is,

$$\Pr(9.9 \leq X \leq 10.1)$$

This may be written in the standardized form

$$\Pr\left(\frac{9.9 - 10}{.2} \leq \frac{X - \mu}{\sigma} \leq \frac{10.1 - 10}{.2}\right)$$
$$= \Pr(-.50 \leq Z \leq .50)$$
$$= .38$$

These calculations confirm our earlier observation in Figure 4-11: although there is any number of normal curves, there is only one standard normal curve. This is fortunate; instead of requiring a whole book of tables, we only need one (Appendix Table IV).

PROBLEMS

4-21 Draw a diagram similar to Figure 4-11 to illustrate (4-14). Shade the area being evaluated.

4-22 If X is normal, calculate:
(a) $\Pr(4.5 \leq X \leq 6.5)$ where $\mu_X = 5$ and $\sigma_X = 1$
(b) $\Pr(X \leq 800)$ where $\mu_X = 400$ and $\sigma_X = 200$
(c) $\Pr(800 \leq X)$ where $\mu_X = 400$ and $\sigma_X = 200$

4-23 Suppose that a population of men's heights is normally distributed with a mean of 68 inches, and standard deviation of 3 inches. Find the proportion of the men who
(a) Are over 6 feet
(b) Are under 5 feet 6 inches
(c) Are between 5 feet 6 inches and 6 feet.
To check your 3 answers, see whether they sum to 1.

Table 4-4   Tabled Form of
$R = g(X) = -X^2 + 4X + 5$

Value of X	Value of $R = g(X)$
0	5
1	8
2	9
3	8

4-6   **A FUNCTION OF A RANDOM VARIABLE**

Considering again the planning of 3 children, suppose for example the cost of sports equipment R is a function of the number of boys X in the family, i.e.,

$$R = g(X)$$

Specifically, suppose[11]

$$R = -X^2 + 4X + 5$$

which is equally well given by Table 4-4.

The values of R are customarily rearranged in order as shown in the third column of Table 4-5. Furthermore, the values of R have certain probabilities which may be deduced from the previous probabilities of

Table 4-5   Mean of R Calculated by First Deriving the Probability Distribution of R

(1) x	(2) $p(x)$	(3) $r = g(x)$	(4) $p(r)$	(5) $r\,p(r)$
0	$\frac{1}{8}$	5	$\frac{1}{8}$	$\frac{5}{8}$
1	$\frac{3}{8}$	8	$\frac{4}{8}$	$\frac{32}{8}$
2	$\frac{3}{8}$	9	$\frac{3}{8}$	$\frac{27}{8}$
3	$\frac{1}{8}$			

$$\mu_R = 8$$

---

[11] A brief justification of this relationship might be: boys tend to use more sports equipment than girls, so that R tends to increase with X. Yet certain savings are possible if all the children are the same sex, so that R finally drops slightly when $X = 3$.

Table 4-6 Mean of R Calculated Directly
from $p(x)$, as an Easier Alternative to Table 4-5

x	$g(x)$	$p(x)$	$g(x)p(x)$
0	5	1/8	5/8
1	8	3/8	24/8
2	9	3/8	27/8
3	8	1/8	8/8

$$\mu_R = 8 \checkmark$$

X (just as the probabilities of X were deduced from the probabilities in our original sample space, in Figure 4-1). Thus, we note that two values of X (1 and 3) give rise to an R value of 8, as shown with arrows in Table 4-5.

R is a random variable; although it has been derived from X, it has all the properties of an ordinary random variable. For example, the mean of R can be computed from its probability distribution, as in Table 4-5, where $\mu_R = 8$.

However, it is often more convenient to omit the distribution of R, and calculate the mean of R directly from the distribution of X, as shown in Table 4-6.

It is easy to see why this works: in a disguised way we are calculating μ_R in the same way as in Table 4-5. For example, the rows for $X = 1$ and $X = 3$ in Table 4-6 appear condensed together as the single row for $R = 8$ in Table 4-5. Similarly, the other rows in Table 4-6 correspond to rows in Table 4-5, so that both tables yield the same value for μ_R. The only difference, really, is that Table 4-6 is ordered according to X values, while Table 4-5 is ordered (and condensed) according to R values.

This example can easily be generalized. If X is a random variable, and g is any function, then $R = g(X)$ is a random variable. μ_R may be calculated either from the probability function of R, or alternatively from the probability function of X according to

$$\mu_R = \sum_x g(x)\, p(x) \tag{4-17a}$$

4-7   **NOTATION**

Some new notation will help us better understand the various viewpoints of the mean. For any random variable X, all the following terms have exactly the same meaning:[12]

$$\mu_X = \text{mean of } X$$
$$= \text{average of } X$$
$$= \text{expectation of } X$$
$$= E(X), \text{ the expected value of } X$$

The term $E(X)$ is introduced because it is useful as a reminder that it represents a weighted sum (E looks like Σ). With this new notation, result (4-17a) can be written

$$E(R) = \sum_x g(x)\, p(x) \tag{4-17b}$$

Finally, we recall that R was just an abbreviation for $g(X)$, so that we may equally well write (4-17b) in an easily remembered form:

$$E[g(X)] = \sum_x g(x)\, p(x) \tag{4-17c}$$

As an example of this notation, we may write

$$E(X - \mu)^2 = \sum_x (x - \mu)^2\, p(x) \tag{4-18}$$

By (4-4),

$$E(X - \mu)^2 = \sigma^2 \tag{4-19}$$

Thus we see that σ^2 may be regarded as just a kind of expectation—namely, the expectation of the random variable $(X - \mu)^2$. In the new notation we may also rewrite (4-5) as[13]

$$\sigma^2 = E(X^2) - \mu^2 \tag{4-20}$$

---

[12]The reason for the plethora of names is historical. For example, gamblers and economists use the term "*expected* gain," meteorologists use the term "*mean* annual rainfall," and teachers use the term "*average* grade."

[13]An interesting corollary to (4-20) is obtained by applying the theory of linear

(cont'd)

PROBLEMS

4-24 For the simple linear function,

$$R = a + bX$$

we have already stated (in Table 4-2) a formula for its mean,

$$\mu_R = a + b\,\mu_X$$

Prove this, using (4-17a).

4-25 Let X be the number of boys in a 4-child family. If $R = -X^2 + 5X + 3$, find $E(R)$
(a) directly from $p(x)$ as in Table 4-6.
(b) by first calculating $p(r)$ as in Table 4-5.

4-26 Again let X be the number of boys in a 4-child family. If $R = |X - 2|$,
(a) find the mean and variance of R.
(b) in Problem 4-24 we proved that for a linear function, the mean follows the same formula as the individual values. Does this hold true for nonlinear functions? In particular, does $\mu_R = |\mu_X - 2|$?

---

transformations. From Table 4-2,

$$\text{if we let } Y = X - a, \text{ then } \sigma_Y^2 = \sigma_X^2 \text{ and } \mu_Y = \mu_X - a \qquad (4\text{-}21)$$

Now (4-20) is true for any random variable, Y in particular. Thus

$$\sigma_Y^2 = E(Y^2) - \mu_Y^2 \qquad (4\text{-}22)$$

Substituting (4-21), we finally obtain

$$\sigma_X^2 = E(X - a)^2 - (\mu_X - a)^2 \qquad (4\text{-}23)$$

The practical application of (4-23) comes from letting a be the rounded value of μ_X, so that the rounding error $e = \mu_X - a$ is small. Thus, $e^2 = (\mu_X - a)^2$ is negligibly small, and

$$\sigma_X^2 \simeq E(X - a)^2 \qquad (4\text{-}24)$$

We conclude that calculating σ^2 around a good approximation of μ (rather than the true μ) introduces very little error; in fact, the error in σ^2 will be merely the squared error in approximating μ (i.e., the last term in (4-23)).

The analogous formula for samples was used extensively in Chapter 2, especially (2-8).

4-27 The time T, in seconds, required for a rat to run a maze, is a random variable with the following probability distribution.

t	2	3	4	5	6	7
$p(t)$	·1	·1	·3	·2	·2	·1

(a) Find the average time.

(b) Suppose the rat is rewarded with 1 biscuit for each second faster than 6. (For example, if he takes just 4 seconds, he gets a reward of 2 biscuits. Of course, if he takes 6 seconds or longer, he gets no reward.) What is the rat's average reward?

(c) Find $E(T^2)$.

(d) Find $E(T - \mu)^2$. Is this related to σ_T^2 in any way?

(e) Find σ_T^2 in an easier way, substituting the answers to parts (a) and (c) into equation (4-20).

Review Problems

4-28 In the 1964 presidential election, 60% voted Democratic, 40% Republican. If Gallup took a sample of 5 voters at random, find

(a) The probability that the sample would be all Democrats.

(b) The probability that the sample would correctly forecast the election winner, i.e., that a majority of the sample would be Democratic.

(c) In what way is a sample of 5 better than a sample of 1?

4-29 Three coins are independently flipped; let X = number of heads. Make a table of the probability distribution and find μ_X and σ_X^2 assuming

(a) The coins are fair.

(b) The last coin is biased, showing heads 3/4 of the time.

4-30 Suppose the amount of cereal in a package cannot be weighed exactly. In fact, it is a normally distributed random variable, with $\mu = 10.10$ oz. and $\sigma = .040$ oz. The claim on the package is "net weight, 10 oz."

(a) What proportion of the packages are underweight?

(b) To what value must the mean μ be raised in order that only .1% of the packages be underweight?

⟹4-31 (The "Sign Test")

Eight volunteers had their breathing capacity measured before and after a certain treatment, as follows:

Person	Breathing Capacity Before	After	Improvement
A	2750	2850	+100
B	2360	2380	+20
C	2950	2800	−150
D	.	.	.
E	.	.	.
.	.	.	.
.	.	.	.
.	.	.	.

Suppose the treatment has no effect whatever, so that the "improvements" represent random fluctuations (resulting from measurement error or minor variation in a person's performance, etc.). Also assume that measurement is so precise that a zero improvement is never observed.

(a) Before any observations are taken, what is the probability of seven or more + signs in such an experiment?

(b) If you were the scientist analyzing this experiment, and you observed that 7 of the 8 observations had + signs, would you question the hypothesis that the treatment has no effect whatever?

4-32 In a learning experiment, a subject attempts a certain task twice in a row. On the first trial, his chance of failure F is 1/3, while his chance of success S is then 2/3.

On the second trial, he learns better from his previous success than his previous failure, in the following sense:

$$\Pr(F/S \text{ on first trial}) = 1/8;$$
$$\Pr(F/F \text{ on first trial}) = 4/8.$$

(a) Find the probability table and mean of X = the total number of failures.

(b) Find the (unconditional) probability of failure on the second trial.

4-33 Another subject runs through the learning experiment in Problem 4-32, with the following difference: on the second trial, he learns equally well from his previous failure as his previous success, i.e.,

$$\Pr(F/F \text{ on first trial}) = \Pr(F/S \text{ on first trial})$$

This common probability, which may be simply called the probability of F on the second trial, is 1/4.

(a) Find the probability table and mean of X = the total number of heads.

(b) Can the second trial be called statistically independent of the first in this problem? In Problem 4-32?

(c) Suppose that in continuing the experiment, for two more trials, he consistently learned so that his probability of failure was 1/5 on the third trial, and 1/6 on the fourth trial. Without taking the trouble to tabulate the distribution of X, can you guess what the mean of X is now?

*4-34 (Requires calculus). Suppose a continuous random variable X has the probability distribution

$$p(x) = 3x^2 \qquad 0 \le x \le 1$$
$$= 0 \qquad \text{otherwise}$$

(a) Graph $p(x)$.

(b) Find the mean, median, and mode. Are they in the order you expect?

(c) Find σ^2.

CHAPTER 5

TWO RANDOM VARIABLES

If you bet on a horse, that's gambling. If you bet you can make three spades, that's entertainment. If you bet cotton will go up three points, that's business. See the difference?

Blackie Sherrod

5-1   **DISTRIBUTIONS**

This first section is a simple extension of the last two chapters. The main problem will be to recognize the old ideas behind the new names. Therefore we give an outline in Table 5-1, as both an introduction and review.

(a) Joint Probability

In the planning of 3 children, let us recall the two random variables:

$$X = \text{number of boys}$$
$$Y = \text{number of changes in sequence}$$

We might be interested in the probability of 2 boys and 1 change of sequence occurring together. As usual, we refer to the sample space of the experiment (in column 1 of Table 5-2), and look for the intersection of these two events, obtaining

$$\Pr(X = 2 \cap Y = 1) = \frac{2}{8} \tag{5-1}$$

For convenience $\Pr(X = 2 \cap Y = 1)$ is abbreviated to $p(2, 1)$ (5-2a)

Table 5-1   Review of Section 5-1, Showing the Origins of the Ideas

Old Idea	Application (new terminology)
$\Pr(G \cap H)$ (3-11) applied to $\Pr(X = 2 \cap Y = 1)$ $\Pr(X = x \cap Y = y)$ in general	*Joint probability distribution* $p(2, 1)$ (5-2a) $p(x, y)$ in general (5-2b)
$\Pr(H/G) = \dfrac{\Pr(H \cap G)}{\Pr(G)}$ (3-22) applied to $\Pr(X = 2/Y = 1)$ $\Pr(X = x/Y = y)$ in general	*Conditional probability function* $p(2/Y = 1)$ $p(x/Y = y)$ or $p(x/y)$ (5-10)

Event F is independent of E if
    $\Pr(F/E) = \Pr(F)$ (3-24)
or $\Pr(E \cap F) = \Pr(E)\,\Pr(F)$ (3-25)
	Variable X is independent of Y if
	    $p(x/y) = p(x)$
	or $p(x, y) = p(x)\,p(y)$ (5-13)

Similarly we could compute $p(0, 0)$, $p(0, 1)$, $p(0, 2)$, $p(1, 2)$ . . . , obtaining in Table 5-3 what is called the *joint (or bivariate) probability distribution of X and Y.* (Actually, it is easier to run down the last two columns of Table 5-2, tabulating all this information into the appropriate cell of Table 5-3. Note that *x* and *y* in Table 5-3 are designated in the lower and left-hand margins; the information in the upper and right-hand margins can be temporarily ignored.)

Table 5-2   Two Random Variables Defined on the Original Sample Space

(1) Outcomes *e*	(2) Corresponding *X* value	(3) Corresponding *Y* value
• BBB	3	0
• BBG	2	1
• BGB	2	2
• BGG	1	1
• GBB	2	1
• GBG	1	2
• GGB	1	1
• GGG	0	0

$X = 2$ $Y = 1$

Table 5-3 $p(x, y)$, The Joint Probability of X
and Y, Summarizing Table 5-2

$p(x)\rightarrow$	1/8	3/8	3/8	1/8	1 ✓
2	0	1/8	1/8	0	2/8
1	0	2/8	2/8	0	4/8
0	1/8	0	0	1/8	2/8
$\uparrow y$ = value of Y x = value of X $\longrightarrow$	0	1	2	3	$\uparrow$ $p(y)$

The formal definition of the joint probability distribution is

$$p(x, y) \triangleq \Pr(X = x \cap Y = y) \tag{5-2b}$$

This general case is illustrated in Figure 5-1. The events $X = 0$, $X = 1$, $X = 2$ . . . form a partition of the sample space, shown schematically as a vertical slicing. Similarly, the events $Y = 0$, $Y = 1$ . . . form a partition shown as a horizontal slicing. The intersection of the slice $X = x$ and the slice $Y = y$ is the event $(X = x \cap Y = y)$. Its probability is collected into the table, and denoted $p(x, y)$.

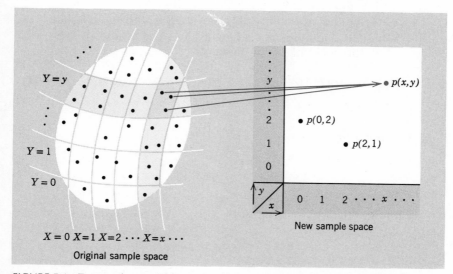

FIGURE 5-1   Two random variables (X, Y), showing their joint probability distribution derived from the original sample space. (Compare to Fig. 4-2.)

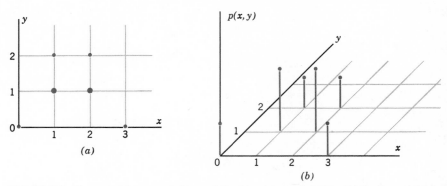

FIGURE 5-2   Two graphic presentations of the bivariate probability distribution of Table 5-3. (a) $p(x,y)$ is represented by the size of the dot; (b) $p(x,y)$ is represented by height.

This table, or specifically Table 5-3, may be graphed. The easiest way is to simply represent the probability by an appropriately sized dot, as shown in Figure 5-2a; or use the three-dimensional presentation of Figure 5-2b, where probability is represented by height.

(b) Marginal Probability Function

Suppose we are interested only in X, yet have to work with the joint probability function of X and Y. How can we compute the probability function of X, for example $p(2) = \Pr(X = 2)$?

It appears that the probability of this event (i.e., the vertical slice $X = 2$ in the schematic sample space of Figure 5-1) is the sum of the probabilities of all those chunks comprising it,

$$p(2) = p(2, 0) + p(2, 1) + p(2, 2) + p(2, 3) + \cdots p(2, y) + \cdots \quad (5\text{-}3)$$
$$= \sum_y p(2, y) \quad (5\text{-}4)$$

and in general, for any given x,

$$p(x) = \sum_y p(x, y) \quad (5\text{-}5)$$

For example, this idea may be applied to Table 5-3. We thus find,

$$p(2) = 0 + \tfrac{2}{8} + \tfrac{1}{8} = \tfrac{3}{8}$$

and place this sum in the upper margin. Similarly, $p(x)$ is computed for every x, thus providing the whole row in the upper margin. This is sometimes called the *marginal* probability distribution of X, to describe how it was obtained. But, of course, it is just the ordinary probability distribution of X (which could have been found without any reference to Y, as indeed it was in Figure 4-1).

In conclusion, the word "marginal" has no specific technical meaning. It simply describes how the probability distribution of X may be calculated when another variable Y is in play; a column sum is calculated and placed "in the margin."

In an identical way we calculate $p(y)$, the (marginal) probability distribution of Y, set out in the marginal column of Table 5-3; each element in this column is the sum of its row.

(c) Conditional Probability Distribution

From Table 5-3, suppose we wish to know the probabilities of various numbers of boys, given one change in sex sequence. In other words, how should we evaluate the conditional distribution of X given $Y = 1$? First, the appropriate ($Y = 1$) row is reproduced in Table 5-4. The problem is that the probabilities in this row sum to only 1/2; hence they cannot represent a true probability distribution. They do, however, give us the *relative* probabilities of various X values. (Thus, if we know $Y = 1$, we know that X cannot be 0 or 3, and X values of 1 or 2 are equally probable.) Therefore, to finally obtain a true probability distribution, we double these probabilities so that they will now sum to 1; the resulting distribution is denoted $p(x/Y = 1)$ in Table 5-4.

Formally, this doubling can be justified rigorously by the theory in Chapter 3, where conditional probability was found to be:

$$\Pr(H/G) = \frac{\Pr(H \cap G)}{\Pr(G)} \qquad \begin{array}{l} (3\text{-}22) \\ \text{repeated} \end{array}$$

For H and G we simply substitute events defined in terms of random variables, as follows:

$$\begin{array}{ll} \text{For } H, \text{ substitute } (X = x) & \\ \text{For } G, \text{ substitute } (Y = 1) & (5\text{-}6) \end{array}$$

Table 5-4   Derivation of the Conditional
Distribution of X, Given $Y = 1$

x	0	1	2	3	
$p(x, 1)$	0	2/8	2/8	0	Sum = Pr $(Y = 1)$ = $p(1)$ = 1/2
$p(x/Y = 1)$	0	1/2	1/2	0	Sum = 1 ✓

Thus

$$Pr(X = x/Y = 1) = \frac{Pr\ (X = x \cap Y = 1)}{Pr\ (Y = 1)}$$

Using new notation

$$p(x/Y = 1) = \frac{p(x,\ 1)}{p(1)} \tag{5-7}$$

In our example, $p(1) = 1/2$, so that (5-7) becomes

$$p(x/Y = 1) = 2p(x, 1) \tag{5-8}$$

thus justifying the doubling in Table 5-4.
    The generalization of (5-7) is clearly

$$p(x/Y = y) = \frac{p(x,\ y)}{p(y)} \tag{5-9}$$

The conditional probability distribution may be further abbreviated to $p(x/y)$, giving

$$p(x/y) = \frac{p(x,\ y)}{p(y)} \tag{5-10}$$

Note how similar this is to equation (3-22).
    Since the conditional distribution is a bona fide distribution, it can be used for example to obtain the conditional mean

$$E(X/Y = y) \text{ or } \mu_{x/y} \overset{\Delta}{=} \sum_{x} x\,p\ (x/y) \tag{5-11}$$

(d) Independence

We define the independence of 2 random variables in terms of the independence of 2 events developed in Chapter 3,

> The random variables X and Y are called independent iff for every x and y, the events $(X = x)$ and $(Y = y)$ are independent. $\tag{5-12}$

The consequences are easily derived. From (3-25) we know that the independence of events $(X = x)$ and $(Y = y)$ means that

$$\Pr(X = x \cap Y = y) = \Pr(X = x)\ \Pr(Y = y)$$

i.e.,

$$p(x, y) = p(x)\ p(y) \tag{5-13}$$

Returning to our example, we easily show that X and Y are not independent. For independence, (5-13) must hold for every (x, y) combination. We ask whether it holds, for example, when $x = 0$ and $y = 0$? The answer is no; from the probabilities in Table 5-3, (5-13) is shown to be violated since

$$\frac{1}{8} \neq \frac{1}{8} \cdot \frac{2}{8}$$

PROBLEMS

5-1 In a family of 4 children, again let
   X = number of boys
   Y = number of changes of sequence
   List the sample space, and then show
   (a) The bivariate probability distribution and its graph.
   (b) The (marginal) probability function of X.
   (c) The mean and variance of X.
   (d) The conditional probability function $p(x/Y = 2)$.
   (e) The conditional mean and variance of X, given $Y = 2$.
   (f) Are X and Y independent?
5-2 Suppose X and Y have the following joint probability distribution

6	.10	.15
4	.20	.30
2	.10	.15
y / x	5	10

Answer the same questions as in Problem 5-1.

5-3 Suppose X and Y have the following bivariate distribution

3	0	.1	.1
2	.1	.4	.1
1	.1	.1	0
y			
x	0	1	2

Answer the same questions as in Problem 5-1.

5-2   A FUNCTION OF TWO RANDOM VARIABLES

In Section 4-6, we analyzed a derived random variable R which was some function of a random variable X,

$$R = g(X) \tag{5-14}$$

In this chapter we shall similarly analyze a derived variable R which is some function of a *pair* of random variables X, Y,

$$R = g(X, Y) \tag{5-15}$$

The concepts and proofs of this section will therefore run parallel to those of the previous chapter, the main difference being that the joint probability distribution $p(x, y)$ will replace the probability distribution $p(x)$. We shall be particularly interested in the distribution and mean of R.

Following the usual procedure, we develop the argument first in terms of a simple example, the sample space for a family of 3 children as shown in Figure 5-3. Suppose, for example, that excess clothing costs are simply the sum[1] of X and Y,

$$R = g(X, Y) = X + Y \tag{5-16}$$

In Figure 5-3, we show how $p(r)$ may be derived directly from the original sample space, or indirectly by means of $p(x, y)$. In either case, the result is the same.

———————————

[1] The sum $X + Y$ would reflect excess clothing costs if, for example, boys were more expensive to clothe than girls, and if changes in sex sequence interfered with the convenient passing-on of clothing.

	x	y	$r = x + y$	Reordered r	$p(r)$
• (GGG)	0	0	0	0	$\frac{1}{8}$
• (GGB)	1	1	2	1	0
• (GBG)	1	2	3	2	$\frac{2}{8}$
• (GBB)	2	1	3	3	$\frac{4}{8}$
• (BGG)	1	1	2	4	$\frac{1}{8}$
• (BGB)	2	2	4		
• (BBG)	2	1	3		
• (BBB)	3	0	3		

(a)

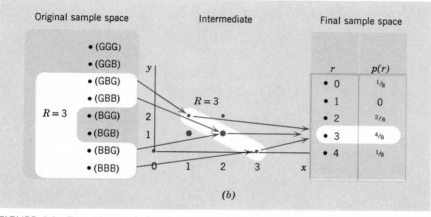

(b)

FIGURE 5-3 Two views of the derivation of the probability function of $R = X + Y$ (a) Directly (b) Using $p(x,y)$ as an intermediate condensation.

On the one hand, consider the direct derivation in panel (a). We note that the event $R = 3$, for example, consists of four of the eight equiprobable outcomes. Hence, $p(3) = \text{Pr}(R = 3)$ is 4/8. On the other hand, in panel (b) we derive $p(3)$ indirectly, using $p(x, y)$ in the intermediate sample space.

The expectation $E(R)$ may similarly be derived in two ways. On the one hand, applying (4-3) to the probability distribution of R, we have by definition,

$$E(R) = \sum r\,p(r)$$

$$= 0(\tfrac{1}{8}) + 1(0) + 2(\tfrac{2}{8}) + 3(\tfrac{4}{8}) + 4(\tfrac{1}{8}) \qquad (5\text{-}17)$$

$$= 2\tfrac{1}{2}$$

On the other hand, let us try to arrive at the same result[2] by using $p(x, y)$ in an extension of (4-17c):

$$E(R) = E(X + Y) = \sum_x \sum_y (x + y)\,p(x, y)$$

$$= (0 + 0)\tfrac{1}{8} + (0 + 1)0$$
$$+ (1 + 0)0 + (1 + 1)\tfrac{2}{8} \cdots$$
$$+ (1 + 2)\tfrac{1}{8} + (2 + 1)\tfrac{2}{8} + (3 + 0)\tfrac{1}{8} \qquad (5\text{-}18)$$
$$= 2\tfrac{1}{2} \text{ again}$$

So (5-18) does in fact work, and it is easy to see why. The last line of (5-18), for example, amounts to

$$3(\tfrac{1}{8} + \tfrac{2}{8} + \tfrac{1}{8}) = 3(\tfrac{4}{8})$$

which is the same as the second last term of (5-17). Continuing in this fashion, we see that (5-18) is just a disguised form of the more condensed form (5-17).

This example can be easily generalized. If $R = g(X, Y)$ is a function of two random variables, then

$$E(R) = E[g(X, Y)] = \sum_x \sum_y g(x, y)\,p(x, y) \qquad \begin{array}{c}(5\text{-}19)\\ \text{like } (4\text{-}17c)\end{array}$$

PROBLEMS

5-4 Let

$$R = X(X + Y)$$
$$T = (X - 8)(Y - 4)$$

where X and Y have the same joint distribution as in Problem 5-2.

---

[2]Although the calculations in (5-17) and (5-18) (and indeed throughout this chapter) are displayed in a long line for typographical reasons, in practice it is better to carry out the computations in tabular form, as in Table 4-1 for example.

(a) Find the mean of R using (5-19).

(b) Find the mean of R, by finding first its distribution, and then using (5-17).

(c) Find $E(T)$.

(5-5) Repeat Problem 5-4, where

$$R = XY$$

$$T = (X - 1)(Y - 2) \tag{5-20}$$

and X and Y have the same joint distribution as in Problem 5-3.

5-3   COVARIANCE AND CORRELATION

(a) Covariance

In this section, we shall develop a measure of the degree to which two variables are linearly related. As an example, consider the joint distribution of Table 5-5, graphed in Figure 5-4. We notice some tendency

Table 5-5   Joint Probability $p(x,y)$

FIGURE 5-4   Definition of new variables $(X - \mu_X)$ and $(Y - \mu_Y)$—i.e., translation of axes into new (dotted) position.

for these two variables to move together (i.e., a large x tends to be associated with a large y; and a small x with a small y).

Our measure of how the variables move together should be independent of where the variables happen to be centered. We therefore consider the deviations from the mean

$$(x - \mu_X) \quad \text{and} \quad (y - \mu_Y) \tag{5-21}$$

which are shown in Figure 5-4 for a typical point; the geometric interpretation of (5-21) is the (dotted) translation of the axes. Now let us multiply the deviations, obtaining the product

$$(x - \mu_X)(y - \mu_Y) \tag{5-22}$$

For any point in the NE (North East) quadrant of Figure 5-4, both deviations are positive, (since x exceeds μ_X, and y exceeds μ_Y); hence their product (5-22) is also positive. Similarly, for any point in the SW quadrant, both deviations are negative, so their product is positive. However, for points in the other two quadrants, the product is negative. When we sum all of these products, attaching the appropriate probability weight to each, we obtain a good measure of how the variables move together,[3] i.e.,

---

[3]The computation of σ_{XY} may often be simplified by using

$$\sigma_{XY} = E(XY) - \mu_X \mu_Y \tag{5-25}$$

For example, in Problem 5-5, $E(T)$ was just σ_{XY} in disguise, and was calculated from the definition (5-24) as $E(X - 1)(Y - 2) = .2$. On the other hand, σ_{XY} can be calculated from (5-25) as $E(XY) - (1)(2) = 2.2 - 2 = .2$. Formula (5-25), and its proof, is analogous to

$$\sigma_X^2 = E(X^2) - \mu_X^2 \qquad \text{from (4-5)}$$

proof of (5-25)   Beginning with (5-23),

$$\sigma_{XY} = \sum_x \sum_y (x - \mu_X)(y - \mu_Y)\, p(x, y)$$

$$= \sum_x \sum_y (xy - x\mu_Y - y\mu_X + \mu_X\mu_Y)\, p(x, y)$$

$$= \sum_x \sum_y xy\, p(x, y) - \mu_Y \sum_x \sum_y x\, p(x, y) - \mu_X \sum_x \sum_y y\, p(x, y) + \mu_X\mu_Y \sum_x \sum_y p(x, y) \tag{5-26}$$

(cont'd)

$$\text{covariance, } \sigma_{XY} \triangleq \sum_x \sum_y (x - \mu_X)(y - \mu_Y) \, p(x, y) \tag{5-23}$$

As in (4-19), we may rewrite this[4] as

$$\sigma_{XY} = E(X - \mu_X)(Y - \mu_Y) \tag{5-24}$$

In our example, because the heavier probability weights occur in the NE and SW quadrants where the product (5-22) is positive, we obtain a positive covariance,

$$\sigma_{XY} = (-4)(-2)(.1) + (-2)(-1)(.2) + \cdots = +2.0$$

which confirms the tendency of the variables to move together positively. Alternatively, if the larger probabilities had occurred in the NW and SE quadrants, the covariance would be negative, indicating the

---

In the second term, we find that

$$\sum_x \sum_y x \, p(x, y) = \sum_x x \left[\sum_y p(x, y) \right]$$

and by (5-5),

$$= \sum_x x \, p(x) = \mu_X \tag{5-27}$$

Similarly, in the third term of (5-26),

$$\sum_x \sum_y y \, p(x, y) = \mu_Y$$

Finally, in the last term of (5-26),

$$\sum_x \sum_y p(x, y) = 1$$

Thus (5-26) reduces to

$$\sigma_{XY} = \sum_x \sum_y xy \, p(x, y) - \mu_Y(\mu_X) - \mu_X(\mu_Y) + \mu_X\mu_Y$$

$$= E(XY) - \mu_X\mu_Y \tag{5-25} \text{ proved}$$

[4]We recognize the variance of X in (4-19) as just a special case of the covariance (5-24), setting $Y = X$.

tendency for X and Y to move in opposite directions. Finally, had the probabilities been evenly distributed in the four quadrants, there would be no discernible tendency for X and Y to move together and, as expected, their covariance would be zero.

(b) Correlation

The covariance can still be improved. As it now stands, it depends upon the units in which X and Y are measured. If X were measured, for example, in feet instead of inches, each x-deviation in (5-22), and hence σ_{XY} itself, would unfortunately change by a factor of 12. An indicator of how two variables move together which is unaffected by the (irrelevant) unit of measurement is:

$$\text{correlation, } \rho_{XY} \triangleq \frac{\sigma_{XY}}{\sigma_X \sigma_Y} \tag{5-28}$$

In the example of Table 5-5

$$\rho_{XY} = \frac{2}{\sqrt{5.6} \sqrt{1.4}} = .71$$

This does in fact work: measuring X in terms of feet rather than inches still changes σ_{XY} in the numerator by a factor of 12; but this is exactly cancelled by the fact that σ_X in the denominator is also changed by the same factor 12. Since (5-28) similarly neutralizes any change in the scale of Y, the correlation coefficient ρ is, as desired, completely independent of the units of measurement of either variable.

Another reason that ρ is a very useful measure[5] of the relation between X and Y is that it is always bounded by

$$-1 \leq \rho \leq +1 \tag{5-29}$$

Whenever X and Y have a perfect positive linear relation, (as would be the case if the entire distribution in Figure 5-4 were located on a straight line running SW to NE), then ρ takes on the limiting value of $+1$; similarly if there is a perfect negative linear relation (i.e., the entire distribution is on a straight line running NW to SE), then ρ would be -1. Furthermore,[6]

---

[5]Proofs of (5-29) and later statements, as well as more interpretations of ρ, are given in Chapter 14.

[6]**proof**   If X and Y are independent, then from (5-13),

$$p(x, y) = p(x)\, p(y)$$

(cont'd)

> If X and Y are independent, then they are uncorrelated, i.e., $\sigma_{XY} = \rho_{XY} = 0$.
> $$\text{(5-30)}$$

Finally, it is often useful to express correlation as an expectation:

$$\rho_{XY} = E\left(\frac{X - \mu_X}{\sigma_X}\right)\left(\frac{Y - \mu_Y}{\sigma_Y}\right) \tag{5-31}$$

which is similar to covariance in (5-24) except that the divisors σ_X and σ_Y are required as in the definition (5-28).

PROBLEMS

5-6 For the following joint probability table

y		
2	0	.4
1	.2	.2
0	.2	0
x	0	1

(a) Calculate σ_{XY} from the definition (5-23).
(b) Calculate σ_{XY} from the easier formula (5-25).
(c) Calculate ρ_{XY}.

(5-7) Repeat Problem 5-6, for the following joint probability distribution:

Thus (5-23) becomes

$$\sigma_{XY} = \sum\sum (x - \mu_X)(y - \mu_Y)\, p(x)\, p(y)$$

$$= \left[\sum (x - \mu_X)\, p(x)\right]\left[\sum (y - \mu_Y)\, p(y)\right]$$

Since, for any distribution, the (appropriately weighted) sum of deviations from the mean must equal zero,

$$\sigma_{XY} = 0 \cdot 0 = 0 \tag{5-30 proved}$$

From (5-28) ρ_{XY} must also be zero.

y \ x	0	1	2
2	.4	0	0
1	0	.2	.2
0	0	0	.2

5-8 Suppose X and Y have the following joint distribution:

y \ x	1	2	3
2	.10	.05	.05
1	.40	.20	.20

(a) Are X and Y independent?
(b) What is σ_{XY}?
(c) What is ρ_{XY}?
5-9 Referring to Problems 5-4 and 5-5, is it true that $E(T) = \sigma_{XY}$?
5-10 Referring to Problem 5-1,
(a) What is σ_{XY}?
(b) Are X and Y independent?
(c) Looking beyond this particular example, which statements are true for any X and Y?
(1) If X and Y are independent, then they must be uncorrelated.
(2) If X and Y are uncorrelated, then they must be independent.
⇒5-11 In a certain gambling game, a pair of honest three-sided dice are thrown. Let
X = number on first die
Y = number on the second die
The joint probability distribution of X and Y is, of course

y \ x	1	2	3
3	1/9	1/9	1/9
2	1/9	1/9	1/9
1	1/9	1/9	1/9

and the total number of dots S is,

$$S = X + Y$$

(a) Find the distribution of S, and its mean and variance.
(b) Find the mean and variance of X and of Y.
(c) Do you see the relation between (a) and (b)?

⇒5-12 Suppose the gambling game of Problem 5-11 is complicated by using loaded dice, as follows:

x	$p(x)$
1	.4
2	.3
3	.3

y	$p(y)$
1	.5
2	.4
3	.1

Assuming that the dice are tossed independently, tabulate the joint distribution of X and Y, and then answer the same questions as in Problem 5-11.

5-4   LINEAR COMBINATION OF TWO RANDOM VARIABLES

In this section we shall find easy ways to analyze the sum of two random variables,

$$S = X + Y \tag{5-32a}$$

and, more generally, the weighted sum

$$W = aX + bY \tag{5-32b}$$

where a and b may be any coefficients, called *weights*. This is also called a linear combination (or linear function) of X and Y. S is seen to be just the special case of W where $a = b = 1$. As another example, the average of two random numbers X and Y is $(X + Y)/2 = \frac{1}{2}X + \frac{1}{2}Y$, which is just a weighted sum with weights $1/2$. Similarly, any weighted average is just a linear combination with a and b satisfying $a + b = 1$.

To illustrate, suppose a couple is drawn at random from a certain population of working couples. In thousand dollar units, let

$$X = \text{man's income}$$
$$Y = \text{woman's income}$$

Then $S = X + Y = \text{couple's total income}$

Suppose the tax rates on X and Y are fixed at 20% and 30% respectively; then the couple's income after taxes is the weighted sum

$$W = .8X + .7Y \qquad (5\text{-}33)$$

Of course, since X and Y are random variables, so also are S and W. How can we find their moments easily?

(a) Mean

Continuing our example, if we know that

$$E(X) = 12 \quad \text{and} \quad E(Y) = 9$$

it is natural to guess that

$$E(S) = 12 + 9 = 21$$

This guess is correct, because it is always true[7] that

$$\overline{\underline{E(X + Y) = E(X) + E(Y)}} \qquad (5\text{-}34)$$

(This is the same result that was guessed and confirmed in Problems 5-11 and 5-12.) Similarly, it is natural to guess that

$$E(W) = .8(12) + .7(9) = 15.9$$

_____

[7]**proof**   For $g(X, Y) = X + Y$, (5-19) becomes

$$E(X + Y) = \sum_x \sum_y (x + y)\, p(x, y)$$

$$= \sum_x \sum_y x\, p(x, y) + \sum_x \sum_y y\, p(x, y)$$

Considering the first term, we may write it as

$$\sum_x \sum_y x\, p(x, y) = \sum_x x \left[\sum_y p(x, y) \right]$$

by (5-5) $\qquad\qquad\qquad = \sum_x x\, p(x)$

$$= E(X)$$

Similarly the second term reduces to $E(Y)$, so that

$$E(X + Y) = E(X) + E(Y) \qquad \qquad (5\text{-}34) \text{ proved}$$

This guess is also correct, because it is always true[8] that

$$E(aX + bY) = a\,E(X) + b\,E(Y) \tag{5-35}$$

Statisticians often refer to this important property as the "additivity" or "linearity" of the expectation operator.

To appreciate the simplicity of (5-35), we should compare it to (5-19). Both formulas provide a means of calculating the expected value of a function of X and Y. However, (5-19) applies to *any* function of X and Y, whereas (5-25) is restricted to *linear* functions only. But when we are dealing with this restricted class of linear functions, (5-35) is generally preferred to (5-19) because it is much simpler. Whereas evaluation of (5-19) involves working through the whole joint probability distribution of X and Y, (5-35) requires only the marginal distributions of X and Y.

(b) Variance

The variance of a sum is a little more complicated[9] than its mean:

$$\text{var}\,(X + Y) = \text{var}\,X + \text{var}\,Y + 2\,\text{cov}\,(X, Y) \tag{5-36}$$

where var and cov are abbreviations for variance and covariance, of course. Similarly, for a weighted sum,[10]

$$\text{var}\,(aX + bY) = a^2\,\text{var}\,X + b^2\,\text{var}\,Y + 2ab\,\text{cov}\,(X, Y) \tag{5-37}$$

---

[8] Since the proof parallels the proof of (5-34), it is left as an exercise.

[9] **proof of (5-36)**   It is time to simplify our proofs by using brief notation such as $E(W)$ rather than the awkward $\sum w p(w)$, or the even more awkward $\sum_x \sum_y w(x, y)\,p(x, y)$. First, from (4-19),

$$\text{var}\,S = E(S - \mu_S)^2$$

Substituting for S and μ_S,

$$\begin{aligned}
\text{var}\,S &= E[(X + Y) - (\mu_X + \mu_Y)]^2 \\
&= E[(X - \mu_X) + (Y - \mu_Y)]^2 \\
&= E[\underbrace{(X - \mu_X)^2} + \underbrace{2(X - \mu_X)(Y - \mu_Y)} + \underbrace{(Y - \mu_Y)^2}]
\end{aligned}$$

each of these is a random variable

Realizing that (5-34) holds for *any* random variables (in particular, each of the above),

$$\begin{aligned}
\text{var}\,S &= E(X - \mu_X)^2 + 2E(X - \mu_X)(Y - \mu_Y) + E(Y - \mu_Y)^2 \\
&= \text{var}\,X + 2\,\text{cov}\,(X, Y) + \text{var}\,Y \tag{5-36 proved}
\end{aligned}$$

[10] Since the proof parallels the proof of (5-36), it is left as an exercise.

Table 5-6 The Mean and Variance of Various Functions
of Two Random Variables

Function of X and Y	Mean and Variance Derived by:	Mean	Variance
1. Any function $g(X, Y)$		$E[g(X, Y)] =$ $\sum_x \sum_y g(x, y) p(x, y)$ <div style="text-align:right">(5-19)</div>	
2. Linear combination $aX + bY$	Row 1	$E(aX + bY)$ $= aE(X) + bE(Y)$ <div style="text-align:right">(5-35)</div>	var $(aX + bY)$ $= a^2$ var $X + b^2$ var Y $+ 2ab$ cov (X, Y) <div style="text-align:right">(5-37)</div>
3. Simple sum $X + Y$	Setting $a = b = 1$ in row 2	$E(X + Y)$ $= E(X) + E(Y)$ <div style="text-align:right">(5-34)</div>	var $(X + Y)$ $=$ var $X +$ var Y $+ 2$ cov (X, Y) <div style="text-align:right">(5-36)</div>
4. Function of one variable, aX	Setting $b = 0$ in row 2	$E(aX) = aE(X)$ (Table 4-2)	var $(aX) = a^2$ var X (Table 4-2)

For example, suppose that for our randomly selected couple,

$$\text{var } X = 16, \quad \text{var } Y = 10, \quad \text{and} \quad \text{cov } (X, Y) = 8 \quad (5\text{-}38)$$

Then

$$\text{var } S = 16 + 10 + 2(8) = 42 \qquad (5\text{-}39)$$
$$\text{var } W = (.8)^2(16) + (.7)^2(10) + 2(.8)(.7)(8) = 24.1 \qquad (5\text{-}40)$$

There is a simple intuitive reason for the covariance term in (5-36). A positive covariance (as in (5-38) for example) means that when X is high, Y tends to be high as well. Then the sum $X + Y$ tends to be very high. (Similarly, when X is low, Y tends to be low, making the sum tend to be very low.) These extreme values of S make its variance high (as borne out in the formula (5-39), for example).

A very simple and common case occurs when X and Y are uncorrelated, i.e., $\sigma_{XY} = 0$. Then (5-36) reduces to

$$\text{var } (X + Y) = \text{var } X + \text{var } Y \qquad (5\text{-}41)$$

Since independence assures us that X and Y are uncorrelated according to (5-30), we may finally conclude,

If X and Y are independent,

$$\text{var}(X + Y) = \text{var}\,X + \text{var}\,Y \qquad (5\text{-}42)$$

Similarly,

$$\text{var}(aX + bY) = a^2\,\text{var}\,X + b^2\,\text{var}\,Y \qquad (5\text{-}43)$$

For example, the independent dice thrown in Problems 5-11 and 5-12 obeyed the simple rule (5-42).

The theorems of this chapter are summarized in Table 5-6 for future reference. The general function $g(X, Y)$ is dealt with in the first row, while the succeeding rows represent increasingly simpler special cases.

PROBLEMS

5-13 According to (5-36), the variance of $(X + Y)$ is reduced if cov (X, Y) is negative. Give an intuitive explanation.

5-14 In a small community of ten working couples, yearly income (in thousands of dollars) has the following distribution:

Couple	Man's Income X	Wife's Income Y
1	10	5
2	15	15
3	15	10
4	10	10
5	10	10
6	15	5
7	20	10
8	15	10
9	20	15
10	20	10

A couple is drawn by lot to represent the community at a convention. Let X and Y be the (random) income of the man and wife respectively. Find

(a) The bivariate probability distribution, and its graph.

(b) The distribution of X, and its mean and variance.

(c) The distribution of Y, and its mean and variance.

(d) The covariance σ_{XY}.

(e) $E(Y/X = 10)$ and $E(Y/X = 20)$. Note that as X increases, the conditional mean of Y increases too. This is another expression of the "positive relation" between X and Y.

(f) If S is the total combined income of the couple, what is its mean and variance?

(g) Suppose that $W = .6X + .8Y$ is the couple's income after taxes; what is its mean and variance?

(h) To measure the degree of sexual discrimination against wives, a certain organization is interested in the difference $D = X - Y$. What is the mean and variance of D?

Incidentally, do you think $E(D)$ is a good measure of sexual discrimination?

5-15 Continuing Problem 5-14, we shall consider some alternative schemes for collecting the tax T on the couple's income S. Find the mean and variance of T:

(a) If S is taxed at a straight 20%, i.e.,

$$T = .20 \ S$$

(b) If S is taxed according to the formula

$$T = .5(S - 12)$$

(c) If S is taxed according to the following progressive tax table:

Combined Income S	Tax T
10	1
15	2
20	3
25	5
30	7
35	10
40	13

*(d) Remembering that T is the tax on the representative couple (the couple drawn at random), compare the 3 tax schemes above, according to the following three virtues:

(1) Which scheme yields the most revenue to the government?

(2) Which scheme is most egalitarian, in the sense of resulting in the smallest variance in net income left after taxes?

(3) Which of these schemes has the smallest marginal tax rate at high income levels? I.e., which takes the smallest tax bite out of the last dollar earned by a rich couple ($S = 35$), and hence provides the strongest incentive for such a couple to continue working?

5-16 The students of a certain large class wrote 2 exams, obtaining a distribution of grades with the following characteristics:

	Class Mean μ	Standard Deviation σ	Variance σ^2	
1st exam, X_1	50	20	?	covariance
2nd exam, X_2	80	20	?	$\sigma_{12} = 50$
(a) Average, $\bar{X}$	?	?	?	
(b) Weighted average W	?	?	?	

Fill in the blanks in the table, assuming

(a) The instructor calculated a simple average of the two grades, $\bar{X} = (X_1 + X_2)/2$

(b) The instructor thought the second exam was twice as important, so took a weighted average

$$W = \tfrac{1}{3}X_1 + \tfrac{2}{3}X_2$$

5-17 Repeat Problem 5-16

(i) if the covariance $\sigma_{12} = -200$. How might you interpret such a negative covariance? What has it done to the variance of the average grade?

(ii) if the covariance $\sigma_{12} = 0$.

(5-18) Continuing Problems 5-11 and 5-12, suppose the pair of 3-sided dice are not only loaded, but dependent, so that the joint probability function of the 2 numbers is

3	.1	.2	.1
2	.1	.1	.1
1	.1	.1	.1
X_2 / X_1	1	2	3

(a) Find the distribution of S (the total number of dots), and its mean and variance.

(b) Find the mean and variance of X_1 and of X_2.

(c) Find the covariance of X_1 and X_2, and then verify that (5-34) and (5-36) hold true.

Review Problems

5-19 When a coin is fairly tossed 3 times, let

$$X = \text{number of heads on the first two coins}$$
$$Y = \text{number of heads on the last coin}$$
$$S = \text{total number of heads}$$

(a) Are X and Y independent? What is their covariance?

(b) For each of X, Y, and S, find the distribution, mean, and variance.

(c) Verify that (5-34) and (5-36) hold true.

(5-20) Repeat Problem 5-19 for a coin which is not fairly tossed, having in fact the sample space given in Problem 3-26.

5-21 Ten football players in a certain junior high school have the following heights and weights

Player	Height (inches) H	Weight (pounds) W
A	70	150
B	65	140
C	65	150
D	75	160
E	70	150
F	70	140
G	65	140
H	75	150
I	75	160
J	70	160

For a player drawn by lot, as a representative to the students council, find:

(a) The bivariate probability distribution of H and W, and its dot graph.

(b) The distribution of H, and its mean and variance.

(c) The distribution of W, and its mean and variance.

(d) The covariance, σ_{HW}.

(e) $E(W/H = 65)$, $E(W/H = 70)$, and $E(W/H = 75)$.
(As height increases, the conditional mean weight increases, which is another view of the positive covariance of H and W.)
(f) Are H and W independent?
(g) If a size index I is defined by the coach as:

$$I = 2H + 3W$$

find the mean, variance and standard deviation of I; then find the distribution of I and verify directly.

⟹5-22 A bowl contains 3 chips numbered 2, 6 and 7. One chip is selected at random, replaced, and then a second is selected (random sampling with replacement). Let X_1 and X_2 be the first and second numbers drawn.
(a) Tabulate the joint distribution of X_1 and X_2.
(b) Tabulate the (marginal) distribution of X_1, and of X_2.
(c) Are X_1 and X_2 independent? What is their covariance?
(d) Find the mean and variance of X_1, and of X_2.
(e) Find the mean and variance of $S = X_1 + X_2$. Then find the distribution of S and verify directly.
(f) How would your answers above be different if the bowl contained 1000 chips of each kind? Is it correct to conclude:

In sampling with replacement, the important issue is the *relative* frequency of the various kinds of chips. The *absolute* frequency is immaterial.

⟹5-23 Repeat Problem 5-22 with the following change. The first chip is kept out when the second is drawn (random sampling without replacement; equally well, the two chips could be drawn simultaneously).

⟹5-24 Continuing Problem 5-22, if 10 chips are sampled with replacement, let us define the sum $S = X_1 + X_2 + \cdots X_{10}$.
(a) What are the mean and variance of S?
(b) What is the range of possible values of S?

Review Problems (Chapters 1–5)

5-25 Suppose the number of defects X in a new TV set has the following probability distribution

x	$p(x)$	$c(x)$
0	.2	0
1	.4	$15
2	.3	$20
3	.1	$25

The last column lists the cost of repairing the set (honoring the guarantee). Since the cost consists of a fixed fee ($10) plus a variable component ($5 per defect), it could equally well be given by the formula

$$c(x) = 0 \qquad \text{if } x = 0$$
$$ = 10 + 5x \qquad \text{if } x > 0$$

(a) Find the average number of defects.

(b) Find the average cost of repair.

(c) Find the standard deviation of the number of defects.

5-26 Three factories produce cars, including some lemons, according to the following schedule:

	Proportion of All Output	Rate of Producing Lemons
Factory A	40%	1/100
Factory B	40%	1/25
Factory C	20%	1/10
Total	100%	

If you go to a dealer and buy a car at random, what is the probability that it is produced by factory C

(a) if you have no further information?

(b) if it turns out to be a lemon?

(c) if it turns out *not* to be a lemon?

5-27 (a) Suppose a secretary spills 3 different form letters and their envelopes; she so hopelessly scrambles them that, in despair, she stuffs each letter in an envelope at random, and then mails them. Let S = number of people who receive the right letter; thus $S = 0$, 1, 2, 3. Find the mean of S.

(b) Repeat (a), if the 3 letters are not all different: instead, 2 of the letters are identical.

*(c) Repeat (a), if there are n different letters, instead of 3.

*(d) Repeat (b), if there are n letters, k of which are identical, while the remaining $(n - k)$ are all different.

5-28 Two baskets are taken on a cookout. The first contains 2 ham and 5 cheese sandwiches; the second contains 6 ham and 3 cheese. In the confusion of darkness, a basket is picked at random.

(a) If a sandwich is drawn from this basket, what is the chance it is a ham sandwich?

(b) If a second sandwich is drawn from the same basket, what is the conditional probability that this second sandwich also will be ham, if the first is ham?

5-29 A submarine fires 3 torpedoes at a ship, with the following chances of hitting:

For the first torpedo, 1/3.

For the other torpedoes,

1/2 if the previous torpedo is a hit.

1/4 if the previous torpedo is a miss.

(a) Tabulate the probability distribution for the total number of hits X.

(b) Find the mean and variance of X.

(c) What is $\Pr(X \geq 2 / X \geq 1)$?

(d) What is the probability of at least 2 hits, given that the first shot was a hit?

(e) Suppose that the damage D to the ship depends on the number of hits X according to:

$$D = 5X^2 \text{ (in millions of dollars)}$$

Find the expected damage.

(f) On which shot is the unconditional probability of a hit the greatest?

5-30 "When the cards are dealt at bridge, there is a probability 1/4 that I shall hold the ace of spades, and a probability 1/3 that my partner will hold it if I do not. Hence the total probability that between us we hold it is 7/12." Comment. (From the Oxford University examinations, Trinity term, 1962.)

5-31 In putting up a new building, suppose there are two consecutive stages, surveying and construction. The times, in years, required to complete the surveying (S) and construction (C), are two independent random variables, with the following probability distributions:

$$p(s) = (.8)(.2)^{s-1} \qquad s = 1, 2, 3, \ldots$$
$$p(c) = (.5)(.5)^{c-2} \qquad c = 2, 3, 4, \ldots$$

The total building time is $T = S + C$, of course.

A penalty is incurred if completion takes more than $T = 4$ years. What is the probability of incurring this penalty?

5-32 Answer Problem 5-31, if S and C are now dependent, and normally distributed, as follows:

Random Variable	Mean	Variance	Covariance
S	1	.09	.10
C	2	.16	

Hint. Look ahead to (6-13).

5-33 A certain millionaire devised the following "sure-fire" sequential scheme for making $1000 by selecting the right color (black or red) at roulette.

The first time, bet $1000. If you win, stop. If you lose, double your bet.

If you win this second time, stop. If you lose, double your bet, and continue in this way until you win—at which point your net winning will be $1000. What do you think of this idea?

CHAPTER 6

SAMPLING

*THE
NORMAL
LAW OF ERROR
STANDS OUT IN THE
EXPERIENCE OF MANKIND
AS ONE OF THE BROADEST
GENERALIZATIONS OF NATURAL
PHILOSOPHY ◆ IT SERVES AS THE
GUIDING INSTRUMENT IN RESEARCHES
IN THE PHYSICAL AND SOCIAL SCIENCES AND
IN MEDICINE AGRICULTURE AND ENGINEERING ◆
IT IS AN INDISPENSABLE TOOL FOR THE ANALYSIS AND THE
INTERPRETATION OF THE BASIC DATA OBTAINED BY OBSERVATION AND EXPERIMENT*

W. J. Youden

I know of scarcely anything so apt to impress the imagination as the wonderful form of cosmic order expressed by the "Law of Frequency of Error." The law would have been personified by the Greeks and deified, if they had known it.

Sir Francis Galton

6-1 **INTRODUCTION**

In the last three chapters we have studied probability and random variables, so that now we can answer the basic deductive question in statistics: What can we expect of a random sample drawn from a known population?

We have already met several examples of sampling: the poll of voters sampled from the population of all voters; the sample of light bulbs drawn from the whole production of bulbs; a sample of men's heights drawn from the whole population; a sample of 2 chips drawn from a bowl of chips. As defined earlier, a random sample is one in which each individual in the population is equally likely to be sampled. There are several ways to actually carry out the physical process of random sampling. For example, suppose a random sample is to be drawn from the population of students in the classroom.

1. The most graphic method is to record each person on a cardboard chip, mix all these chips in a large bowl and then draw the sample.

2. A more practical method is to assign each person a number, and then draw a random sample of numbers. For example, for a population of less than a hundred, a random sample may be obtained by consulting a table of random numbers (Appendix Table IIa) and reading off a pair of digits for each individual required in the sample.

These two sampling methods are mathematically equivalent. The random number method is simpler to employ, hence is common in practical sampling. However, the bowlful of chips is conceptually easier; consequently in our theoretical development of random sampling, we shall often visualize drawing chips from a bowl.

(a) Example

As an example, suppose a population of a million men's heights has the distribution shown in Table 6-1 and Figure 6-1. For future reference, we also compute μ and σ^2, and call them the mean and variance of X, where X represents the *parent population* of men's heights. Random sampling from this population is equivalent mathematically to placing the million chips of column 2 in a bowl. Then the first chip selected at random can take on any of the x values shown in column 1, with probabilities shown in column 3. This first random draw is denoted by X_1; the second draw is denoted by X_2, and so on. But each of these

Table 6-1   A Population of Men's Heights[1], and the
Calculation of μ and σ^2

(1) Height (Midpoint of Cell) x	(2) Frequency	(3) Relative Frequency, also $p(x)$	(4) $x\,p(x)$	(5) $(x - \mu)^2\,p(x)$
60	10,000	.01	.60	.81
63	60,000	.06	3.78	2.16
66	240,000	.24	15.84	2.16
69	380,000	.38	26.22	0
72	240,000	.24	17.28	2.16
75	60,000	.06	4.50	2.16
78	10,000	.01	.78	.81
	$N = 1,000,000\checkmark$	$1.00\checkmark$	$\mu = 69.00$	$\sigma^2 = 10.26$
				$\sigma = \;\;3.20$

---

[1]We approximate each height by the cell midpoint to keep concepts simple. To be more precise, we ought to have used a very fine subdivision of height into so many cells that we would closely approximate the continuous distribution shown in Figure 6-1.

Of course, the calculation of μ and σ^2 could have been simplified by coding, as in Table 2-5.

FIGURE 6-1   Population of men's heights. (a) Histogram of Table 6-1, and its continuous approximation. (b) Bowl-of-chips equivalent.

random variables $X_1, X_2, \ldots X_n$ (together constituting our sample of n chips) has the same probability distribution—the distribution of the parent population,

$$p(x_1) = p(x_2) = \cdots p(x_n) = \text{population distribution, } p(x) \quad (6\text{-}1)$$

Thus we have characterized random sampling very simply. Every chip drawn at random can be regarded as a random variable whose possible values range over the whole population, with probabilities $p(x)$ given by the relative frequencies in the population.

(b) Sampling With or Without Replacement

In large populations, such as the million heights in Table 6-1, it makes practically no difference whether or not we replace each chip before drawing the next. After all, what is one chip in a million? It cannot substantially change the relative frequencies, $p(x)$.

However, in small populations, replacement of each sampled chip is an important issue. In Problems 5-22 and 5-23 this difference was made clear. When the first chip X_1 was replaced, it restored the population to exactly its original state, so that X_2 was completely independent of whatever X_1 happened to be. On the other hand, when the first chip X_1 was not replaced, the population was significantly changed. That is, the distribution of X_2 was dependent on what X_1 happened to be.

In general, then, we see that the random observations $X_1, X_2 \ldots X_n$ will be independent if we sample with replacement. And in large populations, even if we sample without replacement, it is practically the same as with replacement, so that we still essentially have independence. All these cases in which observations are assumed to be independent are very easy to analyze, and are therefore called *simple random sampling*.

(c) Conclusion

We may restate the definition of simple random sampling in more mathematical terms for future reference:

A *simple random sample* is a sample whose n observations $X_1, X_2 \ldots X_n$ are independent. The distribution of each X_i is the population distribution $p(x)$, (with mean μ and variance σ^2). $\qquad$ (6-2)

The only exception to this is sampling from a small population, without replacement. This case is more difficult, and is deferred to Section 6-7. Everywhere else, we shall assume simple random sampling.

6-2 $\qquad\qquad\qquad\qquad\qquad\qquad\qquad\qquad\qquad\qquad$ **SAMPLE SUM**

We are now ready to bring to bear the theory we have developed in Chapters 3 to 5. In taking a random sample from a population, consider the sample sum,

$$S \triangleq X_1 + X_2 + \cdots + X_n \qquad (6\text{-}3)$$

Being the sum of random variables, S itself will also be a random variable. How does it fluctuate? In particular, what is its mean and variance?

By applying[2] (5-34) to (6-3) we can easily calculate the mean,

$$E(S) = E(X_1) + E(X_2) + \cdots + E(X_n)$$

---

[2] Extending (5-34) and (5-42) to cover the sum of more than two variables is left as an exercise.

In (6-1) we noted that each observation X_i has the population distribution $p(x)$, with expectation μ, so that

$$E(S) = \mu + \mu + \cdots + \mu \tag{6-4}$$

$$\overline{E(S) = n\mu} \tag{6-5}$$

Similarly, we obtain the variance of S; because all its component variables are independent, (5-42) may be applied to (6-2), yielding

$$\text{var } S = \text{var } (X_1) + \text{var } (X_2) + \cdots + \text{var } (X_n) \tag{6-6}$$

Again we note that each observation X_i has the population distribution $p(x)$, with variance denoted by σ^2, so that

$$\text{var } S = \sigma^2 + \sigma^2 + \cdots + \sigma^2$$
$$\text{var } S = n\,\sigma^2 \tag{6-7}$$

$$\overline{\sigma_S = \sqrt{n}\,\sigma} \tag{6-8}$$

This is our first important deduction: we have deduced the behavior of a *sample* sum from knowledge of the parent *population*.

For example, suppose a sample of $n = 4$ observations is drawn from the population of heights in Figure 6-1. The sample sum would fluctuate around

$$E(S) = n\mu = 4\mu \qquad \text{(6-5) applied}$$

with standard deviation

$$\sigma_S = \sqrt{n}\,\sigma = 2\sigma \qquad \text{(6-8) applied}$$

This distribution of the sample sum is shown on the right-hand side of Figure 6-2, as compared to the distribution of the population (in black).

As another example, suppose a machine produces a large population of bicycle chain links with average length $\mu = .40$ inch and standard deviation $\sigma = .02$ inch. A chain is made by joining together a random sample of 100 of these links. Its length S is a random variable, with

$$E(S) = n\mu = 100(.40) = 40.0 \text{ inches} \qquad \text{(6-5) applied}$$
$$\sigma_S = \sqrt{n}\,\sigma = 10(.02) = .20 \text{ inch} \qquad \text{(6-8) applied}$$

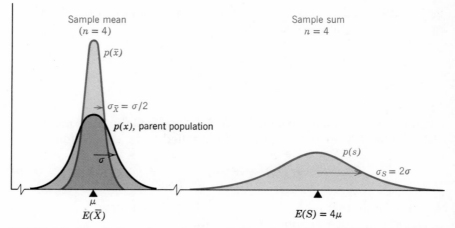

FIGURE 6-2 Distribution of sample mean (left) and sample sum (right) compared to parent population.

This allows us to interpret (6-5) and (6-8) intuitively. It was no surprise that μ_S was n times μ. But why should σ_S be only $\sqrt{n}$ times σ? Typically, a sample sum (e.g. chain) will include some individuals (links) which are oversized, and some which are undersized so that some cancellation occurs. While the fluctuation in the chain (σ_S) does exceed the fluctuation in the individual link (σ), it is substantially less than it would be if the fluctuations in all the links were accumulated without cancellation ($\sigma + \sigma + \cdots + \sigma = n\sigma$).

6-3   THE SAMPLE MEAN

From the sample sum, it is easy to derive the sample mean:

$$\bar{X} \triangleq \frac{1}{n}(X_1 + X_2 + \cdots + X_n) \qquad \text{(2-1a) repeated}$$

$$= \frac{1}{n} S \qquad\qquad\qquad\qquad \text{(6-9)}$$

In this form $\bar{X}$ is recognized to be just a linear transformation of S; hence $\bar{X}$ can easily be analyzed in terms of S. Applying Table 4-2 to (6-9) yields the expectation,

$$E(\bar{X}) = \frac{1}{n} E(S)$$

From (6-5)

$$= \frac{1}{n}(n\mu)$$

$$\overline{\underline{E(\overline{X}) = \mu}}$$ (6-10)

Similarly, by applying Table 4-2 to (6-9) we obtain the variance

$$\text{var } \overline{X} = \left(\frac{1}{n}\right)^2 \text{var } S$$

From (6-7)

$$= \left(\frac{1}{n}\right)^2 n \sigma^2$$

$$\text{var } \overline{X} = \frac{\sigma^2}{n}$$ (6-11)

$$\overline{\underline{\sigma_{\overline{X}} = \frac{\sigma}{\sqrt{n}}}}$$ (6-12)

This standard deviation of $\overline{X}$ is also called the *standard error* of the mean. For example, consider once again the sample of 4 observations drawn from the population of heights in Figure 6-1. The sample mean $\overline{X}$ fluctuates around

$$E(\overline{X}) = \mu$$ (6-10) applied

with standard deviation

$$\sigma_{\overline{X}} = \frac{\sigma}{\sqrt{n}} = \frac{\sigma}{2}$$ (6-12) applied

This is illustrated in the left side of Figure 6-2. It is also intuitively clear: $\overline{X}$ fluctuates around the same central value as an individual observation, but with less deviation because of "averaging out." In other words, whereas you might get a 7-foot man in an individual observation from the population, you would be far less likely to get a 7-foot average in a sample of 4 men. Even if you get a 7-foot observation in your sample, it will be cancelled out by a small observation; or at least its effect will be moderated because it is averaged in with other (more typical) observations.

6-1 True or false? If false, correct the errors:

If 10 men were randomly sampled from the population of Table 6-1, and then laid end to end, the expectation of the total length would be $n\mu = 690$ inches. The total length would vary (from sample to sample) with a standard deviation of $n\sigma = 32$ inches.

On the other hand, if the 10 men in the random sample were averaged, the expectation of the average would be $\mu = 69$ inches, and its standard deviation would be $\sigma = 3.2$ inches. This is how the long and short men in the sample tend to "average out," making $\overline{X}$ fluctuate less than a single observation.

6-2 The population of employees in a certain large office building has weights distributed around a mean of 150 pounds, with a standard deviation of 20 pounds. A random group of 25 employees get in the elevator each morning. Find the mean and variance of:

(a) The total weight S.

(b) The average weight $\overline{X}$.

6-3 A bowl contains six chips, numbered 1 to 6. A sample of 2 chips is drawn, with replacement.

(a) By tabulating the joint distribution of X_1 and X_2, calculate the distribution of $S = X_1 + X_2$.

(b) From its distribution, calculate the mean and variance of S.

(c) Find the population mean and variance, and hence verify (b).

(d) How is this problem different from tossing two dice and recording the total number of dots?

6-4 Continuing Problem 6-3, graph the distribution of S. By rescaling the axis, show the distribution of $\overline{X}$. Then answer true or false; if false, correct it:

(a) $\overline{X}$ fluctuates around $3\frac{1}{2}$, as does an individual observation X. This illustrates $E(\overline{X}) = \mu$.

(b) $\overline{X}$ ranges from 1 to 6, as does an individual observation X. However, the extreme values of $\overline{X}$ are rare (probability 1/36, compared to probability 1/6 for an extreme value of an individual observation X.) Thus, $\overline{X}$ has a smaller standard deviation than X. This illustrates $\sigma_{\overline{X}} = \sigma/\sqrt{n}$.

Incidentally, this also illustrates why the range is a better measure of spread than the standard deviation.

⟹6-5 A bowl is full of many chips, one-third marked 2, one-third marked 4, and one-third marked 6.

(a) When one chip is drawn, let X be its number. Find μ and σ, (the population mean and standard deviation.)

(b) When a sample of 2 chips is drawn, let $\bar{X}$ be the sample mean. Find

    (1) The probability table of $\bar{X}$.

    (2) From this calculate $\mu_{\bar{X}}$ and $\sigma_{\bar{X}}$; check your answers using (6-10) and (6-12).

(c) Repeat (b) for a sample of 3 chips.

(d) Graph $p(\bar{x})$ for each case above, i.e., for sample size $n = 1, 2, 3$. Comparison is facilitated by using probability density, i.e., by using a bar graph with probability = area = (height) × (width).

As n increases, notice that $p(\bar{x})$ becomes more concentrated around μ. What else is happening to the *shape* of $p(\bar{x})$?

6-4 THE CENTRAL LIMIT THEOREM

In the preceding section we found the mean and standard deviation of $\bar{X}$. Now we shall investigate the *shape* of its distribution.

(a) The Distribution of $\bar{X}$ from a Normal Population

When the parent population is normal, then $\bar{X}$ is normal too, as illustrated in the left side of Figure 6-2. This will follow from a theorem on linear combinations, which we quote without proof:

> If X and Y are normal, then any linear combination $Z = aX + bY$ is also a normal random variable.   (6-13)

When the parent population is normal, each observation in the sample $X_1, X_2 \ldots X_n$ has this same normal distribution. Now let us write the sample mean $\bar{X}$ as a linear combination of these normal variables,

$$\bar{X} = \frac{1}{n} X_1 + \frac{1}{n} X_2 \cdots + \frac{1}{n} X_n \tag{6-14}$$

so that (6-13) establishes that $\bar{X}$ is normal.

(b) The Distribution of $\bar{X}$ from a Nonnormal Population

Across the top of Figure 6-3 we show 3 different examples of a nonnormal population; in each case successive graphs reading down the column show how the distribution of the sample mean changes shape as sample size n increases. These three examples display an astonishing pattern—*the sample mean becomes normally distributed as n grows, no*

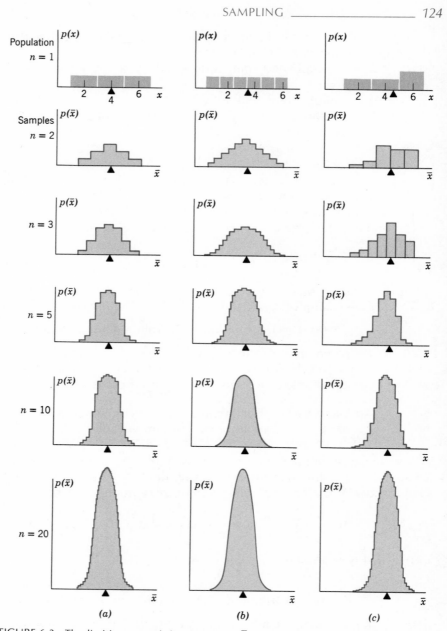

FIGURE 6-3 The limiting normal distribution of $\bar{X}$ where parent population is (a) Bowl of three kinds of chips.[2] (b) Bowl of six kinds of chips (or die). (c) Bowl of three kinds of chips of different frequency.

[2]The sampling in panel (a) was already discussed in Problem 6-5, and panel (b) in Problem 6-4. Panel (c) could be similarly worked out, for $n = 2$ at least, as an exercise.

matter what the parent population is. This is especially remarkable in the third example, where even a skewed population generates the symmetric normal distribution for the sample mean. This pattern is of such central importance that mathematicians have formulated it as

---

the central limit theorem   As the sample size *n* increases, the distribution of the mean, $\overline{X}$, of a random sample taken from practically[3] any   (6-15) population approaches a *normal* distribution, (with mean μ and standard deviation $\sigma/\sqrt{n}$).

The central limit theorem is not only remarkable, but very practical as well. For it completely specifies the distribution of $\overline{X}$ in large samples, and is therefore the key to large-sample statistical inference. In fact, as a rule of thumb it has been found that usually when the size *n* reaches about 10 or 20, the distribution of $\overline{X}$ is practically normal. This is certainly the case in the 3 examples of Figure 6-3.

In conclusion, we can assume that $\overline{X}$ is normal for samples of any size taken from a normal population, and for large samples taken from practically any population. With our previous conclusions on the mean and standard deviation of $\overline{X}$, we can now be very specific in our deduction about a sample mean taken from a known population.

Example   Consider the marks of a large class of students on a statistics test. If the marks have a normal distribution with a mean of 72 and standard deviation of 9, let us compare (1) the probability that any one student will have a mark over 78 with (2) the probability that a sample of 10 students will have an average mark over 78.

1. The probability that a single student will have a mark over 78 is found by standardizing the normal population

$$\text{Pr}\,(X > 78) = \text{Pr}\left(\frac{X - \mu}{\sigma} > \frac{78 - 72}{9}\right)$$
$$= \text{Pr}\,(Z > .67) = .2514.$$

2. Now consider the distribution of the sample mean. From the central limit theorem we know it is normal, with mean $\mu = 72$ and standard deviation $\sigma/\sqrt{n} = 9/\sqrt{10}$. Using these moments to standardize

---

[3]The one qualification is that the population have finite variance. For a proof of this theorem, see for example, P. Hoel, *Introduction to Mathematical Statistics,* 3rd ed., pp. 143–5, John Wiley & Sons, 1962.

FIGURE 6-4   Comparison of probabilities for a single observation and for a sample mean.

again, we calculate the probability of a sample mean exceeding 78,

$$\Pr\left(\bar{X} > 78\right) = \Pr\left(\frac{\bar{X} - \mu}{\sigma/\sqrt{n}} > \frac{78 - 72}{9/\sqrt{10}}\right)$$
$$= \Pr\left(Z > 2.11\right)$$
$$= .0174 \tag{6-16}$$

Hence, although there is a reasonable chance (about 1/4) that a single student will get over 78, there is very little chance (about 1/60) that a sample average of ten students will perform this well. This is shown in Figure 6-4.

PROBLEMS

6-6 The weights of packages filled by a machine are normally distributed about a mean of 25 ounces, with a standard deviation of 2 ounces. What is the probability that n packages from the machine will have an average weight of less than 24 ounces if
(a) $n = 1$
(b) $n = 4$
(c) $n = 16$
(d) $n = 64$

6-7 Suppose that the education level among adults in a certain country has a mean of 11.1 years, and a variance of 9. What is the probability that in a random survey of 100 adults you will find an average level of schooling between 10 and 12 years?

6-8 Does the central limit theorem (6-15) also hold true for the sample sum? Justify briefly.

6-9 An elevator is designed with a load limit of 2000 lb. It claims a capacity of 10 persons. If the weights of all the people using the elevator are normally distributed with a mean of 185 lb and a standard deviation of 22 lb, what is the probability that a group of 10 persons will exceed the load limit of the elevator?

6-10 Suppose that bicycle chain links have lengths distributed around a mean $\mu = .50$ cm, with a standard deviation $\sigma = .04$ cm. The manufacturer's standards require the chain to be between 49 and 50 cm long.

(a) If chains are made of 100 links, what proportion meets the standards?

(b) If chains are made of only 99 links, what proportion now meets the standards? How many links should be put in a chain?

(c) Using 99 links, to what value must σ be reduced (how much must the quality control on the links be improved) in order to have 90% of the chains meet the standards?

(6-11) The amount of pocket money that persons in a certain city carry has a nonnormal distribution with a mean of $9.00 and a standard deviation of $2.50. What is the probability that a group of 225 individuals will be carrying a total of more than $2100?

6-12 In each of Problems 6-6 to 6-11, what crucial assumption did you implicitly make? Suggest some circumstances where it would be seriously violated. Then how would the correct answer differ?

*6-13 A farmer has 9 wheatfields planted. The distribution of yield from each field has a mean of 1000 bushels and variance 20,000. Furthermore, the yields of any 2 fields are correlated, because they share the same weather conditions, weed control, etc; in fact the correlation is .59. Letting S denote the total yield from all 9 fields, find

(a) The mean and variance of S. [*Hint.* How must (6-6) be adjusted?]

(b) Pr $(S < 8,000)$. [*Hint.* S is approximately normal].

⟹6-14 The number of completed years of college had the following distribution, in a large class of statistics students:

x = Number of Completed Years	$p(x)$ = Relative Frequency
0	.30
1	.30
2	.40

(a) Find the population mean and variance.

(b) If 10 students were randomly sampled, what is Pr $(\bar{X} \le .50)$?

(c) The 10 best marks in the class came from freshmen and sophomores, in fact a group of students having $\bar{X} = .50$. This led the instructor to claim that the younger students were doing unusually well; the dean then replied that a sample of only 10 students provided too little evidence for any firm conclusion. How would you settle the dispute?

⇒6-15 In a recent election, each voter was asked how many votes he had cast for the Democratic candidate. Since this was an honest election, he had to reply either 0 or 1. Thus the following distribution was recorded for the population:

x = Number of Democratic Votes Cast	$p(x)$ = Relative Frequency
0	.44
1	.56

(a) What is the population mean? What is the proportion of Democratic voters?

(b) What is the population variance?

(c) When 10 voters were randomly polled, they gave the following answers:

$$1, 0, 1, 0, 0, 1, 1, 0, 1, 1.$$

What is the sample sum? The sample mean? The sample proportion of Democrats?

(d) Of course, the sample sum in part (c) is a random variable, and could be anywhere from 0 to 10. Roughly tabulate its probability distribution. (*Hint.* Problem 4-28.) What is its mean and variance?

6-5   **0 — 1 VARIABLES**

(a) Introduction

In this chapter, we shall draw heavily on Problem 6-15, where we considered a population of voters. For each voter we defined

$$X = \text{number of Democratic votes cast} \qquad (6\text{-}17)$$

If this seems a strange way to define such a simple variable, we could explicitly define it with the formula

$$X = 0 \text{ if not a Democrat} \tag{6-18}$$
$$= 1 \text{ if a Democrat}$$

Since X provides a simple means of counting the number of Democrats, it is called a *counting variable* (also, a dummy variable, a $0 − 1$ variable, switching variable, off-on variable, or Bernoulli variable.) To illustrate: suppose the following X values were observed in a random sample of 10 Americans:

$$1, 1, 0, 1, 0, 1, 1, 0, 1, 1$$

Then the sample sum $S = 7$ is just the sampled number of Democrats.

$$\text{sample sum } S = \text{number of Democrats} \tag{6-19}$$

Furthermore, the sample mean $\overline{X} = S/n = 7/10$ is just the sample proportion of Democrats,

---

$$\text{sample mean } \overline{X} = \text{sample proportion } P \tag{6-20}$$

Thus we have found a very easy way to handle proportions: they are simply averages of counting variables. The general theory of sampling can now be applied directly to answer questions like "How does the sample proportion P fluctuate around the true population proportion π?" But first we must fully describe the population by calculating its moments.

(b) The Population

In Table 6-2 we calculate the mean and variance for a population whose proportion of Democrats is (a) 56%, for example, (b) π, in general. It turns out that just as the sample mean was the sample proportion in (6-20), so

$$\text{population mean } \mu = \text{population proportion } \pi \tag{6-21}$$

Calculation in Table 6-2 also established that

$$\text{population variance } \sigma^2 = \pi(1 − \pi). \tag{6-22}$$

Table 6-2 Population Mean and Variance for a Counting Variable, when the Proportion of Democrats is (a) 56%, for Example (b) π, in General

(a)

x = Number of Democratic Votes an Individual Casts	$p(x)$ = Relative Frequency = Population Proportion	$x\,p(x)$	$(x - \mu)$	$(x - \mu)^2 p(x)$
0	.44	0	$-.56$	$(-.56)^2(.44)$
1	.56	.56	.44	$(.44)^2(.56)$
		$\mu = .56$		$\sigma^2 = .246$

(b)

x = Number of Democratic Votes an Individual Casts	$p(x)$ = Relative Frequency = Population Proportion	$x\,p(x)$	$(x - \mu)$	$(x - \mu)^2 p(x)$
0	$(1 - \pi)$	0	$-\pi$	$(-\pi)^2(1 - \pi)$
1	π	π	$1 - \pi$	$(1 - \pi)^2\pi$
		$\mu = \pi$		$\sigma^2 = \pi(1 - \pi)$

(c) The Sample Sum S

As first noted in Problem 4-28 and in Table 4-3 the total number of Democrats in n observations (the sample sum S) is just a binomial random variable (the total number of successes S in n trials). Thus, this section will provide a more extended development of the binomial distribution, including calculation of its mean and variance, and a convenient normal approximation.

The mean of S is found by substituting (6-21) into (6-5),

$$\text{Binomial mean, } E(S) = n\pi \tag{6-23}$$

Similarly, the variance of S is found by substituting (6-22) into (6-7),

$$\text{Binomial variance, } \sigma_S^2 = n\pi(1 - \pi) \tag{6-24}$$

Furthermore, in a large sample the distribution is approximately normal,[4] so that we can compute probabilities very easily.

_____

[4] By the central limit theorem, which holds equally well for a sample sum as for a sample mean. A useful rule of thumb is that n should be large enough to make $n\pi > 5$ and $n(1 - \pi) > 5$. If n is large, yet π is so small that $n\pi \le 5$, then there is a better approximation than the normal, called the "Poisson distribution for rare events."

For example, let us find the probability that there will be at least 30 Democrats in a sample of 50 voters, when the population proportion $\pi = .56$.

$$\Pr(S \geq 30) = \Pr\left(\frac{S - \mu_S}{\sigma_S} \geq \frac{30 - n\pi}{\sqrt{n\pi(1 - \pi)}}\right)$$

$$= \Pr\left(\frac{S - \mu_S}{\sigma_S} \geq \frac{30 - (50)(.56)}{\sqrt{50(.56)(.44)}}\right)$$

$$= \Pr(Z \geq .57) = .28 \tag{6-25}$$

This is graphed in Figure 6-5, where the continuous normal curve used to evaluate (6-25) is seen to be an excellent approximation[5] to the exact, discrete binomial. Moreover it is easy to see how hopelessly complicated an evaluation of all the binomial bars in this graph would be.[6]

(d) Sample Proportion P

We now turn to the final major issue of this section: what is the distribution of the sample P around the population proportion π? The expected value of P is found by recognizing that it is a sample mean; then substituting (6-20) and (6-21) into (6-10):

$$E(P) = \pi \tag{6-26}$$

---

[5]There is one additional improvement that will make this approximation even better. Figure 6-5 clearly indicates that we should evaluate the area under the normal curve above 29.5, not 30. This peculiarity arises from trying to approximate a discrete variable with a continuous one, and is therefore called the *continuity correction*. The better approximation is therefore

$$\Pr(S \geq 29.5) = \Pr\left(\frac{S - \mu_S}{\sigma_S} \geq \frac{29.5 - 50(.56)}{\sqrt{50(.56)(.44)}}\right) = \Pr(Z \geq .43) = .334$$

To keep the analysis uncluttered, this continuity correction will henceforth be ignored, except in the problems where answers with the continuity correction (w.c.c.) are given, as well as answers with no continuity correction (n.c.c.).

[6]The exact binomial answer would be

$$\Pr(S \geq 30) = \sum_{s=30}^{50} \binom{50}{s} (.56)^s (.44)^{50-s}$$

There are 21 terms (i.e., bars in Figure 6-5) to evaluate, each one a major computational effort; (binomial tables like Appendix Table IIIc do not include n as large as 50).

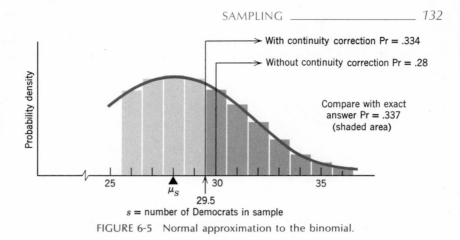

s = number of Democrats in sample

FIGURE 6-5 Normal approximation to the binomial.

Its variance is obtained by substituting (6-20) and (6-22) into (6-11):

$$\text{var}\,(P) = \frac{\pi(1 - \pi)}{n} \qquad (6\text{-}27)$$

Again the central limit theorem assures us that, in large samples, the distribution is approximately normal.

To illustrate, let us reconsider the sample of 50 voters from a population that has Democratic proportion $\pi = .56$. What is the probability that the sample proportion of Democrats will be at least .60? We find[7]

$$\text{Pr}\,(P \geq .60) = \text{Pr}\left(\frac{P - \mu_P}{\sigma_P} \geq \frac{.60 - \pi}{\sqrt{\pi(1 - \pi)/n}}\right)$$

$$= \text{Pr}\left(\frac{P - \mu_P}{\sigma_P} \geq \frac{.60 - .56}{\sqrt{(.56)(.44)/50}}\right)$$

$$= \text{Pr}\,(Z \geq .57) = .28 \qquad \text{(6-25) confirmed}$$

PROBLEMS

(Note that if you want high accuracy in your answers, you should make continuity corrections, especially for small samples).

_____

[7] Again, the continuity correction gives an even better approximation. Of course, since this correction involves half a bar of the histogram, and each bar now has width 1/50, the computation is

$$\text{Pr}\left(P \geq .60 - \left(\frac{1}{2}\right)\left(\frac{1}{50}\right)\right) = \text{Pr}(P \geq .59) = \cdots = .334 \text{ again}$$

6-16 In the 1964 Presidential election, 60% voted Democratic (as in Problem 4-28). If prior to the election Gallup took a random sample of 25 voters, find the probability that the sample would correctly forecast the election winner, i.e., a majority would be Democratic.

6-17 The central limit theorem states that the sample sum becomes approximately normal. Illustrate this by graphing the distribution of the binomial S. Use $\pi = .40$ and $n = 1, 2, 3, 5,$ and 10. (You may use Appendix Table IIIb.) Compare with Figure 6-3.

6-18 If a fair die is rolled 100 times, what is the probability that at least one quarter of these are aces? Answer two ways:
(a) $\Pr(P \geq \frac{1}{4})$
(b) $\Pr$ (total number of aces ≥ 25)

(6-19) What is the chance that of the first 100 babies born in the New Year, more than 60 will be boys?

6-20 What is the chance that of the first 10 babies born in the New Year, more than 6 will be boys? Answer two ways:
(a) Exactly, using the binomial distribution.
(b) Approximately, using the normal distribution.

6-6   SUMMARY OF SAMPLING THEORY

(b) Sampling with a 0 − 1 Variable

If we take a large sample (say as large as 10 or 20) from a large population, we may write

$$\overline{X} \sim N\left(\mu, \frac{\sigma^2}{n}\right) \tag{6-28}$$

which means, "$\overline{X}$ is approximately normally distributed, with mean μ and variance σ^2/n." If the population itself is nearly normal, then (6-28) is true for *any* sample size.

(b) Sampling with a 0 − 1 Variable

General sampling theory can be applied to a special population—chips coded 0 and 1, (or any variable that takes only the values 0 and 1). Then the sample sum S is just the binomial S (number of successes in n trials); for large n

$$S \sim N\left(n\pi, n\pi(1 - \pi)\right) \tag{6-29}$$

Moreover, the sample proportion of successes P is just a disguised $\overline{X}$, and the population proportion π is just a disguised μ, so that for large n,

$$P \sim N\left(\pi, \frac{\pi(1 - \pi)}{n}\right) \tag{6-30}$$

PROBLEMS

6-21 Five men, selected at random from a normal population with mean weight $\mu = 160$ lb and $\sigma = 20$ lb, get on an elevator. What is the probability that
(a) All five men weigh more than 170?
(b) The average weight is more than 170?
(c) The total weight is more than 850?
(d) Give an intuitive reason why your answers are related as they are.

⇒6-22 Fill in the blanks.
(a) Suppose that in a certain election, the U.S. and California are alike in their proportion of Democrats, π, the only difference being that the U.S. is about 10 times as large a population. In order to get an equally reliable sampling estimate of π, the U.S. sample should be _____ as large as the California sample.
(b) A certain length is measured with an error, which we suppose for simplicity to be $+2''$ or $-2''$, equally likely. A sample of n independent measurements is taken. The sample sum S *could possibly be* in error as much as _____. However, S is *likely* (95%) to be in error by no more than _____. For example, for $n = 100$, these two errors are
Worst possible error = _____.
Likely error $\leq$ _____.

6-23 Let $\overline{X}$ be the sample mean when a die is thrown 1000 times. Intuitively we feel "fairly certain" that $\overline{X}$ is "quite close" to μ. More precisely, calculate

$$\Pr\left(\mu - .1 < \overline{X} < \mu + .1\right)$$

6-24 (a) In adding up his assets, an accountant rounds to the nearest 10 cents. If there are 200 items, what is the chance that the rounding error will exceed $1.00?
(b) Briefly state the assumptions you made in part (a).

SMALL-POPULATION SAMPLING

In (6-2) we defined simple random sampling to be sampling where the observations $X_1, X_2 \ldots X_n$ are independent. In this section we shall analyze one exception to this—when we sample without replacement from a small population (often called simply "small-population sampling").

To be concrete, suppose we are drawing a sample of 2 chips from a bowl containing three chips, marked 2, 6, and 7 (as in Problem 5-23). The joint distribution of X_1 and X_2 is displayed in Table 6-3, from which the marginal distributions are derived. Since the joint distribution is symmetric, the marginal distribution of X_1 and of X_2 must always be exactly the same.

This is also intuitively clear: if we have no knowledge of X_1, then X_2 will have the population distribution, just as X_1 has the population distribution. For example, suppose the deal of a poker hand is interrupted after 2 cards have been dealt face down. Which card is likely to be better? Obviously both cards have the *same* distribution of possible values—the population of 52 cards in the deck. Similarly, all successive cards that are dealt (sampled) have the same population distribution, so that we may write

$$p(x_1) = p(x_2) = \cdots = p(x_n) = \text{population distribution} \qquad (6\text{-}31)$$
$$\text{like (6-1)}$$

Table 6-3 Joint Distribution of Two Chips Drawn without Replacement from a Bowl with 3 Chips (Marked 2, 6, and 7)

$\overrightarrow{p(x_1)}$	1/3	1/3	1/3	1✓
7	1/6	1/6	0	1/3
6	1/6	0	1/6	1/3
2	0	1/6	1/6	1/3
$\uparrow x_2$	2	6	7	$p(x_2)\uparrow$
$x_1 \longrightarrow$				

*This is a starred section, and like a starred problem, it is optional; the student may skip it without loss of continuity.

(a) Expectation

As a consequence of (6-31), all observations have the same mean and variance, so that many of the formulas for simple random sampling still hold true. For example, the formulas for expectation have exactly the same proof as before, so that we arrive at the same result,

$$E(S) = n\mu \qquad\qquad (6\text{-}32)$$
$$\text{like (6-5)}$$

$$E(\overline{X}) = \mu \qquad\qquad (6\text{-}33)$$
$$\text{like (6-10)}$$

(b) Variance

We have already noted that the *marginal* distribution of X_1 is the same as X_2, both being the distribution of the population. However, the *conditional* distribution of X_2, given X_1, is not the same. Since the first chip X_1 is not replaced, the remaining population and hence the conditional distribution of X_2 is different. That is, the distribution of X_2 is dependent on what X_1 happens to be. In fact, X_1 and X_2 have a negative correlation: when X_1 is low, then the remaining chips (possible values for X_2) tend to be high.

This negative correlation can also be seen from the joint distribution of X_1 and X_2 in Table 6-3. The main diagonal is zero, reflecting the impossibility of drawing the same chip twice. This leaves the probability (in the white region) with a negative tilt, so that cov (X_1, X_2) is slightly negative. (Numerical computation bears this out.) When we substitute into

$$\text{var } S = \text{var } (X_1 + X_2) = \text{var } X_1 + \text{var } X_2 + 2 \text{ cov } (X_1, X_2)$$
$$\text{(5-36) repeated}$$

we note that var S is slightly reduced by the negative covariance.

It could similarly be proved in general, for a sample of n observations drawn from a population of N individuals, that the variance of S is reduced by an amount that can be expressed as

$$\text{the reduction factor} = \left(\frac{N-n}{N-1}\right) \qquad\qquad (6\text{-}34)$$

Thus, (6-7) becomes

$$\text{var } S = n\sigma^2 \left(\frac{N - n}{N - 1} \right) \tag{6-35}$$

Because $\overline{X}$ is simply S/n, if S fluctuates less, so will $\overline{X}$—by a proportionate amount, i.e., $\overline{X}$ will be similarly reduced in variance. Thus, (6-11) becomes

$$\text{var } \overline{X} = \frac{\sigma^2}{n} \left(\frac{N - n}{N - 1} \right) \tag{6-36}$$

Certain special sample sizes shed a great deal of light on the variance of $\overline{X}$:

1. When there is only $n = 1$ chip sampled, it does not matter whether or not it is replaced. This is reflected in the reduction factor (6-34) becoming 1, making var $\overline{X}$ without replacement the same as with replacement. [If you have wondered where the 1 came from in the denominator of (6-34), you can see that it is necessary, in order to logically make (6-36) and (6-11) equivalent, as they must be, for a sample size of one.]
2. When $n = N$, the sample coincides with the whole population, every time. Hence every sample mean must be the same—the population mean. The variance of the sample mean, being a measure of its fluctuation, must be zero. This is reflected in (6-36) becoming zero.
3. On the other hand, when n is much smaller than N, (e.g., when 200 men are sample from one million), then (6-34) is practically 1; i.e., as we have already remarked, it makes very little difference whether or not the observations are replaced before continuing sampling.

Finally, we give a simple example to make this all intuitively clear. Suppose we sample 10 of the heights of the male students on a small college campus; suppose further that the first student we sample is the star of the basketball team at 7 feet. Clearly, we now face the problem of a sample average that is too high. If we replace, then in the next 9 men chosen, the star *could* turn up again, thus distorting our sample mean for the second time. But if we don't replace, then we don't have to worry about this tall individual again. In summary, sampling without replacement yields a more reliable sample mean (i.e., $\overline{X}$ has less variance), because extreme values once sampled, cannot return to haunt us again.

PROBLEMS

*6-25 In the game of bridge, cards are allotted points as follows:

Cards	Points
All cards below jack	0
Jack	1
Queen	2
King	3
Ace	4

(a) For the population of 52 cards, find the mean number of points, and the variance.

(b) In a randomly dealt hand of 13 cards, the total number of points S is a random variable. What are the mean and variance of S? (Bridge players beware: no points counted for distribution).

(c) What is $\Pr(S \geq 13)$? (*Hint.* The distribution shape is approximately normal, as we might hope from the central limit theorem).

*6-26 Rework Problem 6-9, assuming the population of people using the elevator is no longer very large, but rather

(a) $N = 500$.

(b) $N = 50$.

*6-27 Rework Problem 6-16, assuming the population is no longer very large, but rather

(a) $N = 5000$

(b) $N = 100$

*6-28 True or False? Correct if false:

When sampling from a finite population (without replacement), the variance (of S or $\bar{X}$) contains the reduction factor $(N - n)/(N - 1)$. However, if the population is large relative to the sample, this factor may be ignored just as if the population were infinite. (To be specific, if $N \geq 100n$, then the reduction factor is between .99 and 1.00, and so changes the variance less than 1%).

Review Problems

6-29 A man at a carnival pays $1 to play a game (roulette) with the following payoff:

Y = Gross Winning	Net Winning = $Y - 1$	Probability
0	-1	20/38
$2	$+1$	18/38

(a) What is the average net winning in a game?

(b) What is his approximate chance of ending up a loser (net loss) if he plays the game:

(1) 5 times?

(2) 25 times?

(3) 125 times?

(c) How could you get an exact answer for (b)1?

(d) How many times should he play if he wants to be 99% certain of losing?

6-30 Suppose there are five men in a room, whose heights in inches are 62, 65, 68, 65, 65. One man is drawn at random, and his height is denoted X.

(a) Graph the probability distribution of X, i.e., the population distribution. Find its mean μ, and variance σ^2.

Suppose a sample of two men is drawn, with replacement, and the sample mean $\bar{X}$ is calculated. Then,

(b) Construct a table of the probability function of $\bar{X}$.

(c) Graph the probability function of $\bar{X}$.

(d) Find the mean and variance of $\bar{X}$ from its probability distribution.

(e) Check your answers to (d) using the equations of this chapter.

(f) Is the following statement valid for this problem? If not, correct it.

$\bar{X}$ fluctuates around μ—sometimes larger, sometimes smaller, but its expectation is exactly μ. Being the average of 2 observations, $\bar{X}$ does not fluctuate as much as a single observation, however. This is reasonable, because in a sample, a large observation will often be "cancelled out" by a small observation.

*6-31 Repeat Problem 6-30 for a sample of 2 men drawn *without* replacement. Why is this sampling without replacement preferable?

6-32 In Chapter 3 it was implied that in a finite, but very large sample, relative frequency is "very likely" to be "close to" probability. To make this statement precise, for the rolling of a die for example, let P denote the proportion of aces in 10,000 throws, and calculate

$$\Pr\left(\tfrac{1}{6} - .01 < P < \tfrac{1}{6} + .01\right)$$

ESTIMATION I

The only way to save yourself from the pain of lost illusions is to have none.

Charles Marriott

7-1   **CONFIDENCE INTERVALS**

Before beginning statistical induction, we pause in Table 7-1 to review the concepts of sample and population. It is essential to remember that the population mean μ and variance σ^2 are constants (though generally unknown). These are called population *parameters*.

By contrast, the sample mean $\bar{X}$ and sample variance s^2 are random variables, varying from sample to sample, with a certain probability distribution. For example, the distribution of $\bar{X}$ was found to be $\bar{X} \sim N$ $(\mu, \sigma^2/n)$ in (6-15). A random variable such as $\bar{X}$ or s^2 which is calculated from the observations in a sample is given the technical name *sample statistic*. In Table 7-1 and throughout the rest of the text, we shall color the sample red and the population gray, in order to keep the distinction clear.

As a specific example of statistical inference, suppose we wish to estimate the average height of the men on a large midwestern campus. This population mean μ is a fixed, but unknown parameter. We estimate it by taking a sample of 25 men, say; suppose the sample mean $\bar{X}$ turns out to be 68 inches. We shall see in the next section that this is our best single estimate or "point estimate" of μ. But we also know from

Table 7-1   Review of Sample versus Population

A *Random Sample* is a Random Subset of *the Population*	
Relative frequencies f_i/n are used to compute $\overline{X}$ and s^2, which are examples of random statistics or estimators	Probabilities $p(x)$ are used to compute μ and σ^2, which are examples of fixed parameters or targets

sampling theory, that unless we are extremely lucky this estimate $\overline{X}$ will not be exactly on target, but rather a bit high or a bit low; ($\overline{X}$ is distributed around μ as shown in the left-hand side of Figure 6-2.) If we want to be reasonably confident that our inference is correct, we cannot claim that μ is precisely equal to our observed $\overline{X}$; instead we must make an allowance—known as a *confidence interval* or *interval estimate*—of the following form:

$$\mu = \overline{X} \pm \text{a sampling error} \tag{7-1}$$

The crucial issue is: How wide must the sampling allowance be? We shall find that we can be very specific in our interval estimate of μ, because we were very specific about the distribution of $\overline{X}$ around μ in the previous chapter. This distribution is reviewed in Figure 7-1.

First we must decide how confident we wish to be that our interval

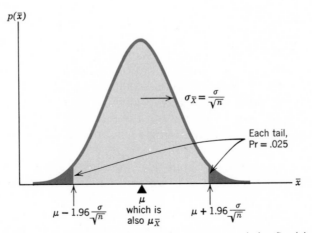

FIGURE 7-1   Normal distribution of the sample mean around the fixed but unknown parameter μ.

estimate is right—that it does indeed bracket μ. It is common to choose 95% confidence; in other words, we will be using a technique that will give us, in the long run, a correct interval estimate 19 times out of 20.

To get a confidence level of 95%, we select the smallest range under the normal distribution of $\overline{X}$ that will just enclose a 95% probability. Obviously, this is the middle chunk, leaving $2\frac{1}{2}\%$ probability excluded in each tail, as shown in Figure 7-1. From our normal tables, we note that this involves going above and below the mean by 1.96 standard deviations of $\overline{X}$. We therefore write

$$\Pr\left(\mu - 1.96\frac{\sigma}{\sqrt{n}} < \overline{X} < \mu + 1.96\frac{\sigma}{\sqrt{n}}\right) = 95\% \qquad (7\text{-}2)$$

The bracketed inequalities may be solved for μ, "turned around" so to speak, obtaining the equivalent statement:[1]

$$\Pr\left(\overline{X} - 1.96\frac{\sigma}{\sqrt{n}} < \mu < \overline{X} + 1.96\frac{\sigma}{\sqrt{n}}\right) = 95\% \qquad (7\text{-}3)$$

We must be exceedingly careful not to misinterpret (7-3). μ has *not* changed its character in the course of this algebraic manipulation. It has not become a variable; it remains a population constant. Equation (7-3), like (7-2), is a probability statement about the random variable $\overline{X}$, or more precisely, the "random interval" $\overline{X} - 1.96(\sigma/\sqrt{n})$ to $\overline{X} + 1.96(\sigma/\sqrt{n})$. *It is this interval that varies, not μ.*

To appreciate this fundamental point, let's return to the problem of constructing an interval estimate of average men's heights on the large midwestern campus. Moreover, to clearly illustrate what is going on, suppose we have some supernatural knowledge of the population μ (which we know to be 69 inches) and σ (which we know to be 3.2 inches.) Now let us just observe what happens when the statistician (poor mortal that he is) tries to estimate μ using (7-3) above. Just for

---

[1]To prove (7-3) more directly, we could begin by standardizing $\overline{X}$, which then has the standard normal distribution. Thus from the standard normal tables,

$$\Pr\left(-1.96 < \frac{\overline{X} - \mu}{\sigma/\sqrt{n}} < 1.96\right) = 95\% \qquad (7\text{-}4)$$

In (7-4) the bracketed inequalities may be solved for μ, obtaining the equivalent inequalities

$$\Pr\left(\overline{X} - 1.96\frac{\sigma}{\sqrt{n}} < \mu < \overline{X} + 1.96\frac{\sigma}{\sqrt{n}}\right) = 95\% \qquad (7\text{-}3) \text{ proved}$$

the sake of illustration, let's suppose he makes 20 such interval estimates, each time from a different random sample of 36 men. Figure 7-2 illustrates his typical experience.

First, in the top panel we illustrate equation (7-2): $\bar{X}$ is distributed around $\mu = 69$, with a 95% probability that it lies as close as

$$\pm 1.96 \frac{\sigma}{\sqrt{n}} = \pm 1.96 \frac{(3.2)}{\sqrt{36}} = \pm 1.0 \qquad (7\text{-}5)$$

That is, there is a 95% probability that any $\bar{X}$ will fall in the range 68 to 70 inches.

But the statistician does not know this; he blindly takes his first random sample, from which we suppose he computes the first mean $\bar{x}$ to be 69.5. From (7-3) he calculates[2] the appropriate 95% confidence interval for μ:

$$69.5 \pm 1.96 \frac{\sigma}{\sqrt{n}} \qquad (7\text{-}6)$$

$$69.5 \pm 1.96 \frac{3.2}{\sqrt{36}} \qquad (7\text{-}7)$$

$$= 69.5 \pm 1.0$$

$$= 68.5 \text{ to } 70.5 \qquad (7\text{-}8)$$

This interval estimate for μ is the first one shown in Figure 7-2. We note that in his first effort, the statistician is right; μ is enclosed in this interval.

In his second sample, the statistician happens to draw a shorter group of individuals, and duly computes $\bar{x}$ to be 68.6 inches. From a similar evaluation of (7-3) he comes up with his second interval estimate shown in the diagram, and so on. We observe that nineteen of these twenty estimates bracket the constant μ. Only one missed the mark, and was wrong.

We can easily see why he was right most of the time. For each interval estimate he is simply adding and subtracting 1 inch to his sample mean; but this is the same ± 1 inch that appears in (7-5) and defines the range

_____

[2]We gloss over one difficulty here. In evaluating (7-3) the statistician has an observed value for $\bar{X}$ and knows that sample size n is 36. But he does *not* know σ, the population standard deviation. All he can do is guess at it, and his best guess is the sample standard deviation s, which we suppose he computes to be 3.2 inches. We deal with this problem in detail in Section 8-2; but for now we can rest assured that s is a reasonable approximation for σ in this problem.

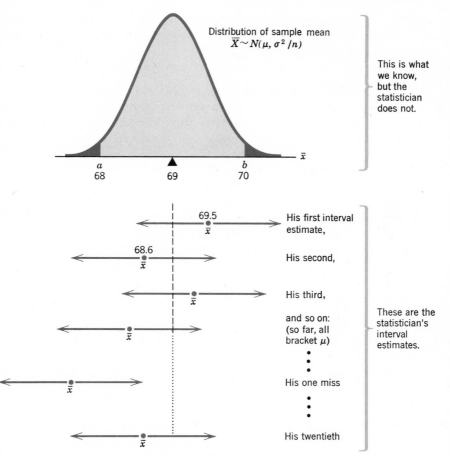

FIGURE 7-2   Construction of twenty interval estimates: typical results.

ab around μ. Thus, if and only if he observes a sample mean within the range *ab*, will his interval estimate bracket μ. Nineteen of his twenty sample means do fall in the range *ab*, and in all these instances his interval estimate was right. He was wrong only in the one instance when he observed a sample mean outside *ab*.

In practice, of course, a statistician would not take many samples—he only takes one. And once this interval estimate is made, he is either right or wrong; this interval brackets μ or it does not. But the important point to recognize is that the statistician is using a method with a 95% probability of success; this follows because there is a 95% probability that his observed $\overline{X}$ will fall within the range *ab*, and as a consequence his interval estimate will bracket μ. This is what is meant by a 95% confidence interval: the statistician knows that in the long run, 95% of the intervals he constructs in this way will bracket μ.

To review, we briefly emphasize the main points:

1. The population parameter μ is constant, and remains constant. It is the interval estimate that is a random variable, because $\overline{X}$ is a random variable. As long as $\overline{X}$ is a random variable that can take on a whole range of values, it is referred to as an "estimator" of μ.
2. But once the sample has been observed and $\overline{X}$ takes on one specific value (e.g., $\overline{x} = 69.5$ inches) it is then called an "estimate"[3] of μ. Since it is no longer a random variable, probability statements are no longer strictly valid. For this reason when the estimate $\overline{x}$ is substituted into (7-3), it is no longer called a 95% probability statement, but rather a 95% confidence statement,

$$\overline{x} - 1.96\frac{\sigma}{\sqrt{n}} < \mu < \overline{x} + 1.96\frac{\sigma}{\sqrt{n}} \qquad (7\text{-}9)$$

Thus, our deduction in (7-3) that $\overline{X}$ is close to μ has been "turned around" into the induction that μ is close to the observed $\overline{x}$. Sometimes (7-9) is abbreviated to

95% confidence interval,

$$\mu = \overline{x} \pm z_{.025}\frac{\sigma}{\sqrt{n}} \qquad (7\text{-}10)$$

where $z_{.025}$ is the critical value leaving 2.5% probability in the upper tail of the standard normal distribution.

To recapitulate, once $\overline{X}$ is observed to be $\overline{x}$, then the "die is cast," and the interval estimate (7-9) is either dead right or dead wrong.

3. Because of our omniscience, we know the one time that the statistician erred. But *he* does not know which confidence intervals, if any, are wrong. All he knows is that he will be right 95% of the time, in the long run.

_____

[3] For emphasis, the *estimate* is denoted by the lower case letter $\overline{x}$, while the random *estimator* is denoted by the capital letter $\overline{X}$. We might call $\overline{x}$ the realized value, and $\overline{X}$ the potential value.

4. As sample size is increased, the distribution of $\overline{X}$ becomes more concentrated around μ (as n increases, $\sigma/\sqrt{n}$ decreases), and the confidence interval becomes more narrow and precise.
5. If we wish to be more confident—e.g., 99% confident—of our conclusions, then we must leave less of the probability in each tail in Figure 7-2; thus the range ab increases. Hence our interval estimate becomes less precise. Note how this point and the one preceding verify our casual observations in Chapter 1.
6. An inference about the population parameter μ was feasible because we knew the distribution of the estimator $\overline{X}$. This raises an interesting question, "Is it not possible that there are other statistics (for example, the sample median) that could be used to estimate μ? Why did we use the sample mean?" Intuitively, it seems preferable to estimate a mean with a mean. But there are stronger reasons, given in the next section.

PROBLEMS

7-1 An anthropologist measured the heights (in inches) of a random sample of 100 men from a certain population, and found the sample mean and variance to be 71 and 9 respectively.
(a) Find a 95% confidence interval for the mean height μ of the whole population.
(b) Find a 99% confidence interval.

7-2 A research study examines the consumption expenditures (in thousands of dollars) of a random sample of 50 American families (all at the same income and asset level). The sample mean is 5.2 and the standard deviation is .72. Construct a 95% confidence interval for the mean consumption of all American families (at this income and asset level).

7-3 The reaction times of 150 randomly selected drivers were found to have a mean of .83 sec and standard deviation of .20 sec. Find a 95% confidence interval for the mean reaction time of the whole population of drivers.

7-4 From a very large class in statistics, the following 40 marks were randomly selected:

71	74	65	72	64	42	62	62	58	82
49	83	58	65	68	60	76	86	74	53
78	64	55	87	56	50	71	58	57	75
58	86	64	56	45	73	54	86	70	73

Construct a 95% confidence interval for the average mark of the whole class. (*Hint.* Reduce your work to manageable proportions by grouping into cells of width 5. Coding also helps.)

7-5 A scientist computed a 95% confidence interval for each of 3 different parameters. What is the probability that all three intervals are correct,

(a) if they are independent?

*(b) if they are not independent?

If an exact answer is not possible, at least give the bounds within which the answer must lie.

7-6 What is the probability that a statistician who constructs 20 independent 95% confidence intervals will err:

(a) Not at all?

(b) Once (as in our example in Section 7-1)?

(c) More than once?

7-2   **DESIRABLE PROPERTIES OF ESTIMATORS**

So far we have considered two kinds of estimates of μ: the point estimate $\bar{x}$, which is our best single estimate, but must almost certainly be slightly in error; and the preferable interval estimate which is constructed around it,

$$\bar{x} \pm z_{.025} \frac{\sigma}{\sqrt{n}}$$ (7-10) repeated

In the next chapter we shall return to the construction of various interval estimates; but in the balance of this chapter we shall examine the characteristics of point estimators.

To be perfectly general, we consider any population parameter θ, and denote an estimator for it by $\hat{\theta}$. (In our special example in the preceding section, μ is the population parameter θ, and $\bar{X}$ is its estimator $\hat{\theta}$). We would like the random variable $\hat{\theta}$ to vary within a narrow range around its fixed target θ. We develop this notion of closeness in several ways.

(a) No Bias

An unbiased estimator is one that is, *on the average*, right on target, as shown in Figure 7-3a. Formally, we state the definition,

$\hat{\theta}$ is an unbiased estimator of θ if $E(\hat{\theta}) = \theta$ (7-11)

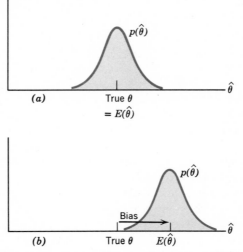

FIGURE 7-3   Comparison of (a) unbiased estimator, and (b) biased estimator.

For example, $\overline{X}$ is an unbiased estimator of μ, because

$$E(\overline{X}) = \mu \qquad \text{(6-10) repeated}$$

Of course, an estimator $\hat{\theta}$ is called biased if $E(\hat{\theta})$ is different from θ; in fact, bias is defined as this difference,

$$\text{Bias} \triangleq E(\hat{\theta}) - \theta \qquad (7\text{-}12)$$

Bias is illustrated in Figure 7-3b. The distribution of $\hat{\theta}$ is "off target"; since $E(\hat{\theta})$ exceeds θ, there will be a tendency for $\hat{\theta}$ to over-estimate θ.

As an example of a biased estimator, the sample mean squared deviation

$$\text{MSD} = \frac{1}{n} \sum (X_i - \overline{X})^2 \qquad \begin{array}{l}(7\text{-}13)\\ (2\text{-}5a) \text{ repeated}\end{array}$$

will on the average underestimate σ^2, the population variance.[4] But if

_____

[4]This underestimation can be seen very easily in the case of $n = 1$. Then $\overline{X}$ coincides with X_i, so that (7-13) gives MSD = 0, which is an obvious underestimate of σ^2.

On the other hand, (7-14), when $n = 1$, gives $s^2 = 0/0$, which is undefined. But this is not a drawback; in fact, it gives a good warning that since a sample of just one observation has no "spread," it cannot estimate the population variance σ^2 (assuming μ is unknown, of course).

we inflate it just a little, by dividing by $n - 1$ instead of n, we obtain the sample variance

$$s^2 = \frac{1}{n - 1} \sum (X_i - \overline{X})^2 \qquad (7\text{-}14)$$

$$(2\text{-}6a) \text{ repeated}$$

which has been proved an unbiased estimator of σ^2. (When we say "has been proved," we mean that it has been proved in advanced texts. If it has been proved in *this* text, we shall usually say "we have proved.") If you were puzzled by the divisor $n - 1$ used in defining s^2 in Chapter 2, you can now see why: we want to use this sample variance as an unbiased estimator of the population variance.

Both the sample mean and median are unbiased estimators of μ in a normal population; thus, in judging which is to be preferred, we must examine their other characteristics.

(b) Efficiency

As well as being on target on the average, we should also like the distribution of an estimator $\hat{\theta}$ to be highly concentrated, that is, to have a small variance. This is the notion of efficiency, shown in Figure 7-4.

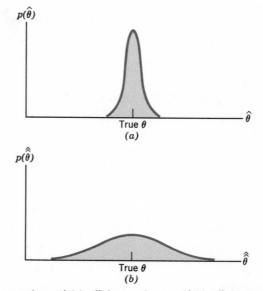

FIGURE 7-4   A comparison of (a) efficient estimator; (b) inefficient estimator (both are unbiased).

We describe $\hat{\theta}$ as more efficient because it has smaller variance. Formally, the relative efficiency of two unbiased[5] estimators is defined as

$$\text{Relative efficiency of } \hat{\theta} \text{ compared to } \hat{\hat{\theta}} \triangleq \frac{\text{var } \hat{\hat{\theta}}}{\text{var } \hat{\theta}} \qquad (7\text{-}15)$$

An estimator which is more efficient than any other is called absolutely efficient, or simply "efficient."

Finally, we are in a position to pass judgement on the merits of the sample mean and median as estimators of μ. *In sampling from a normal population*, $\overline{X}$ has been proved to be the efficient estimator of μ. We have already established that its variance is σ^2/n. On the other hand, the sample median has been shown to have a variance of approximately[6]

$$(\pi/2)(\sigma^2/n) \qquad (7\text{-}16)$$

Hence the relative efficiency of the sample mean compared to the sample median is derived from (7-15) as approximately

$$\frac{(\pi/2)(\sigma^2/n)}{\sigma^2/n} = \frac{\pi}{2} = 157\% \qquad (7\text{-}17)$$

Because it is 57% more efficient, $\overline{X}$ is preferred. It will give us a point estimate that will tend to be closer to the target μ; or, it will give us a more precise (smaller range) interval estimate. Of course, by increasing sample size n we can reduce the variance of either estimator. Therefore, an alternative way of looking at the greater efficiency of the sample mean is to recognize that the sample median will yield as accurate a point or interval estimate only if we take a larger sample, (specifically, 57% larger.) Hence, using the sample mean is more efficient, because it costs less to sample; note how the economic and statistical definitions of efficiency coincide.

---

[5] For biased estimators, the definition of efficiency is

$$\frac{E(\hat{\hat{\theta}} - \theta)^2}{E(\hat{\theta} - \theta)^2}$$

which is (7-15) if both estimators have 0 bias.

[6] (7-16) and (7-17) are approximations that become better and better as sample size increases. They are therefore called "large-sample," or "limiting," or "asymptotic" formulas.

(c) Consistency

Roughly speaking, a consistent estimator is one that concentrates completely on its target as sample size increases indefinitely, as sketched in Figure 7-5. In the limiting case, as the sample size becomes infinite, a consistent estimator $\hat{\theta}$ will provide a perfect point estimate of the target θ.

We now state consistency more precisely. Just as the variance was a good measure of the spread of a distribution about its mean, so the

$$\text{mean squared error} \triangleq E(\hat{\theta} - \theta)^2 \qquad (7\text{-}18)$$

is a good measure of how the distribution of $\hat{\theta}$ is spread about its target value θ. Consistency requires this to be zero in the limit; thus we define,[7]

FIGURE 7-5   A consistent estimator, showing how the distribution of $\hat{\theta}$ concentrates on its target θ as n increases.

---

[7]Definition (7-19) is sometimes called "consistency in mean-square." It implies a condition called "consistency in probability": for any positive δ (no matter how small),

$$\Pr(|\hat{\theta} - \theta| < \delta) \to 1 \qquad (7\text{-}20)$$

$$\text{as } n \to \infty$$

This is usually taken as the definition of consistency by mathematical statisticians.

$$\hat{\theta} \text{ is consistent iff}^8 \ E(\hat{\theta} - \theta)^2 \to 0 \qquad (7\text{-}19)$$
$$\text{as } n \to \infty$$

Mean squared error is related to bias and variance by the following theorem,[9]

$$E(\hat{\theta} - \theta)^2 = (\text{bias } \hat{\theta})^2 + \text{var } \hat{\theta} \qquad (7\text{-}21)$$

which has the important corollary,

$\hat{\theta}$ is a consistent estimator iff[8] its bias and
variance *both* approach zero, as $n \to \infty$. $\qquad$ (7-22)

If the bias approaches zero, the estimator is called "asymptotically unbiased"—a condition that is clearly weaker than[10] consistency.

The sample mean $\overline{X}$, for example, is a consistent estimator of μ. This follows from (7-22) and the fact that

$$\text{bias } \overline{X} = 0 \text{ for any } n \qquad \begin{array}{l}(7\text{-}23)\\ (6\text{-}10) \text{ repeated}\end{array}$$

$$\text{var } \overline{X} = \frac{\sigma^2}{n} \to 0 \text{ as } n \to \infty \qquad \begin{array}{l}(7\text{-}24)\\ (6\text{-}11) \text{ repeated}\end{array}$$

Consistency does not guarantee that an estimator is a good one. For example, as an estimator of μ in a normal population, the sample median is consistent.[11] But it is not the best estimator; the sample mean is preferred because it is both consistent *and* efficient.

---

[8] Recall that iff is an abbreviation for "if and only if."

[9] **proof** $\quad$ Letting $\mu = E(\hat{\theta})$, we may write

$$\begin{aligned}
E(\hat{\theta} - \theta)^2 &= E[(\hat{\theta} - \mu) + (\mu - \theta)]^2 \\
&= E(\hat{\theta} - \mu)^2 + 2(\mu - \theta) \underbrace{E(\hat{\theta} - \mu)}_{=0} + (\mu - \theta)^2 \\
&= \text{var } \hat{\theta} + 0 + (\mu - \theta)^2 \\
&= \text{var } \hat{\theta} + (\text{Bias } \hat{\theta})^2.
\end{aligned}$$

[10] Asymptotic unbiasedness is also a weaker condition than unbiasedness—since the latter applies for all n, not just $n \to \infty$.

[11] To prove consistency, we again use (7-22), noting that the sample median has zero bias, and a variance given by (7-16) which approaches zero.

As a final example, the sample MSD is a consistent estimator of σ^2. It is true that it is a biased estimator; but as $n \to \infty$, this bias disappears, i.e., it is asymptotically unbiased.[12] Since it can also be proven that its variance approaches zero, the conditions of corollary (7-22) are satisfied. This concept of a biased, yet consistent estimator is a very important one—for example, in econometrics.

PROBLEMS

7-7 True or false? If false, correct it.

(a) The sample proportion P is an unbiased estimator of the population proportion π.

(b) μ is a random variable (varying from sample to sample), and is used to estimate the parameter $\overline{X}$.

(c) In sampling from a normal population, the sample median and sample mean are both consistent. The difference is that the sample median is biased, whereas the sample mean is unbiased.

7-8 Suppose two economists estimate μ (the average expenditure of American families on food), with two different (and statistically independent) estimates $\overline{X}_1$ and $\overline{X}_2$. The first economist is more careful than the second—he manages to keep the standard deviation of $\overline{X}_1$ down to 1/5 the standard deviation of $\overline{X}_2$. When asked how to combine $\overline{X}_1$ and $\overline{X}_2$ to get a publishable overall estimate, a certain group of statisticians comes up with 4 proposals:

(1) $\hat{\mu}_1 = \frac{1}{2}(\overline{X}_1 + \overline{X}_2)$

(2) $\hat{\mu}_2 = (\frac{4}{5})\overline{X}_1 + (\frac{1}{5})\overline{X}_2$

(3) $\hat{\mu}_3 = (\frac{5}{6})\overline{X}_1 + (\frac{1}{6})\overline{X}_2$

(4) $\hat{\mu}_4 = \overline{X}_1$

(a) Rank these estimators in decreasing order of efficiency.

*(b) Find an even more efficient estimate of μ, or else prove that your answer to (a) is the most efficient linear combination possible. (Requires calculus.)

*(c) Find the efficiency of each $\hat{\mu}_i$ relative to the most efficient estimate found in (b).

---

[12] To establish this, we note that

$$\text{MSD} = \left(\frac{n-1}{n}\right) s^2$$

Thus $\text{MSD} \to s^2$ as $n \to \infty$. Since s^2 is unbiased (for any n), it follows that MSD is unbiased as $n \to \infty$.

7-9 Based on a random sample of 2 observations, consider two estimators of μ:

$$\bar{X} = (\tfrac{1}{2})X_1 + (\tfrac{1}{2})X_2$$

and

$$W \triangleq (\tfrac{1}{3})X_1 + (\tfrac{2}{3})X_2$$

(a) Prove they are unbiased.

(b) What is the efficiency of W relative to $\bar{X}$? Which estimator is better?

7-10 Based on a random sample of 100 observations, consider two estimators of μ:

$$\bar{X}_{100} \triangleq \frac{1}{100}(X_1 + X_2 + \cdots + X_{100})$$

and

$$\bar{X}_{90} \triangleq \frac{1}{90}(X_1 + X_2 + \cdots + X_{90})$$

What is the efficiency of $\bar{X}_{90}$ relative to $\bar{X}_{100}$?

7-11 Discuss the following statements:

(a) In both Problems 7-9 and 7-10 we see an example of a relatively inefficient estimator (an estimator with relative efficiency of only 90%). In Problem 7-10, this inefficiency was obvious, because 10% of the observations were thrown away in calculating $\bar{X}_{90}$. In Problem 7-9, the inefficiency was more subtle, because it was caused merely by an inefficient analysis, using the wrong weights for W. However, in terms of results (producing an estimator with more variance than necessary), we can say that both inefficiencies are the same; in other words, the man who uses an inefficient analysis is getting the same results as a man who throws away data.

In view of this, what advice would you give to a researcher who spends $100,000 collecting data, and $100 analyzing it?

(b) In Problem 7-8, the inefficiency of $\hat{\mu}_1$ (only 15% efficient relative to the optimum linear estimator) was very surprising. Here is an example of an estimator which might seem reasonable to some people; (the two conflicting parties are simply "splitting their difference"). Yet it is just as damaging to use this as to throw away 85% of the observations in a simple random sample.

7-12 Consider a bowl full of many chips—one-third marked 2, one-third marked 4, and one-third marked 6. The population moments were found in Problem 6-5 to be $\mu = 4$ and $\sigma^2 = 8/3$. When a sample of 2 chips is drawn, construct the probability table of $\overline{X}$, and hence

(a) Show (once more) that $\overline{X}$ is an unbiased estimator of μ.

(b) Is $(2\overline{X} + 1)$ an unbiased estimator of $(2\mu + 1)$?

(c) Is $(\overline{X})^2$ an unbiased estimator of μ^2?

(d) Is $1/\overline{X}$ an unbiased estimator of $1/\mu$?

(e) How could you have answered parts (a), (b) and (c) theoretically, without going through all the computations?

7-13 To illustrate bias very concretely, consider again the sample of $n = 2$ chips in Problem 7-12. We shall study sample estimators in 3 ways.

(a) *Empirical approach* (Monte-Carlo technique). Repeat the sampling experiment many times. (You can simulate the drawing of 2 chips with the random digits of Appendix Table II. If each student does it, say, 5 times, and the results from the class are pooled, this would save work.) The result will be a table like:

Sample of 2 Chips	$\overline{X}$	MSD	s^2
(2,6)	4	4	8
(4,2)	3	1	2
(6,6)	6	0	0
⋮	⋮	⋮	⋮
Averages	?	?	?

It may be convenient to array the data in relative frequency tables.

(1) Does $\overline{X}$ average close to μ?

(2) Does s^2 average close to σ^2?

(3) Does MSD average close to σ^2?

(b) *Analytical approach*. In (a), if the experiment were repeated endlessly, the relative frequencies would settle down to probabilities, which you can use to calculate whether

(1) $E(\overline{X}) \overset{?}{=} \mu$

(2) $E(s^2) \overset{?}{=} \sigma^2$

(3) $E(\text{MSD}) \overset{?}{=} \sigma^2$

(c) *Theoretical approach*. Find the references in the text that give the same answers as part (b)—only more generally, for any sample size and population.

*7-14 A farmer has a square field, whose area he wants to estimate. When he measures the length of the field, he makes a random error, so that his *observed length* X_1 is a normal variable centered at 200 (the true but unknown value) with $\sigma = 20$. Worried about his possible error, he decides to take a second independent observation X_2 and average. But he is in a dilemma as to how to proceed:

(1) Should he average X_1 and X_2, and then square? or
(2) Should he square first, and then average?
Mathematically, it's a question whether

$$\left(\frac{X_1 + X_2}{2}\right)^2 \quad \text{or} \quad \left(\frac{X_1^2 + X_2^2}{2}\right) \text{ is best}$$

(a) Are methods (1) and (2) really different, or are they just 2 different ways of saying the same thing? (*Hint.* Try a couple of actual values, like $X_1 = 100$ and $X_2 = 200$.)

(b) If they are different, which has less bias? (*Hints.* This problem will actually be easier if you avoid arithmetic by generalizing from a length of 200 feet to a length of μ, and also use general σ. Furthermore, the *normality* is irrelevant to questions of expectation. Finally, try using equation (4-20).)

(c) Generalize answer (b) to a sample of n measurements.

7-3   AN INTRODUCTION TO NONPARAMETRIC ESTIMATION

In this section we shall consider nonnormal populations; however, they will all be perfectly symmetric, with the mean, median, and mode all coinciding exactly at the center of symmetry c, shown in Figure 7-6a. To estimate this, suppose that the statistician has taken the sample of 9 observations shown in Figure 7-6b. How shall he use this sample efficiently to estimate c? (For simplicity, we shall simply look for a point estimate, while postponing the preferred, but more complicated, interval estimate to Chapter 16.)

Of course, the sample of 9 random observations will not be perfectly symmetric like the population, so that the *sample* mean and median will differ. Which is the better point estimator of c?

One statistician, noting that c happens to be the population mean, might recommend using the sample mean as in Section 7-1. But another statistician, noting that c is the population median, might recommend the sample median. In the particular sample shown in Figure 7-6b, the sample median happens to be closer than the sample mean to the target c, but in other samples the reverse might be true. To choose between them, we should look at their relative efficiency, as defined by (7-15).

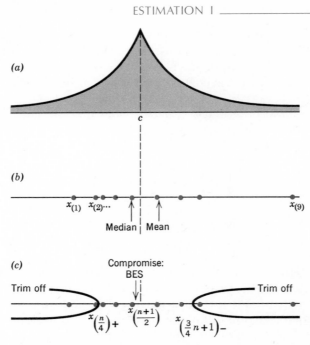

FIGURE 7-6   Robust estimation of the population center c. (a) Symmetrical population distribution. (b) Sample of 9 observations. (c) BES (best easy systematic) estimate.

If the population is normal, we already know from (7-17) that the sample mean is about[13] 57% more efficient than the sample median. Unfortunately, this advantage is not maintained for many nonnormal populations. For example, consider the Cauchy distribution, whose formula[14] is

$$p(x) = \frac{1}{\pi[(x - c)^2 + 1]} \tag{7-25}$$

Although this distribution looks bell-shaped, it has tails that are much thicker than the normal. For a random sample from a Cauchy population, the sample mean has approximately *zero* efficiency relative to the sample median.[15]

We have already emphasized that the population from which we are

---

[13] Remember that (7-17) (like all the other numerical estimates of efficiency of this section) applies for large samples; but it is a reasonable approximation for small sample efficiencies as well.

[14] In this formula, π represents the mathematical constant 3.1416.

[15] In fact, the sample mean is just as variable as a single observation. This is because a wildly deviant observation is likely to occur in the sample, pulling the mean way off target. On the other hand, the median is unaffected by one wild observation.

sampling is a mystery, in the sense that its mean and variance are unknown. But now we see that there is another problem: when its *shape* (normal, Cauchy, or whatever) is unknown, it is no longer clear which estimator is best. Hence a strong argument can be made for using an estimator that is reasonably efficient for *any* kind of population shape; such an estimator, that is free of the assumption that the population is normal, is called "robust," or "distribution-free," or "nonparametric."[16]

These remarks on the Cauchy distribution suggest that the sample median is more robust than the sample mean. Yet when one considers all possible population shapes, neither is really satisfactory: the sample median uses too few observations (only the middle one), while the sample mean uses too many observations (all of them, including the problem outliers.) Is it not possible to compromise, and find something better? One suggestion is to "trim off" a quarter of the observations from each end of the sample, thus getting rid of possible wild outliers. In this trimmed sample, average just the 2 end and 2 middle values. The result may be called the Best Easy Systematic (BES) estimate. (Its efficiency is very good, but not quite best in the mathematical sense of surpassing everything else in every population.) The explicit formulas are

for *n* even,

$$\text{BES} \triangleq \frac{1}{4} \left[x_{\left(\frac{n}{4}\right)+} + x_{\left(\frac{n}{2}\right)} + x_{\left(\frac{n}{2}+1\right)} + x_{\left(\frac{3}{4}n+1\right)-} \right] \qquad (7\text{-}26a)$$

for *n* odd,[17]

$$\text{BES} \triangleq \frac{1}{4} \left[x_{\left(\frac{n}{4}\right)+} + x_{\left(\frac{n+1}{2}\right)} + x_{\left(\frac{n+1}{2}\right)} + x_{\left(\frac{3}{4}n+1\right)-} \right] \qquad (7\text{-}26b)$$

---

[16] The term "nonparametric" has an interesting origin. The normal is often referred to as the "parametric" distribution, since it is completely specified by the two parameters μ and σ; hence "nonparametric" means nonnormal, or more specifically, estimation that is perfectly valid in a population that may be nonnormal.

Although the term "distribution-free" is used synonymously with "non-parametric," the term "robust" is commonly used in a slightly weaker sense—estimation that remains *almost* valid in a non-normal population.

[17] In this case, we may find it instructive to rewrite (7-26b) as

$$\text{BES} = \frac{1}{4} \left[x_{\left(\frac{n}{4}\right)+} + 2x_{\left(\frac{n+1}{2}\right)} + x_{\left(\frac{3}{4}n+1\right)-} \right] \qquad (7\text{-}26c)$$

$$= \frac{1}{2} \left\{ x_{\left(\frac{n+1}{2}\right)} + \left[\frac{x_{\left(\frac{n}{4}\right)+} + x_{\left(\frac{3}{4}n+1\right)-}}{2} \right] \right\} \qquad (7\text{-}26d)$$

(cont'd)

where $x_{(i)}$ = the ith ordered observation, i.e., $x_{(1)}$ has the smallest numerical value, $x_{(2)}$ the next smallest, etc. (see Figure 7-6b). (This must be distinguished from our previous usage where X_1, with no brackets on the subscript, was the first value to be sampled, X_2 the second, and so on.) For subscripts involving fractions, + means round up to the nearest integer, while − means round down.

Finally, let us compare the above estimators of the center of a symmetric population with unknown shape. In increasing order of robustness they are

1. sample mean
2. sample median
3. BES (best easy systematic) estimator given by (7-26).

Thus if the population shape is unknown, BES may be the preferred estimator. But for most of the book we shall return to the sample mean, not only because it is best if the population is known to be normal (or nearly normal), but also because of its attractive mathematical properties and its more easily constructed confidence intervals.

This section therefore should be regarded as a warning that the assumption of population normality often may not hold—and when it does not, an estimator from the large array of nonparametric statistics may be preferred.

PROBLEMS

7-15 (a) Take a sample of size 10 from a normal population (using rounded numbers from Appendix Table IIb). Derive the mean, median, and BES estimate. Which provides the best point estimate of μ in this specific case?

(b) Repeat this procedure on a second random sample. Which is best in this case?

(c) Which would outperform the others if this procedure were to be repeated many times?

7-16 In each of the samples below, calculate the most efficient point estimate of μ (sample mean, median, or BES), explaining why it is preferred.

In the form (7-26d) we see that the BES estimate is just the average of (1) the median and (2) the average of the two quartiles (in square brackets).

For the normal, Cauchy, and double exponential distributions, the efficiency of the BES estimator has been shown to be at least 80% relative to the very best estimator that you could possibly use (even if you *knew* the shape of the population).

(a) A chemist takes the following 12 measurements:

$$8.9 \quad 7.2 \quad 8.5 \quad 8.3 \quad 7.3 \quad 7.8$$
$$7.6 \quad 7.5 \quad 8.6 \quad 7.9 \quad 9.4 \quad 7.9$$

(Assume these observations differ only because of a normally distributed measurement error.)

(b) Suppose that 5 government departments independently estimate U.S. plant and equipment expenditures in 1970 to be (in $ billions):

$$79.9 \quad 80.2 \quad 80.0 \quad 79.5 \quad 80.0$$

(Assume these values differ only because of a normally distributed estimation error.)

(c) An anthropologist measured the width (in centimeters) of 9 skulls from a certain tribe:

$$13.3, \ 14.2, \ 13.5, \ 16.7, \ 11.1, \ 13.1, \ 13.0, \ 12.2, \ 13.0$$

Unfortunately, his measurement technique occasionally erred, being out by several centimeters. Since he was unaware of his blunders, however, he does not know which of the above measurements are invalid.

(d) In a survey of educational attainment, the number of years of schooling was recorded for a random sample of 1000 people. In preparing the data for analysis, there is a possibility that the key-puncher will occasionally misplace a decimal point.

Assuming the distribution of years of education is approximately normal, how should the computer be programmed to estimate the mean μ? Can you suggest anything even better than the mean, median or BES?

ESTIMATION II

Reconnaissance is as important in the art of politics as it is in the art of war—or the art of love.

Henry Durant

8-1   **DIFFERENCE IN TWO MEANS**

In Section 7-1 of the previous chapter, we used a sample mean to construct an interval estimate of a population mean. In this chapter we will develop several other similar examples of how a sample statistic is used to construct an interval estimate of a population parameter.

For example, two population means may be compared by estimating their difference:

$$\mu_1 - \mu_2 \tag{8-1}$$

A reasonable estimate of this difference in population means is the difference in sample means

$$\bar{X}_1 - \bar{X}_2 \tag{8-2}$$

Again, because of sampling fluctuation in point estimates, we are typically interested in an interval estimate. Its development is comparable to the argument in Section 7-1, and involves two steps: the distribution of the estimator $(\bar{X}_1 - \bar{X}_2)$ must be deduced; then this can be turned around to make an inference about the population parameter $(\mu_1 - \mu_2)$.

163

First, how is the estimator $(\bar{X}_1 - \bar{X}_2)$ distributed? Let us assume large samples, so that from (6-15) we know that the first sample mean $\bar{X}_1$ is approximately normally distributed,

$$\bar{X}_1 \sim N(\mu_1, \sigma_1^2/n_1) \tag{8-3}$$

where σ_1^2 represents the variance of the first population, and n_1 the size of the sample drawn. Similarly

$$\bar{X}_2 \sim N(\mu_2, \sigma_2^2/n_2)$$

Independence of the two sampling procedures will ensure that the two random variables $\bar{X}_1$ and $\bar{X}_2$ are independent. Hence, from (5-35) and (5-43), the moments of $(\bar{X}_1 - \bar{X}_2)$ will be

$$E(\bar{X}_1 - \bar{X}_2) = E(\bar{X}_1) - E(\bar{X}_2)$$
$$= \mu_1 - \mu_2 \tag{8-4}$$

$$\text{var}\,(\bar{X}_1 - \bar{X}_2) = (+1)^2 \, \text{var}\, \bar{X}_1 + (-1)^2 \, \text{var}\, \bar{X}_2$$
$$= \frac{\sigma_1^2}{n_1} + \frac{\sigma_2^2}{n_2} \tag{8-5}$$

Since the distribution will be approximately normal, according to (6-13), we may summarize by writing

$$(\bar{X}_1 - \bar{X}_2) \sim N\left(\mu_1 - \mu_2, \frac{\sigma_1^2}{n_1} + \frac{\sigma_2^2}{n_2}\right) \tag{8-6}$$

as shown in Figure 8-1.

In an exercise similar to the derivation of equation (7-10), this knowledge of how the estimator $(\bar{X}_1 - \bar{X}_2)$ behaves can now be turned around to construct the confidence interval,

---

95% confidence interval for the difference in means,

$$(\mu_1 - \mu_2) = (\bar{X}_1 - \bar{X}_2) \pm 1.96 \sqrt{\frac{\sigma_1^2}{n_1} + \frac{\sigma_2^2}{n_2}} \tag{8-7}$$

When σ_1 and σ_2 have a common value, say σ, the 95% confidence interval becomes

$$(\mu_1 - \mu_2) = (\bar{X}_1 - \bar{X}_2) \pm 1.96\, \sigma \sqrt{\frac{1}{n_1} + \frac{1}{n_2}} \tag{8-8}$$

Standard deviation of $(\bar{X}_1 - \bar{X}_2)$ is $\sqrt{\frac{\sigma_1^2}{n_1} + \frac{\sigma_2^2}{n_2}}$

$(\mu_1 - \mu_2)$

$(\bar{x}_1 - \bar{x}_2)$

FIGURE 8-1   Distribution of $(\bar{X}_1 - \bar{X}_2)$.

The variances of the two populations, σ_1^2 and σ_2^2 in (8-7), are usually not known; the best the statistician can do is guess at them, with the variances s_1^2 and s_2^2 he observed in the two samples. Provided the samples are large, this is an accurate enough approximation; but with small samples, this introduces a new source of error. You will recall that this same problem was encountered in estimating a single population mean in Section 7-1. In the next section we shall give a solution for these problems of small-sample estimation.

PROBLEMS

8-1 A random sample of 100 workers in one large plant took an average of 12 minutes to complete a task, with a standard deviation of 2 minutes. A random sample of 50 workers in a second large plant took an average of 11 minutes to complete the task, with a standard deviation of 3 minutes. Construct a 95% confidence interval for the difference between the two population mean completion times.

8-2 Two samples of 100 seedlings were grown with two different fertilizers. One sample had an average height of 10 inches and a standard deviation of 1 inch. The second sample had an average height of 10.5 inches and a standard deviation of 3 inches. Construct a confidence interval for the difference between the average population heights $(\mu_1 - \mu_2)$
(a) At the 95% level of confidence.
(b) At the 90% level of confidence.

8-3 A random sample of 60 students was taken in each of two different universities. The first sample had an average mark of 77 and a standard deviation of 6. The second sample had an average mark of 68 and a standard deviation of 10.
(a) Find a 95% confidence interval for the difference between the mean marks in the two universities.

(b) What increase in the sample size would be necessary to cut the sampling allowance by 1/2?

(c) What increase in the sample size would be necessary to reduce the sampling allowance to 1.0?

8-2　　　　SMALL SAMPLE ESTIMATION: THE t DISTRIBUTION

We shall assume in this section that parent populations are normal; otherwise the t distribution that we now introduce will be only approximately valid.

(a) One Mean, μ

In estimating a population mean μ with a sample mean $\bar{X}$, the statistician generally has no information on the population standard deviation σ; hence he uses the estimator s, the sample standard deviation. Substituting this into (7-10), he estimates the 95% confidence interval for μ as,

$$\mu = \bar{X} \pm z_{.025} \frac{s}{\sqrt{n}}$$

Provided his sample is large (at least 25–50, depending on the precision required), this will be a reasonably accurate approximation. But with a smaller sample size, this substitution introduces an appreciable source of error. Hence if he wishes to remain 95% confident, his interval estimate must be broadened. How much?

Recall that $\bar{X}$ has a normal distribution; when σ was known, we formed the standardized normal variable,

$$Z = \frac{\bar{X} - \mu}{\sigma/\sqrt{n}} \tag{8-9}$$

By analogy, we introduce "Student's t" variable,[1]

$$t = \frac{\bar{X} - \mu}{s/\sqrt{n}} \tag{8-10}$$

---

[1] This t variable was first introduced by Gosset writing under the pseudonym "Student," and later proved valid by R. A. Fisher. We make no attempt to develop the proof because it is not very instructive. It can be found in almost any mathematical statistics text.

The similarity of these two variables is immediately evident. The only difference is that Z involves σ, which is usually unknown; but t involves s, which can always be calculated from the sample. The distribution of t is compared to Z in Figure 8-2, and is tabulated in Appendix Table V.

(At this point of the text, we have come to an unavoidable break in notation. Until now, capital letters denoted random variables, while small letters denoted their realized values. But from now on, in order to conform to common usage, we shall entirely forget this convention. For some variables, like t or s, we shall use small letters for either the random variable *or* its realized values; for other variables like X, $\bar{X}$, P, etc. we shall use capital letters in either case.)

As expected, the t distribution is more spread out than the normal, since the use of s rather than σ introduces a degree of uncertainty. Moreover, while there is one standard normal distribution, there is a whole family of t distributions. With small sample size, this distribution is considerably more spread out than the normal; but as sample size increases, the t distribution approaches the normal, and for samples of about 50 or more, the normal becomes a very accurate approximation.

The distribution of t is not tabled according to sample size n, but rather according to the divisor in s^2, which is now called "degrees of freedom."[2] In calculating s^2 in (2-6) we used the divisor,

$$\text{degrees of freedom, d.f.} = n - 1 \tag{8-11}$$

For example, for a sample with $n = 3$, then d.f. $= 2$, and we find from Appendix Table V that the critical t value which leaves $2\frac{1}{2}\%$ probability in the upper tail is

$$t_{.025} = 4.30$$

---

[2] The phrase "degrees of freedom" is explained in the following intuitive way:

Originally there are n degrees of freedom in a sample of n observations. But one degree of freedom is used up in calculating $\bar{X}$, leaving only $n - 1$ degrees of freedom for the residuals $(X_i - \bar{X})$ to calculate s^2.

For example, consider a sample of two observations, 21 and 15, say. Since $\bar{X} = 18$, the residuals are $+3$ and -3, the second residual necessarily being just the negative of the first. While the first residual is "free," the second is strictly determined; hence there is only 1 degree of freedom in the residuals.

Generally, for a sample of size n, it may be shown that while the first $n - 1$ residuals are free, the last residual is strictly determined by the requirement that the sum of all residuals be zero, i.e., $\Sigma(X_i - \bar{X}) = 0$.

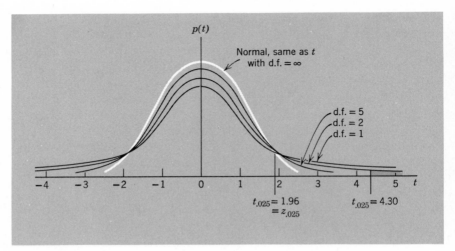

FIGURE 8-2   The standard normal distribution and the t distribution compared.

This is shown in Figure 8-2. By symmetry, it follows that for any observed t,

$$\Pr(-4.30 < t < 4.30) = 95\% \tag{8-12}$$

Substituting for t according to (8-10),

$$\Pr\left(-4.30 < \frac{\bar{X} - \mu}{s/\sqrt{n}} < 4.30\right) = 95\% \tag{8-13}$$

This deduction can now be turned around as usual to produce an inference: for a sample of size 3, the 95% confidence interval for μ is

$$\mu = \bar{X} \pm 4.30 \frac{s}{\sqrt{n}} \tag{8-14}$$

For example, suppose that from a large class, a sample of 3 grades was drawn and analyzed as in Table 8-1. Substituting into (8-14), we obtain the 95% confidence interval for the whole class mean,

$$\mu = 60 \pm 4.30 \frac{\sqrt{93}}{\sqrt{3}}$$
$$= 60 \pm 24$$

For a general sample size n, we obtain

95% confidence interval for the population mean,

$$\mu = \bar{X} \pm t_{.025}\frac{s}{\sqrt{n}}$$

(8-15)

---

where $t_{.025}$ is the critical t value leaving $2\frac{1}{2}$% of the probability in the upper tail, with $n - 1$ degrees of freedom.

To sum up, we note the similarity of t estimation in (8-15) and normal estimation in (7-10). The only difference is that the observed sample value s is substituted for σ, and as a consequence the critical t value must be substituted for the critical z value.

An important practical question is: When do we use the t distribution and when do we use the normal? If σ is known, the normal distribution is appropriate; if σ is unknown, then the t distribution is appropriate—regardless of sample size. However, if the sample size is large, the normal is an accurate enough approximation[3] of the t. So in practice the t distribution is used only for small samples when σ is unknown— and the normal is used otherwise.

As sample size n decreases, estimation becomes less precise (i.e., interval estimates become wider). The two reasons for this are clearly distinguished in (8-15). First, the divisor $\sqrt{n}$ becomes smaller. This appears in (7-10) as well as in (8-15); thus even if σ is known and

Table 8-1 Student's t Analysis of One Sample

Observed Grade X_i	$(X_i - \bar{X})$	$(X_i - \bar{X})^2$
56	-4	16
71	11	121
53	-7	49
$\bar{X} = \dfrac{180}{3}$ $= 60$	0✓	$s^2 = \dfrac{186}{2} = 93$

---

[3]This may be verified from Table V. For example, a 95% confidence interval with d.f. $= 60$ should use a critical t value of 2.00; but the use of the normal value of 1.96 as an approximation involves very little error (just 2%).

As we scan down the $t_{.025}$ column in Table V, these critical values approach $z_{.025} = 1.96$, shown in the last row. This verifies Figure 8-2, where the t distributions approach the normal.

inference is based on the normal distribution, the sampling allowance increases and the interval estimate becomes wider as a consequence. The secondary reason for loss of precision occurs if s must be substituted for an unknown σ. The smaller the sample, the more the appropriate t distribution will depart from the normal; and the more spread the t distribution, the broader the interval estimate.

(b) Difference in Two Means ($\mu_1 - \mu_2$), Independent Samples

We shall assume, as often occurs in practice, that even though the two populations may have different means, they have a common variance σ^2. When σ^2 is known, (8-8) is appropriate. When unknown, σ^2 must be estimated. The appropriate estimate is to add up all the squared deviations from both samples, and then divide by the degrees of freedom $(n_1 - 1) + (n_2 - 1)$, to obtain an unbiased estimator called the pooled sample variance:

$$s_p^2 = \frac{1}{(n_1 + n_2 - 2)}\left[\sum_{i=1}^{n_1}(X_{1i} - \bar{X}_1)^2 + \sum_{i=1}^{n_2}(X_{2i} - \bar{X}_2)^2\right] \quad (8\text{-}16)$$

where X_{1i} (or X_{2i}) represents the ith observation in the first (or second) sample. Substitution of s_p for σ in (8-8) requires also that the t distribution be used, obtaining

---

95% confidence interval for the difference in means,

$$(\mu_1 - \mu_2) = (\bar{X}_1 - \bar{X}_2) \pm t_{.025}\, s_p\sqrt{\frac{1}{n_1} + \frac{1}{n_2}} \quad (8\text{-}17)$$

---

where $t_{.025}$ is the critical t value with d.f. $= n_1 + n_2 - 2$.

For example, suppose that from two large classes, samples of grades were drawn and analyzed as in Table 8-2. Then, from (8-16),

$$s_p^2 = \frac{1}{(4 + 3 - 2)}[398 + 186] = \frac{584}{5} = 117$$

d.f. $= 5$.

Substituting into (8-17), we obtain the 95% confidence interval for the difference in the 2 class means,

$$(\mu_1 - \mu_2) = (74.0 - 60.0) \pm 2.57\sqrt{117}\sqrt{\frac{1}{4} + \frac{1}{3}}$$

$$= 14.0 \pm 21.1 \quad (8\text{-}18)$$

Table 8-2   Analysis of 2 Independent Samples

Class 1			Class 2		
Observed X_{1i}	$X_{1i} - \bar{X}_1$	$(X_{1i} - \bar{X}_1)^2$	Observed X_{2i}	$(X_{2i} - \bar{X}_2)$	$(X_{2i} - \bar{X}_2)^2$
64	−10	100	56	−4	16
66	−8	64	71	11	121
89	15	225	53	−7	49
77	3	9			
$\bar{X}_1 = \dfrac{296}{4}$	0✓	398	$\bar{X}_2 = \dfrac{180}{3}$	0✓	186
$= 74.0$			$\doteq 60.0$		

Thus, we see that the large difference in sample means is obscured by an even larger sampling allowance (due primarily to the smallness of the samples). This procedure not only requires that the variance of grades be the same in the two classes but also that the two samples be independently drawn; (e.g., we do not sample a pair of individuals studying together, one from each class, since they might be very similar in their study habits, and perhaps in their exam results as well).

As another example, consider just one class of students, examined at two different times—say fall and spring terms. The fall and spring population of grades could then be sampled and compared using (8-17)—provided, of course, that the two samples are independently drawn (e.g., we do not make a point of canvassing the same students twice).

(c) Difference in Two Means ($\mu_1 - \mu_2$), Paired Samples

Suppose in our comparison of fall and spring grades that we *do* wish to use the same students twice in both samples; then (8-17), which requires independent samples, can no longer be applied.[4]

The paired values for a sample of four students are set out in Table 8-3. The natural first step is to see how each student changed, that is, calculate the difference $D = X_1 - X_2$ for each student.[5] Once these differences are calculated (in red), then the original data, having served their purpose, can be discarded. We proceed to treat the differences D now *as a single sample*, and we analyze them just as we analyze any other single sample (for example, the sample in Table 8-1). First, we

---

[4] (8-17) was derived from (8-8), (8-7), and (8-6), which in turn used (5-43)—and this crucially required independence.

[5] Or, leading to the same conclusion, the difference $X_2 - X_1$.

Table 8-3   Analysis of 2 Paired Samples

| Student | Observed Grades | | Difference | | |
	X_1 (spring)	X_2 (fall)	$D = X_1 - X_2$	$(D - \bar{D})$	$(D - \bar{D})^2$
A	64	54	10	-4	16
B	66	54	12	-2	4
C	89	70	19	5	25
D	77	62	15	1	1
			$\bar{D} = \dfrac{56}{4}$	0✔	$s_D^2 = \dfrac{46}{3}$
			$= 14.0$		$= 15.3$

calculate the average difference $\bar{D}$ and then use this appropriately in (8-15) to construct a 95% confidence interval for the equivalent population parameter Δ, i.e.,

average difference between two populations,

$$\Delta = \bar{D} \pm t_{.025} \frac{s_D}{\sqrt{n}} \tag{8-19}$$

$$= 14.0 \pm 3.18 \frac{\sqrt{15.3}}{\sqrt{4}}$$

$$= 14.0 \pm 6.2 \tag{8-20}$$

Of course, Δ is also recognized to be the difference in the two population averages,[6] $\mu_1 - \mu_2$, so that our problem is solved.

It is interesting to compare (8-20) with (8-18). The sampling fluctuation for the paired data is much reduced ($\sqrt{15.3}$ vs. $\sqrt{117}$). Although there are several reasons for this, the most important is intuitively clear: the differences in the two samples are not obscured by the second sample of students being entirely different (independent) from the first. In other words, this pairing (matching) of observations is a desirable feature to design into the sampling experiment, whenever possible. It allows us to get more leverage on the problem at hand (difference in fall vs. spring) because we have been able to keep "other things equal" (i.e., the stu-

---

[6]This can be seen in the samples as well as the populations: the average difference $\bar{D} = 14.0$ is just the difference in averages $\bar{X}_1 - \bar{X}_2 = 74 - 60 = 14$.

dents the same); as we shall see in many other contexts later, this is a very useful procedure.

8-4 Two classes were independently sampled, yielding the following grades:

Sample 1	Sample 2
75	52
70	60
60	42
75	58

Calculate a 95% confidence interval for
(a) The difference in class means $\mu_1 - \mu_2$.
(b) Each class mean (μ_1, then μ_2).
(c) In view of the fact that the two confidence intervals in (b) overlap, do you want to revise your answer to (a)?

8-5 Sixteen weather stations at random locations in a state measure rainfall. In 1967, they recorded an average of 10 inches and standard deviation of 1.5 inch. For the mean rainfall for the state,
(a) Construct a 95% confidence interval.
(b) Construct a 99% confidence interval.

8-6 100 cars on a thruway were clocked at an average speed of 69 m.p.h., with a standard deviation of 4 m.p.h. Construct a 95% confidence interval for the mean speed of all cars on this thruway.

8-7 A random sample of 4 students in a large statistics course received the following marks: 56, 70, 55, 59. Construct a 95% confidence interval for the average mark of all students in the course.

8-8 (a) From a sample of five random normal numbers from Appendix Table IIb (rounded to one decimal place), find an 80% confidence interval for the mean of the population.
(b) About what proportion of the students in your class will make a correct inference? An incorrect one?

8-9 Five people selected at random had their breathing capacity measured before and after a certain treatment, obtaining the data in the table on the next page. Let μ_X (and μ_Y) be the mean capacity of the whole population before (and after) treatment. Construct a 95% confidence interval for ($\mu_Y - \mu_X$).

Breathing Capacity Person	Before (X)	After (Y)
A	2750	2850
B	2360	2380
C	2950	2930
D	2830	2860
E	2250	2320

8-10 In a random sample of 10 football players, the average age was 27 and the sum of squared deviations was 300. In a random sample of 20 hockey players, the average age was 25 and the sum of squared deviations was 450. Estimate, with a 95% confidence interval, the difference in the population means, assuming $\sigma_1 = \sigma_2$.

8-11 Given the following random samples from 2 populations,

$$n_1 = 25 \qquad \bar{X}_1 = 60.0 \qquad s_1 = 12$$
$$n_2 = 15 \qquad \bar{X}_2 = 68.0 \qquad s_2 = 10$$

and assuming $\sigma_1 = \sigma_2$,

find a 95% confidence interval for $(\mu_1 - \mu_2)$.

8-12 (a) Derive the confidence interval (8-14) from (8-13). (*Hint.* Use practically the same method as in the footnote to equation (7-3).)

(b) Derive the confidence interval (8-7) from (8-6).

8-3   **ESTIMATING PROPORTIONS**

(a) Large Samples

In Chapter 6-5, we saw that a sample proportion P is just a disguised sample mean $\bar{X}$ drawn from a 0–1 population. For example, if we observe 4 Democrats in a sample of 10, then

$$P = \bar{X} = \tfrac{1}{10}(1 + 1 + 0 + 0 + 0 + 1 + 0 + 1 + 0 + 0) = \tfrac{4}{10}$$

Similarly, the population proportion π is just the disguised mean μ in this same sort of population. The simplest method of deriving an interval estimate for a proportion is therefore to modify (7-10), the interval estimate for a mean. Thus with a large sample, the 95% confidence interval for π is

$$\pi = P \pm z_{.025}\sqrt{\frac{\pi(1 - \pi)}{n}} \qquad (8\text{-}21)$$

We confirm that (8-21) is just a recasting of (7-10). $\bar{X}$ is replaced by P, and σ^2 (the population variance) is replaced by $\pi(1 - \pi)$ from (6-22).

But we seem to have reached an impasse; the unknown π appears in the right-hand side of (8-21). Fortunately, the situation has a remedy: substitute the sample P for π in the right side of (8-21). This is a strategy we have used before, when we substituted s for σ in the confidence interval for μ. Again, this approximation introduces another source of error; but with a large sample size, this is no great problem. Thus

---

95% confidence interval for the proportion, for large n,

$$\pi = P \pm z_{.025}\sqrt{\frac{P(1 - P)}{n}}$$

$\qquad (8\text{-}22)$

---

where $z_{.025}$ is the critical value leaving $2\frac{1}{2}\%$ of the probability in the upper tail. As an example, the voter poll in Chapter 1 used this formula.

(b) Moderately Large Samples

For moderately large samples (roughly, $50 < n < 100$) there are several options. The crudest[7] is to substitute $t_{.025}$ for $z_{.025}$ in (8-22), just as we did in (8-15).

A more conservative alternative is to allow for the worst that could happen in (8-21). Since the maximum value[8] of $\pi(1 - \pi)$ is $1/4$, the maximum value of the sampling allowance in (8-21) is

$$\pm 1.96\sqrt{\frac{1/4}{n}} = \pm\frac{.98}{\sqrt{n}} \qquad (8\text{-}23)$$

---

[7]This method is not exactly valid, because the t distribution assumes a normal population, rather than a 0–1 population. However, this is still better than using the z value.

[8]The simplest proof is with calculus, setting the derivative of $\pi(1 - \pi)$ equal to zero. To prove it without calculus, we may simply graph $f(\pi) = \pi(1 - \pi)$, as follows:

Note that for either extreme value of π (1 or 0) the value of $f(\pi)$ is zero; and if $\pi = 1/2$, then $\pi(1 - \pi)$ reaches its maximum value because of symmetry of the parabola.

Thus the conservative 95% confidence interval is

$$\pi = P \pm \frac{.98}{\sqrt{n}} \qquad (8\text{-}24)$$

But this is assuming the worst; if, in fact, π is not $1/2$, then $\pi(1 - \pi)$ is less than $1/4$, and our interval estimate need not be this wide; or to restate, (8-24) is an interval estimate for π with *at least* a 95% level of confidence. For example, this very simple formula is sometimes used in political polls where it is known on the basis of historical experience that the proportion of Democrats is close to $1/2$. In these circumstances (8-24) becomes a very accurate approximation.

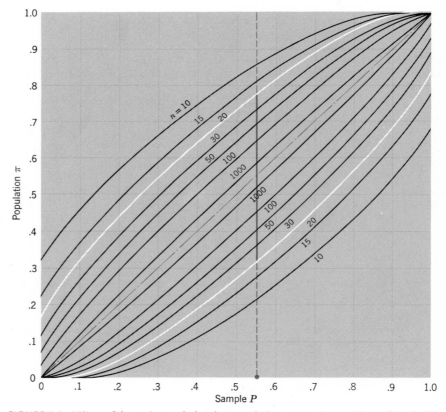

FIGURE 8-3 95% confidence intervals for the population proportion π. [Reproduced with the permission of Professor E. S. Pearson from C. J. Clopper and E. S. Pearson, "The Use of Confidence or Fiducial Limits Illustrated in the Case of the Binomial," *Biometrika* 26, (1934), p. 404.]

(c) Small Samples

There is yet another way to find an interval estimate for π, which works for all sample sizes, large and small.

This method, based on Figure 8-3, is extremely easy to use. For example, suppose we observe 11 Democrats in a sample of 20. We first calculate $P = 11/20 = .55$ as usual. Then on Figure 8-3 we locate the two curves reading $n = 20$, and see where they contain the vertical line through $P = .55$. This is our confidence interval, shown in red. It may be expressed numerically, if desired, as

$$.31 < \pi < .77 \tag{8-25}$$

Although this method is easy to use, it is rather complicated to justify. Nevertheless, we shall work through the derivation, not only for its own sake, but also to shed light on the meaning of confidence intervals in general.

The first step is the mathematical deduction of how the variable estimator P is distributed, for any population π. This is shown for a sample size $n = 20$ in Figure 8-4. Thus, for example, if $\pi = .4$, then the sample P has the pink distribution shown in this diagram, and there is a 95% probability that any P calculated from a random sample of 20 will lie in the interval ab. For each possible value of π, such a probability distribution of P defines two critical points like a and b. When all such points are joined, the result is the two curves enclosing a 95% probability band.

This deduction of how the statistic P is related to the population π

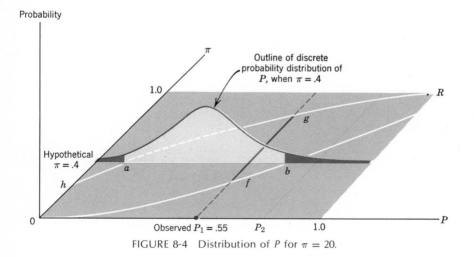

FIGURE 8-4   Distribution of P for $\pi = 20$.

is now turned around to draw a statistical inference about π from a given sample P. For example, if we have observed a sample proportion $P_1 = 11/20 = .55$, then the 95% confidence interval for π is defined by the interval *fg* contained within this probability band above P_1, i.e.,

$$.31 < \pi < .77 \qquad \text{(8-25) repeated}$$

Whereas the (deduced) probability interval is defined in the horizontal direction of the P axis, the (induced) confidence interval is defined in the vertical direction of the π axis.

To see why this works suppose, for example, that the true value of π is .4. Then the probability is 95% that a sample P will fall between a and b. *If and only if it does* (e.g., P_1) will the confidence interval we construct bracket the true π of .4. We are therefore using an estimation procedure that is 95% likely to bracket the true value of π, and thus yield a correct statement. But we must recognize the 5% probability that the sample P will fall beyond a or b (e.g., P_2); in this case our interval estimate will not bracket $\pi = .4$, and our conclusion will be wrong.

This is a more general theory of confidence intervals than we have encountered before. In previous instances (e.g., estimating μ) we constructed a confidence interval *symmetrically* about the point estimate $\overline{X}$. But in estimating π, no such symmetry is generally involved.[9] For example, with the observed sample proportion $P_1 = .55$, the confidence interval for π in (8-25) was *not* symmetric about the point estimate .55.

(d) Difference in Two Proportions, $\pi_1 - \pi_2$

Just as we derived (8-7), similarly we could derive the confidence interval to compare two population proportions

---

95% confidence interval for the difference in proportions, for large n_1 and n_2,

$$(\pi_1 - \pi_2) = (P_1 - P_2) \pm 1.96 \sqrt{\frac{P_1(1 - P_1)}{n_1} + \frac{P_2(1 - P_2)}{n_2}} \qquad (8\text{-}26)$$

---

[9]You may wonder why the 95% probability band does not converge on the two end points O and R. It is true that one half of this band (made up of all points similar to b) does intersect the P axis at 0; this means that if π is zero (e.g., no Socialists in the U.S.), then any sample P must also be zero (no Socialists in the sample). But the other half of this band does not intersect the π axis at 0; instead it intersects at h. This means that an observed P of zero (e.g., no Socialists in a sample) does *not* necessarily imply that π is zero (no Socialists in the U.S.).

8-13 In a poll of 1063 college students in 1970, the American Institute of Public Opinion (Gallup Poll) found that 49% of those interviewed believed that change in America is likely to occur in the next 25 years through relatively peaceful means (rather than a revolution).

(a) Construct a 95% confidence interval for the population proportion π.

(b) Repeat (a), assuming that the same sample proportion .49 was observed in a sample of 100. Compare.

8-14 In response to the question in 8-13, the same affirmative reply was given by 50% of students 18 years old and under, and 69% of those 24 years old and over.

(a) If we assume that there were 300 students sampled in each group, construct a 99% confidence interval for the difference in population proportions.

(b) Suppose the same sample P_1 and P_2 had been observed in a sample of 500 from the first group (18 and under) and a sample of 100 from the second group (24 and over). Again construct a 99% confidence interval for the difference in population proportions. Is this more or less precise than the interval you constructed in (a)?

8-15 In the same poll, 13% of the male students and 11% of the female students indicated that they had worked for a political party in the 1970 campaign. If roughly half of the students polled (say, 533) were men, construct a 95% confidence interval for the difference in proportions of all college men and women working for a political party.

(8-16) In the same poll, 7% of the students placed themselves on the "far left" in the political spectrum.

(a) Construct a 95% confidence interval for the population proportion on the far left.

(b) Repeat (a), if the sample size had been 100.

(8-17) In the same poll, 44% of the students believed that violence is sometimes justified to bring about change in American society. Construct a 95% confidence interval for the proportion of all students with this view.

8-18 In a random sample of tires produced by a certain company, 20% did not meet the company's standards. Construct a 95% confidence interval for the proportion π (in the whole population of tires) which does not meet the standards,

(a) If the sample size $n = 10$.

(b) If $n = 25$.

(c) If $n = 2500$.

8-19 In a survey of U.S. consumer intentions, 498 families in a random sample of 2500 indicated that they intended to buy a new car within a year. Construct a 95% confidence interval for the proportion of all U.S. families intending a new car purchase,

(a) Using the usual formula (8-22).

(b) Using the simplified formula (8-24).

8-20 If $\pi = .2$, what is the percentage error introduced by using (8-24)? Does this suggest that (8-24) is a reasonable approximation, provided $.2 \leq \pi \leq .8$?

8-21 A sample of 100 cars was taken in each of 2 cities. In one city, 72 of the cars passed the safety test; in the second only 66 passed. Construct a 95% confidence interval for the difference between the proportions of safe cars in the two cities.

8-4   ESTIMATING THE VARIANCE OF A NORMAL POPULATION

We give one further example of a confidence interval, interesting not so much for its practical value[10] as for the insight it provides.

Consider a normal population $N(\mu, \sigma^2)$ with both μ and σ^2 unknown. So far we have estimated σ^2 with s^2 only as a means of finding a confidence interval for μ. Now suppose, on the other hand, that our primary interest is in σ^2, rather than μ. For example, we may wish to ask "How much variance is there in Japan's balance of payments?" in order to get some indication of the country's requirement of foreign exchange reserves. Or, we may ask "What is the variance of farm income?" in order to evaluate whether a policy aimed at stabilizing farm income is necessary.[11] To estimate variance we shall assume that the population is normally distributed; if so, how do we proceed?

We have already seen following (7-14) that s^2 is an unbiased estimator of σ^2; to construct an interval estimate for σ^2 we must further ask: "How is the estimator s^2 distributed around σ^2?" To answer this, it is customary

---

[10] One reason that the confidence interval for σ^2 is of limited practical use is that it is not robust, i.e., it depends crucially on the assumption that the parent population is normal. By contrast, most of the confidence intervals for means are robust.

[11] Income stabilization policies are almost always designed to stabilize income around a reasonably high level. Thus they aim both at reducing variance σ^2 and raising average income μ. Here we concentrate only on the variance problem.

to define a variable, called the modified chi-square,

$$C^2 \triangleq \frac{s^2}{\sigma^2} \tag{8-27}$$

Of course, when $s^2 = \sigma^2$, this ratio is 1; thus our question can be rephrased: "How is C^2 distributed around 1?" It has been proved that the distribution of C^2 is that of Figure 8-5. Critical values are given in Appendix Table VIb, tabulated according to d.f. $= n - 1$, like[12] Student's t.

Since its numerator s^2 and denominator σ^2 are both positive, the variable C^2 is also always positive, with its distribution falling to the right of zero in Figure 8-5. For small sample values we note that it is also skewed to the right; but as n gets large, this skewness disappears and the C^2 distribution approaches normality. Since s^2 is an unbiased estimator of σ^2, this implies that the expected value of each of these C^2 distributions is 1. Moreover as sample size increases C^2 becomes more and more heavily concentrated near 1, indicating that s^2 is becoming an increasingly accurate estimator of σ^2.

With this deduction of how the estimator s^2 is distributed around its target σ^2, we may now infer a 95% confidence interval for σ^2 using our now-familiar technique. We illustrate with sample size $n = 11$ (d.f. $= 10$). From Figure 8-5, or more precisely from Table VIb, we find the critical points cutting off $2\frac{1}{2}\%$ of the distribution in each tail; thus

$$\Pr\left(.325 < \frac{s^2}{\sigma^2} < 2.05\right) = 95\%$$

Solving for σ^2, we obtain the equivalent statement

$$\Pr\left(\frac{s^2}{2.05} < \sigma^2 < \frac{s^2}{.325}\right) = 95\% \tag{8-29}$$

---

[12] C^2 is comprised of the constant parameter σ^2, and the variable s^2. Thus it has the same degrees of freedom as s^2 [explained in the footnote to equation (8-11)]. The justification of the same degrees of freedom for t is similar: t also uses s^2.

Modified chi-square (C^2, in Table VIb) is related to ordinary chi-square (χ^2, in Table VIa) according to

$$C^2 = \frac{\chi^2}{d.f.} \tag{8-28}$$

The χ^2 distribution historically was used first, because of its many applications to goodness-of-fit tests. This separate topic, along with other χ^2 applications, are described in Chapter 17.

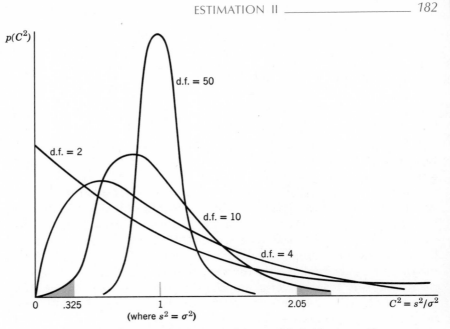

FIGURE 8-5   Some distributions of the modified chi square, C^2.

If the observed value of s^2 turns out to be 3.6, for example, then the 95% confidence interval for σ^2 is

$$1.76 < \sigma^2 < 11.1 \qquad (8\text{-}30)$$

We note that this is another example of an asymmetrical confidence interval.

In general, the upper and lower critical values of C^2 are denoted $C^2_{.025}$ and $C^2_{.975}$, and the 95% confidence interval for σ^2 is written

$$\frac{s^2}{C^2_{.025}} < \sigma^2 < \frac{s^2}{C^2_{.975}} \qquad (8\text{-}31)$$

PROBLEMS

8-22 If a sample of 25 IQ scores from a certain population has $s^2 = 120$, construct a 95% confidence interval for the population σ^2.

8-23 Construct a 95% confidence interval for σ^2, using
(a) the first sample in Problem 8-4

   (b) the second sample

   (c) the combined sample (use s_p^2 with d.f. $= n_1 + n_2 - 2$)

Review Problems

8-24 Two machines are used to produce the same good. In 400 articles produced by machine A, 16 were substandard. In the same length of time, the second machine produced 600 articles, and 60 were substandard. Construct 95% confidence intervals for

   (a) π_1, the true proportion of substandard articles from the first machine.

   (b) π_2, the true proportion of substandard articles from the second machine.

   (c) The difference between the two proportions $(\pi_1 - \pi_2)$.

8-25 To determine the effectiveness of a certain vitamin supplement, the following data were obtained:

Weight Increases for Two Groups
of Mice

Control Group	Treated Group
12	18
19	16
14	23
	20
	23

   Assuming that $\sigma_1 = \sigma_2$, construct a 95% confidence interval for the "vitamin effect," $\mu_2 - \mu_1$.

8-26 Suppose a psychologist runs 6 people through a certain experiment. In order to find the effect on heart rate, he collects the following data:

Heart Rate / Person	Before Experiment	After Experiment
Smith	71	84
Jones	67	72
Gunther	71	70
Wilson	78	85
Pestritto	64	71
Seaforth	70	81

Suppose that it is known that people as a whole have an average heart rate approximately normally distributed, with mean 73. Calculate a 95% confidence interval for the effect of the experiment on heart rate.

8-27 A certain scientist concluded his study in fertility control as follows: "So far one result has emerged from the before-and-after survey, and it is a key measure of the outcome: at the end of 1962, 14.2% of the women in the sample were pregnant, and at the end of 1963 (after the birth-control campaign) 11.4% of the women (in a second independent sample) were pregnant, a decline of about one fifth."

If the samples (both before and after) included 2500 women, what statistical qualification would you add to the above statement, in order to make its meaning clearer?

8-28 In the poll cited in Problem 8-13, 19% of the students whose parents' income was $15,000 and over considered themselves on the right (i.e., either "right" or "far right" in their political views); at the same time 21% of the students whose parents had incomes under $7,000 placed themselves in this category. Construct a 95% interval estimate for the difference in population proportions. Assume $n_1 = 350$ and $n_2 = 300$.

8-29 To measure the effect of an aerial spray treatment against a certain insect, 300 trees were selected at random from a stand of timber. Each tree was measured both before and after treatment, and then classified in one of the 4 cells of the following table.

Table 1

After Before	Not Infected	Infected	Subtotals
Not infected	220	3	223
Infected	32	45	77
Subtotals	252	48	300 total

If we let π_X be the infected proportion in the population of trees *before* treatment, and let π_Y be the infected proportion in the population of trees *after* treatment, find a 95% confidence interval for $(\pi_Y - \pi_X)$, the change in infection rates.

Hint. For each of the 300 trees, let X be a counting variable to measure whether or not the tree is infected *before* treatment, and Y a counting variable to measure *after* treatment. Then as an alternative to Table 1, the data could have been recorded as follows:

Table 2   Tree-by-Tree
Detail of Table 1

Tree #	X	Y
1	1	0
2	0	0
3	0	0
4	1	1
5	1	0
6	0	0
.	.	.
.	.	.
.	.	.

Note that trees #2, 3, 6, . . . , will be among the 220 trees classified in the upper left cell of Table 1; trees #1, 5, . . . will be among the 32 trees classified in the lower left cell, etc.

Recording the data in the detail of Table 2 yields a conceptual advantage: in this form, it is obviously a matched sample, so that (8-19) may be used.

8-30 For entrance to a certain university an interview is required, at either the West Coast Board (W) or the East Coast Board (E). In order to test whether the two boards have the same standards, the university subjected 100 candidates (chosen at random from the large population of all candidates) to an interview by both boards. The following frequency table summarizes the result.

Board W / Board E	Accepted	Rejected	Totals
Accepted	48	5	53
Rejected	12	35	47
Totals	60	40	100

At first glance, Board E seems to have stricter standards, because its rejection rate in the sample is 47%, while the rejection rate of Board W is only 40%.

(a) Analyze further.

(b) Can you suggest improvements or possible criticisms of the experimental design?

8-31 Of the 453 boys released from a detention home for delinquents, there were 150 boys for whom sufficient information was available, both for the period before and the period after detention. The behavior record of these 150 boys is as follows.

Before Detention	After Detention Good	Fair	Bad	Totals
Good	18	9	2	29
Fair	49	33	15	97
Bad	10	4	10	24
Totals	77	46	27	150

(Abridged from the Oxford University examinations, Trinity term, 1964.)

(a) We would like to know, on the average, how the stay at the detention home changes behavior. One possible way to analyze the data is, for each boy, to ascribe to bad behavior the value zero, to good behavior the value 1, and to fair behavior some intermediate value, say 1/2. For each boy, therefore, a numerical improvement can be calculated. The 150 improvements constitute a sample from a population; calculate a 95% confidence interval for the mean of this population. (Although this coding is somewhat arbitrary, it allows a simple and powerful analysis that can't be too far wrong. The analysis is then very similar to Problem 8-29.)

(b) In what way does your analysis in part (a) show, or fail to show, how the detention home changes behavior?

Chapter 9

hypothesis testing

Say not, "I have found the truth," but rather, "I have found a truth."

Kahlil Gibran

$$\displaystyle\int$$

9-1 INTRODUCTION: THE EQUIVALENCE OF HYPOTHESIS TESTING AND CONFIDENCE INTERVALS

Recall from Chapter 8 the example of student grades, where the 95% confidence interval for the difference in average grades between spring and fall terms was approximately

$$\Delta = 14 \pm 6 \tag{9-1}$$
$$\text{(8-20) repeated}$$

that is, $\qquad\qquad 8 < \Delta < 20$

This means that with 95% confidence, we estimate Δ to be between 8 and 20.

These values of Δ are called *acceptable* at the 95% confidence level (or 5% significance level, α); all other values outside the confidence interval may be rejected. Thus

> A confidence interval may be regarded as just the set of acceptable hypotheses.[1]   (9-2)

---
[1]This is discussed in greater detail in Appendix 9-2.

The value $\Delta = 0$ is of particular interest; since it represents no difference (in average grades) whatsoever, it is called the *null hypothesis* H_0. Since it lies outside the confidence interval (9-1), we reject it. In so doing, we establish the important claim that there is indeed a difference between spring and fall grades; hence we call our results *statistically significant*.

Statistical significance simply means that enough data have been collected to establish that a difference does exist. It does *not* mean that the difference is necessarily important. For example, in another test based on very large samples from nearly identical populations, the 95% confidence interval, instead of (9-1), might be

$$\Delta = .014 \pm .006$$

This difference is so miniscule that we could dismiss it as being of no real interest, even though it is statistically as significant as (9-1). In other words, *statistical* significance is a technical term, with a far different meaning than *ordinary* significance.[2]

PROBLEMS

9-1 For each of the review Problems 8-25 to 8-31, state whether the results are statistically significant at the 95% confidence level (5% significance level).

⟹9-2 A manufacturing process has, for many years, produced TV tubes with a mean life $\mu = 1200$ hours, and standard deviation $\sigma = 300$ hours. A new process is tried on a sample of 100 tubes, producing a new average $\overline{X} = 1245$ hours. (The standard deviation is assumed to remain unchanged.) Is the new process different from the old? Specifically, is the sample mean $\overline{X} = 1245$ statistically significant (i.e., significantly different from the H_0 value of 1200) at a confidence level of

(a) 99%
(b) 95%
(c) 90%
(d) 80%
(e) 50%

---

[2] It is unfortunate, perhaps, that the words *statistically significant* have become so entrenched in the literature. Perhaps a phrase such as *statistically discernable* would be less likely to mislead the layman.

9-2   PROB-VALUE ✓

The solution to Problem 9-2 is outlined in Fig. 9-1*a*; in this diagram and those that follow, *hypothetical* population values are outlined in white—while the sample continues to be in red. It is clear from this figure that as the confidence level falls lower and lower, significance is finally reached and maintained. Thus the weakness of this approach is seen to be the arbitrary specification of the level of confidence (or, alternatively, of α). The important issue is not *whether or not* statistical significance is achieved, but rather at *what level* it is achieved. The level at which we cross over from insignificance to significance may be called the *most impressive confidence level*, or more simply, the *critical confidence level*—with a corresponding critical α level. From Figure 9-1*a* it is clear that this crossover occurs between 90% and 80%. Now let us calculate it precisely. From (7-10), an interval estimate is seen to involve

$$\pm z\,\frac{\sigma}{\sqrt{n}} \qquad\qquad (9\text{-}3)$$

FIGURE 9-1 Comparison of hypothesis tests given prespecified confidence levels, with calculation of prob-value.

which is cut off on either side of the observed $\bar{X}$. In Figure 9-1 we see that the critical confidence interval involves setting this length equal to $|1245 - 1200| = 45$; i.e.,

$$|z|\frac{\sigma}{\sqrt{n}} = 45 \tag{9-4}$$

with z the unknown in this equation. Solving

$$|z|\frac{300}{\sqrt{100}} = 45$$

$$|z| = \frac{45}{300/\sqrt{100}} = 1.5 \tag{9-5}$$

The probability contained between $z = \pm 1.5$ is found from Appendix Table IV,

$$\text{critical confidence level} = 87\% \tag{9-6}$$

and the critical significance level $\alpha = 13\%$. When the critical value of α is solved for in this way, it is often referred to as the probability-value, or simply

$$\text{prob-value} = 13\% \tag{9-7}$$

An alternative way to define the prob-value is to imagine the experiment being repeated, while the null hypothesis H_0 is true. Then

$$\text{Prob-value} \triangleq \text{Pr}\left(\begin{array}{c}\text{the sample value would be as}\\ \text{extreme as the value we actually}\\ \text{observed, assuming } H_0\end{array}\right) \tag{9-8}$$

This is verified as the same prob-value we understood in (9-7), by evaluating (9-8) for our example:

$$\text{Prob-value} = \text{Pr}\left(|\bar{X} - \mu_0| \geq |1245 - 1200|\right) \tag{9-9}$$

where μ_0 represents the null hypothesis population mean. Now this can be written in standardized form as

$$\text{Prob-value} = \Pr\left(\left|\frac{\bar{X} - \mu_0}{\sigma/\sqrt{n}}\right| \geq \frac{45}{300/\sqrt{100}}\right) \qquad (9\text{-}10)$$

$$= \Pr(|z| \geq 1.5) \qquad (9\text{-}11)$$

$$= 13\%, \text{ as before}$$

This calculation is illustrated in Figure 9-2, which shows the distribution of the sample mean *if H_0 is true.* Note that the more extreme the observed $\bar{X}$ (i.e., the further from the null hypothesis μ_0), the smaller the prob-value. Since small prob-value means small credibility for H_0, *the prob-value is an excellent way to measure the credibility of the null hypothesis.*

9-3   ONE-SIDED PROB-VALUE

It often happens that the only interesting or possible alternatives to H_0 lie all on one side. For example, suppose that *even before collecting any data,* the production engineer could be sure that the new process was at least as good as the old. He will still test the null hypothesis (no difference), i.e.,

$$H_0: \mu = 1200 \qquad (9\text{-}12)$$

but now it will be against the one-sided alternative hypothesis (H_1) that the new process is better, i.e.,

$$H_1: \mu > 1200 \qquad (9\text{-}13)$$

FIGURE 9-2   Prob-value $\triangleq$ Pr (sample mean $\bar{X}$ would be as extreme as the one we observed, if H_0 were true).

Or he may be even more specific in his alternative, say

$$H_1: \mu = 1240$$

For either form of H_1, the calculation of prob-value should now be one sided.[3] Following our definition of a two-sided prob-value in (9-8), we define

One-sided prob-value $\overset{\Delta}{=}$ Pr $\begin{pmatrix} \text{the sample value would be } as \\ large \text{ as the value we actually} \\ \text{observed, assuming } H_0. \end{pmatrix}$ (9-15)

In Figure 9-3 we immediately see that the analysis is entirely similar to the two-sided problem in Figure 9-2, except that we are now calculating probability in only the upper tail. The algebraic calculation is similar to (9-9), except that the absolute value sign is, of course, omitted so that we find

$$\text{One-sided prob-value} = Pr(\overline{X} - \mu_0 \geq 1245 - 1200)$$
$$= 6\tfrac{1}{2}\% \qquad (9\text{-}16)$$

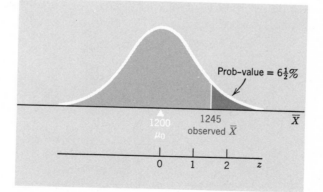

FIGURE 9-3   One sided prob-value $\overset{\Delta}{=}$ Pr (sample mean $\overline{X}$ would be as large as the one we observed, if H_0 were true). Compare with Figure 9-2.

---

[3]Compare this with the two-sided prob-value in Section 9-2, appropriate there because the alternative hypothesis was the two-sided hypothesis that the new process is different, i.e.,

$$H_1: \mu \neq 1200 \qquad (9\text{-}14)$$

This means that, if in fact the new process is no better, there would be only a $6\frac{1}{2}\%$ probability of observing a sample result this large.

A one-sided rather than two-sided prob-value is often the appropriate calculation. It is recognized by some sort of asymmetrical phrase like "more than, at least, better . . . ." Or "less than, no more than, worse . . . ," in which case a similar one-sided calculation involving probability only in the lower tail is of course required.

PROBLEMS

9-3 For each of the review Problems 8-25 to 8-31, calculate the two-sided prob-value. Use a diagram similar to Figure 9-2. Also note that if the sample is small, and the population variance is estimated with s^2, z should be replaced with t.

9-4 For Problems 8-25 to 8-27, calculate the one-sided prob-value. Use a diagram similar to Figure 9-3. In each case state clearly what assumption you are making a priori to justify it.

9-5 Suppose that an auto firm has been using brake linings with a stopping distance of 90 feet. The firm is considering a switch to another type of lining, which is similar in all other respects, but alleged to have a shorter stopping distance. In a test run the new linings are installed on 64 cars; the average stopping distance is 87 feet, with a standard deviation of 16 feet. In your job of quality control, you are asked to evaluate whether or not the new lining is better. What would you say?

9-4   CLASSICAL TESTING

(a) Prob-value Versus the Classical Hypothesis Test

The calculation of prob-value, as described above, is an approach favored by applied statisticians. We shall now compare it to the classical accept-or-reject method, which involves an arbitrary prespecification of the significance level α, usually 5%. Although this will shed additional light on several important issues, it does involve serious drawbacks.

With our previous quality control example we now illustrate the three steps involved in the classical hypothesis test:

1. The null hypothesis ($H_0: \mu = 1200$) and the alternative ($H_1: \mu > 1200$, for example, $\mu = 1240$) are formally stated. At the same time, the sample size (e.g., 100) and the level of significance of the test (e.g., $\alpha = 5\%$) are set.

2. We now assume temporarily that the null hypothesis is true. And

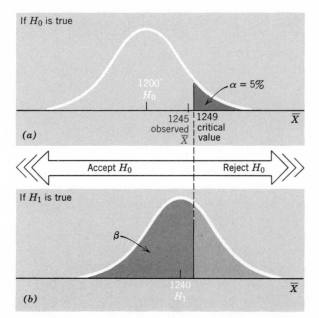

If H_0 is true

1200°
H_0

$\alpha = 5\%$

1245
observed
$\overline{X}$

1249
critical
value

$\overline{X}$

(a)

⟪⟨ Accept H_0 | Reject H_0 ⟩⟫

If H_1 is true

β

1240
H_1

$\overline{X}$

(b)

FIGURE 9-4   A standard hypothesis test with α set at 5%. (a) If H_0 is true then $\alpha =$ prob-ability of erring by rejecting the true hypothesis H_0. (b) If H_0 is false (i.e., H_1 true), then $\beta =$ probability of erring by accepting the false hypothesis H_0.

we ask, what can we expect of a sample statistic (in our example, a sample mean) drawn from this sort of world? Its specific distribu-tion is again shown in Figure 9-4a, just as it was in Figure 9-3. But there is one important difference in these two diagrams: whereas in Figure 9-3 the shaded prob-value was calculated from the ob-served $\overline{X}$, in Figure 9-4a the shaded area α is arbitrarily set (and with it the critical range for rejecting the null hypothesis)—even before any data are observed.

3. The sample is now taken; if the observed $\overline{X}$ falls in the reject area in Figure 9-4a, then it is judged sufficiently in conflict with the null hypothesis H_0 to allow its rejection in favor of H_1. Otherwise H_0 is acceptable.

The critical value for this 5% significance test is $\overline{X} = 1249$, calculated by noting from Appendix Table IV that a z value of 1.64 cuts a 5% tail off the normal distribution; i.e.,

$$\text{critical } z = \frac{\overline{X} - \mu_0}{\sigma/\sqrt{n}} = 1.64 \tag{9-17}$$

$$\text{critical } \frac{\overline{X} - 1200}{300/\sqrt{100}} = 1.64$$

$$\text{critical } \overline{X} = 1249 \qquad (9\text{-}18)$$

In our example, our observed $\overline{X} = 1245$ leads us to call H_0 acceptable.[4]

In summary, there is another way of looking at this testing procedure. If we get an observed $\overline{X}$ exceeding 1249, there are two explanations:

1. H_0 is true, but we have been exceedingly unlucky and got a very improbable sample $\overline{X}$. (We're born to be losers; even when we bet with odds of 19 to 1 in our favor, we still lose); or
2. H_0 is *not* true after all; thus it is no surprise that the observed $\overline{X}$ was so high.

Being reasonable, we opt for the second explanation. Although the first explanation is conceivable, it is not as plausible as the second. But we are left in some doubt; it is just possible that the first explanation is the correct one. For this reason we qualify our conclusion "to be at the 5% significance level."

(b) Type I and Type II Errors

In the decision-making process discussed above, we run the risk of committing two distinct kinds of error. The first is shown in Figure 9-4a,

_____

[4]The relation to prob-value may be seen in the figure below. The prob-value (6.5%,

from (9-16)) is greater than α, and the observed $\overline{X}$ is correspondingly in the acceptable region. Similarly, whenever the prob-value is less than α, the observed $\overline{X}$ is correspondingly in the rejection region, i.e.,

_____

$$\text{reject } H_0 \text{ iff prob-value} \leq \alpha \qquad (9\text{-}19)$$

_____

To restate this, we recall that the prob-value is a measure of the credibility of H_0; if this credibility sinks below α, then H_0 is rejected.

Table 9-1   Possible Results of Hypothesis Testing

Decision / State of the World	Accept H_0	Reject H_0
If H_0 is true	Correct decision. Probability $= 1 - \alpha$; corresponds to "confidence level"	Type I error. Probability $= \alpha$; also called "significance level"
If H_0 is false (H_1 true)	Type II error. Probability $= \beta$	Correct decision. Probability $= 1 - \beta$; also called "power"

which shows what the world looks like if H_0 is true. In this event, there is a 5% probability that we may observe $\overline{X}$ in the shaded region, and thus erroneously reject the true H_0. Rejecting H_0 when it is true is called a type I error, with its probability of course being α, the level of significance of the test.

But suppose the null hypothesis is false (i.e., the alternative H_1 is true). Then we are living in a different sort of world; the quite different distribution of $\overline{X}$ around H_1 is shown in Figure 9-4b. The correct decision in this case would be to reject the false H_0; an error would occur if $\overline{X}$ were to fall in the H_0 acceptance region. Such acceptance of H_0 when it is false is called a type II error; its probability is called β, and is shown as the shaded area in Figure 9-4b.

The terminology of hypothesis testing is reviewed in Table 9-1. Note that the probabilities in each row must sum to 1; this must follow, so long as we decide either[5] to accept or reject H_0.

PROBLEMS

⇒9-6 (a) In the test shown in Figure 9-4, what is β? (For the alternate hypothesis, $\mu = 1240$, $\sigma = 300$, while $n = 100$)

(b) If you reduce α, what happens to β?

(c) With the $\overline{X}$ observed to be 1245, we have already noted that our decision is to accept H_0. But now suppose you had designed

---

[5]Of course other more complicated decision rules may be used. For example, the statistician may decide to suspend judgement if the observed $\overline{X}$ is in the region around 1240 (say $1230 < \overline{X} < 1250$). If he observes an ambiguous $\overline{X}$ in this range, he would then undertake a second stage of sampling—which might yield a clear-cut decision, or might lead to further stages of sequential sampling.

this new process, and you were convinced it was better than the old; specifically, on the basis of sound engineering principles you really believed $H_1: \mu = 1240$. Would it still be correct to accept H_0? Explain your answer.

(d) Suppose sample size is doubled, while you keep $\alpha = 5\%$ and you continue to observe $\overline{X}$ to be 1245; what would your decision be then? Is it therefore true to say that your problem may have been inadequate sample size?

(e) Suppose now that your sample size is increased by 10,000 times, and in that huge sample you observed $\overline{X} = 1201$. Such an improvement of only 1 unit over the old process is of no economic significance (i.e., does not justify retooling, etc.); but is it statistically significant? Is it therefore true to say that a sufficiently large sample size may provide the grounds for rejecting any specific H_0—no matter how nearly true it may be—simply because it is not *exactly* true?

9-7 Fill in the blanks.

Consider the problem facing a radar operator whose job is to detect enemy aircraft. When something irregular appears on the screen, he must decide between

H_0: all is well; only a bit of interference on the screen.

H_1: an attack is coming.

In this case, the type ⎯⎯⎯ error is a "false alarm," and the type ⎯⎯⎯ error is a "missed alarm." To reduce both α and β, the electronic equipment is made as reliable and sensitive as possible.

9-8 A coffee shop sells on the average 320 cups of coffee per day, with a standard deviation of 40. After advertising, they find that on 7 days they sell an average of 350 cups.

(a) Has advertising left their business unchanged? Calculate the prob-value.

(b) If the owner of the coffee shop specifies that the type I error of the test (significance level) is to be 5%, do you reject the hypothesis that business is unchanged?

(c) If coffee sales can be observed for 25 days, what would the average sales have to be in order to justify a statement that business had improved, at the 5% significance level?

(d) What assumptions have you implicitly made above? Under what conditions are they questionable?

9-9 Records show that in a random sample of 100 hours a machine produced an hourly average of 678 articles with a standard deviation of 25. After a control device was installed, in a random sample of 500 hours the machine produced an hourly average of 674 articles with a standard deviation of 5. Pointing to the drop of 4 articles per hour in the sample mean, management claimed the control device was reducing production. The union countered that the drop of 4 articles was "merely statistical fluctuation."

To objectively summarize the evidence on whether production is left unchanged, calculate the prob-value.

9-10 If, in Problem 9-9, the arbitration board decides that $\alpha = 1\%$ is a fair level of significance (type I error), do they rule in favor of management or union?

9-11 (Acceptance Sampling). Suppose the purchaser of inexpensive waterproof gloves cannot afford statistical advice. So he decides on a very simple rule-of-thumb: In a random sample of 10 gloves, if more than one is defective, return them; otherwise accept them.

(a) Suppose his null hypothesis is that there is the same proportion of defectives (5%) as a competing brand. What is the type I error probability α (level of significance)?

(b) Suppose the purchaser learns that the supplier recently produced a bad lot: of 10,000 gloves, 2000 were defective. For the alternate hypothesis (that his sample is from this bad lot), what is the type II error probability β?

9-5   **CLASSICAL TESTING RECONSIDERED**

(a) Reducing α and β

Problem 9-6 above is important enough for us to set out the solution in Figure 9-5. Figure 9-5a is a condensed version of Figure 9-4. It shows that the probability of a type II error is 62%, calculated by first recalling from (9-18) that the critical $\overline{X}$ value is 1249. Thus,

$$\beta = \Pr(\overline{X} < 1249/H_1) \tag{9-20}$$

$$= \Pr\left(\frac{\overline{X} - \mu_1}{\sigma/\sqrt{n}} < \frac{1249 - 1240}{300/\sqrt{100}}\right)$$

where $\mu_1 = 1240$ is, of course, the H_1 value. Then

$$\beta = \Pr(z < .30)$$
$$= 62\%$$

In panel (b) of this diagram, we illustrate how decreasing α (by moving the critical point to the right to, say, 1270) will at the same time increase

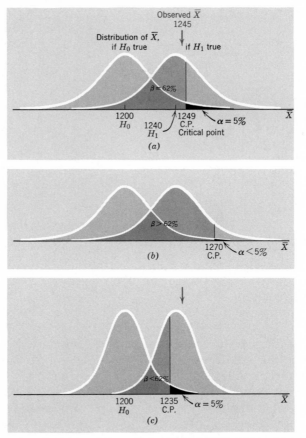

FIGURE 9-5(a) Hypothesis test of Figure 9-4, with probability of type I (α) and type II (β) errors. (b) How a reduction in α increases β, other things being equal. (c) How an increase in sample size allows one error probability (β) to be reduced, while holding the other (α) constant.

β, or vice versa. In statistics, as in economics, the problem is trading off conflicting objectives. There is an interesting legal analogy: in a murder trial, the jury is being asked to decide between H_0, the hypothesis that the accused is innocent, and the alternate H_1, that he is guilty. A type I error is committed if an innocent man is condemned, while a type II error occurs if a guilty man is set free. The judge's admonition to the jury that "guilt must be proved beyond a reasonable doubt" means that α should be kept very small. There have been many legal reforms (for example, in limiting the evidence that can be used against an accused man) which have been designed to reduce α, the probability that an innocent man will be condemned. But these same reforms have increased β, the probability that a guilty man will evade punishment. There is no way of pushing α down to zero (insuring absolutely against convicting an innocent man) without raising β to 1 (letting every defendent go free and making the trial meaningless). The one way that α and β can *both* be reduced is by improved crime detection—i.e., by increased available evidence brought to bear on H_0.

Similarly, in our quality control example, we see by comparing panels (a) and (c) in Figure 9-5, how more information improves our test. Increased sample size n will decrease $\sigma/\sqrt{n}$, and hence decrease the spread of the distribution of $\overline{X}$ in panel (c). This allows a reduction in both α and β; or alternatively, as shown in this figure, an even larger reduction in β, with α held constant at 5%.

(b) Some Difficulties

This example illustrates the difficulties that may be encountered in applying a classical reject-or-accept hypothesis test at a prespecified level of significance α. In Figure 9-5(a) the observation of $\overline{X} = 1245$ was not quite extreme enough to allow rejection of H_0, so we accepted it. But if we had set $\alpha = 10\%$, then H_0 could have been rejected. This illustrates once again the crucial nature of the arbitrary specification of α. But the problem is deeper than this: our decision to accept H_0 may be most unfortunate, especially if we had prior grounds for believing H_1, i.e., expecting that the new process would yield 1240. In this case our prior belief in the new process is not only supported by the sample observation of 1245—it is confirmed in spades. Yet we have used this confirming sample result (in this classical hypothesis test) to conclude that the new process is no better. It is true that this is an extreme example of how badly a classical hypothesis test can go astray, and most such tests cannot be subjected to such strong criticism; in fact, in Chapter 13 we discuss cases in which accepting H_0 in a classical hypothesis test is the appropriate decision. Nevertheless, this section may be regarded as a warning of the serious potential problem that may exist whenever a small sample[6] is used in a classical test to accept a null hypothesis.

---

[6]We may be prevented from confirming a true H_1 simply because of inadequate sample size. To illustrate, suppose H_1 is true in Figure 9-5, and we continue to observe $\overline{X}$ to be about 1245. Whereas the sample size in panel (a) would not allow us to establish H_1 (by rejecting H_0), the larger sample size in panel (c) would. (In other words, an observed $\overline{X}$ of 1245 is not quite in the black-tailed region for rejecting H_0 in panel (a), but in panel (c) it is.)

(cont'd)

We conclude that although statistical theory provides a rationale for rejecting H_0, it provides no formal rationale for accepting[7] H_0. As this illustration makes clear, the null hypothesis may sometimes be uninteresting, and one that we neither believe nor wish to establish; it is selected because of its simplicity. In such cases, it is the alternative H_1 that we are trying to establish, and we prove H_1 by rejecting H_0. We can see now why statistics is sometimes called "the science of disproof." H_0 cannot be proved, and H_1 is proved by disproving (rejecting) H_0. It follows that if we wish to prove some proposition, we will often call it H_1 and set up the contrary hypothesis H_0 as the "straw man" we hope to destroy. And of course if H_0 is only such a straw man, then it becomes absurd to accept it in the face of a small sample result that really supports H_1.

(c) Conclusions

Since there are great dangers in accepting H_0, the decision instead should often be simply to "not reject H_0", i.e., reserve judgment. This means that type II error in its worse form may be avoided; but it also means you may be leaving the scene of the evidence with nothing in hand. It is for this reason that either the construction of a confidence interval or the calculation of prob-value is preferred, since either provides a summary of the information provided by the sample, useful to sharpen up your knowledge of what the underlying population is really like.

If, on the other hand, a simple accept-or-reject hypothesis test is desired, then we must look to a far more sophisticated technique. Specifically, we must explicitly take account not only of the sample data used in any standard hypothesis test (along with the adequacy of the sample size), but also:

Yet at the other extreme, a huge sample size may lead us into another kind of error—namely, the error of rejecting an H_0 which, although essentially true, is not *exactly* true (and, of course, no specific hypothesis is ever exactly true.) This was illustrated in Problem 9-6(e); in that case our huge sample confirmed that H_0 was essentially (but not exactly) true. But the sample was also huge enough to reduce the standard error of estimate $(\sigma/\sqrt{n})$ to the point where even the small observed difference became statistically significant, hence the essentially true H_0 was rejected.

[7]This is why we were careful in Section 9-1 to call H_0 "accept*able*", rather than accepted.

In conclusion, sample size is obviously an important consideration in hypothesis testing. If the sample is very large, rejecting H_0 may be unwise; on the other hand, if the sample is very small, accepting H_0 is dangerous (and this is the more critical problem for economists and other social scientists, with their limited available information.) This is discussed further in Chapters 13 and 15.

1. Prior belief. How much confidence do we have in the engineering department that has assured us that the new process is better? Is their vote divided? Have they ever been wrong before?
2. Loss involved in making a wrong decision. If we make a type I error (i.e., decide to reject the old process in favor of the new, even though the old is as good), what will be the costs of retooling, etc.?

This is, in fact, Bayesian decision theory, discussed in detail in Chapter 15. Its further advantage over the standard hypothesis test is that it does not require that α be arbitrarily prespecified; instead, one can interpret the Bayesian approach as a means of explicitly taking account of (1) and (2) above in order to determine the appropriate α level.

PROBLEMS

⇒9-12 Consider a very simple example, in order to keep the philosophical issues clear. Suppose that you are gambling with a die, and lose whenever the die shows ace. After 100 throws you notice that you have suffered an inordinate number of losses—20 aces. This makes you suspect that your opponent is using a loaded die; specifically, you begin to wonder whether this is one of the crooked dice recently advertised as giving aces one-quarter of the time.
(a) Set up an hypothesis test at a 95% confidence level. What is α? β? Illustrate this test with a diagram similar to Figure 9-5a.
(b) With your observation of 20 aces, what is your decision? Are you entirely happy with that decision? If not, why not?
(c) Suppose you are playing against a strange character you have just met on a Mississippi steamboat. Are you still happy with your decision? Suppose a friend passes you a note indicating that this stranger cheated him at poker last night; and you are playing for a great deal of money. Still happy?
(d) What is the prob-value?
(e) If you halve α, what happens to β?

⇒9-13 To see whether a die has a fair number of aces, using $n = 100$ consider the test, at the 5% significance level, of

$$H_0: \pi = .167$$
$$\text{versus } H_1: \pi = .300$$

Compared with the test developed in Problem 9-12 above,
(a) Is the critical value different?
(b) Is α different?
(c) Is β different?

Review Problems

9-14 Four coins are tossed together 144 times. The average number of heads is 2.2. To answer a gambler who fears the coins are biased towards heads, calculate the prob-value for the null hypothesis of fair coins.

9-15 A sample of 784 men and 820 women in 1962 showed that 30% of the men and 22% of the women stated they were against the John Birch Society. The majority had no opinion.

(a) Letting π_M and π_W be the population proportion of men and women respectively who are against the Society, construct a 95% confidence interval for the difference $(\pi_M - \pi_W)$.

(b) What is the prob-value for the null hypothesis that $(\pi_M - \pi_W) = 0$?

(c) At the 5% significance level, is the difference between men and women statistically significant? (i.e., do you reject the null hypothesis)?

(d) Would you judge this difference to be of *sociological* significance?

9-16 Of 400 randomly selected townspeople in a certain city, 184 favored a certain presidential candidate. Of 100 randomly selected students in the same city, 40 favored the candidate.

(a) To judge whether the student population and town population have the same proportion favoring the candidate, calculate the prob-value.

(b) Is the difference in the students and townspeople statistically significant, at the 5% level?

9-17 To complete a certain task a sample of 100 workers in one plant took an average of 12 minutes, and a standard deviation of 2.5 minutes. A sample of 100 workers in a second plant took an average of 11 minutes, and a standard deviation of 2.1 minutes.

(a) Construct a 95% confidence interval for the difference in the two population means.

(b) Calculate the prob-value for the null hypothesis that the two population means are the same.

(c) Is the difference in the two sample means statistically significant at the 5% level?

9-18 By talking to a random sample of 50 students, suppose you find that 28% support a certain candidate for student government. To what extent does this invalidate the claim that only 20% of all the students support the candidate?

9-19 Suppose you are gambling on the throw of a die: when it turns up 5 or 6, you lose, and otherwise you win. A sequence of 50 throws yielded the following frequency graph for the 6 faces. Is your opponent cheating?

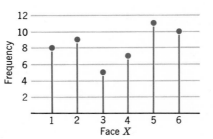

*APPENDIX 9-1 β and the Power Function

Problems 9-12 and 9-13 are important enough that we set out the solutions in Figure 9-6. The details of the calculations are as follows: The null hypothesis of a fair die is expressed mathematically as

$$H_0: \pi = \frac{1}{6} = .167 \qquad (9\text{-}21)$$

which is tested against the alternative

$$H_1: \pi = .25 \qquad (9\text{-}22)$$

FIGURE 9-6   Calculation of β, the probability of type II error, for a composite hypothesis.

The critical value of P for the 5% significance test is calculated to be, as in (9-18),

$$\text{critical } z = \frac{P - \mu_P}{\sigma_P} = \frac{P - \pi_0}{\sqrt{\dfrac{\pi_0(1 - \pi_0)}{n}}} = 1.64 \qquad (9\text{-}23)$$

$$\text{critical } z = \frac{P - .167}{\sqrt{\dfrac{.167(.833)}{100}}} = 1.64 \qquad (9\text{-}24)$$

$$\text{critical } P = .228 \qquad (9\text{-}25)$$

From this, we calculate the probability of the type II error, as in (9-20),

$$\beta = \Pr(P < .228 / H_1) = \Pr\left(\frac{P - \pi_1}{\sqrt{\dfrac{\pi_1(1 - \pi_1)}{n}}} < \frac{.228 - .25}{\sqrt{\dfrac{.25(.75)}{100}}}\right) \qquad (9\text{-}26)$$

$$= \Pr(z < -.51) = 31\% \qquad (9\text{-}27)$$

The distribution of P if $\pi = .25$ is shown as the left-hand curve in Figure 9-6. Thus if π is .25 there is a probability $\beta = 31\%$ that an observed P will be less than our critical value of .228—and we will erroneously conclude that the die is fair (accept H_0).

But this whole analysis is based on the assumption that there is only one way the die can be crooked. If, in fact, there are many ways in which it can be crooked then H_1 should not be the *simple* alternative (9-22), but rather the composite alternative

$$H_1: \mu > .167 \qquad (9\text{-}28)$$

which embraces not only (9-22) but also

$$H_1: \mu = .17 \qquad (9\text{-}29)$$
$$\mu = .18$$
$$\vdots$$

For each of these alternatives, there is a different hypothetical distribution of P, each giving a different β. As an example, the distribution of P for $\pi = .30$, as in Problem 9-13, is shown as the right-hand curve in Figure 9-6, with its corresponding $\beta = 6\%$ enclosed to the left of the critical .228.

Table 9-2 shows a whole set of possible values of π; the corresponding

Table 9-2 β and the Power Function for the Test of a Fair Die, at the 5% Level of Significance, with $n = 100$.

(1) Possible Values of π	(2) Probability of (Erroneously) Accepting H_0 β	(3) Probability of Correctly Rejecting H_0 Power $= 1 - \beta$
1.00	0%	100%
$\vdots$	$\vdots$	$\vdots$
.32	2	98
.30	6	94
.28	12	88
.26	23	77
.24	39	61
.22	58	42
.20	76	26
.18	89	11
.17	94	6
$\vdots$	$\vdots$	$\vdots$
Limit (.167)	(95%)	(5% $= \alpha$)

β values are shown in column 2, and the power of the test $(1 - \beta)$ is shown in column 3; this power is the probability that we will correctly reject a crooked die. If a dishonest gambler uses a die which always turns up an ace, he knows he will be quickly found out, and the game abandoned; the more crooked the die he uses, the greater your "power" to uncover him as a cheat. The less crooked the die, (i.e., as we move down this column), the more difficult it becomes to reject it. The dishonest gambler will recognize this, and will prefer to get you to play against a slightly crooked die; then our test has little power, and it

FIGURE 9-7   Graph of the power function of Table 9-2, for the test of a fair die at the 5% significance level, with $n = 100$.

becomes almost impossible to distinguish between the two conflicting hypotheses. This is confirmed from the last, limiting line in Table 9-2. Here the value of π approaches H_0; then the probability of rejecting H_0 is $\alpha = 5\%$ by definition.

The power function is graphed in Figure 9-7. Clearly we should like a power function that begins very close to the baseline, since its initial height is α, the level of significance, which we wish to keep low. At the same time, we wish the power function to be very steep; the more rapidly it rises, the greater is our power to distinguish between competing hypotheses.

PROBLEMS

*9-20 A certain type of seed has always grown to a mean height of 8.5 inches. A sample of 100 seeds grown under new conditions has a mean height of 8.8 inches and a standard deviation of 1 inch.
(a) At the 5% significance level, test the hypothesis that the new conditions grow no better plants.
(b) Graph the power function of this test.

*9-21 Whereas the power function of our die test involved graphing all the $(1 - \beta)$ values in column 3 of Table 9-2, an "operating characteristics curve" (OCC) is defined by graphing all β values (column 2). Draw the operating characteristics curve for this test, and compare it with the power function in Figure 9-7. What is the most desirable shape for an OCC?

*9-22 What is the power function of the rule-of-thumb acceptance test of gloves in Problem 9-11?

* APPENDIX 9-2   Proof of the Equivalence of Interval Estimation
                                          and Hypothesis Testing

In this section we shall establish a very important conclusion, used earlier in (9-2): a confidence interval can be used to test *any* hypothesis; in fact the two procedures are equivalent.

(a) Two-sided Hypothesis Tests

We illustrate with an example: suppose a firm has been producing a light bulb with an average life of 800 hours. It wishes to test a new bulb. A sample of 25 new bulbs has an average life $\overline{X}$ of 810 hours, with a standard deviation s of 30 hours. Because σ is unknown and the sample is small, we should use the t, rather than the normal distribution. We have two options:

1. Test the hypothesis

$$H_0: \mu = 800 \qquad (9\text{-}30)$$

against the two-sided alternative (that the new bulb is better *or* worse)

$$H_1: \mu \neq 800 \qquad (9\text{-}31)$$

Whereas the one-sided hypothesis test in Figure 9-4(a) involved calculating a critical value by cutting off 5% in one tail, we now require a two-sided critical value, cutting off $2\frac{1}{2}$% in each tail. Thus, if

$$\text{observed } |t| = \left| \frac{\bar{X} - \mu_0}{s/\sqrt{n}} \right| \geq t_{.025}$$

then μ_0 is rejected. On the other hand, if

$$\text{observed } |t| = \left| \frac{\bar{X} - \mu_0}{s/\sqrt{n}} \right| < t_{.025} \qquad (9\text{-}32)$$

then μ_0 is acceptable. This condition may be rewritten: H_0 is acceptable at the 5% level of significance iff

$$\mu_0 - t_{.025} \frac{s}{\sqrt{n}} < \bar{X} < \mu_0 + t_{.025} \frac{s}{\sqrt{n}}.$$

Given the sample s, along with the hypothesis μ_0, this condition becomes: H_0 is acceptable iff

$$788 < \bar{X} < 812 \qquad (9\text{-}33)$$

Since the observed $\bar{X}$ (810) does fall within this interval, μ_0 is acceptable. This is shown in Figure 9-8a.

2. Alternatively, the sample could be used to construct a confidence interval for μ. Using the same 95% level of confidence, this confidence interval is, according to (8-15),

$$\mu = \bar{X} \pm t_{.025} \frac{s}{\sqrt{n}} \qquad (9\text{-}34)$$

$$798 < \mu < 822 \qquad (9\text{-}35)$$

This is shown in Figure 9-8b.

FIGURE 9-8   Comparison of two-sided hypothesis test with confidence interval (using a sample with $\overline{X} = 810$ and $s = 30$). (a) Test of H_0: $\mu = 800$ versus H_1: $\mu \neq 800$. (b) Confidence interval for μ.

To sum up Figure 9-8: in the hypothesis test shown in panel (a), the observed $\overline{X} = 810$ falls in the region calling for the acceptance of μ_0. At the same time, in panel (b), μ_0 falls within the confidence interval.

This is the key point: if and only if μ_0 falls within this confidence interval, will it be an acceptable hypothesis. This is clear from the diagram, since the interval we use is the same length in both cases: it is constructed by adding and subtracting precisely the same error allowance ($t_{.025} s/\sqrt{n} = 12$). Provided the sample mean $\overline{X}$ and μ_0 differ by less than this, μ_0 will fall in the confidence interval, and will also be an acceptable hypothesis. This holds for any μ_0.

It can be proven, in general, that

H_0 is acceptable if and only if the relevant confidence interval contains H_0 (9-36)

---

noting, of course, that the level of confidence (e.g., 95%) must match the level of type I error (level of significance, 5%).[8]

(b) One-sided Hypothesis Tests

Equation (9-36) remains true for a one-sided test of a hypothesis, provided, of course, that we use the appropriate,

---

95% one-sided confidence interval,

$$\mu > \bar{X} - t_{.05}\frac{s}{\sqrt{n}} \tag{9-38}$$

---

which is, of course, just the one-sided equivalent of the two-sided interval (9-34). Substituting,

$$\mu > 810 - 1.71\frac{30}{\sqrt{25}}$$

$$> 799.7$$

This is shown in Figure 9-9. In panel (*b*) we show this confidence interval, with $\mu_0 = 800$ just barely falling within it. At the same time in panel (*a*) we define the equivalent one-tailed hypothesis test, with μ_0 judged acceptable (because $\bar{X}$ falls barely within the acceptance range). This illustrates once more that H_0 is acceptable if and only if the confidence interval contains H_0.

The reasons for one-sided hypothesis tests have been established in Section 9-3. These same reasons justify the use of one-sided confidence

---

[8] Just as we proved (9-36) for the case of the *t* test in Figure 9-8, we shall now prove it for the *Z* test also, to help show its generality.

Consider the basis of both the confidence interval and hypothesis test: With 95% probability,

$$|z| = \left|\frac{\bar{X} - \mu}{\sigma/\sqrt{n}}\right| < 1.96 \tag{9-37}$$

In deciding whether the null hypothesis μ_0 is acceptable, we first fix μ_0, and then see whether the observed $\bar{X}$ satisfies this inequality. If it does, then μ_0 is acceptable.

In constructing a confidence interval, we first observe $\bar{X}$; then the values of μ which satisfy (9-37) form our confidence interval. μ_0 will be in the confidence interval if and only if the hypothesis μ_0 is accepted, for in both cases we have

$$\left|\frac{\bar{X} - \mu_0}{\sigma/\sqrt{n}}\right| < 1.96$$

intervals too. Thus, the one-sided confidence interval (9-38) would be appropriate if we were trying to establish that the new bulb was *better* than the old (not merely *different* from the old). This one-sided confidence interval shaves a little closer at the lower end, at the cost of being completely vague (open-ended) at the upper end.

As another example where a one-sided interval is appropriate, suppose the federal government is considering construction of a dam. To get an idea of benefits, suppose we run a careful calculation of the operation of a random sample of 25 farmers in the river basin, and estimate that the net profit (per 100 acres) will increase on the average by $810, with a standard deviation of $30. (To simplify the exposition, we have used the same numbers as in Figures 9-8 and 9-9, except that $\bar{X}$ and μ now refer to the average increase in profit.)

The best point estimate of μ (average profit increase) is 810. But if we use this in our benefit calculations, we will take no account of its

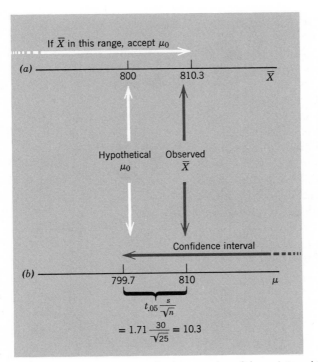

FIGURE 9-9 Comparison of one-sided hypothesis test and confidence interval (using same sample result as Fig. 9-8). (a) Test of $H_0: \mu_0 = 800$ versus $H_1: \mu > 800$. (b) Confidence interval for μ.

reliability; i.e., it may be way too high, or way too low. Now consider the alternative estimate of $799.7, the critical point in our one-sided confidence interval in Figure 9-9. We can be 95% confident that the true figure is greater than this. We do not know by how much, but this doesn't matter; the point is that we are almost certain that $799.7 underestimates benefits. From a policy point of view this is a much stronger conclusion than that the "best estimate" of benefits is $810, since the reliability of this estimate remains a mystery. Thus, suppose the cost turns out to be $750; since this is less than the minimum benefit of 799.7, the dam is clearly justified.

By "cooking the case" against our conclusion, it has been strengthened. Economists often apply this general philosophy in another way, by selecting adverse assumptions in order to strengthen a policy conclusion; they may use one-sided confidence intervals in the future for the same reason.

PROBLEMS

*9-23 Three different sources claim that the average income in a certain profession is $7200, $6000, and $6400 respectively. You find from a sample of 16 persons in the profession that their mean salary is $6030 and the standard deviation is $570.

(a) At the 5% significance level, test each of the three hypotheses, one at a time.

(b) Construct a 95% confidence interval for μ. Then test each of the 3 hypotheses by simply noting whether it is included in the confidence interval. Is this easier than (a)?

*9-24 A sample of 8 students made the following marks: 3, 9, 6, 6, 8, 7, 8, 9. Assume the population of marks is normal. At a 5% level of significance, which of the following hypotheses about the mean mark (μ) would you reject?

(a) $\mu_0 = 8$.

(b) $\mu_0 = 6.3$.

(c) $\mu_0 = 4$.

(d) $\mu_0 = 9$.

CHAPTER 10
ANALYSIS of VARIANCE

Nothing is good or bad but by comparison.

Thomas Fuller

In Chapter 7 we made inferences about one population mean, and in Chapter 8 we compared two means. Now we shall compare r means, using techniques called analysis of variance. Since rigorous proofs would be quite complicated and mathematical, we shall largely forego them in favor of an intuitive description of what is involved.

10-1   ONE-FACTOR ANALYSIS OF VARIANCE

As an example, suppose that three machines are being compared. Because these machines are operated by men, and for other inexplicable reasons, output per hour is subject to chance fluctuation. In the hope of "averaging out" and thus reducing the effect of chance fluctuation, a random sample of 5 hours is obtained from each machine and set out in Table 10-1, along with the mean of each sample. Of the many questions which might be asked, the simplest are set out in Table 10-2.

(a) Hypothesis Test

The first question is "Are the machines really different?" That is, are the sample means $\bar{X}_i$ in Table 10-1 different because of differences in

Table 10-1 Sample Output of Three Machines

Machine, or Sample Number	Sample from Machine i	$\overline{X}_i$
$i = 1$	48.4 49.7 48.7 48.5 47.7	48.6
$= 2$	56.1 56.3 56.9 57.6 55.1	56.4
$= 3$	52.1 51.1 51.6 52.1 51.1	51.6

Average $\overline{X} = \overline{\overline{X}} = 52.2$

Table 10-2

Question	How It Is Answered
(a) Are the machines different?	Analysis of Variance Table 10-6 (test of hypothesis)
(b) *How much* are the machines different?	Multiple Comparisons Table 10-7 (simultaneous confidence intervals)

the underlying population means μ_i (where μ_i represents the lifetime performance of machine i)? Or may these differences in $\overline{X}_i$ be reasonably attributed to chance fluctuations alone? To illustrate, suppose we collect three similar samples, but now from just one machine, as shown in Table 10-3. As expected, sample statistical fluctuations cause small differences in $\overline{X}_i$ even though the μ_i in this case are identical. So the question may be rephrased, "Are the differences in $\overline{X}_i$ of Table 10-1 of the same order as those of Table 10-3 (and thus attributable to chance fluctuation), or are they large enough to indicate a difference in the underlying μ_i?" The latter explanation seems more plausible; but how do we develop a formal test?

The hypothesis of "no difference" in the population means is, as usual, called the null hypothesis,

$$H_0: \mu_1 = \mu_2 = \mu_3 \qquad (10\text{-}1)$$

Table 10-3 Three Samples of the Output of One Machine

Sample Number	Sample Values	$\overline{X}_i$
$i = 1$	51.7 53.0 52.0 51.8 51.0	51.9
$= 2$	52.1 52.3 52.9 53.6 51.1	52.4
$= 3$	52.8 51.8 52.3 52.8 51.8	52.3

$\overline{\overline{X}} = 52.2$

A plausible test of this hypothesis first requires a numerical measure of the degree to which the sample means differ. We therefore take the three sample means in the last column of Table 10-1 and calculate their variance. Using (2-6a) (and being very careful to note that we are calculating the variance of the sample means and *not* the variance of all values in the table), we have

$$s_{\bar{X}}^2 = \frac{1}{(r-1)} \sum_{i=1}^{r} (\bar{X}_i - \bar{\bar{X}})^2 \tag{10-2}$$

$$= \tfrac{1}{2}[(48.6 - 52.2)^2 + (56.4 - 52.2)^2 + (51.6 - 52.2)^2]$$

$$= 15.5 \tag{10-3}$$

where r = number of rows (the number of sample means), and

$$\bar{\bar{X}} = \text{average } \bar{X} = \frac{1}{r} \sum_{i=1}^{r} \bar{X}_i = 52.2 \tag{10-4}$$

Yet $s_{\bar{X}}^2$ does not tell the whole story; for example, consider the data of Table 10-4, which has the same $s_{\bar{X}}^2$ as Table 10-1, yet more erratic machines that produce large chance fluctuations within each row. The implications of this are shown in Figure 10-1. In panel (a), the machines are so erratic that all samples could be drawn from the same population—i.e., the differences in sample means may be explained by chance. On the other hand, the (same) differences in sample means can hardly be explained by chance in panel (b), because the machines in this case are *not* erratic.

We now have our standard of comparison. In panel (b) we concluded the μ's are different—and reject H_0—because the variance in sample means $(s_{\bar{X}}^2)$ is large *relative to* the chance fluctuation.

How can we measure this chance fluctuation? Intuitively, we seem to be interpreting it as the spread (or variance) of observed values *within*

Table 10-4   Samples of the Production of Three Different Machines

Machine	Sample Output from Machine i					$\bar{X}_i$
$i = 1$	54.6	45.7	56.7	37.7	48.3	48.6
$= 2$	53.4	57.5	54.3	52.3	64.5	56.4
$= 3$	56.7	44.7	50.6	56.5	49.5	51.6

$$\bar{\bar{X}} = 52.2$$

FIGURE 10-1

each sample. Thus we compute the variance within the first sample in Table 10-1,

$$s_1^2 = \frac{1}{(n-1)} \sum_{j=1}^{n} (X_{1j} - \overline{X}_1)^2 = \frac{(48.4 - 48.6)^2 + \cdots}{4}.$$

$$= .52 \tag{10-5}$$

where X_{1j} is the jth observed value in the first sample.

Similarly we compute the variance or chance fluctuation within the second (s_2^2) and third samples (s_3^2). The simple average of these

$$s_p^2 = \frac{1}{r} \sum_{i=1}^{r} s_i^2 = \frac{.52 + .87 + .25}{3} = .547 \tag{10-6}$$

becomes the measure of chance fluctuation—and is referred to as "pooled variance." From each of the r samples, we have a sample variance with $(n - 1)$ degrees of freedom, so that the pooled variance s_p^2 has $r(n - 1)$ degrees of freedom.

The key question can now be stated. Is $s_{\bar{X}}^2$ large relative to s_p^2? In practice, we examine the ratio,

$$F = \frac{ns_{\bar{X}}^2}{s_p^2} \qquad (10\text{-}7)$$

called the "variance ratio." n is introduced into the numerator so that, whenever H_0 is true, this ratio will have, on the average, a value near 1; however, because of statistical fluctuation, it will sometimes be above 1, and sometimes below.

If H_0 is not true (and the μ's are not the same) then $ns_{\bar{X}}^2$ will be relatively large compared to s_p^2, and the F value in (10-7) will be greater than 1. Formally, H_0 is rejected if the computed value of F is significantly greater than 1.

To interpret this F ratio further, suppose that our samples are drawn from three normal populations with the same variance. If, in addition, H_0 is true, and the three population means are the same, then the division of our data into three samples is rather artificial—all observations could be viewed as one large sample drawn from a single population. Now consider two alternative ways of estimating σ^2, the variance of that population:

1. Average the variances within each of the three samples as in (10-5) and (10-6). This is the s_p^2 in the denominator of (10-7).
2. Or, infer σ^2 from $s_{\bar{X}}^2$, the observed variance of sample means. Recall from Chapter 6 how the variance of sample means is related to the variance of the population:

$$\sigma_{\bar{X}}^2 = \frac{\sigma^2}{n} \qquad (10\text{-}8)$$
$$(6\text{-}12) \text{ repeated}$$

Thus

$$\sigma^2 = n\sigma_{\bar{X}}^2 \qquad (10\text{-}9)$$

This suggests estimating σ^2 with $ns_{\bar{X}}^2$, which is recognized as the numerator of (10-7).

To review, we note that if H_0 is true, we can estimate σ^2 by two valid methods; since the two will be about equal, their ratio F will fluctuate around 1. But if H_0 is not true, then the numerator of (10-7) will blow up because the difference in population means will result in a spread in the sample means (large $s_{\bar{X}}^2$); at the same time, the denominator will still reflect only chance fluctuation, consequently the F ratio will be large.

The formal test of H_0 exploits this distribution of the test statistic F. When H_0 is true, the exact distribution is shown in Figure 10-2. The critical $F_{.05}$ value, cutting off 5% of the upper tail of the distribution, is also shown. To test at the 5% significance level, we reject H_0 whenever F exceeds this critical value 3.89. Thus, if H_0 is true there is only a 5% probability that we would observe an F value exceeding 3.89, and con-sequently reject H_0. It is conceivable, of course, that H_0 is true and we were very unlucky; but we choose the more plausible explanation that H_0 is false.

To illustrate this procedure, let us reconsider the three sets of sample results shown in Tables 10-1, 10-3, and 10-4, and in each case ask whether the machines exhibit differences that are statistically significant. In other words, in each case we test H_0: $\mu_1 = \mu_2 = \mu_3$ against the alternative that they are not equal. For the data in Table 10-3, an evaluation of (10-7) yields

$$F = \frac{ns_{\bar{X}}^2}{s_p^2} = \frac{.35}{.547} = .64 \tag{10-10}$$

Since this is below the critical $F_{.05}$ value of 3.89, H_0 is acceptable. In this case the observed differences in means can reasonably be explained by chance fluctuations. This is no surprise; recall that we generated these three samples in Table 10-3 from the same machine.

Similarly, for the data in Table 10-4,

$$F = \frac{77.4}{35.7} = 2.17 \tag{10-11}$$

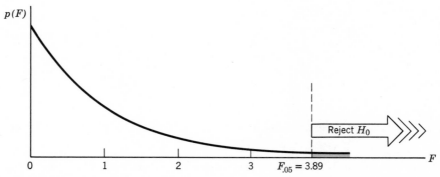

FIGURE 10-2 The distribution of F when H_0 is true (with 2, 12 degrees of freedom).

Since this is also below $F_{.05}$, H_0 is again acceptable. In this case, the difference between sample means (and consequently the numerator) is much greater. But so is the chance fluctuation (reflected in a large denominator).

However, for the data in Table 10-1,

$$F = \frac{77.4}{.547} = 141 \tag{10-12}$$

Since this exceeds $F_{.05}$, H_0 is rejected. In this case, the difference in sample means is very large relative to the chance fluctuation.

These three formal tests confirm our earlier intuitive conclusions. Table 10-1 provides the only case in which we conclude that the underlying populations have different means, at the 5% significance level.

(b) The F Distribution

The F distribution shown in Figure 10-2 is only one of many; there is a different distribution depending on degrees of freedom $(r - 1)$ in the numerator, and degrees of freedom $[r(n - 1)]$ in the denominator. Intuitively, we can see why this is so. The more degrees of freedom in calculating both numerator and denominator, the closer these two estimates of variance will likely be to their target σ^2; thus the more closely their ratio will concentrate around 1. This is illustrated in Figure 10-3.

Critical points for the F distributions are tabulated in Table VII of the appendix. From this table, we confirm the critical point of 3.89 used in Figure 10-2.

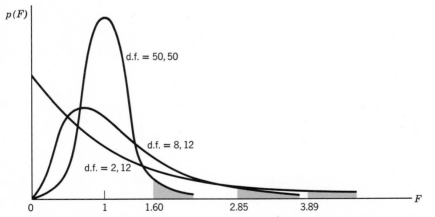

FIGURE 10-3   The F distribution, with various degrees of freedom in numerator and denominator. Note how the 5% critical point (beyond which we reject H_0) moves toward 1 as degrees of freedom increase.

(c) The ANOVA Table

This section merely presents a convenient and customary way to lay out the calculations already described. But first, the model is summarized in Table 10-5. We confirm in column 2 that all samples are assumed drawn from normal[1] populations with the same variance σ^2—but, of course, means that may differ. (Indeed it is the possible differences in means that are being tested).

The ensuing calculations are conveniently laid out in Table 10-6, called the ANOVA table—an obvious shorthand for ANalysis Of VAriance. This is mostly a bookkeeping arrangement, with the first row showing calculations of the numerator of the F ratio, and the second row the denominator. In part (b) of this table we evaluate the specific example of the three machines in Table 10-1.

In addition, this table provides two handy intermediate checks on our calculations. One is on degrees of freedom in column 3. The other check is on sums of squares in column 2; the sum of squares *between* rows plus the sum of squares *within* rows should add up to the total sum of squares.[2] Each sum of squares is also called *variation;* when divided by the appropriate degrees of freedom, it yields *variance* in column 4.

Table 10-5   Summary of Assumptions

(1) Population	(2) Assumed Distribution	(3) Observed Sample Values	
1	$N(\mu_1, \sigma^2)$	X_{1j}	$(j = 1\cdots n)$
2	$N(\mu_2, \sigma^2)$	X_{2j}	$(j = 1\cdots n)$
$\vdots$	$\vdots$	$\vdots$	
i	$N(\mu_i, \sigma^2)$	X_{ij}	$(j = 1\cdots n)$
$\vdots$	$\vdots$	$\vdots$	
r	$N(\mu_r, \sigma^2)$	X_{rj}	$(j = 1\cdots n)$

null hypothesis $H_0: \mu_1 = \mu_2 = \cdots = \mu_i = \cdots \mu_r$

The variance *between* rows is "explained" by the fact that the rows may come from different parent populations (e.g., machines that perform differently). The variance *within* rows is "unexplained" because it is the random or chance variation that cannot be systematically explained (by

---

[1] Just as for the t distribution in Section 8-2, our results usually remain approximately true even if the populations are nonnormal.

[2] **Proof:** The difference, or deviation of any observed value X_{ij} from the mean of all observed values $\bar{\bar{X}}$, can be broken down into two parts:

(cont'd on p. 222)

Table 10-6

(a) ANOVA Table, General

(1) Source of Variation	(2) Variation; Sum of Squares (SS)	(3) d.f.	(4) Variance; Mean Sum of Squares (MSS)	(5) F ratio
Between rows; "EXPLAINED" by differences in $\bar{X}_i$	$n \sum_{i=1}^{r} (\bar{X}_i - \bar{\bar{X}})^2 = SS_r$	$(r-1)$	$MSS_r = SS_r/(r-1)$ $= n s_{\bar{X}}^2$	$\dfrac{\text{explained variance}}{\text{unexplained variance}} = F$
Within rows; residual variation, resulting from chance fluctuation, "UNEXPLAINED"	$\sum_{i=1}^{r} \sum_{j=1}^{n} (X_{ij} - \bar{X}_i)^2 = SS_u$	$r(n-1)$	$MSS_u = SS_u/r(n-1)$ $= s_p^2$	
Total	$\sum_i \sum_j (X_{ij} - \bar{\bar{X}})^2$	$(nr-1)$		

(b) ANOVA Table, for Observations Given in Table 10-1

(1) Source of Variation	(2) Variation	(3) d.f.	(4) Variance	(5) F ratio	(6) prob-value
Between machines; "EXPLAINED"	154.8	2	77.4	$\dfrac{77.4}{.547} = 141$	$p \ll .001$
Within machines; "UNEXPLAINED"	6.56	12	.547		
Total	161 ✓	14 ✓			

differences in machines). Thus F is sometimes referred to as the variance ratio,

$$F = \frac{\text{explained variance}}{\text{unexplained variance}} \tag{10-17}$$

This suggests a possible means of strengthening the F test. Suppose, for example, that these three machines are sensitive to differences in

Total deviation = explained deviation + unexplained deviation

$$(X_{ij} - \bar{\bar{X}}) = (\bar{X}_i - \bar{\bar{X}}) + (X_{ij} - \bar{X}_i) \tag{10-13}$$

Thus, using Table 10-1 as an example, the third observation in the second sample (56.9) is 4.7 greater than $\bar{X} = 52.2$. This total deviation can be broken down,

$$(56.9 - 52.2) = (56.4 - 52.2) + (56.9 - 56.4)$$
$$4.7 = 4.2 + .5$$

Thus most of this total deviation is explained by the machine (4.2), while very little (.5) is unexplained, due to random fluctuations. Clearly (10-13) must always be true, since the two occurrences of $\bar{X}_i$ cancel.

Square both sides of (10-13) and sum over all i and j:

$$\sum_i \sum_j (X_{ij} - \bar{\bar{X}})^2 = \sum_i \sum_j (\bar{X}_i - \bar{\bar{X}})^2 + 2 \sum_i \sum_j (\bar{X}_i - \bar{\bar{X}})(X_{ij} - \bar{X}_i) + \sum_i \sum_j (X_{ij} - \bar{X}_i)^2 \tag{10-14}$$

On the right side, the middle (cross product) term may be written as

$$2 \sum_{i=1}^{r} \left[(\bar{X}_i - \bar{\bar{X}}) \underbrace{\sum_{j=1}^{n} (X_{ij} - \bar{X}_i)}_{\updownarrow} \right], \text{ which must be zero since}$$

the algebraic sum of deviations about the mean is always zero. Furthermore, the first term on the right side of (10-14) is:

$$\sum_{j=1}^{n} \left[\underbrace{\sum_{i=1}^{r} (\bar{X}_i - \bar{\bar{X}})^2}_{\text{independent of } j} \right] = n \sum_{i=1}^{r} (\bar{X}_i - \bar{\bar{X}})^2 \tag{10-15}$$

Substituting these two conclusions back into (10-14), we have:

$$\sum_i \sum_j (X_{ij} - \bar{\bar{X}})^2 = n \sum_i (\bar{X}_i - \bar{\bar{X}})^2 + \sum_i \sum_j (X_{ij} - \bar{X}_i)^2 \tag{10-16}$$

Total variation = explained variation + unexplained variation.

the men operating them. Why not introduce the operator explicitly into the analysis? If some of the previously unexplained variation can now be explained by differences in operator, the denominator of (10-17) will be reduced. With the larger F value that results, we will have a more powerful test of the machines (i.e., we will be in a stronger position to reject H_0). Thus our ability to detect whether one factor (machine) is important is strengthened by introducing another factor (operator) to help explain variance. (This introduces two-factor ANOVA in Section 10-2.)

Finally, although it is common to test H_0 at the arbitrary significance level of 5%, we have already pointed out in Chapter 9 that it is more meaningful to state the prob-value (most impressive significance level). This can be approximated by interpolating the F table. For example, for $F = 141$, given in column 5 of Table 10-6 (based on 2 and 12 d.f.), the closest critical value is $F_{.001} = 13.0$. We therefore conclude that

$$\text{prob-value} \ll .001 \tag{10-18}$$

where $\ll$ means "is much less than."

As another example, in (10-11) we found $F = 2.17$, with 2 and 12 d.f. The closest critical values are $F_{.10} = 2.81$ and $F_{.25} = 1.56$. Thus

$$.10 < \text{prob-value} < .25 \tag{10-19}$$

By crude interpolation,[3] we would guess that

$$\text{prob-value} \simeq .15 \tag{10-20}$$

(d) Confidence Intervals

Other limitations of hypothesis tests cited in Chapter 9 also hold in ANOVA. It may not be too enlightening to ask *whether* population means differ; by increasing sample size enough, statistical significance can nearly always be established—even though the population difference may be too small to be of any practical or economic importance. It is therefore more important to find out "by *how much* do population means differ?"

It is easy to compare only two machines in Table 10-1 by constructing

_____

[3] Interpolating by eye gives a reasonable approximation. Rules for careful interpolation, worthwhile for important data, are given in Appendix Table X.

a confidence interval for $(\mu_1 - \mu_2)$ using $(\overline{X}_1 - \overline{X}_2)$ and the t distribution:

$$(\mu_1 - \mu_2) = (\overline{X}_1 - \overline{X}_2) \pm t_{.025}\, s_p \sqrt{\frac{1}{n} + \frac{1}{n}} \qquad (10\text{-}21)$$
$$(8\text{-}17) \text{ repeated}$$

In (8-17), s_p^2 was the variance pooled from the two samples. However, it is more reasonable to use all the information available, and pool the variance from all three samples as in (10-6), obtaining $s_p^2 = .547$ with $4 + 4 + 4 = 12$ degrees of freedom. Thus the 95% confidence interval is

$$(\mu_1 - \mu_2) = (48.6 - 56.4) \pm 2.179 \sqrt{.547}\, \sqrt{\tfrac{1}{5} + \tfrac{1}{5}}$$

Similar confidence intervals for $(\mu_1 - \mu_3)$ and for $(\mu_2 - \mu_3)$ may be constructed, for a total of three intervals; in our example, these intervals are:

$$\left. \begin{array}{ll} (\mu_1 - \mu_2) = -7.8 \pm 1.0 & (a) \\ (\mu_1 - \mu_3) = -3.0 \pm 1.0 & (b) \\ (\mu_2 - \mu_3) = +4.8 \pm 1.0 & (c) \end{array} \right\} \qquad (10\text{-}22)$$

(e) Simultaneous Confidence Intervals: Multiple Comparisons

There is just one difficulty with the above approach. Although we can be 95% confident of each individual statement such as (10-22a), we can be far less confident that the whole *system* of statements (10-22) is true; there are three ways (three statements) where this could go wrong.[4]

The level of confidence in the system (10-22) would be reduced to $(.95)^3 = .857$, if the three individual statements were independent.[5] But in fact they are not; for example, they all involve the common term s_p. Thus if our observed s_p is high, all three interval estimates in (10-22) will be broad as a consequence. The problem is how to allow for this dependence in order to obtain the correct *simultaneous* confidence coefficient for the whole system. In fact, this problem is usually stated the other way around: how much wider must the *individual* intervals in (10-22) be in order to yield a 95% level of confidence that all are simultaneously true?

---

[4]To emphasize this point, suppose there were 100 individual confidence intervals comprising (10-22) instead of merely 3. Then we would expect, with average luck, for 95 of them to be right, and 5 of them to be wrong; hence the system of statements as a whole would be wrong.

[5]See Problem 7-5, if necessary.

Of the many solutions, we quote without proof the simplest;[6] with 95% confidence, *all* the following statements are true.

$$(\mu_1 - \mu_2) = (\overline{X}_1 - \overline{X}_2) \pm \sqrt{F_{.05}}\, s_p\sqrt{\frac{(r-1)}{n}2} \quad (a)$$

$$(\mu_1 - \mu_3) = (\overline{X}_1 - \overline{X}_3) \pm \sqrt{F_{.05}}\, s_p\sqrt{\frac{(r-1)}{n}2} \quad (b) \Bigg\} \quad (10\text{-}23)$$

$$(\mu_2 - \mu_3) = (\overline{X}_2 - \overline{X}_3) \pm \sqrt{F_{.05}}\, s_p\sqrt{\frac{(r-1)}{n}2} \quad (c)$$

where $F_{.05}$ = The critical value of F (with $r-1$ and $r(n-1)$ d.f.) leaving 5% in the upper tail.

s_p^2 = the pooled sample variance, as calculated in Table 10-6 or equation (10-6)

r = number of rows (means) to be compared.

n = each sample size.

For the machines in Table 10-1, the actual simultaneous confidence intervals are

i.e.,

$$\mu_1 - \mu_2 = (48.6 - 56.4) \pm \sqrt{3.89}\,(.74)\sqrt{\tfrac{2}{5}(2)}$$

$$\begin{aligned}
\mu_1 - \mu_2 &= -7.8 \pm 1.3 \quad (a) \\
\mu_1 - \mu_3 &= -3.0 \pm 1.3 \quad (b) \\
\mu_2 - \mu_3 &= +4.8 \pm 1.3 \quad (c)
\end{aligned}\Bigg\} \qquad (10\text{-}24)$$

As expected, (10-22) and (10-24) are similar, except that the width of the confidence interval is greater in (10-24); (compare 1.3 versus 1.0). Indeed, it is this increased width (vagueness) that makes us 95% confident that *all* statements are true.

The results in (10-24) are summarized in Table 10-7. For those intervals which do not enclose the null value of zero, the difference in means is statistically significant, indicated with a star. Note how a machine can quickly be evaluated by examining its row: thus the positive (starred)

---

[6]H. Scheffé's method, in his *The Analysis of Variance*, pp. 66–73, New York: Wiley, 1959. Not only are the 3 statements in (10-23) covered by 95% confidence, but some other statements as well—as we shall see in (10-29). In fact if we were interested *only* in the three comparisons of means in (10-23), our interval estimates could be made slightly narrower.

Table 10-7   Differences in Population Means
$(\mu_i - \mu_I)$ Estimated from Sample Means $(\overline{X}_i - \overline{X}_I)$.
For 95% *simultaneous* confidence intervals, take
the listed value ± 1.3. Statistically significant
differences are starred. (Data from Table 10-1).

i \ I	1	2	3
1	0	-7.8^*	-3.0^*
2	7.8^*	0	$+4.8^*$
3	3.0^*	-4.8^*	0

differences in row 2 indicate how machine 2 (significantly) outperforms the other two machines.[7]

As a bonus, the theory from which (10-23) is derived can be used to make any number of comparisons of means, called "contrasts." A "contrast of means" is defined as a linear combination, or weighted sum, with weights that add to zero:

$$\sum_{i=1}^{r} C_i \mu_i$$

provided

$$\sum_{i=1}^{r} C_i = 0 \qquad (10\text{-}25)$$

For example, the simplest contrast is the difference

$$\mu_1 - \mu_2 = (+1)\mu_1 + (-1)\mu_2 + (0)\mu_3 \qquad (10\text{-}26)$$

It was this contrast that was estimated in (10-24a). Another interesting contrast is the difference between μ_1 and the average of μ_2 and μ_3:

$$\mu_1 - \frac{(\mu_2 + \mu_3)}{2} = (+1)\mu_1 + (-\tfrac{1}{2})\mu_2 + (-\tfrac{1}{2})\mu_3 \qquad (10\text{-}27)$$

There is no limit to the number of contrasts. It is no surprise that each contrast of the population means will be estimated by the same contrast

---

[7] Any column shows these comparisons in reverse: thus column 1 indicates how machine 1 is *outperformed by* the other two machines.

of the sample means, plus or minus an error allowance. (10-24a) is one example. As another example, the contrast of means given in (10-27) is estimated as

$$\mu_1 - \tfrac{1}{2}\mu_2 - \tfrac{1}{2}\mu_3 = (\overline{X}_1 - \tfrac{1}{2}\overline{X}_2 - \tfrac{1}{2}\overline{X}_3) \pm \sqrt{F_{.05}}\, s_p \sqrt{\frac{(r-1)}{n}\frac{3}{2}} \quad (10\text{-}28)$$

The general statement, from which (10-24) and (10-28) were derived, is:

With 95% simultaneous confidence, *all* contrasts are bracketed by the bounds:

$$\sum C_i \mu_i = \sum C_i \overline{X}_i \pm \sqrt{F_{.05}}\, s_p \sqrt{\frac{(r-1)}{n}\left(\sum C_i^2\right)} \qquad (10\text{-}29)$$

---

provided only that $\sum C_i = 0$ to satisfy the definition of "contrast." As before, s_p^2 is pooled variance, and $F_{.05}$ is the critical value of F.

When we examine (10-29) more carefully, we discover that this defines a set of 95% simultaneous confidence intervals that includes not only the three statements in (10-23) but also statements like (10-28), and indeed an infinite number of contrasts that could be constructed. You may justifiably wonder "How can we be 95% confident of an infinite number of statements?" The answer is: because these statements are dependent. Thus, for example, once we have made the first two statements in (10-24), our intuition tells us that the third is likely to follow. Moreover, once these three statements are made, intervals like (10-28) tend to follow, and can be added with little damage to our level of confidence. As the number of statements or contrasts grows and grows, each new statement tends to become simply a restatement of contrasts already specified, and essentially no damage is done to our level of confidence. Thus, it can be mathematically confirmed that the entire (infinite) set of contrasts in (10-29) are all simultaneously estimated at a 95% level of confidence.[8]

---

[8] If all possible simultaneous contrasts are not desired (but just the differences in means), then it is possible to construct three 95% simultaneous confidence intervals in a much simpler way than (10-23). For example, following the principles of Problem 7-5, set the probability of error for each interval equal to 5%/3, i.e.,

$$\Pr(E_i) = 1.67\% \qquad (i = 1, 2, 3) \qquad (10\text{-}30)$$

Then

$$\Pr(\text{some error}) = \Pr(E_1 \text{ or } E_2 \text{ or } E_3) \qquad (10\text{-}31)$$

(con't on p. 229)

Table 10-8 Modification of ANOVA Table 10-6, for Unequal Sample Sizes, $n_1, n_2, \ldots, n_i \ldots$

(1) Source of Variation	(2) Variation; Sum of Squares (SS)	(3) d.f.	(4) Variance; Mean Sum of Squares (MSS)	(5) F ratio
Between rows; "EXPLAINED" by differences in $\bar{X}_i$	$\sum\limits_{i=1}^{r} n_i(\bar{X}_i - \bar{\bar{X}})^2 = SS_r$	$(r-1)$	$MSS_r = SS_r/(r-1)$ $= ns_{\bar{X}}^2$	$\dfrac{\text{explained variance}}{\text{unexplained variance}} = F$
Within rows; residual variation, resulting from chance fluctuation, "UNEXPLAINED"	$\sum\limits_{i=1}^{r}\sum\limits_{j=1}^{n_i}(X_{ij} - \bar{X}_i)^2 = SS_u$	$\sum\limits_{i=1}^{r}(n_i - 1)$	$MSS_u = SS_u/\sum(n_i - 1)$ $= s_p^2$	
Total	$\sum\limits_{i}^{n_i}\sum\limits_{j}(X_{ij} - \bar{\bar{X}})^2$	$\sum n_i - 1$		

(f) Unequal Sample Sizes

The commonest and most efficient way to collect observations is to make all samples the same size n. However, when this is not feasible (e.g., because the data have already been observed in different sample sizes, $n_1, n_2, \ldots n_i \ldots$), it is still possible to modify the ANOVA calculations to allow for this. The necessary modifications of Table 10-6 are given in Table 10-8.

PROBLEMS

⇒10-1   Twelve plots of land are randomly divided into 3 groups. The first is held as a control group while fertilizers A and B are applied to the other 2 groups. Yield is observed to be:

Control, C	60	64	65	55
A	75	70	66	69
B	74	78	72	68

(a) Does fertilizer affect yield? Calculate the ANOVA table.
(b) Construct a table of differences in means, similar to Table 10-7, starring the differences that are statistically significant.

If these events are mutually exclusive:

$$= Pr\,(E_1) + Pr\,(E_2) + Pr\,(E_3) \tag{10-32}$$

But since in general these events need not be mutually exclusive

$$Pr\,(\text{some error}) \leq 1.67\% + 1.67\% + 1.67\% = 5\% \tag{10-33}$$

Thus   the simultaneous confidence level $\geq 95\%$ (10-34)

The specification of, say, the first interval in (10-30) can be achieved by simply using (10-21) with a new t value. Since the two-sided probability required is .0167, we should use $t_{.0083}$, which is found by interpolation to be 2.8. Thus (10-21) becomes

$$\left. \begin{array}{l} \mu_1 - \mu_2 = -7.8 \pm 1.3 \\ \mu_1 - \mu_3 = -3.0 \pm 1.3 \\ \mu_2 - \mu_3 = 4.8 \pm 1.3 \end{array} \right\} \tag{10-35}$$

Similarly

which is the same as (10-24), at least to 2 significant figures. In other examples, we would usually find the intervals in (10-35) to be slightly narrower than in (10-24). This suggests that our admitted approximation in (10-33) has resulted in an estimator (10-35) which is more efficient than (10-24). This is, in fact, the case, provided we limit ourselves only to two-at-a-time comparisons. (10-24) becomes more efficient only if we want the bonus of all possible comparisons (10-29).

We might say that (10-29) allows us to hunt legitimately for interesting contrasts that may be turned up by the data (but need not be specified a priori). In this sense, the greater width of (10-29) may be regarded as the "cost" of this "hunting licence."

(c) Do the two fertilizers have a different effect?

(d) What is the difference between a contrast of means, and a weighted average of means?

10-2 A sample of 4 workers was drawn at random from each of two different industries, with their annual income (in $100) recorded as follows:

Industry A	66	62	65	63
Industry B	58	56	53	61

(a) Using first a t test (as in Chapter 8) and then an ANOVA F test, calculate the prob-value for the null hypothesis (no difference in industries).

(b) Are the t and F tests exactly equivalent? Can you see why the t^2 distribution is often referred to as the F distribution with 1 degree of freedom in the numerator?

(c) Using first the t distribution (8-17), and then the F distribution (10-23), construct a 95% confidence interval for the difference in mean incomes in the two industries.

⟹10-3 The annual income (in $100) of a random sample of men and women in a certain occupation was found to be:

Women	Men
48	60
56	70
50	62
54	48

(a) What is the prob-value for the null hypothesis that mean income is the same for men and women?

(b) Construct a 95% confidence interval for the difference in the two means.

Since this problem is important later in Chapter 13 we state its solution. It may be solved with the 2 sample t distribution, or with ANOVA as follows:

(a)   ANOVA Table

Source	Variation	d.f.	variance	F ratio	prob-value
Between sexes	128	1	128	$F = \dfrac{128}{48}$	$.10 < p < .25$
Residual	288	6	48	$= 2.67$	
Total	416	7			

where $\bar{\bar{Y}}_1 = 52$ $\bar{\bar{Y}}_2 = 60$ $\bar{\bar{Y}} = 56$

(b) Evaluate the first equation in (10-23); or, more simply (10-21), noting that $t_{.025} = \sqrt{F_{.05}}$

$$(\mu_1 - \mu_2) = (52 - 60) \pm 2.45\sqrt{48}\sqrt{2/4}$$
$$= -8 \pm 12$$

This also confirms the answer in (a); since this interval includes zero, it is not statistically significant.

10-4 For the data in Table 10-4, calculate the ANOVA table, and a table of differences in means similar to Table 10-7.

10-5 Suppose that the number of years of school completed by a sample of adult Americans was:

White	14	8	9	12	13	12	10	14	13	12	13	11	15
Negro	10	9	8	11	10	8	7						

At a 5% level of significance, does race make a difference? What is the prob-value?

10-6 Referring to the machine example of Table 10-1 and its ANOVA Table 10-6(b), use equation (10-29) to incidentally solve the following problem:

Suppose one factory is to be outfitted entirely with machines of the first type. Suppose a second factory is to be outfitted with machines of the second and third types, in the proportions 30% and 70%. Find a confidence interval for the difference in mean production for the 2 factories.

10-7 Following equation (10-7), we gave two alternate methods of estimating σ^2, (the variance of the population from which all samples are taken). Is there not a third, even more direct way of estimating σ^2? Why isn't it used in (10-7), i.e., why instead did we use the two indirect estimates?

10-8 From each of four very large classes, 50 students were sampled, with the following results:

Class	Average Grade $\bar{X}$	Standard Deviation, s
A	68	11
B	74	12
C	70	8
D	68	10

Test whether the classes are equally good at a 5% significance level. If they are not, construct a table of differences in the means, similar to Table 10-7.

10-9 A sample of American workmen in selected industries reported the following hourly earnings in 1969:

Durables manufacturing	$3.30	3.65	3.45	3.50	3.15	3.40	3.35
Nondurables manufacturing	3.10	2.70	2.85	2.90	2.85	3.00	
Construction	4.80	4.80	5.20	4.85	4.55		
Retail trade	2.20	2.25	2.50	2.40	2.35	2.10	

Can you establish that these industries display statistically significant differences in income? What is the prob-value for the null hypothesis ("no differences")?

10-2   TWO-FACTOR ANALYSIS OF VARIANCE

(a) The ANOVA Table

We have already suggested that the F test on the differences in machines given in (10-17) would be strengthened if the unexplained variance could be reduced by taking into account other factors. Suppose, for example, that the sample outputs given in Table 10-4 were produced by five different operators—with each operator producing one of the sample values on each machine. This data, reorganized according to a two-way classification (by machine *and* operator), is shown in Table 10-9. It is necessary to complicate our notation somewhat. We are now interested in the average of each operator (each column average $\overline{X}_{.j}$) as well as the average of each machine (each row average $\overline{X}_{i.}$).[9]

Now the picture is clarified; some operators are efficient (the first and fourth), some are not. The machines are not that erratic after all; there is just a wide difference in the efficiency of the operators. If we can explicitly adjust for this, it will reduce our unexplained (or chance) variation in the denominator of (10-17); since the numerator will remain unchanged, the F ratio will be larger as a consequence, perhaps allowing us to reject H_0. To sum up, it appears that another influence (difference in operators) was responsible for a lot of extraneous noise in our simple one-way analysis in the previous section; by removing this noise, we hope to get a much more powerful test of the machines.

The analysis is an extension of the one-factor ANOVA, and is summarized in Table 10-10a. Of course, the small letter c represents the

[9]The dot indicates the subscript over which summation occurs. For example, the dot suppresses the subscript j in $\overline{X}_{i.} = \dfrac{1}{n} \sum_{j} X_{ij}$

Table 10-9   Samples of Production (X_{ij}) of Three Different Machines (as given in Table 10-4, but now arranged according to machine operator)

Machine	Operator $j = 1$	2	3	4	5	Machine Mean $\bar{X}_{i.}$
$i = 1$	56.7	45.7	48.3	54.6	37.7	48.6
2	64.5	53.4	54.3	57.5	52.3	56.4
3	56.7	50.6	49.5	56.5	44.7	51.6
						$52.2 = \bar{\bar{X}}$
Operator Mean $\bar{X}_{.j}$	59.3	49.9	50.7	56.2	44.9	$52.2 = \bar{\bar{X}}$

number of columns in Table 10-9, and replaces n in Table 10-6. As before, the component sources of variation shown in column 2 of Table 10-10(a) sum to the total variation at the bottom of this column, i.e.,

$$\sum_{i=1}^{r} \sum_{j=1}^{c} (X_{ij} - \bar{\bar{X}})^2 = c \underbrace{\sum_{i=1}^{r} (\bar{X}_{i.} - \bar{\bar{X}})^2}_{\text{Total variation} = \text{machine (row)} \atop \text{variation}} + r \underbrace{\sum_{j=1}^{c} (\bar{X}_{.j} - \bar{\bar{X}})^2}_{\text{+ operator (column)} \atop \text{variation}}$$

$$+ \underbrace{\sum_{i=1}^{r} \sum_{j=1}^{c} (X_{ij} - \bar{X}_{i.} - \bar{X}_{.j} + \bar{\bar{X}})^2}_{\text{+ random variation}} \quad (10\text{-}36)$$

We note that operator variation is defined like machine variation; the only difference is that this is defined as the variation exhibited by *column* means. (10-36) is established by a complex set of manipulations, parallel to those used to establish (10-16) in the simpler case. (The last term—the random variation—in (10-36) may seem a bit puzzling; it will be interpreted below.)

(b) Testing Hypotheses

With the total variation broken down into components in (10-36), we can now test whether there is a significant difference in machines, *or* whether there is a significant difference in operators; in either test the extraneous influence of the other factor will be taken into account.

On the one hand, we test for differences in machines by constructing the ratio

$$F = \frac{\text{MSS}_r}{\text{MSS}_u} = \frac{\text{variance explained by machines}}{\text{unexplained variance}} \quad (10\text{-}37)$$

Table 10-10a Two-Way ANOVA, General

(1) Source	(2) Variation; Sum of Squares (SS)	(3) d.f.	(4) Variance; Mean Sum of Squares (MSS)	(5) F
Between rows; EXPLAINED by differences in machines, i.e. differences in $\bar{X}_{i.}$	$SS_r = c \sum_{i=1}^{r} (\bar{X}_{i.} - \bar{\bar{X}})^2$	$r - 1$	$MSS_r = \dfrac{SS_r}{r-1} = cs_{\bar{X}_{i.}}^2$	$\dfrac{MSS_r}{MSS_u}$
Between columns; EXPLAINED by differences in operators, i.e., differences in $\bar{X}_{.j}$	$SS_c = r \sum_{j=1}^{c} (\bar{X}_{.j} - \bar{\bar{X}})^2$	$c - 1$	$MSS_c = \dfrac{SS_c}{c-1} = rs_{\bar{X}_{.j}}^2$	$\dfrac{MSS_c}{MSS_u}$
UNEXPLAINED, i.e., residual variation, resulting from chance fluctuation.	$SS_u = \sum_{i=1}^{r} \sum_{j=1}^{c} (X_{ij} - \bar{X}_{i.} - \bar{X}_{.j} + \bar{\bar{X}})^2$	$(r - 1)(c - 1)$	$MSS_u = \dfrac{SS_u}{(r-1)(c-1)} = s^2$	
Total	$SS = \sum_{i=1}^{r} \sum_{j=1}^{c} (X_{ij} - \bar{\bar{X}})^2$	$rc - 1$		

Table 10-10b   Two-Way ANOVA, for Observations Given in Table 10-9

(1) Source	(2) Variation; (SS)	(3) d.f.	(4) Variance; (MSS)	(5) F Ratio	(6) Prob-value for H_0
Between machines	154.8	2	77.4	13.1	$p < .01$
Between operators	381.6	4	95.4	16.2	$p < .001$
Residual	47.3	8	5.9		
Total	583.7✓	14✓			

which, if H_0 is true, has an F distribution. Our calculations are shown in full in Table 10-10b, where (10-37) is evaluated as,

$$F = \frac{77.4}{5.9} = 13.1 \qquad (10\text{-}38)$$

Since this exceeds the critical $F_{.05}$ value of 4.46, we reject the null hypothesis that the machines are similar, at the 5% significance level. Better still, we find the prob-value $< .01$. It is interesting to compare this with the F test in (10-11), where we could not reject the null hypothesis. The numerator has remained unchanged, but the chance variation in the denominator is much smaller, since the effect of differing operators has been netted out. This has given us greater statistical leverage,[10] allowing rejection of the null hypothesis.

Similarly, we might test the null hypothesis that the operators perform equally well. Once again F is the ratio of an explained to an unexplained variance; but this time, of course, the numerator is the variance estimated from column differences. Thus

$$F = \frac{\text{variance explained by operators}}{\text{unexplained variance}} = \frac{MSS_c}{MSS_u} = \frac{95.4}{5.9} = 16.2$$
$$(10\text{-}39)$$

In this case, the machine "noise" has been isolated; as a consequence we get a strong test of how operators compare. Since our observed F value of 16.2 exceeds the critical $F_{.05}$ value of 3.84, we reject the null hypothesis, concluding that machinists do differ at the 5% significance level.

---

[10]Strictly speaking, we have a stronger test because we have gained more by reducing unexplained variance than we have lost because our degrees of freedom in the denominator have been reduced by 4. (If we are already short of degrees of freedom—i.e., if we are near the top of F Table VII, loss of degrees of freedom may be serious.)

There is one issue that we passed over quickly, that still requires clarification. In our one-factor test we calculated unexplained variation by looking at the spread of n observed values within a category, i.e., within a whole row in Table 10-4. But in the two-way test Table 10-9 we have split our observations columnwise, as well as rowwise; this has left us with only one observation within each category. Thus, for example, there is only a single observation (57.5) of how much output is produced by operator 4 on machine 2. Variation can no longer be computed within that cell. What should we do?

We ask: If there were no random error, how would we predict the output of operator 4 on machine 2? We note, informally, that this is a better-than-average machine ($\overline{X}_{2.} = 56.4$) and a relatively efficient operator ($\overline{X}_{.4} = 56.2$). On both counts we would predict output to be above average. This strategy can easily be formalized to predict $\hat{X}_{2,4}$. We can do this for each cell, with the random element estimated as the difference between the observed value X_{ij} and the corresponding predicted value $\hat{X}_{ij}$. This yields a whole set of random elements, whose sum of squares is precisely the unexplained variation[11] SS_u (the last term in (10-36), also appearing in column 2 of Table 10-10a); divided by d.f.,

---

[11] Predicted value $\hat{X}_{ij}$ is defined as

$$\hat{X}_{ij} = \overline{\overline{X}} + \text{adjustment reflecting machine performance} + \text{adjustment} \quad (10\text{-}40)$$
$$\text{reflecting operator performance}$$

$$= \overline{\overline{X}} + (\overline{X}_{i.} - \overline{\overline{X}}) + (\overline{X}_{.j} - \overline{\overline{X}}) \quad (10\text{-}41)$$

Specifically, in our example

$$\hat{X}_{24} = 52.2 + (56.4 - 52.2) + (56.2 - 52.2)$$
$$= 52.2 + 4.2 + 4.0 = 60.4$$

Thus, our prediction of the performance of operator 4 on machine 2 is calculated by adjusting average performance (52.2) by the degree to which this machine is above average (4.2) and the degree to which this operator is above average (4.0).

Cancelling $\overline{\overline{X}}$ values in (10-41):

$$\hat{X}_{ij} = \overline{X}_{i.} + \overline{X}_{.j} - \overline{\overline{X}} \quad (10\text{-}42)$$

and the random element, being the difference between the observed and expected, becomes:

$$X_{ij} - \hat{X}_{ij} = X_{ij} - \overline{X}_{i.} - \overline{X}_{.j} + \overline{\overline{X}} \quad (10\text{-}43)$$

We emphasize that this random element is output left unexplained after adjustment for both machine i and operator j.

In our example

$$X_{24} - \hat{X}_{24} = 57.5 - 60.4 = -2.9 \quad (10\text{-}44)$$

(cont'd)

this becomes the unexplained variance used in the denominator of both tests in this section.

One final warning: in computing predicted output $\hat{X}_{ij}$, we assume that there is no interaction between the two factors as would occur, for example, if certain operators like some machines, and dislike others; such interaction would require a more complex model, and more sample observations. The two-way analysis of variance developed in this section is based on the assumption that interaction does not exist.

(c) Multiple Comparisons

Turning from hypothesis tests to confidence intervals, we may write a statement for two-factor ANOVA which is quite similar to (10-29):

With 95% simultaneous confidence, all contrasts in row means fall within the bounds:

$$\sum C_i \mu_i = \sum C_i \bar{X}_{i.} \pm \sqrt{F_{.05}}\, s \sqrt{\frac{(r-1)}{c}\left(\sum C_i^2\right)} \qquad (10\text{-}45)$$

---

where

$F_{.05}$ = the critical value of F, with $(r-1)$ and $(r-1)(c-1)$ d.f.
$s = \sqrt{MSS_u}$, as calculated in Table 10-10a, column 4
r = number of rows
c = number of columns

Note that (10-45) differs from (10-29) primarily because its unexplained variance s^2 is now smaller, making the confidence interval more precise.

As an example, consider the machines of Table 10-9, analyzed in ANOVA Table 10-10b. With 95% confidence, all the following statements are true:

$$\mu_1 - \mu_2 = (48.6 - 56.4) \pm \sqrt{4.46}\sqrt{5.9}\sqrt{\tfrac{2}{5}(2)}$$

i.e.,

$$\left.\begin{aligned}
\mu_1 - \mu_2 &= -7.8 \pm 4.5^* \\
\mu_1 - \mu_3 &= -3.0 \pm 4.5 \\
\mu_2 - \mu_3 &= 4.8 \pm 4.5^*
\end{aligned}\right\} \qquad (10\text{-}46)$$

and all other possible contrasts

Thus, this observed output is 2.9 units below what we expected, and must be left un-explained—the result of random influences.

Unexplained variation (SS_u) is recognized to be the sum of squares of all random elements as defined in (10-43).

Table 10-11   Differences in Operator Means
$\mu_j - \mu_J$ Estimated from the Sample Means
$(\overline{X}_{.j} - \overline{X}_{.J})$. For 95% simultaneous confidence
intervals, take the listed value ±7.8. Statistically
significant differences are starred.

j \ J	1	2	3	4	5
1	0	9.4*	8.6*	3.1	14.4*
2	−9.4*	0	−.8	−6.3	5.0
3	−8.6*	.8	0	−5.5	5.8
4	−3.1	6.3	5.5	0	11.3*
5	−14.4*	−5.0	−5.8	−11.3*	0

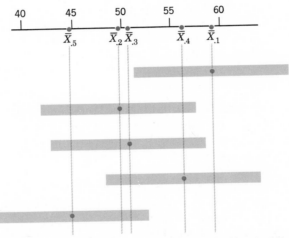

FIGURE 10-4   Differences in operator means, with each colored bar (±7.8) providing tests of significance. For example, the means that lie outside the top bar ($\overline{X}_{.2}, \overline{X}_{.3}, \overline{X}_{.5}$) are significantly different from $\overline{X}_{.1}$; those that lie outside the second bar are significantly different from $\overline{X}_{.2}$; and so on.

Again the intervals that do not overlap zero are starred to indicate statistical significance. Compare this with the corresponding analysis before operators were taken into account (Problem 10-4); note how the error allowance has been decreased, and hence the strength of the test increased.

Of course, we could contrast the column means equally well, by simply interchanging r and c in (10-45). As an example, how do the operators of Table 10-9 compare, as analyzed in ANOVA Table 10-10b? With 95% confidence, all the following statements are true:

$$\mu_1 - \mu_2 = (59.3 - 49.9) \pm \sqrt{3.84}\sqrt{5.9}\sqrt{\tfrac{4}{3}(2)}$$

i.e.,

$$\mu_1 - \mu_2 = 9.4 \pm 7.8*$$
$$\mu_1 - \mu_3 = 8.6 \pm 7.8*$$
$$\mu_1 - \mu_4 = 3.1 \pm 7.8$$
$$\mu_1 - \mu_5 = 14.4 \pm 7.8*$$
$$\mu_2 - \mu_3 = -0.8 \pm 7.8$$
$$\vdots$$

and all other possible contrasts, of the form   (10-47)

$$\sum C_j\mu_j = \sum C_j\bar{X}_j \pm 5.5\sqrt{\sum C_j^2}$$

For example, we might wish to compare the three best performers in Table 10-9 with the two worst:

$$\frac{\mu_1 + \mu_3 + \mu_4}{3} - \frac{\mu_2 + \mu_5}{2} = (55.4 - 47.4) \pm 5.5\sqrt{5/6}$$
$$= 8.0 \pm 5.0*$$

The first part of equation (10-47)—differences in means—is presented more concisely in Table 10-11. A graphic method of quickly testing for the statistical significance of the difference in any pair of means is presented in Figure 10-4.

PROBLEMS

10-10 To refine the experimental design of Problem 10-1, suppose the twelve plots of land are on 4 farms (3 plots on each). Moreover, you suspect that there may be a difference in fertility between farms. You now retabulate the data in Problem 10-1, according to fertilizer and farm as follows.

Fertilizer \ Farm	1	2	3	4
Control C	60	64	65	55
A	69	75	70	66
B	72	74	78	68

(a) Calculate the ANOVA table to determine whether fertilizers differ, and whether farms differ.

(b) Construct a table of differences in fertilizers similar to Table 10-11, starring differences that are statistically significant; also construct a table of differences in farms, and a graph similar to Figure 10-4 showing tests of significance.

10-11 Three men work on an identical task of packing boxes. The number of boxes packed by each in 3 selected hours is shown in the table below.

Hour \ Man	A	B	C
11–12 A.M.	21	18	21
1–2 P.M.	22	22	25
4–5 P.M.	17	16	18

(a) Calculate the ANOVA table.

(b) For the factors which are statistically significant at the 5% level, construct a table of simultaneous 95% confidence intervals as in Table 10-11.

10-12 Five children were tested for pulse rate before and after a certain television program, with the following results:

Child \ Time	Before	After
A	96	104
B	102	112
C	108	112
D	89	93
E	85	89

(a) Using first a paired t test, and then an ANOVA F test, calculate the prob-value for the null hypothesis (no difference in times).

(b) Are the t and F tests exactly equivalent?

(c) Using first the t distribution and then the F distribution, construct a 95% confidence interval for the difference in mean pulse rate, before and after.

Review Problems (Chapters 6–10)

10-13 A certain population of men has heights that are normally distributed, with mean 66″ and standard deviation 5″. What proportion
of these men are over 6′ (72″)?

10-14 Continuing Problem 10-13, suppose a random sample of 4 men
were chosen. What is the chance that the sample mean would
exceed 6′ (72″)?

10-15 Suppose a 95% confidence interval for a population mean was
calculated to be $\mu = 170 \pm 20$. From the following select the best
interpretation, and criticize the others.

(a) Any hypothesis in the interval $150 < \mu < 190$ is called the null
hypothesis, while any hypothesis outside this interval is called the
alternate hypothesis.

(b) The population mean is a random variable with expectation
170 and standard deviation 20.

(c) If this sampling experiment were repeated many times, and
each time a confidence interval were similarly constructed, 95%
of these confidence intervals would cover $\mu = 170$.

(d) The sample mean is a random variable with expectation 170
and standard deviation 10.2.

(e) Any hypothesis in the interval $150 < \mu < 190$ may be called
acceptable at the 5% significance level.

10-16 An anthropologist collected a random sample of 100 men from
among the large population of men on a certain island. Their
heights in inches were as follows:

Height x (cell midpoints)	Frequency
75	1
72	6
69	20
66	39
63	24
60	8
57	0
54	2

Does this throw any light on the theory that some anthropologists
have put forward that they have the same physical characteristics
as North Americans (as given in Table 2-4).

10-17 In Chapter 1 the notion of a biased sample was introduced, and in Chapter 7 the notion of a biased estimator. In order to see how these two ideas are related, consider the following vastly simplified example:

A certain population consists of two classes of people:

> 70% are poor people earning $4,000 each;
> 30% are rich people earning $20,000 each.

A politician records the incomes of 100 visitors to his office during a week when each rich person is twice as likely as each poor person to visit the office, thus making the sample mean a biased estimator of the population mean.

(a) How much is this bias, in dollars?

(b) What would be the bias in part (a) if
  (1) the sample size were 25 (instead of 100)?
  (2) the split between poor and rich were 60%–40% (instead of 70%–30%).

10-18 In a certain county, suppose the electorate is 80% urban, 20% rural; 70% of the urban voters, and only 25% of the rural voters, vote for D in preference to R. In a certain straw vote conducted by a small town newspaper editor, each rural voter has a 6 times larger chance of being selected than each urban voter. This bias in the sampling will cause the sample proportion to be a biased estimator of the population proportion in favor of R.

(a) How much is this bias?

(b) Is the bias large enough to cause the average sample to be wrong (in the sense that the average sample "elects" a different candidate from what the population elects)?

10-19 Turning now from the omniscient viewpoint of 10-18 to the more limited viewpoint of the newspaper editor, to be realistic we cannot suppose that the population proportion π favoring D is known. However, we can suppose that the 80%–20% urban-rural split in the population is known, through census figures, for example. Suppose the editor then obtains the following data from a biased sample of 500 voters:

Location \ Vote	For D	For R	Totals
Urban	210	92	302
Rural	80	318	398
Totals	290	410	700

The simple-minded and biased estimate of π is the simple proportion $290/700 = 41\%$. Calculate an *unbiased* estimate of π. Incidentally, such a technique based on several population strata (urban, rural) whose proportions are known and allowed for, is an example of *"stratified* sampling."

10-20 Suppose that in 1968, the annual income of a sample of Americans with various levels of education achievement was:

Elementary school only	$3,200	5,100	4,800	5,300	5,000	6,900	4,700
High school (4 years)	5,900	7,800	8,100	7,800	9,400	9,000	8,200
	7,600	7,900	8,100	7,000	9,200	8,000	
University (4 years)	9,400	12,000	11,500	12,100	12,200	11,800	

Does education have a statistically significant effect on income? Can you see any reason why this test might be biased?

10-21 In a certain freshman statistics course, there are 4 sections. From each section a sample of 6 grades was drawn, with the following results:

Section	Random Sample of 6 Grades from Each Section	Sample Mean $\bar{X}$
A	63, 87, 64, 69, 78, 65	71
B	77 etc.	70
C		50
D		81

ANOVA Table (partial)

Source	Variation (sum of squares)
Between sections	3036
Within sections	2080
Total	5116

(a) Construct 95% simultaneous confidence intervals for all differences in section means.

(b) Sections A and C were taught by Professor Jones, while sections B and D were taught by Professor Koestler. Therefore the contrast

$$\left[\frac{\mu_B + \mu_D}{2}\right] - \left[\frac{\mu_A + \mu_C}{2}\right]$$

is of interest. Construct a confidence interval for it.

(c) What level of confidence do you have in statement (b)?

(d) Does answer (b) prove (statistical proof at a certain level of confidence, not logical proof) that Professor Koestler is better than Professor Jones, in the restricted sense that Koestler can get students to perform better on exams?

(e) Suppose that sections B and C were taught at 8:00 a.m., while sections A and D were taught at 10:00 p.m. It therefore makes sense to array the sample means in the following 2-way table:

Time Professor	8:00	10:00
Jones	50	71
Koestler	70	81

Analyze this as a 2-factor experiment.

10-22 An instructor wished to compare the grades in his large statistics class of 810 students. From the 220 students who attended class less than half the time (the "absentees" A) he took a random sample of 10 students. From the remaining 590 students who attended at least half the time (the "participants" P) he took an independent random sample of 10 students also.

The following data were obtained:

	Population Size	Sample Size	Sample Mean	Sample Variance
Absentees A	220	10	53.2	280
Participants B	590	10	71.2	170

Construct a 95% confidence interval for the difference Δ in the mean grade between the two groups of students.

10-23 In a certain problem of determining confidence limits of a positive population parameter θ, suppose F is a quantity computed from a random sample of size n, for which it is known that

$$Pr\left\{\frac{1}{3.51} < \frac{F}{1 + 5\theta} < 2.45\right\} = .95$$

What is the 95% confidence interval for θ, if F turns out to be 6.0?

10-24 A random sample of 100 people were asked, both before and after a major policy speech, whether or not they approved of the President's policies. The number of responses in each category were:

After \ Before	Not Approve	Approve
Not Approve	57	13
Approve	2	28

To what extent has approval in the population changed? Answer with a 95% confidence interval.

iNTRODUCTION
TO REGRESSION

The cause is hidden, but the result is known.

Ovid

Our first example of statistical inference (in Chapter 7) was estimating the mean of a single population. This was followed (Chapter 8) by a comparison of two population means. Finally (Chapter 10) r population means were compared, using analysis of variance. We now consider the question "Can the analysis be improved if the r populations do not fall in unordered categories, but are ranked numerically?"

For example, it is easy to see how the analysis of variance could be used to examine whether wheat yield depended on 7 different *kinds* of fertilizer.[1] Now we wish to consider whether yield depends on 7 different *amounts* of fertilizer; in this case, fertilizer application is defined in a numerical scale. If yield Y that follows from various fertilizer applications X is plotted, a scatter similar to Figure 11-1 might be observed. From this scatter it is clear that fertilizer does affect yield. Moreover, it should be possible to describe *how*, by an equation relating Y to X. Estimating an equation is of course equivalent geometrically to fitting a curve through this scatter. This is called the regression of Y on X; as

---

[1] By extending Problem 10-1.

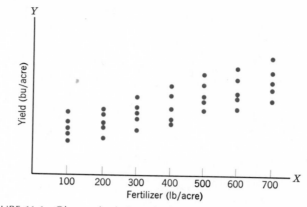

FIGURE 11-1   Observed relation of wheat yield to fertilizer application.

a simple mathematical model, it will be useful as a brief and precise description, or as a means of predicting the yield Y for a given amount of fertilizer X. This chapter is devoted exclusively to how a straight line may best be fitted.

11-1

AN EXAMPLE

Since yield depends on fertilizer, it is referred to as the "dependent" variable Y; since fertilizer application is not dependent on yield, but instead is determined by the experimenter, it is referred to as the "independent" variable X. Suppose funds are available for only seven experimental observations, so that the experimenter sets X at seven different

FIGURE 11-2   Yields at various levels of fertilizer application.

Table 11-1 Experimental Data
Relating Yield to the Amount of
Applied Fertilizer, as in Figure 11-2

X Fertilizer (Pound/Acre)	Y Yield (Bushel/Acre)
100	40
200	45
300	50
400	65
500	70
600	70
700	80

values, taking only one observation Y in each case, shown in Figure 11-2 and Table 11-1.

First, note that if all the points were exactly in a line, as in Figure 11-3a, then the fitted line could be drawn in with a ruler "by eye" perfectly accurately. Even if the points were *nearly* in a line, as in Figure 11-3b, fitting by eye would be reasonably satisfactory. But in the highly scattered case, as in Figure 11-3c, fitting by eye is too subjective and too inaccurate. We need to find a more objective method, which can also be easily computerized and extended to handle much more difficult problems where fitting by eye is out of the question. The following sections, therefore, set forth various algebraic methods for fitting a line.

11-2 POSSIBLE CRITERIA FOR FITTING A LINE

It is time to ask more precisely, "What is a good fit?" The answer surely is "a fit that makes the total error small." One typical error is shown in Figure 11-4. It is defined as the vertical distance from the observed

FIGURE 11-3 Various degrees of scatter.

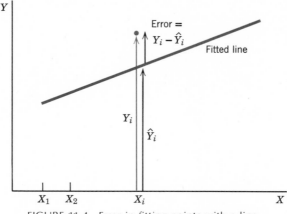

FIGURE 11-4   Error in fitting points with a line.

Y to the fitted line—that is $(Y_i - \hat{Y}_i)$, where $\hat{Y}_i$ is the "fitted value of Y" or the ordinate of the line. We note that the error is positive when the observed Y_i is above the line and negative when the observed Y_i is below the line.

1. As our first tentative criterion, consider a fitted line that minimizes the sum of all these errors,

$$\sum_{i=1}^{n} (Y_i - \hat{Y}_i) \tag{11-1}$$

   Unfortunately, this works badly. Using this criterion, the two lines shown in Figure 11-5 fit the observations equally well, even though the fit in (a) is intuitively a good one, and the fit in (b) a very bad one. The problem is one of sign; in both cases, positive errors just offset negative errors, leaving their sum equal to zero. This criterion must be rejected, since it provides no distinction between bad fits and good ones.

2. There are two ways of overcoming the sign problem. The first is to minimize the sum of the *absolute* values of the errors,

$$\sum |Y_i - \hat{Y}_i| \tag{11-2}$$

   Since large positive errors are not allowed to offset large negative ones, this criterion would rule out bad fits like Figure 11-5*b*. However, it still has a drawback. It is evident in Figure 11-6 that the fit in (*b*) satisfies this criterion better than the fit in (a); $(\sum |Y_i - \hat{Y}_i|$

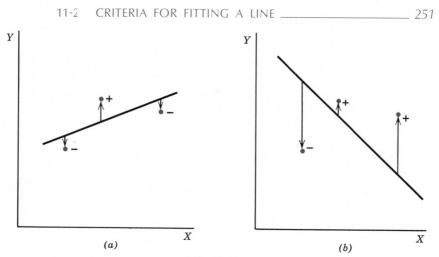

FIGURE 11-5

is 3, rather than 4). In fact, you can satisfy yourself that the line in (b) joining the two end points satisfies this criterion better than *any* other line. But it is perhaps not the best solution to the problem, because it pays no attention whatever to the middle point. The fit in (a) may be preferable because it takes account of all points.

3. As a second way to overcome the sign problem, we finally propose to minimize the sum of the squares of the errors,

$$\sum (Y_i - \hat{Y}_i)^2 \qquad (11\text{-}3)$$

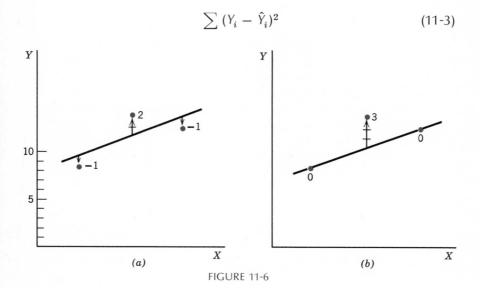

FIGURE 11-6

This is the famous "least squares" criterion; its justifications include:

(a) Squaring overcomes the sign problem by making all errors positive.

(b) Squaring emphasizes the large errors, and in trying to satisfy this criterion large errors are avoided if at all possible. Hence, all points are taken into account, and the fit in Figure 11-6a is selected by this criterion in preference to Figure 11-6b.

(c) The algebra of least squares is very manageable.

(d) There are two important theoretical justifications for least squares: the Gauss-Markov theorem (discussed in Chapter 12), and the maximum likelihood criterion (in Chapter 18).

11-3 THE LEAST SQUARES SOLUTION

Our scatter of observed X and Y values from Table 11-1 is graphed again in Figure 11-7a. Our objective is to fit a line

$$Y = a_0 + bX \tag{11-4}$$

This involves three steps:

STEP 1. Translate X into deviations from its mean; that is, define a new variable x, so that:

$$x = X - \overline{X} \tag{11-5}$$

This is equivalent to a geometric translation of axis, as shown in Figure 11-7b; the Y axis has been shifted from 0 to $\overline{X}$. The new x value becomes positive or negative, depending on whether X was above or below $\overline{X}$. There is no change in the Y values. The intercept a differs from the original a_0, but the slope b remains the same.[2]

One of the advantages of measuring X_i as deviations from their central value is that we can more explicitly ask the question: "How is Y affected when X is unusually large, or unusually small?" In addition, the mathematics will be simplified because the sum of the new x values equals zero,[3] that is,

$$\sum x_i = 0 \tag{11-6}$$

⎯⎯⎯⎯⎯⎯⎯⎯

[2]The geometry of lines and planes (including the concepts of intercept, slope, etc.) is reviewed in Appendix 13-1.

[3]Although this was proved in (2-3) essentially, we shall repeat the proof because of its simplicity and importance:

(cont'd)

FIGURE 11-7   Translation of axis. (a) Regression using original variables. (b) Regression, translating X.

$$\sum x_i = \sum (X_i - \bar{X})$$

$$= \sum X_i - n\bar{X}$$

Noting that $\bar{X}$ is defined as $\sum X_i/n$, it follows that $\sum X_i = n\bar{X}$ and

$$\sum x_i = n\bar{X} - n\bar{X} = 0 \qquad\qquad \text{(11-6) proved}$$

STEP 2. Fit the line in Figure 11-7b; that is, fit the line

$$Y = a + bx \tag{11-7}$$

to this scatter by selecting the values for a and b that satisfy the least squares criterion: select those values of a and b that minimize

$$\sum (Y_i - \hat{Y}_i)^2 \tag{11-8}$$

Since each fitted value $\hat{Y}_i$ is on our estimated line (11-7),

$$\hat{Y}_i = a + bx_i \tag{11-9}$$

When this is substituted into (11-8) the problem becomes one of selecting a and b to minimize the sum of squares,

$$S(a, b) = \sum (Y_i - a - bx_i)^2 \tag{11-10}$$

The notation $S(a, b)$ is used to emphasize that this expression depends on a and b. As a and b vary (i.e., as various lines are tried), $S(a, b)$ will vary too, and we ask at what value of a and b it will be a minimum. This will give us our optimum (least squares) line.

The simplest minimization technique is calculus, and it will be used in the next paragraph. [Readers without calculus can minimize (11-10) with the more cumbersome algebra of Appendix 11-1, and rejoin us where the resulting theorems (11-13) and (11-16) are set out in the box below.]

Minimizing $S(a, b)$ requires setting its partial derivatives with respect to a and b equal to zero. In the first instance, setting the partial derivative with respect to a equal to zero:

$$\frac{\partial}{\partial a} \sum (Y_i - a - bx_i)^2 = \sum 2(-1)(Y_i - a - bx_i)^1 = 0 \tag{11-11}$$

Dividing through by -2 and rearranging:

$$\sum Y_i - na - b \sum x_i = 0 \tag{11-12}$$

Noting that $\sum x_i = 0$ by (11-6), we can solve for a:

$$a = \frac{\sum Y_i}{n} \quad \text{or} \quad a = \bar{Y} \tag{11-13}$$

Thus, our least squares estimate of a is simply the average value of Y; referring back to Figure 11-7, we see that this ensures that our fitted regression line must pass through the point $(\overline{X}, \overline{Y})$, which may be interpreted as the center of gravity of the sample of n points.

It is also necessary to set the partial derivative of (11-10) with respect to b equal to zero,

$$\frac{\partial}{\partial b} \sum (Y_i - a - bx_i)^2 = \sum 2(-x_i)(Y_i - a - bx_i)^1 = 0 \quad (11\text{-}14)$$

Cancelling -2,

$$\sum x_i(Y_i - a - bx_i) = 0 \quad (11\text{-}15)$$

Rearranging

$$\sum x_i Y_i - a \sum x_i - b \sum x_i^2 = 0$$

Noting that $\sum x_i = 0$, we can solve for b:

$$b = \frac{\sum x_i Y_i}{\sum x_i^2} \quad (11\text{-}16)$$

Our results[4] in (11-13) and (11-16) are important enough to restate:

With x values measured as deviations from their mean, the least squares values of a and b are

$$a = \overline{Y} \quad (11\text{-}13)$$

$$b = \frac{\sum x_i Y_i}{\sum x_i^2} \quad (11\text{-}16)$$

For the example in Table 11-1, a and b are calculated in the first five columns in Table 11-2; (the last three columns may be ignored until the next chapter). It follows that the least squares equation is:

$$Y = 60 + .068x \quad (11\text{-}17)$$

This fitted line is graphed in Figure 11-7b.

---

[4] To be rigorous, it can be proved with second partial derivatives or other techniques, that we actually do have a minimum sum of squares—rather than a maximum or saddle point.

Table 11-2   Least Squares Calculations (Data from Table 11-1)

(1) X_i	(2) Y_i	(3) $x_i = X_i - \bar{X}$ $= X_i - 400$	(4) $x_i Y_i$	(5) x_i^2	(6) $\hat{Y}_i = a + bx_i$ $= 60 + .068x_i$	(7) $Y_i - \hat{Y}_i$	(8) $(Y_i - \hat{Y}_i)^2$
100	40	−300	−12,000	90,000	39.6	.4	.16
200	45	−200	−9,000	40,000	46.4	−1.4	1.96
300	50	−100	−5,000	10,000	53.2	−3.2	10.24
400	65	0	0	0	60.0	5.0	25.00
500	70	100	7,000	10,000	66.8	3.2	10.24
600	70	200	14,000	40,000	73.6	−3.6	12.96
700	80	300	24,000	90,000	80.4	−.4	.16

$\sum X_i = 2,800$ $\sum Y_i = 420$ $\sum x_i = 0 \checkmark$ $\sum x_i Y_i = 19,000$ $\sum x_i^2 = 280,000$

$$\bar{X} = \frac{\sum X_i}{n}$$
$$= \frac{2,800}{7}$$
$$= 400$$

$$\bar{Y} = \frac{\sum Y_i}{n}$$
$$= \frac{420}{7}$$
$$= 60$$

$$\boxed{a = 60}$$

$$b = \frac{\sum x_i Y_i}{\sum x_i^2}$$
$$= \frac{19,000}{280,000}$$

$$\boxed{b = .068}$$

$$\sum(Y_i - \hat{Y}_i)^2 = 60.72$$

$$s^2 = \frac{1}{n-2}\sum(Y_i - \hat{Y}_i)^2$$
$$= 12.14$$

and $\boxed{s = 3.48}$

STEP 3. If desired, this regression can now be retranslated back into our original frame of reference in Figure 11-7a. Express (11-17) in terms of the original X values:

$$Y = 60 + .068(X - \bar{X})$$
$$= 60 + .068(X - 400)$$
$$= 60 + .068X - 27.2$$
$$Y = 32.8 + .068X \tag{11-18}$$

This fitted line is graphed in Figure 11-7a.

A comparison of (11-17) and (11-18) confirms that the slope of our fitted regression ($b = .068$) remains the same; the only difference is in the intercept. Moreover, we note how easily the original intercept ($a_0 = 32.8$) may be recovered.

An estimate of yield for any given fertilizer application is now easily derived from our least squares equation (11-18). For example, if 350 lb of fertilizer is to be applied, our estimate of yield is:

$$Y = 32.8 + .068(350) = 56.6 \text{ bushels/acre}$$

The alternative least squares equation (11-17) yields exactly the same result. When $X = 350$, then $x = -50$, and

$$Y = 60 + .068(-50) = 56.6$$

PROBLEMS

(Save your work in the next three chapters, for future reference.)

11-1 Suppose a random sample of five families had the following income and saving:

Family	Income Y	Saving S
A	$ 8,000	$ 600
B	11,000	1200
C	9,000	1000
D	6,000	700
E	6,000	300

(a) Estimate and graph the regression line of saving S on income Y.

(b) Interpret the intercepts a and a_0.

11-2 Use the data of Problem 11-1 to regress consumption C on income Y, where $C = Y - S$.

11-3 To interpret the regression slope b, use equation (11-18) to answer the following questions:

(a) About how much is the yield increased for every pound of fertilizer applied—that is, what is the marginal physical product of fertilizer?

(b) If the value of the crop is $2 per bushel, what is the marginal revenue product of fertilizer? (i.e., by how much is revenue increased because one more pound of fertilizer is applied?) If fertilizer costs $0.25 per pound, would it be economic to apply?

⇒11-4 Translate both X and Y into deviations x and y (just as X was translated in Figure 11-7b)

(a) What is the new y-intercept? Does the slope remain the same? Does this imply that the fitted regression equation is simply

$$y = bx?\qquad\qquad(11\text{-}19a)$$

Draw a diagram similar to Figure 11-7b to illustrate this procedure.

(b) Prove that $\Sigma\, x_i y_i = \Sigma\, x_i Y_i$; hence we may alternatively calculate b as

$$b = \frac{\Sigma\, x_i y_i}{\Sigma\, x_i^2}\qquad\qquad(11\text{-}19b)$$

(c) Using this procedure show how the original intercept ($a_0 = 32.8$) may be recovered.

11-5 Suppose that four firms had the following profits and research expenditures.

Firm	Profit, P (Thousands of Dollars)	Research Expenditure, R (Thousands of Dollars)
1	50	40
2	60	40
3	40	30
4	50	50

(a) Fit a regression line of P on R.

(b) Does this regression line "show how research generates profits"? Criticize.

*11-6 (Requires calculus). Suppose X is left in its original form, rather than being translated into x (deviations from the mean).

(a) Write out the sum of squared deviations as in (11-10), in terms of a_0 and b.

(b) Set equal to zero the partial derivatives with respect to a_0 and b, thus obtaining two so-called "normal" equations.

(c) Evaluate these two normal equations using the data in Problem 11-1 and solve for a_0 and b. Do you get the same answer?

(d) Compare this method of solution with the one used in the text.

APPENDIX 11-1   An Alternative Derivation of Least
                                          Squares Estimates of a and b,
                                          Without Calculus

Before estimating a and b, it is necessary to solve the theoretical problem of minimizing an ordinary quadratic function of one variable b, of the form

$$f(b) = k_2 b^2 + k_1 b + k_0 \qquad (11\text{-}20)$$

where k_2, k_1, k_0 are constants, with $k_2 > 0$.

With a little algebraic manipulation, (11-20) may be written as

$$f(b) = k_2\left(b + \frac{k_1}{2k_2}\right)^2 + \left(k_0 - \frac{k_1^2}{4k_2}\right)$$

Note that b appears in the first term, but not in the second. Therefore, our hope of minimizing the expression lies in selecting a value of b to minimize the first term. Being a square and hence never negative, the first term will be minimized when it is zero, that is, when

$$b + \frac{k_1}{2k_2} = 0 \qquad (11\text{-}21)$$

i.e.,

$$b = \frac{-k_1}{2k_2} \qquad (11\text{-}22)$$

This result is shown graphically in Figure 11-8. To restate: a *quadratic function of the form* (11-20) *is minimized by setting*

$$b = -\frac{(\text{coefficient of first power})}{2(\text{coefficient of second power})} \qquad (11\text{-}23)$$

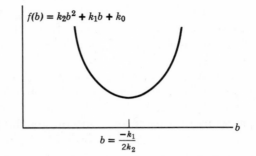

FIGURE 11-8   The minimization of a quadratic function.

With this theorem in hand, let us return to the problem of selecting values for a and b to minimize

$$S(a, b) = \sum [(Y_i - a) - bx_i]^2 \tag{11-24}$$

It will be useful to manipulate this, as follows:

$$S(a, b) = \sum [(Y_i - a)^2 - 2bx_i(Y_i - a) + b^2x_i^2] \tag{11-25}$$

$$= \sum (Y_i - a)^2 - 2b \sum x_i(Y_i - a) + b^2 \sum x_i^2 \tag{11-26}$$

In the middle term, consider

$$\sum x_i(Y_i - a) = \sum x_i Y_i - a \sum x_i$$

$$= \sum x_i Y_i + 0$$

Using this to rewrite the middle term of (11-26) we have:

$$S(a,b) = \sum (Y_i - a)^2 - 2b \sum x_i Y_i + b^2 \sum x_i^2 \tag{11-27}$$

This is a useful recasting of (11-24), because the first term contains a alone, while the last two terms contain b alone. To find the value of a that minimizes (11-27) only the first term is relevant. This may be written

$$\sum (Y_i - a)^2 = \sum Y_i^2 - 2a \sum Y_i + na^2$$

According to (11-23), this is minimized when

$$a = \frac{-(-2\sum Y_i)}{2n} = \frac{\sum Y_i}{n} = \bar{Y} \qquad \text{(11-13) proved}$$

To find the value of b that minimizes (11-27), only the last two terms are relevant. According to (11-23), this is minimized when

$$b = \frac{-(-2\sum x_i Y_i)}{2\sum x_i^2} = \frac{\sum x_i Y_i}{\sum x_i^2} \qquad \text{(11-16) proved}$$

REGRESSION THEORY

*Models are to be used,
but not to be believed.*

Henri Theil

12-1   THE MATHEMATICAL MODEL

So far we have only mechanically fitted a line. This is just a description of the sample observations; now we wish to make inferences about the parent population from which this sample was drawn. Specifically, we must consider the mathematical model that allows us to run tests of significance on a and b.

Turning back to the example in the previous chapter, suppose that the experiment could be repeated many times at a fixed value of x. Even though fertilizer application is fixed from experiment to experiment, we would not observe exactly the same yield each time. Instead, there would be some statistical fluctuation of the Y's, clustered about a central value. We can think of the many possible values of Y forming a population; the probability distribution of Y for a given x we shall call $p(Y/x)$. Moreover, there will be a similar probability distribution for Y at any other experimental level of x. One possible sequence of Y populations is shown in Figure 12-1a. There would obviously be mathematical problems involved in analysing such populations. To keep the problem manageable, we make several assumptions about the regularity of these populations, as shown in Figure 12-1b. We assume the probability distributions $p(Y_i/x_i)$:

263

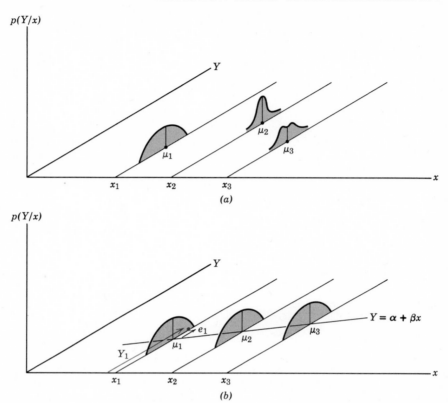

FIGURE 12-1 (a) General populations of Y, given x. (b) The special form of the populations of Y assumed in simple linear regression.

1. Have the same variance σ^2 for all x_i.
2. Have the means $E(Y_i)$ lying on a straight line, known as the true (population) regression line:

$$E(Y_i) = \mu_i = \alpha + \beta x_i \qquad (12\text{-}1)$$

The population parameters α and β specify the line; they are to be estimated from sample information. We also assume that

3. The random variables Y_i are statistically independent. For example, a large value of Y_1 does not tend to make Y_2 large; that is, Y_2 is "unaffected" by Y_1.

These assumptions may be written more concisely as:

The random variables Y_i are statistically independent, with

$$\text{mean} = \alpha + \beta x_i$$

and

$$\text{variance} = \sigma^2$$

(12-2)

On occasion, it is useful to describe the deviation of Y_i from its expected value as the error or disturbance term e_i, so that the model may alternatively be written

$$Y_i = \alpha + \beta x_i + e_i$$

(12-3)

where the e_i are independent random variables, with

$$\text{mean} = 0$$

and

$$\text{variance} = \sigma^2$$

(12-4)

We note that the distributions of Y and e are identical, except that their means differ. In fact, the distribution of e is just the distribution of Y translated onto a zero mean. In Figure 12-1b we show one possible observed value of Y, along with the corresponding value for the error term e.

No assumption is made about the *shape* of the distribution of e (normal or otherwise) provided it has a finite variance. We therefore refer to assumptions (12-4) as the "weak set"; we shall derive as many results as possible from these, before adding a more restrictive normality assumption later.

12-2   THE NATURE OF THE ERROR TERM

Now let us consider in more detail the "purely random" part of Y_i, the error or disturbance term e_i. Why does it exist? Or, why doesn't a precise and exact value of Y_i follow, once the value of x_i is given?

The error may be regarded as the sum of two components:

1. *Measurement error.* There are various reasons why Y may be measured incorrectly. In measuring crop yield, there may be an error resulting from sloppy harvesting or inaccurate weighing. If the example is a study of the consumption of families at various income

levels, the measurement error in consumption might consist of budget and reporting inaccuracies.

2. *Stochastic error* occurs because of the inherent irreproducibility of biological and social phenomena. Even if there were no measurement error, continuous repetition of an experiment using exactly the same amount of fertilizer would result in different yields; these differences are unpredictable and are called stochastic differences. They may be reduced by tighter experimental control—for example, by holding constant soil conditions, amount of water, etc. But *complete* control is impossible—for example, seeds cannot be duplicated. Stochastic error may be regarded as the influence on Y of many omitted variables, each with an individually small effect.

In the social sciences, controlled experiments are usually not possible. For example, an economist cannot hold U.S. national income constant for several years while he examines the effect of interest rate on investment. Since he cannot neutralize extraneous influences by holding them constant, his best alternative is to take them explicitly into account, by regressing Y on x *and* the extraneous factors. This is a useful technique for reducing stochastic error; it is called "multiple regression" and is discussed fully in the next chapter.

12-3   **ESTIMATING α AND β**

Suppose that our true regression $Y = \alpha + \beta x$ is the black line shown in Figure 12-2. This will remain unknown to the statistician, whose job it is to estimate it as best he can by observing x and Y. If at the first level x_1, the stochastic error e_1 takes on a negative value, as shown in the diagram, he will observe Y_1. Similarly, suppose his only other two observations are Y_2 and Y_3, resulting from positive values of e. Furthermore, suppose the statistician estimates the true line by fitting a least squares line, applying the method of Chapter 11 to the only information he has—the sample values Y_1, Y_2, and Y_3. He would come up with the red estimating line in this figure. In Chapter 11 we called this fitted least squares line $Y = a + bx$; now we rename it $Y = \hat{\alpha} + \hat{\beta}x$, to emphasize that $\hat{\alpha}$ is our estimator of α, and $\hat{\beta}$ our estimator of β.

Figure 12-2 is a critical diagram. Before proceeding, you should be sure that you can clearly distinguish between: (1) the true regression and its surrounding e distribution; since these are population values and cannot be observed they are shown in black. (2) the Y observations and the resulting fitted regression line; since these are sample values, they are known to the statistician and shown in red.

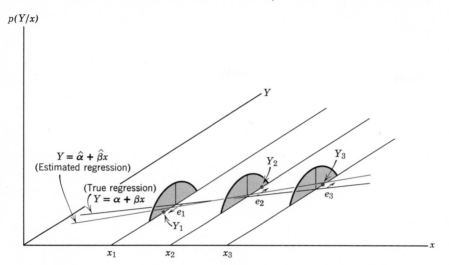

FIGURE 12-2   True (population) regression and estimated (sample) regression.

Unless the statistician is very lucky indeed, it is obvious that his estimated line will not be exactly on the true population line. The best he can hope for is that the least squares method of estimation will be close to the target. Specifically, we now ask: How is the estimator $\hat{\alpha}$ distributed around its target α, and $\hat{\beta}$ around its target β?

12-4   THE MEAN AND VARIANCE OF $\hat{\alpha}$ AND $\hat{\beta}$

We shall show that the random estimators $\hat{\alpha}$ and $\hat{\beta}$ have the following moments:

$$E(\hat{\alpha}) = \alpha \tag{12-5}$$

$$\text{var}(\hat{\alpha}) = \frac{\sigma^2}{n} \tag{12-6}$$

$$E(\hat{\beta}) = \beta \tag{12-7}$$

$$\text{var}(\hat{\beta}) = \frac{\sigma^2}{\sum x_i^2} \tag{12-8}$$

where σ^2 is the variance of the error e (the variance of Y around the regression line).

Because of its greater importance, we shall concentrate on the slope estimator $\hat{\beta}$, rather than $\hat{\alpha}$, for the rest of the chapter.

proof of (12-7) and (12-8)   The formula for $\hat{\beta}$ in (11-16) may be rewritten as

$$\hat{\beta} = \sum \left\{ \frac{x_i}{k} \right\} Y_i \tag{12-9}$$

where

$$k = \sum x_i^2 \tag{12-10}$$

Thus,

$$\hat{\beta} = \sum w_i Y_i = w_1 Y_1 + w_2 Y_2 \cdots + w_n Y_n \tag{12-11}$$

where

$$w_i = \frac{x_i}{k} \tag{12-12}$$

Thus from (12-11) we establish the important conclusion:

$\hat{\beta}$ is a weighted sum (i.e., a linear combination)   (12-13)
of the random variables Y_i

Hence by (5-35) we may write

$$E(\hat{\beta}) = w_1 E(Y_1) + w_2 E(Y_2) \cdots + w_n E(Y_n) = \sum w_i E(Y_i) \tag{12-14}$$

Moreover, noting that the variables Y_i were assumed independent, it follows from (5-43) that

$$\text{var}(\hat{\beta}) = w_1^2 \text{ var } Y_1 + \cdots + w_n^2 \text{ var } Y_n = \sum w_i^2 \text{ var } Y_i \tag{12-15}$$

For the mean, from (12-14) and (12-1),

$$E(\hat{\beta}) = \sum w_i [\alpha + \beta x_i] \tag{12-16}$$

$$= \alpha \sum w_i + \beta \sum w_i x_i \tag{12-17}$$

and noting (12-12)

$$E(\hat{\beta}) = \frac{\alpha}{k} \sum x_i + \frac{\beta}{k} \sum (x_i)x_i \qquad (12\text{-}18)$$

but $\sum x_i$ is zero, according to (11-6). Thus

$$E(\hat{\beta}) = 0 + \frac{\beta}{k} \sum x_i^2$$

From (12-10)

$$E(\hat{\beta}) = \beta \qquad (12\text{-}7) \text{ proved}$$

Thus $\hat{\beta}$ is an unbiased estimator of β.

For the variance, from (12-15) and (12-2),

$$\text{var}(\hat{\beta}) = \sum w_i^2 \sigma^2 \qquad (12\text{-}19)$$

$$= \sum \frac{x_i^2}{k^2} \sigma^2 \qquad (12\text{-}20)$$

$$= \frac{\sigma^2}{k^2} \sum x_i^2 \qquad (12\text{-}21)$$

Again, noting (12-10),

$$\text{var}(\hat{\beta}) = \frac{\sigma^2}{\sum x_i^2} \qquad (12\text{-}8) \text{ proved}$$

A similar derivation of the mean and variance of $\hat{\alpha}$ is left as an exercise.

We observe from (12-12) that in calculating $\hat{\beta}$, the weight w_i attached to the Y_i observation is proportional to the deviation x_i. Hence, outlying observations exert a relatively heavy influence in the calculation of $\hat{\beta}$.

12-5   THE GAUSS-MARKOV THEOREM

This is the major justification for using the least squares method in the linear regression model.

Gauss-Markov Theorem.

Within the class of linear unbiased estimators of β (or α),   (12-22) the least squares estimator has minimum variance.

This theorem is important because it follows even from the weak set of assumptions (12-4), and hence requires no assumption about the shape of the distribution of the error term. A proof is given in most mathematical statistics texts.

To interpret this important theorem, consider $\hat{\beta}$, the least squares estimator of β. We have already seen in (12-13) that it is a linear estimator, and we restrict ourselves to linear estimators because they are easy to analyse and understand. We restrict ourselves even further, as shown in Figure 12-3; within this set of linear estimators we consider only the limited class that is unbiased. The least squares estimator not only is in this class, according to (12-7); of all the estimators in this class, it has the minimum variance. Therefore, it is often referred to as BLUE, the "best linear unbiased estimator."

The Gauss-Markov theorem has an interesting corollary. As a special case of regression, we might ask what happens if we are explaining Y, but $\beta = 0$ in (12-2), so that no independent variable x comes into play. From (12-2), α is the mean of the Y population (μ). Moreover, from (11-13) its least squares estimator is $\bar{Y}$. Thus, the least squares estimator of a population mean (μ) is the sample mean ($\bar{Y}$), and the Gauss-Markov theorem fully applies: the sample mean is the "best linear unbiased estimator" of a population mean.

It must be emphasized that the Gauss-Markov theorem is restricted, applying only to estimators that are both linear and unbiased. It follows that there may be a nonlinear estimator that is better (i.e., has smaller variance) than the least squares estimator. For example, to estimate a population mean, the sample median is a nonlinear estimator that is better than the sample mean for certain kinds of nonnormal populations. This issue is discussed in more detail in Chapter 16.

12-6   **THE DISTRIBUTION OF** $\hat{\beta}$

With the mean and variance of $\hat{\beta}$ established in (12-7) and (12-8), we now ask: What is the shape of the distribution of $\hat{\beta}$? If we add (for the first time) the strong assumption that the Y_i are normal, and recall that $\hat{\beta}$ is a linear combination of the Y_i, it follows that $\hat{\beta}$ will also be normal from (6-13). But even without assuming the Y_i are normal, as sample size increases the distribution of $\hat{\beta}$ will usually approach normality; this can be justified by a generalized form[1] of the central limit theorem (6-15).

---

[1] The central limit theorem (6-15) proved the large sample normality of the sample mean $\bar{X}$. In Problem 6-8 it was seen to apply equally well to the sample sum S. It applies also to a *weighted* sum of random variables such as $\hat{\beta}$ in (12-13), under most conditions. See for example, D. A. S. Fraser, *Nonparametric Statistics*, New York: John Wiley, 1957. Similarly the normality of $\hat{\alpha}$ is justified.

FIGURE 12-3   Diagram of the restricted class of estimators considered in the Gauss-Markov theorem.

We are now in a position to graph the distribution of $\hat{\beta}$ in Figure 12-4, in order to develop a clear intuitive idea of how this estimator varies from sample to sample. First, of course, we note that (12-7) established that $\hat{\beta}$ is an unbiased estimator,[2] so that the distribution of $\hat{\beta}$ is centered on its target β.

The interpretation of its variance (12-8) is more difficult. Suppose that the experiment has been badly designed with the X_i's close together. This makes the deviations x_i small; hence Σx_i^2 small. Therefore, $\sigma^2/\Sigma x_i^2$, the variance of $\hat{\beta}$ from (12-8) is large and $\hat{\beta}$ is a comparatively unreliable estimator. To check the intuitive validity of this, consider the scatter diagram in Figure 12-5a. The bunching of the X's means that the small part of the line being investigated is obscured by the error e, making the slope estimate $\hat{\beta}$ very unreliable. In this specific instance,

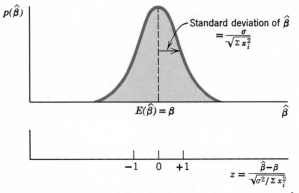

FIGURE 12-4   The probability distribution of the estimator $\hat{\beta}$.

[2]We must emphasize that this conclusion depends heavily on the regression assumptions (12-4). In practical situations, if these assumptions do not hold, the regression line of Y on X may be quite inappropriate; for example, see Figure 12-9.

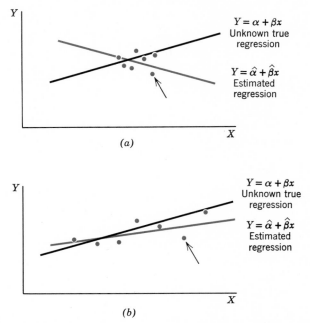

FIGURE 12-5 (a) Unreliable estimate when X_i are very close. (b) More reliable fit because X_i are spread out.

our estimate has been pulled badly out of line by the errors—in particular the one indicated by the arrow.

By contrast, in Figure 12-5b we show the case where the X's are reasonably spread out. Even though the errors e remain the same, the estimate $\hat{\beta}$ is much more reliable, because errors no longer exert the same leverage.

As a concrete example, suppose we wish to examine how sensitive Canadian imports (Y) are to the international value of the Canadian dollar (x). A much more reliable estimate should be possible using the periods when the Canadian dollar was floating (and took on a range of values) than in the periods when this dollar was fixed (and only allowed to fluctuate within a very narrow range).

12-7   CONFIDENCE INTERVALS AND TESTING
                         HYPOTHESES ABOUT β

With the mean, variance, and normality of the estimator $\hat{\beta}$ established, statistical inferences about β are now in order. First standardize $\hat{\beta}$, obtaining

$$z = \frac{\hat{\beta} - \beta}{\sqrt{\sigma^2/\sum x_i^2}} \qquad (12\text{-}23)$$

where z is normally distributed, with mean 0 and variance 1, as shown in Figure 12-4.

Since σ^2, the variance of Y is generally unknown, it is estimated with

$$s^2 = \frac{1}{n-2} \sum (Y_i - \hat{Y}_i)^2 \qquad (12\text{-}24)$$

where $\hat{Y}_i$ is the fitted value of Y on the estimated regression line; that is,

$$\hat{Y}_i = \hat{\alpha} + \hat{\beta}x_i \qquad (12\text{-}25)$$

s^2 is often referred to as "residual variance," a term similarly used in analysis of variance. The divisor $(n-2)$ is used in (12-24) rather than n in order to make s^2 an unbiased estimator[3] of σ^2. When this substitution of s^2 for σ^2 is made, the standardized $\hat{\beta}$ is no longer normal, but instead has the slightly more spread out t distribution[4].

$$t = \frac{\hat{\beta} - \beta}{\sqrt{s^2/\sum x_i^2}} \qquad (12\text{-}26)$$

where t has $(n-2)$ degrees of freedom, like s^2. For easy reference, (12-26) may be rewritten as

$$t = \frac{\hat{\beta} - \beta}{s_{\hat{\beta}}} \qquad (12\text{-}27)$$

where

$$s_{\hat{\beta}} = \frac{s}{\sqrt{\sum x_i^2}} \qquad (12\text{-}28)$$

---

[3] Using an argument similar to the one used in the footnote to (8-11). But in the present calculation of s^2, two estimators $\hat{\alpha}$ and $\hat{\beta}$ are required; thus two degrees of freedom are lost for s^2. Hence $(n-2)$ is the divisor in s^2, and also the degrees of freedom of the subsequent t distribution in (12-26).

[4] For the t distribution to be strictly valid, we require the strong assumption that the distribution of Y_i is normal; but even if it is not, t may still be a good approximation.

s_β is often called the *standard error* of $\hat\beta$ (or estimated standard deviation).

From (12-26) we may now proceed to construct a confidence interval or test an hypothesis.

(a) Confidence Intervals

Let $t_{.025}$ denote the t value that leaves $2\frac{1}{2}\%$ of the distribution in the upper tail, that is,

$$\Pr\left(-t_{.025} < t < t_{.025}\right) = .95 \tag{12-29}$$

Substituting t from (12-27)

$$\Pr\left(-t_{.025} < \frac{\hat\beta - \beta}{s_\beta} < t_{.025}\right) = .95 \tag{12-30}$$

The inequalities within the bracket may be reexpressed:

$$\Pr\left(\hat\beta - t_{.025}\, s_\beta < \beta < \hat\beta + t_{.025}\, s_\beta\right) = .95 \tag{12-31}$$

which yields the 95% confidence interval

$$\beta = \hat\beta \pm t_{.025}\, s_\beta \tag{12-32}$$

Substituting s_β from (12-28) yields

95% confidence interval for the slope,

$$\beta = \hat\beta \pm t_{.025} \frac{s}{\sqrt{\sum x_i^2}} \tag{12-33}$$

where $t_{.025}$ has $(n - 2)$ degrees of freedom.[5]

For the example of crop yield in the previous chapter, the confidence interval for β (the effect of fertilizer on yield) is computed as follows: s as given by (12-24) is evaluated in the last three columns of Table 11-2.

---

[5] Using a similar argument, and noting (12-6), the 95% confidence interval for α is:

$$\alpha = \hat\alpha \pm t_{.025} \frac{s}{\sqrt{n}} \tag{12-34}$$

Also noting the values for $\hat{\beta}$ and $\sum x_i^2$ calculated in that table, the 95% confidence interval (12-33) becomes

$$\beta = .068 \pm 2.571 \frac{3.48}{\sqrt{280,000}}$$

$$= .068 \pm .017$$

$$.051 < \beta < .085 \qquad\qquad (12\text{-}35)$$

Since this interval excludes the null hypothesis ($\beta = 0$, that is, fertilizer has no effect on yield), we reject it in favor of the alternate hypothesis that fertilizer does affect yield.

(b) Prob-Value

If we are sure that any effect fertilizer may have on yield must be favourable, then it is appropriate to calculate the one-sided prob-value. If $H_0 (\beta = 0)$ were true, then (12-26) becomes:

$$\text{test statistic } t = \frac{\hat{\beta}}{\sqrt{s^2 / \sum x_i^2}} \qquad\qquad (12\text{-}36)$$

$$= \frac{.068}{3.48 / \sqrt{280,000}}$$

$$= 10.3$$

Referring this to the t tables, we find the one-tailed

$$\text{prob-value} \ll .001$$

In other words, if fertilizer has no effect, then there is less than one chance in a thousand we would get a sample result as extreme as the one we observed. This then is very strong evidence that fertilizer does favourably affect yield.

PROBLEMS

12-1 Construct a 95% confidence interval for the regression coefficient β in
 (a) Problem 11-1
 (b) Problem 11-2
 (c) Problem 11-5
12-2 Which of the following hypotheses does the data of Problem 11-1

prove to be unacceptable at the 5% level of significance? (Use 2-sided test.)

(a) $\beta = 0$
(b) $\beta = 1/2$
(c) $\beta = .1$
(d) $\beta = -.1$

*12-3 Suppose in Problem 11-1 we are sure that saving cannot decrease with income. Construct therefore a one-sided 95% confidence interval for β, and test the same hypotheses as in Problem 12-2.

12-8   INTERPOLATION (CONFIDENCE INTERVALS AND PREDICTION INTERVALS)

In the previous section we considered the broad aspects of the model, namely, the position of the whole line (determined by α and β). In this section, we shall consider two narrower problems:

(a) For a given, perhaps new, value of x, say x_0, what is the interval that will predict the *mean* value of Y_0, [i.e., the confidence interval for $E(Y_0)$ or μ_0]? In our fertilizer problem, we may wish, for example, an interval estimate of the mean yield resulting from the application of 550 lb of fertilizer. (Note that we are not deriving an interval estimate of mean yield by observing repeated applications of 550 lb of fertilizer; in that case, we could apply the simpler technique of estimating a population mean with the sample mean. Instead we are observing only seven *different* applications of fertilizer. This is clearly a more difficult problem.)

(b) What is the interval that will predict a *single observed* value of Y_0 (referred to as the prediction interval for an individual Y_0). Again using our example, what would we predict a single yield to be from an application of 550 lb of fertilizer? This individual value is clearly less predictable than the mean value in (a). We now consider both in detail.

(a) The Confidence Interval for the Mean μ_0

First we find the point estimator, $\hat{\mu}_0$, then construct an interval estimate around it. The appropriate estimator of μ_0 is just the point on our estimated regression line above x_0,

$$\hat{\mu}_0 = \hat{\alpha} + \hat{\beta}x_0 \tag{12-37}$$

But as a point estimate, this will almost certainly involve some error, because of errors made in the estimates $\hat{\alpha}$ and $\hat{\beta}$. Figure 12-6 illustrates the effect of these errors; the true regression is shown, along with an estimated regression. Note how $\hat{\mu}_0$ underestimates in this case. In Figure 12-7, the true regression is again shown, along with several estimated

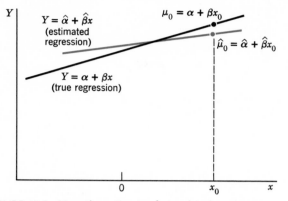

FIGURE 12-6 How the estimator $\hat{\mu}_0$ is related to the target μ_0.

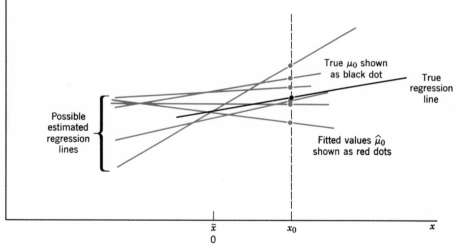

FIGURE 12-7 $\hat{\mu}_0$ as an unbiased estimator of μ_0.

regressions fitted from several possible sets of sample data. The fitted red dot is sometimes too low, sometimes too high, but on average it seems just right. To verify this, we note that $\hat{\mu}_0$ in (12-37) is a linear combination of the random variables[6] $\hat{\alpha}$ and $\hat{\beta}$. Thus, from (5-35),

$$E(\hat{\mu}_0) = E(\hat{\alpha}) + x_0 E(\hat{\beta})$$

_____

[6] Recall that each is a random variable, fluctuating around its target.

From (12-5) and (12-7),

$$= \alpha + x_0 \beta = \mu_0$$

$$\overline{E(\hat{\mu}_0) = \mu_0} \tag{12-38}$$

Thus $\hat{\mu}_0$ is indeed an unbiased estimator of μ_0.

Consider next its variance. Because $\hat{\alpha}$ and $\hat{\beta}$ are uncorrelated,[7] from (5-43),

$$\text{var}\,(\hat{\mu}_0) = \text{var}\,\hat{\alpha} + x_0^2 \,\text{var}\,\hat{\beta}$$

From (12-6) and (12-8),

$$= \frac{\sigma^2}{n} + x_0^2 \frac{\sigma^2}{\sum x_i^2}$$

$$\overline{\text{var}\,(\hat{\mu}_0) = \sigma^2 \left(\frac{1}{n} + \frac{x_0^2}{\sum x_i^2} \right)} \tag{12-39}$$

where of course x_0 is the new specified x value, while the x_i are the originally observed x's. To interpret (12-39), we note that this variance (or uncertainty) of $\hat{\mu}_0$ has two components, resulting from the variance (uncertainty) of $\hat{\alpha}$ and of $\hat{\beta}$ respectively. The uncertainty term resulting from $\hat{\beta}$ increases as x_0^2 increases, that is, the further x_0 is from the central value 0. This also can be seen from Figure 12-7: if x_0 were further to the right, then our estimates $\hat{\mu}_0$ would be spread out over an even wider range. On the other hand, if x_0 were further to the left (i.e., closer to zero), then our estimates $\hat{\mu}_0$ would be less spread.

Finally, we note that since $\hat{\alpha}$ and $\hat{\beta}$ are normal (as established at the beginning of Section 12-6), it follows from (6-13) that $\hat{\mu}_0$ is also normal. Thus the 95% confidence interval for μ_0 is

$$\mu_0 = \hat{\mu}_0 \pm z_{.025}\, \sigma \sqrt{\frac{1}{n} + \frac{x_0^2}{\sum x_i^2}}$$

or in the usual case where an unknown σ must be replaced with s:

$$\overline{\text{95\% confidence interval}}$$

$$\mu_0 = \hat{\mu}_0 \pm t_{.025}\, s \sqrt{\frac{1}{n} + \frac{x_0^2}{\sum x_i^2}} \tag{12-40}$$

[7] One reason for redefining the X variable as a deviation from the mean was to make the covariance of $\hat{\alpha}$ and $\hat{\beta}$ zero. The proof, straightforward but tedious, is omitted.

Again, the appropriate t distribution has $(n - 2)$ degrees of freedom. When x_0 is set at its central value of 0, note how this confidence interval reduces simply to the confidence interval for α in (12-34). In this case there is no uncertainty introduced by estimating β.

For the fertilizer example in Table 11-2, the average yield for 550 pounds of fertilizer application is estimated as

$$
\begin{aligned}
\hat{\mu}_0 &= \hat{\alpha} + \hat{\beta}x_0 \\
&= 60 + .068(550 - 400) \\
&= 70.2 \text{ bushels/acre}
\end{aligned}
$$

This is the point estimate of average yield. The 95% confidence interval using (12-40) is

$$
\mu_0 = 70.2 \pm 2.571(3.48)\sqrt{\frac{1}{7} + \frac{150^2}{280,000}} \tag{12-41}
$$

$$
= 70.2 \pm 4.2
$$

i.e., $\quad\quad\quad\quad 66.0 < \mu_0 < 74.4$

(b) The Prediction Interval for an Individual Y_0

In predicting a single observed Y_0, once again the best estimate is the point on the estimated regression line above x_0. In other words, the best *point* prediction for Y_0 is

$$
\hat{Y}_0 = \hat{\alpha} + \hat{\beta}x_0 = \hat{\mu}_0 \tag{12-42}
$$

When we try to find the *interval* estimate for Y_0, we will face all the problems involved in the interval for the mean, μ_0. Now, in addition, we face a problem because we are trying to estimate only one observed Y, rather than the more stable average of all the possible Y's. Hence, to our previous variance (12-39), we must now add the inherent variance σ^2 of an individual Y observation, obtaining

$$
\sigma^2\left(\frac{1}{n} + \frac{x_0^2}{\sum x_i^2}\right) + \sigma^2 = \sigma^2\left(\frac{1}{n} + \frac{x_0^2}{\sum x_i^2} + 1\right) \tag{12-43}
$$

Except for this larger variance, the prediction interval for Y_0 can be proved to be the same as the confidence interval for μ_0, i.e.,

95% prediction interval for an individual Y observation

$$Y_0 = \hat{\mu}_0 \pm t_{.025}\, s \sqrt{\frac{1}{n} + \frac{x_0^2}{\sum x_i^2} + 1} \qquad (12\text{-}44)$$

with the t distribution again having $(n-2)$ degrees of freedom.

Again using the fertilizer example, suppose we wish to predict a single crop yield if 550 lb/acre of fertilizer is applied. With a 95% chance of being right, we would predict:

$$Y_0 = 70.2 \pm 2.571(3.48)\sqrt{\frac{1}{7} + \frac{150^2}{280{,}000} + 1} \qquad (12\text{-}45)$$

$$= 70.2 \pm 9.9$$

$$60.3 < Y_0 < 80.1 \qquad (12\text{-}46)$$

We note, as expected, that this is a wider interval than (12-41).

The relationship of prediction and confidence intervals is shown in Figure 12-8. The two potential sources of error in a confidence interval for the mean are shown in panels (a) and (b); these are combined to form the red band in panel (c). The wider pink band in (c) gives the prediction intervals for individual Y observations. Note how both bands expand as x_0 moves farther away from its central value of zero; this reflects the fact that x_0^2 appears in both variances.

We emphasize that in formulas (12-40) and (12-44), x_0 may be *any* value of x. If x_0 lies *among* the values $x_1 \cdots x_n$, the process is called interpolation. (If x_0 is one of the values $x_1 \cdots x_n$, the process might be called, "using also the other values of x to sharpen our knowledge of this one population at x_0".) If x_0 is out beyond the observed x's, then the process is called extrapolation. The techniques developed in this section may be used for extrapolation, but only with great caution as we shall see in the next section.

12-9   DANGERS OF EXTRAPOLATION

There are two risks in extrapolation, which we might call "mathematical" and "practical." In both cases, there is no sharp division between safe interpolation and dangerous extrapolation. Rather, there is *continually* increasing danger of misinterpretation as x_0 gets further and further from its central value.

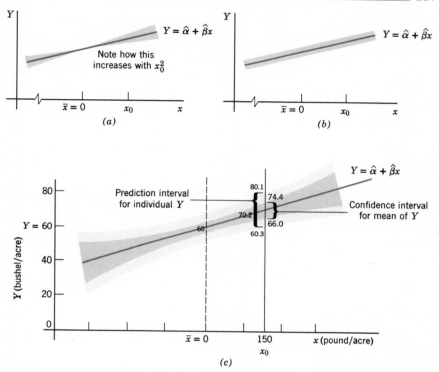

FIGURE 12-8 (a) Interval estimate of the mean of Y, if there were error only in estimating β. (b) Interval estimate of the mean of Y, if there were error only in estimating α. (c) Interval estimate for mean of Y and prediction interval for individual Y.

(a) Statistical Risk

It was emphasized in the previous section that prediction intervals get larger as x_0 moves away from $\bar{x}$. This is true, even if all the assumptions underlying our mathematical model hold exactly.

(b) Risk of Invalid Model

In practice it must be recognized that a mathematical model is never absolutely correct. Rather, it is a useful approximation. In particular, one cannot take seriously the assumption that the population means are strung out in an *exactly* straight line. If we consider the fertilizer example, it is likely that the true relation increases initially, but then bends down eventually as a "burning point" is approached, and the crop is overdosed. This is illustrated in Figure 12-9, which is an extension of Figure 11-2 with the scale appropriately changed. In the region of interest, from 0 to 700 lb, the relation is *practically* a straight line, and no great harm

FIGURE 12-9 Comparison of linear and nonlinear models.

is done in assuming the linear model. However, if the linear model is extrapolated far beyond this region of experimentation, the result becomes meaningless. In such cases a nonlinear model should be considered.

12-10   **CONCLUDING OBSERVATIONS**

Two points warrant emphasis. First, the theory of this chapter—and in particular the Gauss-Markov justification of least squares—requires no assumption of normality of the error term (i.e., normality of Y). The one exception occurred in Sections 12-6 to 12-8, where the normality assumption was required only for small sample estimation—and this because of a quite general principle that small sample estimation requires a normally distributed parent population to validate the t distribution. But even here, t may be a reasonably good approximation in some nonnormal populations.

Second, the independent variable x has been assumed to take on a given set of fixed values (for example, fertilizer application was set at certain specified levels). But in many cases x cannot be controlled in this way. Thus, if we are examining the effect of rainfall on yield, it must be recognized that x (rainfall) is a random variable, completely outside our control. The surprising thing is that most of this chapter remains valid whether x is fixed *or* a random variable, provided we assume, as well as (12-4), that:

x is independent of α, β, and σ^2; and	(12-47)
x and the error e are independent	(12-48)

This greatly generalizes the application of the regression model.

12-4 Using the data of Problem 11-1, what is your 95% prediction interval for the saving of a family with an income of
   (a) $6000
   (b) $8000
   (c) $10,000
   (d) $12,000
   (e) Which of these four intervals is least precise? Most precise? Why?
   (f) How is the answer to (b) related to the confidence interval found from (12-34)?

12-5 Repeat Problem 12-4 calculating instead a confidence interval for the *average* saving of all families at each income level. Compare.

12-6 (a) Suppose you are trying to explain how the interest rate (i) affects investment (I) in the U.S. Would you prefer to take observations of i and I over a period in which the authorities were trying to hold interest constant, or a period in which it is allowed to vary widely?
   (b) Suppose you have estimated the regression of consumption (C) on income (Y) using data from families in the $8000 to $16,000 income range. Would you prefer to predict the future consumption of a family with an $8000 income, or a family with a $10,000 income? Why?

Review Problems

12-7 In collecting data for a regression $Y = \hat{\alpha} + \hat{\beta}X$, suppose a scientist faces a choice between,
   Design (i): X values spread uniformly between $X = 10$ and $X = 20$, using n_1 observations, or
   Design (ii): X values spread uniformly between $X = 10$ and $X = 50$, using $n_2 = 100$ observations.
   Suppose there are no problems of nonlinearity (such as in Figure 12-9), and in fact all the standard assumptions (12-2) are valid. In order to make design (i) yield an estimator $\hat{\beta}$ with as little variance as design (ii), how large should n_1 be, compared to n_2?

12-8 A class of 150 registered students wrote two tests, the grades being denoted X_1 and X_2. The instructor calculated the following summary statistics:

$$\bar{X}_1 = 60 \qquad \bar{X}_2 = 70$$

$$\sum (X_1 - \bar{X}_1)^2 = 36{,}000 \qquad \sum (X_2 - \bar{X}_2)^2 = 24{,}000$$

$$\sum (X_1 - \bar{X}_1)(X_2 - \bar{X}_2) = 30{,}000$$

The instructor then discovered that there was one more student, unregistered; worse yet, one of this student's grades (X_1) was lost, although the other grade was discovered $(X_2 = 85)$. The instructor was told by the Dean to estimate the missing grade X_1 as closely as possible. What should his estimate be?

12-9 In order to estimate this year's inventory, a tire company sampled 6 dealers, in each case getting inventory figures for both this year and last:

X = Inventory Last Year	Y = Inventory This Year
70	60
260	320
150	230
100	120
20	50
60	60

Summary statistics are $\bar{X} = 110$, $\bar{Y} = 140$, $s^2 = 860$

$$\sum x^2 = 36{,}400 \qquad \sum y^2 = 61{,}800 \qquad \sum xy = 46{,}100$$

(a) Calculate the least-squares line showing how this year's inventory (Y) is related to last year's (X).

(b) Suppose that a complete inventory of all dealers is available for last year (but not for this year). Suppose also that the mean inventory for last year was found to be $\mu_X = 180$ tires per dealer. On the graph below we show this population mean μ_X and sketch the population scatter (although this scatter remains unknown to the company, because Y values are not yet available). On this graph plot the six observed points, along with $\bar{X}$, $\bar{Y}$, and the estimated regression line.

(c) Indicate on the graph how μ_Y should be estimated. Construct a 95% confidence interval for μ_Y.

(d) Construct a 95% confidence interval for μ_Y, if last year's data X had been unavailable or ignored (i.e., using only Y values).

(e) Comparing (c) to (d), state in words the value of exploiting prior knowledge on last year's inventory.

Multiple
REGRESSION

> *"The cause of lightning," Alice said very decidedly, for she felt quite sure about this, "is the thunder—no, no!" she hastily corrected herself, "I meant it the other way."*
>
> *"It's too late to correct it," said the Red Queen, "When you've once said a thing, that fixes it, and you must take the consequences."*
>
> Lewis Carroll

13-1   **INTRODUCTION**

Multiple regression is the extension of simple regression, to take account of the effect of more than one independent X variable on the dependent variable Y. It is obviously the appropriate technique when we want to investigate the effects on Y of several variables simultaneously. Yet, even if we are interested in the effect of only one variable on Y, it is usually wise to include the other variables influencing Y in a multiple regression analysis, for two reasons:

1. To reduce stochastic error (discussed in Section 12-2); the objective here, as in introducing a second factor in ANOVA, is to increase the strength of our statistical tests.
2. Even more important, to eliminate bias that might result if we were just to ignore an uncontrolled variable that substantially affects Y.

For example, suppose that the fertilizer and yield observations in Chapter 11 were taken at seven different agricultural experiment stations across the country. If soil conditions and temperature were essentially the same in all these areas, we still might ask whether part of the fluctuation in Y (i.e., the disturbance term e) can be explained by varying levels

Table 13-1   Observed Yield, Fertilizer Application,
and Rainfall

Y Wheat Yield (Bushels/Acre)	X Fertilizer (Pounds/Acre)	Z Rainfall (Inches)
40	100	36
45	200	33
50	300	37
65	400	37
70	500	34
70	600	32
80	700	36

of rainfall in different areas. A better prediction of yield may be possible if *both* fertilizer and rainfall are examined. The observed levels of rainfall are shown in Table 13-1, along with the original observations of yield and fertilizer from Table 11-1.

13-2   THE MATHEMATICAL MODEL

Yield Y is now to be regressed on the two independent variables, or "regressors," fertilizer X and rainfall Z. Let us suppose that this relationship is of the form

$$E(Y_i) = \alpha + \beta x_i + \gamma z_i \tag{13-1}$$
$$\text{like (12-1)}$$

with both regressors x and z measured as deviations from their means. Geometrically this equation is a plane[1] in the three dimensional space shown in Figure 13-1. For any given combination of rainfall and fertilizer (x_i, z_i), the expected yield $E(Y_i)$ is the point on this plane directly above, shown as a hollow dot. Of course, the observed value of Y is very unlikely to fall precisely on this plane. For example, our particular observed Y_i at this fertilizer/rainfall combination is somewhat greater than its expected value, and is shown as the red dot lying directly above this plane.

The difference between the observed and expected value of Y_i is the stochastic or error term e_i. Thus, any observed value Y_i may be expressed as its expected value plus this disturbance term

$$Y_i = \alpha + \beta x_i + \gamma z_i + e_i \tag{13-2}$$

with our assumptions about e the same as in Chapter 12.   like (12-3)

---

[1]It is a plane because it is linear in x and z, as shown in Appendix 13-1.

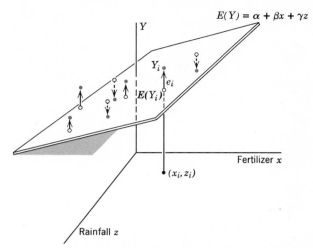

FIGURE 13-1   Scatter of observed points about the true regression plane.

β is geometrically interpreted as the slope of the plane as we move in a direction parallel to the (x, Y) plane, keeping z constant; thus β is the marginal effect of fertilizer x on yield Y. Similarly γ is the slope of the plane as we move in a direction parallel to the (z, Y) plane, keeping x constant; thus γ is the marginal effect of z on Y. This is explained in detail in Appendix 13-1.

13-3   LEAST SQUARES ESTIMATION

Least squares estimates are derived by selecting the estimates of α, β, and γ that minimize the sum of the squared deviations between the observed Y's and the fitted Y's; that is, minimize

$$\sum (Y_i - \hat{\alpha} - \hat{\beta}x_i - \hat{\gamma}z_i)^2 \tag{13-3}$$

like (11-10)

where $\hat{\alpha}$, $\hat{\beta}$, and $\hat{\gamma}$ are, of course, our estimators of α, β, and γ. This is done with calculus by setting the partial derivatives of this function with respect to $\hat{\alpha}$, $\hat{\beta}$, and $\hat{\gamma}$ equal to zero (or algebraically by a technique similar to that used in Appendix 11-1). The result is the following three estimating equations (sometimes called normal equations),

$$\left. \begin{aligned} \hat{\alpha} &= \bar{Y} \\ \sum x_i Y_i &= \hat{\beta} \sum x_i^2 + \hat{\gamma} \sum x_i z_i \\ \sum z_i Y_i &= \hat{\beta} \sum x_i z_i + \hat{\gamma} \sum z_i^2 \end{aligned} \right\} \tag{13-4}$$

Table 13-2 Least Squares Estimates for Multiple Regression of Y on X and Z

Y_i	X_i	Z_i	$x_i = X_i - \bar{X}$	$z_i = Z_i - \bar{Z}$	$x_i Y_i$	$z_i Y_i$	x_i^2	z_i^2	$x_i z_i$	$\hat{Y}_i = 60 + .0689x + .603z$
40	100	36	-300	1	-12,000	40	90,000	1	-300	39.9
45	200	33	-200	-2	-9,000	-90	40,000	4	400	45.0
50	300	37	-100	2	-5,000	100	10,000	4	-200	54.3
65	400	37	0	2	0	130	0	4	0	61.2
70	500	34	100	-1	7,000	-70	10,000	1	-100	66.3
70	600	32	200	-3	14,000	-210	40,000	9	-600	72.0
80	700	36	300	1	24,000	80	90,000	1	300	81.3
$\sum Y_i$	$\sum X_i$	$\sum Z_i$	0	0	$\sum x_i Y_i$	$\sum z_i Y_i$	$\sum x_i^2$	$\sum z_i^2$	$\sum x_i z_i$	
= 420	= 2800	= 245			= 19,000	= -20	= 280,000	= 24	= -500	
$\hat{a} = \bar{Y} = 60$	$\bar{X} = 400$	$\bar{Z} = 35$								

Estimating equations (13-4) $\begin{cases} 19{,}000 = 280{,}000\hat{\beta} - 500\hat{\gamma} \\ -20 = -500\hat{\beta} + 24\hat{\gamma} \end{cases}$

Solution $\begin{cases} \hat{\beta} = .0689 \\ \hat{\gamma} = .603 \end{cases}$

Thus our regression is $Y = \hat{a} + \hat{\beta}x + \hat{\gamma}z$

$$= 60 + .0689x + .603z$$

Or, in terms of the original X and Z,

$$Y = 60 + .0689(X - \bar{X}) + .603(Z - \bar{Z})$$
$$= 60 + .0689(X - 400) + .603(Z - 35)$$

$$Y = 11.33 + .0689X + .603Z$$

Again, note that the intercept estimate $\hat{\alpha}$ is the average $\overline{Y}$. The second and third equations may be solved for $\hat{\beta}$ and $\hat{\gamma}$. These calculations are shown in Table 13-2, and yield the fitted multiple regression equation.

PROBLEMS

13-1 Suppose a random sample of five families yielded the following data (an extension of Problem 11-1):

Family	Saving S	Income Y	Assets W
A	$ 600	$ 8,000	$12,000
B	1,200	11,000	6,000
C	1,000	9,000	6,000
D	700	6,000	3,000
E	300	6,000	18,000

(a) Estimate the multiple regression equation of S on Y and W.

(b) Does the coefficient of Y differ from the answer to Problem 11-1? Which coefficient better illustrates the relation of S to Y?

(c) For a family with assets of $5000 and income of $8000, what would you predict saving to be?

(d) If a family had a $2,000 increase in income, while assets remained constant, estimate by how much their saving would increase.

(e) If a family had a $1,000 increase in income, and a $3,000 increase in assets, estimate by how much their saving would increase.

(f) Calculate the residual sum of squares, and residual variance s^2.

(g) Are you satisfied with the degrees of freedom you have for s^2 in this problem? Explain.

(13-2) Suppose a random sample of five families yielded the following data (another extension of Problem 11-1):

Family	Saving S	Income Y	Number of Children N
A	$ 600	$ 8,000	5
B	1,200	11,000	2
C	1,000	9,000	1
D	700	6,000	3
E	300	6,000	4

(a) Estimate the multiple regression of S on Y and N.

(b) For a family with five children and income of $6000, what would you predict saving to be?

*13-3 Suppose the data in Problems 13-1 and 13-2 apply to exactly the same families. Then this can be combined to obtain the following table:

Family	Saving S	Income Y	Assets W	Number of Children N
A	$ 600	$ 8,000	$12,000	5
B	1,200	11,000	6,000	2
C	1,000	9,000	6,000	1
D	700	6,000	3,000	3
E	300	6,000	18,000	4

Measuring the independent variables as deviations from the mean, we wish to estimate the regression equation

$$S = \alpha + \beta y + \gamma w + \psi n$$

(a) Generalizing (13-4), use the least squares criterion to derive the system of four equations needed to estimate the four parameters.

(b) Using a table such as Table 13-2, calculate the estimates of the four parameters.

13-4   MULTICOLLINEARITY

(a) In Simple Regression

In Figure 12-5a it was shown how the estimate $\hat{\beta}$ became unreliable if the X_i's were closely bunched, that is, if the regressor X had little variation. It will be instructive to consider the limiting case, where the X_i's are concentrated on one single value $\bar{X}$, as in Figure 13-2. Then $\hat{\beta}$ is not determined at all. There are any number of differently sloped lines passing through $(\bar{X}, \bar{Y})$ which fit equally well: for each line in Figure 13-2, the sum of squared deviations is the same, since the deviations are measured vertically from $(\bar{X}, \bar{Y})$. This geometric fact has an algebraic counterpart. If all $X_i = \bar{X}$, then all $x_i = 0$, and the term involving $\hat{\beta}$ in (11-10) is zero; hence, the sum of squares does not depend on $\hat{\beta}$ at all. It follows that any $\hat{\beta}$ will do equally well in minimizing the sum of squares. An alternative way of looking at the same problem is that since all x_i are zero, $\sum x_i^2$ in the denominator of (11-16) is zero, and $\hat{\beta}$ is not defined.

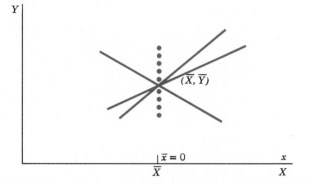

FIGURE 13-2   Degenerate regression, because of no spread (variation) in X.

In conclusion, when the values of X show little or no variation, then the effect of X on Y can no longer be sensibly investigated. But if the problem is *predicting* Y—rather than investigating Y's dependence on X—this bunching of the X values does not matter *provided* we limit our prediction to this same value of X. All the lines in Figure 13-2 predict Y equally well. The best prediction is $\bar{Y}$, and all these lines give us that result.

(b) In Multiple Regression

Again consider the limiting case where the values of the independent variables X and Z are completely bunched up on a line L, as in Figure 13-3. This means that all the observed points in our scatter lie in the vertical plane running up through L. You can think of the three-dimensional space as a room in a house; our observations are not scattered throughout this room, but instead lie embedded in an extremely thin pane of glass standing vertically on the floor.

In explaining Y, multicollinearity makes us lose one dimension. In the earlier case of simple regression, our best fit for Y was not a line, but rather a point $(\bar{x}, \bar{Y})$; in this multiple regression case our best fit for Y is not a plane, but rather the line F. To get F, we just fit the least squares line through the points on the vertical pane of glass. The problem is identical to the one shown in Figure 11-2; in one case a line is fitted on a flat pane of glass, in the other case, on a flat piece of paper. This regression line F is, therefore, our best fit for Y. As long as we stick to the same *combination* of X and Z—that is, so long as we confine ourselves to predicting Y values on that pane of glass—no special problems arise. We can use the regression F on the glass to predict Y in exactly the same way as we did in the simple regression analysis of Chapter 11.

FIGURE 13-3   Multicollinearity.

But there is no way to examine how X affects Y. Any attempt to define β, the marginal effect of X on Y (holding Z constant), involves moving off that pane of glass, and we have no sample information whatsoever on what the world out there looks like. Or, to put it differently, if we try to explain Y with a plane—rather than a line F—we find there are any number of planes running through F (e.g. π_1 and π_2) which do an equally good job. Since each passes through F, each yields an identical sum of squared deviations; thus each provides an equally good fit. This is confirmed in the algebra in the estimating equations (13-4). When X is a linear function of Z, (i.e., when x is a linear function of z) it may be shown that the last two equations are dependent, and cannot be solved uniquely[2] for $\hat{\beta}$ and $\hat{\gamma}$.

Now let's be less extreme in our assumptions and consider the near-limiting case, where Z and X are almost on a line (i.e., where all our observations in the room lie very close to a vertical pane of glass). In this case, a plane may be fitted to our observations, but the estimating procedure is very unstable; it becomes very sensitive to random errors, reflected in large variances of the estimators $\hat{\beta}$ and $\hat{\gamma}$. Thus, even though

---

[2]Two linear equations can usually be solved for two unknowns, but not always. For example, suppose that John's age (X) is twice Harry's (Y). Then we can write

$$X = 2Y$$
$$5X = 10Y \tag{13-5}$$

Note that these two equations tell us the same thing. We have two equations in two unknowns, but they don't generate a unique solution, because they don't provide independent information.

X may really affect Y, its statistical significance may not be established because the standard error of $\hat{\beta}$ is so large. This is analogous to the argument in the simple regression case in Section 12-6.

When the independent variables X and Z are collinear, or nearly so (i.e., highly correlated), it is called the problem of multicollinearity.[3] As indicated earlier this does not raise problems in predicting Y provided there is no attempt to predict for values of X and Z removed from their line of collinearity. But structural questions cannot be answered—the influence of X alone (or Z alone) on Y cannot be sensibly investigated.

Example 1 In our wheat yield example, suppose that X is (as before) the amount of fertilizer measured in pounds per acre, and that the statistician makes the incredibly foolish error of defining another independent variable Z as the amount of fertilizer measured in ounces per acre. Since any weight measured in ounces must be sixteen times its measurement in pounds,

$$Z = 16X \tag{13-6}$$

exactly. Thus, all combinations of X and Z must fall on this straight line, and we have an example of perfect collinearity. Now if we try to fit[4] a regression plane to the observations of yield and fertilizer given in Table 11-1, one possible answer would be the original regression given in (11-18):

$$Y = 32.8 + .068X + 0Z \tag{13-7}$$

But an equally satisfactory solution would follow from substituting $X = \frac{1}{16}Z$:

$$Y = 32.8 + 0X + .00425Z$$

Another equivalent answer would be to make a partial substitution for X into (13-7) with arbitrary weight λ,

$$
\begin{aligned}
Y &= 32.8 + .068[\lambda X + (1 - \lambda)X] \\
&= 32.8 + .068[\lambda X + (1 - \lambda)(\tfrac{1}{16})Z] \\
Y &= 32.8 + .068\lambda X + .00425(1 - \lambda)Z
\end{aligned}
\tag{13-8}
$$

_____

[3]Actually, it would be more accurate to call it the problem of *collinearity*, and reserve the term *multicollinearity* if there are many regressors $X, Z, \ldots$ that are highly correlated.

[4]Since a computer program would probably break down, suppose the calculations are done by hand.

(13-8) is a whole family of planes depending on the value assigned to λ. In fact, all these three dimensional planes are equivalent expressions for the simple two dimensional relationship between fertilizer and yield. While all give the same correct prediction of Y, no meaning can be attached to whatever coefficients of X and Z we may come up with.

Example 2 While the previous extreme example may have clarified some of the theoretical issues, no statistician would make that sort of error in model specification. Instead, more subtle difficulties arise. For example, suppose demand for a group of goods is being related to prices and income, with the overall price index being the first independent variable. Suppose aggregate income measured in money terms is the second independent variable. If this is real income multiplied by the same price index, the problem of multicollinearity may become a serious one. The solution is to use real income, rather than money income, as the second independent variable. This is a special case of a more general warning: in any multiple regression in which price is one independent variable, beware of other independent variables measured in prices.

The problem of multicollinearity may be solved if there happens to be prior information about the relation of β and γ. For example, if it is known a priori that

$$\gamma = 5\beta \tag{13-9}$$

then this information will allow us to uniquely determine the regression plane, even in the case of perfect collinearity. This is evident from the geometry of Figure 13-3. Given a fixed relation between the two slopes (β and γ), there is only one regression plane π that can be fitted to pass through F. This is confirmed algebraically. Using (13-9), the model (13-2) can be written

$$Y_i = \alpha + \beta x_i + 5\beta z_i + e_i \tag{13-10}$$
$$= \alpha + \beta(x_i + 5z_i) + e_i \tag{13-11}$$

It is natural to define a new variable

$$w_i = x_i + 5z_i \tag{13-12}$$

Thus, (13-11) becomes

$$Y_i = \alpha + \beta w_i + e_i \tag{13-13}$$

and a regression of Y on w will yield estimates $\hat{\alpha}$ and $\hat{\beta}$. Finally, if we wish an estimate of γ, it is easily computed using (13-9):

$$\hat{\gamma} = 5\hat{\beta} \qquad (13\text{-}14)$$

13-5   CONFIDENCE INTERVALS AND STATISTICAL TESTS

As in simple regression, the true relation of Y to X is measured by the unknown population parameter β; we estimate it with the sample estimator $\hat{\beta}$. Although the unknown β is fixed, our estimator is a random variable, differing from sample to sample. The properties of $\hat{\beta}$ may be established, just as in the previous chapter. Thus $\hat{\beta}$ may be shown to be normal—again provided the sample size is large, or the error term is normal. $\hat{\beta}$ can also be shown to be unbiased, with its mean equal to β. The fluctuation of $\hat{\beta}$ is measured by its standard error; this is very complicated to calculate, even in this relatively simple case with only two regressors.[5] It is customarily calculated by an electronic computer using a library program; then the user has no need whatever to know the formula. Instead he needs to understand the *meaning* of the standard error, which is quite analogous to the simple regression case.

For example in Table 13-3 we reproduce the computer output for the wheat-yield data of Table 13-2. In successive columns the computer prints, for each regressor,

Table 13-3   Computer Output for Wheat Yield Multiple Regression (data in Table 13-1)

MULTIPLE REGRESSION EQUATION				
VARIABLE	COEFFICIENT	STD. ERROR	T VALUE	PARTIAL COR.
YIELD =				
CONST	11.33	27.04	0.4189	
FERT	0.0689	.00696	9.896	0.9802
RAIN	0.6028	0.7524	0.8012	0.3719
RESIDUAL VARIANCE =		13.08		

---

[5]With only two regressors X and Z, the

$$\text{standard error of } \hat{\beta} = s_{\hat{\beta}} = \frac{s}{\sqrt{\sum x_i^2 - \left(\sum x_i z_i\right)^2 / \sum z_i^2}} \qquad (13\text{-}15)$$

where s^2 is the residual variance, as usual. This is similar in form to (12-28). With three regressors, the formula is three times as long. The notation (but not the calculations) may be greatly simplified by using matrices. (See, for example, our *Econometrics* text, Chapter 13.) Matrices are also used in the computer programs.

(1) the name
(2) the estimated coefficient
(3) the standard error
(4) the t statistic, calculated easily from (2) and (3) above; for example, for the coefficient β,

$$t = \frac{\hat{\beta}}{s_{\hat{\beta}}} \qquad\qquad (13\text{-}16)$$
$$= \frac{.0689}{.00696} = 9.896 \qquad \text{like (12-36)}$$

with d.f. $= n - k - 1$, where k is the number of regressors
(5) the partial correlation; this concept is explained in Chapter 14, and may be ignored for now.

From these basic quantities we may then easily run tests and confidence intervals, as follows:

(a) Student's t statistic is used to test the null hypothesis that a coefficient is zero. For example, in Table 13-3, to test whether Y is affected by fertilizer application, we note that the observed t value is 9.896 with d.f. $= 7 - 2 - 1 = 4$. Referring to Appendix Table V,

$$\text{prob-value} < .001$$

so that the effect of fertilizer on yield is highly significant.
(b) For each coefficient, a 95% confidence interval may be constructed analogous to (12-32); for example, for β, the 95% confidence interval is:

$$\beta = \hat{\beta} \pm t_{.025}\, s_{\hat{\beta}} \qquad\qquad (13\text{-}17)$$

where $t_{.025}$ is the critical t value, with d.f. $= n - k - 1$. Thus, in our example, the effect of fertilizer has the 95% confidence interval,

$$\beta = .0689 \pm (2.776)(.00696)$$
$$= .0689 \pm .0193$$

It is customary to rearrange the information of Table 13-3 in equation form as follows:

	YIELD = 11.33	+ .0689 FERTILIZER	+ .603 RAINFALL	
standard error	27.04	.00696	.752	
t-value	.419	9.90	.801	(13-18)
prob-value		.001	$\approx.25$	
confidence interval		$\pm.0193$	±2.088	

13-6 HOW MANY REGRESSORS SHOULD BE RETAINED?

We have already seen that the t-value for fertilizer in Table 13-3 would lead us to reject H_0, thus retaining fertilizer X as a statistically significant variable, and this raises no problems. But if we run a standard hypothesis test for rainfall, H_0 cannot be rejected; if we use this evidence to accept H_0 (no effect of rainfall), and thus drop rainfall as a regressor, we may encounter the same difficulty discussed in Section 9-5. Since this is so important in regression analysis, the argument is briefly reviewed for emphasis.

Although it is true that our t coefficient (.8) for rainfall Z is not "statistically significant," this does *not* prove there is no relationship between Z and Y. It is easy to see why. We have strong biological grounds for believing that yield Y is positively related to rainfall Z. In (13-18) this belief is confirmed by the positive coefficient $\hat{\gamma} = .603$. Thus our statistical evidence is consistent with our prior belief (even though it is not as strong a confirmation as we might like).[6] To accept the null hypothesis $\gamma = 0$ and conclude that Z does not affect Y, would be in direct contradiction to both the (strong) prior belief and the (weak) statistical evidence. We would be reversing a prior belief even though the statistical evidence weakly confirmed it. And this remains true for any positive t value, although as t becomes smaller, our statistical confirmation becomes weaker. Only if t is zero or negative, do the statistical results contradict our prior belief.

It follows from this, that if we had strong prior grounds for believing that Z is positively related to Y, it should not be dropped from the estimating equation (13-18); instead it should be retained, with all the pertinent information on its t value, confidence interval, etc.

On the other hand, what if our prior belief is that H_0 is approximately true? (Of course, we would never believe that a specific H_0 is *exactly*

---

[6]Perhaps because of too small a sample. Thus, .603 may be a very accurate description of how Y is related to Z; but our t value is not statistically significant because our sample is small, and the standard error of our estimator ($s_{\hat{\gamma}} = .752$) is relatively large as a consequence.

true; hence the question becomes whether or not we accept H_0 as a *working* hypothesis.) Then the decision to drop or retain a variable becomes quite different. For example, a weak observed relationship (such as $t = .8$) would be in some conflict with our prior expectation of no relationship. But it is so minor a conflict, that it is easily explained by chance (prob-value $\simeq .25$). Hence resolving it in favor of our prior expectation and continuing to use H_0 as a working hypothesis might be a reasonable judgment.

In the case of regression, there is another argument that may lead a statistician who has very weak prior belief (in either H_0 or H_1) to accept H_0 when the data are insignificant: it keeps the model simple, and conserves degrees of freedom to strengthen tests on other regressors.[7] (When a regressor is dropped, the equation involving the fewer remaining regressors must be recalculated; then since the number of regressors k is reduced, d.f. $= n - k - 1$ are increased.)

We conclude once again, that classical statistical theory alone does not provide absolutely firm guidelines for accepting H_0; acceptance must be based also on extrastatistical judgment. Thus prior belief plays a key role, not only in the initial specification of which regressors should be in the equation, but also in the decision on which should be dropped in the light of the statistical evidence, and finally in the decision on how the model will eventually be used.

Prior belief plays a less critical role in the rejection of an hypothesis; but it is by no means irrelevant. Suppose, for example that although you believed Y to be related to three variables, you didn't really expect it to be related to a fourth; someone had just suggested that you "try on" the fourth at a 5% level of significance. This means that if H_0 (no relation) is true, there is a 5% chance of ringing a false alarm. If this is the *only*

---

[7]A more sophisticated argument for accepting H_0 in these circumstances goes like this. Even though you know that the estimate that $\beta = 0$ (i.e., accepting H_0 and dropping this regressor) must be somewhat wrong, you know that $\beta = \hat{\beta}$ (rejecting H_0, and retaining the regressor) is somewhat wrong too but in a different way: whereas the estimate 0 has some bias but no variance (it was arbitrarily prespecified), the estimate $\hat{\beta}$ has no bias but some variance. Which is more wrong? The best criterion, that combines bias and variance, is the mean squared error (7-21). This leads you to accept H_0 if

(a) you think its bias is small (if H_0 was considered near the truth, a priori), and/or
(b) $\hat{\beta}$ has a lot of variance, either because of a small sample, or multicollinearity problems.

These are recognized as the two conditions for accepting H_0 we have already encountered above.

variable "tried on," then this is a risk you can live with. However, if many similar variables are included in a multiple regression by someone who is "bag-shaking" (i.e., trying on everything in sight), then the chance of a false alarm increases dramatically.[8] Of course, this risk can be kept small by reducing the level of error for each t test from 5% to 1% or less. This has led some authors to suggest a 1% level of significance with the variables just being "tried on," and a 5% level of significance with the other variables expected to affect Y.

To sum up, hypothesis testing should not be done mechanically. It requires:

1. Good judgment, and good prior theoretical understanding of the model being tested.
2. An understanding of the assumptions and limitations of the statistical techniques.

PROBLEMS

13-4 Suppose a multiple regression of Y on three independent variables yields the following estimates, based on a sample of $n = 30$:

$$Y = 25.1 \quad + \quad 1.2X_1 + 1.0X_2 - .50X_3$$

Standard error	(2.1)	(1.5)	(1.3)	(.06)
t-value	(11.9)	( )	( )	( )
Prob-value	($\ll$.001)	( )	( )	( )
95% CI	($\pm$4.3)	( )	( )	( )

(a) Fill in the blanks.

(b) True or false? If false, correct it.

(1) The coefficient of X_1 is estimated to be 1.2. Other scientists might collect other samples and calculate other estimates. The distribution of these estimates would be centered around the true value of 1.2. Therefore, the estimator is called unbiased.

(2) If there were strong prior reasons for believing that X_1 does not influence Y, it is reasonable to reject the null hypothesis $\beta_1 = 0$ at the 5% level of significance.

(3) If there were strong prior reasons for believing that X_2 does influence Y, it is reasonable to use the estimated coefficient 1.0 rather than accept the null hypothesis $\beta_2 = 0$.

---

[8] Suppose, for simplicity, that the t tests for the significance of the several variables (say k of them) were independent. Then the probability of no error at all is $(.95)^k$. For $k = 10$, for example, this is .60, which makes the probability of some error (some false alarm) as high as .40.

13-5 Suggest possible additional regressors that might be used to improve the multiple regression analysis of wheat yield.

13-6 Give an example of a multiple regression of Y on X_1 and X_2 in which you would drop X_1 from the equation, but retain X_2 even though its coefficient had a lower t value.

13-7 True or false? If false, correct it: Multicollinearity occurs when the regressors are highly correlated. This means that some regression coefficients will have large standard errors. Some regressors may therefore become statistically insignificant; if these regressors are also regarded a priori as unimportant, they may be dropped from the model. Then when the new regression equation is calculated, the multicollinearity problem will be reduced.

13-8 Suppose your roommate is a bright student, but he has studied no economics, and not much statistics. (Specifically, he understands only simple—but not multiple—regression). In trying to explain what influences the U.S. price level he has regressed U.S. prices on 100 different economic variables one-at-a-time (i.e., in 100 simple regressions). Moreover, he apparently selected these variables in a completely haphazard way without any idea of potential cause-and-effect relations. Using a 95% level of confidence he discovered 5 variables that were statistically significant, and concluded that each of these has an influence on U.S. prices.

(a) Explain to him in simple terms what reservations, if any, you have about his conclusion.

(b) If he had uncovered 20 "statistically significant" variables, would your criticism remain the same? How would you suggest he improve his analysis?

13-7   INTERPRETATION OF REGRESSION:
                               "OTHER THINGS BEING EQUAL"

The coefficients in a linear regression model have a very simple but important interpretation, which we shall now consider. (The same interpretation is given geometrically in Appendix 13-1, for readers who want it).

(a) Simple Regression Reviewed

Recall the simple regression model of Chapter 12

$$Y = \alpha + \beta x \tag{13-19}$$
$$\text{(12-3) essentially}$$

(In this discussion the error term e is ignored, since we are interested in interpreting β both for models with and without a stochastic error term.) It is often very useful to interpret β as

$$\beta = \text{increase in } Y \text{ if } x \text{ is increased by one unit} \qquad (13\text{-}20)$$

For example, in the relation of wheat yield Y to fertilizer x, β is the increase in yield when fertilizer is increased one unit (called "marginal physical product" of fertilizer, in Problem 11-3).

To prove (13-20), let us consider what happens when x is increased by 1 unit, say from the initial x_0 to $(x_0 + 1)$. Then the increase in yield Y can be found by solving for Y in (13-19) both before and after the increase in x:

$$\begin{aligned} \text{initial } Y &= \alpha + \beta x_0 \\ \text{new } Y &= \alpha + \beta(x_0 + 1) \\ \hline \text{difference} = \text{increase in } Y &= \beta \end{aligned} \qquad (13\text{-}20) \text{ proved}$$

(b) Nonlinear Regression

To appreciate the linear model, it is useful to contrast it with a more complicated model, for example, the quadratic model,

$$Y = \alpha + \beta x + \gamma x^2$$

When the marginal product of x is calculated as before, by increasing x one unit, then

$$\begin{aligned} \text{initial } Y &= \alpha + \beta x_0 + \gamma x_0^2 \\ \text{new } Y &= \alpha + \beta(x_0 + 1) + \gamma(x_0 + 1)^2 \\ \hline \text{difference} = \text{increase in } Y &= \beta + 2\gamma x_0 + \gamma \end{aligned} \qquad (13\text{-}21)$$

Thus in this case the marginal productivity of x is no longer simply the coefficient β. It also involves the coefficient γ, and the level x_0. Thus a major advantage of the linear model is that β has such a clear and direct interpretation.

(c) Multiple Regression

Consider again the multiple regression model

$$Y = \alpha + \beta x + \gamma z \qquad (13\text{-}22)$$

for example, where wheat yield Y depends on both fertilizer x and rainfall z. The interpretation of β is now

$$\beta = \text{the increase in } Y \text{ if } x \text{ is increased}$$
$$\text{one unit, } \textit{while } z \textit{ is held constant} \qquad (13\text{-}23)$$

To prove this, we keep z constant (say at z_0), while we increase x from x_0 to $(x_0 + 1)$. Then from (13-22),

$$\begin{aligned}
\text{initial } Y &= \alpha + \beta x_0 + \gamma z_0 \\
\text{new } Y &= \alpha + \beta(x_0 + 1) + \gamma z_0 \\
\hline
\text{increase in } Y &= \beta
\end{aligned} \qquad (13\text{-}23) \text{ proved}$$

For the general linear model

$$Y = \alpha + \beta_1 x_1 + \beta_2 x_2 + \cdots + \beta_k x_k \qquad (13\text{-}24)$$

it may be confirmed that the interpretation of each coefficient is similar:

$$\beta_i = \text{the increase in } Y \text{ if } x_i \text{ is increased one unit}$$
$$\text{while all other } x \text{ variables are held constant} \qquad (13\text{-}25)$$

13-8   **SIMPLE AND MULTIPLE REGRESSION COMPARED**

In order to evaluate the benefits of a proposed irrigation scheme in a certain region, suppose the relation of yield Y to rainfall R is investigated over several years. The data are given in the first 3 columns of Table 13-4. From it we could calculate the simple regression equation,

$$Y = 60 - 1.67\, r \qquad (13\text{-}26)$$
$$(s_\beta = 4.0)$$

But the negative coefficient (implying that increased rainfall *reduces* yield) strongly suggests that something in this analysis has gone very wrong. Actually, even before we calculated the regression (13-26) we should have known it might be wrong, because it only measures the simple relation of Y to R. What we really need to know is how yield is related to rainfall, *while all other important variables are held constant*. According to (13-25), therefore, we should carry out a multiple regression of yield on rainfall and any other important variables, such as temperature; hence temperature was included along with rainfall in

Table 13-4. Yield, Rainfall and Temperature
Over Several Years.

Year	Yield, Y (bu./acre)	Total Spring Rainfall R (inches)	Average Spring Temperature T (° Fahr.)
1963	60	8	56
1964	50	10	47
1965	70	11	53
1966	70	10	53
1967	80	9	56
1968	50	9	47
1969	60	12	44
1970	40	11	44

a computation of the multiple regression equation

$$Y = 60 + \underset{(s_{\hat\beta} = 2.68)}{5.71\ r} + \underset{(s_{\hat\gamma} = .69)}{2.95\ t} \tag{13-27}$$

This regression yields a much more reasonable conclusion. Rainfall R does have a positive relation to yield when T is held constant.[10] This is the positive *direct relation*, shown in Figure 13-4.

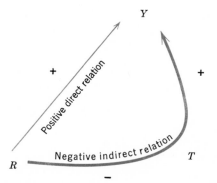

FIGURE 13-4 In applying simple regression to a multiple regression problem, the indirect relation may cause bias.

---

[10] The magnitude of the rainfall coefficient (5.71) is also important: it estimates the productivity of water, which can then be compared to the cost of water in order to determine whether irrigation is worthwhile.

Although temperature was introduced into the regression equation primarily to clarify the relation of yield to rainfall, the temperature coefficient is of some interest in its own right. We note that it is positive, and even more significant than rainfall.

To see why (13-26) yields the wrong sign, we must realize that in the data from which it was calculated, T is *not* held constant. In fact, T has a negative correlation with R; for example, in 1970 high rainfall occurs with low temperature. Low temperature in turn results in low yields (because of the positive coefficient of t in (13-27)). Thus high rainfall, via low temperature, may be associated with low yields. This is the negative *indirect relation*, shown in Figure 13-4. If the indirect relation predominates, then it will determine the sign of the simple regression coefficient. This apparently is what happened in (13-26). Even in situations less spectacular than this,[11] the simple regression coefficient will still be biased to some extent by the indirect effect of an omitted regressor (whenever the omitted regressor is correlated with the other variables, of course). This is the great advantage of multiple regression —*to avoid bias.*[12]

Another advantage of multiple regression is to reduce the residual variance;[13] this reduces the standard error of the coefficient of r, from 4.0 in (13-26) to 2.68 in (13-27). Hence statistical tests and confidence intervals are strengthened.

In conclusion, we have illustrated the advantages first mentioned in Section 13-1: multiple regression reduces bias and residual variance. Of course, the addition of other regressors (as well as R and T) might further reduce bias and residual variance.[14]

---

[11]When a wrong sign appears on a regression coefficient, it is sometimes called a "nonsense regression" or "nonsense correlation." It would be more accurate to call it a "severely biased" regression. This is further discussed in Section 14-2(f).

[12]The bias of the indirect effect illustrated in Figure 13-4 may be stated more precisely:

simple regression coefficient = direct effect + indirect effect (bias)

$$b_{Yr} = b_{Yr/t} + b_{Yt/r} \, b_{tr} \tag{13-28}$$

where
  b_{Yr} = simple regression coefficient of Y on r
  b_{tr} = simple regression coefficient of t on r
  $b_{Yr/t}$ = multiple regression coefficient of Y on r (holding t fixed)
  $b_{Yt/r}$ = multiple regression coefficient of Y on t (holding r fixed).

[13]The residual variance is reduced from $s^2 = 194$ in (13-26) to $s^2 = 50$ in (13-27). (These values were calculated by computer, at the same time as (13-26) and (13-27).)

[14]Many computer programs for multiple regression add one variable at a time (one "step" at a time; thus the program is called "stepwise" regression). At each step the reduction in residual variance is noted. When enough regressors have been added so that further significant reduction is impossible, the calculation stops. As noted in Section 13-6, however, such a mechanical procedure should not be used blindly; instead the issues of statistical significance should always be interpreted in the light of what is reasonable *a priori*.

PROBLEMS

13-9 Suppose a psychologist computed the following multiple regression on the basis of a random sample of 60 observations from a large population:

$$Y = 64 + 16X_1 - 1.2X_2$$

Standard error	(1.06)	(3.0)	(1.7)
95% C I	($\pm$ 2.12)	($\pm$ 6.0)	($\pm$ 3.4)

Select the statement that is most appropriate for the coefficient $\hat{\beta}_1 = 16$ (and criticize the other statements):

(a) $\hat{\beta}_1$ estimates the total increase in Y that would accompany a unit increase in X_1 and the associated increase in X_2.

(b) $\hat{\beta}_1$ estimates the total increase in Y that would be caused by a unit increase in X_1 (while X_1 caused simultaneously an estimated decrease of 1.2 units in X_2).

(c) $\hat{\beta}_1$ estimates the increase in Y that would accompany a unit increase in X_1, if X_2 were held constant.

(d) $\hat{\beta}_1$ is a fixed parameter that estimates the sample coefficient β_1, with a mean of 16 and a variance of 9.

(e) The null hypothesis ($\hat{\beta}_1 = 0$) should be accepted at the 95% confidence level.

13-10 What further criticism do you now have of your roommate's analysis in Problem 13-8(a)?

13-11 Cigarette smokers have a life expectancy about 5 years less than nonsmokers. Is all of this necessarily caused by their smoking? Which way do you think the bias is (if any)?

13-12 True or false? If false, correct it:

(a) The simple regression equation (13-26) can occasionally be useful. For example, in the absence of any information on temperature, it would correctly lead us to hope for a year with low rainfall.

(b) In view of the positive multiple regression coefficients in (13-27), however, it would be even better to hope for a year with low rainfall and then irrigate.

13-13 (a) Suppose there was a positive correlation between R and T in Figure 13-4. Would there be a bias in simple regression? If so, in which direction?

(b) Now suppose there were no correlation between R and T in Figure 13-4 (or to use a mathematical term, suppose R and T were orthogonal). Would there be a bias in simple regression? If so, in which direction?

(c) True or false? If false, correct it:
Applying simple regression to a multiple regression problem will introduce bias if the independent variables are uncorrelated.

13-14 Note the similarity of the coefficient for X calculated in the simple regression (11-18) and calculated in the multiple regression (last line in Table 13-2).

(a) What does this imply about the correlation of X and Z?

(b) Do you find your answer to (a) intuitively surprising? Explain.

13-15 (a) From Table 13-4 calculate the regression coefficient of T on R.

(b) Using also the regression coefficients calculated in (13-26) and (13-27), verify (13-28).

13-9   DUMMY VARIABLES

(a) Introductory Example

Suppose we wish to investigate how the public purchase of government bonds (B) is related to national income (Y). A hypothetical scatter of annual observations of these two variables is shown for Canada in Figure 13-5 and in Table 13-5. It is immediately evident that the relationship of bonds to income follows two distinct patterns—one applying in wartime (1940–1945), the other in peacetime.

The normal relation of B to Y (say L_0) is subject to an upward shift (to L_1) during wartime; heavy bond purchases in those years is explained not by Y alone, but also by the patriotic wartime campaign to induce public bond purchases. B therefore should be related to Y and another

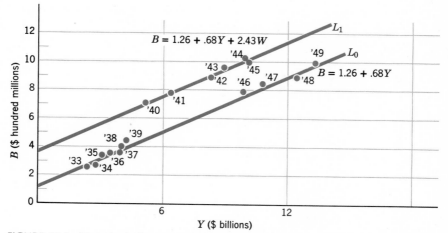

FIGURE 13-5 Hypothetical scatter of public purchases of bonds (B) and national income (Y).

Table 13-5 Calculations for Regression of B on Y and W, where W is a Dummy Variable.

Year	B	Y	W	$y = Y - \bar{Y}$	$w = W - \bar{W}$	yw	By	Bw	y^2	w^2
1933	2.6	2.4	0	−4.44	−.35	1.55	−11.54	−.91	19.71	.12
1934	3.0	2.8	0	−4.04	−.35	1.41	−12.12	−1.05	16.32	.12
1935	3.6	3.1	0	−3.74	−.35	1.31	−13.46	−1.26	13.99	.12
1936	3.7	3.4	0	−3.44	−.35	1.20	−12.73	−1.29	11.83	.12
1937	3.8	3.9	0	−2.94	−.35	1.03	−11.17	−1.33	8.64	.12
1938	4.1	4.0	0	−2.84	−.35	0.99	−11.64	−1.43	8.07	.12
1939	4.4	4.2	0	−2.64	−.35	0.92	−11.62	−1.54	6.97	.12
1940	7.1	5.1	1	−1.74	.65	−1.13	−12.35	4.62	3.03	.42
1941	8.0	6.3	1	−.54	.65	−.35	−4.32	5.20	.29	.42
1942	8.9	8.1	1	1.26	.65	.82	11.21	5.78	1.59	.42
1943	9.7	8.8	1	1.96	.65	1.27	19.01	6.30	3.84	.42
1944	10.2	9.6	1	2.76	.65	1.79	28.15	6.63	7.62	.42
1945	10.1	9.7	1	2.86	.65	1.86	28.89	6.56	8.18	.42
1946	7.9	9.6	0	2.76	−.35	−.97	21.80	−2.77	7.62	.12
1947	8.7	10.4	0	3.56	−.35	−1.25	30.97	−3.05	12.67	.12
1948	9.1	12.0	0	5.16	−.35	−1.81	46.96	−3.19	26.63	.12
1949	10.1	12.9	0	6.06	−.35	−2.12	61.21	−3.53	36.72	.12

(War years: 1940–1945)

$$\sum B = 115 \qquad \sum Y = 116.3 \qquad \sum W = 6$$

$$\bar{B} = \frac{\sum B}{17} \qquad \bar{Y} = \frac{\sum Y}{17} \qquad \bar{W} = \frac{6}{17}$$

$$= 6.76 \qquad\qquad = 6.84 \qquad\qquad = .35$$

$$\sum yw \qquad \sum By \qquad \sum Bw \qquad \sum y^2 \qquad \sum w^2$$

$$= 6.52 \qquad = 147.25 \qquad = 13.74 \qquad = 193.72 \qquad = 3.84$$

Estimating equations (13-4)
$$\begin{cases} \sum By = \hat{\beta}\sum y^2 + \hat{\gamma}\sum yw \\ \sum Bw = \hat{\beta}\sum yw + \hat{\gamma}\sum w^2 \end{cases}$$

or
$$\begin{cases} 147.25 = \hat{\beta}193.72 + \hat{\gamma}6.52 \\ 13.74 = \hat{\beta}6.52 + \hat{\gamma}3.84 \end{cases}$$

Solution:
$$\begin{cases} \hat{\beta} = .68 \\ \hat{\gamma} = 2.43 \end{cases}$$

Thus our estimated regression is: $B = 6.76 + .68y + 2.43w$

Or, expressed in terms of the original variables: $B = 6.76 + .68(Y - \bar{Y}) + 2.43(W - \bar{W})$

$$= 6.76 + .68(Y - 6.84) + 2.43(W - .35)$$

$$\overline{B = 1.26 + .68Y + 2.43W}$$

variable—war W. W does not have a whole range of values, but only two: we arbitrarily set its value at 1 for all wartime years and at 0 for all peacetime years.[15] (Since W is either "on" or "off," it is a dummy variable of the kind we encountered in Section 6-5.) Our model is therefore

$$B = \alpha + \beta Y + \gamma W + e \qquad (13\text{-}29)$$

where $W = 0$ for peacetime years, and
$\qquad = 1$ for wartime years.
This single equation is seen to be equivalent to the following two equations:

$$B = \alpha + \beta Y + e \qquad \text{for peacetime} \qquad (13\text{-}30)$$
$$B = \alpha + \beta Y + \gamma + e \qquad \text{for wartime} \qquad (13\text{-}31)$$

We note that γ represents the effect of wartime on bond sales; and β represents the effect of income changes. (The latter is assumed to remain the same in war or peace.) The important point to note is that one multiple regression of B on Y and W as in (13-29) will yield the *two* estimated lines shown in Figure 13-5; L_0 is the estimate of the peacetime function (13-30), and L_1 is the estimate of the wartime function (13-31).

Complete calculations for our example are set out in Table 13-5, and the procedure is interpreted in Figure 13-6. Since all observations are at $W = 0$ or $W = 1$, the scatter is confined to the two vertical planes π_0 and π_1. The estimated regression plane,

$$B = \hat{\alpha} + \hat{\beta} Y + \hat{\gamma} W \qquad (13\text{-}32)$$

may be viewed as a plane resting on two supporting buttresses L_0 and L_1; some of the observed dots of course lie above this fitted plane, and others below it. The slopes of L_0 and L_1 are (by assumption) equal[16] to the common value $\hat{\beta}$, and $\hat{\gamma}$ is the estimated wartime shift.

_____

[15] Actually, this 0-1 coding is not entirely arbitrary; it is motivated by the simplicity it brings to the multiple regression analysis. In particular, when the coefficient of W is given the customary interpretation (13-25), it gives the increase in the response (bond sales) if W is increased one unit (as we go from peace 0 to war 1), if the other variable (income) were held constant. This is just the distance between lines L_0 and L_1 in Figure 13-5, as we soon confirm in the text following (13-31).

[16] This restriction means that L_0 and L_1 are *not* independently fitted. In other words, our least squares plane (13-29) is fitted first; L_0 and L_1 are simply "read off" this plane.
(cont'd)

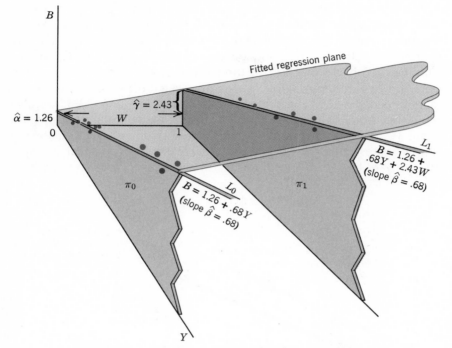

FIGURE 13-6   Multiple regression with a dummy variable (W).

Thus L_0 does *not* represent a least squares fit to the left-hand scatter, nor does L_1 represent a least squares fit to the right-hand scatter.

This dummy variable method of fitting a single multiple regression plane and then reading off L_0 and L_1, can be compared to the alternative method of independently fitting two simple regression lines to the two scatters in Figure 13-6. This model would be:

$$B = \alpha_1 + \beta_1 Y + e_1 \qquad \text{for wartime}$$
$$B = \alpha_2 + \beta_2 Y + e_2 \qquad \text{for peacetime}$$

and the estimated slopes ($\hat{\beta}_1$ and $\hat{\beta}_2$) would generally not be the same.

Estimates of four parameters are required for this model, rather than the three in the dummy variable model (13-29); thus one advantage of the dummy model is that it conserves one extra degree of freedom. Its disadvantage is that it requires an additional prior restriction—that the two slopes are equal. But this is not always a disadvantage. For instance, in our example it may be better to assume the two slopes equal than to independently fit a wartime function to only five observations. The very small wartime sample may yield a very unreliable estimate of slope, and it may make better sense to pool all the data to estimate one slope coefficient.

In a dummy variable model—as in any regression model—we can see how ignoring one variable would invite bias, as well as an increased residual variance. For example, consider what happens if W is ignored, so that the scatter involves only the two dimensions B and Y. Geometrically, this involves projecting the three-dimensional scatter in Figure 13-6 onto the two-dimensional B-Y plane, as in Figure 13-7a. This is immediately recognized as the same scatter plotted in Figure 13-5; we also reproduce from that diagram L_0 and L_1, the estimated multiple regression using W as a dummy variable. Now if we erroneously calculate the simple regression of B on Y, L_2 say, it clearly has too great a slope. This upward bias results from the fact that war years tended to be high

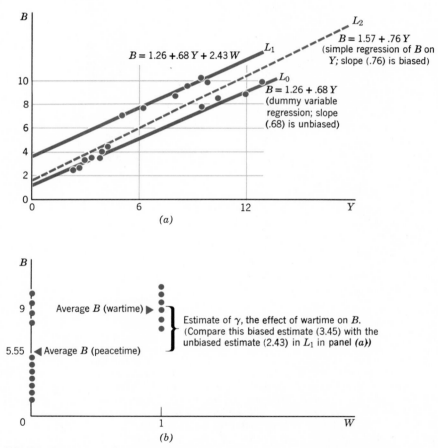

FIGURE 13-7 Error when one explanatory variable is ignored. (a) Biased estimate of slope (the effect of Y) because the categorical variable W is ignored. (b) Biased estimate of the effect of W because the numerical variable Y is ignored.

income years: thus, on the right-middle side of this scatter, higher bond sales that should be attributed in part to wartime would be (erroneously) attributed to income alone.

A similar error is to be expected in any investigation of B and W that ignores Y. With no Y dimension, our scatter in Figure 13-6 would be projected onto the B-W plane, as in Figure 13-7b. In this diagram the only way to estimate the wartime effect is to look at the difference in sample means,[17] which is too large. This upward bias comes from the same cause: higher bond sales that should be attributed in part to higher income would be (erroneously) attributed to wartime alone.

PROBLEMS

13-16 Consider the estimated multiple regression of personal income Y as a function of age A, number of years of education E, and sex S (where sex is coded 0 for male, 1 for female):

$$Y = \hat{\alpha} + \hat{\beta}_1 A + \hat{\beta}_2 E + \hat{\beta}_3 S$$

Select the most appropriate statement (and criticize the others): The coefficient $\hat{\beta}_3$ may be interpreted as the estimate of
(a) the amount of income that the average man earns more than the average woman;
(b) the amount of income that a woman would earn more than a man of the same age and education;
(c) the amount of further age and education the average woman would need in order to earn as much as the average man.

13-17 Referring to the bond sales example, estimate what bond sales would have been in 1946 if the war had lasted till then, rather than 1945.

13-18 (a) What would the estimate of bond sales in 1950 be, given a national income of $13.6 billion?
(b) What is the equivalent point estimate, using a simple regression of B on Y (ignoring W)? Explain why this estimate is inferior.

13-19 (a) Referring to Figures 13-5 and 13-7a, suppose the last four years were missing. In a simple regression of B on Y, will the bias of the slope be less or greater than before (when all the years were used)? Why?
(b) Repeat (a), assuming instead that the first seven years are missing. What will the bias be then? Explain.

_____

[17] This is equivalent to a simple regression of B on W. Because of the peculiar scatter involved, this regression line would pass through these two means; thus their difference represents the effect of W on B.

13-10   **REGRESSION, ANALYSIS OF VARIANCE,
                                               AND ANALYSIS OF COVARIANCE**

(a) Regression with Dummies Equivalent to ANOVA

If all the independent variables are categorical (dummy) variables, then regression analysis is essentially the familiar analysis of variance (ANOVA). This can be proved in general; but it is more instructive to illustrate it in the simplest case of one independent dummy variable. In Problem 10-3 we applied analysis of variance to the problem of whether the income (Y) of men and women differs. Dummy regression could alternatively have been used, with a model of the form:

$$Y = \alpha + \beta G + e$$

where

$$G = 0 \text{ for men}$$
$$= 1 \text{ for women.}$$

The data is analyzed in Table 13-6. We find the same value ($\hat{\beta} = -8$) for the difference in groups that we found in Problem 10-3 ($\overline{Y}_1 - \overline{Y}_2 = -8$). Note also that in both tests the residual variance (48) is the same; so is the standard error of estimate ($\sqrt{48}\ \sqrt{1/2}$). Hence the two procedures are seen to be identical.

The example of bond sales (13-29) was a regression on a numerical variable (income) and a dummy variable (wartime). This could alternatively be described as a combination of standard regression analysis and analysis of variance. Technically, this combination is referred to as analysis of covariance (ANOCOVA), although this term is often reserved for cases in which the effect of the dummy variable (wartime) is of prime interest and the other variable (income) is explicitly introduced only to remove its noise effects (i.e., to remove the bias shown in Figure 13-7b, and to reduce the residual variance).

Another application of the analysis of covariance might be a study of the effects of racial discrimination on income; here the major concern would be the effect on income of the dummy variable (black versus white), with a simultaneous regression on other numerical variables (years of experience, education, etc.) simply a means of keeping these other influences from biasing the result.

(b) Summary

Multiple regression is an extremely useful tool with many broad applications. We define three special cases, distinguished by the nature of the independent variables:

Table 13-6 Regression Using Only a Categorical Variable, Being then Equivalent to the Analysis of Variance

Y	G	$g = G - \bar{G}$	Yg	g^2	$\hat{Y} = 56 - 8g$	$Y - \hat{Y}$	$(Y - \hat{Y})^2$
60	0	$-1/2$	-30	$1/4$	60	0	0
70	0	$-1/2$	-35	$1/4$	60	10	100
62	0	$-1/2$	-31	$1/4$	60	2	4
48	0	$-1/2$	-24	$1/4$	60	-12	144
48	1	$1/2$	24	$1/4$	52	-4	16
56	1	$1/2$	28	$1/4$	52	4	16
50	1	$1/2$	25	$1/4$	52	-2	4
54	1	$1/2$	27	$1/4$	52	2	4

$\bar{Y} = 56$ $\bar{G} = 4/8 = 1/2$ $\sum Yg = -16$ $\sum g^2 = 2$ $\sum (Y - \hat{Y})^2 = 288$

$$\hat{\beta} = \frac{\sum Yg}{\sum g^2} = -16/2 = -8$$

$$s^2 = \frac{1}{6}\sum (Y - \hat{Y})^2 = 48$$
(This is residual variance, also appearing in solution table in Problem 10-3)

$$|t| = \frac{\hat{\beta}}{s/\sqrt{\sum g^2}} = \frac{8}{\sqrt{48}/\sqrt{2}} = 1.63$$

which is less extreme than the critical t value of 2.45, therefore not statistically significant.

1. *"Standard regression"* is regression on only numerical variables.
2. *Analysis of Variance (ANOVA)* is equivalent to regression on only categorical (dummy) variables.
3. *Analysis of Covariance (ANOCOVA)* is regression on both categorical and numerical variables.

These three techniques are compared using the hypothetical data of Figures 13-8 to 13-11, which show the possible ways that mortality may be analyzed.

The hypothetical data in Figure 13-8 shows a sample of observations of the mortality of American men. Applying standard regression, we would reject the hypothesis that the true slope $\beta = 0$; thus we conclude that age does affect the mortality rate. In the process, we derive a useful estimate $\hat{\beta}$, of *how* age affects mortality.

If the data is collected into three groups, the result is the scatter shown in Figure 13-9. Note that this is exactly the same set of mortality (Y) observations as in Figure 13-8. The only difference is that we are no longer as detailed about the age (X) variable. But with the data now assembled in three classifications, ANOVA can be applied[18] to test whether the means of these three scatters are significantly different. Once again, the conclusion is that age affects mortality. However, ANOVA does not tell us *how* age affects mortality, unless we extend it to multiple comparisons.

So long as X is numerical, as in Figures 13-8 and 13-9, we conclude that standard regression can be applied and is often the preferred tech-

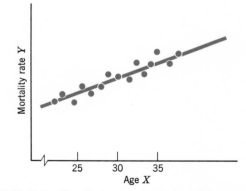

FIGURE 13-8   "Standard regression," since X is numerical.

---

[18] Standard regression could also be applied, with a line fitted to the scatter in Figure 13-9. However, if this technique is to be applied, it is more efficient to use the ungrouped data of Figure 13-8.

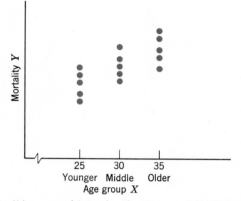

FIGURE 13-9   X is grouped into classifications, and ANOVA may be used.

nique. But when X is categorical, it cannot be applied. For example, in Figure 13-10 we graph some hypothetical data on how mortality depends on nationality;[19] our X variable ranges over various categories, (American, British, etc.) and there is no natural way of placing these on a numerical scale—or even ordering them. Hence, standard regression is out of the question,[20] and ANOVA must be used.

If mortality is dependent on income as well as nationality, the analysis of covariance shown in Figure 13-11 is appropriate. This uses nationality

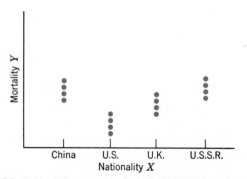

FIGURE 13-10   X is categorical, and ANOVA must be used.

---

[19] In Figures 13-10 and 13-11, all samples are assumed drawn from a single age group; we consider only the other factors influencing mortality.

[20] To confirm, note that a standard linear regression line fitted to the scatter in Figure 13-10 would yield $\hat{\beta} \simeq 0$ (i.e., no evidence that nationality matters). Yet, if China is graphed last rather than first, $\hat{\beta} \not\simeq 0$ and it would be concluded that nationality does matter. Thus, the conclusion would depend on the arbitrary ordering of the nationality variable.

FIGURE 13-11   Analysis of covariance for a categorical variable (nationality) and numerical variable (income).

dummies, with the numerical variable income explicitly introduced to eliminate the error that it might otherwise cause. We confirm that this has greatly improved our analysis. Whereas it appeared in Figure 13-10 that a national characteristic of the British was a lower mortality rate than the Chinese, we see in Figure 13-11 that it is not this simple. The height of the fitted lines for China and the United Kingdom are practically the same. The lower U.K. mortality rate is explained solely by higher income.

In summary, standard regression is the more powerful tool whenever the independent variable X is numerical and the dependence of Y on X can be described by a simple function. Analysis of variance is appropriate if the independent variable is a set of unordered categories.

PROBLEMS

13-20 Construct a confidence interval for β using the data in Table 13-6. Compare this with the answer to Problem 10-3*b*.

13-21 The following is the result of a test of gas consumption on a sample of 6 cars:

	Miles Per Gallon	Engine Horsepower
Make A	21	210
	18	240
	15	310
Make B	20	220
	18	260
	15	320

(a) Determine the difference in the performance (miles per gallon) of the two makes, allowing for horsepower differences.

(b) Graph your results as in Figure 13-11.

*13-22 Using the data in Problem 10-1, estimate the regression of yield on fertilizer type, using two dummies. Compare with your answer to Problem 10-1. (*Hint.* Let

$$D_1 = 1 \text{ if fertilizer } A \text{ is used}$$
$$= 0 \text{ otherwise}$$
$$D_2 = 1 \text{ if fertilizer } B \text{ is used}$$
$$= 0 \text{ otherwise.})$$

Review Problems

13-23 A sociologist computed a regression of mobility M as a function of family income X_1

$$M = b_0 + b_1 X_1$$

Then he realized that family size X_2 was also relevant, and so calculated the multiple regression

$$M = c_0 + c_1 X_1 + c_2 X_2$$

Under what conditions will the coefficients of X_1 in the two regressions be equal ($b_1 = c_1$)?

13-24 (a) Based on the following sample information, use the analysis of covariance to describe how education is related to father's income and place of residence.

(b) Graph your results.

	Years of Formal Education (E)	Father's Income (F)
Urban sample	15	$8,000
	18	11,000
	12	9,000
	16	12,000
Rural sample	13	$5,000
	10	3,000
	11	6,000
	14	10,000

13-25 A sociologist collected a random sample of 1000 men to see how divorce rates are related to religion, income, region, and degree of urbanization. Outline how you would analyze the data.

APPENDIX 13-1   **Lines and Planes; Elementary Geometry**

(a) Lines

The definitive characteristic of a straight line is that it continues forever in the *same constant direction*. In Figure 13-12 we make this idea precise. In moving from one point P_1 to another point P_2, we denote the horizontal distance by ΔX (where Δ means change, or difference) and the vertical distance by ΔY. Then the slope[21] is defined as

$$\text{slope} = \frac{\Delta Y}{\Delta X} \tag{13-33}$$

The characteristic of a straight line is that this slope remains the same everywhere, i.e.,

$$\frac{\Delta Y}{\Delta X} = b \text{ (a constant)} \tag{13-34}$$

For example, the slope between P_3 and P_4 is the same as between P_1 and P_2, as calculation will verify:

$$P_1 \text{ to } P_2: \quad \frac{\Delta Y}{\Delta X} = \frac{3}{6} = .50$$

$$P_3 \text{ to } P_4: \quad \frac{\Delta Y}{\Delta X} = \frac{2}{4} = .50 \tag{13-35}$$

A very instructive case occurs when X increases just one unit; then (13-34) yields

$$\text{when } \Delta X = 1, \quad \Delta Y = b \tag{13-36}$$

In words, "b is the increase in Y that accompanies a unit increase in X," which agrees with the regression interpretation (13-20).

It is now very easy to derive the equation of a line, if we know its

---

[21] Also called the gradient, the slope is a concept useful in engineering as well as mathematics. For example, if a highway rises 12 feet over a distance of 200 feet, its slope is $12/200 = 6\%$.

FIGURE 13-12 A straight line is characterized by constant slope, $\Delta Y / \Delta X = b$.

slope b and any one point on the line. Suppose the one point we know is P_0, the Y-intercept; since its coordinates as shown in Figure 13-13 are 0 and a_0, it is denoted $P_0 (0, a_0)$. In moving to any other point $P(X, Y)$ on the line, we may write

$$\text{slope, } \frac{\Delta Y}{\Delta X} = \frac{Y - a_0}{X - 0} \tag{13-37}$$

For the line to be straight, we insisted in (13-34) that this slope must equal the constant b:

$$\frac{Y - a_0}{X - 0} = b$$

$$Y - a_0 = bX$$

$$\overline{Y = a_0 + bX} \tag{13-38}$$

$$\text{(11-4) proved}$$

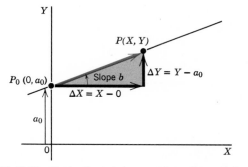

FIGURE 13-13 Derivation of the equation of a straight line.

Hence the value of Y is seen to depend on the Y-intercept a_0, the slope b, and the value of X (i.e., how far along this line you are).

(b) Planes

In Figure 13-14, we show a plane in the 3-dimensional (X, Y, Z) space. Let L_{XY} denote the line where this plane cuts the XY plane; then we may think of the plane as a grid of lines parallel to L_{XY} with slope b, or equally well, as a grid of lines parallel to L_{ZY} with slope c.

Now suppose we start at point P_1. If we hold Z constant and move to P_2, then we are moving along one of the grid lines parallel to L_{XY} (with slope $= b$). Thus, by analogy with (13-36)

$$
\begin{array}{ll}
\text{If } Z \text{ is held constant,} & \\
\quad \text{when } \Delta X = 1, \quad \Delta Y = b &
\end{array}
\tag{13-39}
$$

In words, "b is the increase in Y that accompanies a unit increase in X, while Z is held constant," which agrees with the regression interpretation (13-23).

Similarly we can interpret a move from P_1 to P_3:

$$
\begin{array}{ll}
\text{If } X \text{ is held constant,} & \\
\quad \text{when } \Delta Z = 1, \quad \Delta Y = c &
\end{array}
\tag{13-40}
$$

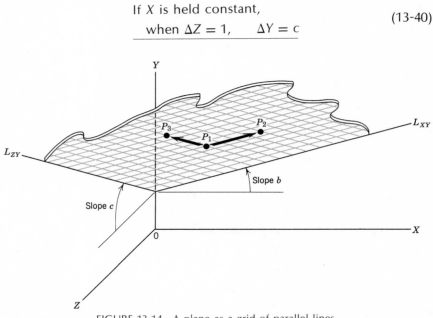

FIGURE 13-14 A plane as a grid of parallel lines.

FIGURE 13-15   Derivation of the equation of a plane.

In words, "c is the increase in Y that accompanies a unit increase in Z, while X is held constant."

It is now very easy to derive the equation of a plane. Referring to Figure 13-15, let us start at the Y-intercept P_0 $(0, 0, a_0)$. Let us move to the typical point $P(X, Z, Y)$ in two steps: (1) along the line L_{ZY} to an intermediate point I, and then (2) parallel to L_{XY} to finally reach P. Then we find Y (the height of P) as follows.

1. Just as (13-38) gives the height as a function of X, so we analogously find that the height of I as a function of Z is

$$a_0 + cZ \qquad (13\text{-}41)$$

2. To move from I to P, note that our intercept at I is now $(a_0 + cZ)$ as given in (13-41); note also that we will be moving along a grid line parallel to L_{XY} with slope b. Applying (13-38),

$$Y = (a_0 + cZ) + bX$$
$$\overline{Y = a_0 + bX + cZ} \qquad (13\text{-}42)$$

This is the equation of the plane, which agrees with (13-2) (except for notational changes, of course).

Chapter 14

CORRELATION

*Q. What is the difference between capitalism and
socialism?*

*A. Under capitalism, man exploits man. Under so-
cialism, it's just the opposite.*

Anonymous

14-1   SIMPLE CORRELATION

Simple regression analysis showed us *how* variables are linearly related; correlation analysis will only show us to which *degree* variables are linearly related. In regression analysis, a whole mathematical function is estimated (the regression equation); but correlation analysis yields only one number—an index designed to give an immediate picture of how closely two variables move together. Although correlation is a less powerful technique than regression, the two are so closely related mathematically that correlation often becomes a useful aid in interpreting regression analysis; in fact, this is the major reason for studying it.

(a) The Population Correlation Coefficient ρ (rho)

In (5-28) we have already defined the population correlation,

$$\rho = \frac{\sigma_{XY}}{\sigma_X \sigma_Y} \tag{14-1}$$

or, noting (5-24)

$$\rho = \frac{E(X - \mu_X)(Y - \mu_Y)}{\sigma_X \sigma_Y} \tag{14-2}$$

It is useful to reexpress this in terms of the standardized X and Y,

$$\rho = E\left(\frac{X - \mu_X}{\sigma_X}\right)\left(\frac{Y - \mu_Y}{\sigma_Y}\right) \tag{14-3}$$

(b) The Sample Correlation Coefficient r

By analogy with (14-3), the sample correlation is

$$r_{XY} \triangleq \frac{1}{n-1} \sum_{i=1}^{n} \left(\frac{X_i - \bar{X}}{s_X}\right)\left(\frac{Y_i - \bar{Y}}{s_Y}\right) \tag{14-4}$$

An intuitive development of this is shown in Figure 14-1, closely parallel-ing the development of population correlation in Section 5-3b. Panel (a) shows the scatter of marks on a verbal (Y) and mathematical (X) test scored by a sample of eight college students; these data are also set out in the first two columns in Table 14-1. To ensure that our resulting index will be independent of the choice of origin, we shift both axes in panel (b) with x and y now defined as deviations from the mean. Values of these translated variables are given in columns 3 and 4 of Table 14-1.

Suppose we multiply the x and y coordinate values for each student, and sum them all. This $\Sigma\, xy$ gives us a good measure of how math and verbal results tend to move together. Whenever an observation such as P_1 falls in the first quadrant in Figure 14-1b, both its x and y coordinates will be positive, and their product xy positive. This also holds true for any observation in the third quadrant, with both coordinates negative. The product is negative only for observations such as P_2 in the second or fourth quadrant, (one coordinate positive, the other negative). If X and Y move together, most observations will fall in the first and third quadrants; consequently most products xy will be positive, as will their sum—a reflection of the positive relationship between X and Y. But if X and Y are negatively related, (i.e., when one rises the other falls), most observations will fall in the second and fourth quadrants, yielding a negative value for our $\Sigma\, xy$ index. We conclude that as an index of correlation, $\Sigma\, xy$ at least carries the right sign. Moreover, when there is no relationship between X and Y, and our observations are distributed evenly over the four quadrants, positive and negative terms will cancel, and this index will be zero.

There are just two ways that $\Sigma\, xy$ can be improved. First, it is depend-

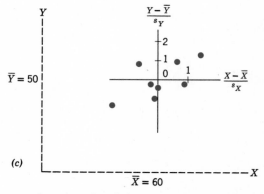

FIGURE 14-1 Scatter of math and verbal scores. (a) Original observations. (b) Axes shifted. (c) Axes rescaled to standard units.

Table 14-1   Math Score (X) and Corresponding Verbal Score (Y) of a Sample of Eight Students Entering College.

(1) X	(2) Y	(3) $x = X - \bar{X}$	(4) $y = Y - \bar{Y}$	(5) xy	(6) x^2	(7) y^2	Regression of Y on X			Regression of X on Y		
							(8) $\hat{Y} = \bar{Y} + bx$	(9) $Y - \hat{Y}$	(10) $(Y - \hat{Y})^2$	(11) $\hat{X} = \bar{X} + b_\bullet y$	(12) $X - \hat{X}$	(13) $(X - \hat{X})^2$
36	35	−24	−15	360	576	225	37.96	−2.96	8.76	48.27	−12.27	150.55
80	65	20	15	300	400	225	60.03	4.97	24.70	71.73	8.27	68.39
50	60	−10	10	−100	100	100	44.99	15.01	225.30	67.82	−17.82	317.55
58	39	−2	−11	22	4	121	49.00	−10.00	100.00	51.39	6.61	43.69
72	48	12	−2	−24	144	4	56.02	−8.02	64.32	58.44	13.56	183.87
60	44	0	−6	0	0	36	50.00	−6.00	36.00	55.31	4.69	22.00
56	48	−4	−2	8	16	4	47.99	.01	.00	58.44	−2.44	5.95
68	61	8	11	88	64	121	54.01	6.99	48.86	68.61	−.61	.37

$\sum X$
$= 480$
$\bar{X} = 60$

$\sum Y$
$= 400$
$\bar{Y} = 50$

$\sum x = 0$

$\sum y = 0$

$\sum xy$
$= 654$

$\sum x^2$
$= 1304$

$\sum y^2$
$= 836$

Regression of Y on X:

$$\hat{\beta} = \frac{\sum xy}{\sum x^2}$$
$$= .5015$$

Regression of X on Y:

$$\hat{\beta}_\bullet = \frac{\sum xy}{\sum y^2}$$
$$= .782$$

$$\sum (Y - \hat{Y})^2$$
$$= 508$$

$$s^2 = \frac{\sum (Y - \hat{Y})^2}{n - 2}$$
$$= \frac{508}{6}$$
$$= 84.7$$
$$s = 9.20$$

$$\sum (X - \hat{X})^2$$
$$= 792.37$$

$$s_\bullet^2 = \frac{\sum (X - \hat{X})^2}{n - 2}$$
$$= \frac{792}{6}$$
$$= 132$$
$$s_\bullet = 11.5$$

ent on sample size. (Suppose we observed exactly the same sort of scatter from a sample of double the size; our index would also double, even though the picture of how these variables move together remained the same.) To avoid this problem we divide by the sample size—actually[1] by $(n-1)$—to yield the index

$$\text{sample covariance} = s_{XY} \triangleq \frac{\sum xy}{n-1} \qquad (14\text{-}5)$$

$$= \frac{1}{n-1} \sum (X_i - \bar{X})(Y_i - \bar{Y}) \qquad (14\text{-}6)$$
like (5-24)

This is a highly useful concept in statistics. But it does have one remaining weakness: it depends on the units in which x and y are measured. (Suppose the math test had been marked out of 50 instead of 100; x values and our index would be only half as large—even though the degree to which verbal and mathematical performance is related would not have changed.) This difficulty is avoided by measuring both variables in terms of standard units; both x and y are divided by their observed standard deviations. This step is shown in Figure 14-1c, with the resulting index being the sample correlation coefficient (14-4).

Finally, to simplify calculations (14-4) is often reduced to:

$$r = \frac{\sum (X_i - \bar{X})(Y_i - \bar{Y})}{\sqrt{\sum (X_i - \bar{X})^2 \sum (Y_i - \bar{Y})^2}}$$

$$= \frac{\sum xy}{\sqrt{\sum x^2 \sum y^2}} \qquad (14\text{-}7)$$

For example the data in columns (5) to (7) of Table 14-1 are applied to (14-7) to calculate the correlation coefficient between the math and verbal scores of a sample of eight students,

$$r = \frac{654}{\sqrt{(1304)(836)}} = .62 \qquad (14\text{-}8)$$

---

[1]The divisor is $(n-1)$ rather than n so that it will cancel in (14-4) with the divisor $\sqrt{n-1}$ appearing in both s_X and s_Y.

Some idea of how *r* behaves is given in Figure 14-2; especially note panel (*b*). When there is a perfect linear association, the product of the coordinates in every case is positive; thus, their sum (and the resulting coefficient of correlation) is as large as possible. The same argument holds for the perfect *inverse* relation of Y and X shown in panel (*d*).

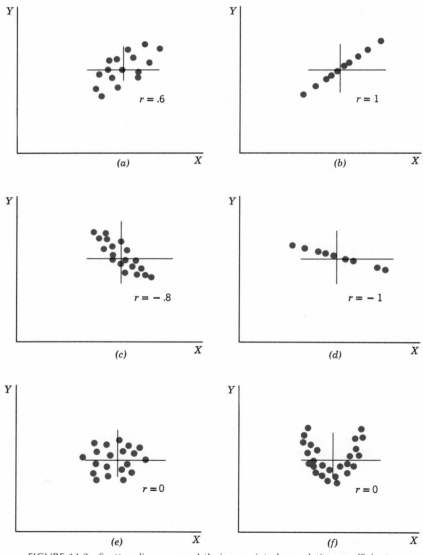

FIGURE 14-2   Scatter diagrams and their associated correlation coefficients.

This suggests that r has an upper limit of $+1$ and a lower limit of -1. (This is proved in Section 14-2c below.)

Finally compare panels (e) and (f). Our calculation of r in either case is zero, because positive products of the coordinates are offset by negative ones. Yet when we examine the two scatters, no relation between X and Y is confirmed in (e)—but a strong relation is evident in (f); in this case a knowledge of X will tell us a great deal about Y. A zero value for r therefore does not imply "no relation"; rather, it means "no linear relation." Thus correlation is a measure of *linear relation* only; it is of no use in describing nonlinear relations. This brings us to the next critical question: In calculating r, what can we infer about the underlying population ρ?

(c) Inference from r to ρ

Before we can draw any statistical inference about ρ from our sample statistic r, we must clarify our assumptions about the parent population from which our sample was drawn. In our example, this would be the math and verbal marks scored by *all* college entrants.

This population might appear as in Figure 14-3, except that there would, of course, be many more dots in this scatter, each representing another student. If we subdivide both X and Y into class intervals, the area in our diagram will be divided up in a checkerboard pattern. From the relative frequency (sampling probability) in each of the squares, the histogram in Figure 14-4 is constructed.[2] If this histogram is rescaled to relative frequency *density*, and then approximated by a smooth surface, the result is the continuous function shown in Figure 14-5, representing the probability density of any X and Y combination.

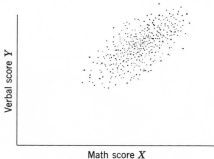

Math score X

FIGURE 14-3   Bivariate population scattergram (math and verbal scores).

_____

[2]Our example is of a finite population, but a similar argument would apply for an infinite population.

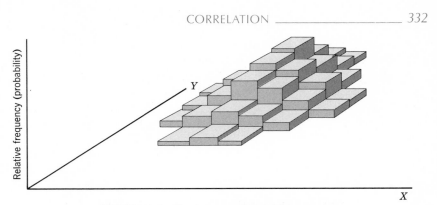

FIGURE 14-4 Bivariate population histogram.

A special kind of joint distribution of X and Y is assumed in making statistical inferences in simple correlation analysis—a bivariate normal distribution. Bivariate, because both X and Y are random variables; one is not fixed, as was the fertilizer in Chapter 11. Normal, because the conditional distribution of X or of Y is always normal. Specifically, if we slice the surface at any value of Y, (say Y_0), the shape of the resulting cross section is normal. Similarly, if we select any X value (say X_0) and slice the surface in this other direction, the resulting cross section is also normal.

It is worthwhile pausing briefly to consider the alternative way that the bivariate normal population shown in three dimensions in Figure 14-5 can be graphed in two dimensions. Instead of slicing the surface vertically as we did in that diagram, slice it horizontally as in Figure 14-6. The resulting cross section is an ellipse, representing all X, Y combinations with the same probability density. This "isoprobability" curve is

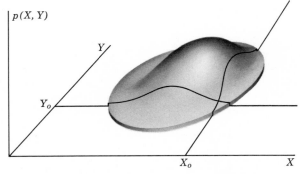

FIGURE 14-5 Bivariate normal distribution.

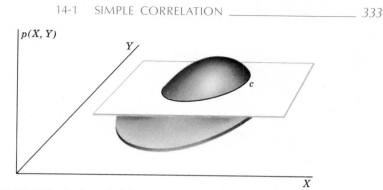

$p(X, Y)$

FIGURE 14-6   An isoprobability ellipse from a bivariate normal surface.

marked "c" in the two dimensional X, Y space in Figure 14-7; isoprobability ellipses defined when this surface is sliced horizontally at higher and lower levels are also shown. (Social scientists will recognize this as the familiar technique of forcing a three-dimensional function into a two-dimensional space by showing one variable as a set of isoquants, isobars, or whatever.) It will also be useful in Figure 14-7 to mark the major axis d common to all these isoprobability ellipses. If the bivariate normal distribution concentrates about its major axis, ρ increases. Several examples of populations, and their associated correlation coefficients ρ are shown in Figure 14-8.

Provided that the parent population is bivariate normal, inferences about the population ρ can easily be made from a sample correlation r. Recall the inferences about π from P in Chapter 8. Using the same reasoning that established Figure 8-3, Figure 14-9 is constructed. Thus from any sample r, a 95% confidence interval for the population ρ can

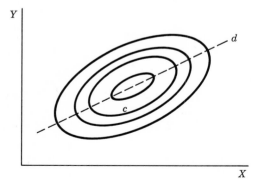

FIGURE 14-7   The bivariate normal distribution shown as a set of isoprobability ellipses.

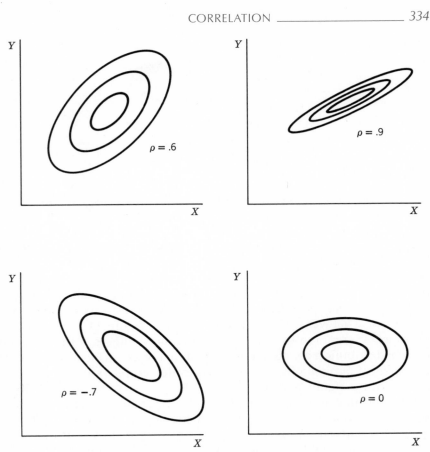

FIGURE 14-8   Examples of population correlations.

be found. For example, if a sample of 10 students has $r = .6$, we show in red the 95% confidence interval for ρ, read vertically as

$$-.05 < \rho < .87 \qquad (14\text{-}9)$$

Because of space limitations, we shall concentrate in the balance of this chapter on sample correlations, and ignore the corresponding population correlations. But each time a sample correlation is introduced, it should be recognized that an equivalent population correlation is defined similarly, and inferences may be made about it from the sample correlation.

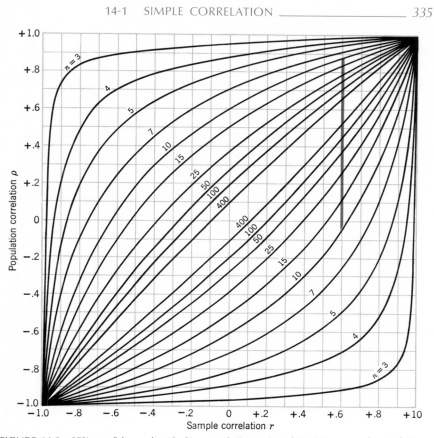

FIGURE 14-9 95% confidence bands for correlation ρ in a bivariate normal population, for various sample sizes n. Reproduced with the permission of Professor E. S. Pearson from F. N. David, *Tables of the Ordinates and Probability Integral of the Distribution of the Correlation Coefficient in Small Samples*, Cambridge University Press, 1938.)

PROBLEMS

14-1

Son's Height (inches)	Father's Height (inches)
68	64
66	66
72	71
73	70
66	69

From the above random sample of 5 son and father heights, find
(a) The sample correlation r;
(b) The 95% confidence interval for the population correlation ρ;
(c) At the 5% significance level, can you reject the hypothesis that $\rho = 0$?

⇒14-2 From the following sample of student grades,

Student	First Test X	Second Test Y
A	80	90
B	60	70
C	40	40
D	30	40
E	40	60

(a) Calculate r; and find a 95% confidence interval for ρ;
(b) Calculate the regression of Y on X, and find a 95% confidence interval for β;
(c) Graph the 5 data points and the estimated regression line;
(d) At the 5% significance level, can you reject
   (1) The null hypothesis $\rho = 0$?
   (2) The null hypothesis $\beta = 0$?

14-2   CORRELATION AND REGRESSION

(a) Relation of $\hat{\beta}$ to r

If regression and correlation analysis were both applied to the same scatter of math (X) and verbal (Y) scores, how would they be related? From (11-19b)

$$\hat{\beta} = b = \frac{\sum xy}{\sum x^2} \tag{14-10}$$

and repeating (14-7),

$$r = \frac{\sum xy}{\sqrt{\sum x^2}\sqrt{\sum y^2}} \tag{14-11}$$

When (14-10) is divided by (14-11)

$$\frac{\hat{\beta}}{r} = \frac{\sqrt{\sum x^2}\sqrt{\sum y^2}}{\sum x^2} = \sqrt{\frac{\sum y^2}{\sum x^2}} \qquad (14\text{-}12)$$

If we divide both the numerator and denominator inside the square root sign by $(n - 1)$,

$$\frac{\hat{\beta}}{r} = \frac{\sqrt{\sum y^2/(n-1)}}{\sqrt{\sum x^2/(n-1)}} = \frac{s_Y}{s_X} \qquad (14\text{-}13)$$

or

$$\hat{\beta} = r\frac{s_Y}{s_X} \qquad (14\text{-}14)$$

This close correspondence of $\hat{\beta}$ and r will play an important role in the argument later. Note that if either r or $\hat{\beta}$ is zero, the other will also be zero.

(b) Explained and Unexplained Variation

In Figure 14-10, we reproduce the sample of math (X) and verbal (Y) scores, along with the fitted regression of Y on X, calculated in a straight-forward way from the information set out in Table 14-1. Now, if we wished to predict a student's verbal score Y without knowing X, then the best prediction would be the average observed value $\bar{Y}$. At x_i, it is clear from this diagram that we would make a very large error—

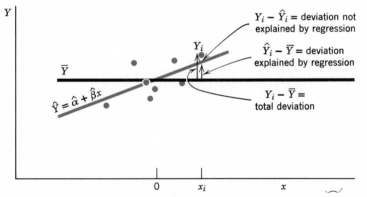

FIGURE 14-10   The value of regression in reducing variation in Y.

namely $(Y_i - \overline{Y})$, the deviation of Y_i from its mean. However, once our regression equation has been calculated, we predict Y to be $\hat{Y}_i$. Note how this reduces our error, since $(\hat{Y}_i - \overline{Y})$—a large part of our deviation—is now "explained." This leaves only a relatively small "unexplained" deviation $(Y_i - \hat{Y}_i)$. The total deviation of Y_i is the sum:

$$(Y_i - \overline{Y}) = (\hat{Y}_i - \overline{Y}) + (Y_i - \hat{Y}_i), \text{ for any } i \qquad (14\text{-}15)$$
$$\text{total deviation} = \text{explained deviation} + \text{unexplained deviation}$$

It follows that

$$\sum (Y_i - \overline{Y}) = \sum (\hat{Y}_i - \overline{Y}) + \sum (Y_i - \hat{Y}_i) \qquad (14\text{-}16)$$

What is surprising is that this same equality holds true when these deviations are squared, and we obtain a result[3] very similar to ANOVA in Chapter 10,

$$\sum (Y_i - \overline{Y})^2 = \sum (\hat{Y}_i - \overline{Y})^2 + \sum (Y_i - \hat{Y}_i)^2 \qquad (14\text{-}17)$$

$$\text{total variation} = \text{explained variation} + \text{unexplained variation}$$

where variation is defined as the sum of squared deviations.

---

[3] *Proof* is very similar to the proof of (10-16): Square both sides of (14-15), and sum over all values of i,

$$\sum (Y_i - \overline{Y})^2 = \sum [(\hat{Y}_i - \overline{Y}) + (Y_i - \hat{Y}_i)]^2$$

$$= \sum (\hat{Y}_i - \overline{Y})^2 + \sum (Y_i - \hat{Y}_i)^2 + 2 \sum (\hat{Y}_i - \overline{Y})(Y_i - \hat{Y}_i)$$
$$\qquad (14\text{-}18)$$

The last term can be rewritten using (14-19)

$$2\hat{\beta} \sum x_i (Y_i - \hat{Y}_i)$$

But this sum vanishes; in fact, it was set equal to zero in equation (11-15) used to estimate our regression line. Thus, the last term in (14-18) disappears, and (14-17) is proved. This same theorem can similarly be proved in the general case of multiple regression.

A further justification of the least squares technique (not mentioned in Chapter 11) is that it results in this useful relation between explained, unexplained, and total variation.

Since we may write, according to (11-19a)

$$(\hat{Y}_i - \bar{Y}) = \hat{y}_i = \hat{\beta}x_i \tag{14-19}$$

it is often convenient to rewrite (14-17) as

$$\sum (Y_i - \bar{Y})^2 = \hat{\beta}^2 \sum x_i^2 + \sum (Y_i - \hat{Y}_i)^2 \tag{14-20}$$

total variation = variation explained by X + unexplained variation

This equation makes clear that explained variation is the variation accounted for by the estimated regression coefficient $\hat{\beta}$. This procedure of decomposing total variation and analysing its components is called "analysis of variance applied to regression." The components of variance are displayed in the ANOVA Table 14-2; it is very important to note that variance is variation divided by degrees of freedom. From this, a null hypothesis test on β may be constructed; the question is whether the

Table 14-2   Analysis of Variance Table for Linear Regression

(a) General

Source of Variation	Variation	Degrees of Freedom (d.f)	Variance
Explained (by regression)	$\sum(\hat{Y}_i - \bar{Y})^2$ or $\hat{\beta}^2\sum x_i^2$	1	$\dfrac{\hat{\beta}^2\sum x_i^2}{1}$
Unexplained (residual)	$\sum(Y_i - \hat{Y}_i)^2$	$n - 2$	$s^2 = \dfrac{\sum(Y_i - \hat{Y}_i)^2}{n - 2}$
Total	$\sum(Y_i - \bar{Y})^2$	$n - 1$	

(b) For Sample of Verbal and Math Scores (Table 14-1)

Source of Variation	Variation	Degrees of Freedom (d.f.)	Variance	F ratio
Explained (by regression)	328	1	328	3.87
Unexplained (residual)	508	6	84.7	
Total	836 ✓	7 ✓		

ratio of the explained variance to unexplained variance is sufficiently large to reject the hypothesis that Y is unrelated to X. Specifically, a test of the hypothesis

$$H_0: \beta = 0 \tag{14-21}$$

involves forming the ratio

$$F = \frac{\text{variance explained by regression}}{\text{unexplained variance}}$$

$$= \frac{\hat{\beta}^2 \sum x_i^2}{s^2} \tag{14-22}$$

A 5% significance test involves finding the critical F value that leaves 5% of the distribution in the right-hand tail. If the sample F value calculated in (14-22) exceeds this, reject the hypothesis.

We must emphasize that this is just an alternative way of testing the null hypothesis (14-21). The first method—using the t statistic[8] as in (12-36)—is usually preferable.

Now the F and t distributions are related, in general, by

$$\overline{F = t^2} \tag{14-23}$$

where there is one degree of freedom in the numerator of F. Since the F calculated in (14-22) is just the t^2 of (12-36), the ANOVA F-test of this section is justified.

Example In Table 14-2*b*, the ANOVA calculations are presented for the verbal and math score example. (The necessary computational details are shown in Table 14-1.) To test $\beta = 0$, (14-22) is evaluated to be

$$F = \frac{328}{84.7} = 3.87 \tag{14-24}$$

Since this falls short of 5.99, the critical 5% point of F (see Appendix Table VII), we do not reject the null hypothesis.

Equivalently, $\beta = 0$ could be tested using (12-36):

$$t = \frac{\hat{\beta}}{s_{\hat{\beta}}} = \frac{.50}{9.2/\sqrt{1304}} = \frac{.50}{.254} = 1.97 \tag{14-25}$$

---

[8] Except that in this case it is two-tailed rather than one-tailed.

Since this falls short of 2.45, (the critical value leaving a total of 5% in both tails of the t distribution), the null hypothesis is not rejected. Again note that $t^2 = F$ (both for the calculated and for the critical values) so that the same conclusion must follow from both tests.

Alternatively, a 95% confidence interval for β could be constructed using (12-32),

$$\beta = .50 \pm (2.45).254$$
$$= .50 \pm .62 \tag{14-26}$$

This includes the value $\beta = 0$, once more confirming that H_0 cannot be rejected.

(c) Coefficient of Determination, r^2

The variations in Y will now be related to r. It follows from (14-12) that

$$\hat{\beta} = r \sqrt{\frac{\sum y_i^2}{\sum x_i^2}} \tag{14-27}$$

Substituting this value for $\hat{\beta}$ in (14-20)

$$\sum (Y_i - \bar{Y})^2 = r^2 \sum y_i^2 + \sum (Y_i - \hat{Y}_i)^2 \tag{14-28}$$

Noting that $\sum y_i^2$ is by definition $\sum (Y_i - \bar{Y})^2$, the solution for r^2 is

$$\frac{\sum (Y_i - \bar{Y})^2 - \sum (Y_i - \hat{Y}_i)^2}{\sum (Y_i - \bar{Y})^2} = r^2 \tag{14-29}$$

Finally, we can reexpress the numerator by noting (14-17). Thus

$$r^2 = \frac{\sum (\hat{Y}_i - \bar{Y})^2}{\sum (Y_i - \bar{Y})^2} = \frac{\text{explained variation of } Y}{\text{total variation of } Y} \tag{14-30}$$

This equation provides a clear intuitive interpretation of r^2. Note that this is the *square* of the correlation coefficient r, and is often called the coefficient of determination. *It is the proportion of the total variation in Y explained by fitting the regression.* Since the numerator cannot exceed the denominator, the maximum value of the right-hand side of (14-30) is 1; hence the limits on r are ± 1. These two limits were illustrated in Figure 14-2: in panel (*b*), $r = 1$ and all observations lie on a straight line running uphill; in panel (*d*), $r = -1$ and this perfect inverse correlation reflects the fact that all observations lie on a straight line running downhill. In either case, a regression fit will explain all the variation in Y.

When $r = r^2 = 0$, the explained variation of Y is zero and a regression line explains nothing; that is, the regression line will be parallel to the X axis, with $\hat{\beta} = 0$. Thus $r = 0$ and $\hat{\beta} = 0$ are seen to be equivalent ways of formally stating "no observed linear relation between X and Y."

(d) Regression Applied to a Bivariate Normal Population

In Table 14-1, a regression of Y on X was calculated for sample values assumed taken from a bivariate normal population. We now ask: Is the $\hat{\beta}$ we calculated an estimator of a population β, or does β even exist? (For a bivariate normal population, does there exist a true regression line of Y on X?) It will now be shown that the answer is yes.

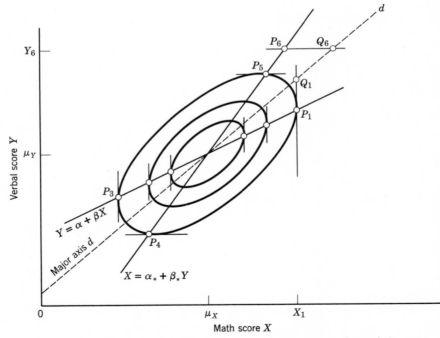

FIGURE 14-11 The two regression lines in a bivariate normal population.

Our assumed bivariate normal population is shown in Figure 14-11 as a set of isoprobability ellipses, with major axis d. Now consider the straight line $Y = \alpha + \beta X$, defined by joining points of vertical tangency such as P_1 and P_3. Each of these vertical tangents defines a cross-section slice of Y which is normal. Concentrating on the slice through $P_1 Q_1$, for example, we see that the mean of these Y values occurs at the point of tangency P_1; at this point our vertical line touches its highest iso-probability ellipse, and the highest point on any normal curve is at the mean. Thus, we see that the means of the Y populations lie on the straight line $Y = \alpha + \beta X$. Next, the variance of the Y populations can be shown to be constant.[4] Thus, the assumptions of the *regression* model (12-2) are satisfied by a bivariate normal (*correlation*) population. The line $Y = \alpha + \beta X$ may, therefore, be regarded as a true linear regression of Y on X.

Thus, if we know a student's math score and we wish to predict his verbal score, this regression line would be appropriate, (e.g., if his math score were X_1, we would predict his verbal score to be P_1). It is important to fully understand why we would *not* predict Q_1; that is, we do *not* use the major axis of the ellipse (line d) for prediction, even though this represents "equivalent" performance on the two tests. Since this student is far above average in mathematics, an equivalent verbal score seems too optimistic a prediction. Recall that there is a large random element involved in performance. There are a lot of students who will do well in one exam, but poorly in the other; in other words, ρ is less than 1 for this population. Therefore, instead of predicting at Q_1, we are more moderate and predict at P_1—a sort of average[5] of "equivalent" performance Q_1 and "average" performance μ_Y.

This is the origin of the term regression. Whatever a student's score in math, there will be a tendency for his verbal score to "regress" towards

---

[4] This may seem like a curious conclusion, since in Figure 14-5 the size of each cross-section slice differs depending on the value of X_0. However, each slice $p(X_0, Y)$ must be adjusted by division by $p(X_0)$ in order to define the conditional distribution of Y, as shown in (5-10). Thus the conditional distribution is

$$p(Y/X_0) = \frac{p(X_0, Y)}{p(X_0)}$$

This adjustment makes all the conditional distributions of Y "look alike," and thus have the same variance.

[5] P_1 is in fact a weighted average of Q_1 and μ_Y, with weights depending on ρ and $(1 - \rho)$. Thus, in the limiting case in which $\rho = 1$, X and Y are perfectly correlated, and we would predict Y at Q_1. At the other limit, in which $\rho = 0$, we can learn nothing about likely performance on one test from the result of the other, and we would predict Y at μ_Y. But for all cases between these two limits, we predict using both Q_1 and μ_Y.

mediocrity (i.e., the average).[6] It is evident from Figure 14-11 that this is equally true for a student with a math score below average; in this case, the predicted verbal score regresses upward toward the average.

Another interesting observation is that the correlation coefficient between X and Y is unique (i.e., ρ_{XY} is identically ρ_{YX}); but there are two regressions, the regression of Y on X *and* the regression of X on Y. This is immediately evident if we ask how we would predict a student's math score (X) if we knew his verbal score (e.g., Y_6). Then equivalent performance (point Q_6 on line d) is a bad predictor; since he has done very well in the verbal test, we would expect him to do less well in math, although still better than average. Thus, the best prediction is P_6 on the line $X = \alpha_* + \beta_* Y$, the regression of X(math) or Y(verbal). This is the direct analogue to our regression of Y on X, but in this case our regression is defined by joining points $(P_5, P_4$, etc.) of *horizontal*, rather than vertical tangency. Each of these horizontal tangents defines a normal conditional distribution of X, given Y; each of these distributions has the same variance, with its mean lying on this regression line, thus satisfying our conditions of a true regression of X on Y; hence, least squares values $\hat{\alpha}_*$ and $\hat{\beta}_*$ can be used to estimate α_* and β_*.

Example The sample of eight student's scores shown in Figure 14-1 and Table 14-1 was, by assumption, drawn from a bivariate normal population as shown in Figure 14-11. We have already estimated ρ with

$$r = .62 \qquad \text{(14-8) repeated.}$$

And from Table 14-1, we estimated $Y = \alpha + \beta X$ with

$$Y = 50 + .50x \qquad \text{(14-31)}$$
$$= 50 + .50(X - \bar{X})$$
$$= 20 + .50X \qquad \text{(14-32)}$$

We now estimate $X = \alpha_* + \beta_* Y$. The coefficients in this simple regression of X on Y are calculated in Table 14-1; this involves using the estimating equations (11-13) and (11-16), taking care to interchange X and Y throughout.

---

[6]The classical case, encountered by Pearson & Lee (*Biometrika,* 1903) involved trying to predict a son's height from his father's height. If the father is a giant, the son is likely to be tall; but there are good reasons for expecting him to be shorter than his father. (For example, how tall was his mother? And his grandparents? And so on.) So the prediction for the son was derived by "regressing" his father's height toward the population average.

Thus

$$X = 60 + .78y \qquad (14\text{-}33)$$
$$= 60 + .78(Y - \bar{Y})$$
$$= 21 + .78Y \qquad (14\text{-}34)$$

The two estimated regressions (14-32) and (14-34) are shown in Figure 14-12. Thus, for example, a student with a math result of 90 has a predicted verbal score of 65; and a student with a verbal result of 30 has a predicted math score of 44.

(e) When Correlation, When Regression?

Both the standard regression and correlation models require that Y be a random variable. But the two models differ in the assumptions made about X. The regression model makes few assumptions about X, but the more restrictive correlation model of this chapter requires that X be a random variable, having with Y a bivariate normal distribution. We therefore conclude that the standard regression model has wider application. It may be used for example to describe the fertilizer-yield problem in Chapter 11 where X was fixed at prespecified levels, or the bivariate normal population of X and Y in this chapter; however, the standard correlation model describes only the latter. (It is true that r^2 can be *calculated* even when X is prespecified, as an indication of how effectively regression reduces variation in (14-30); but r cannot be used for inferences about ρ in Figure 14-9.)

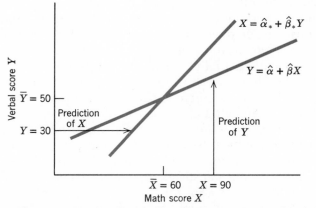

FIGURE 14-12   The two regression lines estimated from a sample of verbal and math scores.

In addition, regression answers more interesting questions. Like correlation, it indicates if two variables move together; but it also estimates how. Moreover, it can be shown that a key issue in correlation analysis—the test of the null hypothesis

$$H_0: \rho = 0 \tag{14-35}$$

can be answered directly from regression analysis by testing the equivalent null hypothesis

$$H_0: \beta = 0 \tag{14-36}$$

Thus, rejection of $\beta = 0$ implies rejection of $\rho = 0$, and yields the conclusion that correlation does exist between X and Y. If this is the only correlation question, then it can be answered by the regression test (14-36), and there is no need to introduce correlation analysis at all.

Since regression answers a broader and more interesting set of questions, (and some correlation questions as well), it becomes the preferred technique; correlation is useful primarily as an aid to understanding it, and as an auxiliary tool.

(f) "Nonsense" Correlations

In interpreting correlation and regression, one must keep firmly in mind that absolutely no claim is made that this necessarily indicates cause and effect. For example, the correlation of teachers' salaries and the consumption of liquor over a period of years turned out to be .9. This does not prove that teachers drink; nor does it prove that liquor sales increase teachers' salaries. Instead, both variables moved together, because both are influenced by a third variable—long-run growth in national income and population. If only third factors of this kind could be kept constant—or their effects fully discounted—then correlation would become more meaningful. This is the objective of multiple regression, or equivalently *partial correlation* in the next section.

Correlations such as the above are often called "nonsense" correlations. It would be more accurate to say that the observed mathematical correlation is real enough, but any naive inference of cause and effect is nonsense. Moreover as we have already suggested, the same charge can also be leveled at the conclusions sometimes drawn from regression analysis. For example, a regression applied to teachers' salaries and liquor sales would also yield a statistically significant $\hat{\beta}$ coefficient. Any inference of cause and effect from this would still be nonsense. Although correlation and regression cannot be used as *proof* of cause and effect, these techniques are very useful in two ways. First, they may provide *further confirmation* of a relation that theory tells us should exist (e.g., prices depend on wages). Second, they are often helpful in *suggesting* causal relations that were not previously suspected. For example, when cigarette smoking was found to be highly correlated with lung cancer, causal links between the two were investigated further.

PROBLEMS

14-3 For the following random sample of five shoes, find:
(a) The proportion of the variation in Y explained by its regression on X.
(b) The proportion unexplained.
(c) Whether Y depends on X, at the 5% significance level. Answer this in three alternate ways using the F test, t test, and a 95% confidence interval.

X = Cost of Shoe	Y = Months of Wear
10	8
15	10
10	6
20	12
20	9

14-4 Suppose a bivariate normal distribution of scores is perfectly symmetric in X and Y, with $\rho = .50$ and with isoprobability ellipses as follows:

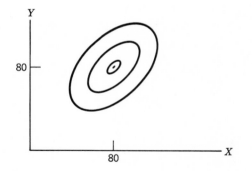

True or False? If false, correct it.
(a) The regression line of Y on X is

$$Y = 80 + .5(X - 80)$$

(b) The regression line of Y on X has the following graph:

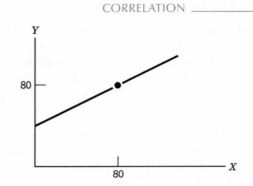

(c) The variance of Y is $1/4$ the variance of X.

(d) The proportion of the Y variation explained by X is only $1/4$.

(e) Thus, the residual Y values (after fitting X) would have $3/4$ the variation of the original Y values.

(f) For a student with a Y score of 70, the predicted X score is also 70.

14-5 Let $\hat{\beta}$ and $\hat{\beta}_*$ be the sample regression slopes of Y on X, and X on Y, for any given scatter of points.

True or false? If false, correct it.

(a) $\hat{\beta} = r\dfrac{s_Y}{s_X}$

(b) $\hat{\beta}_* = r\dfrac{s_X}{s_Y}$

(c) $\hat{\beta}\hat{\beta}_* = r^2$

(d) If $\hat{\beta} > 1$, then $\hat{\beta}_* < 1$ necessarily.

(e) If $\hat{\beta} < 1$, then $\hat{\beta}_* > 1$ necessarily.

14-6 In the following graph of four students' marks, find geometrically

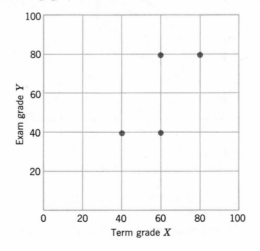

(without doing any algebraic calculations):
(a) The regression line of Y on X.
(b) The regression line of X on Y.
(c) The correlation r (*Hint.* Problem 14-5c).
(d) The predicted Y-score of a student with X-score of 70.
(e) The predicted X-score of a student with Y-score of 70.

14-3   **PARTIAL AND MULTIPLE CORRELATION**

(a) Partial Correlation

In a multiple regression equation, the statistical significance of each regressor is indicated by the t value,

$$t = \frac{\hat{\beta}}{s_{\hat{\beta}}}$$ (13-16) repeated

The same information is sometimes expressed by the *partial correlation*, which is defined as the correlation of the regressor and the response, while all other regressors are kept constant. From the partial correlation the prob-value can be computed. Of course, this prob-value coincides exactly with the prob-value computed from the t statistic,[7] so that the

_____

[7] In fact, the prob-value for the partial correlation is usually calculated by first calculating the t value, and then using this to read off the prob-value in the t table (Table V).

If desired, the partial correlation can be expressed in terms of the simple correlations. Although the general case is so complicated that it must be expressed in matrix form, the case of two regressors has a manageable formula for the partial correlation of Y and X, given Z fixed:

$$r_{YX/Z} = \frac{r_{YX} - r_{YZ}r_{XZ}}{\sqrt{1 - r_{XZ}^2}\sqrt{1 - r_{YZ}^2}}$$ (14-37)

where r_{YZ} represents the simple correlation of Y and Z, etc. This formula shows explicitly that there need be no close correspondence between the partial and simple correlation coefficient; however, in the special case that both X and Y are completely uncorrelated with Z (i.e., $r_{XZ} = r_{YZ} = 0$), then (14-37) reduces to

$$r_{YX/Z} = r_{YX}$$

that is, the partial and simple correlation coefficients are the same. It is also instructive to note what happens at the other extreme when X becomes perfectly correlated with Z. In this case $r_{YX/Z}$ cannot be calculated since $r_{XZ} = 1$ and the denominator of (14-37) becomes zero as a consequence. This is recognized as the problem of perfect multicollinearity in Chapter 13, where the corresponding multiple regression estimate $\hat{\beta}$ could not be defined.

partial correlation coefficient adds nothing here; it is quoted in computer programs (for example in Table 13-3) for the benefit of those who are familiar with correlation coefficients and their intuitive meaning.

(b) Multiple Correlation, R

Whereas the partial correlations measure the significance of regressors one by one, the multiple correlation R measures the significance of all the regressors at once. R is derived by first calculating the fitted values $\hat{Y}$ using all the regressors; for example, when there are two regressors,

$$\hat{Y} = \hat{\alpha} + \hat{\beta}X + \hat{\gamma}Z \tag{14-38}$$

Then the multiple correlation R is defined as the ordinary (simple) correlation between the fitted $\hat{Y}$ and the observed Y:

$$R \overset{\Delta}{=} r_{\hat{Y}Y} \tag{14-39}$$

This has all the nice algebraic properties of any simple correlation. In particular, we note (14-30), which takes the form

$$R^2 = \frac{\sum (\hat{Y}_i - \overline{Y})^2}{\sum (Y_i - \overline{Y})^2} = \frac{\text{variation of } Y \text{ explained by all regressors}}{\text{total variation of } Y} \tag{14-40}$$

Note that this is identical to r^2 if there is only one regressor.

Thus, as we add additional explanatory variables to our model, by watching how fast R^2 increases we can immediately see in (14-40) how helpful the additional variables are in improving the explanation of Y. Our conclusion is the same as in simple correlation: the major value of calculating R^2 is to clarify how successfully the regression explains the variation in Y.

It remains, finally, to relate this to the t test of regression coefficients (as given, for example, in Table 13-3). To cover the multiple regression case, (14-20) can be generalized,

total variation = variation explained by first regressor(s) $(X_1 \cdots X_{k-1})$
    + additional variation explained by last regressor (X_k)
    + unexplained variation $\tag{14-41}$

Then we construct the variance ratio (similar to (14-22)),

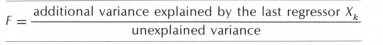

$$F = \frac{\text{additional variance explained by the last regressor } X_k}{\text{unexplained variance}}$$

(14-42)

Then using (14-23), we calculate finally

$$t = \pm \sqrt{F}$$

(14-43)

where the sign of t is taken to agree with the coefficient of the last regressor.

Since the order of the regressors is arbitrary, they can be reordered to place a new regressor last. Then the t statistic is calculated for the new regressor, by repeating the steps given above. In this way the computer calculates the t value for each regressor in turn.

PROBLEMS

14-7 For the data of Problem 13-1 relating saving S to income Y and assets W, find:

(a) r_{SY}, the simple correlation of S and Y.

(b) R, the multiple correlation of S on Y and W.

(c) The proportion of the variation of S which is

(1) explained by Y alone

(2) explained by Y and W

(3) explained by the addition of W as a regressor, after Y.

(4) left unexplained by Y and W.

(d) For the addition of the regressor W, calculate F as the ratio of items (3) and (4) in part (c), appropriately dividing by d.f. Then calculate t from (14-43).

(e) Repeat parts (a) through (d), replacing Y with W (and W with Y).

(f) Write out the regression equation of S on Y and W in the form (13-18), in the following steps:

(1) Write down the t values calculated in parts (d) and (e).

(2) Calculate the prob-values using Table V.

(3) Calculate the standard errors, using (13-16).

(4) Calculate the confidence intervals, using (13-17).

(5) Star the regressors that are statistically significant at the 95% confidence level.

(14-8) Repeat Problem 14-7, using the data of Problem 13-2 and substituting N for W throughout.

14-9 Prove that multiple regression will yield the same coefficient (for the first regressor) as simple regression if the regressors have zero correlation.

Review Problems (Chapters 11–14)

14-10 Five students were selected at random from a certain class and their grades on the first test (X) and second test (Y) were recorded:

Student	X	Y
S. B.	23	12
T. N.	24	28
J. F.	40	50
S. M.	22	25
H. V.	36	50

To simplify the arithmetic, the summary statistics have been calculated:

$$\bar{X} = 29 \qquad \bar{Y} = 33$$
$$s_X^2 = 70 \qquad s_Y^2 = 277$$
$$s_{XY} = 128$$

(a) What is the equation of the estimated regression line you would use to predict Y from X?

(b) Graph the 5 points and their regression line.

(c) If the regression line of Y on X were computed for the whole class of 600 students, in what range do you think (with 95% confidence) you would find the slope β?

(d) Calculate the prob-value for the null hypothesis H_0: X and Y have no positive correlation.

14-11 In a sample of 30 students, achievement score Y and aptitude score X have a correlation coefficient $r = .4$. The variances are $s_X^2 = 100$, $s_Y^2 = 150$. Is there sufficient data to calculate the slope $\hat{\beta}$ in the regression model $Y = a_0 + \beta X$? If so, what is it?

14-12 A random sample of 4 men from a certain peculiar tribe had their heights and weights recorded, as follows

H, Height (in.)	W, Weight (lb)
68	170
70	190
71	180
67	140
$\overline{H} = 69$	$\overline{W} = 170$

Variance of $H = 3.33$

Variance of $W = 467$

After W was regressed on H, the residual variance of W about the regression line was calculated to be 200.

(a) What is the least-squares regression line of weight as a function of height?

(b) Suppose the weight of a man 71″ tall is to be predicted. In order to give the prediction a 95% chance of being correct, by how much should the value predicted from the least squares line be "hedged"?

14-13 (a) Referring to the math and verbal scores of Table 14-1, suppose that only the students with math score exceeding 65 were admitted to college. For this subsample of three students, calculate the correlation of the X and Y scores.

(b) For the other subsample of five remaining students, calculate the correlation of the X and Y scores.

(c) Are these two correlations in the subsamples greater or less than the correlation in the whole sample?

14-14 Give two examples of meaningless or nonsense correlation. Explain in each case what is causing the variables to move together.

14-15 True or false? If false, correct it.

(a) In simple regression, it is assumed that

$$Y_i = \alpha + \beta X_i + e_i$$

where the e_i are independent, with nonzero mean and decreasing variance.

(b) The least squares estimators $\hat{\alpha}$ and $\hat{\beta}$ are biased, consistent estimators of α and β in the simple regression model.

(c) In simple regression, the more distant X_0 is from $\overline{X}$, the greater the error in predicting Y, given X_0.

(d) One severe limitation of multiple regression is that it cannot include factors that are categorical (nonnumerical, e.g., sex, region).

(e) $R^2 = \dfrac{\text{variation of } Y, \text{ explained by all regressors}}{\text{total variation of } Y}$

(f) Multicollinearity of X and Z occurs when $r_{xz} = 0$; then we can get a more reliable estimate of the regression of Y on X and Z.

(g) Multicollinearity is often a problem in the social sciences, when the regressors have high correlation. On the other hand, in the experimental sciences the values of the regressors can usually be designed so as to avoid multicollinearity.

14-16 (a) A physician investigated the number of hours of sleep required, comparing men and women. He collected a random sample of 5 men, and an independent random sample of 5 women, with the following results:

Hours of Sleep
per Day

Men	Women
10	8
9	10
11	11
7	10
8	11

Analyze appropriately.

(b) A second physician suspected that age was relevant, and so reexamined the two samples, recording their ages as follows:

Men

Y = Hours of Sleep per Day	X = Age
10	40
9	35
11	50
7	20
8	30

Women

Y = Hours of Sleep per Day	X = Age
8	35
10	55
11	60
10	50
11	65

Outline how you would analyze this data. (Do not carry out the computations; merely state what method you would use, and refer to the relevant pages, formulas, or analogous examples in the text.)

Graph Y against X, and so roughly state how your conclusions would differ from (a).

(c) Which method is better, (a) or (b)? Why?

14-17 An economist fitted quarterly unemployment figures from 1968 to 1970 with the following very simple model

$$U = a + bT + cD$$

where U = unemployment, in %

   T = time (in quarter years, starting with $T = 1$ for the first quarter of 1968)

   $D = 1$ for first quarter (winter)

   $ = 0$ otherwise

Select the most appropriate statement (and criticize the others):

The coefficient c is interpreted as

(a) the 3-year trend in first-quarter unemployment—specifically, the slope of this trend, measured in percentage points per year.

(b) the number of months that serious unemployment lasts each year, due to the severe winter season.

(c) the average increase in unemployment (in percentage points) in the first quarter compared to the rest of the year, allowing for trend.

(d) the rise in unemployment that occurs every first quarter.

(e) the fall in unemployment that occurs every first quarter.

14-18 A random sample of 10 workers in a certain population were classified according to income Y, educational background E, and sex, with the following data obtained.

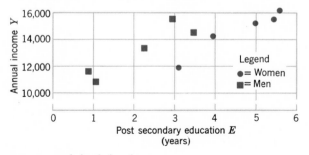

Assume a model of the form,

$$\text{men: } Y = a_M + bE + \text{error}$$
$$\text{women: } Y = a_W + bE + \text{error}$$

Roughly sketch in the graph whatever you find helpful. Then select the most appropriate conclusion that you would roughly estimate to be true of the population (and criticize the others).

(a) There is no evidence of sexual discrimination, since men earn less than women, on average.

(b) Men earn about $2000 a year more than women with the same education, on the average.

(c) The number of degrees of freedom in the model left for estimating residual variance is only 4. This is too small to make any conclusion.

14-19 Suppose that all the firms in a certain industry recorded their profits P (after tax) in 1969 and again in 1970, as follows:

The least-squares regression line is also shown in the graph. From it we would predict, for example, that a firm making a profit of 12% in 1969 would make a profit of 10% in 1970; and that a firm making a profit of 4% in 1969 would make a profit of 6% in 1970. That is, the outstandingly prosperous firms in 1969, and the outstandingly poor firms in 1969 too, tended to become less outstanding in 1970. Select the most appropriate statement (and criticize the others).

(a) This shows that the firms tended to become more homogeneous (more stable) in their profits in 1970—fewer risks were run.

(b) This indicates, but does not prove, that some factor (perhaps a too progressive taxation policy, or a more conservative outlook by businessmen, etc.) caused profits to be much less extreme in 1970 than in 1969.

(c) This shows, among other things, how difficult it is to stay at the top, or near the top, from year to year (from 1969 to 1970, specifically).

(d) To predict the 1970 profit for a firm making a 1969 profit of 12%, we ought to use the 45° line and hence get the prediction $P_{1970} = P_{1969} = 12\%$.

*14-20 Given a bivariate distribution with $\mu_X = \mu_Y = 0$, $\sigma_X = 2$, $\sigma_Y = 1$, and a coefficient of correlation between X and Y of 0.5, what is the coefficient of correlation between $(X - Y)$ and Y?

*14-21 Suppose the regression model (equation (12-3) in the text) is changed slightly, as follows: e_i has variance σ_i^2 (no longer a constant σ^2). The least squares estimator

$$\hat{\beta} = \frac{\sum x_i Y_i}{\sum x_i^2}$$

may still be calculated, although it may no longer have the optimal properties it enjoyed formerly. What are the mean and variance of $\hat{\beta}$?

*14-22 Suppose there are 7 observations generated by a standard simple regression model, with the X values ordered $X_{(1)} < X_{(2)} < \cdots < X_{(6)} < X_{(7)}$, and $Y_1, Y_2 \ldots$ being the associated Y values. A quick estimate of the slope β can be obtained from using only the first two and last two observations:

$$B = \frac{(Y_7 + Y_6) - (Y_2 + Y_1)}{(X_{(7)} + X_{(6)}) - (X_{(2)} + X_{(1)})}$$

(a) What is the bias of B? (Hint. Regard the $X_{(i)}$ as fixed constants, and see (12-14).)

(b) Calculate B for the wheat and fertilizer data of Table 11-1. In this specific example, how does the variance of B compare to the variance of the least-squares estimator $\hat{\beta}$?

(c) In general, how does the variance of B compare to the variance of $\hat{\beta}$?

14-23 A certain drug (e.g., tobacco, alcohol, marijuana) is taken by a proportion of the American population. To investigate its effect on health (for example, mortality rate), suppose certain people are to be studied for a five-year period, at the end of which each person's "mortality" will be recorded as follows:

$$M = 0 \text{ if he lives}$$
$$= 1 \text{ if he dies}$$

For each person, also let D represent his average monthly dose of the drug, and let subscripts 1 and 2 refer to drug users and nonusers respectively.

Criticize the scientific merit of the following five proposals. (If you like, you may comment on their ethical and political aspects too.) Which proposal do you think is scientifically soundest? Can you think of a better proposal of your own?

1. Draw a random sample of n persons. For each person, record the drug dose D that he chooses to take, and his mortality M after five years. From these n points, calculate the regression line of M against D, interpreting the coefficient of D as the effect of the drug.

2. Again, draw a random sample of n persons. For each person record such characteristics as age, sex, grandparents' longevity, etc., as well as drug dose D and mortality M after five years. Then calculate the multiple regression of M on all the other variables, interpreting the coefficient of D as the effect of the drug.

3. Once again draw a random sample of n persons. Then construct a 95% confidence interval for the difference in mortality rates between drug users and nonusers, using (8-17):

$$\text{drug effect, } (\mu_1 - \mu_2) = (\bar{M}_1 - \bar{M}_2) \pm t_{.025} \, s_p \sqrt{(1/n_1) + (1/n_2)}$$

where n_1 and n_2 are the numbers of drug users and nonusers respectively (so that $n_1 + n_2 = n$, the size of the random sample), and s_p^2 is the pooled sample variance.

4. Ask for volunteers who have never used the drug. Suppose there are too many volunteers, so that we may select from among them a random sample of n volunteers (where n is even, $n = 2m$ say). Divide the volunteer sample at random into two equal groups (control and treatment), each group being of size m.

The control group of volunteers is allowed no drug, while the treatment group is given a standard dose, over the five-year period. Then a 95% confidence interval for the difference between drug users and nonusers would be, using (8-17) again,

$$\text{drug effect } (\mu_1 - \mu_2) = (\bar{M}_1 - \bar{M}_2) \pm t_{.025}\, s_p\, \sqrt{(1/m) + (1/m)}.$$

5. Again, ask for volunteers who have never used the drug. Suppose there are too many volunteers, so that we may select from among them a group of m *matched* pairs now—each pair consisting of two volunteers of similar age, sex, grandparents' longevity, etc. From each pair select at random (for example by the flip of a coin) one of the two volunteers to go into the treatment group, while the other volunteer of course goes into the control group.

The control group is allowed no drug, while the treatment group is given a standard dose, over the five-year period. Then a 95% confidence interval for the difference between drug users and nonusers would be,

$$\text{drug effect, } (\mu_1 - \mu_2) = (\bar{M}_1 - \bar{M}_2) \pm t_{.025}\, s_p\, \sqrt{(1/m) + (1/m)}.$$

PART 2

selected topics

bayesian decision Theory

If I toss a coin and get two heads, does that mean it is two-headed?

Anonymous

In Chapters 9 and 13 it became clear that prior belief about a parameter may play a key role in its estimation. Bayesian theory is the means of formally taking such prior information into account. It is not only useful for its own sake, but it also sharpens our understanding of the limitations of classical statistics.

15-1   PRIOR AND POSTERIOR DISTRIBUTIONS

In a certain country, suppose it rains 40% of the days and shines 60% of the days.[1] A barometer manufacturer, in testing his instrument, has found that it sometimes errs: on rainy days it erroneously predicts "shine" 10% of the time, and on shiny days it erroneously predicts "rain" 20% of the time.

The best prediction of tomorrow's weather *before* looking at the barometer would be the prior distribution in Table 15-1. But *after* looking at the barometer and seeing it predict "rain," what is the poste-

---

[1]This is just Problem 3-23b repeated.

Table 15-1   Prior Probabilities, $p(\theta)$

State θ	Rain (θ_1)	Shine (θ_2)
Prior probability $p(\theta)$	.40	.60

rior distribution? That is, with this new information in hand, can't we quote better odds on rain than Table 15-1?

The answer is, of course, yes. To see why, we first formally set out the reliability of the barometer in Table 15-2. This information is combined with the prior probabilities in Table 15-1 to define the sample space shown as the entire large rectangle in Figure 15-1. It has four subdivisions, each representing the probability of a specific state of nature, and a barometric prediction. Thus, for example, the probability of the state of nature θ being rain and the barometric prediction X being "rain" is, according to (3-23),

$$p(\theta_1, X_1) = p(\theta_1)\, p(X_1/\theta_1) \tag{15-1}$$
$$= (.4)(.9) = .36 \tag{15-2}$$

Similarly, the probability of the state shine, and the prediction "rain" is

$$p(\theta_2, X_1) = p(\theta_2)\, p(X_1/\theta_2) \tag{15-3}$$
$$= (.6)(.2) = .12 \tag{15-4}$$

Of course, after "rain" has been predicted, the whole sample space is no longer relevant. It is replaced by the new sample space, shown shaded in Figure 15-1; rain is seen to be three times as probable as shine (.36 versus .12). This produces the posterior distribution in Table 15-3. Comparing this with Table 15-1, we see how the odds on rain improve once the barometer has predicted it.

Table 15-2   Conditional Probabilities, $p(X/\theta)$

Prediction X \ State θ	Rain (θ_1)	Shine (θ_2)
"Rain" (X_1)	.90	.20
"Shine" (X_2)	.10	.80
$\sum$	1.00	1.00

Table 15-3   Posterior Probabilities, $p(\theta/X)$

State θ	Rain (θ_1)	Shine (θ_2)
Posterior probability $p(\theta/\text{"rain"})$	.75	.25

Since Table 15-3 is so important, we now write down its formal confirmation. From (15-2) and (15-4)

$$p(\text{prediction "rain"}) = p(X_1) = .36 + .12 = .48 \qquad (15\text{-}5)$$

According to (3-22),

$$p(\theta_1/X_1) = \frac{p(\theta_1, X_1)}{p(X_1)} = \frac{.36}{.48} = .75$$

Similarly $\qquad\qquad\qquad\qquad\qquad\qquad\qquad\qquad\qquad\qquad (15\text{-}6)$

$$p(\theta_2/X_1) = \frac{p(\theta_2, X_1)}{p(X_1)} = \frac{.12}{.48} = .25$$

This is often written in a more convenient and general form, known as Bayes' theorem,

$$p(\theta/X) = \frac{p(\theta, X)}{p(X)} = \frac{p(\theta)p(X/\theta)}{p(X)} \qquad (15\text{-}7)$$

To keep the mathematical manipulations in perspective, we repeat the physical interpretation for emphasis. Before the evidence (barometer)

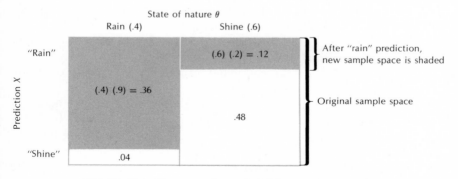

FIGURE 15-1   How posterior probabilities are determined.

is seen, the prior probabilities $p(\theta)$ give the proper betting odds on the weather. But after the evidence is in, we can do better; the posterior probabilities $p(\theta/X)$ now give the proper betting odds. (This may be intuitively grasped by appealing to the relative frequency interpretation. Of all the times the barometer registers "rain," in what proportion will rain actually occur? The answer: 75%.) As a simple summary, we note that the prior probability distribution is adjusted by the empirical evidence to yield the posterior distribution. Schematically:

| Prior probabilities | and | probability of empirical evidence | yields → | posterior probabilities |

| $p(\theta)$ | | $p(X/\theta)$ | | $p(\theta/X)$ |

PROBLEMS

15-1 Suppose another barometer is used: on shiny days it erroneously predicts "rain" 30% of the time, but on rainy days it always correctly predicts "rain."
(a) With the prior probabilities in Table 15-1, calculate the posterior probability of rain, once this barometer has predicted "rain." What is the posterior probability of shine?
(b) True or false? If false, correct it:
    Since the barometer always predicts "rain" when it does rain, a "rain" prediction means that it is dead certain that it will rain.
(c) Explain why the posterior probability of rain is now *less* than in Table 15-3, even though this new barometer is a better predictor when it rains.

15-2 Suppose you are in charge of the nationwide leasing of a specific car model. Your service agent in a certain city has not been perfectly reliable: he has shortcut his servicing in the past about 1/10 of the time. The effect of such shortcutting is to increase the probability that an individual will cancel his lease from .2 to .5.
(a) If an individual has cancelled his lease, what is the probability that he received shortcut servicing?
(b) Suppose this had happened in a city with a service agent of even more questionable reputation (you have learned from his previous employer that he is in the habit of shortcutting half the time). What is your answer to (a) in this case?

15-3 A factory has three machines $(\theta_1, \theta_2,$ and $\theta_3)$ making bolts. The newer the machine, the larger and more accurate it is, according to the following table:

Machine ⟶	θ_1 (Oldest)	θ_2	θ_3 (Newest)
Proportion of total output produced by this machine	10%	40%	50%
Rate of defective bolts it produces	5%	2%	1%

Thus, for example, θ_3 produces half of the factory's output, and of all the bolts it produces, 1% are defective.

(a) Suppose a bolt is selected at random; *before* it is examined, what is the chance it was produced by machine θ_1? by θ_2? by θ_3?

(b) Suppose the bolt is examined and found to be defective; *after* this examination, what is the chance it was produced by machine θ_1? by θ_2? by θ_3?

⇒15-4 Suppose a man is drawn at random from a group of ten people, whose heights θ have the following distribution:

θ (Inches)	$p(\theta)$
70	.1
71	.3
72	.2
73	.2
74	.1
75	.1

(a) Graph this (prior) distribution of θ.

(b) Suppose also that a crude measuring device is available that makes errors with the following distribution:

e (Error in Inches)	p(e)
−2	.1
−1	.2
0	.4
1	.2
2	.1

Surely this can help us a little in estimating the man's height. For example, suppose his measured height using this crude device is $X = 74''$. We now have further information about θ; that is, this measurement changes the probabilities for θ from the prior distribution $p(\theta)$ to a posterior distribution $p(\theta/X = 74)$. Calculate and graph this posterior distribution.

15-2   **OPTIMAL DECISIONS**

(a) Example

Suppose a salesman regularly sells umbrellas or lemonade on Saturday afternoons at football games. To keep matters simple, suppose he has just three possible options (actions, a_i):

$$a_1 = \text{sell only umbrellas.}$$
$$a_2 = \text{sell some umbrellas, some lemonade.}$$
$$a_3 = \text{sell only lemonade.}$$

(15-8)

If he chooses a_1 and it rains, his profit is \$20; but if it shines, he loses \$10. It will be more convenient to describe everything as a loss (negative profit); thus his losses will be -20 or $+10$ respectively.

If he chooses action a_2 or a_3, there will also be certain losses. All this information may be assembled conveniently in the following loss table:

Table 15-4   Loss Function $l(a, \theta)$

Action a	State θ Rain (θ_1)	Shine (θ_2)
a_1	-20	10
a_2	5	5
a_3	25	-7

Suppose further that the probability distribution (long-run relative frequency) of the weather is:

Table 15-5   Probability Distribution of θ

State θ	Rain (θ_1)	Shine (θ_2)
Probability $p(\theta)$	.20	.80

If the salesman wants to maximize long-run profits, what is the best action for him to take? (You are urged to work this out, before reading on; it will be easier that way.)

solution   If he chooses a_1, what would his loss be, on the average? Intuitively, we calculate the average (expected) loss if he chooses a_1

$$L(a_1) = -20(.20) + 10(.80) = 4 \qquad (15\text{-}9)$$

Formally, the expected loss is[3]

$$L(a_1) = l(a_1, \theta_1)\, p(\theta_1) + l(a_1, \theta_2)\, p(\theta_2) = \sum_\theta l(a_1, \theta)\, p(\theta) \quad (15\text{-}10)$$

Similarly, we evaluate

$$L(a_2) = 5(.20) + 5(.80) = 5 \qquad (15\text{-}11)$$

and

$$L(a_3) = 25(.20) - 7(.80) = -.6 \qquad (15\text{-}12)$$

In general

$$L(a) = \sum_\theta l(a, \theta)\, p(\theta) \qquad (15\text{-}13)$$

The optimal action is seen to be a_3, which minimizes the expected loss; in fact, this is the only option that allows any expected profit. All our information and calculations are summarized in Table 15-6.

Table 15-6   Calculation of the Optimal Action a

$p(\theta)$	.20	.80	
θ / a	θ_1	θ_2	$L(a)$ = expected loss
a_1	−20	10	4
a_2	5	5	5
a_3	25	−7	−.6 ←—minimum

Loss function
$l(a, \theta)$

[3] Equation (15-10) is just the expected value, or mean, given essentially in (4-3). Recall the following relative frequency interpretation: in, say, 100 days the salesman would get about 20 rainy days at −$20 each, yielding −$400; and about 80 shiny days, at +$10 each, yielding +$800; the sum is about +$400 in 100 days, or an average of $4 per day.

(b) Generalization

Of course this problem can be generalized to any number of states θ or actions a (even an infinite number, as in the next section). The objective remains the same: to minimize expected loss. We now pause to reconsider in detail:

1. The probabilities $p(\theta)$.
2. The loss function $l(a, \theta)$.

1. *The probabilities $p(\theta)$*, of course, should represent the best possible intelligence on the subject. For example, suppose the salesman moves to another state, with weather probabilities as given in Table 15-1. If he has no barometer, he will have to use the (prior) probabilities in this table. But if he can consult the barometer (described in Table 15-2) then, of course, the posterior probabilities $p(\theta/X)$ in Table 15-3 should be used.

   The logic of Bayesian inference is laid out in a block diagram in Figure 15-2. Incidentally, in the calculation of the average loss $L(a)$ in (15-13) it would not hurt to use $kp(\theta)$ instead of $p(\theta)$ as weights, where k is any constant (independent of θ and a). This is because $kp(\theta)$ would generate losses $kL(a)$, which would rank

FIGURE 15-2   The logic of Bayesian decisions to minimize expected loss.

in the same order as the true losses $L(a)$, and hence point to the same correct optimizing action. This is a very useful observation; for example, our umbrella salesman need not undertake the last step in calculating the posterior probabilities of rain in (15-6); he can forget about the denominator $p(X_1)$, and use (15-2) and (15-4) instead—without affecting his decision.[4]

2. *The loss function, $l(a, \theta)$*. In our example, we assumed that monetary loss is the appropriate consideration. This may be valid enough if the stakes are small and the decision is made ("game is played") over and over again: whatever minimizes the expected loss in each game will minimize total expected loss in the long run.

Yet there are some decisions that are made once for large stakes; then expected monetary loss may not be the right criterion. To illustrate: suppose you were offered (tax-free) a choice between

$$\left.\begin{array}{l} \text{(a)} \ \$100{,}000 \text{ for sure, or} \\ \text{(b)} \ \text{a } 1/2 \text{ chance (lottery ticket) on a } \$210{,}000 \text{ prize} \end{array}\right\} \ (15\text{-}14)$$

Most people would prefer choice (a), even though the expected monetary value of choice (a),

$$\left.\begin{array}{c} \$100{,}000 \ (1) = \$100{,}000 \\ \\ \text{is less than that of choice (b),} \\ \\ \$210{,}000 \left(\dfrac{1}{2}\right) = \$105{,}000 \end{array}\right\} \qquad (15\text{-}15)$$

The reason is that most people value their first hundred thousand more than their second. (You can easily speculate on how you would spend the first hundred thousand. But once these purchases have been made, there would be less exciting opportunities for spending the second hundred thousand; the sports car has already been bought, and so on.) Such a decision should be based not on money itself as in (15-15), but rather on a subjective valuation of money, or the "utility" of money. As an illustration, Figure 15-3 shows one author's subjective evaluation[5] $U(M)$. Since utility is the

---

[4] That is, attaching weights of .36 and .12 to his losses would yield the same optimum action as weights of .75 and .25.

[5] This utility curve is highly personal, and temporary. It is defined empirically for an individual by asking him a sequence of questions about which bets he prefers. In other words, many bets like (15-14) may be used to discover an individual's utility curve.

FIGURE 15-3   Author's subjective evaluation of money.

more appropriate measure, the decision should be based on *expected utility*, rather than expected money. Using Figure 15-3, the expected utilities of the two choices are:

$$\left.\begin{array}{l} \text{(a) } u_1(1) = u_1 \\ \text{(b) } u_2(\tfrac{1}{2}) = 1.4u_1(\tfrac{1}{2}) = .7u_1 \end{array}\right\} \tag{15-16}$$

which is a clear victory for choice (a).

In conclusion, in decision situations, the loss function $l(a, \theta)$ should represent *loss of utility*; hereafter we shall interpret losses in this way.

PROBLEMS

15-5 Using the losses of Table 15-4, calculate the optimal action if:
(a) The only available probabilities are the prior probabilities of Table 15-1.
(b) The barometer reads "rain" (so that the posterior probabilities of Table 15-3 are relevant).
(c) The barometer reads "shine."
(d) Is the following a true or false summary of parts (a) to (c) above? If false, correct it.

   If the salesman must choose his action (order his merchandise) before consulting a barometer, then a_2 (umbrellas and lemonade) is best.

   However, if the barometer can be consulted first, then the salesman should

Choose a_1 (umbrellas) if the barometer predicts "rain."
Choose a_3 (lemonade) if the barometer predicts "shine."

But a bright salesman could have seen this obvious solution without going to all the trouble of learning about Bayesian decisions.

15-6 A farmer has to decide whether to sell his corn for use A or use B. His losses depend on its water content, (determined by the mill during processing, after the farmer's decision has been made) according to the following loss table:

State θ Action a	Dry	Wet
Use A	−10	30
Use B	20	10

(a) If his only additional information is that, through long past experience his corn has been classified as dry one third of the time, what should his decision be?

(b) Suppose he has developed a rough-and-ready means of determining whether it is wet or dry—a method which is correct 3/4 of the time regardless of the state of nature. If this indicates that his corn is "dry" what should his decision be?

*(c) How much is the method of part (b) worth, that is, how much does it reduce his expected loss?

15-7 You wish to invest $10,000 for a year, but you are undecided between three options: (1) a conservative portfolio of bonds; (2) a selection of both bonds and stocks; and (3) an aggressive portfolio of stocks. An advisor quotes you his best estimate of how each will perform, depending on business conditions:

Business Condition Portfolio Option	Stagnation	Moderate Growth	Rapid Growth
All bonds	10,600	10,500	10,500
Bonds and stocks	9,500	10,800	11,700
All stocks	8,600	11,000	12,500

(a) If an economist has advised you that his odds on these three conditions are 1/3, 1/3, 1/3, which portfolio would you select? Why?

(b) True or false. "A change in your evaluation of money may lead you to alter your investment portfolio." Illustrate, using the example above.

⇒15-8 A warehouse is to be built to service 25 retail stores, all of the same size, and strung out (distributed) along a single main street. In order to minimize total transportation cost, where should the warehouse be located (at the mean, median, mode, or midrange)?

Arbitrary
origin, 0

(a) If the transportation cost is zero for the stores right at the warehouse, and a constant value (irrespective of distance) for the other stores.

(b) If the transportation cost for each store is strictly proportional to its distance from the warehouse; thus we wish to minimize

$$\sum |X_i - a|$$

*(c) If there are not only transportation costs but also costs involved in servicing and inventory delays that increase sharply with distance from the warehouse. Specifically, suppose the cost is proportional to the square of the distance; thus we wish to minimize

$$\sum (X_i - a)^2$$

⇒15-9 Suppose the judge at a beauty contest is asked, as a preliminary diversion, to guess the height or some other dimension of the first contestant, who will be picked at random from a group of 10 contestants. First, the judge wisely takes the time to find the relative frequency (probability) distribution of heights of the contestants, as given below.

θ (inches)	$p(\theta)$
64	.1
65	.1
66	.2
67	.2
68	.3
69	.1

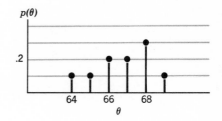

In order to give the judge an incentive, suppose he is subject to certain fines if he guesses wrong. How should he guess,
(a) if the fine is $1 for a mistake (no matter how large or small)—"a miss is as good as a mile";
(b) If the fine is a little more severe, being equal to the size of the mistake, i.e., $x for a mistake of x inches;
*(c) if the fine is even more severe, being equal to the square of the mistake, i.e., x^2 for a mistake of x inches?

15-3   ESTIMATION AS A DECISION

In our earlier example the states θ (rain and shine) and actions a were categorical (i.e., nonnumerical). But this was not an essential part of the theory; in this section we consider some numerical problems.

Consider, for example, Problems 15-8 and 15-9. Although they differ slightly in content, they are entirely similar in form; so let us translate one of them, Problem 15-9, into the familiar language of decision theory: the girl's height is the state of nature θ, and the guessed height (estimate) is the action a to be taken. The fine the judge must pay is the loss function $l(a, \theta)$; since a and θ are numerical, the loss function is most conveniently given by a formula, rather than a table. Each of the three loss functions, along with its corresponding optimal estimator[6], is shown in Table 15-7.

_____
[6]Each of the three optimal estimators can be established by setting out the loss function in tabular form. For example, in the context of Problem 15-9, the mean is shown to be appropriate for the quadratic loss function as follows:

$p(\theta)$		.1	.1	.2	.2	.3	.1	
State of Nature (Height) θ Action (Estimator) a		64	65	66	67	68	69	$L(a) =$ Expected Loss
Mode	68	16	9	4	1	0	1	3.60
Median	67	9	4	1	0	1	4	2.20
Try	66.9	8.41	3.61	.81	.01	1.21	4.41	2.17
Mean	66.8	7.84	3.24	.64	.04	1.44	4.84	2.16 ◄ min
Try	66.7	7.29	2.89	.49	.09	1.69	5.29	2.17
Try	66	4	1	0	1	4	9	2.70

Loss function $l(a, \theta) = (a - \theta)^2$

(cont'd)

Table 15-7   How the Optimal Estimator of θ
Depends on the Loss Function

If the Loss Function $l(a, \theta)$ is:	Then the Corresponding Optimal Estimator a is:	
(a) $\begin{cases} 0 \text{ if } a = \theta \text{ exactly,} \\ 1 \text{ otherwise} \end{cases}$	Mode of $p(\theta)$	(15-17)
(b) $\lvert a - \theta \rvert$	Median	(15-18)
(c) $(a - \theta)^2$ \quad (quadratic)	Mean	(15-19)

The quadratic loss function (c) is the one that is usually used in decision theory. It is graphed in Figure 15-4. It is justified not only by its intuitive appeal but also by its attractive mathematical properties. For example, it is easily differentiated (an important requirement in minimization problems); on the other hand, (a) obviously cannot be differentiated, nor can (b), since it is an absolute value function.

We emphasize that the probability distribution $p(\theta)$ used in the decision process ought to reflect the best available information. Thus we may be forced to use the prior distribution $p(\theta)$ if we have not yet collected any data. But after data is collected, the posterior distribution $p(\theta/X)$ is appropriate.

FIGURE 15-4   The quadratic loss function.

The first element (16) in this table results from squaring the difference between the estimator (i.e., the mode = 68) and the state of nature (64); the total expected loss from using the mode as estimator involves weighting each of the losses in this row by the probability of each state of nature above. Thus the mode as estimator results in an expected loss of

$$16(.1) + 9(.1) + 4(.2) + \cdots = 3.6$$

Of all the possible estimators (rows), the mean is seen to be best (i.e., it generates the minimum expected loss).

Of course, to prove this rigorously, a more general proof involving algebra and calculus would be required.

PROBLEMS

15-10 Suppose you have to guess the height of the man drawn in Problem 15-4, with only the prior distribution $p(\theta)$ known. Find the optimal estimate of θ, assuming in succession the 3 loss functions of Table 15-7.

15-11 Repeat Problem 15-10, *after* the man's height has been crudely measured as $X = 74$, so that the posterior distribution $p(\theta/X)$ is relevant, as calculated in Problem 15-4b.

15-4   **BAYESIAN VERSUS CLASSICAL ESTIMATION**

(a) Example, in a Normal Population

We shall use an extended example to compare these techniques. Suppose it is essential to estimate the length θ of a beetle accidentally caught in a delicate piece of machinery. A measurement X is possible, using a device that is subject to some error: X is normally distributed about the true value θ, with $\sigma^2 = 10$. Suppose a sample of 10 such observations yields an average $\bar{X} = 20$.

Question 1. What is the classical 95% confidence interval for θ?

solution   From (7-10)

$$\theta = \bar{X} \pm 1.96 \frac{\sigma}{\sqrt{n}}$$

$$= 20 \pm 1.96 \tag{15-20}$$

and, of course,

$$\text{point estimate of } \theta = \bar{X} = 20 \tag{15-21}$$

Question 2. Suppose we find out from a biologist that the population of all beetles has a normally distributed length, with mean $\theta_0 = 25$ and variance $\sigma_0^2 = 4$. How can this be used to determine the posterior distribution of θ?

solution   It will be useful to develop a general formula applying for any θ_0, σ_0, etc., and then use it on this specific example. Since the prior distribution is normal,

$$p(\theta) = N(\theta_0, \sigma_0^2) \tag{15-22}$$

and the distribution of the empirical evidence $\bar{X}$ is normal too,

$$p(\bar{X}/\theta) = N\left(\theta, \frac{\sigma^2}{n}\right)$$

(15-23)

(6-28) repeated

it can be shown[7] that the posterior distribution is also normal:

$$p(\theta/\bar{X}) = N\left(\frac{w_1\bar{X} + w_2\theta_0}{w_1 + w_2}, \frac{1}{w_1 + w_2}\right)$$

(15-24)

---

[7] Using (4-12), we may write (15-22) and (15-23) explicitly as

$$p(\theta) = K_1 e^{-(1/2\sigma_0^2)(\theta-\theta_0)^2}$$

(15-25)

$$p(\bar{X}/\theta) = K_2 e^{-(n/2\sigma^2)(\bar{X}-\theta)^2}$$

(15-26)

where K_1 and K_2 and other similar constants introduced in this footnote are independent of θ and, hence, of a form not critical to the argument. Since

$$p(\bar{X}, \theta) = p(\theta)\, p(\bar{X}/\theta)$$

(15-27)

we can use (15-25) and (15-26) to write

$$p(\bar{X},\theta) = K_1 K_2 e^{-(1/2)[(1/\sigma_0^2)(\theta^2-2\theta\theta_0+\theta_0^2)+(n/\sigma^2)(\bar{X}^2-2\bar{X}\theta+\theta^2)]}$$

(15-28)

Now consider only the exponent, which may be rearranged to

$$-\frac{1}{2}\left[\theta^2\left(\frac{1}{\sigma_0^2} + \frac{n}{\sigma^2}\right) - 2\theta\left(\frac{\theta_0}{\sigma_0^2} + \frac{n\bar{X}}{\sigma^2}\right) + K_3\right]$$

(15-29)

Let

$$\left.\begin{aligned}\frac{1}{\sigma_0^2} + \frac{n}{\sigma^2} &= \frac{1}{a}\\[2mm]\frac{\theta_0}{\sigma_0^2} + \frac{n\bar{X}}{\sigma^2} &= b\end{aligned}\right\}$$

(15-30)

Using these definitions, the exponent (15-29) can be written

$$-\frac{1}{2}\left[\frac{\theta^2}{a} - 2b\theta + K_3\right]$$

(15-32)

$$= -\frac{1}{2a}[(\theta - ab)^2 + K_5]$$

(15-33)

Finally we use this to write (15-28) as

$$p(\bar{X}, \theta) = K_6 e^{-(1/2a)(\theta-ab)^2}$$

(15-34)

(cont'd)

where w_1 and w_2 are the "weights" to be attached, respectively, to the observed mean $\bar{X}$ and the prior mean θ_0. To determine the appropriate weights for each, we note that the smaller the variance, the more reliable the information, and the more it should be weighted; hence the weight for the observed mean is inversely related to its variance,

and similarly

$$\left.\begin{array}{c} w_1 = \dfrac{1}{\sigma^2/n} \\[2em] w_2 = \dfrac{1}{\sigma_0^2} \end{array}\right\}$$
(15-38)

Now apply this to our example. Since

$$\sigma^2 = 10, \qquad n = 10, \qquad \sigma_0^2 = 4 \tag{15-39}$$

the weights are

$$w_1 = \frac{1}{10/10} = 1, \qquad w_2 = \frac{1}{4} \tag{15-40}$$

Applying these weights to (15-24), we find that the posterior distribution of θ is normal, with

$$\text{mean} = \frac{1(20) + 1/4(25)}{1 + 1/4} = 21 \tag{15-41}$$

and

$$p(\theta/\bar{X}) = \frac{p(\bar{X}, \theta)}{p(\bar{X})} = K_7\, e^{-(1/2a)(\theta - ab)^2} \tag{15-35}$$

This means that θ, given $\bar{X}$, has the normal distribution

$$N(ab, a) \tag{15-36}$$

Now, from (15-30) and (15-38),

$$\left.\begin{array}{c} \dfrac{1}{a} = w_1 + w_2 \\[1em] b = w_1\bar{X} + w_2\theta_0 \end{array}\right\}$$
(15-37)

Substituting (15-37) into (15-36) yields (15-24).

and
$$\text{variance} = \frac{1}{1 + 1/4} = .8 \tag{15-42}$$

To summarize

$$p(\theta/\overline{X}) = N(21,.8) \tag{15-43}$$

Question 3. With the posterior distribution (15-43) now in hand, defining a Bayesian estimate of θ requires only a loss function. Suppose this is the quadratic loss function; what is the Bayesian point estimator of θ? Find also the 95% probability interval for θ.

solution According to (15-19), for a quadratic loss function

$$\text{optimum estimator} = \text{the posterior mean} \tag{15-44}$$
$$= 21$$

(Note that because $p(\theta/\overline{X})$ is normal, this is also the posterior median and mode, so that all the loss functions in Table 15-7 yield the same answer.)

To construct a 95% probability interval, we know from (15-43) that there is a 95% probability that θ will fall in the interval

$$21 \pm 1.96\sqrt{.8}$$
$$= 21 \pm 1.76$$

This is not only centered better than the classical interval (15-20), it is also narrower[8] (more precise). This is illustrated in Figure 15-5. Note how the prior information is given only 1/4 the weight of the observed

---

[8]To see why the Bayesian interval is narrower in general, we see from (15-36) that

$$\text{posterior variance} = a$$

Moreover
$$\frac{1}{a} = \frac{1}{\sigma^2/n} + \frac{1}{\sigma_0^2} \tag{15-30 repeated}$$

Thus, provided $\sigma_0^2 \neq \infty$ (i.e., provided prior information is not useless)

$$\frac{1}{a} > \frac{1}{\sigma^2/n} \tag{15-45}$$

hence
$$a < \sigma^2/n \tag{15-46}$$

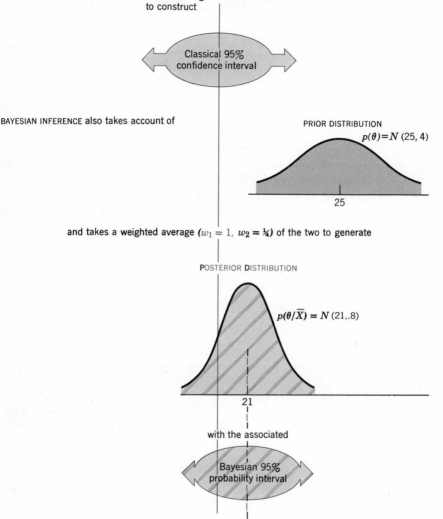

CLASSICAL INFERENCE uses   OBSERVED STATISTIC

$\overline{X}$

20

and knowledge of its distribution
to construct

Classical 95%
confidence interval

BAYESIAN INFERENCE also takes account of   PRIOR DISTRIBUTION

$p(\theta) = N(25, 4)$

25

and takes a weighted average $(w_1 = 1, \ w_2 = \frac{1}{4})$ of the two to generate

POSTERIOR DISTRIBUTION

$p(\theta/\overline{X}) = N(21, .8)$

21

with the associated

Bayesian 95%
probability interval

FIGURE 15-5   Classical versus Bayesian estimation, for the example in the text.

evidence according to (15-40); as a result the posterior mean (21) is only
1/4 as close to the prior mean (25) as it is to the observed mean (20).
Thus the Bayesian posterior distribution is seen to be an intuitively
reasonable compromise between observed and prior information.

(b) Limiting Bayes Estimators

It is interesting to see what happens to Bayesian estimates if the prior information becomes so vague as to become useless—i.e., as the prior variance σ_0^2 becomes infinite. Then we see in (15-38) that as $\sigma_0^2 \to \infty$

$$w_2 \to 0 \tag{15-47}$$

Thus in (15-24)

$$p(\theta/\overline{X}) \to N\left(\frac{w_1\overline{X}}{w_1}, \frac{1}{w_1}\right) = N\left(\overline{X}, \frac{\sigma^2}{n}\right) \tag{15-48}$$

Thus the Bayes estimate approaches the classical estimate, if prior information becomes infinitely vague. The same conclusion holds if the empirical evidence becomes overwhelmingly reliable, i.e., if the sample size[9] $n \to \infty$. Table 15-8 provides a summary of this argument, showing how in either of the above limiting cases, classical and Bayesian estimates coincide.

(c) Is θ Fixed or Variable?

In this chapter we regard the target to be estimated as a random variable—for example, the beetle's length θ in Figure 15-5. Yet in all preceding chapters, we have regarded the target as a fixed parameter—for

Table 15-8   Relation of Classical and Bayesian Estimation. (Although Normality is Assumed, Results are Instructive for Other Cases Too)

Procedure to Estimate θ		Requires, Along With Observed $\overline{X}$	And Gets the Answer:	
			In Our Example, ($n = 10$)	In the Limit, as $n \to \infty$ or $\sigma_0^2 \to \infty$
Classical	Point estimate		20	$\overline{X}$
	Confidence interval	$p(\overline{X}/\theta)$	20 ± 1.96	$\overline{X} \pm 1.96\dfrac{\sigma}{\sqrt{n}}$
Bayesian	Point estimate	$p(\overline{X}/\theta), p(\theta)$ and loss function	21	Same as classical
	Probability interval	$p(\overline{X}/\theta), p(\theta)$	21 ± 1.76	Same as classical

---

[9] As $n \to \infty$, the weight $w_1 \to \infty$; hence the relative weight of w_2 approaches 0, just as in (15-47). Then the same conclusion (15-48) follows.

example, the average height μ of American men. Nevertheless, we may often find it useful to think of μ as having a *subjective* probability distribution—with this being a description of the betting odds we would give that μ is bracketed by any two given values (see the description of subjective probability in Problem 3-36). In the problem of men's heights it may be helpful to boil down our best prior knowledge of μ into a prior subjective distribution of μ. Then the posterior subjective distribution of μ would reflect how the sampling data changed the betting odds.

PROBLEMS

15-12 For the beetle example described in this section, suppose that:

$$\sigma_0^2 = 100 \qquad \sigma^2 = 10$$
$$\theta_0 = 25 \qquad n = 100$$
$$\bar{X} = 20$$

(a) Calculate the Bayesian point estimate for θ, the length of the beetle. Explain intuitively why this estimate is closer to the observed value of 20 than the Bayesian estimate in Figure 15-5.
(b) Calculate the Bayesian 95% probability interval for θ.

15-13 Before investigating the heights of a certain population of men, an anthropologist was asked what he thought the mean would be. His best guess was 70″, but he was reluctant to be so specific. Finally he agreed that his prior distribution was approximately as follows:

A random sample of 100 men was then taken, with a mean height of 71″, and variance 9 ($\sigma^2 \simeq s^2 = 9$).
(a) What is the Bayes estimate of μ?
(b) What is the 95% Bayes interval for μ?
(c) How and why does (b) differ from the classical interval given in Problem 7-1a?

15-14 Select the most appropriate statement (and criticize the others):
Bayesian estimation of a parameter θ differs from classical estimation as follows:

(a) Bayesian estimation combines the data, a prior distribution of θ, and a loss function, whereas classical estimation uses only the data.

(b) As sample size increases, the difference between the classical estimate and the Bayesian estimate grows without limit.

(c) Classical estimates are harder to compute than Bayesian estimates.

15-5   CRITIQUE OF BAYESIAN METHODS

(a) Strength

Bayesian inference is the optimal statistical method (in the sense of minimizing loss of utility) if there is a known prior distribution $p(\theta)$ and loss function $l(a, \theta)$. Compared to classical methods, Bayesian methods often yield shorter interval estimates, more credible point estimates, and more appropriate hypothesis tests. Bayesian methods are particularly useful in the social sciences and business, where sample size is often very small, and Bayesian methods therefore differ considerably from the classical methods.

(b) Weakness

The major criticism of Bayesian estimation is that it is highly subjective. The prior $p(\theta)$ and loss function $l(a, \theta)$ are usually not known[10] nor is there often any hope at all of specifying them exactly. For example, what is the loss function for an economist measuring a population's unemployment rate, with inevitable statistical error? We have already seen that this is not as serious a difficulty as it seems at first glance, since in many problems any of the three loss functions of Table 15-7 lead to the same Bayes estimator. Then selecting the "wrong" loss function would still lead to the right estimator.

The other information required—the prior distribution $p(\theta)$—usually remains unknown too. Moreover, there are often difficulties in interpreting it as relative frequency. For example, an economist usually cannot regard the unemployment rate θ as having a relative frequency distribution as though it were drawn from a bowlful of chips. Instead he must

---

[10] The other required information for Bayesian inference is the distribution of the sample statistic, e.g., $p(\overline{X}/\theta)$. But this can be borrowed from classical statistics, as for example in (15-23).

think of $p(\theta)$ as a subjective distribution reflecting his prior betting odds on θ. But he may not view even this as entirely satisfactory.

Since Bayesian techniques require a rough-and-ready specification of these unknown functions, they do indeed involve subjective judgments. The interesting observation however, is that classical methods which require no such *explicit* specifications, are by no means free of the same subjective elements. One of the major contributions of the Bayesian method has been to lay bare the assumptions implicit in classical techniques. As we shall next show, some of these fare badly when exposed; in extreme cases *any* intelligent guess is substantially better.

(c) Classical Estimators as Peculiar Bayesian Estimators

Suppose that in a small poll of 12 students taken on a college campus, only 1 student is a Democrat. To estimate the population proportion π, the classical estimator is the sample proportion

$$P = \frac{S}{n} = \frac{1}{12} = 8\% \qquad (15\text{-}50)$$

It could be shown that a Bayesian would arrive at the same answer, if he used the quadratic loss function, and the prior distribution shown in Figure 15-6a. This prior distribution is very peculiar indeed—it means that there is very likely a huge majority of Democrats ($\pi \approx 1$) or Republicans ($\pi \approx 0$). It would be more reasonable to guess "complete ignorance," as specified by the flat prior distribution shown in Figure 15-6b. It has been proved that this leads to the Bayesian estimator

$$\frac{S+1}{n+2} = \frac{2}{14} = 14\% \qquad (15\text{-}51)$$

But anyone with any knowledge of politics can do better than this; for example, consider the prior distribution shown in Figure 15-6c, which implies that it is very unlikely that there is a huge majority of Democrats or Republicans. This leads to the Bayesian estimator

$$\frac{S+3}{n+6} = \frac{4}{18} = 22\% \qquad (15\text{-}52)$$

Now the same flawless logic is used in deriving all three estimators (15-50) to (15-52). They must be judged, therefore, by their differing prior distributions, with the classical estimator (15-50) being the least satisfactory.

We therefore conclude that in cases like this involving a small sample

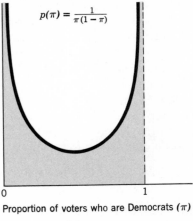

$$p(\pi) = \frac{1}{\pi(1-\pi)}$$

0   1

Proportion of voters who are Democrats (π)

(a)

$p(\pi)$

0   1 π

(b)

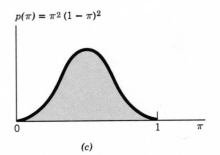

$$p(\pi) = \pi^2(1-\pi)^2$$

0   1 π

(c)

FIGURE 15-6 (a) The peculiar prior distribution that yields the classical estimator $P = S/n$ (assuming the quadratic loss function). (b) A less absurd (but still not very useful) prior distribution, yielding the estimator $(S+1)/(n+2)$. (c) A more plausible prior distribution, yielding the estimator $(S+3)/(n+6)$.

and relatively strong prior belief, a classical estimate may be quite inappropriate, and should be replaced by a Bayesian estimate.

15-6   HYPOTHESIS TESTING AS A BAYESIAN DECISION

(a) Example

Suppose there are two species of beetle. Species S_0 is harmless, while species S_1 is a serious pest, requiring an expensive insecticide. A beetle is sighted in a new, as yet uninfested territory; but this sighting provides no information useful in establishing whether the beetle was S_0 or S_1. Should insecticide be used or not?

To answer this question, we need to know the costs $l(a, \theta)$ of a wrong decision, and the probabilities $p(\theta)$ of it being one species or the other; these are given in Table 15-9. Obviously action a_0 (don't spray) is appropriate if the state of nature is S_0 (harmless beetle) while a_1 is appropriate if the state is S_1.

Question 1. Should we spray, or not?

solution   It will be convenient to generalize the loss table, calling $l(a_i, \theta_j) = l_{ij}$, for short. As always, we calculate the expected losses $L(a)$, by weighting elements in each row of this table by their appropriate probabilities:

$$
\left.
\begin{aligned}
L(a_0) &= p(\theta_0)\, l_{00} + p(\theta_1)\, l_{01} \\
       &= (.7)\, 5 + (.3)\, 100 = 33.5 \\[2mm]
\text{and} \\[1mm]
L(a_1) &= (.7)\, 15 + (.3)\, 15 = 15 \leftarrow \text{min}
\end{aligned}
\right\}
\tag{15-53}
$$

Thus the optimal action is a_1 (spray).

Table 15-9 Probabilities of States of Nature, and Loss Function

Probability $p(\theta)$	.7	.3
State θ Action a	S_0 (Harmless Species)	S_1 (Harmful Species)
a_0 (don't spray)	5	100
a_1 (spray)	15	15

We see that this problem may be expressed in terms of hypothesis testing: action a_0 (don't spray) may be interpreted as accepting H_0 (harmless beetle), while action a_1 (spray) may be interpreted as accepting H_1 (harmful beetle).

Question 2. Suppose that prior information about the beetles is that species S_0 is 9 times as common as S_1. Given this new information about $p(\theta)$, what is the optimum action?

solution Don't spray, as shown in Table 15-10.

In this case the harmful species is so rare, that it is better to "take the risk," that is, assume the beetle is harmless as our working hypothesis.

Question 3. So far we have assumed no statistical information on the beetle that has been sighted. Now suppose it has been captured, with its length measured as 27 mm. Suppose further that the two species are distinguishable by their lengths, which are normal random variables with $\sigma = 4$, and means $\theta_0 = 25$ and $\theta_1 = 30$ respectively. What now is the best action, a posteriori? [Assume $p(\theta)$ and losses given in Table 15-9.]

solution It will be most instructive to develop a general solution, leaving substitution of particulars to the end. Losses are calculated as in (15-53), using the appropriate posterior probabilities $p(\theta/X)$:

$$L(a_0) = p(\theta_0/X)\, l_{00} + p(\theta_1/X)\, l_{01} \tag{15-54}$$

Similarly

$$L(a_1) = p(\theta_0/X)\, l_{10} + p(\theta_1/X)\, l_{11} \tag{15-55}$$

We choose action a_0 iff

$$L(a_0) < L(a_1) \tag{15-56}$$

Table 15-10   Calculation of optimal action

$p(\theta)$	.9	.1	
State θ / Action a	S_0 (H_0)	S_1 (H_1)	$L(a)$
a_0 (don't spray)	5	100	14.5 ← min
a_1 (spray)	15	15	15

Substituting (15-54) and (15-55) into (15-56), and collecting like terms, we obtain the criterion: choose a_0 iff

$$p(\theta_1/X)\,[l_{01} - l_{11}] < p(\theta_0/X)\,[l_{10} - l_{00}] \tag{15-57}$$

The bracketed quantities

$$r_0 \triangleq l_{10} - l_{00} \tag{15-58}$$

and

$$r_1 \triangleq l_{01} - l_{11} \tag{15-59}$$

are called regrets. It is easy to see why: the regret if the beetle is harmless (r_0) is the extra loss incurred if we use the wrong action—that is, spray (a_1), rather than not spray (a_0). Evaluating (15-58) we see that r_0 is $15 - 5 = 10$, the difference in column elements in Table 15-9. Our much larger regret $r_1 = 100 - 15$ represents our net loss if we employ the wrong action (don't spray) on a beetle that turns out to be harmful.

Returning to (15-57), it may now be written in terms of regrets:

$$p(\theta_1/X)\,r_1 < p(\theta_0/X)\,r_0 \tag{15-60}$$

that is

$$\frac{p(\theta_1/X)}{p(\theta_0/X)} < \frac{r_0}{r_1} \tag{15-61}$$

The posterior probabilities in this equation can now be expressed in full using (15-7), and noting that $p(X)$ cancels,

$$\frac{p(\theta_1)\,p(X/\theta_1)}{p(\theta_0)\,p(X/\theta_0)} < \frac{r_0}{r_1} \tag{15-62}$$

Recall that this is our criterion for action a_0 (don't spray), interpreted as acceptance of H_0: (beetle harmless, $\theta = \theta_0$). An appropriate cross-multiplication in (15-62) leads us to an important theorem,

Bayesian Likelihood-Ratio Criterion:

Accept H_0 iff
$$\frac{p(X/\theta_1)}{p(X/\theta_0)} < \frac{r_0\,p(\theta_0)}{r_1\,p(\theta_1)} \tag{15-63}$$

where r_i is the regret if θ_i is true, $p(\theta_i)$ is the prior distribution, and $p(X/\theta_i)$ is the probability distribution of the observed data, sometimes called the "likelihood" function.

This criterion is certainly reasonable. If θ_1 is a sufficiently implausible explanation of the data [i.e., $p(X/\theta_1)$ is sufficiently less than $p(X/\theta_0)$], then the likelihood ratio will be small enough to satisfy this inequality. Thus H_0 will be accepted, as it should be.

To illustrate further, consider the very simple case in which the regrets (penalties for error) are assumed equal, and the prior probabilities $p(\theta_0)$ and $p(\theta_1)$ are also assumed equal. The right-hand side of (15-63) becomes 1; thus H_0 is accepted if the likelihood of θ_0 generating the sample $[p(X/\theta_0)]$ is greater than the likelihood of θ_1 generating the sample $[p(X/\theta_1)]$. Otherwise, the alternative H_1 is accepted. In simplest terms: we accept the hypothesis which is more likely to generate the observed X, as shown in Figure 15-7a. In Figure 15-7b we make the further as-

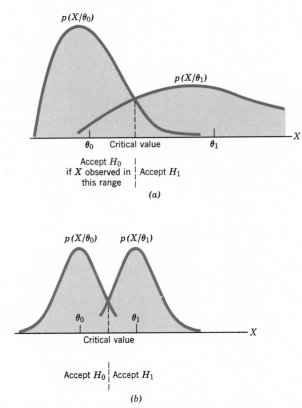

FIGURE 15-7 Hypothesis testing, using the Bayesian likelihood ratio [special case when $r_0 = r_1$ and $p(\theta_1) = p(\theta_0)$]. (a) For any $p(X/\theta_i)$. (b) If $p(X/\theta_i) = N(\theta_i, \sigma^2)$.

sumption that the two likelihood functions (centered on θ_0 and θ_1 respectively) have the same normal[11] distribution. Then (15-63) reduces to the very reasonable criterion

Accept H_0 iff X is observed closer to θ_0 than θ_1 (15-64)

Evaluating (15-63) when $r_0 \neq r_1$ or $p(\theta_0) \neq p(\theta_1)$ is obviously a more complicated matter. To keep things simple, we assume that $\theta_0 < \theta_1$, and that $p(X/\theta_0)$ and $p(X/\theta_1)$ are normal with a common σ. Then (15-63)—our criterion for accepting H_0—becomes

$$\frac{e^{-(1/2\sigma^2)(X-\theta_1)^2}}{e^{-(1/2\sigma^2)(X-\theta_0)^2}} < \frac{r_0 p(\theta_0)}{r_1 p(\theta_1)} \tag{15-65}$$

This may be reduced[12] to: accept H_0 iff

$$X < \frac{\sigma^2}{\theta_1 - \theta_0} \log\left[\frac{r_0 p(\theta_0)}{r_1 p(\theta_1)}\right] + \frac{\theta_1 + \theta_0}{2} \tag{15-66}$$

(The logarithms used throughout this section are natural logarithms, to the base e. The common logarithms of Appendix Table Ib can be converted to natural logarithms by multiplying by 2.30.) We note that the right-hand side of (15-66) is independent of X; as in all hypothesis tests, this can be evaluated prior to observing X. At the same time (15-66) does depend, as expected, on background information $p(\theta)$ and regrets.

---

[11] In fact, normality is not required; the two distributions need only have the same unimodal symmetric shape.

[12] **proof**   taking logarithms of (15-65):

$$-\frac{1}{2\sigma^2}(X - \theta_1)^2 + \frac{1}{2\sigma^2}(X - \theta_0)^2 < K$$

where

$$K = \log\left[\frac{r_0 \, p(\theta_0)}{r_1 \, p(\theta_1)}\right]$$

Rearranging

$$\frac{1}{2\sigma^2}(2\theta_1 X - 2\theta_0 X - \theta_1^2 + \theta_0^2) < K$$

$$2(\theta_1 - \theta_0)X - (\theta_1^2 - \theta_0^2) < 2\sigma^2 K$$

that is, accept H_0 iff:

$$X < \frac{\sigma^2}{\theta_1 - \theta_0} K + \frac{(\theta_1^2 - \theta_0^2)}{2(\theta_1 - \theta_0)} \tag{15-66} \text{ follows}$$

Moreover, when $r_0 = r_1$ and $p(\theta_0) = p(\theta_1)$, then the log term disappears and this reduces to the special case (15-64).

Finally, the particular problem of the beetle spray can now be solved. Substituting the information given in question 3 and Table 15-9 into (15-66) yields: accept H_0 iff

$$X < \frac{16}{5} \log\left[\frac{10(.7)}{85(.3)}\right] + 27.5 \qquad (15\text{-}67)$$

$$X < 3.2 \log\left(\frac{7}{25.5}\right) + 27.5$$

$$X < 3.2(-1.29) + 27.5$$

$$X < 23.4 \qquad (15\text{-}68)$$

Since we observed a 27 mm beetle, this condition is violated, and we reject H_0. But what does seem strange is the critical value in (15-68): even if the beetle were 25 mm—exactly θ_0, the length we would expect of a *harmless* beetle—we would still spray. With further thought we see that this answer is, after all, reasonable. The heavy damage involved if the beetle turns out to be harmful induces us to spray to avoid this risk. [From (15-67) we confirm that it is in fact the relative size of the two regrets that explains this result.]

(b) Comparison with Classical Methods

Bayesian methods are more complicated than classical methods, yet often more satisfactory. This is as true for testing as it was for confidence intervals. A Bayesian test uses all the information in a classical test, and also exploits the prior distribution $p(\theta)$ and regrets (the loss function). A classical test sets the level of significance (probability of type I error) at 5% or 1%—sometimes arbitrarily, sometimes with implicit reference to vague considerations of loss and prior belief. Bayesians would argue that these considerations should be explicitly introduced—with all the assumptions exposed, and open to criticism and improvement.

PROBLEMS

15-15 Suppose a psychiatrist has to classify people as sick or well (hospitalized or not) on the basis of a psychological test. The test scores are normally distributed, with $\sigma = 8$, and mean $\theta_0 = 100$ if they are well or $\theta_1 = 120$ if they are sick. The losses (regrets) of a wrong classification are obvious: if a healthy person is hospitalized, resources are wasted and the person himself may even be hurt by the treatment. Yet the other loss is even worse: if a sick person is not hospitalized, he may do damage, conceivably fatal. Suppose this second loss is considered roughly five times as serious. From past records it has been found that of the people taking the test, 60% are sick and 40% are healthy.

(a) (1) What should be the critical score above which the person is classified as sick? Then

(2) What is α? (Probability of type I error).

(3) What is β? (Probability of type II error).

(b) (1) If a classical test is used, arbitrarily setting $\alpha = 5\%$, what will be the critical score? then

(2) What is β?

(3) By how much has the average loss increased by using this less-than-optimal method?

(c) What would we have to assume the ratio of the two regrets to be in order to arrive at a Bayesian test having $\alpha = 5\%$? Do you think it is reasonable?

15-16 (a) Using $p(\theta)$ and losses given in Table 15-10, reconstruct the hypothesis test of question (3) which appears just before (15-54). With your measurement of 27 mm, what would you do? Why does our previous argument (spray even if beetle is 25 mm) no longer hold?

(b) Suppose that species S_0 and S_1 were equally frequent. Would that alter your decision?

(c) How frequent would species S_1 have to be in order to justify spraying?

Review Problems

15-17 Suppose an archaeologist has to classify skulls as "tribe A" or "tribe B," on the basis of their width. The populations of skull widths are normally distributed as follows:

Tribe	Mean	Standard Deviation
A	12 cm.	2 cm.
B	15 cm.	2 cm.

Tribe A is 5 times as numerous as tribe B. Misclassifying an A skull as a B is considered equally unfortunate as misclassifying a B skull as an A. How would you advise an archaeologist to classify each of the ten skulls whose widths are as follows:

11.6	14.2
15.9	15.1
16.8	18.6
13.5	14.0
13.9	15.0

State clearly the basis for your decision.

15-18 After reading this chapter, a biologist wryly observed that a scientist was not a business man—his job was to discover the truth, not minimize costs. Do you agree?

15-19 To help decide whether or not to drill for oil in a certain location off the west coast, an oil company gets their geologists to list the possibilities, as follows:

Possible Outcome	Value of Oil	Probability
Dry well	0	.6
Wet well	$200,000	.4

We shall suppose that utility is proportional to money, for such a small operation as this.

(a) If the cost of drilling is $50,000 (whether the well is wet or dry), should the company risk it?

(b) If the well is wet, there is a 5% chance that it will get out of hand and cause pollution of the shore. If this happens, how large a fine should the government impose in order to just barely discourage drilling?

15-20 A farmer has to decide whether or not to cut his hay crop before the weekend, and is worried lest it rain. He estimates the value of his crop (in dollars) under various circumstances, as follows:

His Action \ State of Nature	Rain	Shine
Cut now	400	700
Wait	800	500

Of course, if he *knew* it was going to rain, he would wait. Or if he *knew* it was going to shine, he would cut before the weekend.

Unfortunately he does not know for certain—the best information he has is the weather broadcast, which predicts rain with probability 4/10, shine with probability 6/10. What should he do—cut now, or wait?

15-21 Suppose your firm has just purchased a major piece of machinery, and your engineers have judged it to be substandard. You know that the firm that produced it often substitutes inferior domestic components for the standard imported components (1/4 of the time, at random). You further know that such substitution of domestic components increases the probability that the machine will be substandard from .2 to .3. What is the probability that your machine has imported components?

*15-22 A biologist collected many moths by random sampling in a certain region, and found there were 2 species, beneficial (S_B) and harmful (S_H). He further found that these two species were easily (but imperfectly) distinguishable on the basis of their antenna lengths, which were distributed as follows:

(These figures represent smoothed histograms, and you may take them as adequate representations of the populations; note from the areas enclosed by the two curves that species S_B is much more common than S_H.)

Consider the following classification rule for a randomly caught moth:

1. Classify the moth as S_B if antenna length $< c$
2. Classify the moth as S_H if antenna length $\geq c$

The biologist asks us to find the optimal value of the critical length c. Of course we must take into account the relative regrets for the two misclassification errors, which we denote as

r_0 = regret for type I error (misclassifying an S_B moth as an S_H)

r_1 = regret for type II error (misclassifying an S_H moth as an S_B)

Since much of your information is graphic, your solution will have to be graphic and approximate also.

Find the optimum value for c if

(a) $r_0 = r_1$

(b) $r_0 = (1/4)r_1$

(c) $r_0 = 4r_1$

CHAPTER 16
NONPARAMETRIC STATISTICS

Public agencies are very keen on amassing statistics—they collect them, add them, raise them to the nth power, take the cube root and prepare wonderful diagrams. But what you must never forget is that every one of those figures comes in the first instance from the village watchman, who just puts down what he damn pleases.

Sir Josiah Stamp

16-1 INTRODUCTION

Many of the classical statistics we have so far considered (like Student's t) require the assumption of population normality. If this assumption does not hold, then these statistics become more or less invalid—depending on the particular application. Thus, when the population is suspected to be nonnormal, it becomes appropriate to consider nonparametric statistics (like the BES introduced in Section 7-3), which require no normality assumption. There may be two reasons for preferring a nonparametric test:

1. The corresponding classical test may be invalid.
2. But even in applications where the classical test is reasonably valid, a nonparametric estimator may be much more efficient (have smaller variance); in fact, this is the more important reason for using nonparametric estimators.

For nearly every parametric test (e.g., t test, ANOVA) there are usually several corresponding nonparametric tests; a description of all of these would fill several volumes. We begin by developing two: the sign test, which corresponds to the 1 sample t test (8-15), and the W test, which corresponds to the 2 sample t test (8-17).

16-2 **THE SIGN TEST**

(a) Confidence Interval for the Median, Small Samples

Suppose the median income of families in a certain city is claimed to be \$11,000 by the Chamber of Commerce. But in a random sample of 9 families, 8 have an income below \$11,000, while only one has an income over \$11,000. Does this evidence allow us to reject the claim?

Suppose these 9 observations are ordered according to size as in Table 16-1 and Figure 16-1. The null hypothesis is

$$H_0: \text{median, } \nu = \$11,000 \tag{16-1}$$

That is, half the population incomes lie below \$11,000; or if an observation is randomly drawn, the probability that it lies below \$11,000 is

$$H_0: \pi = 1/2 \tag{16-2}$$

We recognize (16-2) as being just like the hypothesis that a coin is fair. To state it more explicitly, we have two events which are mathematically equivalent:

random observation will fall below the median
= a coin will show heads   (16-3)

If H_0 is true, the sample of $n = 9$ observations is just like tossing a coin 9 times. The total number of successes S (families below \$11,000) will have the binomial distribution, and H_0 may be rejected if S is too far away from its expected value to be reasonably explained by chance.

Table 16-1	Random Sample of Nine Incomes
$X_{(1)} =$	6,900
$X_{(2)} =$	7,200
$X_{(3)} =$	8,300
$X_{(4)} =$	8,700
$X_{(5)} =$	8,900
$X_{(6)} =$	9,800
$X_{(7)} =$	10,100
$X_{(8)} =$	10,800
$X_{(9)} =$	12,000

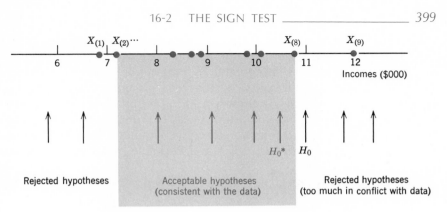

FIGURE 16-1   Nine ordered observations of income.

Now suppose the alternative hypothesis is that the Chamber of Commerce estimate is wrong (i.e., too high or too low). Since this is a two-sided alternative, the test should also be two-sided. Therefore, using (9-8), we calculate the two-sided prob-value, i.e., given H_0, the probability that we would observe an S as extreme as 8 (that is, either 0, 1, 8, or 9). Thus

$$\text{prob-value} = 2 \Pr(S \geq 8) \tag{16-4}$$

which, in Appendix Table IIIc, is seen to be

$$= 2(.0195) \tag{16-5}$$
$$= .039 \tag{16-6}$$

Or, if we had used a Classical hypothesis test, setting the level of significance at say $\alpha = .04$, we would just barely reject[1] H_0. Of course, it is evident from Figure 16-1 that any hypothesis above $X_{(8)} = 10,800$ would be rejected for the same reasons. Rejected hypotheses like this (e.g., $\nu = 11,900$, $\nu = 12,300$) are shown as black arrows in Figure 16-1.

On the other hand, consider an hypothesis below $X_{(8)} = 10,800$, such as

$$H_0^*: \text{median}, \nu = \$10,500 \tag{16-7}$$

Since there are now 7 rather than 8 "heads" (incomes below the median), (16-4) becomes

$$\text{prob-value} = 2 \Pr(S \geq 7)$$
$$= 2(.0898) = .1796 \tag{16-8}$$

_____

[1] Recall from (9-19) that we reject H_0 iff prob-value $\leq \alpha$.

Since this now exceeds $\alpha = .04$, H_0^* is an acceptable hypothesis. By the same logic, even lower hypotheses such as $\nu = 10{,}000$ or $\nu = 9100$, are also acceptable. These acceptable hypotheses are shown as colored arrows in Figure 16-1. Of course, at the very low end of the range we again encounter rejected hypotheses, in strong conflict with the observed data; (in a symmetric two-tailed test, if $X_{(8)}$ is one critical cutoff point between acceptance and rejection, then by symmetry $X_{(2)}$ must be the other). Finally, we note that the set of acceptable hypotheses form an interval.

Now we recall the crucial connection between hypothesis testing and confidence intervals:

> A confidence interval may be regarded as just the set of acceptable hypotheses

(16-9)

(9-2) repeated

Thus in Figure 16-1 we have constructed a confidence interval for the population median, the level of confidence being $1 - \alpha = 96\%$. In algebraic language, the 96% confidence interval for the population median, when $n = 9$, is

$$X_{(2)} \leq \nu \leq X_{(8)} \qquad (16\text{-}10)$$

i.e.,
$$7200 \leq \nu \leq 10800 \qquad (16\text{-}11)$$

Note that since the binomial distribution is discrete, confidence levels are discrete too. For example, if we considered (16-11) as having a higher confidence level (96%) than necessary, the next possible level would be[2] 82%. Of course, as sample size increases, the binomial becomes nearly continuous and this problem tends to disappear.

(b) Generalization

Consider a sample of n ordered observations $X_{(1)}, X_{(2)} \ldots X_{(n)}$ from a population with unknown median ν. The confidence interval is defined by counting off q observations from each end,

$$\overline{X_{(q)} \leq \nu \leq X_{(r)}} \qquad (16\text{-}12)$$

where q and r are symmetrically chosen, i.e.,

$$r = n - q + 1 \qquad (16\text{-}13)$$

---

[2] Using (16-8), it follows that $X_{(3)} \leq \nu \leq X_{(7)}$ has confidence level $1 - 2(.0898) \simeq 82\%$; actually, a 95% confidence interval can be approximated by interpolating between $X_{(2)}$ and $X_{(3)}$, and between $X_{(7)}$ and $X_{(8)}$.

The problem then is to solve for the significance level α, which may be obtained from the binomial distribution, using $\pi = 1/2$ in Table IIIc. For S successes in n trials,

$$\alpha = 2 \Pr(S \geq r) \qquad (16\text{-}14)$$

(c) Confidence Interval for the Median, Large Samples

Suppose a large sample of 100 incomes is taken in order to find a confidence interval for the median. With this larger sample, it is evident that there is no longer any great problem of discreteness, so that it becomes convenient to use the standard technique of first arbitrarily setting the confidence level, and then solving for the interval. If the confidence level is set at 95% (i.e., $\alpha = .05$), then (16-14) becomes,

$$\Pr(S \geq r) = .025 \qquad (16\text{-}16)$$

where S is binomial with $\pi = 1/2$. The problem now is to solve for r. Note that in a large sample, S becomes approximately normal with

$$\mu_S = n\pi = 50 \qquad \begin{array}{c}(16\text{-}17)\\ (6\text{-}23) \text{ repeated}\end{array}$$

and

$$\sigma_S = \sqrt{n\pi(1 - \pi)} = 5 \qquad \begin{array}{c}(16\text{-}18)\\ (6\text{-}24) \text{ repeated}\end{array}$$

Now (16-16) may be restated in standardized form as

$$\Pr\left(\frac{S - \mu_S}{\sigma_S} \geq \frac{r - 50}{5}\right) = .025 \qquad (16\text{-}19)$$

From the standard normal tables,

$$\Pr(Z \geq 1.96) = .025 \qquad (16\text{-}20)$$

Comparing these two equations yields

$$\frac{r - 50}{5} = 1.96$$

$$r = 60 \qquad (16\text{-}21)$$

Substituting into (16-13) yields $q = 41$; hence the approximate 95% confidence interval is, from (16-12),

$$X_{(41)} \leq \nu \leq X_{(60)} \qquad (16\text{-}22)$$

A numerical evaluation of (16-22) requires only sorting (by hand, machine, or computer) through the sample for observations $X_{(41)}$ and $X_{(60)}$. Note that the sample median will be near (but not exactly on) the center of this confidence interval; and, of course, if we wanted a point estimate (rather than an interval estimate) of the population median it would be natural to use the sample median.

(d) Two Matched Samples

Consider an example similar to Problems 4-31 and 8-9: suppose a small sample of 8 men had their motor capacity measured before and after a certain treatment; the results are shown in Table 16-2. Let us test the null hypothesis that the treatment has no effect on average over the whole population. Suppose the alternate hypothesis is two-sided.

The original matched pairs can be forgotten, once the differences have been found. These differences D form a single sample, to which we shall now apply the sign test. The null hypothesis ("no affect of treatment") is

$$H_0: \text{median}, \nu = 0 \qquad (16\text{-}27)$$

i.e., $$\pi = \Pr(\text{observing positive}^4 D) = 1/2 \qquad (16\text{-}28)$$

The question is: are the observed 6 positive D's (i.e., 6 "heads") in a sample of 8 observations ("tosses") consistent with H_0? The probability of this is

Table 16-2   Motor Capacity of Eight Patients,
Before and After Treatment

X (Before)	Y (After)	Difference $(D = Y - X)$
2750	2850	+100
2360	2380	+ 20
2950	2930	− 20
2830	2860	+ 30
2250	2300	+ 50
2680	2740	+ 60
2720	2760	+ 40
2810	2800	− 10

---

[4]Negative D could equally well serve as the criterion in (16-28) but positive D is the custom. It should also be noted that any observation that occurs right on the hypothetical median (i.e., any D observed to be exactly zero) should be discarded immediately, and not be counted in any way.

$$\text{prob-value} = 2 \Pr(S \geq 6)$$
$$= 2(.1445) = .29 \qquad (16\text{-}29)$$

which does not call for rejecting H_0.

The origin of the term "sign test" should now be clear. It is a test based on the binomial distribution, where the test statistic is the number of positive differences ("heads").

PROBLEMS

16-1   Random Sample of Heights of 8
                        Brother-Sister Matched Pairs

Men's Heights (M)	Women's Heights (W)
65	63
68	62
69	64
70	65
71	68
74	66
75	71
76	69

Construct a 93% nonparametric confidence interval for the population median of
(a) men's heights
(b) women's heights
(c) Calculate the prob-value for the null hypothesis H_0 that men's median height is 69.5 inches.
(d) Is H_0 in part (c) acceptable at the 10% level of significance?

16-2 Consider, for each pair in Problem 16-1, the difference $D = M - W$.
(a) Construct a 93% nonparametric confidence interval for the population median of D.
(b) By interpolating the t table, construct a 93% parametric confidence interval for the population mean of D. What crucial assumption are you making? What does this assumption gain you?
(c) When are the population mean and median of D the same?

16-3 Suppose a statistician has used the data in Table 16-1 to construct the following confidence intervals for the median. What is his level of confidence for each?
(a) $6,900 \leq \nu \leq 12,000$
(b) $8,300 \leq \nu \leq 10,100$

THE *W* TEST FOR TWO SAMPLES

(a) Small Sample

The Wilcoxon-Mann-Whitney (*W-M-W*, or *W*) test is used for two independent samples (in contrast to the last section, which used matched pairs). The objective again is to detect whether the two underlying populations are centered differently. For example, suppose independent random samples of income were taken from two different states and ordered as follows:

State *X*	State *Y*
6,300	7,500
6,900	8,200
7,200	8,900
7,900	12,000
$m = 4$	27,000
	46,000
	$n = 6$

Let us test the null hypothesis that the two underlying populations are identical. Suppose the alternate hypothesis is that state *X* is poorer, so that a one-sided test is appropriate.

We first rank the combined *X* and *Y* observations, as shown in Table 16-3.

Table 16-3   Combined Ranking Yields the
W Statistic

Combined Ordered Observations		Combined Ranks	
X	*Y*	*X*	*Y*
6300		1	
6900		2	
7200		3	
	7500		4
7900		5	
	8200		6
	8900		7
	12000		8
	27000		9
	46000		10

$$W = 11$$

The actual income levels are now discarded in favor of this ranking, providing a test that is not affected by skewness, or any other distributional peculiarity—in other words, a distribution-free test. Then W is defined as the sum of all the X ranks; in this case,

$$W = 1 + 2 + 3 + 5 = 11 \qquad (16\text{-}30)$$

Obviously, the lower this value, the stronger the evidence for rejecting H_0. For our data, the one-sided prob-value is found in Appendix Table VIII to be .010, which is strong evidence of a lower average income level in state X.

(b) Generalization

In general, suppose there are m observations in the smaller sample (call them $X_1, X_2 \ldots X_m$) and $n \geq m$ observations in the larger sample (call them $Y_1, Y_2 \ldots Y_n$). For a one-sided test, start counting from the end where the X's predominate (or more precisely, where the X's would tend to predominate if H_1 were true. This keeps the X ranks low.) Adding up all the X ranks yields the rank sum W.

Appendix Table VIII gives the corresponding one-sided prob-value, for $n \leq 7$ and prob-value $\leq .25$. For samples larger than those covered by this table, W is approximately normal[5] (if H_0 is true), with

$$\left.\begin{array}{l} E(W) = \dfrac{1}{2}m(m + n + 1) \\[2mm] \text{var}\,(W) = \dfrac{1}{12}\,mn(m + n + 1) \end{array}\right\} \qquad (16\text{-}31)$$

To illustrate, suppose we had taken two larger samples of income from the two states, as shown in Table 16-4a.

---

[5] It is remarkable that just as the binomial statistic is normally distributed, so is W, and in fact all the other test statistics we shall study in this chapter. The proof consists of generalizing the central limit theorem.

The approximately normal distribution for W must not be confused with the parent distribution of the X's and Y's, which may be very nonnormal.

Table 16-4a W Statistic, Large-Sample

Combined Ordered Observations		Combined Ranks	
X	Y	X	Y
4200		1	
	5100		2
5300		3	
6700		4	
	8700		5
	8800		6
8900		7	
	11300		8
	11800		9
	11900		10
	26000		11
	28000		12

$$W = 15$$

Substituting $n = 8$ and $m = 4$ into (16-31),

$$\left. \begin{array}{l} E(W) = 26 \\ \text{var}(W) = 34.7 \end{array} \right\} \tag{16-32}$$

To test the null hypothesis,

$$\text{prob-value} \triangleq \Pr(W \le 15) \tag{16-33}$$

$$= \Pr\left(\frac{W - \mu_W}{\sigma_W} \le \frac{15 - 26}{\sqrt{34.7}}\right) \tag{16-34}$$

$$= \Pr(Z \le -1.87)$$

$$= .031 \tag{16-35}$$

Hence, at a 5% level of significance H_0 may be rejected in favor of the alternate hypothesis that income is lower in state X.

(c) Ties

Tied observations should be given the same rank—their average rank. Unless most of the observations are tied, we can then continue as usual. For example, suppose the 12 observations of Table 16-4a were slightly different with several ties occurring. Then we assign ranks as shown in Table 16-4b.

Table 16-4*b*   *W* Statistic, When Ties Occur

Combined Ordered Observations		Combined Ranks	
X	Y	X	Y
4200		1	
5200	5200	2.5	2.5
6700		4	
8800	8800,8800	6	6,6
	11300		8
	11800		9
	11900		10
	26000		11
	28000		12

$$W = 13.5$$

$E(W)$ and var (W) may still be approximated by (16-31); the prob-value, taken from the normal tables, is

$$\text{prob-value} \overset{\Delta}{=} \Pr(W \leq 13.5) \tag{16-36}$$

$$= \Pr\left(\frac{W - \mu_W}{\sigma_W} \leq \frac{13.5 - 26}{\sqrt{34.7}}\right) \tag{16-37}$$

$$= \Pr(Z \leq -2.12)$$

$$= .017 \tag{16-38}$$

PROBLEMS

16-4 Two makes of cars were randomly sampled, to determine the mileage (in thousands) until the brakes required relining. Calculate the prob-value for the null hypothesis that the two populations are equal. (Use a two-sided alternative hypothesis).

Make *A*	Make *B*
30	22
41	26
48	32
49	39
61	

16-5 A random sample of 8 men's heights and an independent random sample of 8 women's heights were observed, and ordered as follows:

Men's Heights (M)	Women's Heights (W)
65	62
68	63
69	64
70	65
71	66
74	68
75	69
76	71

(a) Calculate the prob-value for the null hypothesis H_0 that the two population distributions are the same. (Although it may be unrealistic, let the alternate hypothesis be two-sided throughout this problem.)

(b) Calculate the prob-value for the hypothesis that men's heights are distributed 2″ higher than women's heights. (*Hint.* If this hypothesis were true, then by subtracting 2″ from each man's height, we would obtain a sample from the same distribution as the women's heights.)

(c) Construct a 93% nonparametric confidence interval for the population differences in men's and women's heights. (*Hint.* Consider many possible shifts as in part (b) and retain only those that are acceptable at the 7% significance level).

(d) Note that the tabled numbers in this problem are the same as in Problem 16-1, although the way they were obtained is different. How does the confidence interval in this problem compare to the one in Problem 16-2. Why?

(e) By interpolating the t table, construct a 93% parametric confidence interval for the population difference in men's and women's heights. What assumption are you making? Does it seem reasonable? What does it gain you?

16-6 Recalculate the prob-value in Problem 16-4
(a) using the large sample formula (16-31), just to see how well it works.
(b) using the large sample formula (16-31), with continuity correction (w.c.c.). Do you think the c.c. is worthwhile?

*16-7 (a) Recalculate the prob-value in (16-33) w.c.c.
(b) Recalculate the prob-value in (16-36) w.c.c., (Hint: when there are ties, how wide are the bars in the probability distribution of W?)

16-4   TESTS FOR RANDOMNESS

(a) Runs Test

One of the most crucial assumptions (even more important than the normality assumption) that we have relied upon in previous chapters is the assumption that our sampling is random.[6] Now we shall develop a test for even that assumption.

By definition, a random sample consists of observations that are *independently* drawn from a *common* population (identically distributed). Thus, if the observations are graphed in the order in which they were sampled, the graph should look somewhat like Figure 16-2a. On the other hand, if the observations are correlated, they will display some "tracking" as in Figure 16-2b. Or if the observations come from 2 different populations, they may appear to be displaced as in Figure 16-2c. How can we quantify the differences that are obvious to the eye in this figure, and find some numerical measure to test the null hypothesis of randomness? We note that when H_0 is true, the path of the observations crosses the median line quite frequently; but when H_0 is not true, this happens much less frequently. This is the basis for the runs test.

For example, in Figure 16-2b we mark observations H (for high) or L (for low), depending on whether they fall above or below the sample median. With slashes indicating the crossovers, this sequence is

$$\text{L L L/H H H H H/L L L L/H H}\tag{16-39}$$

The number of runs R is defined as the number of blocks separated by slashes; in this case $R = 4$. The more tracking, the fewer runs there are.

Let us suppose in general that there are n observations.[7] When H_0 is true, the distribution of R is approximately normal with

$$E(R) \simeq \frac{n}{2} + 1$$

$$\text{var } R \simeq \frac{n(n-2)}{4(n-1)} \simeq \frac{(n-1)}{4}\tag{16-40}$$

---

[6] For example, independent observations were crucial in developing the variance of S in (6-6), hence the variance of $\bar{X}$ in (6-11), which played a key role in estimating μ.

[7] If the sample size is odd, the median line will pass through the median observation, which should be counted neither L nor H. Instead it should be discarded, and let n refer to the even number of observations remaining. When the sample size is even, this issue does not arise, if the population distribution is continuous.

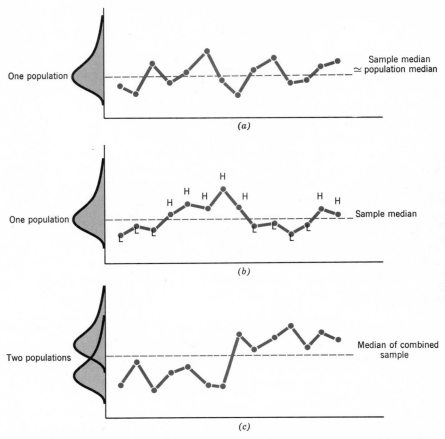

FIGURE 16-2 Sample sequence of (a) independent observations from one population; (b) correlated observations from one population; (c) observations from two populations.

To calculate the prob-value for the null hypothesis of randomness, note that the usual alternative hypothesis results in too few runs (i.e., the observations are positively correlated, as in Figure 16-2b, or drawn from different populations as in Figure 16-2c). Thus a one-sided prob-value is usually appropriate. For the example in Figure 16-2b, $n = 14$, so that (16-40) yields

$$E(R) = \frac{14}{2} + 1 = 8 \qquad (16\text{-}41)$$

$$\text{var }(R) \simeq \frac{(14 - 1)}{4} = 3.25 \qquad (16\text{-}42)$$

Using the normal approximation,

$$\text{prob-value} = \Pr(R \le 4) \tag{16-43}$$

$$= \Pr\left(\frac{R - \mu_R}{\sigma_R} \le \frac{4 - 8}{\sqrt{3.25}}\right) \tag{16-44}$$

$$= \Pr(Z \le -2.22) = .014 \tag{16-45}$$

which is strong evidence that the sample is not random.

(b) Mean-Square Successive Difference

An alternative test for randomness will now be developed that exploits the difference between observations, $(X_i - X_{i-1})$. In fact, let us square to get rid of the sign, obtaining $(X_i - X_{i-1})^2$. Now average over the sample, thus defining the *mean squared successive difference*,

$$\text{MSSD} \overset{\Delta}{=} \frac{1}{n-1} \sum_{i=2}^{n} (X_i - X_{i-1})^2 \tag{16-46}$$

If H_0 (sample is random) is true, the expected value[8] is,

$$E(\text{MSSD}) = 2\sigma^2 \tag{16-47}$$

Now if we knew σ^2, we could appropriately divide by it, obtaining

$$E\left(\frac{\text{MSSD}}{\sigma^2}\right) = 2 \tag{16-48}$$

But since σ^2 is unknown, it is reasonable to divide instead by the unbiased estimator s^2. We finally define, therefore,

$$d \overset{\Delta}{=} \frac{\text{MSSD}}{s^2}$$

---

[8]**proof**   First, we derive the expected value of one individual squared successive difference.

$$E(X_i - X_{i-1})^2 = E[(X_i - \mu) - (X_{i-1} - \mu)]^2$$
$$= E(X_i - \mu)^2 + E(X_{i-1} - \mu)^2 - 2 \operatorname{cov}(X_i, X_{i-1})$$
$$= \sigma^2 + \sigma^2 - 0 = 2\sigma^2$$

Now the expected value of the average of all of these is also $2\sigma^2$ as given in (16-47), since the sample mean is an unbiased estimator of the "population" mean $2\sigma^2$.

i.e.,

$$d = \frac{\sum\limits_{i=2}^{n} (X_i - X_{i-1})^2}{\sum\limits_{i=1}^{n} (X_i - \bar{X})^2} \tag{16-49}$$

Small observed values of d call for rejection of the randomness hypothesis. For example, in Figure 16-2b, the terms in the numerator of (16-49) will tend to be small, since X_i tends to closely follow X_{i-1}. And in Figure 16-2c, the terms in the denominator will tend to be large, since each block of X_i's is so far removed from the sample mean.

To illustrate, suppose we drew the following sequence of 14 observations (similar to Figure 16-2b, except that they have been drawn from a normal population):

$$18, 19, 18, 21, 22, 24, 23, 21, 21, 19, 17, 18, 18, 21 \tag{16-50}$$

Substituting into (16-49), and using $\bar{X} = 20$, we calculate:

$$d = \frac{(19 - 18)^2 + (18 - 19)^2 + (21 - 18)^2 + \cdots}{(18 - 20)^2 + (19 - 20)^2 + \cdots}$$

$$= \frac{44}{60} = .73 \tag{16-51}$$

Finally, we must calculate the prob-value, i.e., interpret $d = .73$ in terms of the distribution of all possible values of d. If the sample is taken from a normal population[9] in which H_0 is true,

$$E(d) \simeq 2 \tag{16-52}$$

like (16-48)

and

$$\text{var}(d) \simeq \frac{n-2}{n^2} \tag{16-53}$$

---

[9] Strictly speaking, then, this is *not* a nonparametric test. However, since most tests of randomness are nonparametric, and this is a test of randomness, in common usage this is often (rather inaccurately) called nonparametric.

In our example (16-50), $n = 14$, so that

$$\text{var}(d) = \frac{14 - 2}{14^2}$$

$$= .0612 \tag{16-54}$$

$$\text{prob-value} = \Pr(d \le .73) \tag{16-55}$$

$$= \Pr\left(\frac{d - \mu_d}{\sigma_d} \le \frac{.73 - 2}{\sqrt{.0612}}\right) \tag{16-56}$$

$$= \Pr(Z \le -5.13)$$

$$\ll .001$$

which provides extraordinarily strong evidence of nonrandomness.

PROBLEMS

16-8

The above graph shows a sample of 12 air pollution readings, taken every 10 minutes over a period of 2 hours. To what extent can we claim these are statistically independent observations from a fixed (rather than drifting) population? Answer by calculating the prob-value for the null hypothesis,

(a) using the runs test

(b) using the mean square successive difference.

(c) What are the advantages and disadvantages of method (a) relative to method (b)?

16-5   **THE ADVANTAGES OF NONPARAMETRIC TESTS**

(a) Validity

(i) Introduction

A test is said to be valid if its prob-values and confidence levels are correct, as specified. Consider a very simple and familiar example: a valid 95% confidence interval for a normal population μ is

$$\mu = \bar{X} \pm t_{.025} \frac{s}{\sqrt{n}} \qquad (16\text{-}57)$$
$$(8\text{-}15) \text{ repeated}$$

But if we carelessly use $z_{.025}$ instead of $t_{.025}$, obtaining

$$\mu = \bar{X} \pm 1.96 \frac{s}{\sqrt{n}} \qquad (16\text{-}58)$$

the test becomes invalid for small samples. For example, if $n = 6$ so that d.f. $= 5$, the interval (16-58) is not only narrower than the correct 95% confidence interval, it is even narrower than the correct 90% confidence interval:

$$\mu = \bar{X} \pm t_{.05} \frac{s}{\sqrt{n}} \qquad (16\text{-}59)$$

$$= \bar{X} \pm 2.015 \frac{s}{\sqrt{n}}$$

Thus in a sample of 6 the true confidence level of (16-58) is less than 90%, rather than specified 95%.

A 95% confidence interval may be invalid for either of two reasons:

1. Its true confidence level may be really lower than 95%, as in the example above. Such a case is called *unsafe*. Thus, this problem can be viewed as an overstatement of confidence level; alternatively, one might say that the interval is unjustifiably narrow.
2. Its true confidence level may be really higher than 95%. Such a case is called *too safe,* or *conservative.* Such confidence intervals are wider (vaguer) than necessary.

(ii) t Tests Versus Nonparametric Tests

The single-sample *t* test for the population mean may be invalid if the population is very nonnormal; (this is especially true of the small-sample, one-tailed *t* test in a skewed population). On the other hand,

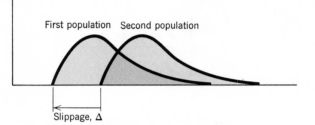

First population   Second population

Slippage, Δ

FIGURE 16-3   Slippage assumption of two-sample tests.

the sign test for the population median is perfectly valid for *any* population whatsoever.

In two-sample tests the *t* and the *W* test make one common assumption: that the two populations are identically shaped, their only possible difference being in location. This is illustrated in Figure 16-3; the difference in location is called the "slippage" or "difference" Δ, and is given as

$$\Delta = \nu_1 - \nu_2 = \mu_1 - \mu_2 \tag{16-60}$$

If this assumption does not hold, both the *t* test and *W* test may be invalid. Thus, we see that even nonparametric tests require some assumptions, even though they are free of the normality assumption.

The two-sample *t* test also nominally assumes the populations are normal. If this assumption does not hold, however, the *t* test remains nearly valid, and is therefore called *robust*. To find the essential difference between the *t* test and *W* test, therefore, we must look beyond their validity, and consider their efficiency.

(b) Efficiency

(i) *Introduction*

Efficiency was first considered in Section 7-2; recall that in estimating the center of a normal distribution, the efficiency of the sample mean relative to the sample median was given by the ratio of their variances as:

$$\frac{(\pi/2)(\sigma^2/n)}{\sigma^2/n} = \frac{\pi}{2} = 157\% \tag{16-61}$$
$$\text{(7-17) repeated}$$

It is evident that these two variances can be equalized by increasing the sample size for the median (i.e., increasing *n* in the numerator) by

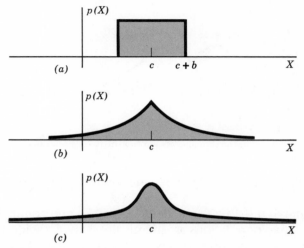

FIGURE 16-4 Three symmetric distributions. (a) Short-tailed rectangular. (b) Long-tailed two-tailed exponential. (c) Extremely long-tailed Cauchy.

57%. Thus the relative efficiency of two estimators may be viewed as the ratio of sample sizes required to make them equally accurate. In the same way we shall define:

> the relative efficiency of two *tests*[10] is the ratio of sample sizes required to give equally accurate tests, i.e., tests with the same probability of type I and type II errors

(ii) Comparisons

In Table 16-5 efficiencies are compared; but first, a few words of explanation. Since the sign test is for the population median v, while the t test is for the population mean μ, comparisons make sense only for symmetric distributions where the median and the mean coincide:

$$v = \mu = c, \text{ say} \tag{16-62}$$

Thus we chose 3 symmetric distributions as well as the normal, as a basis of comparison; their graphs are given in Figure 16-4, and their formulas are as follows.

---

[10]Similarly we define the relative efficiency of two confidence intervals as the ratio of sample sizes required to give equally accurate intervals, i.e., intervals with the same confidence level and the same length.

(a) The rectangular distribution has no tails. Its formula is

$$p(X) = \frac{1}{2b} \qquad c - b < X < c + b \qquad (16\text{-}63)$$

(b) The two-tailed exponential has longer and thicker[11] tails than the normal. Its formula is

$$p(X) = \frac{1}{2b} e^{\frac{-|X - c|}{b}} \qquad (16\text{-}64)$$

(c) The Cauchy distribution has extremely long tails, so long in fact that its variance does not exist.[12] Its formula is

$$p(X) = \left(\frac{b}{\pi}\right) \frac{1}{(X - c)^2 + b^2} \qquad (16\text{-}65)$$

(iii) Conclusions

From the details of Table 16-5, we may draw two brief conclusions.

1. Although the t test is somewhat more efficient for the normal distribution, it is very much less efficient for the long-tailed distributions.
2. The W test shows up exceptionally well. This explains its growing popularity.

(c) Outliers

Outliers are defined to be observations that are so far away from the rest of the sample that they should be discarded, or at least modified somehow. They may occur, for example, because of a clerical error such as misplacement of a decimal point, or because an observation was left blank and then counted as zero by a computer, or because of a wild measurement, such as a ridiculously false reply to a questionnaire ("What is your income?" "$10 million a year"). Outliers are particularly dangerous if data are impersonally analyzed, with no human eye to catch the outlier.

The problem is that we can never be certain whether or not an extreme

---

[11]More precisely, "thicker at its extremities," since both distributions extend to infinity. Henceforth, we shall use the simple abbreviation "longer tails."

[12]Even its mean μ does not exist, in a strict mathematical sense. Thus it is no surprise that the sample mean $\bar{X}$ is a pretty useless estimator of the center c; note that the t test has zero relative efficiency in Table 16-5.

Table 16-5 Nonparametric Tests Compared to t Tests
(in symmetric populations where mean and median coincide)

Test		Population Parameter	Tested by Sample	Assumptions about Population Required for Validity[a]	Asymptotic[b] Relative[c] Efficiency When the Normal Assumption is True[d]	Asymptotic[b] Relative[c] Efficiency When the Normal Assumption is False, and Instead the Population Is		
						(a) Rectangular	(b) Two-tailed Exponential	(c) Cauchy
1 Sample	Sign Test	median, ν	median, $X\left(\frac{n+1}{2}\right)$		64%	33%	200%	∞
1 Sample	t Test	mean, μ	mean, $\bar{X}$	normal[f]				
2 Sample	W Test	slippage $\Delta = \nu_1 - \nu_2$ $= \mu_1 - \mu_2$	rank sum W	populations which are identical except for different locations	95%	100%	150%	∞
2 Sample	t Test	$\mu_1 - \mu_2$	$\bar{X}_1 - \bar{X}_2$	populations which are nominally[e] normal, and identical except for different locations				

[a] I.e., to make confidence level $(1 - \alpha)$ as claimed. Of course, in all tests we make the standard assumption that the sample is *random*, as specified by (6-2).

[b] In small samples, relative efficiencies differ slightly from those given in this table.

[c] "Relative" means the efficiency of the nonparametric test relative to the efficiency of the t test.

[d] In the normal case for which it was developed, the t test is absolutely efficient, i.e., more efficient than any other test. (However, note that the W test is a close competitor.)

[e] As mentioned previously, the two-sample t test is robust, i.e., is very nearly valid even for nonnormal populations.

[f] As mentioned previously, the one-sample t test is fairly robust, i.e., is nearly valid even for a nonnormal population—except for one-tailed tests in a skewed population.

FIGURE 16-5 Is the extreme observation an outlier? (a) Probably, (b) probably not, (c) maybe. What should be done? (i) Discard (ii) keep as is, or (iii) transform.

observation is an outlier. (If we knew for sure a *priori*, we could just drop it from the sample, and there would be no problem.) For example, in Figure 16-5 we show three possible positions for the right-hand observation: in panel (a) it seems obviously an outlier; in panel (b) it seems obviously not; and in panel (c) we have the common case where it is not at all clear. Should this extreme observation be (i) discarded (trimming the sample), (ii) kept as is, or (iii) transformed to a more useful form? (Transformation is a compromise, and often the wisest choice.)

First, we must briefly build a mathematical model of the outliers. We suppose the whole population of possible outliers forms a probability distribution that is very disperse; in a sense this "contaminates" the regular distribution, as shown in Figure 16-6. All the possible observations, both those from the regular distribution (to be estimated) and from

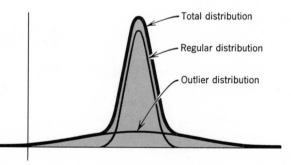

FIGURE 16-6 Outliers form a widespread distribution that contaminates the regular distribution.

the confusing or "noisy" outlier distribution, form the total distribution. Since outliers are innocently slipped into the sample with the rest of the observations, the observer in practice faces the undifferentiated total distribution, with such long tails that it is wise, in view of the efficiency results in Table 16-5, to use a nonparametric test such as the *W* test, rather than the *t* test.

Ranking observations as in the *W* test may be viewed simply as a way of transforming the outliers. (It is true that we transform all the observations to ranks, but it is the outliers that are changed most.) For example, if the observations in Figure 16-5 are ranked, we see that in all three panels the right-hand observation counts the same—its rank is 7. Thus we have taken the outlier in the first or third panel and "pulled it in" toward the rest of the distribution. On the other hand, the *t* test, which uses $\overline{X}$, would give the right-hand observation far more influence in the first panel—the very case in which it is most likely to be an outlier deserving less influence.

An alternative way to treat the outliers was described in Section 7-3—the best easy systematic estimator (BES), where the upper and lower quarters of the sample were simply trimmed off.[13] However, BES was only a point estimate. In this chapter, we have discussed the more crucial issue of interval estimates, and tests.

(d) Conclusions

The advantages of nonparametric statistics, in decreasing order of importance, are:

1. Greater efficiency in long-tailed distributions, including the case of outlier contamination.
2. Validity, in the sense that their confidence level (or type I error level) really is exactly as specified.
3. Easier computation in some cases.

Review Problems

16-9 Two samples of children were randomly selected to test two art education programs, A and B. At the end, each child's best painting was collected, to be judged by an independent artist. In terms of creativity, he ranked them as follows:

_____
[13]This is not quite the same as saying that these end observations are entirely useless. It is true that their specific values are ignored; but their presence tells us which are the more reliable central observations.

Rank of Child	1	2	3	4	5	6	7	8	9	10	11	12	13	14	15	16
His Art Program	B	A	B	B	B	A	B	B	A	B	A	B	A	A	A	A

Test whether program B (the intensive program) is better than program A.

16-10 Is the following true or false? Where false, correct it. If true, elaborate on it:

(a) If you have prior knowledge that the distribution is normal (or nearly normal), you gain by exploiting this in using the t test. However, if your prior knowledge is false, the t test you have used may cost you dearly. A nonparametric test, especially a test like the W test, is a relatively risk-free alternative to the t test.

(b) Non-parametric tests are invaluable for data that are ordered, from best to worst for example (on an ordinal scale), rather than for data given a numerical value (on an interval scale).

16-11 A production manager wishes to test whether soft background music will increase labor productivity on an assembly line. Suppose you find the following effect on a sample of 8 workers (each observed with and without music).

Per Hour Output

Without Music	With Music
27	29
32	29
23	36
28	29
23	27
27	29
25	26
30	34

(a) Calculate the prob-value of H_0 (no favorable effect of music), using a nonparametric test, and then the t test.

(b) If the normality assumption is a reasonable one, what can you say about the

(1) validity

(2) relative efficiency

of each of these tests?

(c) Repeat (b), if the normality assumption cannot be made (and if the parent population is like the two-tailed exponential or Cauchy distribution).

*16-12 Suppose you have observed the following sequence of interest rates, and bankruptcies in the construction industry.

	Interest Rate (X)	Bankruptcies (Y)
First year	5%	3300
Second year	6	3000
Third year	5	2600
Fourth year	7	4200
Fifth year	7	3800
Sixth year	6	4000
Seventh year	6	3600
Eighth year	10	4300

(a) Calculate the regression of Y on X, and the correlation coefficient.

(b) If you believe it is likely that the last observation is an outlier, explain why the analysis in (a) is unsatisfactory. Then recalculate part (a), dropping the last observation.

(c) Rank all X values numerically, from smallest to largest. Do the same for Y. Then calculate a "rank correlation," using all the ranks. Compare with (a) and (b), and explain.

Chapter 17

chi-SQUARE TESTS

> *The age of chivalry is gone; that of sophisters, econo-*
> *mists, and calculators has succeeded.*
>
> Edmund Burke

Chi square (χ^2) is a very popular form of hypothesis testing, and one subject to substantial abuse. Besides the type I and type II errors already encountered in Chapter 9, we now must face yet another kind of error: the error of asking the wrong question. Statisticians unaware of it may commit this error wholesale—and chi-square tests are likely to be their favorite vehicle. We shall therefore spend considerable effort in giving alternatives to chi square that are more appropriate under certain conditions.

17-1 χ^2 TESTS FOR GOODNESS OF FIT

(a) Example

Suppose we wish to test the null hypothesis that births in Sweden occur equally often throughout the year. Suppose that the only available data is a random sample of 88 births distributed over the year, but grouped into seasons of differing length. These observed frequencies O_i are given in column 1 of Table 17-1.

Table 17-1   Distribution of $n = 88$ Births Among 4 Cells
(seasons of the year)

i	Season	(1) Observed Frequency O_i	(2) Probability (if H_0 true) π_i	(3) Expected Frequency $E_i = n\pi_i$	(4) Deviation $(O_i - E_i)$	(5) Deviation Squared and Weighted $(O_i - E_i)^2/E_i$
1	Spring		$91/365$	$.25(88)$	$27 - 22$	$25/22$
	Apr–June	27	$= .25$	$= 22.0$	$= +5.0$	$= 1.13$
2	Summer					
	July–Aug	20	.17	15.0	+5.0	1.67
·3	Fall					
	Sept–Oct	8	.167	14.7	−6.7	3.05
4	Winter					
	Nov–Mar	33	.413	36.3	−3.3	.30
		$n = 88$	$1.00\checkmark$	$88\checkmark$	$0\checkmark$	$\chi^2 = 6.15$
						prob-value $\simeq .105$

How well does the data fit the hypothesis? The notion of goodness of fit may now be developed in several steps.

1. First consider the implications of H_0, the null hypothesis that every birth is likely to occur in any given season with a probability proportional to the length of that season. Spring is defined to have 3 months, or 91 days; thus π_1—the probability (given H_0) of a birth occurring in the first period, spring—is $91/365 = .25$. Similarly, all the other probabilities π_i are calculated in column (2).
2. Now calculate what the expected frequencies in each cell (season) would be if the null hypothesis were true. For example, consider the first cell; if H_0 were true, $\pi_1 = .25 = 25\%$, so that the expected frequency would be 25% of 88 = 22 births. Similarly, column (3) displays the calculation of all other expected frequencies[1] E_i:

$$E_i = n\pi_i \tag{17-1}$$

3. The question now is: "By how much does the observed frequency deviate from the expected frequency?" For example, in the first cell, this deviation is $27 - 22 = 5$. Similarly, all the other deviations

_____

[1] Formula (17-1) is just a restatement of the formula (6-23) for the mean of a binomial distribution. In order to use Table VI(a) with assurance, it is necessary that $E_i \geq 5$ in each cell. If this condition is not met, then this table should be used only with considerable reservation. Better still, cells should be redefined more broadly until this condition is met.

$(O_i - E_i)$ are set out in column (4). Left in this form, the deviations would always sum algebraically to 0, so this is not a useful criterion. This problem is avoided by taking the square[2] of the deviations:

$$(O_i - E_i)^2 \tag{17-2}$$

4. To show its *relative* importance, each squared deviation must somehow be compared to the expected frequency in its cell, E_i. We therefore calculate the ratio $(O_i - E_i)^2/E_i$, as shown in the last column of Table 17-1.
5. Finally, sum the contributions from all cells, to obtain an overall measure of how the observations deviate from the null hypothesis; this is denoted as the

$$\text{chi-square goodness-of-fit statistic, } \chi^2 = \sum_{i=1}^{k} \frac{(O_i - E_i)^2}{E_i} \tag{17-3}$$

$$= 6.15 \tag{17-4}$$

This whole argument obviously has strong similarities to that used in developing ANOVA; specifically, the χ^2 statistic is very similar to the F statistic (10-7), which also measured discrepancy from a null hypothesis. Hence the χ^2 statistic may be analyzed in a similar way.

First, χ^2 is a random variable that fluctuates from sample to sample—with this fluctuation in χ^2 occurring because of the fluctuation in the observed cell frequencies O_i that comprise it. In passing, note that these frequencies are not independent: since $O_1 + O_2 + O_3 + O_4 = n$, any one of them may be expressed in terms of the other. For example, $O_4 = n - (O_1 + O_2 + O_3)$; thus, the last cell is determined by the previous three. Therefore, in this case χ^2 has only 3 degrees of freedom, which is indicated by a subscript, χ_3^2; and in general, with k cells there are $k - 1$ degrees of freedom.

If H_0 is true, the χ_3^2 distribution is shown approximately[3] in Figure 17-1,

---

[2] This squaring of the deviations likewise occurred in the definition of

$$\text{MSD} = \sum (X_i - \bar{X})^2 \left(\frac{f_i}{n}\right) \tag{2-5b repeated}$$

Also note the weighting by relative frequency (f_i/n); a similar weighting will be used in defining χ^2.

[3] This approximation is like the normal approximation to the binomial—adequate, but not perfect. Perhaps this issue may be clarified by distinguishing between the χ^2
(cont'd)

with the critical points (10%, 5%, etc.) given in Appendix Table VI(a). By interpolating Table VI(a) we find that the approximate prob-value for H_0 (births evenly distributed) is about 10.5% as shown in Figure 17-1. Finally, several other χ^2 distributions with various other degrees of freedom are shown in Figure 17-2, with the critical points also given in Table VI(a).

(b) Limitations of χ^2

Continuing the example in (a), suppose we gather a very large sample; in fact, *all* the births in Sweden in 1935 are shown in Table 17-2. With a little stretch of the imagination, this may be considered a random sample from an infinite conceptual population. χ^2 is calculated to be 128.47, which exceeds our last tabular value by so much that we conclude that the prob-value $\ll .001$. At any reasonable level of significance, H_0 is rejected.[4]

At this point, the χ^2 test is seen to be quite inappropriate; it asks the

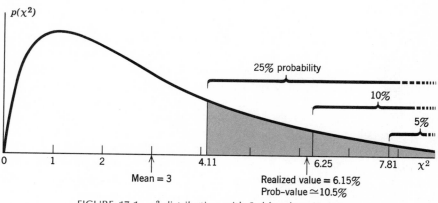

FIGURE 17-1 χ^2 distribution with 3 d.f., when H_0 is true.

---

goodness-of-fit statistic (17-3), and the χ^2 *distribution* in Figure 17-1. The χ^2 *distribution* with r d.f. is defined rigorously as the distribution of the sum of r independent standard normal variables squared, thus is easily tabulated. It is used for many purposes, including confidence intervals for σ^2 in (8-31), and in this chapter as an approximation to the distribution of the χ^2 goodness-of-fit statistic (17-3) and the χ^2 statistic to test independence, (17-20) below.

The definition of the χ^2 goodness-of-fit statistic was justified by intuitive arguments in Section 17-1(a); but this is not enough, since alternative measures—equally appealing on intuitive grounds—could have been devised. The χ^2 goodness-of-fit statistic is really justified because its distribution is very well approximated by the known χ^2 distribution.

[4] For any given level of significance α, H_0 is rejected if prob-value $\leq \alpha$. See (9-19).

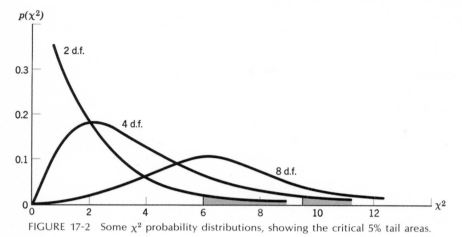

FIGURE 17-2 Some χ^2 probability distributions, showing the critical 5% tail areas.

wrong question. To see why, recall H_0: births occur with probability proportional to the length of the season. Even before *any* data were gathered, we knew H_0 could not be *exactly* the truth—a good approximation, perhaps, but not exactly true. So when the data call for rejection of H_0, the only sensible reaction is, "So what?—I could have told you so beforehand. All you have to do to reject *any* specific null hypothesis is collect a large enough sample."

On these same grounds, we wonder: Is not the χ^2 test with the small sample of $n = 88$ observations in example (a) also irrelevant? It tells us little we do not already know about whether H_0 is true or false (we know

Table 17-2 Distribution of $n = 88,273$ Births Among 4 Cells (seasons of the year), Sweden, 1935

i	Season	(1) Observed Frequency O_i	(2) Probability (if H_0 true) π_i	(3) Expected Frequency $E_i = n\pi_i$	(4) $(O_i - E_i)$	(5) $(O_i - E_i)^2/E_i$
1	Spring Apr–June	23,385	.24931	22,008	1,377	86.16
2	Summer July–Aug	14,978	.16986	14,994	−16	.02
3	Fall Sept–Oct	14,106	.16712	14,752	−646	28.29
4	Winter Nov–Mar	35,804	.41371	36,519	−715	14.00
		88,273	1.00000✓	88,273✓	0✓	$\chi^2 = 128.47$

prob-value $\ll$ .001

before any test that H_0 must be slightly false, at least); thus, about all that the χ^2 test really tells us is that the sample was too small to enable us to reject H_0.

(c) Alternative to χ^2: Confidence Intervals

With the relevancy of χ^2 hypothesis tests in question, what then *is* relevant? The reason this question is so seldom asked is that there is no single answer that will work in all cases. However, we shall give one possible answer to illustrate an important principle: an imaginative and common sense use of confidence intervals may yield more information than a routine χ^2 hypothesis test.

Let us continue to regard the 88,273 observed births in Table 17-2 as a very large sample from an infinite conceptual population. Now consider P, the sample proportion of births observed in the first season, spring:

$$P = \frac{23{,}385}{88{,}273} = .265$$

Next, use this to construct a 95% confidence interval for the corresponding population proportion (probability of spring births): from (8-22),

$$\text{true } \pi = .265 \pm 1.96 \sqrt{\frac{(.265)(.735)}{88{,}273}} \tag{17-7}$$

$$= .265 \pm .0029$$

Now compare this to the probability of births in the spring if H_0 were true: since spring is defined to have 91 of the 365 days of the year,

$$\text{null } \pi = \frac{91}{365} = .249 \tag{17-8}$$

as shown in column (2) of Table 17-2. Consider the ratio

$$\frac{\text{true } \pi}{\text{null } \pi} = \frac{(.265 \pm .0029)}{.249}$$

$$= 1.063 \pm .012 \tag{17-9}$$

This is easy to interpret: in spring, births were about 6% above normal—more precisely, somewhere between 5.1% and 7.5% above normal, with 95% confidence. The darkly shaded bands in Figure 17-3 illustrate (17-9) and similar estimates for the other 3 seasons.

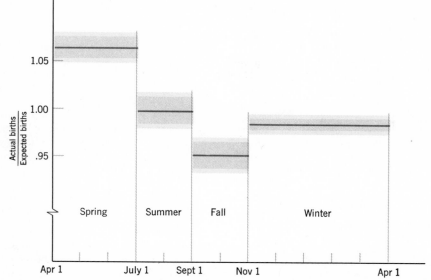

FIGURE 17-3   Ratio of actual births to expected births if H_0 were true. Darker shading shows individual 95% confidence intervals. Lighter shading shows *simultaneous* 95% confidence intervals.

Finally, we come to a problem already encountered in the ANOVA chapter: although we can be 95% confident of each individual interval in Figure 17-3, we can be far less confident that the whole system of intervals is true; there are 4 ways (intervals) where we could go wrong. How can we construct a system of confidence intervals that are all *simultaneously* true with 95% confidence, analogous to the multiple comparisons in (10-24)? One very simple solution is to cut the error rate of each interval from 5% to 5%/4 = 1.25%. Then the overall error rate will be at most (1.25%)4 = 5%, as required.[5] This solution, shown as

_____

[5] A more rigorous proof is as follows. Let E_i be the event that the *i*th confidence interval is in error. Then we may develop the same argument used in ANOVA, (10-30) to (10-35):

$$Pr(E_1 \text{ or } E_2) = Pr(E_1) + Pr(E_2) - Pr(E_1 \cap E_2) \qquad \text{(3-14) repeated}$$
$$\leq Pr(E_1) + Pr(E_2)$$

Similarly, $Pr(E_1 \text{ or } E_2 \text{ or } E_3 \text{ or } E_4) \leq Pr(E_1) + Pr(E_2) + Pr(E_3) + Pr(E_4)$

$$\leq (1.25\%) \, 4 = 5\%$$

i.e., $$Pr(\text{any error at all}) \leq 5\%$$

i.e., $$Pr(\text{all correct}) \geq 95\%$$

the lightly shaded bands in Figure 17-3, is overly conservative but effective.[6]

17-1 Throw a fair die 30 times (or simulate it with random digits in Table II(a)).

_____

[6]A more refined and exact solution is to construct a 95% confidence region, using χ^2 in the following unusual way. Noting (17-3) and (17-1), we can state with 95% probability that

$$\sum \frac{(O_i - n\pi_i)^2}{n\pi_i} \leq \chi^2_{.05} \tag{17-10}$$

With O_i, n, and $\chi^2_{.05}$ known, this defines a 95% confidence region for the unknown set of population probabilities $(\pi_1, \pi_2 \ldots \pi_k)$. It must be emphasized that in (17-10) the π_i's are not fixed by a rigid null hypothesis; instead, they are unknown parameters to be solved for. The solution is a statement about all π_i's simultaneously, so that the confidence region is of the same simultaneous type as the multiple comparisons in (10-24).

The major difficulty with (17-10) is a technical one: it is hard to graph, and impossible to express as a set of k individual inequalities (intervals) like (10-24). About the best that can be done is the following approximation.

In (17-10), as n increases, O_i approaches $n\pi_i$, so that for large enough samples this substitution in the denominator yields the following approximate 95% confidence region:

$$\sum \frac{(O_i - n\pi_i)^2}{O_i} \leq \chi^2_{.05} \tag{17-11}$$

By appropriately dividing by n, we may reexpress this as

$$\sum \frac{[(O_i/n) - \pi_i]^2}{(O_i/n)} \leq \frac{\chi^2_{.05}}{n} \tag{17-11b}$$

This form, called *relative* χ^2, is recognized as a quadratic function of π_i, and hence an ellipsoidal region in $(k - 1)$ dimensions; [when $k - 1$ of the π_i are specified, the last π_k of course is determined].

In our example, the 95% confidence ellipsoid is defined as all those combinations of π_1, π_2, and π_3 satisfying

$$\frac{(.265 - \pi_1)^2}{.265} + \frac{(.169 - \pi_2)^2}{.169} + \frac{(.160 - \pi_3)^2}{.160} + \frac{(.405 - \pi_4)^2}{.405} \leq .000089$$

where $\pi_4 = 1 - \pi_1 - \pi_2 - \pi_3$.

(a) Use χ^2 to test H_0 (that it is a fair die) at the 25% significance level.

(b) If each student in a large class correctly carries out the test in (a), calculate (if you can) the proportion that will reject H_0 (i.e., what is the probability that any one student will reject H_0?). What is this probability called?

17-2 Repeat Problem 17-1 for an unfair die. (Since you do not have an unfair die available, use the table of random numbers to simulate a die that is biased towards aces; for example, let the digit 0 as well as 1 represent the ace, so that the ace has twice the probability of any other face.)

17-3 Is there a better test than χ^2 for the die in Problem 17-2 that is suspected of being biased toward aces? If so, use it to recalculate Problem 17-2.

17-4 The data of Table 17-2 is a condensation of the following table of monthly births in Sweden, 1935:

Table 17-3   Monthly
Detail on Births

Jan.	7280	July	7585
Feb.	6957	Aug.	7393
Mar.	7883	Sept.	7203
Apr.	7884	Oct.	6903
May	7892	Nov.	6552
June	7609	Dec.	7132
		Total	88273

(a) Calculate a few cells of the χ^2 test of the null hypothesis (H_0: births are equally likely to occur on all days of the year).

(b) Analyze a few cells of the data in a more appropriate way, as in Figure 17-3.

(c) What are the advantages and disadvantages of using monthly data instead of seasonal data?

*17-5 Prove that the expectation of χ^2 in (17-3) is $(k-1)$. (Hint. use (5-35) and (6-24). This is another interpretation of d.f.)

*(d) Test of Distribution Shape: χ^2 with Estimated Parameters

χ^2 is often used to determine whether a sample is drawn from a normal or some other kind of population distribution. As a simple example, Table 17-4 displays a sample distribution of male offspring in families of 4 children; suppose we wish to test the null hypothesis

H_0: the population distribution is binomial   (17-12)

To calculate χ^2, the first step is to derive the cell probabilities π_i, assuming H_0 is true—where π_i represents the probability of i boys in 4 births. These probabilities will be binomial, with $n = 4$; but what value of π (i.e., the probability of a male in a single birth) should be used? If π is set at .50, we would be testing too narrow a null hypotheses, H_0': the distribution is binomial, with $\pi = .50$. But (17-12) calls for no restrictions whatever on π. Therefore, π is estimated from the data: in 100 families of 4 births each, there are a total of 400 births, of which 220 are males $[220 = 1(17) + 2(49) + 3(27) + 4(6)]$. Thus $\hat{\pi} = 220/400 = .55$. This estimate can now be used to calculate the binomial probabilities; the best way is to use Table III(b). Then these probabilities π_i are entered into column 3 of Table 17-4, and the calculation of χ^2 proceeds as before, obtaining

$$\chi^2 = 8.2 \tag{17-13}$$

The only new twist is the d.f. Recall that in our earlier χ^2 test in (17-4)

$$\text{d.f.} = (\text{number of cells}) - 1$$

But in that case it was possible for the statistician to define the cell probabilities π_i (in column 3 of Table 17-4) directly from H_0; on the other hand, in this present example the cell probabilities π_i could not be defined directly from H_0, but only after π had been estimated. One degree of freedom is lost as a consequence,[7] and in general

$$\text{d.f.} = (\text{number of cells}) - 1 - (\text{number of estimated parameters})$$

$$\tag{17-14}$$

To conclude, our observed $\chi^2 = 8.2$ has $5 - 1 - 1 = 3$ d.f., and slightly exceeds the critical $\chi^2_{.05} = 7.8$ in Table VIa. Thus the evidence contradicts the null hypothesis of a binomial distribution at a 5% level of significance.

----

[7] The loss of a degree of freedom for every parameter that must be estimated beforehand, (first encountered in the footnote to (8-11)), is by now a familiar principle. Because π_i are calculated from the *data* as well as from H_0, E_i fits O_i a little better. This makes χ^2 a little smaller. Therefore the reduction of d.f. is justified. (Note that the critical points of χ^2_3 are lower than those of χ^2_4).

Finally, we confirm that π must be estimated, rather than prespecified. If we had arbitrarily set $\pi = .50$, then we would not know how much of the calculated χ^2 (i.e., how much of the difference between E_i and O_i) was because the observed distribution was not binomial, and how much was because it was not centered on .50.

Table 17-4 Distribution of Males in Completed
Families of 4 Children

(1) Number of Males X_i	(2) Observed Frequency O_i	(3) Probability π_i (based on $\hat{\pi} = .55$)	(4) Expected Frequency $E_i = n\pi_i$	(5) Deviation $(O_i - E_i)$	(6) Deviation Squared and Weighted $(O_i - E_i)^2/E_i$
0	1	.041	4.1	−3.1	2.35
1	17	.200	20.0	−3.0	.45
2	49	.368	36.8	12.2	4.06
3	27	.300	30.0	−3.0	.30
4	6	.091	9.1	−3.1	1.06
		1.000✓	100.0✓	0✓	$\chi^2 = 8.2$

*(e) Alternative to χ^2: Dispersion Test and Confidence Interval

It is time to consider the alternate hypothesis H_1, against which H_0 is being tested. If H_1 is not carefully considered, the result may be a very poor test. In Figure 17-4, we show the H_0 distribution (from column 3 of Table 17-4) as a reference, and several possible alternate distribu-

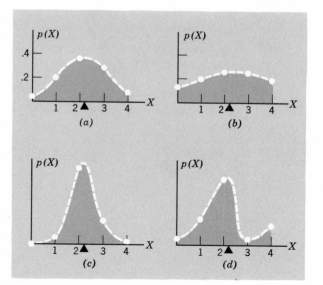

FIGURE 17-4 (a) The null hypothesis (binomial) for the data of Table 17-4. (b), (c), (d) Some alternate hypotheses.

tions. The H_0 binomial distribution in panel (a) is centered at the same place as the data, because π was estimated from the data. The alternate distributions H_1 are also shown centered on the data, because the issue between the competing hypotheses is not where the distributions are centered, but how they are distributed around their center (binomial, or not?). The most natural question is: How much spread is there around the center? In this regard, do the data conform to H_0 or H_1? A good statistic for measuring spread is the sample variance, which is calculated in Table 17-5,

$$s^2 = .687 \tag{17-15}$$

$$\text{d.f.} = n - 1 = 99$$

To see how well s^2 matches H_0, we calculate σ^2, the population variance if H_0 is true,

$$\sigma^2 = m\,\pi\,(1 - \pi) \tag{17-16}$$
$$\text{(6-24) repeated}$$

Noting that m denotes the number of trials (the number of children, 4), and π is estimated to be .55, it follows that

$$\sigma^2 = 4(.55)(.45) \tag{17-17}$$
$$= .990$$

Finally, compare (17-15) to (17-17) by forming the ratio

$$C^2 = \frac{s^2}{\sigma^2} = \frac{.687}{.990} = .694 \tag{17-18}$$

Table 17-5   Dispersion Test for the Data of Table 17-4

X_i	Observed Frequency O_i or f_i	$X_i f_i$	$X_i - \bar{X}$	$(X_i - \bar{X})^2 f_i$
0	1	0	-2.2	4.8
1	17	17	-1.2	24.5
2	49	98	$-.2$	2.0
3	27	81	.8	17.3
4	6	24	1.8	19.4
	$n = 100\checkmark$	$\bar{X} = \dfrac{220}{100}$ $= 2.20$		$\sum (X_i - \bar{X})^2 f_i = 68.0$ from (2-6b), $s^2 = \dfrac{68.0}{99} = .687$

If H_0 is true, the distribution of C^2 is approximately the modified χ^2 with $n - 1 = 99$ d.f., introduced in Section 8-4. From Table VI(b) we therefore find the corresponding one-tailed probability is approximately .005; hence the two-sided prob-value is

$$\text{prob-value} \simeq .01$$

(This must be a two-tailed test, since the competing hypotheses H_1 can involve a dispersion either larger or smaller than the binomial H_0). Since this prob-value is less than the corresponding value of .04 derived in the previous section, this is even stronger evidence against H_0, i.e., this dispersion test is a stronger statistical test of H_0 than the χ^2 test.

Of course, the dispersion test will have particularly high power against an alternate hypothesis with a variance very different from the null hypothesis σ^2. For example, Figure 17-4b shows an alternate hypothesis with a relatively high variance. As another example, Figure 17-4c shows a variance substantially lower than σ^2; in fact, the data probably came from a distribution like this.[8]

On the other hand, the dispersion test will have very little power against an alternate distribution such as Figure 17-4d, which has about the same variance as the null distribution. However, since such an alternative is rare in practice, the dispersion test is generally a more powerful test than the classical χ^2 test.

As has been argued previously, more appropriate than an hypothesis test is the 95% confidence interval, calculated to be

$$\frac{s^2}{C^2_{.025}} < \sigma^2 < \frac{s^2}{C^2_{.975}} \qquad \text{(8-31) repeated}$$

In our example, using interpolated values for $C^2_{.025}$ and $C^2_{.975}$ of approximately 1.3 and .74,

$$\frac{.687}{1.3} < \sigma^2 < \frac{.687}{.74}$$

$$.53 < \sigma^2 < .93$$

Since the null hypothesis value of σ^2 is .99 and so lies well outside this interval, our earlier rejection of H_0 at the 5% level is confirmed. At the same time we see to what extent this variance is less than the binomial variance.

---

[8] Can you explain why this birth data might not be binomial? For a clue, read the title of Table 17-4 carefully.

*17-6 From the data in Table 17-4, calculate the χ^2 test of the null hypothesis that the distribution of males is binomial, with $\pi = 1/2$, (and $n = 4$, of course).

*17-7 At an annual meeting of a large corporation, a sample of 80 stockholders evaluated management performance on a scale 0 to 100 as follows:

Suppose you are considering a goodness-of-fit test for normality, i.e., a test of

H_0: this sample is drawn from a normal population.

Before proceeding, consider:
(a) If H_0 is rejected (at the 5% level say), what will you have shown?
(b) If H_0 is acceptable, what will you have shown? What further use might this information have?
(c) Before running through the calculations, explain how you would proceed to test H_0, indicating which parameters must initially be estimated.
(d) Calculate the χ^2 test of H_0.

*17-8 In Section 17-1(b) we argued that an hypothesis test about births in Sweden was inappropriate because it is known beforehand that H_0 cannot be exactly true. Is it equally inappropriate to test

H_0: population binomial

when we are
(a) observing the number of males in completed families of 4 children (as in Table 17-4)?
(b) observing the number of heads in 4 tosses of a coin?

17-2

CONTINGENCY TABLES

(a) Example

Contingency means dependence, so a contingency table is simply a table that displays how two or more characteristics depend on each other; for example, Table 17-6a shows the dependence of income and region in a sample of 300 U.S. families. To test the null hypothesis of no dependence in the population, χ^2 may again be used in a goodness-of-fit test. In these special circumstances, it is customarily renamed the χ^2 test of independence.

In Table 17-6a, let π_{ij} denote the underlying bivariate probability distribution; for example, π_{14} is the probability that a family is in the north, earning \$15,000 or more. Let π_i and π_j similarly denote the mar-

Table 17-6 (a) Observed Frequencies O_{ij} of 400 Families Classified by Regions and Income, 1964

	j	1	2	3	4		
i	Income (\$000) Region	0–5	5–10	10–15	15 and above	Total Frequency	$\hat{\pi}_i =$ Relative Frequency
1	North	58	91	35	14	198	.660
2	South	47	38	13	4	102	.340
	Total Frequency	105	129	48	18	300	
$\hat{\pi}_j =$	Relative Frequency	.350	.430	.160	.060		1.00

(b) Assuming Independence, Estimated Bivariate Probabilities $\hat{\pi}_{ij} = \hat{\pi}_i \hat{\pi}_j$

i	*j* 1	2	3	4	$\hat{\pi}_i$
1	.230	.284	.106	.040	.66
2	.120	.146	.054	.020	.34
$\hat{\pi}_j$	.350	.430	.160	.060	1.00

Table 17-6   (c) The Difference Between Observed and Expected
Frequencies $(O_{ij} - E_{ij})$, Where $E_{ij} = n\hat{\pi}_{ij}$

i \ j	1	2	3	4
1	$58 - 69.0 = -11.0$	$91 - 85.2 = 5.8$	$35 - 31.8 = 3.2$	$14 - 12.0 = 2.0$
2	$47 - 36.0 = 11.0$	$38 - 43.8 = -5.8$	$13 - 16.2 = -3.2$	$4 - 6.0 = -2.0$

ginal probability distributions. Then the null hypothesis of statistical
independence may be stated precisely:

$$H_0: \pi_{ij} = \pi_i \pi_j \qquad \qquad (17\text{-}19)$$

like (5-13)

To test how well the data fit this hypothesis, we perform the (appropriately adapted) sequence of χ^2 calculations, first introduced in developing (17-3):

(1) First, work out the implications of H_0. The best estimates of
π_i and π_j are the marginal relative frequencies shown in Table
17-6a. Substituting them into (17-19), yields the estimated
probabilities $\hat{\pi}_{ij}$ for each cell,[9] shown in Table 17-6b.

(2), (3) Calculate expected frequencies $E_{ij} = n\hat{\pi}_{ij}$ and then the deviations $(O_{ij} - E_{ij})$, as in Table 17-6c.

(4), (5) Finally, square, weight, and sum the deviations, obtaining

chi-square independence test, $\chi^2 \overset{\Delta}{=} \sum \sum \dfrac{(O_{ij} - E_{ij})^2}{E_{ij}} \qquad (17\text{-}20)$

like (17-3)

$$= \frac{(-11.0)^2}{69.0} + \frac{(5.8)^2}{85.2} + \cdots$$

$$= 9.2 \qquad \qquad (17\text{-}21)$$

Letting r designate the number of rows in the table, and c the number
of columns, the degrees of freedom of this test are,[10]

_____

[9] This step is very much like the fitting of each cell in 2 way ANOVA, except that
here a probability is fitted by multiplying two component probabilities, whereas in ANOVA
a *numerical* response is fitted by *addition* of two component effects, as in (10-40).

[10] The d.f. may be calculated from (17-14). But first, it is necessary to know the number
of estimated parameters, i.e., the number of estimated probabilities. Consider first the r
estimated row probabilities $\hat{\pi}_i$. Once the first $(r - 1)$ are estimated, the last one is strictly

(cont'd)

$$\text{d.f.} = (r - 1)(c - 1) \tag{17-22}$$

$$= (2 - 1)(4 - 1) = 3$$

Finally, the calculated χ^2 in (17-21) is compared to the critical points of the χ^2 distribution with 3 d.f., yielding

$$\text{prob-value} \simeq .027 \tag{17-23}$$

(b) Alternative to χ^2: a Confidence Interval Once Again

A serious drawback of the χ^2 test is that it does not exploit the numerical nature of the income factor. Thus the test completely misses the essential question: *How much* do incomes differ between regions? Even the secondary question of testing may be ineffectively answered by χ^2, since it may have relatively low power. To overcome these faults, the data in Table 17-6a will be reworked: since income is numerical, let us give it a numerical symbol X, and then estimate the difference in means for the two regions.

We calculate $\bar{X}$ and s^2 for each of the two regions, approximating each observation by its cell midpoint; in the last cell, which is open ended and has no midpoint, we arbitrarily use 17.5. Because of the large sample size we may use s_i^2 as a proxy for σ_i^2 in (8-7), obtaining the 95% confidence interval

$$(\mu_1 - \mu_2) = (\bar{X}_1 - \bar{X}_2) \pm 1.96 \sqrt{\frac{s_1^2}{n_1} + \frac{s_2^2}{n_2}} \tag{17-24}$$

$$= (7.63 - 6.22) \pm 1.96 \sqrt{\frac{18.8}{198} + \frac{17.2}{102}}$$

$$= 1.41 \pm 1.96(.512) = 1.41 \pm 1.01$$

$$\text{Mean income differential between North and South} = \$1,410 \pm \$1,010 \tag{17-25}$$

The secondary question of testing H_0 (no difference between regions) may now immediately be answered: H_0 may be rejected, since 0

---

determined, since $\Sigma \hat{\pi}_i = 1$. Thus, there are only $(r - 1)$ independently estimated row probabilities, and by the same argument only $(c - 1)$ column probabilities. Thus

$$\text{d.f.} = (\text{number of cells}) - 1 - (\text{number of estimated parameters})$$
$$= rc - 1 - [(r - 1) + (c - 1)]$$
(17-14) repeated

from which (17-22) follows directly.

does not lie in the confidence interval (17-25). Moreover, since $z = 1.41/.512 = 2.75$, the prob-value $= .006$. Since this is less than the χ^2 prob-value in (17-23), this is a stronger test than χ^2.

Of course, if more than two regions were to be compared, we would use ANOVA and multiple comparisons instead of (17-24). But the conclusion would generally be the same: the χ^2 test is less powerful.

(c) General Alternatives to χ^2 Tests of Independence

The lesson to be drawn from the example above is clear:

Whenever numerical variables appear, they should be analyzed with a tool (such as multiple comparisons or regression) that exploits their numerical nature. A χ^2 hypothesis test fails to do this.	(17-26)

In fact, even if a variable is not naturally numerical, but merely ordered (for example, a variable such as social class, or degree of success), it is often wise to code the various levels of the variable by $0, 1, 2, 3, \ldots$, and then proceed with this new numerical variable. Although this may seem arbitrary, it will usually yield a more powerful test of H_0 than χ^2, and will also give at least a rough-and-ready answer to the question, "*How much* do things differ?" As a special case of this, any variable with just 2 levels can be made numerical by coding it 0 and 1 (i.e., by making it a dummy variable). Problems 17-9 to 17-12 illustrate this.

PROBLEMS

In each of the following problems, a random sample of several hundred Americans was classified according to two characteristics. In each case:

(a) Calculate χ^2 to test whether the two characteristics are independent.
(b) Analyze in a better way, if possible.

17-9

Educational Attainment, by Color, 1964

Color \ Education	Elementary School Attendance	High School Attendance	University Attendance
White	12,835	20,778	9,468
Nonwhite	2,321	1,956	477

17-10

Employment in Various Occupations, by Color, 1965

Occupation / Color	White Collar	Blue Collar	Household and Other Services	Farm Workers
White	95	88	74	85
Nonwhite	5	12	26	15

Note that this sample was designed to have exactly the same number of people (100) in each occupation. Therefore the relative frequency in each occupation is 100/400, and cannot be an estimate of the population proportion. Thus, this sample differs from the simple random sample of Table 17-6.

Nevertheless, it turns out that the standard χ^2 test still remains valid—so go ahead and calculate it. When used in this way, it is often called the χ^2 test of homogeneity. [Are the various occupations homogeneous, i.e., similar in terms of color?] Note that the next three problems are also tests of homogeneity.

17-11

Employment in Selected Industries, by Sex, 1965

Industry / Sex	Manufacturing— Durables	Manufacturing— Nondurables	Mining	Trade
Male	162	124	190	118
Female	38	76	10	82

17-12·

Income, by Sex, 1964

Sex / Income	Male	Female
Less than 5,000	53	90
More than 5,000	47	10

17-13

Classification of 300 Newspaper Readers,
by Social Class

Social Class \ Newspaper	A	B	C
Poor	31	11	12
Lower middle class	49	59	51
middle class	18	26	31
Rich	2	4	6

Review Problems

17-14 Suppose that a certain population is divided in the following proportions:

Region \ Income ($000's)	0–5	5–10	10–15	15 and over
North	.06	.12	.24	.18
South	.12	.16	.08	.04

To test whether both regions have the same distribution of income, use random digits to simulate drawing a random sample of 20 from each region.

(a) Then use χ^2 to calculate the prob-value for H_0 (both regions have the same mean income).

(b) Use a better test to calculate the prob-value.

(c) Use the test of part (b) to construct a 95% confidence interval.

17-15 A large corporation wishes to test whether each of its divisions has equally satisfactory quality control over its output. Suppose the output of each division, along with the number of units rejected and returned by dealers is as follows:

	Division		
	A	B	C
Output	1,200	800	2,000
Rejects	52	60	88

(a) Use χ^2 to test H_0 (no difference in divisions).

(b) Analyse in a better way, if possible.

*17-16 Consider the sample of 200 heights given in Table 2-3 and Figure 2-3. To see whether it may have come from the normal population with $\mu = 69$ and $\sigma = 3.2$ (as given in Figure 6-1), an anthropologist asks you to calculate the prob-values for each of the following hypotheses:

(a) Test whether $\mu = 69$ (using the t test).

(b) Test whether $\sigma = 3.2$ (using the C^2 test).

(c) Test whether the distribution shape is normal (χ^2 test).

(d) Combine parts (a), (b), and (c), by testing whether the population is the specific normal distribution with $\mu = 69$ and $\sigma = 3.2$.

CHAPTER **18**

MAXiMUM
likelihood
ESTiMATiON [mle]

I have set my life upon a cast,
And I will stand the hazard of the die!

Shakespeare, *Richard III*

18-1   **INTRODUCTION**

Maximum likelihood is a technique of estimation often used by statisticians, because it has many of the attractive asymptotic properties (e.g., efficiency, consistency) set out in Section 7-2. The basic idea is to find the population value that best matches the observed sample, i.e., the hypothetical population value that is more likely than any other to generate the observed sample. We shall prove in this chapter that many of the estimators already introduced, in particular the least squares regression estimators, are also maximum likelihood estimators, and so are further justified.

We introduce MLE with an example of sampling from a 0–1 population; to be concrete, suppose we flip a biased coin 10 times in order to estimate π, the population proportion of heads, and get 4 heads. What is the maximum likelihood estimate (MLE) of π?

With 4 out of 10 heads before us, we ask, "Is .1 a reasonable estimate of π?" If π were .1, then the probability of four heads (successes) in our ten tosses (trials) would be, according to the binomial formula[1] (4-7),

---

[1]Note that our earlier convention of using little s to represent a realized value of *S* was dropped in Chapter 8.

$$\binom{n}{S} \pi^S (1 - \pi)^{n-S} = \binom{10}{4}(.1)^4(.9)^6 = .011 \qquad (18\text{-}1)$$

In other words, if $\pi = .1$, there is only about one chance in a hundred that we would get the sample we observed.

Similarly, we might ask ourselves how likely our result of four heads would be if π were .8. You can verify that the probability of getting 4 heads from this sort of population is only .006; again it seems implausible that a population with $\pi = .8$ would yield the sample result we observed.

Similarly, we consider all the other possible values for π, in each case asking how likely it is that this π would yield the sample that we in fact observed. The results are shown in the first column of Table 18-1, and graphed fully in Figure 18-1. We refer to this as the likelihood function,

Table 18-1   Outline of Maximum

	Binomial: Special Case in Text	Binomial: General Case	MLE of μ from a Sample Drawn from a Normal Population, $p(X/\mu)$
Given:	4 successes in 10 trials.	S successes in n trials.	Sample values: X_1, X_2, X_3.
Find:	MLE of π.	MLE of π.	MLE of μ.
As follows:	The probability of 4 heads in 10 trials is $$p(4/\pi) = \binom{10}{4}\pi^4(1 - \pi)^6$$ But in this estimation problem the sample values 10 and 4 have already been observed, hence are given. This is therefore written as a likelihood function of π only:	The probability of S successes in n trials is $$p(S/\pi) = \binom{n}{S}\pi^S(1 - \pi)^{n-S}$$ Since n and S are fixed at their observed values we can write this as a likelihood function of π only: $$L(\pi) = \binom{n}{S}\pi^S(1 - \pi)^{n-S}$$ At what value of π is this function a maximum? Calculus shows that this occurs when $\pi = S/n = P$, the sample proportion.	The probability of our sample resulting from any given μ is $$p(X_1, X_2, X_3/\mu) =$$ $$\prod_{i=1}^{3}\left[\frac{1}{\sqrt{2\pi\sigma^2}}\,e^{-(1/2\sigma^2)(X_i-\mu)^2}\right]$$ But with (X_1, X_2, X_3) fixed at their observed values, the above becomes the likelihood function of μ, $$L(\mu) = \prod_{i=1}^{3}\left[\frac{1}{\sqrt{2\pi\sigma^2}}\,e^{-(1/2\sigma^2)(X_i-\mu)^2}\right]$$ Try out all possible values of μ, selecting that one that maximizes this function. Calculus shows that this is: $$\mu = \tfrac{1}{3}(X_1 + X_2 + X_3)$$ $$= \bar{X}, \text{ the sample mean.}$$
	π | $L(\pi) = \binom{10}{4}\pi^4(1 - \pi)^6$ 0 | 0 .1 | .011 .2 | .088 .3 | .200 .4 | .251 ⟸ max .5 | .205 .6 | .111 .7 | .037 .8 | .006 1.0 | 0		
Conclude:	The MLE of π is .4, the sample proportion P.	Hence, the MLE of π is P.	Thus the MLE of μ is $\bar{X}$.

when the sample values of 4 and 10 are fixed, and the only variable in the function is the hypothetical value of π. For emphasis, we often write this as a function of π alone:

$$L(\pi) = \binom{10}{4} \pi^4 (1 - \pi)^6 \tag{18-2}$$

The maximum likelihood estimate is the value of π maximizing this likelihood function; it turns out to be .4, the sample proportion. In general we define,

> The MLE is the hypothetical population value that maximizes the likelihood of the observed sample. $\tag{18-3}$

Likelihood Estimation (MLE)

MLE of α, β, and γ in the Regression Model $Y = \alpha + \beta x + \gamma z + e$, where each Y has been drawn from a Normal Population	MLE of any Parameter θ from any Population $p(X/\theta)$
Sample values: $Y_1, Y_2, \ldots Y_n$.	Sample values $X_1, X_2, \ldots X_n$.
MLE of α, β, γ.	MLE of θ.
Probability of our sample resulting from any combination of α, β, γ is:	Probability of our sample, for any θ, is:
$p(Y_1, Y_2, \ldots Y_n / \alpha, \beta, \gamma) = \dfrac{1}{(2\pi\sigma^2)^{n/2}} e^{-(1/2\sigma^2)\Sigma[Y_i - (\alpha + \beta x_i + \gamma z_i)]^2}$	$p(X_1, X_2, \ldots X_n / \theta)$ $= p(X_1/\theta)\, p(X_2/\theta) \ldots p(X_n/\theta)$ $= \prod\limits_{i=1}^{n} p(X_i/\theta)$
But with the Y_i, x_i, and z_i fixed at their observed values, the above becomes the likelihood function of α, β, γ, designated $L(\alpha, \beta, \gamma)$. Try out all combinations of α, β, and γ, selecting the combination that maximizes this likelihood function by minimizing the sum of squares in the exponent.	But with $(X_1, X_2, \ldots X_n)$ fixed at their observed values, the above function becomes $L(\theta)$, an expression in θ: $L(\theta) = \prod\limits_{i=1}^{n} p(X_i/\theta)$ Select the value of θ that maximizes this likelihood function.
Thus the MLE is least squares.	

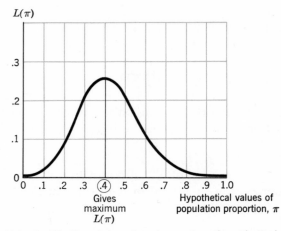

FIGURE 18-1 $L(\pi)$, the likelihood function that various hypothetical population proportions would yield the observed sample of 4 heads in 10 tosses of a coin.

In Figure 18-2 we graph the binomial probabilities $p(S/\pi)$. In Chapter 4 we thought of π fixed and S variable, as in slice a; thus the dotted function shows the probability of various numbers of heads, if the

FIGURE 18-2 The binomial probability function $p(S/\pi)$ plotted against both S and π. $n = 10$.

population proportion were .8, for example. But in this chapter we re-gard S—the observed sample result—as fixed, while the population π is thought of as taking on a whole set of hypothetical values; thus slice b shows the likelihood that various possible population proportions would yield 4 heads. Slices in the a direction are referred to as probability distributions, while slices in the b direction are called likelihood functions.

We next shall generalize maximum likelihood estimation. A summary of our results is shown in Table 18-1 for reference.

18-2   GENERAL BINOMIAL

It is very easy to show that our result in the previous section was no accident, and that the maximum likelihood estimate of the binomial π is *always* the sample proportion P.

Given an observed sample of S successes in n trials, the likelihood function is

$$L(\pi) = \binom{n}{S} \pi^S (1 - \pi)^{n-S} \tag{18-4}$$

With calculus it can easily be shown[2] that the maximum value of this likelihood function occurs when $\pi = S/n = P$. Thus

MLE of π is P, the sample proportion.	(18-5)

[2] To find where $L(\pi)$ is a maximum, set the derivative equal to zero.

$$\frac{dL(\pi)}{d\pi} = \binom{n}{S}[\pi^S(n - S)(1 - \pi)^{n-S-1}(-1) + S\pi^{S-1}(1 - \pi)^{n-S}] = 0 \tag{18-6}$$

Dividing by $\binom{n}{S}\pi^{S-1}(1 - \pi)^{n-S-1}$,

$$-\pi(n - S) + S(1 - \pi) = 0$$
$$-n\pi + S = 0$$
$$\pi = \frac{S}{n}$$

You can easily confirm that this is a maximum (rather than a minimum or inflection point). Actually, this derivation assumed that $0 < S < n$. When $S = 0$, the proof of (18-5) does not even require calculus: from (18-4), when $S = 0$, then $L(\pi) = (1 - \pi)^n$ which is clearly a maximum at the end point $\pi = 0$. (18-5) may be similarly proved valid in the case where $S = n$.

We argued in Chapter 1 that it is reasonable to use the sample proportion to estimate the population proportion; but in addition to its intuitive appeal, we now add the more rigorous justification of maximum likelihood: a population with $\pi = P$ has greatest likelihood of generating the observed sample.

18-3   **MLE OF THE MEAN μ OF A NORMAL POPULATION**

Suppose we have drawn a sample (X_1, X_2, X_3) from a parent population which is $N(\mu, \sigma^2)$; our problem is to find the MLE of the unknown μ. Because the population is normal, the probability[3] of observing any value X, given a population mean μ, is

$$p(X/\mu) = \frac{1}{\sqrt{2\pi\sigma^2}} e^{-(1/2\sigma^2)(X-\mu)^2} \tag{18-7}$$

Specifically, the probability that we would get the value X_1 for the first observation is

$$p(X_1/\mu) = \frac{1}{\sqrt{2\pi\sigma^2}} e^{-(1/2\sigma^2)(X_1-\mu)^2} \tag{18-8}$$

while the probabilities of drawing the values X_2 and X_3 are, respectively

$$p(X_2/\mu) = \frac{1}{\sqrt{2\pi\sigma^2}} e^{-(1/2\sigma^2)(X_2-\mu)^2} \tag{18-9}$$

and

$$p(X_3/\mu) = \frac{1}{\sqrt{2\pi\sigma^2}} e^{-(1/2\sigma^2)(X_3-\mu)^2} \tag{18-10}$$

We assume as usual that X_1, X_2, and X_3 are independent so that the joint probability is the product,

$$p(X_1, X_2, X_3/\mu) = \prod_{i=1}^{3} \left[\frac{1}{\sqrt{2\pi\sigma^2}} e^{-(1/2\sigma^2)(X_i-\mu)^2} \right] \tag{18-11}$$

where $\prod$ means "the product of," just as Σ means "the sum of." But in this estimation problem the sample values X_i are fixed and only μ is

---

[3]Strictly speaking, in the case of a continuous distribution such as the normal we ought to use the phrase "probability density"; but hereafter we abbreviate to "probability."

thought of as varying over hypothetical values; we shall speculate on these various possible values of μ, with a view to selecting the most plausible. Thus (18-11) can be written as the likelihood function of μ,

$$L(\mu) = \prod_{i=1}^{3} \left[\frac{1}{\sqrt{2\pi\sigma^2}}\, e^{-(1/2\sigma^2)(X_i-\mu)^2} \right] \tag{18-12}$$

The MLE of μ is defined as the hypothetical value of μ which maximizes the likelihood function (18-12). Its value may be derived with calculus, but we consider only a geometric interpretation, in Figure 18-3.

We "try out" two hypothetical values of μ. We note that a population with mean μ_* as in Figure 18-3a. is not very likely to yield the sample we observed. Although the probabilities of X_1 and X_2 are large, the probability of X_3 (i.e., the ordinate above X_3) is very small because it is so far distant from μ_*. The product of all three probabilities [i.e., the likelihood of a population with mean μ_* generating the sample (X_1, X_2,

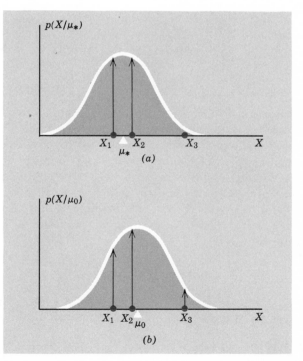

FIGURE 18-3   Maximum likelihood estimation of the mean μ of a normal population, based on three sample observations (X_1, X_2, X_3). (a) Small likelihood $L(\mu_*)$, the product of the three ordinates. (b) Large likelihood $L(\mu_0)$.

X_3)] is therefore quite small. On the other hand a population with mean μ_0 as in Figure 18-3b is more likely to generate the sample values. Since the X values are collectively closer to μ_0, they have a greater joint probability. Thus the likelihood is greater for μ_0 than for μ_*; indeed, very little additional shift in μ_0 is apparently required to maximize the likelihood of the sample. It seems that the MLE of μ might be the sample mean—i.e., the average value of X_1, X_2, and X_3; in fact, it is proved in Problem 18-2 that

---

in a normal population,

MLE of μ is $\overline{X}$

Finally, the reader who has carefully learned that μ is a fixed population parameter may wonder how it can appear in the likelihood function (18-12) as a variable. This is simply a mathematical convenience. The true value of μ is, in fact, fixed. But since it is unknown, in MLE we consider all of its possible, or hypothetical values; the way to do this mathematically is to treat it as a variable.[3]

18-4   **MLE OF PARAMETERS IN A NORMALLY DISTRIBUTED REGRESSION MODEL**

(a) Simple Regression

It was pointed out in Chapter 12 that estimating μ with $\overline{X}$ is, in fact, just the simplest possible special case of least squares. Since it was shown in the previous section that $\overline{X}$ is MLE, we might now ask: "Are least squares estimators still MLE, when they are applied in the full regression model?" The answer to this is, as expected, "yes"—provided that the assumption of normality of the error term (essentially not required in Chapter 12)[4] is now made. Thus, to the standard assumptions of (12-4) we now add that the independent random variables e_i are normally distributed, in the model

$$Y_i = \alpha + \beta x_i + e_i \qquad \text{(12-3) repeated}$$

Estimating α and β using MLE involves selecting those hypothetical population values of α and β more likely than any others to generate

---

[3] Recall that for convenience in the Bayesian analysis of Chapter 15, the population value θ was also treated as a variable.

[4] Except for small sample estimation—and this because of the general principle that small sample estimation requires a normally distributed parent population to strictly validate the t distribution.

the sample values we observed. Before addressing the algebraic derivation, it is best to clarify what is going on with a bit of geometry. To
simplify, assume a sample of only three observations (Y_1, Y_2, Y_3).

First, let us try out the line shown in Figure 18-4a. (Before examining
it carefully, we note that it seems to be a pretty bad fit for our three
observed points.) Temporarily, suppose this were the true regression line;
then the distribution of errors would be centered around it as shown.

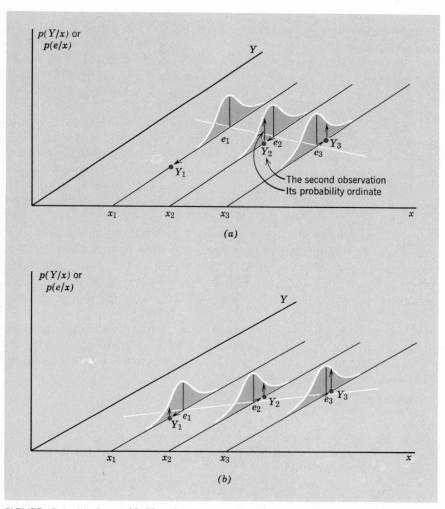

FIGURE 18-4 Maximum likelihood estimation. (a) This is *not* the true population; it is
only a hypothetical population that the statistician is considering. But it is not very likely
to generate the observed Y_1, Y_2, Y_3. (b) Another hypothetical population; this is more likely
to generate Y_1, Y_2, Y_3.

The likelihood that such a population would give rise to the observations in our sample is the probability that we would get the particular set of three e values shown in this diagram. The probability of each e value is shown rising vertically above it. Because our three observations are by assumption statistically independent, the likelihood of all three (i.e., the probability of getting the sample we observed), is the product of these three ordinates. This likelihood seems relatively small, mostly because the very small ordinate above Y_1 reduces the product value. Our intuition that this is a bad estimate is confirmed; such a hypothetical population is not very likely to generate our sample values. We should be able to do better.

In Figure 18-4b it is evident that we can do much better. This hypothetical population is more likely to give rise to the sample we observed. The disturbance terms are collectively smaller, with their probability being greater as a consequence.

The MLE technique is seen to involve speculating on various possible populations. How likely is each to give rise to the sample we observed? Geometrically, our problem would be to try them all out, by moving the population through all its possible values—i.e., *by moving the regression line and its surrounding e distribution through all possible positions in space*. Each position involves a different set of trial values for α and β. In each case the likelihood of observing Y_1, Y_2, Y_3, would be evaluated. For our MLE we choose that hypothetical population which maximizes this likelihood. It is evident that little further adjustment is required in Figure 18-4b to arrive at the MLE. This procedure intuitively seems to result in a good fit; moreover, since it seems similar to the least squares fit, it is no surprise that we shall be able to show that the two coincide.

While geometry has clarified the method, it hasn't provided a precise means of arriving at the specific maximum likelihood estimate. This must be done algebraically. For generality, suppose that we have a sample of size *n*, rather than just 3. We wish to know

$$p(Y_1, Y_2 \cdots Y_n/\alpha, \beta), \tag{18-13}$$

the probability of the sample we observed—expressed as a function of the possible population values of[5] α and β. First, consider the probability of the first value of Y, which is

$$p(Y_1) = \frac{1}{\sqrt{2\pi\sigma^2}}\, e^{-(1/2\sigma^2)[Y_1 - (\alpha + \beta x_1)]^2} \tag{18-14}$$

[5]And also of σ^2. But it turns out that although the likelihood *function* depends on σ^2, the maximum likelihood *estimate* does not; hence σ^2 is ignored in this discussion.

This is simply the normal distribution, with the mean $(\alpha + \beta x_1)$ and variance (σ^2) substituted appropriately into (4-12). [In terms of the geometry of Figure 18-4, $p(Y_1)$ is the ordinate above Y_1.] The probability of the second Y value is similar to (18-14), except that the subscript 2 replaces 1 throughout, and so on, for all the other observed Y values.

The independence of the Y values justifies multiplying all these probabilities together to find (18-13). Thus

$$p(Y_1, Y_2, \ldots Y_n/\alpha, \beta)$$

$$= \left[\frac{1}{\sqrt{2\pi\sigma^2}} \, e^{-(1/2\sigma^2)[Y_1-(\alpha+\beta x_1)]^2} \right] \left[\frac{1}{\sqrt{2\pi\sigma^2}} \, e^{-(1/2\sigma^2)[Y_2-(\alpha+\beta x_2)]^2} \right] \cdots$$

$$= \prod_{i=1}^{n} \left[\frac{1}{\sqrt{2\pi\sigma^2}} \, e^{-(1/2\sigma^2)[Y_i-(\alpha+\beta x_i)]^2} \right] \tag{18-15}$$

where $\displaystyle\prod_{i=1}^{n}$ represents the product of n factors. Using the familiar rule for exponentials,[6] the product in (18-15) can be reexpressed by summing exponents

$$p(Y_1, Y_2 \cdots Y_n/\alpha, \beta) = \left(\frac{1}{\sqrt{2\pi\sigma^2}} \right)^n e^{\Sigma(-1/2\sigma^2)[Y_i-(\alpha+\beta x_i)]^2} \tag{18-16}$$

Recall that the observed Y's are given. We are speculating on various values of α and β. To emphasize this, we rename (18-16) the likelihood function

$$L(\alpha, \beta) = \frac{1}{(2\pi\sigma^2)^{n/2}} \, e^{-(1/2\sigma^2)\Sigma[Y_i-\alpha-\beta x_i]^2} \tag{18-17}$$

We now ask, which values of α and β make L largest? The only place α and β appear is in the exponent; moreover, maximizing a function with a negative exponent involves minimizing the magnitude of the exponent. Hence the MLE estimates are obtained by choosing α and β in order to

$$\text{minimize } \sum [Y_i - \alpha - \beta x_i]^2 \tag{18-18}$$

Since the selection of maximum likelihood estimates of α and β to minimize (18-18) is identical to the selection of least squares estimates a and b to minimize (11-10), a very important conclusion follows:

---

in a normal regression model,
MLE is identical to least squares

---

[6] $e^a e^b = e^{a+b}$ for any a and b.

This establishes a most important theoretical justification of least squares: it is the estimate that follows from applying maximum likelihood techniques to a regression model with normally distributed error.

(b) Multiple Regression

In the multiple regression model

$$Y_i = \alpha + \beta x_i + \gamma z_i + e_i \qquad (18\text{-}19)$$
$$(13\text{-}2) \text{ repeated}$$

maximum likelihood estimates of α, β, and γ are derived in the same way as in the simple regression case; again they coincide with least squares. Algebraically, the argument is similar to the analysis in part (a), and is left as an exercise.[7]

18-5   MLE OF ANY PARAMETER FROM ANY POPULATION

We now state MLE in its full generality. A sample $(X_1, X_2 \cdots X_n)$ is drawn from a population with probability distribution $p(X/\theta)$, where θ is any unknown population parameter that we wish to estimate. From our definition of random sampling (with replacement, or from an infinite population), the X_i are independent, each with the probability distribu-

---

[7]We limit ourselves here to a few brief comments on the geometry of this 3-variable case.

The MLE of α, β and γ involves trying out all possible hypothetical regression planes in Figure 13-1, and selecting the one that is most likely to generate the sample values (red dots) we actually observed.

But first, note that Figure 13-1 involves 3 parameters (α, β, and γ), and 3 variables (Y, x, and z). However, there is one additional variable in our system—$p(Y/x, z)$—which has not yet been plotted. It may appear that there is no way of forcing 4 variables into a three-dimensional space, but this is not so. For example, economists often plot 3 variables (labor, capital, and output) in a two-dimensional labor-capital space by introducing the third output variable as a system of isoquants. Those for whom this is a familiar exercise should have little trouble in graphing four variables [Y, x, z, and $p(Y/x, z)$] in a three-dimensional (Y, x, and z) space by introducing the fourth variable [$p(Y/x, z)$] as a system of isoplanes. Each of these isoplanes represents (Y, x, z) combinations that are equiprobable (i.e., for which the probability density of Y is constant). Thus the complete geometric model is the regression plane shown in Figure 13-1, with isoprobability planes stacked above and below it. Our assumptions about the error term (12-4) guarantee that the isoprobability planes will be parallel to the true regression plane.

For MLE, we introduce the additional assumption that the error configuration is normal. Then we shift a hypothetical regression plane along with its associated set of parallel isoprobability planes. In each position the probability of the observed sample of points is evaluated by examining the isoprobability plane on which each point lies, and multiplying these together. The hypothetical regression that maximizes this likelihood is chosen.

tion $p(X_i/\theta)$; hence the joint probability distribution of the whole sample is obtained by multiplying,

$$p(X_1, X_2 \cdots X_n/\theta) = p(X_1/\theta)\, p(X_2/\theta) \cdots p(X_n/\theta)$$
$$= \prod_{i=1}^{n} p(X_i/\theta) \qquad (18\text{-}20)$$

But we regard the observed sample values as fixed, and ask, "Which of all the hypothetical values of θ maximizes this probability?" This is emphasized by renaming (18-20) the likelihood function:

$$L(\theta) = \prod_{i=1}^{n} p(X_i/\theta) \qquad (18\text{-}21)$$

The MLE is that hypothetical value of θ that maximizes this likelihood function.

18-6   MAXIMUM LIKELIHOOD VERSUS METHOD OF MOMENTS ESTIMATION (MLE VS MME)

In the analysis above, it turned out that a population proportion was estimated with a sample proportion, and a population mean with a sample mean. Why not always use this technique, and estimate any population moment with the corresponding sample moment? This is known as *method of moments estimation* (MME). Its great advantage is that it is very intuitive and easy to understand. Moreover, MLE and MME often coincide.

But suppose the two methods do differ (as in Problem 18-4)? In such a circumstance MLE is usually superior. The intuitive appeal of MME can be matched by an intuitive appeal for MLE: since MLE is the population value most likely to generate the sample values observed, it is in some sense the population value that "best matches" the observed sample. However, the real justification for MLE is that for large samples, it has many of the desirable characteristics of estimation described in Chapter 7-2; under broad conditions MLE has the following asymptotic properties. It is

1. *Efficient*, with smaller variance than any other estimators.
2. *Consistent*, that is, asymptotically unbiased, with variance tending to zero.
3. *Normally distributed*, with easily computed mean and variance; hence it may be readily used to make inferences.

For example, we have already seen that these three properties are true for $\overline{X}$, the MLE of μ in a normal population. [Property 3 follows from

(6-15); Property 2 follows from (6-10) and (6-11); Property 1 is proved in advanced texts, and has been alluded to in (7-17).]

We emphasize that these properties are *asymptotic*, that is, true for large samples as $n \to \infty$. But for the small samples often used by economists for example, MLE is not necessarily best, as we shall see in the next section.

*18-7   MLE AND BAYESIAN ESTIMATION
                                       (Requires Chapter 15 as Background)

Under certain assumptions, MLE will give the same answer as Bayesian methods. Whenever these assumptions are questionable, MLE becomes questionable. This section, therefore, will provide a warning against using MLE too carelessly.

(a) Simplest Case, θ_0 Versus θ_1

Suppose we wish to find the MLE of a parameter θ that is known to have only 2 possible values, θ_0 and θ_1. Then maximum likelihood estimation involves selecting θ_0 rather than θ_1 as the estimator iff

$$L(\theta_0) > L(\theta_1) \tag{18-22}$$

i.e., iff

$$p(X/\theta_0) > p(X/\theta_1) \tag{18-23}$$

(We have in mind that generally $p(X/\theta)$ is interpreted as the probability function of the data X, given θ; but in this context where it represents a likelihood function, X is fixed and θ is variable.)

On the other hand, if we were to use Bayesian techniques to choose between θ_0 and θ_1, we would use the likelihood ratio criterion in (15-63). If the regrets are equal, and also the prior probabilities,[8] then this criterion reduces to:

accept θ_0 rather than θ_1 iff

$$\frac{p(X/\theta_1)}{p(X/\theta_0)} < 1 \tag{18-24}$$

i.e.,

$$p(X/\theta_1) < p(X/\theta_0) \tag{18-25}$$

---

[8] This set of assumptions need not be this restrictive; it is enough that

$$\frac{r_0}{r_1} \cdot \frac{p(\theta_0)}{p(\theta_1)} = 1$$

which is exactly the same as the MLE criterion (18-23), and therefore gives exactly the same answer.

(b) Extension: Continuous θ

Suppose now that θ takes on a continuous range of values. If the statistician has absolutely no prior knowledge about θ, then in desperation he might use (just as in part (a)) the "equiprobable" prior:

$$p(\theta) = c, \quad \text{a constant} \tag{18-26}$$

Further suppose that, rather than using the familiar and attractive quadratic loss function, he opts for the 0-1 loss function. Consequently, according to (15-17) he will estimate θ with the mode of the posterior distribution. This posterior distribution is

$$p(\theta/X) = \frac{p(\theta)p(X/\theta)}{p(X)} \tag{18-27}$$
$$(15\text{-}7) \text{ repeated}$$

which, according to (18-26), reduces to

$$\left[\frac{c}{p(X)}\right] p(X/\theta) \tag{18-28}$$

To find the mode, he finds the value of θ which makes this largest. But since the bracketed term $[c/p(X)]$ does not depend on θ, he only needs to find:

$$\text{the value of } \theta \text{ which makes } p(X/\theta) \text{ largest} \tag{18-29}$$

But this statement is recognized as just the definition of the classical MLE.

From this, we conclude that a classical statistician who uses MLE is getting the same result as a Bayesian using the 0-1 loss function and an "equiprobable" prior. This is not a very flattering description of MLE, since neither this prior nor this loss function is easy to justify. (However, in many cases MLE is not nearly this restrictive. If $p(\theta/X)$ is unimodal and symmetric, as it often is, then its mean, mode, and median coincide; in such circumstances MLE is equivalent to Bayesian estimation using *any* of the three loss functions.)

(c) Bizarre Case: Population Proportion π

As if the discussion of MLE above has not been damaging enough, we recall an even more questionable application—the maximum likelihood estimation[9] of a population proportion π with the sample proportion P. In Section 15-5(c) this was shown to yield the same result as a Bayesian using the quadratic loss function and the hopeless prior distribution shown in Figure 15-6a. This illustrates how strange the maximum likelihood estimate may occasionally be in a small sample.

In conclusion, although MLE has the many attractive large sample properties listed in the previous section, in small sample estimation it should be used with considerable caution.

PROBLEMS

18-1 As in Figure 18-1, graph the likelihood function for a sample of 6 heads in 8 tosses of a coin; show the MLE.

*18-2 Derive the MLE of μ for a normal population, using calculus.

*18-3 (a) Derive the MLE of σ^2 for the normal distribution, assuming μ is known.

(b) Is it unbiased?

*18-4 As $N + 1$ delegates arrived at a convention, they were given successive tags numbered 0, 1, 2, 3, . . . N. In order to estimate the unknown number N, a brief walk in the corridor provided a sample of 5 tags, numbered 37, 16, 44, 43, 22.

(a) What is the MME of N? (Hint: since $\mu = N/2$, set $N/2 = \bar{X}$, i.e., $\hat{N} = 2\bar{X}$) Is it biased?

(b) What is the MLE of N? Is it biased?

(c) If necessary, adjust the MME and MLE to make them unbiased estimators of N.

---

[9] Recall that P has been established as the MLE of π in Section 18-2.

Chapter 19

Time Series Analysis

There's nothing constant in the universe
All ebb and flow, and every shape that's born
Bears in its womb the seeds of change.

Ovid

INTRODUCTION

There are two major categories of statistical information: cross section and time series. To illustrate, econometricians estimating how U.S. consumer expenditure is related to national income ("the consumption function") sometimes use a detailed breakdown of the consumption of individuals at various income levels at one point in time (cross section); other times they examine how total consumption is related to national income over a number of time periods (time series); and sometimes they use a combination of the two. In this chapter we shall use some familiar techniques (especially regression) and develop some new methods to analyze time series. Although our examples will use quarterly data, the techniques are also applicable to monthly data, weekly data, etc.

The main characteristic of a time series (which distinguishes it from a simple random sample) is that its observations have some form of dependence on time. The problem is that there are any number of patterns which this dependence may take. The major ones are illustrated in Figure 19-1. Panel (a) shows a time series with only a trend. Panel (b) shows a time series with only a quarterly pattern, repeated identically every year; thus, for example, the fourth quarter of 1955 is the same as

FIGURE 19-1 Three possible patterns of time dependence in a time series. (a) Trend, (b) seasonal, (c) random tracking.

the fourth quarter of 1956 or any other year. Panel (c) displays a random-tracking time series of autocorrelated or serially correlated terms; that is, each value is related to the preceding values, with a random disturbance added. (There are many examples of "series that follow themselves" outside of business and the social sciences: a machine gun leaves a random-tracking path of bullets along a wall; similarly, an aircraft on a bombing run leaves a tracking path of bombs.)

  If a time series followed only one of these patterns, there would be no problem. In practice, however, it is typically a mixture of all three that is very difficult to unscramble. Consider, for example, the quarterly data on plant and equipment expenditures shown in Figure 19-2. What

FIGURE 19-2   U.S. new plant and equipment expenditures, in durable manufacturing (in billions of dollars). Source: Survey of Current Business, U.S. Department of Commerce.

combination of these three patterns can be perceived? There appears to be some trend, some seasonal influence, and some random element. But how much of each is a mystery.

Time series analysis may be viewed as simply the attempt to break a time series up into these various components. We shall therefore consider each of the patterns in Figure 19-1 in turn.[1]

19-2   TREND

Trend is often the most important element in a time series. It may be linear, as shown in Figure 19-1a, displaying a constant increase in each time period, or it may be exponential (a geometric series), displaying a constant *percentage* increase in each time period; examples might be population growth in a developing country, or the growth of a trust fund over a long period. Then the logarithms of the observations will display a linear trend. The trend may also be a polynomial, or an even more complicated function.

The simplest way to deal with trend is with regression, simultaneously making seasonal adjustment as discussed in the section below. We assume the trend is linear; but if it is not, it may be possible to apply the regression techniques of Chapter 21.

---

[1]To complicate matters even more, there is often a fourth component in a time series: a disturbance that substantially displaces its values. For example, a war will shift bond sales, as shown in Figure 13-6. Such a displacement can often be treated with a dummy variable.

19-3 **SEASONAL**

There may be a seasonal fluctuation in time series as in Figure 19-1*b* for several reasons. A religious holiday, in particular Christmas, results in completely different economic and purchasing patterns. Or the seasons may affect economic activity: in the summer, agricultural production is high, while the sale of ski equipment is low.

(a) Extraction of Trend and Seasonal Components, using dummy Variables

In Figure 19-3*a* and in the first two columns of Table 19-1, we show a spectacular true life example of seasonal fluctuation—jewelry sales. We note both the possibility of a very slight upward trend and an obvious seasonal pattern marked by the sharp rise in sales every fourth quarter because of Christmas. If we made the mistake of trying to estimate only trend, say by a simple linear regression of sales S on time T as shown in Figure 19-3*b*, the result would be a substantial bias.[2] To avoid this, both trend *and* seasonal should be put into the regression model, in order to estimate their separate effects.[3]

The fourth quarter observations may be treated in exactly the same way as the peculiar wartime observations of bond sales in Chapter 13-9—by the use of a dummy variable. Letting Q_4 be the fourth quarter dummy,[4] the model becomes

$$S = \alpha + \beta_1 T + \beta_4 Q_4 + e \qquad (19\text{-}1)$$

---

[2] The upward bias in slope is largely caused by the fact that the last observation is a high, fourth quarter one. (As an exercise, you can confirm that seasonal influences would exert a downward bias on slope if the first observation was for the 4th quarter of 1956 and the last was for the 3rd quarter of 1960.)

[3] Even with this much care, least squares regression may still involve problems, because of random tracking residuals. This issue is discussed in detail in Section 19-8.

[4] There are three points in the analysis at which we might conclude that explicit account should be taken of seasonal swings. We may expect a strong seasonal influence from prior theoretical reasoning. Or, such an influence may be discovered after we plot the series. Finally, it may be discovered by examining residuals after fitting a regression; for example, after the simple regression in Figure 19-3*b* is fitted, we note that the observations indicated by arrows have consistently high residuals. To explain this, we look for something they have in common. Their common property is that they all occur in the fourth quarter. Hence the fourth quarter is introduced as a dummy regressor. This technique of "squeezing the residuals till they talk" is important in every kind of regression, not just time series; used with discretion, it indicates which further regressors may be introduced in order to reduce bias and residual variance.

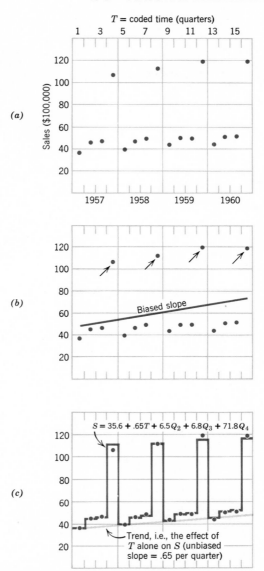

FIGURE 19-3   (a) Canadian jewelry sales. (b) Inadequate simple regression of S on T alone in which trend and seasonal influences are confounded. (c) Multiple regression of S on T and seasonal dummies, which explicitly distinguishes trend and seasonal effects.

Table 19-1   Canadian Department Store Jewelry
Sales and Seasonal Dummies

Time, T (Quarter Years)		Sales, S ($100,000's)	Q_4	Q_3	Q_2
1957	1	36	0	0	0
	2	44	0	0	1
	3	45	0	1	0
	4	106	1	0	0
1958	5	38	0	0	0
	6	46	0	0	1
	7	47	0	1	0
	8	112	1	0	0
1959	9	42	0	0	0
	10	49	0	0	1
	11	48	0	1	0
	12	118	1	0	0
1960	13	42	0	0	0
	14	50	0	0	1
	15	51	0	1	0
	16	118	1	0	0

Source: Dominion Bureau of Statistics, 63-002.

Even this model may not be adequate. If allowance should also be made
for shifts in the other quarters, dummies Q_2 and Q_3 should be added.
A dummy Q_1 is not needed for the first quarter, because Q_2, Q_3, and
Q_4 measure the shift from a first quarter base. (Whether or not to include
the various regressors Q_4, Q_3, Q_2, can be decided on statistical grounds,
by testing for statistical significance. It is common to include them all
in such a test, and reject or accept them as a group. But such a statistical
test on data as extreme as ours would be superfluous.) Our modified
model is now

$$S = \alpha + \beta_1 T + (\beta_4 Q_4 + \beta_3 Q_3 + \beta_2 Q_2) + e \qquad (19\text{-}2)$$

The least squares fit[5] is graphed in Figure 19-3c. Notice that our

---

[5] The least squares fit to this model was calculated by a method similar to that of
Table 13-5. Equation system (13-4) was extended to a system of five estimating equations
for the five unknowns. However, since the calculations are carried out by computer, the
details need not distract us.

seasonal adjustment is exactly the same every year; for example, each year there is the same upward shift ($\hat{\beta}_2$) in our fit between the first and second quarters. The trend is shown as the slope of the bottom line in this diagram.

This is summarized on the left-hand (unshaded) side of Figure 19-4. Panels (a) and (b) show the fitted trend and seasonal components, in sum comprising the fitted regression in panel (d). The difference between this and the observed dots is the residual series, shown in magnified form in panel (c). Thus the total jewelry sales series has been broken down into its three components in panels (a), (b), and (c); except for the block-type artwork, this is the same sort of breakdown as shown in Figure 19-1.

(b) Seasonal Adjustment without Dummies: Moving Average

This section is a brief (and optional) digression to illustrate that dummy variables are not the only means of seasonally adjusting data. Another common method is to take a moving average (over a whole year) of the time series, as shown in Table 19-2. Note how the wild seasonal swing is ironed out in this averaging process (because a fourth quarter observation is included in each average value S'). The trend relation of sales to time could now be estimated by a simple regression of seasonally adjusted S' on T.

It is interesting to compare this method with the dummy variable alternative. An apparent disadvantage is that a total of three observations are lost at the beginning and end of the time series, in order to get the moving average started and finished. However, although it is less evident,

Table 19-2 Moving Average of Canadian Jewelry Sales

Time		S (Unadjusted)		S' (Adjusted by Four Quarter Moving Average)
	1	36		
	2	44	$\frac{1}{4}(36 + 44 + 45 + 106)$	= 57.75
1957	3	45	$\frac{1}{4}(44 + 45 + 106 + 38)$	= 58.25
	4	106		= 58.75
	1	38	$\vdots$	= 59.25
	2	46		= 60.75
1958	3	47		
	4	112		$\vdots$
	$\vdots$	$\vdots$		

FIGURE 19-4 The three components of Canadian jewelry sales, projected with dashed lines. Compare projection of total series in (d) with realized sales (dots). (a) Trend (35.6 + .65T). (b) Seasonal ($6.5Q_2 + 6.8Q_3 + 71.8Q_4$). (c) Serially correlated residual magnified 20 times ($e_t = -.21e_{t-1}$). (d) Total (original) series (as in Figure 19-3a) projected.

468

the same loss is involved in using dummy variables, since three degrees of freedom are lost in estimating the shift coefficients β_2, β_3, and β_4.

An advantage of the moving average method is that it is not necessary to assume a constant seasonal shift; thus the adjustment for any quarter varies from year to year.[6] The advantage of dummy variables is that both seasonal shifts *and* the trend relation of S to T are estimated simultaneously in the same regression. (A moving average adjustment is only the first stage in a two-step process; only after it is completed can trend be estimated by regressing S' on T.) Another advantage is that the dummy coefficients (β_2, β_3, and β_4) give an index of the average seasonal shift, and tests of significance on them can easily be undertaken using standard procedures.

19-4   RANDOM TRACKING (AUTOCORRELATION)

We now return to Figure 19-4: with the trend and seasonal components of the time series removed by regression, this leaves the residual yet to be analyzed.

The simplest model for the random-tracking residual is to linearly relate each value e_t to its previous value e_{t-1}, with a random disturbance[7] v_t added:

$$e_t = \rho e_{t-1} + v_t \qquad (19\text{-}3)$$

To illustrate, we assumed that $\rho = 1$, and the random disturbance v_t was normal; accordingly we drew a sample of 20 independent values of v_t from a table of standard normal deviates (Appendix Table IIb). Then, starting with an initial value of $e_0 = 5$ for example, we used equation (19-3) to generate $e_1, e_2, e_3 \ldots e_{20}$ as shown in Figure 19-5. The positive nature of the autocorrelation is clear; e_t tends to be high whenever the previous value e_{t-1} is high.

In practice, the parameter ρ is typically less than 1; moreover it is generally not known. However, it may be estimated by applying simple regression to (19-3). As an example, the residuals of the jewelry sales

---

[6] A disadvantage of the moving average is that in smoothing out extreme observations, it may make the resulting series S' more cyclical than the original series S.

[7] In previous chapters "error" and "disturbance" may have been used synonymously; but in this chapter it is necessary to make a clear distinction between the original error e_t (which may be autocorrelated), and the further disturbance v_t (which is entirely random).

data in Figure 19-4c were estimated[8] to follow the autoregressive scheme:

$$\hat{e}_t = -.21\hat{e}_{t-1} \qquad (19\text{-}4)$$

This negative estimate of ρ shows that autocorrelation can be negative, as well as positive. In this case, values tend to change sign (a positive value is followed by a negative one), rather than track each other over time—as they did when positively correlated in Figure 19-5. (Inventory series often provide another example of negative serial correlation, if particularly large purchases for inventory result in overstocking, hence smaller purchases in the following period).

In its more general form, (19-3) becomes

$$e_t = \rho_1 e_{t-1} + \rho_2 e_{t-2} \cdots + \rho_k e_{t-k} + v_t \qquad (19\text{-}5)$$

which is sometimes called a kth order autoregression.

19-5

PREDICTION

One of the main reasons for decomposing a time series into its 3 components as in Figure 19-4 is to predict its values into the gray future

---

[8] The hats in (19-4) indicate that the residuals $\hat{e}_t$ are derived from the estimated regression line. That is, $\hat{e}_t$ are the estimated residuals (similar to $y_i - \hat{y}_i$ in column 7 of Table 11-2), whereas e_t are the unobservable true residuals.

The estimate of ρ in (19-4) was calculated to be $-.21$ as follows: $\hat{e}_t$ is given in column (1) below; then column (2) follows directly from it; finally we regress the series in (1) on the series in (2).

Quarter T	Observed: (1) $\hat{e}_t$	Observed: (2) $\hat{e}_{t-1}$	Calculation of $\hat{\rho}$ (3) $\hat{e}_t \cdot \hat{e}_{t-1}$	Calculation of $\hat{\rho}$ (4) $\hat{e}_{t-1}^2$
1	+ .2			
2	+ .7	+ .2	.14	.04
3	+1.0	+ .7	.70	.49
4	−3.6	+1.0	−3.60	1.00
5	− .1	−3.6	.	.
6	.	− .1	.	.
.	.	.	.	.
.	.	.	.	.

From (11-16)

$$\hat{\rho} = \frac{\Sigma \hat{e}_t \cdot \hat{e}_{t-1}}{\Sigma \hat{e}_{t-1}^2}$$
$$= -.21$$

FIGURE 19-5   The construction of a serially correlated error term. (a) Independent disturbance v_t. (b) Generated error: $e_t = e_{t-1} + v_t$.

period in that diagram. A simple method suggested by that analysis is to project each of its components as in the extended dashed lines in panels (a), (b) and (c), and then sum them into the dashed line projection[9] in panel (d).

Although the predicted values for the random tracking residual in

_____

[9] For example, using the equations of Figure 19-4, the 17th and 18th quarters are predicted to be:

Projection of:	T = 17	T = 18
trend $(35.6 + 65T)$	$35.6 + .65(17) = 46.7$	$35.6 + .65(18) = 47.3$
seasonal $(6.5Q_2 + 6.8Q_3 + 71.8Q_4)$	reference quarter = 0	setting $Q_2 = 1$, $6.5(1) = 6.5$
residual $(-.21\hat{e}_{t-1})$	$-.21(.5) = -.1$	$-.21(-.1) = .02$
Total	46.6	53.82

panel (c) are included in the projection in panel (d), they quickly settle down to practically zero, since from (19-4) each is only 1/5 the size of the previous one. This relatively small random tracking element in the total prediction makes good intuitive sense: in this time series it is the least predictable of the three components, and hence makes almost zero predictive contribution beyond the first few quarters. In fact, it sometimes is reasonable enough to set this equal to zero immediately (that is, forget about it), so that only the trend and seasonal are used. This is especially true if computational facilities are scarce, or if only long-run predictions are desired.

To see how well the prediction worked out, we compare it in panel (d) with the actual values the time series took in 1961–1962, shown in dots. Although these values could not be used in the analysis, (they were not yet known), they do provide a good test after the event of how well the prediction turned out. Initially the prediction is not too bad, but it tends to get worse the farther it goes into the future—one more example of the dangers of extrapolation first mentioned in Section 12-9. Thus the shorter the prediction, the better; this suggests that if funds and computing facilities are available, the whole analysis should be recalculated and predictions updated whenever new observations on the variables become available (i.e., delay your predictions for 1962 until the 1961 figures become available; then each of the components in Figure 19-4 can be reestimated).

In our predictions, we have made no attempt to calculate a prediction interval. The reason is not only the great complexity of a three-component time series. As well, the autocorrelation in the tracking residual invalidates prediction intervals like (12-44) that are based on the assumption of independent observations. This issue is discussed more fully in Section 19-8.

19-6

CYCLES

Figure 19-6 illustrates a cycle, showing its three defining characteristics—period, amplitude, and phase. We then define its frequency f as the number of cycles it goes through every quarter (time period). For example, a cycle with period $\tau = 6$ (as in Figure 19-6) makes 1/6 complete cycles every quarter. In general,

$$f \triangleq \frac{1}{\tau} \tag{19-6}$$

Cyclical analysis is the decomposition of a series into cyclical components. (It is also called Fourier analysis. A more practical extension called

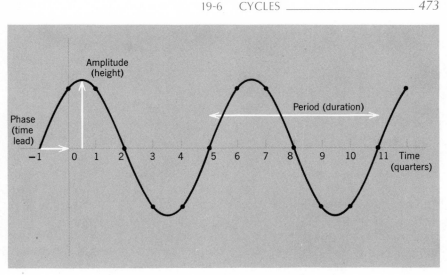

FIGURE 19-6   Defining characteristics of a cycle.

spectral analysis is discussed in the next section). Although cyclical analysis may be applied to any time series, it is usually restricted to residual series, after trend and seasonal components have been extracted. In other words, in Figure 19-4 we split up a time series into its three components—one of which was a residual; in this section we will be further decomposing a *residual* series into its cyclical *subcomponents*.

To keep things simple, in Figure 19-7a we illustrate using only the first six of the residuals from the jewelry sales. With appropriate formulas it is possible to calculate three cycles that, when added up, exactly generate the residual series y. At $T = 4$, for example, the three cyclical values indicated by arrows in panel (b) sum exactly[10] to the value y in panel (a). In general,

---

A time series of length n may be   (19-7)

decomposed into $\frac{n}{2}$ cycles.[11]

---

[10] This is true not only at the integers like $T = 4$, but also at any time in between.

[11] We assume that the series has an even number of terms n, and a zero mean. In order to simplify both theory and computations, the frequencies of the cycles chosen to represent a given series y are uniformly spaced from 0 to 1/2. For example, in Figure 19-7 the frequencies are

$$\frac{1}{6}, \frac{2}{6}, \frac{3}{6}$$ (19-8)

(cont'd)

This can be used to decompose *any* series into a set of cycles. Hence using this analysis to decompose a time series "into its cycles" does not establish that the series was generated by a "cyclical process." Therefore, before attaching much meaning to a specific cycle, we must not only find that its amplitude is relatively large but also establish its economic rationale. This is often difficult to do.

In many ways, the most plausible example of a cycle in business or economics is the replacement cycle. To illustrate, consider the invention of a new consumer good (e.g., TV) that is associated initially with abnormally heavy sales as the public stocks up. This is followed by more or less normal growth (as population and income grow, etc.). But when the original units begin to wear out, this normal growth is usually replaced by a time in which sales are again abnormally high since they now include both normal growth *and* replacement of the original units. Theoretically, this cyclical process could continue, eventually fading out like an echo, (since the lifetime of a product is not very clearly defined). But, in practice, such echoes quickly become dominated by the appearance of new inventions and other disturbances. The same phenomena may apply in capital goods industries as well, initiated by the invention or development of a new kind of machine. (There may be an even more clearly distinct cycle in this case, if the depreciation rate allowed by the tax authorities tends to more clearly establish the lifetime of a machine.) Moreover, it is obvious that cycles are of widely varying duration (i.e., period). For example, a TV cycle will be of short duration compared to the long-term housing cycle that might be initiated by the substantial construction required following a war or a natural disaster.

Since other economic cycles are even harder to define than the replacement cycle, the exercise of decomposing economic series into cycles should be viewed with a healthy degree of skepticism; it's a bit like trying to sort out a set of echoes in a noisy sound chamber.

---

and, in general, to decompose a time series of length n, we use frequencies

$$f = \frac{1}{n}, \frac{2}{n}, \frac{3}{n}, \ldots, \frac{1}{2} \tag{19-9}$$

With these frequencies prespecified, each cycle has two remaining parameters that may be fitted freely, the amplitude and phase. Since there are $n/2$ cycles, this makes n parameters altogether, which can be uniquely determined from the n values of y. This is why any cyclical decomposition (e.g., in Figure 19-7b) will always exactly fit the series (in Figure 19-7a) from which it was derived.

FIGURE 19-7   (a) y = the jewelry sales residual, reproduced from Figure 19-4c. (The first six residuals, shifted slightly because a residual series requires a zero mean.) (b) Its decomposition into three cycles.

19-1 For the following car sales data:

Canadian auto sales (quarterly, 1955–1959). Source: Dominion Bureau of Statistics.

(a) Fit a linear trend by eye.

(b) Shift the linear trend so that it passes as close as possible to the first quarter (reference quarter) points. Then roughly estimate how much higher the second quarters rise, on average, above this reference line. Repeat for the third and fourth quarters.

(c) For this car sales data, the standard least squares (computerized) estimates of trend and seasonal are shown in Figure 19-1a and b. Use them to judge the accuracy of your rough estimates in (a) and (b) above. (Incidentally, the residual in this series is shown in Figure 19-1c; in other words, Figure 19-1 is the complete decomposition of the time series above.)

19-2 As in Figure 19-5 and equation (19-3) (and setting $\rho = 1$), construct a string of ten serially correlated disturbances e_t. (For v_t, use the table of standard normal numbers of Appendix Table IIb, rounded. Start with $e_0 = 0$ for simplicity.)

19-3 True or false? If false, correct it.

If the first observation in a residual time series is negative, then (1) positive serial correlation means that the odds favor (i.e., probability $> .50$) the next observation being negative;

(2) negative serial correlation means that the odds favor the next observation being positive;

(3) no serial correlation (i.e., a purely random residual) means that the next observation is equally likely to be positive or negative.

19-4 True or false? If false, correct it.

(a) A time series may be decomposed into three components:

(1) trend

(2) seasonal pattern

(3) random tracking residual

(b) The fitting of trend and seasonal by eye, as in Problem 19-1, has the advantage of simplicity. However, if computer facilities are available, the least squares estimates have even more advantages, as follows:

(1) they are easy to calculate, since multiple regression is a standard library program;

(2) they are more objective (and hence will not be biased, consciously or subconsciously, by the researcher);

(3) they can be subjected to significance tests.

(c) The fitting of trend by multiple regression, or by moving averages, yields exactly the same result.

(d) The tracking residual may be removed at the same time as the trend, using multiple regression with dummies. This then leaves the seasonal pattern, to be studied further with cyclical analysis.

(e) Only time series generated by some cyclical mechanism can be broken down by cyclical analysis.

19-5 (a) In Figure 19-7, we showed the decomposition of a residual series into its cyclical components. In particular, we showed how the three components add up at $t = 4$. Show this again,

(1) at $t = 2$

(2) at $t = 3$

(3) at even a fractional t, such as $t = 2.5$

(b) Does Figure 19-7 prove that the series in panel (a) was "generated by" the three cyclical processes described in panel (b)?

*19-7   **SPECTRAL ANALYSIS**

Spectral analysis extends the Fourier analysis of Section 19-6, to determine which of the component cycles exert most influence on the original series. In order to give an elementary presentation of this difficult subject, we defer many of the subtleties to the student's manual.

(a) The Variance Spectrum

First, we summarize the cyclical analysis of Figure 19-7 by recording the amplitude of each cycle. This is shown in Figure 19-8a and is called the amplitude spectrum.[12] The variance of each cycle[13] is

$$V = \frac{A^2}{2} \quad \text{except for the last cycle} \quad \text{(19-10)}$$

$$= A^2 \quad \text{for the last cycle} \quad \text{(19-11)}$$

These variances, graphed in Figure 19-8b, are called the *variance spectrum, power spectrum,* or just plain *spectrum.*

The variance spectrum may be regarded as a decomposition of the variance of a time series *y* into its cyclical components—just as ANOVA was regarded as the decomposition of variation into factor components. Specifically, it has been proven that

---

variance of a time series = sum of cycle variances = $\sum V$ (19-12)

---

like (10-36)

For example, from Figure 19-7a we may calculate the variance of the

---

[12] The terminology of spectral analysis has some very interesting origins in the physical sciences. For example, the word "spectrum" is applied to a cyclical analysis of multicolored light. Each particular frequency of light (electromagnetic wave) strikes the eye as a particular color.

The word "harmonic" is applied in the theory of sound and music. When the vibration of a violin string is doubled in frequency (by halving the length of the string), the ear hears it raised an octave. Note that in the three cycles of Figure 19-7, the second is thus an "octave" higher than the first. Thus the three cycles are often called three "harmonics," and Fourier analysis itself is sometimes called "harmonic" analysis.

[13] The variance of a cycle, as for any other sequence, can be found by squaring its deviations from its mean value (in this case zero). Since these deviations are usually less than the amplitude, (see for example cycle 1 in Figure 19-7b), the variance will be less than A^2. In fact, it can be shown with trigonometry that

$$V = \frac{A^2}{2} \quad \text{(19-10) repeated}$$

There is one exception, however—the last cycle, with highest frequency, shown in our example as the last cycle in Figure 19-7b. In this case, we see that the cycle hits its full amplitude at each integer, making

$$V = A^2 \quad \text{(19-11) confirmed}$$

FIGURE 19-8   (a) Amplitude spectrum of the first jewelry sales residuals. (b) Variance spectrum, as given by (19-10) and (19-11).

time series directly:

$$\text{variance}^{14} \text{ of } y = \frac{1}{n} \sum_1^n (y - \bar{y})^2 \tag{19-13}$$

$$= \frac{1}{6}[4^2 + 10^2 + 13^2 + (-32)^2 + 2^2 + 3^2]$$

$$= 220 \tag{19-14}$$

On the other hand, from Figure 19-8b, we find the frequency components approximately sum to

$$\sum V = 81 + 99 + 40 \tag{19-15}$$

$$= 220$$

which verifies (19-12).

_____

[14] Since the mean $\bar{y}$ is set equal to zero rather than estimated, the divisor n is used in calculating variance; otherwise, (19-13) is just like (2-6a), the standard calculation of variance for any set of observations.

So far our illustrations have been very short time series, for reasons of convenience. We shall see, however, that in practice spectral analysis is worthwhile only for long series ($n \geq 50$ or 100). We therefore illustrate, in Figure 19-9a, the spectrum of a long annual series.[15] This spectrum, having half as many components as the time series itself, is so detailed and irregular that "it is hard to see the forest for the trees." Therefore, in Figures 19-9b and c, we have averaged the spectrum lines into cells.

(b) Resolution versus Stability

By comparing Figures 19-9b and c it is evident that the broader we group, the less detail we can see and the less we can distinguish close frequencies; this is called loss of *resolution*. However, for this price we achieve substantial gains: note that the averaging process in panel (c) has given us a very *stable* histogram, whereas in panel (a) we had an enormous amount of statistical fluctuation. This is why a long time series is required: to allow the averaging process to reduce statistical fluctuation.

This stability issue may be expressed precisely. Imagine the time series extending indefinitely, without any change in the generating mechanism. Cut it into chunks of length n, (where n is the size of the observed time series you have in hand), and put all these chunks into a bowl called the *population*. Every chunk has a spectrum like Figure 19-9c that could be calculated; the average of all these spectra is called the *population spectrum* Φ. It is the target that we hope is reasonably well estimated by a single chunk (single time series of length n) drawn at random from the population bowl. It has been shown that for any individual frequency band (as in Figure 19-9c), the ratio

$$\frac{V}{\Phi} \text{ has a } C^2 \text{ distribution} \tag{19-16}$$

$$\text{with d.f.}^{16,17} \simeq 2n(\Delta f) \tag{19-17}$$

---

[15] This spectrum is approximately the spectrum of wheat prices in Europe during the 17th and 18th centuries, with trend removed. Since the data are annual (not quarterly or monthly), there was no seasonal component to be removed.

The spectrum was graphed on a logarithmic scale, to keep the weak frequencies from being entirely obscured.

[16] Note that if $\Delta f = 1/2$, this represents maximum averaging; in fact, since there is only one frequency band, there is no decomposition of variance at all, so that $V = s^2$, which has $(n - 1)$ d.f. From (19-17) we find approximately the same answer: d.f. $\simeq 2n(1/2) = n$.

[17] In the first and last frequency bands, Δf (and consequently d.f.) are only half as large as usual.

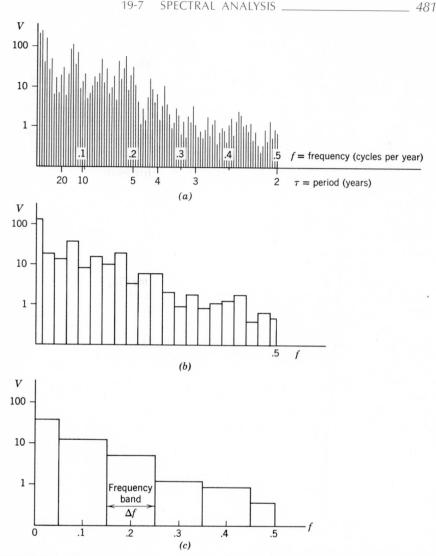

FIGURE 19-9 Variance spectrum of a *long series*. (a) Ungrouped. (b) Grouped into cells covering five frequencies (height of each bar represents average variance of its five cycles). (c) Grouped into cells covering 20 frequencies.

where Δf represents the width of the frequency band. Thus for any frequency band we can construct a 95% confidence interval for Φ, just as we did for σ^2 in Section 8-4, obtaining

$$\frac{V}{C_{.025}^2} < \Phi < \frac{V}{C_{.975}^2}$$

(19-18)
like (8-31)

In Figure 19-10 we show the confidence interval for the variance in each frequency band,[18] using the spectra of Figure 19-9.

Comparing Figures 19-10*b* and *c* we see explicitly how, according to (19-17), a wider frequency band Δf increases d.f., and hence narrows the confidence interval. Thus greater stability is achieved at the price of less resolution.

(c) Computation

In the sections above we have tried by a series of steps to show what the variance spectrum is and how it may be derived. In fact, the actual computer calculations generally follow a shorter and more mysterious route; although it is more difficult to explain, it does involve fewer computations, and this is why it is used. It is worth briefly outlining, so that you may have some knowledge of the terminology used in the computer input and output.

First, the correlogram of the residual series is computed. This involves computing the correlation coefficient of the series y_t with each of its lagged values, as shown in Figure 19-11. Thus, for example, the correlation coefficient[19] between y_t and y_{t-4} is seen in this figure to be .6.

Second, this correlogram of 10 observed correlations can be broken down into its five cycles (Fourier transform) just like we broke down the series of six values in Figure 19-7*a* into its three cycles. The result,

---

[18] The calculations are as follows: it is easiest if we take logarithms of (19-18), obtaining

$$\log V - \log C^2_{.025} < \log \Phi < \log V - \log C^2_{.975} \qquad (19\text{-}19)$$

For $n = 200$, and $\Delta f = 1/40$ as in Figure 19-9*b*, we find from (19-17) that

$$\text{d.f.} = 2(200)\left(\frac{1}{40}\right) = 10$$

except for the first and last frequency bands, where

$$\text{d.f.} = 2(200)\left(\frac{1}{80}\right) = 5$$

and from Table VIb $C^2_{.025} = 2.05$

$$C^2_{.975} = .325$$

$$C^2_{.025} = 2.57$$

$$C^2_{.975} = .166$$

Thus (19-19) becomes

$$\log V - 0.31 < \log \Phi < \log V + .49$$

$$\log V - .41 < \log \Phi < \log V + .78 \qquad (19\text{-}20)$$

In this form, we see yet another advantage in using a logarithmic axis for V.

[19] Covariances, rather than correlations, are sometimes calculated in this first stage.

(a)

(b)

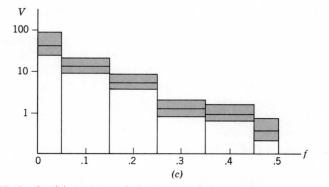

(c)

FIGURE 19-10 Confidence intervals for the population spectrum. (a) Illustration for one frequency band in Figure 19-9*b;* (*b*) For all frequency bands in Figure 19-9*b;* (c) For all frequency bands in Figure 19-9*c.*

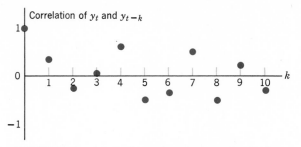

FIGURE 19-11   A typical correlogram for a time series.

strangely enough, is approximately the five-cell variance spectrum[20] of y_t—similar to the variance spectrum we derived in Figure 19-9c.

The reason this short-cut route involves computational saving is because it has been found that even for a y series of say 200 observations, it is only necessary to extend the correlogram in Figure 19-11 to $k = 10$ or 20 usually, which then requires the calculation of only 5 or 10 cycles. It would be much more work to calculate all 100 cycles for the original series of 200 observations; in any case, this detail would be lost in the eventual grouping into 5 or 10 cells.

(d) Conclusions

Anyone who has worked through spectral analysis of a residual series may be tempted to use it for predictive purposes: the idea would be to pick the frequency band with the greatest amplitude, and then use it to predict the residual series. Except for very exceptional circumstances, this is a temptation worth resisting, for several reasons.

In many cases, the estimated spectrum turns out to be jagged and ambiguous, with several peaks. Even if one frequency band does dominate, it is not clear which particular frequency within this band should be used. Moreover, the inevitable statistical error in the point estimate of the population parameter may be much more destructive in a time series than in, say, multiple regression; the reason is that in each successive time period the estimated and true cycle become further and further out of phase (i.e., if the period of the cycle is slightly underes-

---

[20] There is some intuitive justification of this. If y_t is dominated by a strong tendency to repeat itself every four years, then the correlogram peaks periodically, when $k = 0$, 4, 8 ... Then the dominant cycle in the Fourier transform will be the cycle of period 4, (frequency 1/4) as we would hope. Thus, Figure 19-11 does provide a lot of information about the spectrum, at least through periods 1-10. But why it also contains extractable information for the other periods is much more difficult to see.

timated, then the first peak will be a little off target, the second peak a bit more, and so on).

Spectral prediction requires strong prior economic justification. It has already been pointed out that many economic time series that appear to be cyclical may not have been generated by a cyclical process at all; and using apparent cycles for prediction may be much less satisfactory than using the relatively simple estimated autoregressive model (19-3).

PROBLEMS

*19-6 Draw a hypothetical set of observations (similar to Figure 19-3) to show how a cyclical residual can throw the trend estimate off target.

*19-7 Can you guess at the result if you applied spectral analysis to the time series
(a) in Figure 19-1a
(b) in Figure 19-1b
(c) in Figure 19-1c in the special case where the residual is purely random (serially uncorrelated).

*19-8 True or false? If false, correct it.
(a) The seasonal influence can be viewed as a very special cycle.
(b) Just as the seasonal component is removed, so any other cycle whose exact period is known a priori should be removed by using multiple regression. Then conduct a spectral analysis on the residual.

*19-9 Assume you know the amplitude and phase of a cycle exactly, but you don't know its frequency exactly.
(a) Show diagramatically how your prediction of a future value could be completely wrong (i.e., your error in prediction = $2A$)
(b) Repeat (a), assuming you know amplitude and frequency, and err only on its phase.
(c) In a long-term projection, will a small error become more serious in (a) or (b).

*19-8   HOW AUTOCORRELATION AFFECTS THE TREND
                     AND SEASONAL ESTIMATES

(a) Introduction

In our initial analysis of a time series (Sections 19-2 and 19-3) we estimated the trend and seasonal components, leaving a residual series to be analyzed in Section 19-4 for autocorrelation. The problem is that the existence of a positively autocorrelated residual mixed up in the original series will reduce the reliability of our first stage estimate of trend and seasonal (and indeed may reduce the reliability of our estimate of any other influence, for that matter). In this section we discuss this problem and suggest possible solutions. Before plunging into a lot of mathematics, it is important to understand the intuitive idea.

Autocorrelation means that the successive observations are dependent to some extent; thus, with positive autocorrelation, the second (or some later) observation tends to resemble, or repeat, the first observation, and hence gives little new information. Thus n autocorrelated observations give less information about trend (and other influences) than n independent observations would. Consequently, our estimates will be less reliable.

We turn now to the mathematical development. Our regression model is

$$Y_t = \alpha + \beta X_t + e_t \tag{19-21}$$

where X_t represents time T, or seasonal dummies, or any other time series deemed influential in determining Y_t; or for that matter, any combination of these. In addition, the error e_t is assumed to be autocorrelated. Just how e_t is related to its previous values is, of course, unknown, just as α and β are unknown. It's true that we have already estimated it in a very simple way in our example in (19-4); but now we wish to look into its theoretical properties in more detail.

(b) A Simple Example

Just as in Figure 19-5, we again suppose the error term e_t has the simple form of positive serial correlation given by $\rho = 1$ in (19-3); then

$$e_t = e_{t-1} + v_t \tag{19-22}$$

Now we must be even more explicit about the additional disturbance v_t, which is assumed to have the usual characteristics: zero mean, constant variance σ^2, and independence from the other disturbances v_{t-1}, v_{t-2}, etc. The initial value e_0 is also assumed to be random, with mean zero, and variance σ_0^2, say.

Suppose the true regression line (defined by α and β) is as shown in Figure 19-12a. Suppose further that the error terms $e_1, e_2, \ldots$ are those we generated from this same model in Figure 19-5: they are reproduced in Figure 19-12b. Any observed Y (e.g., Y_2) is the sum of its expected value ($\alpha + \beta X_t$) as given by the true regression, plus the corresponding error term (e_2). Since this error e_t is positively correlated, once our observations are above this true regression, they will tend to stay above it (i.e., once e_t is positive, it will be more likely to take on a positive value in the following time period). Similarly, whenever e_t becomes negative, it tends to stay negative.

In Figure 19-12a we can immediately see the difficulties that this serial correlation causes, by observing how badly an ordinary regression through this scatter would estimate the true regression.[21] Specifically, in this sample, β would be underestimated and α overestimated. But in another sample we might have observed precisely the opposite pattern of errors, with e_t initially taking on negative values, followed by positive ones. In this case, we would overestimate β and underestimate α. Either of these two types of estimation error seems equally likely; and there are other possibilities as well. Intuitively, it seems that the problem is not bias, since we are as likely to get an overestimate as an underestimate. Rather, the problem is that estimates may be badly wide of the target. Although unbiased, the estimates have a large variance. Nor is this primarily the fault of the ordinary least squares (OLS) regression procedure; any other estimating procedure (such as fitting by eye) would fit the "tilted" data about the same way. In fact, despite the large variance of its estimators, OLS may still be quite efficient; although there is another more sophisticated technique (Generalized Least Squares, GLS) that is more efficient, the improvement it provides over OLS may be quite small.

We are now in a position to draw our first conclusions.

1. Ordinary least squares estimates of α and β are unbiased $\qquad$ (19-23)
2. OLS may be relatively efficient $\qquad$ (19-24)

However, for an *interval* estimate of β (or α), OLS would be grossly deceptive. There are two reasons for this, which will be seen in comparing the serial correlation of Figure 19-12 to the case of no serial correlation in Figure 19-13. These two figures are alike in all respects other than the serial correlation; in particular, we emphasize that they have the same variance for the error e_t.

---

[21] In the interests of clarity, this argument has been oversimplified, since it is assumed in Figure 19-12a that X_t is increasing over time regularly. Thus the argument holds best if X_t represents simply time T; but it still holds true even if X_t just tends to increase over time. On the other hand, if X_t alternates between low and high values, then our analysis would be complicated; in particular, our later conclusion about the efficiency of ordinary least squares would have to be modified.

FIGURE 19-12   Regression with serially correlated error. (a) True and estimated regression lines. (b) True error terms (from Figure 19-5). (c) Observed error terms.

Since Figure 19-13 satisfies the assumptions of OLS, it will provide a valid confidence interval. But this is not so for the serially correlated data of Figure 19-12; in this case the standard confidence interval

$$\beta = \hat{\beta} \pm t_{.025} \frac{s}{\sqrt{\sum x_i^2}}$$
(19-25)

(12-33) repeated

will err for two reasons:

1. It is likely to be centered at a more erroneous value of $\hat{\beta}$. We might hope that it would allow for this greater error by providing a wider confidence interval.

2. Yet it has a *narrower* confidence interval, because it has a smaller value of s. To establish this, we recall that the variance s^2 is calculated from the observed errors $\hat{e}_t$. In the case of serial correlation, the estimated regression line fits the tracking data rather well, leaving the small errors $\hat{e}_t$ shown in Figure 19-12c.

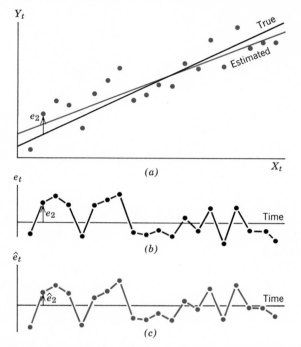

FIGURE 19-13   Regression with independent error (yet same variance as in Figure 19-12). (a) True and estimated regression lines. (b) True error terms. (c) Observed error terms.

To sum up: because the data is tracking, an OLS estimate of β is, in fact, less reliable. But it appears to the statistician to be *more* reliable because tracking data tends to yield smaller observed errors.

(c) Regression of First Differences

To estimate β in the linear regression model (19-21), the remedy for this special case of serial correlation is to transform the data so that it does satisfy the assumptions of OLS. Since (19-21) holds true for any time t, it holds for time $(t - 1)$:

$$Y_{t-1} = \alpha + \beta X_{t-1} + e_{t-1} \tag{19-26}$$

We can now examine the change over time of our variables, by subtracting (19-26) from (19-21),

$$(Y_t - Y_{t-1}) = \beta(X_t - X_{t-1}) + (e_t - e_{t-1}) \tag{19-27}$$

Note from (19-22) that

$$e_t - e_{t-1} = v_t$$

and define

$$\left.\begin{array}{l} Y_t - Y_{t-1} \overset{\Delta}{=} \Delta Y_t \\ X_t - X_{t-1} \overset{\Delta}{=} \Delta X_t \end{array}\right] \qquad (19\text{-}28)$$

which are called "differences." Then (19-27) can be written

$$\underline{\Delta Y_t = \beta \Delta X_t + v_t} \qquad\qquad (19\text{-}29)$$

In this form, the error v_t has all the properties required by OLS. Thus, β may be validly estimated by OLS regression of ΔY on ΔX. However, we must emphasize that this works only for an error of the (usually unrealistic) form of (19-22).

(d) Generalized Differences—an Example of Generalized Least Squares (GLS)

Our original model for the error term (19-3) conforms more realistically to economic and business situations

$$e_t = \rho e_{t-1} + v_t \qquad\qquad (19\text{-}30)$$
$$(19\text{-}3) \text{ repeated}$$

where[22]

$$|\rho| < 1$$

Again the error e_t is the sum of two components: its previous value *attenuated* by the factor ρ, plus the further disturbance v_t. (You can see that in the limiting case where $\rho = 0$, the error e_t reduces to the purely random v_t.)

We continue to assume the linear regression model

$$Y_t = \alpha + \beta X_t + e_t \qquad\qquad (19\text{-}31)$$
$$(19\text{-}21) \text{ repeated}$$

---

[22] If $\rho = 1$ as in (19-22), a major problem arises because the error becomes "explosive"; that is, the variance of e_t increases infinitely with time.

To estimate β, we transform the data in much the same way as before. Equation (19-31) for time $(t-1)$ is multiplied by ρ:

$$\rho Y_{t-1} = \rho\alpha + \rho\beta X_{t-1} + \rho e_{t-1} \qquad (19\text{-}32)$$

Subtracting (19-32) from (19-31)

$$Y_t - \rho Y_{t-1} = \alpha(1-\rho) + \beta(X_t - \rho X_{t-1}) + (e_t - \rho e_{t-1}) \qquad (19\text{-}33)$$

Now define

$$\left. \begin{array}{l} Y_t - \rho Y_{t-1} \overset{\Delta}{=} \Delta Y_t \\ X_t - \rho X_{t-1} \overset{\Delta}{=} \Delta X_t \end{array} \right] \qquad (19\text{-}34)$$

These transformed values are sometimes called "generalized differences," with (19-28) being a special case. Then (19-33) can be written

$$\Delta Y_t = \alpha(1-\rho) + \beta\,\Delta X_t + v_t \qquad (19\text{-}35)$$

In this form, v_t is the error, and has all the properties required by OLS. Thus, after this transformation we may regress ΔY_t on ΔX_t to estimate β. This technique is a form of generalized least squares (GLS).

However, prior to this regression one additional adjustment must be made to the data. The *first* observed values Y_1 and X_1 cannot be transformed by (19-34) since their previous values are not available; instead the appropriate transformation is

$$\begin{array}{l} \sqrt{1-\rho^2}\ Y_1 \overset{\Delta}{=} \Delta Y_1 \\ \sqrt{1-\rho^2}\ X_1 \overset{\Delta}{=} \Delta X_1 \end{array} \qquad (19\text{-}36)$$

This final adjustment is very important; without it, the regression (19-35) may be no better than OLS on (19-21), and perhaps not even as good.[23]

To sum up, if ρ is known, the data is transformed by (19-34) and (19-36), with OLS regression of ΔY_t on ΔX_t in (19-35) providing the estimate of β. The problem with this approach, of course, is that ρ is generally not known, and must be estimated.

---

[23]The transformation (19-36) must be used with some care. It is appropriate if and only if the process (19-30) generating the error has been going on undisturbed for a long time previous to collecting the data. In practice, however, the first observation often is taken just after a war or some other catastrophe, which seriously disturbs the error. In this case, the transformation (19-36) of the first observation may be dropped.

(e) Statistical Estimation of ρ

To estimate ρ, equation (19-30) would be ideal if the true residuals e_t could be observed. Since they cannot, we are forced to use the observed residuals $\hat{e}_t$ that fall out of the OLS regression of Y_t on X_t, as in Figure 19-12c. Thus ρ is estimated by applying OLS to

$$\hat{e}_t = \rho \hat{e}_{t-1} + \text{error} \qquad (19\text{-}37)$$

With this regression, we obtain an estimate r for ρ which is consistent. Yet r has a bias, which can be seen from Figure 19-12c. The estimated residuals $\hat{e}_t$ fluctuate around zero more (and hence have a smaller serial correlation) than do the true residuals[24] e_t. Thus r underestimates ρ on the average.

There are ways to allow for this underestimation; the most popular is *the Durbin-Watson test* for $\rho = 0$, against the alternative $\rho > 0$. Obviously H_0 should be rejected when r is high. What is the critical value of r? Durbin and Watson obtained an equivalent test of $\rho = 0$ by using the statistic[25]

$$D = \frac{\displaystyle\sum_{t=2}^{n} (\hat{e}_t - \hat{e}_{t-1})^2}{\displaystyle\sum_{t=1}^{n} \hat{e}_t^2} \approx 2(1 - r) \qquad (19\text{-}38)$$

which was originally called the "Von Neumann ratio." When r is high, then D is low. Durbin and Watson tabulated the critical value of D, rather than r. This is reproduced in Appendix Table IX. As well as allowing for the bias of r in estimating ρ, Durbin and Watson allowed for the dependence of r upon the configuration of X_t. Thus, there are two limiting values of D tabulated (D_L and D_U), corresponding to the two most extreme configurations of X_t; for any other configuration, the critical value of D will be somewhere between D_L and D_U.

---

[24] In Figure 19-12b the true residuals e_t cross the zero axis only three times. Yet in Figure 19-12c the observed residuals $\hat{e}_t$ bounce around the zero axis, crossing it eight times. Hence, they appear to have very little serial correlation; in fact, in this respect they behave like the uncorrelated residuals in Figure 19-13b which cross the zero axis ten times.

[25] We note that D is defined like d in (16-49). However, since D uses regression residuals $\hat{e}_t$ instead of original observations X_i, its distribution is more complicated. Nevertheless, many similarities remain; for example, when $r = 0$ in (19-38), we approximate (16-48).

(e) Conclusions

When facing time series with an unknown amount of serial correlation, one possible practical procedure is:

1. Apply OLS to (19-21), obtaining estimates $\hat{\alpha}, \hat{\beta}$ and also a time series of observed residuals $\hat{e}_t$; then
2. Estimate ρ from (19-37). If this estimate r is close to 0, there is little evidence that serial correlation is a major problem, and the OLS estimates calculated in 1 can be viewed with considerable confidence.

On the other hand, if r is high, a problem exists and a warning of the possible unreliability of the OLS estimates in 1 is in order. But unfortunately, it may not be possible to come up with anything better. If r is quite high, generalized differencing (19-34) and (19-36) may be applied, substituting r for ρ. But so little is known about the resulting estimates that this becomes a matter of judgment, and there is no guarantee that the result is any better than the OLS result in 1.

*19-9   SEVERAL TIME SERIES

So far we have studied a single time series in isolation. Even more interesting is the relation of two or more time series. In this section we sketch a few of the new issues raised, using two constructed examples. Suppose, for simplicity, that a time series x_t has the very simple form shown in Figure 19-14a; (it is designated with a small x to emphasize that its mean is zero). Suppose also that a new time series is generated from it by the simple formula

$$y_t = \beta x_t = 2x_t \qquad (19\text{-}39)$$

as shown in Figure 19-14b. We could estimate β using OLS,

$$\hat{\beta} = \frac{\sum x_t y_t}{\sum x_t^2} = \frac{10}{5} = 2 \qquad (19\text{-}40)$$
$$(11\text{-}19b) \text{ repeated}$$

which is the correct solution.

As our second example, suppose another series y_t^* is generated by a more complicated relation involving lagged values of x_t,

$$y_t^* = 2x_{t-1} \qquad (19\text{-}41)$$

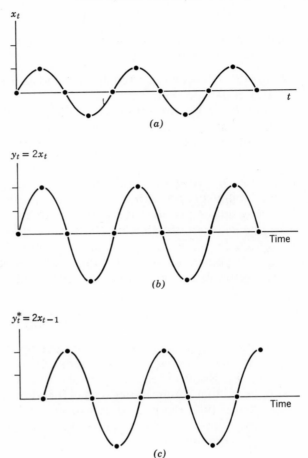

FIGURE 19-14 Two time series in (b) and (c), perfectly related to a given time series x_t in (a).

as shown in Figure 19-14c. If we calculate again the simple regression coefficient of y_t^* on x_t using OLS,

$$\hat{\beta} = \frac{\sum x_t y_t}{\sum x_t^2} = \frac{0}{5} = 0$$

which suggests no relation between x_t and y_t^*, clearly a misleading conclusion.

These two contrasting examples make clear that simple regression will satisfactorily analyze only simple relations. More complicated relations involving time lags, such as (19-41), require a technique that exploits the time dimension of the problem. As an example of such a technique, we might run a multiple regression of y_t on x_t and its lagged values x_{t-1}. If we worked through the appropriate calculations, we would obtain the estimated regression

$$y_t^* = 0x_t + 2x_{t-1}$$

which is the correct solution.

Suppose the relation (19-41) were even more complicated (and realistic), with x_t taking on more subtle values, and an error term included in y_t. In such a situation, "cross-spectral" analysis would be an alternative to multiple regression. This involves finding out how the cycles of the two series are related in amplitude, and also in phase (which series leads, and which lags?). This analysis resembles simple regression analysis, where two variables x and y were related; however, cross-spectral analysis goes further: by taking into account the cyclical nature of each series, it provides a better estimate of how x and y are related. But the reservations about simple spectral analysis expressed in Section 19-7(d) above of course still hold.

PROBLEMS

*19-10 Suppose the serial correlation of the error is more complicated than in (19-30), with every error e_t now depending on its previous *pair* of values, that is,

$$e_t = \rho_1 e_{t-1} + \rho_2 e_{t-2} + v_t \qquad \text{(another special case of (19-5))}$$

where v_t has all the usual, desirable properties of a residual and ρ_1 and ρ_2 are known.
(a) How would you estimate (19-31) in this case? How is this procedure justified?
(b) Suppose ρ_1 and ρ_2 are not known. How might they be estimated?
(c) Will $\hat{e}_t$ be more or less autocorrelated than e_t?
(d) Is it true to say that the problem of a serially correlated error involves not only estimating the ρ's, but also knowing how many nonzero ρ's there are?

*19-11 True or false? If false, correct it.
Unless seasonal influence is taken into account in the analysis, its existence will bias your estimate of trend (as shown in Figure 19-3b). Similarly, the existence of an autocorrelated residual will bias your estimate of trend; but it will raise no problems in your estimate of seasonal.

SIMULTANEOUS EQUATIONS

The chief difficulty Alice found at first was with her flamingo: . . . generally, just as she had got its neck straightened out, and was going to give the hedgehog a blow with its head, it would twist itself around and look up in her face.

Lewis Carroll

INTRODUCTION

Most business and social problems are considerably more complicated than some of the techniques we have introduced so far suggest. Specifically, seldom is a variable determined by a single relationship (equation). Instead, a variable is normally determined simultaneously with many other variables in a whole *system* of simultaneous equations. For example, the price of corn is determined simultaneously with the price of rye, the price of hogs, etc.

An analogy may be useful. The economic or social system may be similar in some sense to the solar system, where the variables (positions of the planets at any point in time) are simultaneously determined by a whole system of equations or relationships (i.e., each indicates how the position of a single planet depends on the position of all the others). Thus, although the position of the moon is most substantially influenced by the position of the earth, it is also influenced to some small degree by the position of the other planets as well. Similarly, the position (sales) of a business firm like Ford Motor Company will depend on the sales of its "closest" competitors like GM and Chrysler and, to a lesser degree, its other competitors as well, like American Motors, Volkswagen, and Toyota.

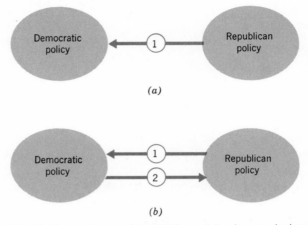

FIGURE 20-1 (a) A single equation model; variables not simultaneously determined. (b) A simultaneous model; variables jointly determined.

Similarly, the position of the Democratic party on a national issue will depend on the position of the Republican party. If the Republican position is determined independently of the Democratic position, then the simple single equation model of previous chapters would suffice: the independent Republican variable can be "plugged into" the Democratic equation, thus determining the Democratic response. This is shown in Figure 20-1a where the arrow indicates the direction of influence. But the *simultaneous* determination of both the Republican and Democratic positions is more likely as shown in Figure 20-1b. Here the Democratic position cannot be determined by plugging a Republican position into relationship (1), since the Republican position is not given; instead it is dependent on the Democrats, according to relationship (2). A single equation model will not work; instead the two-equation model, explaining the simultaneous determination of both variables, is required.

20-2   AN ECONOMIC EXAMPLE

Consider the following, very simple national income model of two equations

$$Y = \alpha + \beta X + e \qquad (20\text{-}1)$$
$$X = Y + I \qquad (20\text{-}2)$$

Equation (20-1) is the standard form of the consumption function that relates consumer expenditure Y to income X. The parameters of this function that must be estimated are α (the intercept) and β (the slope, or marginal propensity to consume[1]). We assume that the error term is well behaved: successive values of e are assumed to be independent and identically distributed, with mean 0 and variance σ^2. Equation (20-2) states that national income is defined as the sum of consumption and investment I. (Since both sides of this equation are, by economic definition, equal, no error term appears in this equation, but the analysis remains the same in any case).

An important distinction must be made between two kinds of variables in our system. By assumption, I is determined *outside* the system of equations; it will often be referred to as "exogenous" or "predetermined." The essential point is that its values are determined elsewhere, and are not influenced by Y, X, or e. In particular, we emphasize that

$$I \text{ and } e \text{ are statistically independent} \qquad (20\text{-}3)$$

On the other hand, X and Y are jointly dependent, or endogenous variables; their values are determined *within* the model and thus are influenced by I and e. Since there are two equations to determine these two endogenous variables, the model is mathematically complete.[2]

Certain oversimplifications in this model are immediately evident. For example, it describes a closed economy with no government sector. The assumption that I is exogenous is also an oversimplification. In fact, I is likely to depend on Y or X. You are invited to experiment in setting up a three-equation model in X, Y, and I; such a system would involve an additional endogenous variable I and an additional equation relating I to another variable that might more reasonably be regarded as exogenous (e.g., the interest rate). Assumptions can always be made more realistic by increasing the size of the model—but then its mathematical complexity also increases. Statisticians constantly must make decisions that involve this sort of trade-off between realism and mathematical manageability. A larger model would also be more difficult to show geometrically. Since this is our next objective, we shall stick to our original two-equation model. (The assumption that only X and Y are jointly determined and that I and other economic variables can be viewed as predetermined is similar to the assumption by the astronomer that the position of the moon may be determined by a simple earth/

---

[1] That is, the additional consumption that would result from a $1 increase in income. See (13-20).

[2] While there must be as many linear equations as unknowns to yield a unique solution, this is not always sufficient; these equations must also be linearly independent.

FIGURE 20-2   The consumption function, and the scatter of observed points around it.

moon model; although other heavenly bodies should theoretically also be included in the model, this simplification yields a good approximation and keeps the mathematics manageable.)

A diagram will be useful in illustrating the statistical difficulties encountered. To highlight the problems the statistician will face, let us suppose that we have some sort of omniscient knowledge, so that we know the true consumption function $Y = \alpha + \beta X$ as shown in Figure 20-2. And let us watch what happens to the statistician—a mere mortal—who does not have this knowledge but must try to estimate this function by observing only Y and X. Specifically, let us show how badly things will turn out if he estimates α and β by fitting a line by ordinary least squares (OLS). To find the sort of scatter of Y and X he will observe, we must remember that all observations must satisfy both equations (20-1) and (20-2).

Consider (20-1) first. Whenever e takes on a zero value, the observation of Y and X must fall somewhere along the true consumption function $Y = \alpha + \beta X$, shown in Figure 20-2. If e takes on a value greater than zero (say + \$50 billion), then consumption is greater as a consequence and the observed Y, X combination will fall somewhere along $Y = \alpha + \beta X + 50$. Similarly, if e takes on a value of -50, he will observe a point on the line $Y = \alpha + \beta X - 50$. According to the standard assumptions, e is distributed about a zero mean. To keep the geometry simple, we further assume that e is equally likely to take on any value between $+50$ and -50. Thus the statistician will observe Y and X falling within this band around the consumption function, darkly shaded in Figure 20-2.

Any observed combination of Y and X must also satisfy (20-2). What does this imply? This condition can be rewritten as

$$Y = X - I \tag{20-4}$$

If I were zero, then Y and X would be equal, and any observation would fall on the 45° line where $Y = X$. Let us suppose that when I is determined by outside factors it is distributed uniformly through a range of 100 to 250. If $I = 100$, then from (20-4) any observation of Y and X must fall along $Y = X - 100$, which is simply the line lying 100 units below the 45° line. Similarly, when $I = 250$, an observation of Y and X would fall along the line $Y = X - 250$. These two lines define the lightly shaded band within which observations must fall to satisfy (20-2).

Since any observed combination of Y and X must satisfy *both* conditions, all observations will fall within the parallelogram $P_1 P_2 P_3 P_4$. To clarify, this parallelogram of observations is reproduced in Figure 20-3. When the statistician regresses Y on X using OLS, the result is shown as $Y = \tilde{\alpha} + \tilde{\beta} X$. When this is compared with the true consumption function ($Y = \alpha + \beta X$), it is clear that the statistician has come up with a bad fit; his estimate of the slope ($\tilde{\beta}$) has an upward bias. What has gone wrong?

The observations around P_2 have "pulled" the estimating line above the true regression; similarly, the observations around P_4 have pulled the estimating line below the true regression. It is the pull on both ends that has tilted this estimated line. Moreover, increasing sample size will not help to reduce this bias. If the number of observations in this parallelogram is doubled, this bias will remain.[3] Hence, OLS is inconsistent; this technique that worked so well in a single equation model is clearly less satisfactory when the problem is to estimate one equation embedded in a system of simultaneous equations.

---

[3]With an increase in sample size, the reliability of $\tilde{\beta}$ as an estimator will be increased somewhat, because its variance will decrease towards zero. But its bias will not be reduced.

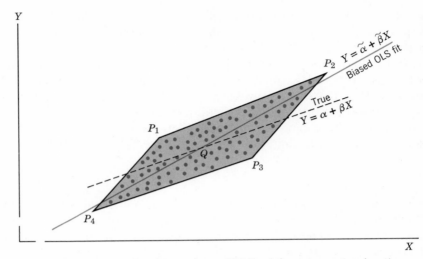

FIGURE 20-3 Biased and inconsistent OLS fit of the consumption function.

The reason is evident: for the single equation model it is assumed, in (12-48), that the error e is independent of the regressor, and this is why OLS works so well. But in a multiple equation model, this assumption no longer holds. Note, for example, in Figure 20-3 how e is positively correlated with X: e tends to be positive (i.e., the observed point lies above the true regression $Y = \alpha + \beta X$) when X is large, and e tends to be negative (with the observed point below the true regression) when X is small.[4] Consequently, the OLS fit has too large a slope. The reason is intuitively clear: in explaining Y, OLS gives as little credit as possible to the error, and as much credit as possible to the regressor X. When the error and regressor are correlated, then some of the effect of the error is wrongly attributed to the regressor.

This then is the problem: the single equation technique of OLS is inconsistent in a simultaneous equations context. A substantial body of econometric research has been devoted to developing more appropriate techniques; increasingly, business statisticians, sociologists, and other social scientists, all of whom must deal with situations of mutual dependence, are likely to turn their attention to these problems. The

---

[4] Note that the reason for this is precisely because of the second equation in the model: thus in Figure 20-2, the observed points are determined not only by equation (20-1); they are also determined, or "pulled" by equation (20-2). And it is this latter pull that results in the positive correlation of X and e.

simplest solution is the use of the instrumental variable technique. Since this is a highly useful statistical method in dealing with other problems as well, we now consider it in some detail.

20-3   **INSTRUMENTAL VARIABLES (IV)**

The instrumental variable technique, sometimes called the "covariance" method, has quite general application. In this section we shall apply it to the simple, single-equation model of Chapter 11, to show that IV yields the same result as OLS. Then in Section 20-4 we shall apply it to the two-equation model ((20-1) and (20-2)) to show that IV yields a consistent result; thus in estimating simultaneous equations, it outperforms OLS.

(a) The Covariance Operator

First, recall from Chapter 14 how we can calculate the covariance of a sample of X and Y observations:

$$s_{XY} \triangleq \frac{\sum xy}{n-1} \qquad (20\text{-}5)$$
$$(14\text{-}5) \text{ repeated}$$

The instrumental variable method involves using this to estimate regression parameters.

To illustrate, consider again the model of Chapter 12,

$$Y = \alpha + \beta X + e \qquad (20\text{-}6)$$

Taking covariances of X with each of the variables in this equation,

$$s_{XY} = \beta s_{XX} + s_{Xe} \qquad (20\text{-}7)$$

To justify this, we recall that the n sample observations of X and Y are assumed in (20-6) to be generated in the following way:

$$\left.\begin{aligned} Y_1 &= \alpha + \beta X_1 + e_1 \\ Y_2 &= \alpha + \beta X_2 + e_2 \\ &\;\vdots \\ Y_n &= \alpha + \beta X_n + e_n \end{aligned}\right\} \qquad (20\text{-}8)$$

We can easily show that with an appropriate translation of both the X and Y axes, the intercept term disappears[5] and we may write

$$\left.\begin{array}{l} y_1 = \beta x_1 + e_1' \\ y_2 = \beta x_2 + e_2' \\ \vdots \\ y_n = \beta x_n + e_n' \end{array}\right] \qquad (20\text{-}10)$$

where the y_i, x_i, and e_i' represent deviations from the sample mean. The first equation is multiplied by x_1, the second by x_2, and so on,

$$\left.\begin{array}{l} x_1 y_1 = \beta x_1 x_1 + x_1 e_1' \\ x_2 y_2 = \beta x_2 x_2 + x_2 e_2' \\ \vdots \\ x_n y_n = \beta x_n x_n + x_n e_n' \end{array}\right] \qquad (20\text{-}11)$$

When we sum all these equations, and divide by $(n - 1)$,

$$\frac{\sum xy}{n-1} = \frac{\beta \sum xx}{n-1} + \frac{\sum xe'}{n-1} \qquad (20\text{-}12)$$

Recalling from (20-9) that e' is just e expressed as deviations from the mean, (20-12) may be written

$$s_{XY} = \beta s_{XX} + s_{Xe} \qquad (20\text{-}7) \text{ proved}$$

(b) The OLS Estimate

In order to estimate β, we divide (20-7) by s_{XX} (the variance of X),

$$\frac{s_{XY}}{s_{XX}} = \beta + \frac{s_{Xe}}{s_{XX}} \qquad (20\text{-}13)$$

---

[5] **proof**   Since

$$Y_i = \alpha + \beta X_i + e_i$$

Taking averages,

$$\bar{Y} = \alpha + \beta \bar{X} + \bar{e}$$

Subtracting,

$$y_i = \beta x_i + e_i' \qquad (20\text{-}10) \text{ proved}$$

where

$$e_i' = e_i - \bar{e} \qquad (20\text{-}9)$$

From the observations of X and Y, s_{XY} and s_{XX} are easily calculated. But e is unobservable, so that s_{Xe} cannot be evaluated. However, if we can assume that s_{Xe} is small enough to neglect, we obtain the estimator

$$\frac{s_{XY}}{s_{XX}} = \hat{\beta} \tag{20-14}$$

which may be referred to as the IV estimator, using X as the instrumental variable. We also recognize this[6] to be the OLS estimator (11-16).

In conclusion, the IV or OLS estimator in (20-14) is seen to be appropriate if we can neglect the last term in (20-13). Provided X and e can be assumed independent (as in our single equation model of Chapter 12) this term can indeed be neglected; in fact, in a large enough sample, this last term will approach zero.[7] Hence the IV or OLS estimator in (20-14) is consistent.

20-4   SIMULTANEOUS EQUATION ESTIMATION

(a) The Inconsistency of OLS Confirmed

Now suppose we try to apply this same technique (i.e., take covariances with respect to X) on the consumption function (20-1). The algebra in equations (20-6) to (20-14) remains the same. Now, however, X and e are no longer uncorrelated, since we are dealing with one equation in a two-equation model (recall how this correlation was established in Figures 20-2 and 20-3). Hence s_{Xe} in (20-13) no longer approaches zero, and the OLS estimator in (20-14) is no longer consistent. Or, to put it another way: using X as an instrument simply does not work, because of its correlation with e.

(b) The Consistency of IV

Since X has been disqualified as an instrumental variable, why not use another variable, say Z, which *is* uncorrelated with e? Taking covariances

---

[6] The OLS estimator may be written, according to (11-19b),

$$\frac{\sum xy}{\sum xx} = \frac{\sum xy/(n-1)}{\sum xx/(n-1)} = \frac{s_{XY}}{s_{XX}}$$

[7] **proof**   In large samples, the sample covariance approaches the population covariance, σ_{Xe}. According to (5-30), independence makes $\sigma_{Xe} = 0$. Of course, it is also necessary to assume that s_{XX} (the variance of X) is nonzero—that is, the X's are spread out (multicollinearity avoided, as in Section 13-4).

of Z with respect to all the variables in (20-6) yields

$$s_{ZY} = \beta s_{ZX} + s_{Ze}$$

To obtain an estimate of β, divide by s_{ZX}

$$\frac{s_{ZY}}{s_{ZX}} = \beta + \frac{s_{Ze}}{s_{ZX}} \tag{20-15}$$

Provided s_{Ze} approaches zero (i.e., Z and e are uncorrelated) while s_{ZX} does not approach zero (i.e., Z and X are correlated), then the last term approaches zero. Disregarding it, therefore, yields the consistent estimator

$$\boxed{\frac{s_{ZY}}{s_{ZX}} = \hat{\beta}} \tag{20-16}$$

OLS is recognized in (20-14) to be just the special case of IV estimation, when X itself is used as the instrumental variable.

(c) Requirements of an Instrumental Variable

From the above analysis it is clear that

> an instrumental variable Z must be
>
> (1) uncorrelated with the error e, and   (20-17)
> (2) correlated with the regressor X.

It is now appropriate to consider the second requirement in more detail. As is evident in (20-15), the higher the covariance s_{ZX}, the smaller will be the term s_{Ze}/s_{ZX}, which is the source of estimation error; hence, the better will be the estimator in (20-16).

As our instrumental variable, therefore, we should look for the most relevant variable (i.e., the instrumental variable most highly correlated with X) to get the most "statistical leverage." Thus, the exogenous variable I (investment) is a natural choice, since it is evident from (20-2) that I has a substantial effect on X. Rainfall in California or even the price of haircuts in Denver might satisfy the theoretical requirements of an instrumental variable; yet either would lack statistical leverage. To state this mathematically, if California rainfall R were used as an instrumental variable, its correlation with X would be so small that the error term s_{Re}/s_{RX} would be large. Only in extremely large samples would this ratio settle down to zero. The consistency of $\hat{\beta}$ in huge samples would be cold comfort for an economist faced with a small sample. Or, to look at it from another point of view, suppose the price of haircuts in Denver were alternatively used as an instrumental variable; since this would also involve a large estimating error, the two small-sample estimates of β might vary widely—even though in an infinitely large sample they would coincide.

In view of this relevancy requirement for an instrument, it is desirable if possible to use as instrumental variables only those exogenous variables that explicitly appear in our model—that is, which appear in at least one of the equations in the system. It is evident that neither this approach, nor any other, entirely overcomes our difficulties; the decision on which variables may be used as instrumental variables is just pushed onto the researcher who specifies the model, and in particular the exogenous variables that are included. Specification of the model remains arbitrary to a degree, and this gives rise to some arbitrariness in statistical estimation. But this cannot be avoided. It can only be concluded that the first task of specifying the original structure of the model is a very important one, since it involves a prior judgment of which variables are "close to" X and Y, and which variables are relatively "far away."

Finally, a note of caution. Estimating simultaneous equations is a very complex issue. Although IV has provided a consistent alternative to OLS, many further problems remain (for example, the "identification problem," introduced in Problem 20-6).

PROBLEMS

20-1 Draw a schematic diagram similar to Figure 20-1 to illustrate:
(a) how the sales of Ford are determined. (For simplicity, assume that the only important variables are the "Big Three" auto manufacturers.)
(b) how consumption and income are determined in (20-1) and (20-2).
20-2 Suppose the true consumption function (20-1) is $Y = 10 + .6X$ and the following combinations of Y, X, and I have been observed:

Y	X	I
46	60	14
31	45	14
61	75	14
58	80	22
43	65	22
73	95	22
70	100	30
55	85	30
85	115	30

(a) Graph the true consumption function and the scatter of (X, Y) observations.

(b) Regress Y on X using OLS, and graph the estimated consumption function. Is it consistent?

(c) Estimate the consumption function using I as an instrumental variable. Graph this estimated consumption function. Is it consistent?

(d) Explain why this small sample is a lucky one. What would you expect if your small sample is less lucky?

20-3 To estimate the consumption model (20-1) suppose the covariance matrix (or table) of X, Y, I has been computed for a sample as follows:

$$\begin{bmatrix} s_{XX} & s_{YX} & s_{IX} \\ s_{XY} & s_{YY} & s_{IY} \\ s_{XI} & s_{YI} & s_{II} \end{bmatrix} = \begin{bmatrix} 130 & 100 & 30 \\ 100 & 80 & 20 \\ 30 & 20 & 10 \end{bmatrix}$$

(a) Find a consistent estimate for the marginal propensity to consume.

(b) Estimate the marginal propensity to consume by applying OLS to the consumption function directly. Is this estimate consistent? Using a diagram, explain this to a student whose statistics is limited to understanding OLS.

20-4 Consider the single equation model,

$$Y = \alpha + \gamma_1 X_1 + \gamma_2 X_2 + e$$

where both regressors (X_1 and X_2) are uncorrelated with the error term e. Show how γ_1 and γ_2 can be estimated,

(a) using OLS;

(b) using X_1 and X_2 in turn as instrumental variables. (Generate one estimating equation using X_1 as an instrumental variable, and a second using X_2). Do IV and OLS yield identical estimators? (This generalizes (20-14).)

20-5 (a) A sociologist observes that the number of children available for adoption Y depends on the number of births X. At the same time, births depend on income Z and on the number of children available for adoption Y. Draw a schematic figure similar to Figure 20-1 illustrating these relationships.

(b) Set up a system of two simultaneous equations similar to (20-1) and (20-2) showing how X and Y might be jointly determined.

(c) Assume that the equations in (b) are of the form,

$$Y = \alpha + \beta X + e \qquad (20\text{-}18)$$
$$X = \delta + \gamma Y + \psi Z + v \qquad (20\text{-}19)$$

where e and v are error terms and Z is exogeneous, of course. Show how β may be consistently estimated. Explain why this technique is consistent. Explain why OLS on (20-18) would not be.

(d) Can equation (20-19) above be consistently estimated? If so, how; if not, why?

*20-6 (This is a brief introduction to the "identification problem.") Consider the following system of two simultaneous equations[8] in the two jointly dependent variables Y_1 and Y_2:

$$Y_1 = \beta_2 Y_2 + e \qquad (20\text{-}20)$$
$$Y_2 = \beta_1 Y_1 + \gamma_1 Z_1 + v \qquad (20\text{-}21)$$

Note that there is only one appropriate instrumental variable, Z_1.

(a) Show that (20-20) can be consistently estimated, but (20-21) cannot.

(We might say that "there are enough instrumental variables in this system (namely, one) to estimate the one parameter in (20-20), but not enough to estimate the two parameters in (20-21)." This is commonly restated as: "There are enough instrumental variables to *identify* the first question, but not the second.")

---

[8] Except for dropping the constants and renaming the variables, this system of equations is like (20-18) and (20-19).

(b) Now suppose from theory that you have prior knowledge that the value of β_1 is unity. Can (20-21) now be identified?

(c) Suppose instead of prior knowledge of β_1 that you know that Y_1 is dependent on Y_2 as before, and also on a new exogenous variable Z_2, that is, (20-20) is replaced by

$$Y_1 = \beta_2 Y_2 + \gamma_2 Z_2 + e \tag{20-20b}$$

Is this equation still identified? Is the other equation in the system (20-21) still not identified?

(d) True or false? If false, correct it.

    (1) Prior knowledge may help to identify an equation.

    (2) An equation is identified by instrumental (exogenous) variables that appear in *other* equations in the system—that is, by exogenous variables *excluded* from the equation to be estimated.

    (3) A requirement for identifying an equation is that the number of exogenous variables excluded from the equation must at least equal the number of endogenous variables included on the righthand side of that equation.

(e) Now suppose (20-20) is replaced by

$$Y_1 = \beta_2 Y_2 + \gamma_2 Z_2 + \gamma_3 Z_3 + e \tag{20-20c}$$

where both Z_2 and Z_3 are exogenous variables. If the other equation (20-21) in the system is to be estimated, are there now too few, too many, or just the right number of instrumental variables? Is it true that (20-21) can now be estimated by selecting any two of the three available instrumental variables? (This surplus of instrumental variables is referred to as *overidentification*.)

Summary. If there are too few instrumental variables in the system, the equation is said to be "unidentified," and estimation is impossible.

If there are just barely enough instrumental variables, the equation is said to be "exactly identified," and IV estimation is straightforward.

Finally, if there is a surplus of instrumental variables, the equation is said to be "overidentified." Then estimation becomes complicated. The difficulty is that there is no longer a unique estimating procedure: any selection of just the right number of instrumental variables from the surplus available will yield a result, and these various results do not coincide (unless the sample is infinitely large). Consequently, a great deal of statistical and econometric research has recently been devoted to asking which selection of instrumental variables is optimal—or better still, how can the large number of instrumental variables be combined, thus reducing their number to just the right size. (For example, a very popular estimating technique called "Two-Stage Least Squares" may be viewed in just this way. The first stage involves combining the available instruments into a new set of just the right number, while the second stage may be interpreted as simply applying these new instruments to yield a unique result).

REGRESSION EXTENSIONS

> *All Mathematics would suggest*
> *A steady straight line as the best,*
> *But left and right alternately*
> *Is consonant with History.*
>
> W. H. Auden

Although our previous regression analysis (Chapters 11 to 14) was devoted exclusively to the linear model, there are many other ways in which Y may depend on X; an example has already been given in Figure 12-9. In this chapter, we analyze some of the many forms nonlinearity may take. It will become evident, even from these few examples, that our standard regression procedure can often still be applied—provided the variables can be redefined, or the form of the equation appropriately transformed.

As examples of how Y may be nonlinearly dependent on X, consider

$$Y = \alpha + \beta X^2 \tag{21-1}$$

or

$$Y = X^\beta \tag{21-2}$$

There is a fundamental difference in these two cases. In (21-1), the only nonlinearity is in the variable X; α and β appear in this equation in the same linear way as in Chapter 12, and as a consequence the techniques developed there can be applied without any difficulty. On the other hand, the nonlinearity in (21-2) directly involves β, the parameter to be estimated; this equation requires a transformation that will make it linear in β, and hence also amenable to standard regression analysis.

21-1   NONLINEARITY IN THE VARIABLES, BUT NOT
                                          THE PARAMETERS

(a) Solution, Requiring Only a Redefinition of Variables

The regressions studied in earlier chapters have been of the linear form

$$Y = \alpha + \beta X + e \qquad (21\text{-}3)$$

Equation (21-3) is linear in both the variable X and the parameters α and β. Now if we closely examine the least squares method in Chapter 11, we note that, as long as α and β appear in a linear way, the estimating equations (11-12) and (11-15) will be linear in the estimates of α and β. Hence, no problems are involved in their solution.

As an illustration, suppose

$$Y = \alpha + \beta Q^2 + e \qquad (21\text{-}4)$$

We simply define

$$X \triangleq Q^2 \qquad (21\text{-}5)$$

When this is substituted into (21-4), our model is transformed into the standard form (21-3), and simple regression of Y on this new X variable gives us the solution.

(b) Example: the U-shaped Cost Curve

When a first-degree term in Q is added to (21-4), the result is the general parabolic model

$$Y = \alpha + \beta Q + \gamma Q^2 + e \qquad (21\text{-}6)$$

This polynomial model might occur in relating a firm's marginal cost Y to its total output Q, for example. At various levels of output Q_i, corresponding marginal costs Y_i are given in columns 1 and 2 of Table 21-1, and graphed in Figure 21-1. Since marginal cost decreases at first and then increases, the parabolic model in (21-6) seems appropriate.

Table 21-1 Multiple Regression Fit of the U-Shaped Marginal Cost Curve,
$$Y_i = \alpha + \beta Q_i + \gamma Q_i^2 + e_i$$

Annotations:
- Translation of Q and Q² into X and Z
- Regression of Y on X and Z
- Retranslation of X and Z back into Q and Q²

(1) Y_i	(2) $X_i = Q_i$	(3) $Z_i = Q_i^2$	(4) $x_i = X_i - \bar{X}$	(5) $z_i = Z_i - \bar{Z}$	(6) $Y_i x_i$	(7) $Y_i z_i$	(8) x_i^2	(9) z_i^2	(10) $x_i z_i$	(11) $\hat{Y}_i = 40.2 - 1.44 x_i + .0366 z_i$
37	10	100	−20	−967	−740	−35,767	400	934,451	19,333	33.6
27	15	225	−15	−842	−405	−22,725	225	708,408	12,625	31.0
31	20	400	−10	−667	−310	−20,667	100	444,449	6,667	30.2
27	25	625	−5	−442	−135	−11,925	25	195,072	2,208	31.2
36	30	900	0	−167	0	−6,000	0	27,779	0	34.1
42	35	1225	5	158	210	6,650	25	25,068	792	38.8
45	40	1600	10	533	450	24,000	100	284,441	5,333	45.3
55	45	2025	15	958	825	52,708	225	918,396	14,375	53.7
62	50	2500	20	1433	1240	88,866	400	2,054,435	28,667	63.8
$\sum Y = 362$	$\sum X = 270$	$\sum Z = 9600$	$\sum x_i = 0$	$\sum z_i = 0$	$\sum Y_i x_i = 1135$	$\sum Y_i z_i = 75,140$	$\sum x_i^2 = 1500$	$\sum z_i^2 = 5,592,500$	$\sum x_i z_i = 90,000$	
$\bar{Y} = 40.22$	$\bar{X} = 30$	$\bar{Z} = 1067$								

$$Y = 40.2 - 1.44(X - \bar{X}) + .0366(Z - \bar{Z})$$
$$\text{or } Y = 44.4 - 1.44X + .0366Z$$
$$\text{i.e. } Y = 44.4 - 1.44Q + .0366Q^2$$

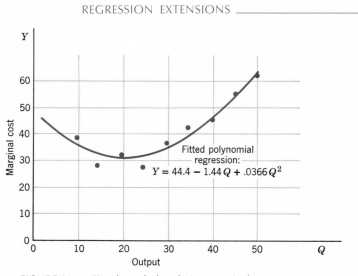

FIGURE 21-1   Fitted parabola relating marginal cost to output.

To find the least squares estimators $\hat{\alpha}$, $\hat{\beta}$, and $\hat{\gamma}$, we define

$$X \triangleq Q \tag{21-7}$$

$$Z \triangleq Q^2 \tag{21-8}$$

When these are substituted into (21-6), we obtain the standard multiple regression equation of Chapter 13,

$$Y = \alpha + \beta X + \gamma Z + e \tag{21-9}$$

We note in passing that although Y is related to only one independent *variable* Q, our fit involves regressing Y on two *regressors*, Q and Q^2. This is the first time that it has been necessary to distinguish between independent variables and regressors, but the distinction now is important. When one variable is used to obtain several regressors, as in this instance, we might wonder if multicollinearity becomes a problem.

Although Z_i and X_i are *functionally* dependent (i.e., one is the square of the other), they are not *linearly* dependent (i.e., one is not, say, three times the other). Geometrically, the points (X_i, Z_i) do lie on a curve as shown in Figure 21-2; the important point is, however, that they do not lie on a line. Thus, the problem of complete multicollinearity is avoided. From a mathematical point of view, the physical or economic source of the X_i and Z_i values is irrelevant; just so long as X and Z are *linearly* independent, the mathematical model of Chapter 13 can be applied.

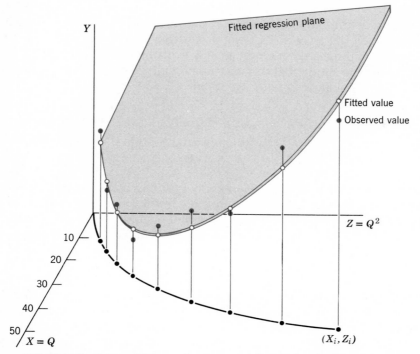

FIGURE 21-2   Polynomial regression as a special case of multiple regression.

We may therefore compute the estimated coefficients $\hat{\alpha}$, $\hat{\beta}$, and $\hat{\gamma}$ using a standard computer program for multiple regression.[1] The results are

$$Y = 44.4 - \quad 1.44\ Q \quad + .0366\ Q^2 \qquad (21\text{-}10)$$
$$\qquad\qquad (t = -3.1) \quad (t = 4.9)$$

_____

[1] It is completely unnecessary in this age of computers to carry out the computations by hand; most canned programs will not only run the regression, but also transform variables beforehand and retransform them afterwards. Nevertheless, in order to explicitly show how this procedure works, we lay out the hand computations in Table 21-1.

Columns 2 and 3 set out the first step: the transformation of Q into X and Z. Columns 4 to 10 set out the second step: the standard regression of Y on X and Z. Our calculations are substituted into the last two estimating equations in (13-4), obtaining

$$1135 = \hat{\beta}(1500) + \hat{\gamma}(90{,}000)$$
$$75{,}140 = \hat{\beta}(90{,}000) + \hat{\gamma}(5{,}592{,}500)$$

These two may be solved,

$$\hat{\beta} = -1.44$$
$$\hat{\gamma} = .0366$$

(21-11)

(cont'd)

When this regression is plotted in Figure 21-1, it raises an interesting question: Is the parabolic model really necessary, or would a straight line suffice? The answer lies in prior knowledge and the statistical significance of the regressor Q^2, as already explained in Chapter 13-6. Since our prior expectation that this was a parabolic relationship is confirmed $(t = 4.9)$ in equation (21-10), we retain Q^2.

21-2   NONLINEARITY IN THE PARAMETERS, REQUIRING A TRANSFORMATION

(a) Example: Population Growth

Figure 21-3a shows U.S. population P during a period of sustained growth, 1860–1900. It curves up in a nonlinear fashion that suggests a constant percentage growth (like compound interest, or unrestrained biological growth). The appropriate model is therefore the exponential,

$$P = Ae^{\beta T} \tag{21-12}$$

with β representing the constant rate of growth.

If it is reasonable to assume that large errors are associated with large values of the dependent variable P, then it is appropriate to treat the error term as multiplicative, rather than additive; then the statistical model is

$$P = Ae^{\beta T} \cdot \overline{u} \tag{21-13}$$

where the errors u have a distribution that fluctuates around 1. Although (21-13) is nonlinear in the parameters A and β, it can easily be linearized by taking natural logarithms, yielding

$$\ln P = \ln A + \beta T + \ln u \tag{21-14}$$

Let us define

$$Y \overset{\Delta}{=} \ln P \tag{21-15}$$
$$\alpha \overset{\Delta}{=} \ln A$$
$$e \overset{\Delta}{=} \ln u \tag{21-16}$$

In the last rows of Table 21-1 we then set out the third step: substituting (21-11), and retranslating X and Z back into Q. This yields (21-10).

In the last column of Table 21-1 we calculate the fitted points, which form the curve in Figures 21-1 and 21-2.

FIGURE 21-3 U.S. population growth, 1860–1900. (a) Its exponential fit, (b) Plotted on semilog paper.

This transformed error term e has a distribution that fluctuates around zero.[2] Thus (21-14) takes the standard linear form,

$$Y = \alpha + \beta T + e \qquad (21\text{-}17)$$

This can be estimated by a standard regression program, which yields

$$Y = 3.90 + .0222t \qquad (21\text{-}18)$$
$$(t = 37)$$

For reference we also show the hand calculations in detail in Table 21-2. The transformed values $Y = \ln P$ in column 3 are graphed in Figure 21-3b, which is seen to be equivalent to graphing the original values P on semilog graph paper. Note how close these observed values are to the fitted regression line (21-18), thus further confirming our selection of the exponential model.

To retransform (21-18) back into the exponential model, we substitute (21-15), obtaining

$$\ln P = 3.90 + .0222t \qquad (21\text{-}19)$$

Table 21-2   Calculation of Exponential Growth Curve, U.S. Population 1860–1900

						Transformation of Equation	Regression of Y on T
						Retransformation	
Year T (1)	Population P (million) (2)	$Y = \ln P$ (3)	$t = T - \bar{T}$ (4)	Yt (5)	t^2 (6)		
1860	31.4	3.45	−20	−69.0	400		
1870	39.8	3.68	−10	−36.8	100		
1880	50.2	3.91	0	0	0		
1890	63.0	4.14	10	41.4	100		
1900	76.0	4.33	20	86.6	400		
$\bar{T} = 1880$		$\bar{Y} = 3.90$		$\sum Yt = 22.2$	$\sum t^2 = 1000$		

$$\hat{a} = \bar{Y} = 3.90$$
$$\hat{\beta} = \frac{\sum tY}{\sum t^2} = \frac{22.2}{1000} = .0222$$

$$Y = 3.90 + .0222t$$
$$\ln P = 3.90 + .0222t$$
$$P = e^{3.90} e^{.0222t}$$
$$P = 49.5\, e^{.022t}$$

taking antilogs

$$P = e^{3.90} e^{.0222t} \qquad (21\text{-}20)$$

i.e., $$P = 49.5 \, e^{.0222t} \qquad (21\text{-}21)$$

For convenience we have left time t in deviation form. Thus the coefficient $\hat{A} = 49.5$ (million) may be interpreted as the estimate of the population in 1880 (when $t = 0$). The coefficient $\hat{\beta} = .0222 = 2.22\%$ is the approximate annual growth rate.

Although a fitted equation like (21-21) may shed a good deal of light on past growth, there is an important final warning against using it for any short-term or long-term prediction of a time series such as population. In this sort of very simple growth model the error u is likely to be serially correlated (when population is unduly high in one period, it may consequently be high in the next period). Then, as we saw in Chapter 19, a short-run prediction that does not explicitly take account of serial correlation of the error, but simply projects a standard regression fit like (21-18), may be very misleading.

The problems are even greater in a longer term projection. So many changes occur in the underlying process determining population growth (wars, the development and acceptance of birth control methods, etc.), that there is no single unchanging relationship to be fitted. Hence, this sort of projection may be a futile exercise; it is far more to the point to try to discover what changes may be expected in the underlying growth process as the population adjusts to the pressures of increasing numbers.

(b) Potential Advantages of a Transformation

Recall that the logarithmic transformation can only be applied provided our error term u in (21-13) can reasonably be assumed multiplicative. But suppose this assumption cannot be made; for example, suppose we know that the error term is additive, so that our model is

$$Y = Ae^{\beta T} + u \qquad (21\text{-}22)$$

Since the log transformation cannot be validly applied, much more complicated and expensive computer fitting techniques would be the only option.

But if the model is in a form like (21-13) that does yield to logarithmic transformation, then this will simultaneously provide a number of advantages. Not only will it (1) linearize the parameters, and (2) make the error term additive; it may also (3) make the error term more normally distributed. This is shown in Figure 21-4: if the distribution of u is skewed

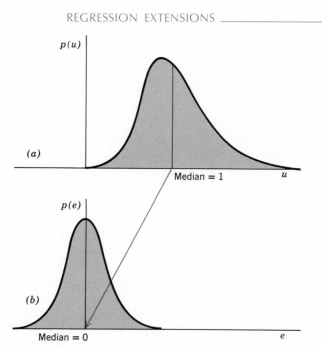

FIGURE 21-4   The error term in the multiplicative model (21-13). (*a*) Original skewed error. (*b*) The more symmetric error after the logarithmic transformation.

to the right, the distribution of ln u is usually more symmetric, hence closer to normal with the advantages (e.g., more valid t-tests, maximum likelihood justification) that population normality brings.

These benefits of a logarithmic transformation are not restricted to regressions on growth models, of course. The log transformation works in multiplicative models generally; for example it can be used in ANOVA.

PROBLEMS

21-1 (a) Fit Y with a second degree polynomial in Q (parabola) for the following data:

Output Q (thousands)	Marginal Cost Y
1	32
2	20
3	20
4	28
5	50

(b) Graph the five points, and the fitted curve.

21-2 In Problem 21-1, what is the estimated Y when $Q = 2.5$?

21-3 For the simple growth model (21-13), construct and plot a hypothetical example of a fitted regression and a serially correlated u to illustrate our statement in the second last paragraph of Section 21-2a: "a short run prediction that does not explicitly take account of serial correlation of the error, but simply projects a standard regression fit like (21-18), may be very misleading."

21-4 The population of the world since 1800 has grown approximately as follows

Year	Population (millions)
1800	960
1850	1,240
1900	1,650
1950	2,570

(a) Graph. Join the dots by a rough curve, and extrapolate to 1960.

(b) Fit an exponential growth model by least squares. Graph it. Extrapolate it to 1960.

(c) Would you use method (a) or (b) to project population in the year 2000? Or would you want to study a number of other questions first? If so, what sort of questions?

21-5 For each of the following models, outline the method you would use to estimate the parameters (Greek letters).

(a) $Y = \alpha + \beta X + \gamma X^2 + \delta X^3$

(b) $Y = \alpha + \beta t + \gamma \sin (2\pi t/12)$ (Linear growth with cycle.)

(c) $Y = \alpha(1 + \beta)^t$

(d) $Y = \alpha\beta^t\gamma^X$

(e) $Y = \alpha + \beta X + \gamma Z + \delta X^2 + \epsilon XZ + \zeta Z^2$

21-6 Suppose that in 1950 a bank balance is left to accumulate at a constant interest rate i.

(a) Assuming no deposits or withdrawals, estimate the original balance B_0 in 1950, and the interest rate, from the following observations;

Time	Balance
1952	$106.09
1953	$109.27
1954	$112.55
1955	$115.92

(b) If bank calculations are error-free (i.e., there is no random disturbance e), would you need all four observations to calculate i and B_0? How many observations are necessary?

21-7 Would it ever make sense to take logarithms of the response before applying ANOVA in Chapter 10? If so, give an example. If not, why not?

*21-8 (a) In the exponential growth model (21-13), is it possible for u to be negative? Why, or why not?

(b) Is it always possible, therefore, to transform according to (21-16)?

(c) What does (a) imply about the skewness of u?

Chapter 22

SAMPLING DESIGNS

There are many in this old world of ours who hold that things break about even for all of us. I have observed for example that we all get the same amount of ice. The rich get it in the summertime and the poor get it in the winter.

Bat Masterson

The simple random sampling of Chapter 6 is conceptually and computationally the most straightforward method of sampling a population. However, alternative procedures do exist which may, in certain cases, be more efficient. Several of these are described in this chapter: each is seen to combine random sampling with some design features aimed at improving efficiency.

22-1   STRATIFIED SAMPLING

(a) Simplified Example

Let us consider first an exaggerated example, where the benefits of stratified sampling are clearest. Suppose a large population is known to be 60% urban, 40% rural, and the problem is to estimate average income. Suppose the unknown income levels are $10,000 for each urban worker and $5000 for each rural worker; accordingly, the population earns a mean income

$$\mu = (10,000)(.6) + (5,000)(.4) = 8000 \qquad (22\text{-}1)$$

Table 22-1   Random versus Stratified Sampling: an Oversimplified
Example

			Various Samples				
Population			Typical Simple Random Samples			Stratified Samples	
Stratum	Proportion (1)	Mean Income (in $1000 units) (2)	(3)	(4)	(5)	(i) Proportional (6)	(ii) Weighted (7)
Urban	.60	10	10 5 10 10	5 5 5 10	5 10 10 5	10 10 10	10
Rural	.40	5.	10	5	10	5 5	5
Total	1.00	$\mu = 10(.6)$ $+5(.4) = 8$					
		Sample Mean	9	6	8	8✓	$10(.6)$ $+5(.4) = 8$✓

How well would a simple random sample estimate μ? Several possible random samples of size 5 are displayed in columns (3), (4) and (5) of Table 22-1. Because the samples are completely random, the number of rural workers fluctuates; this in turn causes the sample mean $\overline{X}$ to fluctuate. Of course, occasionally we will be lucky, as in column (5) when the proportion of rural workers in the sample is exactly the same as in the population.

But if we have prior knowledge of the proportion of urban and rural workers, why depend on luck? Surely it would be wise to design the sampling proportions to be exactly equal to the population proportions. This proportional sampling is shown in column (6); note that the result in this greatly oversimplified case is an estimate that is dead on target. In fact, this same favorable result is guaranteed with a sample of just one observation from each stratum (column (7))—provided, of course, that instead of computing the ordinary mean, each observation is weighted according to the size of its stratum; this "weighted sampling" yields

$$\overline{X} = 10{,}000(.6) + 5000(.4) = 8000 \qquad (22\text{-}2)$$

which, of course, exactly coincides with μ in (22-1); this is the perfect estimator, dead on, with a sample of only two (the number of strata in the population).

But we emphasize that the reason we have been able to do so well in this contrived example is because

1. the weights w_1 and w_2 (i.e., population proportions in each stratum) were known beforehand; and
2. the income of each individual in each stratum was exactly the same (i.e., the variance within each stratum was zero; $\sigma_1^2 = \sigma_2^2 = 0$).

Normally, we would not be so lucky. But this does illustrate the essence of sample design: it is a means of increasing sampling efficiency (i.e., reducing the necessary size of the sample) by the imaginative application of prior information. Of the two components cited above, the more important gain in efficiency generally comes from prior knowledge of weights; this is fortunate because this is the sort of information that is more likely to be available—just as in our example, an independent source like the U.S. population census could be drawn upon for information on urban/rural proportions. Hence, in this analysis it will be assumed throughout that prior knowledge on weights is available. But it cannot be assumed, as in (2) above, that all individuals in each stratum are identical; the next step therefore is to generalize the analysis to take this into account.

(b) General Case

Table 22-2 is a generalization of Table 22-1; the variance within the first stratum is designated σ_1^2, and so on. The most general stratified

Table 22-2   Generalization of Table 22-1

Stratum	Population			Stratified Sample	
	Proportion of Whole Population (weight)	Mean	Variance	Sample Size	Sample Mean
1	w_1	μ_1	σ_1^2	n_1	$\bar{X}_1 = \sum_j X_{1j}/n_1$
2	w_2	μ_2	σ_2^2	n_2	
⋮					
i	w_i	μ_i	σ_i^2	n_i	$\bar{X}_i = \sum_j X_{ij}/n_i$
⋮					
r	w_r	μ_r	σ_r^2	n_r	
	$\sum = 1$	$\mu = \sum \mu_i w_i$		$n = \sum n_i$	$\hat{\mu} = \sum \bar{X}_i w_i$

sample consists of drawing a sample of size n_1 from the first stratum, and so on, so that the total sample size $n = \Sigma\, n_i$. Then calculate the sample mean for each stratum; for example $\bar{X}_1 = \sum_j X_{1j}/n_1$, where X_{1j} represents the jth observation in the given stratum.

Now the population mean is given by

$$\mu = \mu_1 w_1 + \mu_2 w_2 + \cdots = \sum \mu_i w_i \qquad (22\text{-}3)$$
$$\text{like } (22\text{-}1)$$

where the weight w_i is the proportion of the population in the ith stratum. It is natural to estimate μ with

$$\hat{\mu} = \bar{X}_1 w_1 + \bar{X}_2 w_2 \cdots = \sum \bar{X}_i w_i \qquad (22\text{-}4)$$
$$\text{like } (22\text{-}2)$$

Using the rules for linear combinations, we may prove (Problem 22-3) that

$$E(\hat{\mu}) = \mu \qquad (22\text{-}5)$$

that is, (22-4) is an unbiased estimator, and

$$\mathrm{var}\,(\hat{\mu}) = \sum w_i^2 \frac{\sigma_i^2}{n_i} \qquad (22\text{-}6)$$

This leaves the problem of how the n_i are specified; that is, what proportion of the sample should be drawn from each stratum? Three common methods are given below.

(c) Proportional Sampling

The most obvious way to choose n_i is to make n_i proportional to w_i, that is,

proportional sampling requires
$$n_i = w_i n \qquad (22\text{-}8)$$

as illustrated earlier in column (6) of Table 22-1. Then substituting (22-8) into (22-6) yields

$$\mathrm{var}\,(\hat{\mu}) = \frac{1}{n} \sum w_i \sigma_i^2 \qquad (22\text{-}9)$$

(d) Stratification After Sampling

Sometimes it is not possible—or at least extremely inconvenient—to stratify before sampling. For example, suppose it is known that 80% of the population of a city is white and 20% black, and income is being sampled in a house-to-house survey. There is no way of knowing before you knock on the door (i.e., before the sample is taken) whether a household is white or black (i.e., from which stratum this sample value comes).[1] The solution is first to take a simple random sample; then stratify it (i.e., allocate each observation to the appropriate stratum); finally, estimate the mean using the known weights w_i in (22-4).

In a very large sample, the sampling proportions you observe (n_i/n) will be close to the population proportions (w_i), so that

$$n_i \simeq w_i n \tag{22-10}$$

That is, the n_i are approximately what you would have set them if you could have used the prespecified proportional sampling as in (22-8). Thus the variance of $\hat{\mu}$ is approximately the same as in proportional sampling (22-9),

$$\overline{\text{var } \hat{\mu} \simeq \frac{1}{n} \sum_i w_i \sigma_i^2} \tag{22-11}$$

However, in small samples, to the degree that the approximation (22-10) holds less well, the result is a slight loss in efficiency, that is, var ($\hat{\mu}$) exceeds that given in (22-11). This is the only cost of not being able to stratify in advance.

(e) Comparison of Proportional Sampling to Simple Random Sampling

To facilitate the comparison, we quote a formula for the whole population variance σ^2, in terms of the strata:[2]

$$\sigma^2 = \sum w_i (\mu_i - \mu)^2 + \sum w_i \sigma_i^2 \tag{22-12}$$

If we take a simple random sample, the variance for $\overline{X}$ is σ^2/n, which may be expressed according to (22-12) as,

$$\text{var } (\overline{X}) = \frac{\sigma^2}{n} = \frac{1}{n} \sum w_i (\mu_i - \mu)^2 + \frac{1}{n} \sum w_i \sigma_i^2 \tag{22-13}$$

---

[1] Compare this with our earlier urban/rural example, where any household could clearly be specified as urban or rural prior to sampling.

[2] Formula (22-12) may be stated verbally as: total variance = variance between strata + variance within strata. In this form it is analogous to the analysis of variance (10-16), and its proof is similar.

If, on the other hand, we use the more efficient proportional stratified sampling technique, then the variance of the estimator is given by (22-9). This is recognized to be simply the last term in (22-13); thus the second last term in this equation must represent the additional variance (extra cost) involved in simple random sampling. Thus (22-13) can be written

$$
\begin{array}{c}
\text{variance of } \overline{X} \\
\text{in simple random} \\
\text{sampling}
\end{array}
=
\begin{array}{c}
\text{variance that can be} \\
\text{eliminated by using pro-} \\
\text{portional stratified} \\
\text{sampling instead}
\end{array}
+
\begin{array}{c}
\text{variance that} \\
\text{must remain}
\end{array}
$$

$$(22\text{-}14)$$

This leads us to another intuitively appealing conclusion: stratified sampling is seen in (22-13) to be particularly worthwhile when $(\mu_i - \mu)^2$ are large, that is, when differences between strata are large.

(f) Optimal Stratified Sampling

Finally, if the population can be stratified in advance there is an alternative method with even greater efficiency than proportional sampling (i.e., with variance *less* than that given in (22-9)—in fact, with the smallest possible variance). Choose

$$\text{optimum } n_i \text{ proportional to } w_i \sigma_i \qquad (22\text{-}15)$$

Then as an exercise (Problem 22-4) we may prove that the variance is only

$$\text{var } \hat{\mu} = \frac{1}{n} \left(\sum w_i \sigma_i \right)^2 \qquad (22\text{-}16)$$

which is less than (22-9).

The interpretation of (22-15) corresponds to our intuition; a relatively large sample should be taken from a stratum

1. if w_i is large, that is, the stratum is an important part of the population; and
2. if σ_i is large, that is, the stratum is highly varied, and hence requires a large sample to estimate $\overline{X}_i$ accurately. (Or to restate: the smaller the σ_i, the smaller the necessary sample; the limiting case in which

a sample of only one is required in a stratum with zero variance has already been given in the example in column 7 of Table 22-1).

This method has restricted application because σ_i (as well as w_i) must be known beforehand. However, the fact that the sample s_i is a good enough estimator of σ_i—even in fairly small samples—may make it possible to proceed in two stages: as soon as a part of the sample has been taken on a purely random basis, the s_i observed up to that point may be used to estimate the σ_i; these are then used (along with prior information on the w_i) in (22-15) to estimate the optimal n_i, that is, the optimal design for the balance of the sampling. However, the gains from such interim estimation of σ_i tend to be small relative to the gains from prior knowledge of the w_i. Therefore, this procedure tends to be justified only if the sampling must be stopped to allow interim calculations for some other reason as well.

22-2   OTHER SAMPLING DESIGNS

(a) Multistage (Cluster) Sampling

When a population is costly to sample, say because of transportation costs, multistage sampling may provide a way to cut costs. To illustrate, a simple random sample of the political views of 10,000 American men would be extremely costly in terms of time and transportation costs, as the interviewers travelled through thousands of counties, spread over all 50 states. Therefore, it makes sense to merely draw a random sample of, say, 10 states (first stage). Then within each state, draw a random sample of, say, 20 counties (second stage). Finally, within each county, draw a random sample of 50 men (last stage).

Clearly this may provide great savings in cost; but it is also true that this procedure will tend to yield less information. To the extent that the men in a given county think alike, only the first man provides completely new information, while the next 49 tend increasingly to repeat. This loss of information is avoided in simple random sampling, where each observation (man) is independently drawn—thus providing completely new information.

The decision on whether or not multistage cluster sampling is advisable is thus seen to involve an evaluation of how the advantage of reduced sampling costs compares with the disadvantage of information loss.

(b) Systematic Sampling

As an example, we may wish to draw a sample of 20 from a deck of 2000 IBM cards. The most straightforward way is to simply pull every

100th card. Unless strange periodicities occur in the data, this method has about the same precision as simple random sampling; so those formulas may be used as approximations.

The only drawback of systematic sampling is that its precision may badly deteriorate if systematic fluctuations do occur in the data. Although such a misfortune would be compounded by the fact that the sampler might receive no warning, this difficulty rarely arises in practice.

(c) Sequential Sampling

Sequential sampling is simple random sampling, with the sample size n no longer fixed, but rather determined by the information in the observations as they accumulate. For example, in testing the "true die" hypothesis, if it keeps turning up ace each time, a sample of $n = 5$ (or perhaps 10) would suffice to make a decision (to reject the die); a predetermined sample size of 100 is just not necessary. This procedure has already been encountered in the footnote preceding Table 9-1: the idea is to take a small sample, and if the result is unambiguous (as in the case above), the job is done; but if the sample result is ambiguous (i.e., almost 1/6 of the rolls are ace), a second, and perhaps even further stage of sampling is required until the ambiguity is resolved. This procedure is justified if the advantage of the smaller average sample size exceeds the disadvantage of having to sample several times.

22-3   CONCLUSIONS

In this chapter we have discussed a number of imaginative ways of improving on simple random sampling; essentially these involve applying

(a) prior information (e.g., the w_i in stratified sampling), or
(b) information collected in the early stages of sampling (e.g., the initial sample results used in sequential sampling).

The general principle is that the sooner you have this information, the better use can be made of it. Thus in optimal sampling, prior knowledge of σ_i will be more effective than an estimate s_i derived after initial sampling. Of course, if neither (a) nor (b) is available, then the only option is simple random sampling—where information is used only after all the sampling is complete.

The final observation is that, in practice, sampling often combines several of the above techniques. In stratified sampling, for example, cluster sampling may often be used within each stratum.

22-1 In order to investigate student political attitudes, suppose you wish to take a sample of 100 students from your university; how would you take

(a) a simple random sample

(b) a stratified sample

(c) a cluster (multistage) sample?

(d) Which sampling scheme do you think would be most economical (i.e., provide most accuracy for your dollar)?

22-2 Conduct a stratified sample of $n = 10$ students in your class, in order to estimate

(a) mean height

(b) average number of novels read last year

(c) the proportion of car owners

(d) the proportion of cigar smokers

In each case, you must first think of an appropriate division of the student population to serve as the basis of stratification. In each case, do you think the stratification was justified, in the sense of providing a more accurate estimate?

22-3 Prove (22-5) and (22-6).

22-4 Prove (22-16).

22-5 In order to estimate the total inventory of its product being held, a tire company conducts a proportional stratified sample of its dealers, with these dealers being stratified according to their inventory held in the previous year. For a total sample size of $n = 1000$, the following data were obtained:

Stratum (last year's inventory)	Population		Proportional Sample (current inventory)		
	Number of Dealers	Proportion w_i	n_i	$\bar{Y}_i$	s_i^2
0–99	4,000	.20	200	105	1,600
100–199	10,000	.50	500	180	2,500
200–299	5,400	.27	270	270	2,500
300–	600	.03	30	390	5,600
	$N = 20,000$	$\sum w_i = 1$	$n = 1000$		

(a) From this stratified sample, estimate the mean inventory μ, and hence the total inventory.

(b) Estimate the optimum strata sizes n_i, using s_i^2 for σ_i^2 in (22-15).

(c) Again using s_i^2 for σ_i^2, and assuming a fixed sample size of $n = 1000$, estimate the variance of

  (1) $\hat{\mu}$, for the proportional stratified sample in (a);

  (2) $\hat{\mu}$, for the optimal stratified sample in (b);

  (3) $\overline{X}$, for a simple random sample.

(d) Express your answer to (c) in efficiency terms. That is, calculate the efficiency of

  (1) $\hat{\mu}$ (proportional stratified sampling) relative to $\overline{X}$ (simple random sampling);

  (2) $\hat{\mu}$ (optimal stratified sampling) relative to $\overline{X}$.

(e) On the basis of each of the estimators in (c), show how you would construct a 95% confidence interval for the mean inventory μ, and hence for the total inventory. Which of the three confidence intervals is best? Which is worst?

(f) True or false? If false, correct it.

In sampling problems like this tire inventory problem, it is often wise to use proportional stratified sampling. It is true that optimal stratified sampling would be better, but the gains in efficiency that would result—even if full prior knowledge of σ_i^2 were available—are often relatively small.

22-6 Compare the regression analysis in Problem 12-9 with the stratified sampling in Problem 22-5. True or false? If false, correct it.

(a) Both methods involve the use of prior information (on last year's inventory X) to improve the estimate of this year's inventory, Y.

(b) The two methods differ, however, in the way they use the prior information. In the case of regression, prior information on X was used *after* the sample of 6 was taken. It indicated that the sample of 6 dealers was a nontypical X group (i.e., their average inventory for last year $\overline{X}$ was smaller than the population average μ_x); hence, an upward correction was required. On the other hand, the proportional stratified sampling used prior information on last year's inventories *before* sampling to ensure that the sample taken was from a representative X group.

(c) Since stratification after sampling would involve application of knowledge about X after the sample is taken, it provides an even closer analogy to regression.

*(d) Proportional stratified sampling holds three advantages over regression.

(1) It provides a more accurate estimator because prior knowledge is used before the sample is taken, rather than after. (2) It can be applied to either a numerical (e.g., size of inventory) stratification, or a nonnumerical (e.g., male/female) one; but regression can only be used for a numerical stratification. (3) It does not require the assumption that the relation between X and Y is linear (which is required in regression analysis).

*(e) If the knowledge of last year's inventory had been used in the regression analysis of Problem 12-9 to fix X values at appropriate predetermined levels before the sample was taken, then the analogy to proportional stratified sampling would no longer hold.

Chapter 23

index numbers

The time has come, the Walrus said,
To speak of many things.
Of shoes, and ships, and sealing wax,
Of cabbages—and kings.

Lewis Carroll

An index number is a single figure showing how a whole set of related variables has changed over time or differs from place to place. For example, a price index represents the behavior of a set of individual prices. If we ask what has happened to prices over time, it is far more enlightening to reply that the price index has risen by 10%, rather than that the price of eggs is up 20%, the price of TV's down by 10%, etc.

Similarly, if we wish to compare the output of industrial goods in the United States and Canada, it is convenient to state that the industrial output index of Canada is 8% that of the United States, rather than that Canada produces say 9% of the U.S. output of autos, 2% the U.S. output of aircraft parts, etc.

23-1 PRICE INDEXES

(a) Example

To construct the simplest possible price index, consider the hypothetical data in Table 23-1. The problem is to describe with a single index number how the price of this basket of goods has risen. Clearly, an

Table 23-1 Hypothetical Prices of Selected
Items, 1965 and 1970

Prices Items	1965 P_o	1970 P_t	Price Relative $P_t/P_o(100)$
Steak (per pound)	1.00	1.15	115
Pepper (per pound)	2.00	2.20	110
Bread (per loaf)	.20	.27	135

erroneous way would be to sum all the 1970 prices and divide by the
sum of the 1965 prices, thus

$$\frac{\sum P_t}{\sum P_o}(100) = \left(\frac{1.15 + 2.20 + .27}{1.00 + 2.00 + .20}\right)(100) = 113$$

(Note that for convenience, an index value of 100 is customarily assigned
to the base period, i.e., index numbers are expressed in percentage form,
requiring the multiplication by 100.)

The conclusion is that, on average, prices have risen by about 13%.
Why isn't this a good estimate? The answer is that this calculation is
dependent on the arbitrary choice of units in which each good is
measured. Thus, if pepper were measured in ounces rather than pounds,
pepper would play a much less dominant role in this calculation; alternatively, if steak were measured in tons rather than pounds, the resulting
index would be almost exactly 115, that is, completely dominated by
the price of steak.

A simple way to avoid this problem would be to calculate the "price
relative" for each item, as shown in column (3) of Table 23-1; each of
these can be viewed as an index number for the single item involved.
Then a simple average of these price relatives yields

$$\frac{115 + 110 + 135}{3} = 120$$

(b) The Laspeyres and Paasche Indexes

Although the above index is an improvement because it is independent of the unit of measurement of each item, one major flaw
remains. Each item is given equal weight; thus, pepper is assumed to
have as important a price as bread. In fact, of course, it has an insignifi-

cant role in any normal expenditure pattern, hence should be largely disregarded in favor of greater emphasis on the important consumption items of steak and bread. Thus the appropriate index should be a weighted average of the price changes, with the weights being the quantities consumed. Now consider the consumption pattern of the typical consumer, shown in the 1965 column of Table 23-2. When these weights are applied to the prices in Table 23-1, the resulting index is:

$$
\text{Laspeyres price index} \triangleq \frac{\sum P_t Q_o}{\sum P_o Q_o} (100) \tag{23-1}
$$

$$
= \frac{1.15(40) + 2.20(1) + .27(100)}{1.00(40) + 2.00(1) + .20(100)} (100) = 122
$$

with this index depending heavily on prices of bread and steak, but little affected by the price of pepper.

The question then arises, "Why use the base period (i.e., the initial 1965) weights, rather than the weights in the comparison period 1970 (also shown in Table 23-2)?" When the 1970 quantities are used as weights, they yield a different result:

$$
\text{Paasche price index} \triangleq \frac{\sum P_t Q_t}{\sum P_o Q_t} (100) \tag{23-2}
$$

$$
= \frac{1.15(50) + 2.20(1) + .27(90)}{1.00(50) + 2.00(1) + .20(90)} (100) = 120
$$

Although there may be no theoretical reason for preferring one index to the other, there is a practical reason for using the Laspeyres index,

Table 23-2 Hypothetical Quantities Consumed
by the Typical American, 1965 and 1970

Quantities / Items	1965 Q_o	1970 Q_t
Steak (pounds)	40	50
Pepper (pounds)	1	1
Bread (loaves)	100	90

if indexing is to be done for a number of years by hand rather than on a computer: the same base period is used in all calculations, whereas the Paasche index involves changing weights for each calculation.

Clearly, in the application of the Laspeyres index the selection of a base year becomes a crucial issue. For example, the index would become almost meaningless if the initial base period was a wartime year in which steak was rationed, and very little consumed. In this case, steak would essentially disappear from the calculation of price indexes for the later period when it may have been an important item in consumption. Hence, great care must be taken that the base year is a reasonably typical one, free of disasters or other unusual events that would distort consumption patterns.

(c) Fisher's Ideal Index: a Geometric Mean

First we digress to discuss the geometric mean, which is defined as the nth root of the product of n items

$$\text{Geometric mean} \triangleq \sqrt[n]{X_1 X_2 \cdots X_n} \tag{23-3}$$

This mean has many attractive properties, especially for business and economics applications. It is the average that is appropriate in describing rates of increase. To illustrate, suppose the population of a suburban town grew as follows:

	Population	Increase per Decade
1950	1,000	
1960	2,000	2 times
1970	16,000	8 times
Increase overall		16 times

The objective is to describe the average rate of increase per decade. First, note that population increased by a factor of 2 in the first decade, and by a factor of 8 in the second, so that the overall increase was 16 times. The simple arithmetic average of the two,

$$\frac{2 + 8}{2} = 5$$

is clearly seen to be inappropriate; if a fivefold increase occurred over two successive decades, the overall increase would be 25-fold.

On the other hand, the geometric mean

$$\sqrt{(2)(8)} = 4$$

is appropriate; if a fourfold increase occurred over two successive decades, the overall increase would be 16-fold, which agrees with the actual value.

Now, consider the Laspeyres and Paasche indexes. Since they measure rates of change, the geometric mean is the appropriate way to obtain an average of the two. Thus (23-3) can be used to define

---

Fisher's ideal price index $= \sqrt{\text{(Laspeyres Index)(Paasche Index)}}$

$$= \sqrt{\left(\frac{\sum P_t Q_o}{\sum P_o Q_o}\right)\left(\frac{\sum P_t Q_t}{\sum P_o O_t}\right)} (100) \qquad (23\text{-}4)$$

$$= \sqrt{(122)(120)} = 121$$

23-2

FURTHER INDEXES

(a) Quantity Indexes

Suppose in Table 23-2 it is necessary to calculate an index of the change in the physical quantity of goods consumed. Steak purchases have gone up, while bread purchases have gone down; which is more important? This depends on the relative importance of each in the consumer's budget, which in turn depends on the prices (in Table 23-1). Thus, prices should be used as weights in calculating a quantity index, just as quantities were used as weights in calculating a price index. We thus obtain

$$\text{Laspeyres quantity index} \triangleq \frac{\sum Q_t P_o}{\sum Q_o P_o} (100) \qquad (23\text{-}5)$$

$$= \frac{50(1.00) + 1(2.00) + 90(.20)}{40(1.00) + 1(2.00) + 100(.20)} (100) = 113$$

$$\text{Paasche quantity index} \triangleq \frac{\sum Q_t P_t}{\sum Q_o P_t} (100) \qquad (23\text{-}6)$$

$$= \frac{50(1.15) + 1(2.20) + 90(.27)}{40(1.15) + 1(2.20) + 100(.27)} (100) = 111$$

Fisher's ideal quantity index

$$\overset{\Delta}{=} \sqrt{(\text{Laspeyres Index})(\text{Paasche Index})} \tag{23-7}$$

$$= \sqrt{\left(\frac{\sum Q_t P_o}{\sum Q_o P_o}\right)\left(\frac{\sum Q_t P_t}{\sum Q_o P_t}\right)}(100)$$

$$= \sqrt{(113)(111)} = 112$$

(b) The Cost Index

So far, we have defined indexes of quantity as well as price. It would finally seem appropriate to measure *total cost* (monetary value) of the consumer's purchases. Since the cost of one item, such as steak, is

$$\text{item cost} = PQ \tag{23-8}$$

therefore, for all items,

$$\text{total cost} = \sum PQ \tag{23-9}$$

Total costs in the two time periods may be compared by forming their ratio; thus we obtain the

$$\text{cost index} \overset{\Delta}{=} \frac{\sum P_t Q_t}{\sum P_o Q_o}(100) \tag{23-10}$$

$$= \frac{(1.15)(50) + (2.20)1 + (.27)(90)}{(1.00)(40) + (2.00)1 + (.20)(100)}(100) = 135.5$$

Now, if our indexes of price, quantity, and cost are good indexes, they should satisfy the same sort of relation (23-8) that individual items satisfy; that is, we want to check that

$$(\text{price index})(\text{quantity index}) \overset{?}{=} \text{cost index} \tag{23-11}$$

For example, if the price index increases twofold and the quantity index increases threefold, then the cost index should increase sixfold; if not, there must be something wrong with the price and quantity indexes. Unfortunately, this so-called "factor-reversal test" (23-11) is often *not* satisfied, as simple calculation will show:[1]

Laspeyres indexes $(122)(113) \overset{?}{=} 135.5$ (a)

$138 > 135.5$

Paasche indexes $(120)(111) \overset{?}{=} 135.5$ (b)

$133 < 135.5$

Fischer's ideal index $(121)(112) \overset{?}{=} 135.5$ (c)

$135.5 \overset{\checkmark}{=} 135.5$

$$(23\text{-}12)$$

It is easily proved in general[2] that Fisher's ideal index always satisfies the test (23-11); this is one of the properties that justifies the name "ideal."

(c) Further Advantages of Fisher's Ideal Index

We note in (23-12a) that the Laspeyres indexes of price and quantity are both larger than the corresponding ideal indexes; thus their product is larger than it should be (i.e., larger than the cost index). This is not an isolated example; the Laspeyres indexes are too large in nearly all other cases as well, and it is interesting to see why. We shall give the reason in the case of the Laspeyres quantity index (leaving the price index as an exercise).

———————————
[1]To be mathematically correct in (23-11) and later, we ought to express indexes with *percent* signs; for example, in (23-12a), we should actually write

$$(122\%)(113\%) \overset{?}{=} 135.5\%$$

that is

$$(1.22)(1.13) \overset{?}{=} 1.355$$

In dropping the percent signs, we are deferring to customary usage. However, in mathematical proofs such as in (23-12d), we shall find it necessary to put the percent signs back—or even better, delete the factor $100\% = 1$.

[2]**proof**   (Fisher's price index) (Fisher's quantity index)

$$= \sqrt{\left(\frac{\sum P_t Q_o}{\sum P_o Q_o}\right)\left(\frac{\sum P_t Q_t}{\sum P_o Q_t}\right)} \sqrt{\left(\frac{\sum P_o Q_t}{\sum P_o Q_o}\right)\left(\frac{\sum P_t Q_t}{\sum P_t Q_o}\right)} \qquad (23\text{-}12d)$$

Many factors cancel, leaving

$$\frac{\sum P_t Q_t}{\sum P_o Q_o} = \text{cost index}$$

The key to the argument is the numerator, given in (23-5) as $\Sigma\ Q_t P_o$. We see that current quantities are weighted at the old prices. Thus, whatever goods are currently bought in large quantities because they are now relatively cheap, are nonetheless weighted at the old high prices, making the product $Q_t P_o$ too high. Hence the Laspeyres index overstates.

In a similar way we may argue that the Paasche index understates. Consequently the ideal index, being the geometric mean between the Laspeyres and Paasche indexes, is a very useful compromise. (These issues will be proved more rigorously in Section 23-4).

23-3   PRACTICAL CONSIDERATIONS

(a) What's Really Happening to the Cost of Living?

A price index is often popularly known as a "cost of living" index, while a quantity index is often called a "standard of living" or "real income" index. We shall make several important observations about price indexes which are equally true for quantity indexes.

First, it is necessary to select a representative sample of goods, obviously a much larger group than in our very simple example. Furthermore, another difficulty arises. The price of a television will appear in calculating today's cost of living. But suppose this is to be compared to its price in the base year of 1940. Televisions were not part of consumer purchases at that time, hence there is no meaningful price that can be attached to them. Thus, since consumer purchasing patterns are always changing, the base period cannot be too far distant in the past; hence, any extended index series generally involves a number of points in time at which base weights have been changed in recognition of the introduction of new products.

Another problem that arises is that even when data does exist, it is often not comparable. Televisions again provide a good example. Suppose we want to compare prices in 1970 with 1948. Although TV's existed in 1948, they were not at all comparable with the 1970 product. To observe that their price has doubled may be of little consequence; if everyone judges that the increased size of screen, the addition of color, and so on have made a TV now "twice" as good, then isn't this twice the product for twice the price? Have prices changed at all? Unless quality adjustments are accounted for explicitly, such index calculations may not indicate the increase in the cost of living, but rather the increase in the cost of *better* living.

The difficulty with quality judgments is that it is almost impossible to make them. Is the present TV set twice as good, or three times as good as the first model? Autos are another example. At the one extreme there are some who are skeptical that the auto is really any better today than 20 years ago. On the other hand, one might look to specific improvements (safety equipment, disc brakes, automatic choke, etc.) with a view to making a quality adjustment for each. The question is: how much? A specific estimate is feasible: the extra price of each item when it was first introduced as optional equipment. But even this is not satisfactory. From either the producer's or consumer's point of view, the value of a car does not necessarily increase by the sum of a set of options that become standard equipment. For the producer, the cost of these optional items may decrease when they become standard equipment, since they no longer require the special care and attention of "custom items." For the consumer, there may be some items that he simply would not buy if they were options—hence he values them at less than their optional price. (Indeed there may even be items—such as automatic choke—that a lot of buyers would prefer not to have, even if they were *free* options.)

It may be concluded therefore that adjustments for changes in product quality should be made; yet in practice they become extraordinarily difficult. Our example of auto improvements (initially priced as options) is perhaps the most conducive to cold calculation; yet even here, any estimate becomes very difficult to defend. This sort of consideration has led many observers to conclude that, in a world of rapidly changing products, small changes in the cost of living index in the order of say one or two percent may not mean much.

Another important issue is the selection of the base year, that is, the year with which comparisons are to be made. Thus a Republican pointing to Truman's record (1945–1952) would conclude that this Democratic president had a poor record of controlling inflation. Implicitly he is using 1945 as his base year, and one that is quite inappropriate because of its special circumstances; it was at the end of a long period of wartime inflationary pressure held in check only by price controls, difficult or impossible (for any administration) to maintain into the postwar period. Similarly, a Democrat who points to the rapid increase in output during the Roosevelt administration (1932–1945) is biasing his case by the selection of the atypical base year 1932, when employment and production levels were both abnormally low. Clearly, the selection of a base year can load an argument; hence it is crucial that a normal year be chosen. The problem is, of course, that there is no such thing as a perfectly "normal" year; yet some years are more normal than others. In this case, as in many others previously encountered, the good judgment of the statistician becomes crucial.

(b) Price Indexes as Deflators

The money value of U.S. Gross National Product (roughly all goods and services produced each year by Americans) is shown in Figure 23-1. This reflects not only an increase in the physical quantity of goods and services produced but also an increase in their price. Accordingly, to obtain the real (physical) GNP we must deflate money GNP with an

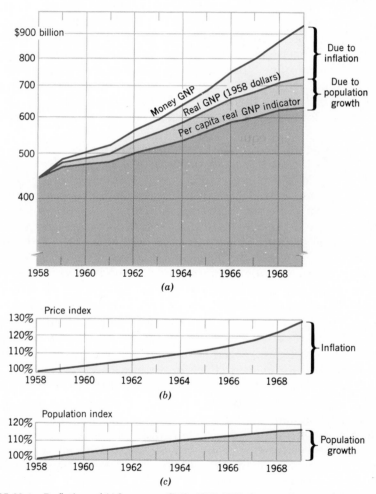

FIGURE 23-1   Deflation of U.S. money GNP, 1958–1969. Source: Survey of Current Business, U.S. Department of Commerce.

appropriate price index.[3] Then we must further deflate this series by population growth if we wish to show the change in *per capita* real GNP (i.e., the improvement in real income[4] of the average American). Both these deflations are shown in Figure 23-1.

If the combination or mix of goods has changed (e.g., more autos, less bread), then any calculation of how an individual's real income has changed may err unless it is based on information about preferences between goods (e.g., between autos and bread.) This subtle problem is addressed in more detail in the next optional section.

PROBLEMS

23-1

Good	Prices		Quantities (per person)	
	1960	1970	1960	1970
Bread (loaves)	$ .25	$ .30	100	80
Steak (pounds)	1.00	1.25	50	40
Milk (quarts)	.30	.35	100	100
Potatoes (pounds)	.05	.05	60	100

From the above data, and using 1960 as the base year:

(a) Calculate the Laspeyres price index for 1970.

(b) Calculate the price relatives for each good, and pick out the smallest and largest. Is the Laspeyres index between them?

(c) Would you guess that the betweenness property of part (b) is true also of the Paasche and Fisher price indexes? Then calculate them to check your guess.

(d) Order the Laspeyres, Paasche, and Fisher price indexes according to size. Is it the same order as in equation (23-12)?

(e) Calculate the three quantity indexes. Order them also according to size. Is it the same order as in equation (23-12)?

(f) Calculate the cost index, and verify which of the three indexes passes the "factor-reversal" test (23-11).

_____

[3]Since this price index is to be used to adjust GNP, it should not be just a consumer price index; instead it is an index of prices of all goods that make up GNP (often called a GNP deflator). Hence it includes prices of investment machinery as well as consumer goods.

[4]Although GNP and national income are not identical concepts, they move together closely enough that changes in per capita GNP can be used to roughly approximate changes in average income.

(g) What difference to the various indexes would it make if all quantities were measured, not on a per person basis, but rather as total national consumption of the good?

(h) Try to generalize the result of (b). That is, either prove that the price index is *always* between the largest and smallest price relative, or else find an example for which it is not true ("counterexample").

23-2

Good	Prices				Quantities (per person)			
	1940	1950	1960	1970	1940	1950	1960	1970
Steak (pounds)	$1.00	$1.20	$1.40	$1.20	40	50	70	50
Bread (pounds)	.10	.20	.40	.20	80	100	110	100

From the above data, answer the following questions.

(a) Using 1940 as the base period, fill in the following table.

Type of Price Index	1940	1950	1960	1970
Laspeyres Paasche Ideal				

(b) Which of the three indexes is simplest to calculate? How important do you think simplicity is, as a practical issue today?

(c) In which decade was there the greatest increase in the cost of living?

(d) Fill in the following table.

Type of Price Index	1960 Index, Using 1950 Base	1970 Index, Using 1960 Base	Product of These 2 Indexes
Laspeyres Paasche Ideal			

Note that in 1970, both prices and quantities reverted to what they were in 1950; that is, during the 1960s, everything that happened in the 1950s was reversed. It would therefore be appropriate if the product of the two indexes, which measures the total change over the two decades, was 1 exactly. This so-called "time reversal test" is passed by which indexes?

23-3 (a) The U.S. Consumer Price Index (CPI) includes about 400 items of food, clothing, rent, medical charges, etc., typically purchased by the U.S. family. It is often used as a "wage deflator." Explain how.

(b) Money wages in a number of U.S. industries are now "tied" to the CPI; that is, escalator clauses in union-management bargains ensure that wage rates automatically adjust for any increase in the CPI. How are these justified? Do you see any problem arising if such escalator clauses become widespread in all (or most) industries?

23-4 Explain why
(a) the Laspeyres price index is usually an overstatement,
(b) the Paasche price index is usually an understatement.

23-5 (a) Would you prefer to spend an (after tax) annual income of $5000 by purchasing *entirely* out of the 1965 Sears catalogue, or *entirely* out of the 1930 Sears catalogue (with its lower prices, but more restricted selection of goods which are also less up-to-date; and of course there will be many goods—like TV's—in the 1965 catalogue that just are not available in the 1930 catalogue.) Assume that not only all goods but also all services (such as medical care and transatlantic trips) are included. In other words, would you prefer to spend your entire income on 1965 goods and services at 1965 prices, or on 1930 goods and services at 1930 prices?

(b) Let us sharpen the answer to (a): how much money do you think you would need to spend in the 1965 catalogue in order to equal the satisfaction you would get by spending $5000 in the 1930 catalogue? This ratio of expenditure (1965 to 1930) might be called the "subjective" price index.

(c) During this period, the U.S. Consumer Price Index actually rose from 58 to 110 (base = 1957–1959). How does this compare to your answer in (b)? In your judgement, therefore, has the CPI overstated or understated price increases?

(d) Repeat (a) to (c) for an income of $500,000 instead of $5000.

23-6 "Indexes may be used for international or interspatial, as well as intertemporal, comparisons." Suppose that the hypothetical data in Tables 23-1 and 23-2 represent comparisons for France and Germany, rather than for 1965 and 1970. With this substitution, interpret the price index (23-1) and the quantity index (23-5).

*23-4   **INDEX COMPARISONS OF REAL INCOME**

In this section a more sophisticated view of index numbers will be developed. This is a starred section, since it becomes a bit more difficult toward the end and requires indifference curve analysis—which will now be very briefly reviewed.

(a) Indifference Curves

Our illustration will focus on changes in quantity (real income), rather than prices. This will involve an examination for a typical consumer of the physical quantities of goods purchased in two time periods using prices as weights.

Figure 23-2 illustrates a typical indifference curve, representing a consumer's preference for two goods X and Y. All points on this curve represent combinations of physical quantities of these two goods which leave the consumer equally satisfied, that is, indifferent—hence the name "indifference curve." Thus this individual is equally happy at Q_1 (with 100 units of X, and 300 of Y), or at Q_2 (with 200 of each); in other words, he is willing to trade 100 units of Y for 100 units of X. However, as he moves from Q_2 to Q_3 the scarceness of Y begins to pinch, and he is reluctant to keep trading Y away, unless he receives more X in return; in fact, for 100 units of Y he now requires 200 units of X. This changing "rate of substitution" simply reflects the fact that the consumer's appetite for a specific good (Y) increases as the good becomes scarce; this in turn implies that the indifference curve will be concave.

Figure 23-3 illustrates a whole set of indifference curves, called an indifference system or map. The curve u_3 is reproduced from Figure 23-2. u_4 is a similar indifference curve, superior to u_3. In other words, any point on u_4 is preferred to any point on u_3.

FIGURE 23-2   An indifference curve.

FIGURE 23-3   An indifference map.

This again illustrates the useful technique often used by economists, of forcing three variables into a two-dimensional diagram. The three variables are Q_y, Q_x, and U, with U representing the consumer's satisfaction (also called "utility" or "real income"). Thus, this indifference mapping represents a "utility hill"; as we move from the origin to the northeast we move up this hill onto higher and higher levels of satisfaction.

Figure 23-4 shows how the consumer will rationally select a combina-

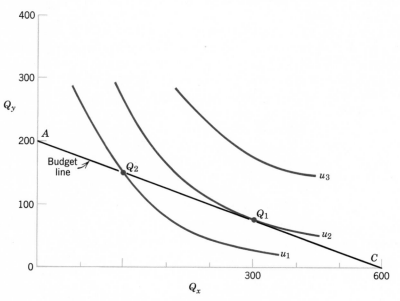

FIGURE 23-4   Consumer equilibrium.

tion of X and Y. He is limited by his budget, which we suppose is $6000. If X costs $10 per unit and Y costs $30, then AC represents his budget limitation. For example, if he buys no Y, he can buy 6000/10 = 600 units of X, at point C. Or, if he buys no X, he can buy 6000/30 = 200 units of Y, at point A. Generally, one can confirm that this budget will just purchase any other combination of X and Y lying on the straight line AC, by noting from (23-9) that

$$P_x Q_x + P_y Q_y = \text{total cost of purchases} \qquad (23\text{-}13)$$
$$= \text{consumer's budget, } B \qquad (23\text{-}14)$$

and in this example

$$10Q_x + 30Q_y = 6000 \qquad (23\text{-}15)$$

which is the equation of a straight line, called the *budget line*. As an exercise you can confirm that the slope of this line is determined by relative prices, that is

$$\text{slope} = \frac{-P_x}{P_y} = \frac{-10}{30} = -.33 \qquad (23\text{-}16)$$

while its distance from the origin is proportional to the size of the consumer's budget B.

He wishes to use this budget to reach the highest level of utility (real income), that is, the highest u curve. It is easy to see that this will occur where his given budget line is tangent to an indifference curve. In our example, the highest indifference curve he can reach is u_2: and he can reach this only by purchasing the quantity of X and Y represented by Q_1. Note how any other set of feasible purchases, say Q_2, must leave him on a lower indifference curve, u_1; at the same time a higher indifference curve, say u_3, simply cannot be reached with his budget.

This very brief introduction to indifference curve analysis can now be used to illuminate the difference between the various index numbers.

(b) Laspeyres Index and Revealed Preference

In the next three sections we shall see how each of the three index numbers measures a change in real income (quantity of goods purchased). For example, in Figure 23-5 let Q_o represent the real income of the consumer in the base period. Do the other four points in this diagram, all representing possible consumption combinations in the later comparison period, represent an increase or decrease in his real income?

FIGURE 23-5   Indexing using the Laspeyres criterion.

It is easy to see that Q_S represents an increase in real income, since the consumer receives more of both goods. Indeed, any point within the angle DQ_oE represents an increase in real income. However, a comparison of each of the other three points with Q_o is much more difficult, since each involves increased consumption of one good, but decreased consumption of the other. The only way that the consumer can be judged better off by moving from Q_o to Q_I, say, is to know what his indifference map looks like; specifically it is necessary to know whether his indifference curve running through Q_o passes above or below Q_I. But how can we possibly discover anything about the specific location of an indifference curve?

The answer comes from "revealed preference"; we can make inferences about an indifference system by examining how the consumer chooses between goods in the face of a specific set of prices. We note that the consumer decided to purchase Q_o with his base year budget B_o when the prices of X and Y were P_{ox} and P_{oy}.

Thus the budget line, from (23-13) is

$$P_{ox}Q_x + P_{oy}Q_y = B_o \tag{23-17}$$

where the first subscript refers to the time, and the second to the good.

This is shown in Figure 23-5 as the line FG, which passes through Q_o with slope given by (23-16) as $-P_{ox}/P_{oy}$. The indifference curve must be tangent to this budget line, and can therefore be roughly sketched in Figure 23-5. Then point Q_o is seen to be superior to all other points on the budget line FG, therefore superior to all points below the budget line. Thus we have shown that Q_o is superior to Q_I.

As well as delimiting the clearly inferior points, the budget line FG

gives a very interesting interpretation of the Laspeyres quantity index: it is precisely the set of comparison points with a Laspeyres index[5] of 100. This is a very natural conclusion, of course, since both the budget line *FG* and the Laspeyres quantity index are based on the same *base* prices P_o. Yet these comparison points on the budget line have been shown to be inferior to Q_o, so that the Laspeyres index (which rates them equal to Q_o) is seen to overstate their utility. This overstatement is even more dramatic in the case of a comparison point slightly above the budget line, such as Q_J: given the indifference curve drawn into Figure 23-5, Q_J represents a reduction in utility from Q_o; but the Laspeyres index erroneously indicates that it is an increase.

Thus we have rigorously proved the point first made in Section 23-2(c): the Laspeyres quantity index *overstates* the utility (real income) of the comparison point.

(c) Paasche Index and Revealed Preference

Although the proof is more difficult,[6] the interpretation of Paasche indexing is similar to Laspeyres, as shown in Figure 23-6. The one differ-

---

[5] **proof**   The Laspeyres index (23-5) may be written in the notation of this section as

$$\text{Laspeyres index} = \frac{P_{ox}Q_{tx} + P_{oy}Q_{ty}}{P_{ox}Q_{ox} + P_{oy}Q_{oy}} \, (100) \tag{23-18}$$

Since the point $Q_o = (Q_{ox}, Q_{oy})$ lies on the budget line, it satisfies the budget equation (23-17)

$$P_{ox}Q_{ox} + P_{oy}Q_{oy} = B_o \tag{23-19}$$

Any comparison point $Q_t = (Q_{tx}, Q_{ty})$ also on the budget line also satisfies equation (23-17)

$$P_{ox}Q_{tx} + P_{oy}Q_{ty} = B_0 \tag{23-20}$$

Substituting (23-19) and (23-20) into (23-18)

$$\text{Laspeyres index} = \frac{B_o}{B_o} \, (100) = 100$$

[6] To rigorously interpret the Paasche index, we first address the question: how does a point such as Q_K in Figure 23-5 compare with Q_o? To answer this, it is necessary to have even more information (i.e., revealed preference) about the shape of the individual's indifference curves.

This information can be obtained from the new budget line, shown in Figure 23-6 as Q_tH, which is sloped according to the new prices P_t and passes through Q_t, the quantity

(cont'd)

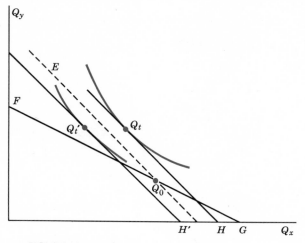

FIGURE 23-6   Indexing using the Paasche criterion.

ence is this: whereas all points with a Laspeyres index of 100 are on the line FQ_o (with slope determined by *old* prices), all points with a Paasche index of 100 are on the line EQ_o (with slope determined by the *new* prices). Finally, whereas the Laspeyres index overstates the utility of any comparison point such as Q'_t, the Paasche index understates it.

(d) Fisher's Ideal Index: a Compromise

In Figure 23-7 we summarize the conclusions of the previous sections. While we may say that Laspeyres indexing, using old prices P_o, is "in

---

of goods actually purchased in the comparison period; (note that Q_o may lie either above or below this line). Of course, all points below this line are inferior to Q_t. If Q_o is such a point, as shown in Figure 23-6, then the issue is decided.

However, if the new quantity consumed is at Q'_t, so that Q_o lies above the budget line $Q'_t H'$, then it is not clear whether Q'_t or Q_o is superior. It is therefore appropriate to draw a line through Q_o, parallel to $Q_t H$, which we denote by $Q_o E$. This line divides the points like Q_t that are clearly superior to Q_o, from the points like Q'_t that are ambiguous.

The new budget line $Q_t H$ gives a very interesting interpretation of the Paasche quantity index: Q_t has a Paasche index of 100 when compared to any base point that lies precisely on $Q_t H$. (This is entirely similar to the interpretation of the Laspeyres index, the only difference being that it is now the *new* prices P_t which give both the slope of the budget line $Q_t H$ and the weights for the Paasche quantity index. The proof is just like the proof for the Laspeyres index in footnote 5.) Yet such a base point on the new budget line is in fact inferior to Q_t; thus the Paasche index (which rates them equal) overstates the utility of the base point relative to the comparison point Q_t.

Turning this statement around, the Paasche index *understates* the utility of the comparison point Q_t relative to the base point Q_o.

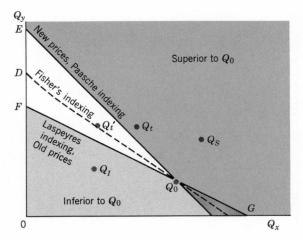

FIGURE 23-7   Using Paasche index, Q_t still superior to Q_0 but Q_t' is not.

the FQ_o direction," Paasche indexing, using new prices P_t, is in the EQ_o direction. Fisher's indexing is the geometric mean, and is therefore in some intermediate direction, say DQ_o, with DQ_o made up of all points with a Fisher index of 100.

Points like Q_I, that are below FQ_o and in fact are inferior to Q_o, are correctly given an index less than 100 by all three indexes—Laspeyres, Paasche, and Fisher's. Similarly, points like Q_t that are above EQ_o and are, in fact, superior to Q_o, are also correctly given an index greater than 100 by all three indexes. However, the wedge EQ_oF is ambiguous. Some points (near the lower line FQ_o) are in fact inferior, while other points (near the top line EQ_o) are in fact superior. The Laspeyres index erroneously overstates them, giving them *all* an index more than 100 while the Paasche index erroneously understates them, giving them all an index of less than 100. On the other hand, Fisher's ideal index splits them, and hence is likely to make fewer errors. To avoid making any errors at all, of course, we would need more complete knowledge of the consumer's indifference map.

(e) Further Difficulties

Several points should be emphasized in conclusion. First, the analysis holds only if the consumer's preferences do not change over time, specifically between the base and comparison periods. Even more important, this discussion has concentrated on evaluating real income changes for an individual, rather than for a group of individuals. The problem that arises in any evaluation of real income for a group, community, or nation, is that an indifference system cannot be defined for a collection of individuals, unless quite restrictive assumptions are made about the similarity of individual preferences.

PROBLEMS

*23-7 In each blank, insert the correct word: Laspeyres, Paasche, or Fisher's.

(a) If the comparison quantities Q_t have _____ index greater than 100, they necessarily have greater utility than the base period quantities.

(b) If the comparison quantities Q_t have _____ index less than 100, they necessarily have less utility than the base period quantities.

(c) The _____ index is always between the other two indexes.

*23-8 Suppose you are omniscient, and you know that a certain consumer's indifference map is the one below.

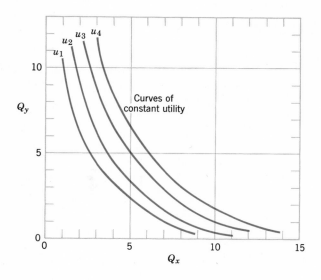

(a) Using the prices in Table A below, graph the budget line for each period, and hence verify the quantities purchased in Table B.

(b) Fill in Tables C, D, and E.

		Base year t_o	Comparison Year t_1	Comparison Year t_2
A.	P_x	$ 300	$ 500	$ 400
	P_y	600	250	200
	Budget	3000	3000	2000
B.	Q_x	8?	3?	2?
	Q_y	1?	6?	6?
C.	Quantity indexes:			
	Laspeyres	100	?	?
	Paasche	100	?	?
	Fisher's	100	?	?
D.	What is the utility change since t_o?		?	?
E.	Which quantity index most accurately measures the utility change since t_o?		?	?

*23-9 Prove the statement made in footnote 6 that Q_t has Paasche quantity index 100 relative to any base point that lies precisely on the new budget line $Q_t H$.

GAME THEORY

Gambling—the sure way of getting nothing for something.

Wilson Mizner

Anyone who has come this far deserves a little recreation. In this last chapter, therefore, we break away from the main theme of statistical inference in order to present game theory—a very simple and entertaining application of elementary probability.

"Games" are simply mathematical models of conflict situations, where the payoffs (outcomes) are determined by the strategies of the players. Because a player can choose his strategy, he has some control over the outcome of the game. But he is not in complete control, since the outcome also depends on the strategy of his opponents.

The simplest game occurs when one player's gain always equals the other player's loss, as in poker for example. Then the total amount won by the players equals zero, and the game is called "zero-sum."

24-1   ZERO SUM GAMES FOR TWO PLAYERS

(a) Strictly Determined Games

In Table 24-1 we illustrate a payoff matrix, representing payments from B to A; for example, if A selects strategy 2 and B selects strategy 1, B

Table 24-1   An Example of a Payoff
Matrix for A (Loss Function for B)

A's Strategies \ B's Strategies	1	2	3
1	25	6	11
2	20	10	18
3	11	7	5

pays A 20 units. A will try to select a strategy to make the outcome as large as possible, while B will try to keep the outcome as small as possible.

Obviously B will have no interest in playing this game as is, since he can do nothing but lose. So a payoff matrix normally involves some positive elements (where B pays A) and some negative ones (where A pays B). Alternatively, in order to induce B to play the game shown in Table 24-1 A might bribe B $12 for each time he plays. This is the assumption we now make, in order to keep our payoff matrix all positive for easier geometric interpretation. The question is "With this $12 side payment, is it in B's interest to play this game?"

If a player can select his strategy after he knows how his opponent has committed himself, his appropriate strategy is obvious and the game becomes a trivial one. For example, if it is known that B has chosen strategy 3, A will just scan column 3, select the largest payoff (18) and then play that strategy 2. The essence of game theory, however, is that each player must commit himself without knowledge of his opponent's decision; he only knows the payoff matrix. We further assume that the game is repeated many times. The only clues a player has about his opponent's strategy must come from observing his past pattern of play.

In these circumstances A finds the continuous play of strategy 1 unattractive. It is true that this row has the largest possible payoff ($25). But this requires B's cooperation in playing his strategy 1, and it is clearly not in B's interest to cooperate. Indeed if B observes that A is continuously playing strategy 1, he will select strategy 2, thus keeping the payoff down to 6. A finds strategy 3 similarly unattractive; B will counter with strategy 3, reducing A's payoff to only 5. A chooses strategy 2; the very best play by B will still yield A a payoff of 10. In conclusion, A calculates the minimum value in each row—and then selected the largest of these minimum values. This *maxim*um of the row *mini*ma is called the "maximin."

Now consider the problem from *B*'s point of view. Recall that he wants to keep the payoff as low as possible. Strategy 1 is ill-advised; when *A* observes him playing this, he will counter with 1, leaving *B* with a loss of $25. Strategy 3 is also rejected—it may cost him $18. He selects strategy 2; the most it can cost him is $10. Note that *B* calculates the maximum value of each column, and then selects the smallest of these. This *minim*um of the column *maxim*a is called the "minimax." Note that in this special case minimax occurs at the same point as maximin; then the game is called "strictly determined."

This is illustrated in Figure 24-1, a diagram of the payoff matrix with each payoff measured vertically. At *X* we note a "saddle point," which is both the largest element in its column and the smallest element in its row. When such a saddle point exists, it is both maximin and minimax.

In this strictly determined game, both *A* and *B* play strategy 2. The payoff (from *B* to *A*) is always 10, so that it is clearly a game *B* will wish to play if he is bribed $12 to do so.

FIGURE 24-1   Payoff matrix in Table 24-1.

PROBLEM

24-1 In each of the following strictly-determined games, the matrix represents payoffs from B to A, as in Table 24-1. What is the appropriate strategy for each opponent, and what is the expected value of the game?

(a)

B / A	1	2	3	4
1	3	−1	0	−2
2	2	2	1	3
3	−2	0	−1	−3

(b)

B / A	1	2	3
1	10	−2	10
2	20	−1	5

(b) Mixed Strategies

Let us now try to apply the theory of part (a) to the game in Table 24-2. A would select strategy 2; this is the row with the largest minimum value (maximin = 4). At the same time B would select strategy 1; this is the column with the smallest maximum value (minimax = 5).

Since A plays strategy 2, while B plays strategy 1, the actual payoff will be 5 (which happens to be the minimax). But since minimax and maximin do not coincide, interesting conflicts will arise if the game is played repeatedly. B will observe that as long as A is playing row 2, he can do better by playing column 2, thus reducing the payoff to 4. But when B switches to column 2, it is now in A's interest to switch to row 1, raising the payoff to 6. As an exercise you can confirm that a whole series of such moves and countermoves are set into play—eventually drawing the players in a circle around to the initial position. Then a new cycle begins. This will continue until the players recognize a fundamental point. Once a player allows his strategy to be predicted, he will be hurt.

Table 24-2   A Game Requiring Mixed Strategies

B / A	1	2	3
1	3	6	2
2	5	4	8

Minimax   Maximin

Thus, for example, when A's strategy becomes clear, he can be hurt by B. What is his defense?

A's best plan is to keep B guessing. Thus if A determines his strategy by a chance process, B will be unable to predict what he will do. For example, A might toss a coin, playing row 1 if heads, or row 2 if tails. He is using a "mixed strategy," weighting each row with a probability of .50. Now B doesn't know what to expect; the only question left for A is whether this 50/50 mix is the best set of odds to use.

The best mix of strategies for A is determined in Figure 24-2. Along the horizontal axis we consider various probabilities p that A may assign to playing row 1. This is all A has to select; once this is determined, then the probability attached to playing row 2 is also determined, as $1 - p$.

Vertically, we plot the expected value of the game—which, of course, not only depends on the probabilities A may select, but also on what B may do. If B plays *only* column 1, then the expected value of the game is a function only of the probability A may select; this appears in this diagram as the line V_1. It is worth examining in detail.

At the extreme left, if A sets $p = 0$ (i.e., never plays row 1, but always plays row 2) then the value of the game V_1 is 5. On the other hand, at the extreme right, if A sets $p = 1$ (and always plays row 1), then $V_1 = 3$. Or if A sets $p = 1/2$, then

$$V_1 = 3\left(\frac{1}{2}\right) + 5\left(\frac{1}{2}\right) = 4 \qquad (24\text{-}1)$$

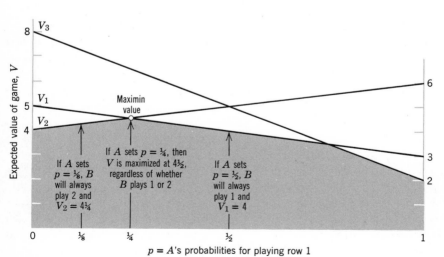

FIGURE 24-2   Determination of A's mixed strategy (for game shown in Table 24-2).

Generally, for any probability p that A may select,

$$V_1 = 3(p) + 5(1 - p) = 5 - 2p \qquad (24\text{-}2)$$

The form of (24-2) confirms that V_1 is a straight line function of p. Similarly, if B plays only column 2, then

$$V_2 = 6p + 4(1 - p) = 4 + 2p \qquad (24\text{-}3)$$

Or, if B plays only column 3, then

$$V_3 = 2p + 8(1 - p) = 8 - 6p \qquad (24\text{-}4)$$

These three equations are graphed in Figure 24-2, for A to examine in order to optimally select p. If he selects $p = 1/8$, his opponent will counter by always playing strategy 2, and keep the expected value of the game at $V_2 = 4\ 1/4$. [This is shown geometrically, and confirmed by evaluating (24-3) for $p = 1/8$.] Or if A selects $p = 1/2$, B will counter with strategy 1, thus keeping the expected value of the game down to $V_1 = 4$. Since A is dealing with an opponent who will be selecting strategies to keep V *low*, the expected value of the game from A's point of view is shown as the shaded area in Figure 24-2. The best A can do, therefore, is to select $p = 1/4$, which guarantees $V = 4\ 1/2$. Since this is the intersection of V_1 and V_2, it is the value of the game regardless of whether B plays 1 or 2. This geometric solution may be verified algebraically by setting $V_1 = V_2$; using (24-2) and (24-3),

$$5 - 2p = 4 + 2p \qquad (24\text{-}5)$$
$$p = \tfrac{1}{4} \qquad (24\text{-}6)$$

Finally, this value of p is substituted back into (24-3) for the value of the game,

$$V_2 = 4 + 2(\tfrac{1}{4}) = 4\tfrac{1}{2} \qquad (24\text{-}7)$$

Thus A decides to assign a probability of 1/4 to playing row 1. (He might, for example, toss 2 coins. If they both come up heads (probability 1/4), then he plays row 1; if not, he plays row 2.) If this game is repeated many times, A will insure that he receives an average payoff which will tend towards $4\tfrac{1}{2}$—and there is nothing B can do to reduce this. All B can hope for is that A has bad luck; (e.g., by the luck of the toss, A plays row 1 when B is playing column 1). This sort of bad luck can reduce

A's average winning below $4\frac{1}{2}$ if the game is played only a few times (or A's good luck can raise his average winnings above $4\frac{1}{2}$); but as the game is played over and over, the element of bad luck tends to average out.

PROBLEM

24-2 (a) Suppose we play a variation on matching coins. Each of us will choose heads or tails, independently and secretly. I'll pay you $30 if I show tails and you show heads. I'll pay you $10 if I show heads and you show tails. Finally, to make it fair, you pay me $20 if we match (i.e., both show heads, or both show tails). Do you want to play? Why?

(b) What are the optimal strategies of the two players in an *ordinary* game of matching pennies? (Recall that in this game, one player gets the pennies if they match, the other gets them if they don't match.) Would you still toss your penny in such a game, rather than secretly selecting a head or tail? Why?

(c) Conclusions

In solving for the best game strategy, the first step is to test whether maximin and minimax coincide. If they do, this is a strictly determined game, and the single strategy to be used by each player is determined.

If minimax and maximin do not coincide, the game is not strictly determined. Mixed strategies are called for, and are determined in simple cases geometrically or algebraically as we have illustrated. In more complex cases, advanced techniques such as linear programming are required; but rather than extending the mathematical solution, it is more important to consider the fundamental philosophy and assumptions underlying game theory:

1. A player using his best mixed strategy can guarantee a certain expected value for the game, regardless of what his opponent may do. However, this is only the value towards which the average of many games will tend. If the game is only played a few times, luck may raise or lower this payoff.
2. Once the optimal mixed strategy is determined (e.g., $p = 1/2$), the play is dictated by a random process (tossing a coin). It is simply not good enough to decide to play each strategy half the time—for example, alternating 1, then 2, then 1, then 2, and so on. Once the opponent observes this pattern, he can predict your next play, and hurt you. Note in the simplest game of matching pennies (Problem

24-2b), how badly a player would be hurt if he alternated heads and tails rather than tossed the coin. Once an intelligent opponent observed this pattern, he could win every time. Each player must be unpredictable, by deciding his play by chance.

3. The theory of games leads to very conservative strategies. It is appropriate if a game is being replayed many times against an intelligent strategist, who is out to get you, knows the payoff matrix, and can observe your strategy mix. If these conditions are not met, you usually can find a better strategy. To illustrate, consider an extreme example with payoff matrix given in Table 24-3.

Table 24-3   When Game Theory May Be Inappropriate

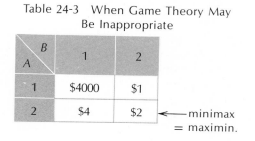

Since maximin and minimax coincide, both A and B should play strategy 2 every time. But suppose on the first play, B plays strategy 1! This means either that he is a fool, or unaware of the payoff matrix (and that $4000 debacle that he faces). It doesn't matter which; in these circumstances, A should drop maximin theory, play row 1 and punish B for his stupidity or ignorance.

Game theory also should not be used in games against nature. As an example, suppose a farmer, in deciding when to plant his crop, has to gamble on whether there will be a spring frost. If he plants early, and a spring frost occurs, the crop will be killed, yielding a zero payoff. This is shown in Table 24-4, along with all the other possible payoffs. If the farmer used game theory, his maximin strategy would be to plant late, yielding a saddlepoint payoff of 100. However, the underlying assumption of a hostile opponent out to minimize the value of the game is obviously false: nature is neutral, with the probability of frost being determined quite independently of what the farmer does. His best strategy therefore is to take account of this probability to obtain the expected value (Bayesian) solution. For example, if spring frost has occurred only one year in ten over a long past period, then planting early (strategy one) yields

$$\text{expected payoff} = 0(.10) + 150(.90) = 135$$

Table 24-4   Payoffs to the Farmer

Farmer \ Nature	Spring Frost	No Spring Frost
1 Plant early	0	150
2 Plant late	100	110

whereas planting late yields

$$\text{expected payoff} = 100(.10) + 110(.90) = 109$$

His expected value solution, therefore, is to plant early. The maximin strategy of planting late would cost him dearly $(135 - 109 = 26)$.

PROBLEMS

24-3 Suppose you are trying to decide whether to hold a banquet indoors or outdoors, with your profit depending on both where the banquet is held and the weather, as follows:

You hold banquet \ Nature	Rain 1	Not Rain 2
Indoors 1	100	0
Outdoors 2	0	1000

(a) According to game theory, what should your strategy, or mix of strategies be? What would your expected profit be? Does this seem like a reasonable solution? If not, why not?

(b) Specifically, suppose past weather records indicate that the probability of rain is 1/5. What action would you take? What is the expected value of this action?

(c) True or false. If false, correct it.

In conclusion, if the "other player's" strategy is determined by a hostile opponent, then game theory is appropriate; but even under these conditions it may be too conservative a line of play, unless the opponent is highly intelligent and informed. On the other hand, if the other player's strategy is determined independently (e.g., rain versus shine), then the expected values of each action indicate which is better.

24-4 Given the following payoff matrix, what strategy should each player choose, and what is the expected value of the game?

A \ B	1	2
1	−20	−4
2	−6	−2
3	1	0

24-5 Suppose you find yourself on a long sea voyage. You wish to match pennies, but your companion wants to play cards. He therefore suggests a compromise. You choose heads or tails while he selects an ace. If you select a head he pays you $15, $4, $−5, and $1 respectively, depending on whether he's chosen the spade, heart, diamond or club ace. If you select a tail, he pays you $−10, $−2, $1, and $−5, again depending on which ace he's chosen.

(a) Do you agree to play? Why? What strategies?

(b) If you were to play this game five times and found you had won $5, what would you conclude?

(c) Are there any two lines in your diagram that do *not* intersect? From both the diagram and the payoff matrix, show that, no matter what the circumstances, it is always preferable for him to select the club ace instead of the heart ace (i.e., the heart strategy is "dominated by" the club strategy). By initially examining the payoff matrix, couldn't he have dropped the heart strategy from all further consideration?

24-2   MORE GENERAL GAMES

If a game is to be used as a model for any sort of realistic conflict situation (aside from parlor games), it obviously has to be much more complicated than the zero-sum, two-person game. For example, three-person games often involve collusion of two players against the third. Even if we confine ourselves to two-person games, the zero-sum restriction is highly unrealistic; a more interesting model would have a payoff matrix for A, and another separate payoff matrix for B, shown in Table 24-5. (For example, we might think of A as management, and B as labor, in a wage dispute. Strategy 1 might represent a hard line, while strategy 2 might represent a more flexible bargaining attitude. When two hard

Table 24-5 A Nonzero-Sum Game

(a) Payoff Matrix for A

B / A	1	2
1	0	100
2	50	110

(b) Payoff Matrix for B

B / A	1	2
1	0	50
2	100	80

lines come into conflict, they result in a long and costly strike that reduces each contestant's payoff to zero). In Table 24-5, A would play strategy 2, because it is better than strategy 1 whatever strategy B may choose. B, seeing that A will choose strategy 2, looks at the relevant second row of his payoff matrix. There he finds his biggest payoff (100) occurs when he chooses strategy 1, and the game is solved.

Most nonzero-sum games, however, do not have such an easy solution; in fact, many have no really satisfactory solution at all. This is one reason that they are less popular to theorists than (the less realistic) two-person, zero-sum games, which always have a solution.

PROBLEM

24-6 In the game of Table 24-5, suppose A is thinking of hiring a bargaining agent. The agent announces loudly (so that both A and B can hear) that he will take the following inflexible schedule of fees from A's payoff matrix

0	10
50	30

(a) What would be A's new (net) payoff matrix?
(b) Should A hire the agent?
(c) Suppose a credible bargaining agent is not available to A. Can he achieve anything by announcing that he is bound he will play strategy 1, no matter what happens.
(d) What happens if B counters A's announcement in (c) with an even louder announcement that he is bound he will play strategy 1, no matter what happens? Is there any circumstance under which this would make B better off?

AppeNdix

LIST OF TABLES

Table Ia Squares and Square Roots

N	N^2	$\sqrt{N}$	$\sqrt{10N}$
1.00	1.0000	1.00000	3.16228
1.01	1.0201	1.00499	3.17805
1.02	1.0404	1.00995	3.19374
1.03	1.0609	1.01489	3.20936
1.04	1.0816	1.01980	3.22490
1.05	1.1025	1.02470	3.24037
1.06	1.1236	1.02956	3.25576
1.07	1.1449	1.03441	3.27109
1.08	1.1664	1.03923	3.28634
1.09	1.1881	1.04403	3.30151
1.10	1.2100	1.04881	3.31662
1.11	1.2321	1.05357	3.33167
1.12	1.2544	1.05830	3.34664
1.13	1.2769	1.06301	3.36155
1.14	1.2996	1.06771	3.37639
1.15	1.3225	1.07238	3.39116
1.16	1.3456	1.07703	3.40588
1.17	1.3689	1.08167	3.42053
1.18	1.3924	1.08628	3.43511
1.19	1.4161	1.09087	3.44964
1.20	1.4400	1.09545	3.46410
1.21	1.4641	1.10000	3.47851
1.22	1.4884	1.10454	3.49285
1.23	1.5129	1.10905	3.50714
1.24	1.5376	1.11355	3.52136
1.25	1.5625	1.11803	3.53553
1.26	1.5876	1.12250	3.54965
1.27	1.6129	1.12694	3.56371
1.28	1.6384	1.13137	3.57771
1.29	1.6641	1.13578	3.59166
1.30	1.6900	1.14018	3.60555
1.31	1.7161	1.14455	3.61939
1.32	1.7244	1.14891	3.63318
1.33	1.7689	1.15326	3.64692
1.34	1.7956	1.15758	3.66060
1.35	1.8225	1.16190	3.67423
1.36	1.8496	1.16619	3.68782
1.37	1.8769	1.17047	3.70135
1.38	1.9044	1.17473	3.71484
1.39	1.9321	1.17898	3.72827
1.40	1.9600	1.18322	3.74166
1.41	1.9881	1.18743	3.75500
1.42	2.0164	1.19164	3.76829
1.43	2.0449	1.19583	3.78153
1.44	2.0736	1.20000	3.79473
1.45	2.1025	1.20416	3.80789
1.46	2.1316	1.20830	3.82099
1.47	2.1609	1.21244	3.83406
1.48	2.1904	1.21655	3.84708
1.49	2.2201	1.22066	3.86005
1.50	2.2500	1.22474	3.87298
N	N^2	$\sqrt{N}$	$\sqrt{10N}$

N	N^2	$\sqrt{N}$	$\sqrt{10N}$
1.50	2.2500	1.22474	3.87298
1.51	2.2801	1.22882	3.88587
1.52	2.3104	1.23288	3.89872
1.53	2.3409	1.23693	3.91152
1.54	2.3716	1.24097	3.92428
1.55	2.4025	1.24499	3.93700
1.56	2.4336	1.24900	3.94968
1.57	2.4649	1.25300	3.96232
1.58	2.4964	1.25698	3.97492
1.59	2.5281	1.26095	3.98748
1.60	2.5600	1.26491	4.00000
1.61	2.5921	1.26886	4.01248
1.62	2.6244	1.27279	4.02492
1.63	2.6569	1.27671	4.03733
1.64	2.6896	1.28062	4.04969
1.65	2.7225	1.28452	4.06202
1.66	2.7556	1.28841	4.07431
1.67	2.7889	1.29228	4.08656
1.68	2.8224	1.29615	4.09878
1.69	2.8561	1.30000	4.11096
1.70	2.8900	1.30384	4.12311
1.71	2.9241	1.30767	4.13521
1.72	2.9584	1.31149	4.14729
1.73	2.9929	1.31529	4.19533
1.74	3.0276	1.31909	4.17133
1.75	3.0625	1.32288	4.18330
1.76	3.0976	1.32665	4.19524
1.77	3.1329	1.33041	4.20714
1.78	3.1684	1.33417	4.21900
1.79	3.2041	1.33791	4.23084
1.80	3.2400	1.34164	4.24264
1.81	3.2761	1.34536	4.25441
1.82	3.3124	1.34907	4.26615
1.83	3.3489	1.35277	4.27785
1.84	3.3856	1.35647	4.28952
1.85	3.4225	1.36015	4.30116
1.86	3.4596	1.36382	4.31277
1.87	3.4969	1.36748	4.32435
1.88	3.5344	1.37113	4.33590
1.89	3.5721	1.37477	4.34741
1.90	3.6100	1.37840	4.35890
1.91	3.6481	1.38203	4.37035
1.92	3.6864	1.38564	4.38178
1.93	3.7249	1.38924	4.39318
1.94	3.7636	1.39284	4.40454
1.95	3.8025	1.39642	4.41588
1.96	3.8416	1.40000	4.42719
1.97	3.8809	1.40357	4.43847
1.98	3.9204	1.40712	4.44972
1.99	3.9601	1.41067	4.46094
2.00	4.0000	1.41421	4.47214
N	N^2	$\sqrt{N}$	$\sqrt{10N}$

N	N²	√N	√10N		N	N²	√N	√10N
2.00	4.0000	1.41421	4.47214		**2.50**	6.2500	1.58114	5.00000
2.01	4.0401	1.41774	4.48330		2.51	6.3001	1.58430	5.00999
2.02	4.0804	1.42127	4.49444		2.52	6.3504	1.58745	5.01996
2.03	4.1209	1.42478	4.50555		2.53	6.4009	1.59060	5.02991
2.04	4.1616	1.42829	4.51664		2.54	6.4516	1.59374	5.03984
2.05	4.2025	1.43178	4.52769		2.55	6.5025	1.59687	5.04975
2.06	4.2436	1.43527	4.53872		2.56	6.5536	1.60000	5.05964
2.07	4.2849	1.43875	4.54973		2.57	6.6049	1.60312	5.06952
2.08	4.3264	1.44222	4.56070		1.58	6.6564	1.60624	5.07937
2.09	4.3681	1.44568	4.57165		2.59	6.7081	1.60935	5.08920
2.10	4.4100	1.44914	4.58258		**2.60**	6.7600	1.61245	5.09902
2.11	4.4521	1.45258	4.59347		2.61	6.8121	1.61555	5.10882
2.12	4.4944	1.45602	4.60435		2.62	6.8644	1.61864	5.11859
2.13	4.5369	1.45945	4.61519		2.63	6.9169	1.62173	5.12835
2.14	4.5796	1.46287	4.62601		2.64	6.9696	1.62481	5.13809
2.15	4.6225	1.46629	4.63681		2.65	7.0225	1.62788	5.14782
2.16	4.6656	1.46969	4.64758		2.66	7.0756	1.63095	5.15752
2.17	4.7089	1.47309	4.65833		2.67	7.1289	1.63401	5.16720
2.18	4.7524	1.47648	4.66905		2.68	7.1824	1.63707	5.17687
2.19	4.7961	1.47986	4.67974		2.69	7.2361	1.64012	5.18652
2.20	4.8400	1.48324	4.69042		**2.70**	7.2900	1.64317	5.19615
2.21	4.8841	1.48661	4.70106		2.71	7.3441	1.64621	5.20577
2.22	4.9284	1.48997	4.71169		2.72	7.3984	1.64924	5.21536
2.23	4.9729	1.49332	4.72229		2.73	7.4529	1.65227	5.22494
2.24	5.0176	1.49666	4.73286		2.74	7.5076	1.65529	5.23450
2.25	5.0625	1.50000	4.74342		2.75	7.5625	1.65831	5.24404
2.26	5.1076	1.50333	4.75359		2.76	7.6171	1.66132	5.25357
2.27	5.1529	1.50665	4.76445		2.77	7.6729	1.66433	5.26308
2.28	5.1984	1.50997	4.77493		2.78	7.7284	1.66733	5.27257
2.29	5.2441	1.51327	4.78539		2.79	7.7841	1.67033	5.28205
2.30	5.2900	1.51658	4.79583		**2.80**	7.8400	1.67332	5.29150
2.31	5.3361	1.51987	4.80625		2.81	7.8961	1.67631	5.30094
2.32	5.3824	1.52315	4.81664		2.82	7.9524	1.67929	5.31037
2.33	5.4289	1.52643	4.82701		2.83	8.0089	1.68226	5.31977
2.34	5.4756	1.52971	4.83735		2.84	8.0656	1.68523	5.32917
2.35	5.5225	1.53297	4.84768		2.85	8.1225	1.68819	5.33854
2.36	5.5696	1.53623	4.85798		2.86	8.1796	1.69115	5.34790
2.37	5.6169	1.53948	4.86826		2.87	8.2369	1.69411	5.35724
2.38	5.6644	1.54272	4.87852		2.88	8.2944	1.69706	5.36656
2.39	5.7121	1.54596	4.88876		2.89	8.3521	1.70000	5.37587
2.40	5.7600	1.54919	4.89898		**2.90**	8.4100	1.70294	5.38516
2.41	5.8081	1.55242	4.90918		2.91	8.4681	1.70587	5.39444
2.42	5.8564	1.55563	4.91935		2.92	8.5264	1.70880	5.40370
2.43	5.9049	1.55885	4.92950		2.93	8.5849	1.71172	5.41295
2.44	5.9536	1.56205	4.93964		2.94	8.6436	1.71464	5.42218
2.45	6.0025	1.56525	4.94975		2.95	8.7025	1.71756	5.43139
2.46	6.0516	1.56844	4.95984		2.96	8.7616	1.72047	5.44059
2.47	6.1009	1.57162	4.96991		2.97	8.8209	1.72337	5.44977
2.48	6.1504	1.57484	4.97996		2.98	8.8804	1.72627	5.45894
2.49	6.2001	1.57797	4.98999		2.99	8.9401	1.72916	5.46809
2.50	6.2500	1.58114	5.00000		**3.00**	9.0000	1.73205	5.47723
N	N²	√N	√10N		N	N²	√N	√10N

N	N²	√N	√10N	N	N²	√N	√10N
3.00	9.0000	1.73205	5.47723	**3.50**	12.2500	1.87083	5.91608
3.01	9.0601	1.73494	5.48635	3.51	12.3201	1.87350	5.92453
3.02	9.1204	1.73781	5.49545	3.52	12.3904	1.87617	5.93296
3.03	9.1809	1.74069	5.50454	3.53	12.4609	1.87883	5.94138
3.04	9.2416	1.74356	5.51362	3.54	12.5316	1.88149	5.94979
3.05	9.3025	1.74642	5.52268	3.55	12.6025	1.88414	5.95819
3.06	9.3636	1.74929	5.53173	3.56	12.6736	1.88680	5.96657
3.07	9.4249	1.75214	5.54076	3.57	12.7449	1.88944	5.97495
3.08	9.4864	1.75499	5.54977	3.58	12.8164	1.89209	5.98331
3.09	9.5481	1.75784	5.55878	3.59	12.8881	1.89473	5.99166
3.10	9.6100	1.76068	5.56776	**3.60**	12.9600	1.89737	6.00000
3.11	9.6721	1.76352	5.57674	3.61	13.0321	1.90000	6.00833
3.12	9.7344	1.76635	5.58570	3.62	13.1044	1.90263	6.01664
3.13	9.7969	1.76918	5.59464	3.63	13.1769	1.90526	6.02495
3.14	9.8596	1.77200	5.60357	3.64	13.2496	1.90788	6.03324
3.15	9.9225	1.77482	5.61249	3.65	13.3225	1.91050	6.04152
3.16	9.9856	1.77764	5.62139	3.66	13.3956	1.91311	6.04979
3.17	10.0489	1.78045	5.63028	3.67	13.4689	1.91572	6.05805
3.18	10.1124	1.78326	5.63915	3.68	13.5424	1.91833	6.06630
3.19	10.1761	1.78606	5.64801	3.69	13.6161	1.92094	6.07454
3.20	10.2400	1.78885	5.65685	**3.70**	13.6900	1.92354	6.08276
3.21	10.3041	1.79165	5.66569	3.71	13.7641	1.92614	6.09098
3.22	10.3684	1.79444	5.67450	3.72	13.8384	1.92873	6.09918
3.23	10.4329	1.79722	5.68331	3.73	13.9129	1.93132	6.10737
3.24	10.4976	1.80000	5.69210	3.74	13.9876	1.93391	6.11555
3.25	10.5625	1.80278	5.70088	3.75	14.0625	1.93649	6.12372
3.26	10.6276	1.80555	5.70964	3.76	14.1376	1.93907	6.13188
3.27	10.6929	1.80831	5.71839	3.77	14.2129	1.94165	6.14003
3.28	10.7584	1.81108	5.72713	3.78	14.2884	1.94422	6.14817
3.29	10.8241	1.81384	5.73585	3.79	14.3641	1.94679	6.15630
3.30	10.8900	1.81659	5.74456	**3.80**	14.4400	1.94936	6.16441
3.31	10.9561	1.81934	5.75326	3.81	14.5161	1.95192	6.17252
3.32	11.0224	1.82209	5.76194	3.82	14.5924	1.95448	6.18061
3.33	11.0889	1.82483	5.77062	3.83	14.6689	1.95704	6.18870
3.34	11.1556	1.82757	5.77927	3.84	14.7456	1.95959	6.19677
3.35	11.2225	1.83030	5.78792	3.85	14.8225	1.96214	6.20484
3.36	11.2896	1.83303	5.79655	3.86	14.8996	1.96469	6.21289
3.37	11.3569	1.83576	5.80517	3.87	14.9769	1.96723	6.22093
3.38	11.4244	1.83848	5.81378	3.88	15.0544	1.96977	6.22896
3.39	11.4921	1.84120	5.82237	3.89	15.1321	1.97231	6.23699
3.40	11.5600	1.84391	5.83095	**3.90**	15.2100	1.97484	6.24500
3.41	11.6281	1.84662	5.83952	3.91	15.2881	1.97737	6.25300
3.42	11.6964	1.84932	5.84808	3.92	15.3664	1.97990	6.26099
3.43	11.7649	1.85203	5.85662	3.93	15.4449	1.98242	6.26897
3.44	11.8336	1.85472	5.86515	3.94	15.5236	1.98494	6.27694
3.45	11.9025	1.85742	5.87367	3.95	15.6025	1.98746	6.28490
3.46	11.9716	1.86011	5.88218	3.96	15.6816	1.98997	6.29285
3.47	12.0409	1.86279	5.89067	3.97	15.7609	1.99249	6.30079
3.48	12.1104	1.86548	5.89915	3.98	15.8404	1.99499	6.30872
3.49	12.1801	1.86815	5.90762	3.99	15.9201	1.99750	6.31664
3.50	12.2500	1.87083	5.91608	**4.00**	16.0000	2.00000	6.32456
N	N²	√N	√10N	N	N²	√N	√10N

N	N²	√N	√10N	N	N²	√N	√10N
4.00	16.0000	2.00000	6.32456	**4.50**	20.2500	2.12132	6.70802
4.01	16.0801	2.00250	6.33246	4.51	20.3401	2.12368	6.71565
4.02	16.1604	2.00499	6.34035	4.52	20.4304	2.12603	6.72309
4.03	16.2409	2.00749	6.34823	4.53	20.5209	2.12838	6.73053
4.04	16.3216	2.00998	6.35610	4.54	20.6116	2.13073	6.73795
4.05	16.4025	2.01246	6.36396	4.55	20.7025	2.13307	6.74537
4.06	16.4836	2.01494	6.37181	4.56	20.7936	2.13542	6.75278
4.07	16.5649	2.01742	6.37966	4.57	20.8849	2.13776	6.76018
4.08	16.6464	2.01990	6.38749	4.58	20.9764	2.14009	6.76757
4.09	16.7281	2.02237	6.39531	4.59	21.0681	2.14243	6.77495
4.10	16.8100	2.02485	6.40312	**4.60**	21.1600	2.14476	6.78233
4.11	16.8921	2.02731	6.41093	4.61	21.2521	2.14709	6.78970
4.12	16.9744	2.02978	6.41872	4.62	21.3444	2.14942	6.79706
4.13	17.0569	2.03224	6.42651	4.63	21.4369	2.15174	6.80441
4.14	17.1396	2.03470	6.43428	4.64	21.5296	2.15407	6.81175
4.15	17.2225	2.03715	6.44205	4.65	21.6225	2.15639	6.81909
4.16	17.3056	2.03961	6.44981	4.66	21.7156	2.15870	6.82642
4.17	17.3889	2.04206	6.45755	4.67	21.8089	2.16102	6.83374
4.18	17.4724	2.04450	6.46529	4.68	21.9024	2.16333	6.84105
4.19	17.5561	2.04695	6.47302	4.69	21.9961	2.16564	6.84836
4.20	17.6400	2.04939	6.48074	**4.70**	22.0900	2.16795	6.85565
4.21	17.7241	2.05183	6.48845	4.71	22.1841	2.17025	6.86294
4.22	17.8084	2.05426	6.49615	4.72	22.2784	2.17256	6.87023
4.23	17.8929	2.05670	6.50384	4.73	22.3729	2.17486	6.87750
4.24	17.9776	2.05913	6.51153	4.74	22.4676	2.17715	6.88477
4.25	18.0625	2.06155	6.51920	4.75	22.5625	2.17945	6.89202
4.26	18.1476	2.06398	6.52687	4.76	22.6576	2.18174	6.89928
4.27	18.2329	2.06640	6.53452	4.77	22.7529	2.18403	6.90652
4.28	18.3184	2.06882	6.54217	4.78	22.8484	2.18632	6.91375
4.29	18.4041	2.07123	6.54981	4.79	22.9441	2.18861	6.92098
4.30	18.4900	2.07364	6.55744	**4.80**	23.0400	2.19089	6.92820
4.31	18.5761	2.07605	6.56506	4.81	23.1361	2.19317	6.93542
4.32	18.6624	2.07846	6.57267	4.82	23.2324	2.19545	6.94262
4.33	18.7489	2.08087	6.58027	4.83	23.3289	2.19773	6.94982
4.34	18.8356	2.08327	6.58787	4.84	23.4256	2.20000	6.95701
4.35	18.9225	2.08567	6.59545	4.85	23.5225	2.20227	6.96419
4.36	19.0096	2.08806	6.60303	4.86	23.6196	2.20454	6.97137
4.37	19.0969	2.09045	6.61060	4.87	23.7169	2.20681	6.97854
4.38	19.1844	2.09284	6.61816	4.88	23.8144	2.20907	6.98570
4.39	19.2721	2.09523	6.62571	4.89	23.9121	2.21133	6.99285
4.40	19.3600	2.09762	6.63325	**4.90**	24.0100	2.21359	7.00000
4.41	19.4481	2.10000	6.64708	4.91	24.1081	2.21585	7.00714
4.42	19.5346	2.10238	6.64831	4.92	24.2064	2.21811	7.01427
4.43	19.6248	2.10476	6.65582	4.93	24.3049	2.22036	7.02140
4.44	19.7136	2.10713	6.66333	4.94	24.4036	2.22261	7.02851
4.45	19.8025	2.10950	6.67083	4.95	24.5025	2.22486	7.03562
4.46	19.8916	2.11187	6.67832	4.96	24.6016	2.22711	7.04273
4.47	19.9809	2.11424	6.68581	4.97	24.7009	2.22935	7.04982
4.48	20.0704	2.11660	6.69328	4.98	24.8004	2.23159	7.05691
4.49	20.1601	2.11896	6.70075	4.99	24.9001	2.23383	7.06399
4.50	20.2500	2.12132	6.70820	**5.00**	25.0000	2.23607	7.07107
N	N²	√N	√10N	N	N²	√N	√10N

N	N²	√N̄	√10N̄	N	N²	√N̄	√10N̄
5.00	25.0000	2.23607	7.07107	5.50	30.2500	2.34521	7.41620
5.01	25.1001	2.23830	7.07814	5.51	30.3601	2.34734	7.42294
5.02	25.2004	2.24054	7.08520	5.52	30.4704	2.34947	7.42967
5.03	25.3009	2.24277	7.09225	5.53	30.5809	2.35160	7.43640
5.04	25.4016	2.24499	7.09930	5.54	30.6916	2.34372	7.44312
5.05	25.5025	2.24722	7.10634	5.55	30.8025	2.35584	7.44983
5.06	25.6036	2.24944	7.11357	5.56	30.9136	2.35797	7.45654
5.07	25.7049	2.25167	7.12039	5.57	31.0249	2.36008	7.46324
5.08	25.8064	2.25389	7.12741	5.58	31.1364	2.34220	7.46994
5.09	25.9081	2.23610	7.13442	5.59	31.2481	2.36432	7.47663
5.10	26.0100	2.25832	7.14143	5.60	31.3600	2.36643	7.48331
5.11	26.1121	2.26053	7.14843	5.61	31.4721	2.36854	7.48999
5.12	26.2144	2.26274	7.15542	5.62	31.5844	2.37065	7.49667
5.13	26.3169	2.26495	7.16240	5.63	31.6969	2.37276	7.50333
5.14	26.4196	2.26716	7.16938	5.64	31.8096	2.37487	7.50999
5.15	26.5225	2.26936	7.17635	5.65	31.9225	2.37697	7.51665
5.16	26.6256	2.27156	7.18331	5.66	32.0356	2.37908	7.52330
5.17	26.7289	2.27376	7.19027	5.67	32.1489	2.38118	7.52994
5.18	26.8324	2.27596	7.19722	5.68	32.2624	2.38328	7.53658
5.19	26.9361	2.27816	7.20417	5.69	32.3761	2.38537	7.54321
5.20	27.0400	2.28035	7.21110	5.70	32.4900	2.38747	7.54983
5.21	27.1441	2.28254	7.21803	5.71	32.6041	2.38956	7.55645
5.22	27.2484	2.28473	7.22496	5.72	32.7184	2.39165	7.56307
5.23	27.3529	2.28692	7.23187	5.73	32.8329	2.39374	7.56968
5.24	27.4576	2.28910	7.23878	5.74	32.9476	2.39583	7.57628
5.25	27.5625	2.29129	7.24569	5.75	33.0625	2.39792	7.58288
5.26	27.6676	2.29347	7.25259	5.76	33.1776	2.40000	7.58947
5.27	27.7729	2.29565	7.25948	5.77	33.2929	2.40208	7.59605
5.28	27.8784	2.29783	7.26636	5.78	33.4084	2.40416	7.60263
5.29	27.9841	2.30000	7.27324	5.79	33.5241	2.40624	7.60920
5.30	28.0900	2.30217	7.28011	5.80	33.6400	2.40832	7.61577
5.31	28.1961	2.30434	7.28697	5.81	33.7561	2.41039	7.62234
5.32	28.3024	2.30651	7.29383	5.82	33.8724	2.41247	7.62889
5.33	28.4089	2.30868	7.30068	5.83	33.9889	2.41454	7.63544
5.34	28.5156	2.31084	7.30753	5.84	34.1056	2.41661	7.64199
5.35	28.6225	2.31301	7.31437	5.85	34.2225	2.41868	7.64853
5.36	28.7296	2.31517	7.32120	5.86	34.3396	2.42074	7.65506
5.37	28.8369	2.31733	7.32803	5.87	34.4569	2.42281	7.66159
5.38	28.9444	2.31948	7.33485	5.88	34.5744	2.42487	7.66812
5.39	29.0521	2.32164	7.34166	5.89	34.6921	2.42693	7.67463
5.40	29.1600	2.32379	7.34847	5.90	34.8100	2.42899	7.68115
5.41	29.2681	2.32594	7.35527	5.91	34.9281	2.43105	7.68765
5.42	29.3764	2.32809	7.56206	5.92	35.0464	2.43311	7.69615
5.43	29.4849	2.33024	7.36885	5.93	35.1649	2.43516	7.70065
5.44	29.5936	2.33238	7.37564	5.94	35.2836	2.43721	7.70714
5.45	29.7025	2.33452	7.38241	5.95	35.4025	2.43926	7.71362
5.46	29.8116	2.33666	7.38918	5.96	35.5216	2.44131	7.72010
5.47	29.9209	2.33880	7.39594	5.97	35.6409	2.44336	7.72658
5.48	30.0304	2.34094	7.40270	5.98	35.7604	2.44540	7.73305
5.49	30.1401	2.34307	7.40945	5.99	35.8801	2.44745	7.73951
5.50	30.2500	2.34521	7.41620	6.00	36.0000	2.44949	7.74597
N	N²	√N̄	√10N̄	N	N²	√N̄	√10N̄

Table Ia   (Continued)

N	N²	√N̄	√10N̄	N	N²	√N̄	√10N̄
6.00	36.0000	2.44949	7.74597	**6.50**	42.2500	2.54951	8.06226
6.01	36.1201	2.45153	7.75242	6.51	42.3801	2.55147	8.06846
6.02	36.2404	2.45357	7.75887	6.52	42.5104	2.55343	8.07465
6.03	36.3609	2.45561	7.76531	6.53	42.6409	2.55539	8.08084
6.04	36.4816	2.45764	7.77174	6.54	42.7716	2.55734	8.08703
6.05	36.6025	2.45967	7.77817	6.55	42.9025	2.55930	8.09321
6.06	36.7236	2.46171	7.78460	6.56	43.0336	2.56125	8.09938
6.07	36.8449	2.46374	7.79102	6.57	43.1649	2.56320	8.10555
6.08	36.9664	2.46577	7.79744	6.58	43.2964	2.56515	8.11172
6.09	37.0881	2.46779	7.80385	6.59	43.4281	2.56710	8.11788
6.10	37.2100	2.46982	7.81025	**6.60**	43.5600	2.56905	8.12404
6.11	37.3321	2.47184	7.81665	6.61	43.6921	2.57099	8.13019
6.12	37.4544	2.47386	7.82304	6.62	43.8244	2.57294	8.13634
6.13	37.5769	2.47588	7.82943	6.63	43.9569	2.57488	8.14248
6.14	37.6996	2.47790	7.83582	6.64	44.0896	2.57682	8.14862
6.15	37.8225	2.47992	7.84219	6.65	44.2225	2.57876	8.15475
6.16	37.9456	2.48193	7.84857	6.66	44.3556	2.58070	8.16088
6.17	38.0689	2.48395	7.85493	6.67	44.4889	2.58263	8.16701
6.18	38.1924	2.48596	7.86130	6.68	44.6224	2.58457	8.17313
6.19	38.3161	2.48797	7.86766	6.69	44.7561	2.58650	8.17924
6.20	38.4400	2.48998	7.87401	**6.70**	44.8900	2.58844	8.18535
6.21	38.5641	2.49199	7.88036	6.71	45.0241	2.59037	8.19146
6.22	38.6884	2.49399	7.88670	6.72	45.1584	2.59230	8.19756
6.23	38.8129	2.49600	7.89303	6.73	45.2929	2.59422	8.20366
6.24	38.9376	2.49800	7.89937	6.74	45.4276	2.59615	8.20975
6.25	39.0625	2.50000	7.90569	6.75	45.5625	2.59808	8.21584
6.26	39.1876	2.50200	7.91202	6.76	45.6976	2.60000	8.22192
6.27	39.3129	2.50400	7.91833	6.77	45.8329	2.60192	8.22800
6.28	39.4384	2.50599	7.92465	6.78	45.9684	2.60384	8.23408
6.29	39.5641	2.50799	7.93095	6.79	46.1041	2.60576	8.24015
6.30	39.6900	2.50998	7.93725	**6.80**	46.2400	2.60768	8.24621
6.31	39.8161	2.51197	7.94355	6.81	46.3761	2.60960	8.25227
6.32	39.9424	2.51396	7.94984	6.82	46.5124	2.61151	8.25833
6.33	40.0689	2.51595	7.95613	6.83	46.6489	2.61343	8.26438
6.34	40.1956	2.51794	7.96241	6.84	46.7856	2.61534	8.27043
6.35	40.3225	2.51992	7.96869	6.85	46.9225	2.61725	8.27647
6.36	40.4496	2.52190	7.97496	6.86	47.0596	2.61916	8.28251
6.37	40.5769	2.52389	7.98123	6.87	47.1969	2.62107	8.28855
6.38	40.7044	2.52587	7.98749	6.88	47.3344	2.62298	8.29458
6.39	40.8321	2.52784	7.99375	6.89	47.4721	2.62488	8.30060
6.40	40.9600	2.52982	8.00000	**6.90**	47.6100	2.62679	8.30662
6.41	41.0881	5.53180	8.00625	6.91	47.7481	2.62869	8.31264
6.42	41.2164	2.53377	8.01249	6.92	47.8864	2.63059	8.31865
6.43	41.3449	2.53574	8.01873	6.93	48.0249	2.63249	8.32466
6.44	41.4736	2.53772	8.02496	6.94	48.1636	2.63439	8.33067
6.45	41.6025	2.53969	8.03119	6.95	48.3025	2.63629	8.33667
6.46	41.7316	2.54165	8.03741	6.96	48.4416	2.63818	8.34266
6.47	41.8609	2.54362	8.04363	6.97	48.5809	2.64008	8.34865
6.48	41.9904	2.54558	8.04984	6.98	48.7204	2.64197	8.35464
6.49	42.1201	2.54755	8.05605	6.99	48.8601	2.64386	8.36062
6.50	42.2500	2.54951	8.06226	**7.00**	49.0000	2.64575	8.36660
N	N²	√N̄	√10N̄	N	N²	√N̄	√10N̄

N	N²	√N	√10N		N	N²	√N	√10N
7.00	49.0000	2.64575	8.36660		**7.50**	56.2500	2.73861	8.66025
7.01	49.1401	2.64764	8.37257		7.51	56.4001	2.74044	8.66603
7.02	49.2804	2.64953	8.37854		7.52	56.5504	2.74226	8.67179
7.03	49.4209	2.65141	8.38451		7.53	56.7009	2.74408	8.67756
7.04	49.5616	2.65330	8.39047		7.54	56.8516	2.74591	8.68332
7.05	49.7025	2.65518	8.39643		7.55	57.0025	2.74773	8.68907
7.06	49.8436	2.65707	8.40238		7.56	57.1536	2.74955	8.69483
7.07	49.9849	2.65895	8.40833		7.57	57.3049	2.75136	8.70057
7.08	50.1264	2.66083	8.41427		7.58	57.4564	2.75318	8.70632
7.09	50.2681	2.66271	8.42021		7.59	57.6081	2.75500	8.71206
7.10	50.4100	2.66458	8.42615		**7.60**	57.7600	2.75681	8.71780
7.11	50.5521	2.66646	8.43208		7.61	57.9121	2.75862	8.72353
7.12	50.6944	2.66833	8.43801		7.62	58.0644	2.76043	8.72926
7.13	50.8369	2.67021	8.44393		7.63	58.2169	2.76225	8.73499
7.14	50.9796	2.67208	8.44985		7.64	58.3696	2.76405	8.74071
7.15	51.1225	2.67395	8.45577		7.65	58.5225	2.76586	8.74643
7.16	51.2656	2.67582	8.46168		7.66	58.6756	2.76767	8.75214
7.17	51.4089	2.67769	8.46759		7.67	58.8289	2.76948	8.75785
7.18	51.5524	2.67955	8.47349		7.68	58.9824	2.77128	8.76356
7.19	51.6961	2.68142	8.47939		7.69	59.1361	2.77308	8.76926
7.20	51.8400	2.68328	8.48528		**7.70**	59.2900	2.77489	8.77496
7.21	51.9841	2.68514	8.49117		7.71	59.4441	2.77669	8.78066
7.22	52.1284	2.68701	8.49706		7.72	59.5984	2.77849	8.78635
7.23	52.2729	2.68887	8.50294		7.73	59.7529	2.78029	8.79204
7.24	52.4176	2.69072	8.50882		7.74	59.9076	2.78209	8.79773
7.25	52.5625	2.69258	8.51469		7.75	60.0625	2.78388	8.80341
7.26	52.7076	2.69444	8.52056		7.76	60.2176	2.78568	8.80909
7.27	52.8529	2.69629	8.52643		7.77	60.3729	2.78747	8.81476
7.28	52.9984	2.69815	8.53229		7.78	60.5284	2.78927	8.82043
7.29	53.1441	2.70000	8.53815		7.79	60.6841	2.79106	8.82610
7.30	53.2900	2.70185	8.54400		**7.80**	60.8400	2.79285	8.83176
7.31	53.4361	2.70370	8.54985		7.81	60.9961	2.79464	8.83742
7.32	53.5824	2.70555	8.55570		7.82	61.1524	2.79643	8.84308
7.33	53.7289	2.70740	8.56154		7.83	61.3089	2.79821	8.84873
7.34	53.8756	2.70924	8.56738		7.84	61.4656	2.80000	8.85438
7.35	54.0225	2.71109	8.57321		7.85	61.6225	2.80179	8.86002
7.36	54.1696	2.71293	8.57904		7.86	61.7796	2.80357	8.86566
7.37	54.3169	2.71477	8.58487		7.87	61.9369	2.80535	8.87130
7.38	54.4644	2.71662	8.59069		7.88	62.0944	2.80713	8.87694
7.39	54.6121	2.71846	8.59651		7.89	62.2521	2.80891	8.88257
7.40	54.7600	2.72029	8.60233		**7.90**	62.4100	2.81069	8.88819
7.41	54.9081	2.72213	8.60814		7.91	62.5681	2.81247	8.89382
7.42	55.0564	2.72397	8.61394		7.92	62.7264	2.81425	8.89944
7.43	55.2049	2.72580	8.61974		7.93	62.8849	2.81603	8.90505
7.44	55.3536	2.72764	8.62554		7.94	63.0436	2.81780	8.91067
7.45	55.5025	2.72947	8.63134		7.95	63.2025	2.81957	8.91628
7.46	55.6516	2.73130	8.63713		7.96	63.3616	2.82135	8.92188
7.47	55.8009	2.73313	8.64292		7.97	63.5209	2.82312	8.92749
7.48	55.9504	2.73496	8.64870		7.98	63.6804	2.82489	8.93308
7.49	56.1001	2.73679	8.65448		7.99	63.8401	2.82666	8.93868
7.50	56.2500	2.73861	8.66025		**8.00**	64.0000	2.82843	8.94427
N	N²	√N	√10N		N	N²	√N	√10N

Table Ia (Continued)

N	N²	√N̄	√10N̄		N	N²	√N̄	√10N̄
8.00	64.0000	2.82843	8.94427		**8.50**	72.2500	2.91548	9.21954
8.01	64.1601	2.83019	8.94986		8.51	72.4201	2.91719	9.22497
8.02	64.3204	2.83196	8.95545		8.52	72.5904	2.91890	9.23038
8.03	64.4809	2.83373	8.96103		8.53	72.7609	2.92062	9.23580
8.04	64.6416	2.83549	8.96660		8.54	72.9316	2.92233	9.24121
8.05	64.8025	2.83725	8.97218		8.55	73.1025	2.92404	9.24662
8.06	64.9636	2.83901	8.97775		8.56	73.2736	2.92575	9.25203
8.07	65.1249	2.84077	8.98332		8.57	73.4449	2.92746	9.25743
8.08	65.2864	2.84253	8.98888		8.58	73.6164	2.92916	9.26283
8.09	65.4481	2.84429	8.99444		8.59	73.7881	2.93087	9.26823
8.10	65.6100	2.84605	9.00000		**8.60**	73.9600	2.93258	9.27362
8.11	65.7721	2.84781	9.00555		8.61	74.1321	2.93428	9.27901
8.12	65.9344	2.84956	9.01110		8.62	74.3044	2.93598	9.28440
8.13	66.0969	2.85132	9.01665		8.63	74.4769	2.93769	9.28978
8.14	66.2596	2.85307	9.02219		8.64	74.6496	2.93939	9.29516
8.15	66.4225	2.85482	9.02774		8.65	74.8225	2.94109	9.30054
8.16	66.5856	2.85657	9.03327		8.66	74.9956	2.94279	9.30591
8.17	66.7489	2.85832	9.03881		8.67	75.1689	2.94449	9.31128
8.18	66.9124	2.86007	9.04434		8.68	75.3424	2.94618	9.31665
8.19	67.0761	2.86182	9.04986		8.69	75.5161	2.94788	9.32202
8.20	67.2400	2.86356	9.05539		**8.70**	75.6900	2.94958	9.32738
8.21	67.4041	2.86531	9.06091		8.71	75.8641	2.95127	9.33274
8.22	67.5684	2.86705	9.06642		8.72	76.0384	2.95296	9.33809
8.23	67.7329	2.86880	9.07193		8.73	76.2129	2.95466	9.34345
8.24	67.8976	2.87054	9.07744		8.74	76.3876	2.95635	9.34880
8.25	68.0625	2.87228	9.08295		8.75	76.5625	2.95804	9.35414
8.26	68.2276	2.87402	9.08845		8.76	76.7376	2.95973	9.35949
8.27	68.3929	2.87576	9.09395		8.77	76.9129	2.96142	9.36488
8.28	68.5584	2.87750	9.09945		8.87	77.0884	2.96311	9.37017
8.29	68.7241	2.87924	9.10494		8.79	77.2641	2.96479	9.37550
8.30	68.8900	2.88097	9.11043		**8.80**	77.4400	2.96648	9.38083
8.31	69.0561	2.88271	9.11592		8.81	77.6161	2.96816	9.38616
8.32	69.2224	2.88444	9.12140		8.82	77.7924	2.96985	9.39149
8.33	69.3889	2.88617	9.12688		8.83	77.9689	2.97153	9.39681
8.34	69.5556	2.88791	9.13236		8.84	78.1456	2.97321	9.40213
8.35	69.7225	2.88964	9.13783		8.85	78.3225	2.97489	9.40744
8.36	69.8896	2.89137	9.14330		8.86	78.4996	2.97658	9.41276
8.37	70.0569	2.89310	9.14877		8.87	78.6769	2.97825	9.41807
8.38	70.2244	2.89482	9.15423		8.88	78.8544	2.97993	9.42338
8.39	70.3921	2.89655	9.15969		8.89	79.0321	2.98161	9.42868
8.40	70.5600	2.89828	9.16515		**8.90**	79.2100	2.98329	9.43398
8.41	70.7281	2.90000	9.17061		8.91	79.3881	2.98496	9.43928
8.42	70.8964	2.90172	9.17606		8.92	79.5664	2.98664	9.44458
8.43	71.0649	2.90345	9.18150		8.93	79.7449	2.98831	9.44987
8.44	71.2336	2.90517	9.18695		8.94	79.9236	2.98998	9.45516
8.45	71.4025	2.90689	9.19239		8.95	80.1025	2.99166	9.46044
8.46	71.5716	2.90861	9.19783		8.96	80.2816	2.99333	9.46573
8.47	71.7409	2.91033	9.20326		8.97	80.4609	2.99500	9.47101
8.48	71.9104	2.91204	9.20869		8.98	80.6404	2.99666	9.47629
8.49	72.0801	2.91376	9.21412		8.99	80.8201	2.99833	9.48156
8.50	72.2500	2.91548	9.21954		**9.00**	81.0000	3.00000	9.48683
N	N²	√N̄	√10N̄		N	N²	√N̄	√10N̄

N	N²	√N	√10N	N	N²	√N	√10N
9.00	81.0000	3.00000	9.48683	**9.50**	90.2500	3.08221	9.74679
9.01	81.1801	3.00167	9.49210	9.51	90.4401	3.08383	9.75192
9.02	81.3604	3.00333	9.49737	9.52	90.6304	3.08545	9.75705
9.03	81.5409	3.00500	9.50263	9.53	90.8209	3.08707	9.76217
9.04	81.7216	3.00666	9.50789	9.54	91.0116	3.08869	9.76729
9.05	81.9025	3.00832	9.51315	9.55	91.2025	3.09031	9.77241
9.06	82.0836	3.00998	9.51840	9.56	91.3956	3.09192	9.77753
9.07	82.2649	3.01164	9.52365	9.57	91.5849	3.09354	9.78264
9.08	82.4464	3.01330	9.52890	9.58	91.7764	3.09516	9.78775
9.09	82.6281	3.01496	9.53415	9.59	91.9681	3.09677	9.79785
9.10	82.8100	3.01662	9.53939	**9.60**	92.1600	3.09839	9.79796
9.11	82.9921	3.01828	9.54463	9.61	92.3521	3.10000	9.80306
9.12	83.1744	3.01993	9.54987	9.62	92.5444	3.10161	9.80816
9.13	83.3569	3.02159	9.55510	9.63	92.7369	3.10322	9.81326
9.14	83.5396	3.02324	9.56033	9.64	92.9296	3.10483	9.81835
9.15	83.7225	3.02490	9.56556	9.65	93.1225	3.10644	9.82344
9.16	83.9056	3.02655	9.57079	9.66	93.3156	3.10805	9.82853
9.17	84.0889	3.02820	9.57601	9.67	93.5089	3.10966	9.83362
9.18	84.2724	3.02985	9.58125	9.68	93.7024	3.11127	9.83870
9.19	84.4561	3.03150	9.58645	9.69	93.8961	3.11288	9.84378
9.20	84.6400	3.03315	9.59166	**9.70**	94.0900	3.11448	9.84886
9.21	84.8241	3.03480	9.59687	9.71	94.2841	3.11609	9.85393
9.22	85.0084	3.03645	9.60208	9.72	94.4784	3.11769	9.85901
9.23	85.1929	3.03809	9.60729	9.73	94.6729	3.11929	9.86408
9.24	85.3776	3.03974	9.61249	9.74	94.8676	3.12090	9.86914
9.25	85.5625	3.04138	9.61769	9.75	95.0625	3.12250	9.87421
9.26	85.7476	3.04302	9.62289	9.76	95.2576	3.12410	9.87927
9.27	85.9329	3.04467	9.62808	9.77	95.4529	3.12570	9.88433
9.28	86.1184	3.04631	9.63328	9.78	95.6484	3.12730	9.88939
9.29	86.3041	3.04795	9.63846	9.79	95.8441	3.12890	9.89444
9.30	86.4900	3.04959	9.64365	**9.80**	96.0400	3.13050	9.89949
9.31	86.6761	3.05123	9.64883	9.81	96.2361	3.13209	9.90454
9.32	86.8624	3.05287	9.65401	9.82	96.4324	3.13369	9.90959
9.33	87.0489	3.05450	9.65919	9.83	96.6289	3.13528	9.91464
9.34	87.2356	3.05614	9.66437	9.84	96.8256	3.13688	9.91968
9.35	87.4225	3.05778	9.66954	9.85	97.0225	3.13847	9.92472
9.36	87.6096	3.05941	9.67471	9.86	97.2196	3.14006	9.92975
9.37	87.7969	3.06105	9.67988	9.87	97.4169	3.14166	9.93479
9.38	87.9844	3.06268	9.68504	9.88	97.6144	3.14325	9.93982
9.39	88.1721	3.06431	9.69020	9.89	97.8121	3.14484	9.94485
9.40	88.3600	3.06594	9.69536	**9.90**	98.0100	3.14643	9.94987
9.41	88.5481	3.06757	9.70052	9.91	98.2081	3.14802	9.95490
9.42	88.7364	3.06920	9.70567	9.92	98.4064	3.14960	9.95992
9.43	88.9249	3.07083	9.71082	9.93	98.6049	3.15119	9.96494
9.44	89.1136	3.07246	9.71597	9.94	98.8036	3.15278	9.96995
9.45	89.3025	3.07409	9.72111	9.95	99.0025	3.15436	9.97497
9.46	89.4916	3.07571	9.72625	9.96	99.2016	3.15595	9.97998
9.47	89.6809	3.07734	9.73139	9.97	99.4009	3.15753	9.98499
9.48	89.8704	3.07896	9.73653	9.98	99.6004	3.15911	9.98999
9.49	90.0601	3.08058	9.74166	9.99	99.8001	3.16070	9.99500
9.50	90.2500	3.08221	9.74679	**10.00**	100.000	3.16228	10.0000
N	N²	√N	√10N	N	N²	√N	√10N

Table Ib   Common Logarithms[a], Log N
(To obtain natural logarithms, multiply by 2.30)

$\overrightarrow{\downarrow N}$	.00	.01	.02	.03	.04	.05	.06	.07	.08	.09
1.0	.0000	.0043	.0086	.0128	.0170	.0212	.0253	.0294	.0334	.0374
1.1	.0414	.0453	.0492	.0531	.0569	.0607	.0645	.0682	.0719	.0755
1.2	.0792	.0828	.0864	.0899	.0934	.0969	.1004	.1038	.1072	.1106
1.3	.1139	.1173	.1206	.1239	.1271	.1303	.1335	.1367	.1399	.1430
1.4	.1461	.1492	.1523	.1553	.1584	.1614	.1644	.1673	.1703	.1732
1.5	.1761	.1790	.1818	.1847	.1875	.1903	.1931	.1959	.1987	.2014
1.6	.2041	.2068	.2095	.2122	.2148	.2175	.2201	.2227	.2253	.2279
1.7	.2304	.2330	.2355	.2380	.2405	.2430	.2455	.2480	.2504	.2529
1.8	.2553	.2577	.2601	.2625	.2648	.2672	.2695	.2718	.2742	.2765
1.9	.2788	.2810	.2833	.2856	.2878	.2900	.2923	.2945	.2967	.2989
2.0	.3010	.3032	.3054	.3075	.3096	.3118	.3139	.3160	.3181	.3201
2.1	.3222	.3243	.3263	.3284	.3304	.3324	.3345	.3365	.3385	.3404
2.2	.3424	.3444	.3464	.3483	.3502	.3522	.3541	.3560	.3579	.3598
2.3	.3617	.3636	.3655	.3674	.3692	.3711	.3729	.3747	.3766	.3784
2.4	.3802	.3820	.3838	.3856	.3874	.3892	.3909	.3927	.3945	.3962
2.5	.3979	.3997	.4014	.4031	.4048	.4065	.4082	.4099	.4116	.4133
2.6	.4150	.4166	.4183	.4200	.4216	.4232	.4249	.4265	.4281	.4298
2.7	.4314	.4330	.4346	.4362	.4378	.4393	.4409	.4425	.4440	.4456
2.8	.4472	.4487	.4502	.4518	.4533	.4548	.4564	.4579	.4594	.4609
2.9	.4624	.4639	.4654	.4669	.4683	.4698	.4713	.4728	.4742	.4757
3.0	.4771	.4786	.4800	.4814	.4829	.4843	.4857	.4871	.4886	.4900
3.1	.4914	.4928	.4942	.4955	.4969	.4983	.4997	.5011	.5024	.5038
3.2	.5051	.5065	.5079	.5092	.5105	.5119	.5132	.5145	.5159	.5172
3.3	.5185	.5198	.5211	.5224	.5237	.5250	.5263	.5276	.5289	.5302
3.4	.5315	.5328	.5340	.5353	.5366	.5378	.5391	.5403	.5416	.5428
3.5	.5441	.5453	.5465	.5478	.5490	.5502	.5514	.5527	.5539	.5551
3.6	.5563	.5575	.5587	.5599	.5611	.5623	.5635	.5647	.5658	.5670
3.7	.5682	.5694	.5705	.5717	.5729	.5740	.5752	.5763	.5775	.5786
3.8	.5798	.5809	.5821	.5832	.5843	.5855	.5866	.5877	.5888	.5899
3.9	.5911	.5922	.5933	.5944	.5955	.5966	.5977	.5988	.5999	.6010
4.0	.6021	.6031	.6042	.6053	.6064	.6075	.6085	.6096	.6107	.6117
4.1	.6128	.6138	.6149	.6160	.6170	.6180	.6191	.6201	.6212	.6222
4.2	.6232	.6243	.6253	.6263	.6274	.6284	.6294	.6304	.6314	.6325
4.3	.6335	.6345	.6355	.6365	.6375	.6385	.6395	.6405	.6415	.6425
4.4	.6435	.6444	.6454	.6464	.6474	.6484	.6493	.6503	.6513	.6522
4.5	.6532	.6542	.6551	.6561	.6571	.6580	.6590	.6599	.6609	.6618
4.6	.6628	.6637	.6646	.6656	.6665	.6675	.6684	.6693	.6702	.6712
4.7	.6721	.6730	.6739	.6749	.6758	.6767	.6776	.6785	.6794	.6803
4.8	.6812	.6821	.6830	.6839	.6848	.6857	.6866	.6875	.6884	.6893
4.9	.6902	.6911	.6920	.6928	.6937	.6946	.6955	.6964	.6972	.6981

Second Decimal Place of N is the heading spanning the .00 through .09 columns.

[a]To find the log of a number outside the range 1 to 10, just shift its decimal place till it falls within the range 1 to 10, then look up the logarithm, and add 1 for each place you shifted the decimal point left. For example, log 2310 = log 2.310 + 3 = .3636 + 3 = 3.3636. Similarly log 0.0231 = log 2.31 − 2 = .3636 − 2 = −1.6364.

Table Ib   (Continued)

↓$\vec{N}$	.00	.01	.02	.03	.04	.05	.06	.07	.08	.09
5.0	.6990	.6998	.7007	.7016	.7024	.7033	.7042	.7050	.7059	.7067
5.1	.7076	.7084	.7093	.7101	.7110	.7118	.7126	.7135	.7143	.7152
5.2	.7160	.7168	.7177	.7185	.7193	.7202	.7210	.7218	.7226	.7235
5.3	.7243	.7251	.7259	.7267	.7275	.7284	.7292	.7300	.7308	.7316
5.4	.7324	.7332	.7340	.7348	.7356	.7364	.7372	.7380	.7388	.7396
5.5	.7404	.7412	.7419	.7427	.7435	.7443	.7451	.7459	.7466	.7474
5.6	.7482	.7490	.7497	.7505	.7513	.7520	.7528	.7536	.7543	.7551
5.7	.7559	.7566	.7574	.7582	.7589	.7597	.7604	.7612	.7619	.7627
5.8	.7634	.7642	.7649	.7657	.7664	.7672	.7679	.7686	.7694	.7701
5.9	.7709	.7716	.7723	.7731	.7738	.7745	.7752	.7760	.7767	.7774
6.0	.7782	.7789	.7796	.7803	.7810	.7818	.7825	.7832	.7839	.7846
6.1	.7853	.7860	.7868	.7875	.7882	.7889	.7896	.7903	.7910	.7917
6.2	.7924	.7931	.7938	.7945	.7952	.7959	.7966	.7973	.7980	.7987
6.3	.7993	.8000	.8007	.8014	.8021	.8028	.8035	.8041	.8048	.8055
6.4	.8062	.8069	.8075	.8082	.8089	.8096	.8102	.8109	.8116	.8122
6.5	.8129	.8136	.8142	.8149	.8156	.8162	.8169	.8176	.8182	.8189
6.6	.8195	.8202	.8209	.8215	.8222	.8228	.8235	.8241	.8248	.8254
6.7	.8261	.8267	.8274	.8280	.8287	.8293	.8299	.8306	.8312	.8319
6.8	.8325	.8331	.8338	.8344	.8351	.8357	.8363	.8370	.8376	.8382
6.9	.8388	.8395	.8401	.8407	.8414	.8420	.8426	.8432	.8439	.8445
7.0	.8451	.8457	.8463	.8470	.8476	.8482	.8488	.8494	.8500	.8506
7.1	.8513	.8519	.8525	.8531	.8537	.8543	.8549	.8555	.8561	.8567
7.2	.8573	.8579	.8585	.8591	.8597	.8603	.8609	.8615	.8621	.8627
7.3	.8633	.8639	.8645	.8651	.8657	.8663	.8669	.8675	.8681	.8686
7.4	.8692	.8698	.8704	.8710	.8716	.8722	.8727	.8733	.8739	.8745
7.5	.8751	.8756	.8762	.8768	.8774	.8779	.8785	.8791	.8797	.8802
7.6	.8808	.8814	.8820	.8825	.8831	.8837	.8842	.8848	.8854	.8859
7.7	.8865	.8871	.8876	.8882	.8887	.8893	.8899	.8904	.8910	.8915
7.8	.8921	.8927	.8932	.8938	.8943	.8949	.8954	.8960	.8965	.9971
7.9	.8976	.8982	.8987	.8993	.8998	.9004	.9009	.9015	.9020	.9025
8.0	.9031	.9036	.9042	.9047	.9053	.9058	.9063	.9069	.9074	.9079
8.1	.9085	.9090	.9096	.9101	.9106	.9112	.9117	.9122	.9128	.9133
8.2	.9138	.9143	.9149	.9154	.9159	.9165	.9170	.9175	.9180	.9186
8.3	.9191	.9196	.9201	.9206	.9212	.9217	.9222	.9227	.9232	.9238
8.4	.9243	.9248	.9253	.9258	.9263	.9269	.9274	.9279	.9284	.9289
8.5	.9294	.9299	.9304	.9309	.9315	.9320	.9325	.9330	.9335	.9340
8.6	.9345	.9350	.9355	.9360	.9365	.9370	.9375	.9380	.9385	.9390
8.7	.9395	.9400	.9405	.9410	.9415	.9420	.9425	.9430	.9435	.9440
8.8	.9445	.9450	.9455	.9460	.9465	.9469	.9474	.9479	.9484	.9489
8.9	.9494	.9499	.9504	.9509	.9513	.9518	.9523	.9528	.9533	.9538
9.0	.9542	.9547	.9552	.9557	.9562	.9566	.9571	.9576	.9581	.9586
9.1	.9590	.9595	.9600	.9605	.9609	.9614	.9619	.9624	.9628	.9633
9.2	.9638	.9643	.9647	.9652	.9657	.9661	.9666	.9671	.9675	.9680
8.3	.9685	.9689	.9694	.9699	.9703	.9708	.9713	.9717	.9722	.9727
9.4	.9731	.9736	.9741	.9745	.9750	.9754	.9759	.9763	.9768	.9773
9.5	.9777	.9782	.9786	.9791	.9795	.9800	.9805	.9809	.9814	.9818
9.6	.9823	.9827	.9832	.9836	.9841	.9845	.9850	.9854	.9859	.9863
9.7	.9868	.9872	.9877	.9881	.9886	.9890	.9894	.9899	.9903	.9908
9.8	.9912	.9917	.9921	.9926	.9930	.9934	.9939	.9943	.9948	.9952
9.9	.9956	.9961	.9965	.9969	.9974	.9978	.9983	.9987	.9991	.9996

Table IIa   Random Digits (blocked merely for convenience)

39 65 76 45 45	19 90 69 64 61	20 26 36 31 62	58 24 97 14 97	95 06 70 99 00
73 71 23 70 90	65 97 60 12 11	31 56 34 19 19	47 83 75 51 33	30 62 38 20 46
72 20 47 33 84	51 67 47 97 19	98 40 07 17 66	23 05 09 51 80	59 78 11 52 49
75 17 25 69 17	17 95 21 78 58	24 33 45 77 48	69 81 84 09 29	93 22 70 45 80
37 48 79 88 74	63 52 06 34 30	01 31 60 10 27	35 07 79 71 53	28 99 52 01 41
02 89 08 16 94	85 53 83 29 95	56 27 09 24 43	21 78 55 09 82	72 61 88 73 61
87 18 15 70 07	37 79 49 12 38	48 13 93 55 96	41 92 45 71 51	09 18 25 58 94
98 83 71 70 15	89 09 39 59 24	00 06 41 41 20	14 36 59 25 47	54 45 17 24 89
10 08 58 07 04	76 62 16 48 68	58 76 17 14 86	59 53 11 52 21	66 04 18 72 87
47 90 56 37 31	71 82 13 50 41	27 55 10 24 92	28 04 67 53 44	95 23 00 84 47
93 05 31 03 07	34 18 04 52 35	74 13 39 35 22	68 95 23 92 35	36 63 70 35 33
21 89 11 47 99	11 20 99 45 18	76 51 94 84 86	13 79 93 37 55	98 16 04 41 67
95 18 94 06 97	27 37 83 28 71	79 57 95 13 91	09 61 87 25 21	56 20 11 32 44
97 08 31 55 73	10 65 81 92 59	77 31 61 95 46	20 44 90 32 64	26 99 76 75 63
69 26 88 86 13	59 71 74 17 32	48 38 75 93 29	73 37 32 04 05	60 82 29 20 25
41 47 10 25 03	87 63 93 95 17	81 83 83 04 49	77 45 85 50 51	79 88 01 97 30
91 94 14 63 62	08 61 74 51 69	92 79 43 89 79	29 18 94 51 23	14 85 11 47 23
80 06 54 18 47	08 52 85 08 40	48 40 35 94 22	72 65 71 08 86	50 03 42 99 36
67 72 77 63 99	89 85 84 46 06	64 71 06 21 66	89 37 20 70 01	61 65 70 22 12
59 40 24 13 75	42 29 72 23 19	06 94 76 10 08	81 30 15 39 14	81 83 17 16 33
63 62 06 34 41	79 53 36 02 95	94 61 09 43 62	20 21 14 68 86	94 95 48 46 45
78 47 23 53 90	79 93 96 38 63	34 85 52 05 09	85 43 01 72 73	14 93 87 81 40
87 68 62 15 43	97 48 72 66 48	53 16 71 13 81	59 97 50 99 52	24 62 20 42 31
47 60 92 10 77	26 97 05 73 51	88 46 38 03 58	72 68 49 29 31	75 70 16 08 24
56 88 87 59 41	06 87 37 78 48	65 88 69 58 39	88 02 84 27 83	85 81 56 39 38
22 17 68 65 84	87 02 22 57 51	68 69 80 95 44	11 29 01 95 80	49 34 35 86 47
19 36 27 59 46	39 77 32 77 09	79 57 92 36 59	89 74 39 82 15	08 58 94 34 74
16 77 23 02 77	28 06 24 25 93	22 45 44 84 11	87 80 61 65 31	09 71 91 74 25
78 43 76 71 61	97 67 63 99 61	80 45 67 93 82	59 73 19 85 23	53 33 65 97 21
03 28 28 26 08	69 30 16 09 05	53 58 47 70 93	66 56 45 65 79	45 56 20 19 47
04 31 17 21 56	33 73 99 19 87	26 72 39 27 67	53 77 57 68 93	60 61 97 22 61
61 06 98 03 91	87 14 77 43 96	43 00 65 98 50	45 60 33 01 07	98 99 46 50 47
23 68 35 26 00	99 53 93 61 28	52 70 05 48 34	56 65 05 61 86	90 92 10 70 80
15 39 25 70 99	93 86 52 77 65	15 33 59 05 28	22 87 26 07 47	86 96 98 29 06
58 71 96 30 24	18 46 23 34 27	85 13 99 24 44	49 18 09 79 49	74 16 32 23 02
93 22 53 64 39	07 10 63 76 35	87 03 04 79 88	08 13 13 85 51	55 34 57 72 69
78 76 58 54 74	92 38 70 96 92	52 06 79 79 45	82 63 18 27 44	69 66 92 19 09
61 81 31 96 82	00 57 25 60 59	46 72 60 18 77	55 66 12 62 11	08 99 55 64 57
42 88 07 10 05	24 98 65 63 21	47 21 61 88 32	27 80 30 21 60	10 92 35 36 12
77 94 30 05 39	28 10 99 00 27	12 73 73 99 12	49 99 57 94 82	96 88 57 17 91

Table IIb Random Normal Numbers, $\mu = 0, \sigma = 1$

.464	.137	2.455	−.323	−.068	.296	−.288	1.298	.241	−.957
.060	−2.526	−.531	−.194	.543	−1.558	.187	−1.190	.022	.525
1.486	−.354	−.634	.697	.926	1.375	.785	−.963	−.853	−1.865
1.022	−.472	1.279	3.521	.571	−1.851	.194	1.192	−.501	−.273
1.394	−.555	.046	.321	2.945	1.974	−.258	.412	.439	−.035
.906	−.513	−.525	.595	.881	−.934	1.579	.161	−1.885	.371
1.179	−1.055	.007	.769	.971	.712	1.090	−.631	−.255	−.702
−1.501	−.488	−.162	−.136	1.033	.203	.448	.748	−.423	−.432
−.690	.756	−1.618	−.345	−.511	−2.051	−.457	−.218	.857	−.465
1.372	.225	.378	.761	.181	−.736	.960	−1.530	−.260	.120
−.482	1.678	−.057	−1.229	−.486	.856	−.491	−1.983	−2.830	−.238
−1.376	−.150	1.356	−.561	−.256	−.212	.219	.779	.953	−.869
−1.010	.598	−.918	1.598	.065	.415	−.169	.313	−.973	−1.016
−.005	−.899	.012	−.725	1.147	−.121	1.096	.481	−1.691	.417
1.393	−1.163	−.911	1.231	−.199	−.246	1.239	−2.574	−.558	.056
−1.787	−.261	1.237	1.046	−.508	−1.630	−.146	−.392	−.627	.561
−.105	−.375	−1.384	.360	−.992	−.116	−1.698	−2.832	−1.108	−2.357
−1.339	1.827	−.959	.424	.969	−1.141	−1.041	.362	−1.726	1.956
1.041	.535	.731	1.377	.983	−1.330	1.620	−1.040	.524	−.281
.279	−2.056	.717	−.873	−1.096	−1.396	1.047	.089	−.573	.932
−1.805	−2.008	−1.633	.542	.250	−.166	.032	.079	.471	−1.029
−1.186	1.180	1.114	.882	1.265	−.202	.151	−.376	−.310	.479
.658	−1.141	1.151	−1.210	−.927	.425	.290	−.902	.610	1.709
−.439	.358	−1.939	.891	−.227	.602	.873	−.437	−.220	−.057
−1.399	−.230	.385	−.649	−.577	.237	−.289	.513	.738	−.300
.199	.208	−1.083	−.219	−.291	1.221	1.119	.004	−2.015	−.594
.159	.272	−.313	.084	−2.828	−.439	−.792	−1.275	−.623	−1.047
2.273	.606	.606	−.747	.247	1.291	.063	−1.793	−.699	−1.347
.041	−.307	.121	.790	−.584	.541	.484	−.986	.481	.996
−1.132	−2.098	.921	.145	.446	−1.661	1.045	−1.363	−.586	−1.023
.768	.079	−1.473	.034	−2.127	.665	.084	−.880	−.579	.551
.375	−1.658	−.851	.234	−.656	.340	−.086	−.158	−.120	.418
−.513	−.344	.210	−.736	1.041	.008	.427	−.831	.191	.074
.292	−.521	1.266	−1.206	−.899	.110	−.528	−.813	.071	.524
1.026	2.990	−.574	−.491	−1.114	1.297	−1.433	−1.345	−3.001	.479
−1.334	1.278	−.568	−.109	−.515	−.566	2.923	.500	.359	.326
−.287	−.144	−.254	.574	−.451	−1.181	−1.190	−.318	−.094	1.114
.161	−.886	−.921	−.509	1.410	−.518	.192	−.432	1.501	1.068
−1.346	.193	−1.202	.394	−1.045	.843	.942	1.045	.031	.772
−1.250	−.199	−.288	1.810	1.378	.584	1.216	.733	.402	.226
.630	−.537	.782	.060	.499	−.431	1.705	1.164	.884	−.298
.375	−1.941	.247	−.491	.665	−.135	−.145	−.498	.457	1.064
−1.420	.489	−1.711	−1.186	.754	−.732	−.066	1.006	−.798	.162
−.151	−.243	−.430	−.762	.298	1.049	1.810	2.885	−.768	−.129
−.309	.531	.416	−1.541	1.456	2.040	−.124	.196	.023	−1.204
.424	−.444	.593	.993	−.106	.116	.484	−1.272	1.066	1.097
.593	.658	−1.127	−1.407	−1.579	−1.616	1.458	1.262	.736	−.916
.862	−.885	−.142	−.504	.532	1.381	.022	−.281	−.342	1.222
.235	−.628	−.023	−.463	−.899	−.394	−.538	1.707	−.188	−1.153
−.853	.402	.777	.833	.410	−.349	−1.094	.580	1.395	1.298

Table IIIa Binomial Coefficients

n	$\binom{n}{0}$	$\binom{n}{1}$	$\binom{n}{2}$	$\binom{n}{3}$	$\binom{n}{4}$	$\binom{n}{5}$	$\binom{n}{6}$	$\binom{n}{7}$	$\binom{n}{8}$	$\binom{n}{9}$	$\binom{n}{10}$
0	1										
1	1	1									
2	1	2	1								
3	1	3	3	1							
4	1	4	6	4	1						
5	1	5	10	10	5	1					
6	1	6	15	20	15	6	1				
7	1	7	21	35	35	21	7	1			
8	1	8	28	56	70	56	28	8	1		
9	1	9	36	84	126	126	84	36	9	1	
10	1	10	45	120	210	252	210	120	45	10	1
11	1	11	55	165	330	462	462	330	165	55	11
12	1	12	66	220	495	792	924	792	495	220	66
13	1	13	78	286	715	1287	1716	1716	1287	715	286
14	1	14	91	364	1001	2002	3003	3432	3003	2002	1001
15	1	15	105	455	1365	3003	5005	6435	6435	5005	3003
16	1	16	120	560	1820	4368	8008	11440	12870	11440	8008
17	1	17	136	680	2380	6188	12376	19448	24310	24310	19448
18	1	18	153	816	3060	8568	18564	31824	43758	48620	43758
19	1	19	171	969	3876	11628	27132	50388	75582	92378	92378
20	1	20	190	1140	4845	15504	38760	77520	125970	167960	184756

Note. $\binom{n}{x} = \dfrac{n(n-1)(n-2) \cdots (n-x+1)}{x(x-1)(x-2) \cdots 3.2.1}$; $\binom{n}{0} = 1$; $\binom{n}{1} = n$.

For coefficients missing from the above table, use the relation

$$\binom{n}{x} = \binom{n}{n-x}, \quad \text{e.g.,} \quad \binom{20}{11} = \binom{20}{9} = 167960.$$

Table IIIb Individual Binomial Probabilities $p(x)$
(If $\pi > .50$, work in terms of the complementary event "failure" instead of "success.")

n	x	.05	.10	.15	.20	.25	$\pi(\rho)$ .30	.35	.40	.45	.50
1	0	.9500	.9000	.8500	.8000	.7500	.7000	.6500	.6000	.5500	.5000
	1	.0500	.1000	.1500	.2000	.2500	.3000	.3500	.4000	.4500	.5000
2	0	.9025	.8100	.7225	.6400	.5625	.4900	.4225	.3600	.3025	.2500
	1	.0950	.1800	.2550	.3200	.3750	.4200	.4550	.4800	.4950	.5000
	2	.0025	.0100	.0225	.0400	.0625	.0900	.1225	.1600	.2025	.2500
3	0	.8574	.7290	.6141	.5120	.4219	.3430	.2746	.2160	.1664	.1250
	1	.1354	.2430	.3251	.3840	.4219	.4410	.4436	.4320	.4084	.3750
	2	.0071	.0270	.0574	.0960	.1406	.1890	.2389	.2880	.3341	.3750
	3	.0001	.0010	.0034	.0080	.0156	.0270	.0429	.0640	.0911	.1250
4	0	.8145	.6561	.5220	.4096	.3164	.2401	.1785	.1296	.0915	.0625
	1	.1715	.2916	.3685	.4096	.4219	.4116	.3845	.3456	.2995	.2500
	2	.0135	.0486	.0975	.1536	.2109	.2646	.3105	.3456	.3675	.3750
	3	.0005	.0036	.0115	.0256	.0469	.0756	.1115	.1536	.2005	.2500
	4	.0000	.0001	.0005	.0016	.0039	.0081	.0150	.0256	.0410	.0625
5	0	.7738	.5905	.4437	.3277	.2373	.1681	.1160	.0778	.0503	.0312
	1	.2036	.3280	.3915	.4096	.3955	.3602	.3124	.2592	.2059	.1562
	2	.0214	.0729	.1382	.2048	.2637	.3087	.3364	.3456	.3369	.3125
	3	.0011	.0081	.0244	.0512	.0879	.1323	.1811	.2304	.2757	.3125
	4	.0000	.0004	.0022	.0064	.0146	.0284	.0488	.0768	.1128	.1562
	5	.0000	.0000	.0001	.0003	.0010	.0024	.0053	.0102	.0185	.0312
6	0	.7351	.5314	.3771	.2621	.1780	.1176	.0754	.0467	.0277	.0156
	1	.2321	.3543	.3993	.3832	.3560	.3025	.2437	.1866	.1359	.0938
	2	.0305	.0984	.1762	.2458	.2966	.3241	.3280	.3110	.2780	.2344
	3	.0021	.0146	.0415	.0819	.1318	.1852	.2355	.2765	.3032	.3125
	4	.0001	.0012	.0055	.0154	.0330	.0595	.0951	.1382	.1861	.2344
	5	.0000	.0001	.0004	.0015	.0044	.0102	.0205	.0369	.0609	.0938
	6	.0000	.0000	.0000	.0001	.0002	.0007	.0018	.0041	.0083	.0156
7	0	.6983	.4783	.3206	.2097	.1335	.0824	.0490	.0280	.0152	.0078
	1	.2573	.3720	.3960	.3670	.3115	.2471	.1848	.1306	.0872	.0547
	2	.0406	.1240	.2097	.2753	.3115	.3177	.2985	.2613	.2140	.1641
	3	.0036	.0230	.0617	.1147	.1730	.2269	.2679	.2903	.2918	.2734
	4	.0002	.0026	.0109	.0287	.0577	.0972	.1442	.1935	.2388	.2734
	5	.0000	.0002	.0012	.0043	.0115	.0250	.0466	.0774	.1172	.1641
	6	.0000	.0000	.0001	.0004	.0013	.0036	.0084	.0172	.0320	.0547
	7	.0000	.0000	.0000	.0000	.0001	.0002	.0006	.0016	.0037	.0078

n	x	.05	.10	.15	.20	.25	π .30	.35	.40	.45	.50
8	0	.6634	.4305	.2725	.1678	.1001	.0576	.0319	.0168	.0084	.0039
	1	.2793	.3826	.3847	.3355	.2670	.1977	.1373	.0896	.0548	.0312
	2	.0515	.1488	.2376	.2936	.3115	.2965	.2587	.2090	.1569	.1094
	3	.0054	.0331	.0839	.1468	.2076	.2541	.2786	.2787	.2568	.2188
	4	.0004	.0046	.0185	.0459	.0865	.1361	.1875	.2322	.2627	.2734
	5	.0000	.0004	.0026	.0092	.0231	.0467	.0808	.1239	.1719	.2188
	6	.0000	.0000	.0002	.0011	.0038	.0100	.0217	.0413	.0703	.1094
	7	.0000	.0000	.0000	.0001	.0004	.0012	.0033	.0079	.0164	.0312
	8	.0000	.0000	.0000	.0000	.0000	.0001	.0002	.0007	.0017	.0039
9	0	.6302	.3874	.2316	.1342	.0751	.0404	.0207	.0101	.0046	.0020
	1	.2985	.3874	.3679	.3020	.2253	.1556	.1004	.0605	.0339	.0176
	2	.0629	.1722	.2597	.3020	.3003	.2668	.2162	.1612	.1110	.0703
	3	.0077	.0446	.1069	.1762	.2336	.2668	.2716	.2508	.2119	.1641
	4	.0006	.0074	.0283	.0661	.1168	.1715	.2194	.2508	.2600	.2461
	5	.0000	.0008	.0050	.0165	.0389	.0735	.1181	.1672	.2128	.2461
	6	.0000	.0001	.0006	.0028	.0087	.0210	.0424	.0743	.1160	.1641
	7	.0000	.0000	.0000	.0003	.0012	.0039	.0098	.0212	.0407	.0703
	8	.0000	.0000	.0000	.0000	.0001	.0004	.0013	.0035	.0083	.0176
	9	.0000	.0000	.0000	.0000	.0000	.0000	.0001	.0003	.0008	.0020
10	0	.5987	.3487	.1969	.1074	.0563	.0282	.0135	.0060	.0025	.0010
	1	.3151	.3874	.3474	.2684	.1877	.1211	.0725	.0403	.0207	.0098
	2	.0746	.1937	.2759	.3020	.2816	.2335	.1757	.1209	.0763	.0439
	3	.0105	.0574	.1298	.2013	.2503	.2668	.2522	.2150	.1665	.1172
	4	.0010	.0112	.0401	.0881	.1460	.2001	.2377	.2508	.2384	.2051
	5	.0001	.0015	.0085	.0264	.0584	.1029	.1536	.2007	.2340	.2461
	6	.0000	.0001	.0012	.0055	.0162	.0368	.0689	.1115	.1596	.2051
	7	.0000	.0000	.0001	.0008	.0031	.0090	.0212	.0425	.0746	.1172
	8	.0000	.0000	.0000	.0001	.0004	.0014	.0043	.0106	.0229	.0439
	9	.0000	.0000	.0000	.0000	.0000	.0001	.0005	.0016	.0042	.0098
	10	.0000	.0000	.0000	.0000	.0000	.0000	.0000	.0001	.0003	.0010

Table IIIc   Cumulative Binomial Probability in Right-Hand Tail
(If $\pi > .50$, work in terms of the complementary event "failure" instead of "success")

n	x_0	.05	.10	.15	.20	.25	.30	.35	.40	.45	.50
2	1	.0975	.1900	.2775	.3600	.4375	.5100	.5775	.6400	.6975	.7500
	2	.0025	.0100	.0225	.0400	.0625	.0900	.1225	.1600	.2025	.2500
3	1	.1426	.2710	.3859	.4880	.5781	.6570	.7254	.7840	.8336	.8750
	2	.0072	.0280	.0608	.1040	.1562	.2160	.2818	.3520	.4252	.5000
	3	.0001	.0010	.0034	.0080	.0156	.0270	.0429	.0640	.0911	.1250
4	1	.1855	.3439	.4780	.5904	.6836	.7599	.8215	.8704	.9085	.9375
	2	.0140	.0523	.1095	.1808	.2617	.3483	.4370	.5248	.6090	.6875
	3	.0005	.0037	.0120	.0272	.0508	.0837	.1265	.1792	.2415	.3125
	4	.0000	.0001	.0005	.0016	.0039	.0081	.0150	.0256	.0410	.0625
5	1	.2262	.4095	.5563	.6723	.7627	.8319	.8840	.9222	.9497	.9688
	2	.0226	.0815	.1648	.2627	.3672	.4718	.5716	.6630	.7438	.8125
	3	.0012	.0086	.0266	.0579	.1035	.1631	.2352	.3174	.4069	.5000
	4	.0000	.0005	.0022	.0067	.0156	.0308	.0540	.0870	.1312	.1875
	5	.0000	.0000	.0001	.0003	.0010	.0024	.0053	.0102	.0185	.0312
6	1	.2649	.4686	.6229	.7379	.8220	.8824	.9246	.9533	.9723	.9844
	2	.0328	.1143	.2235	.3447	.4661	.5798	.6809	.7667	.8364	.8906
	3	.0022	.0158	.0473	.0989	.1694	.2557	.3529	.4557	.5585	.6562
	4	.0001	.0013	.0059	.0170	.0376	.0705	.1174	.1792	.2553	.3438
	5	.0000	.0001	.0004	.0016	.0046	.0109	.0223	.0410	.0692	.1094
	6	.0000	.0000	.0000	.0001	.0002	.0007	.0018	.0041	.0083	.0156
7	1	.3017	.5217	.6794	.7903	.8665	.9176	.9510	.9720	.9848	.9922
	2	.0444	.1497	.2834	.4233	.5551	.6706	.7662	.8414	.8976	.9375
	3	.0038	.0257	.0738	.1480	.2436	.3529	.4677	.5801	.6836	.7734
	4	.0002	.0027	.0121	.0333	.0706	.1260	.1998	.2898	.3917	.5000
	5	.0000	.0002	.0012	.0047	.0129	.0288	.0556	.0963	.1529	.2266
	6	.0000	.0000	.0001	.0004	.0013	.0038	.0090	.0188	.0357	.0625
	7	.0000	.0000	.0000	.0000	.0001	.0002	.0006	.0016	.0037	.0078

Table IIIc   (Continued)

n	x_0	.05	.10	.15	.20	.25	.30	.35	.40	.45	.50
						π					
8	1	.3366	.5695	.7275	.8322	.8999	.9424	.9681	.9832	.9916	.9961
	2	.0572	.1869	.3428	.4967	.6329	.7447	.8309	.8936	.9368	.9648
	3	.0058	.0381	.1052	.2031	.3215	.4482	.5722	.6846	.7799	.8555
	4	.0004	.0050	.0214	.0563	.1138	.1941	.2936	.4059	.5230	.6367
	5	.0000	.0004	.0029	.0104	.0273	.0580	.1061	.1737	.2604	.3633
	6	.0000	.0000	.0002	.0012	.0042	.0113	.0253	.0498	.0885	.1445
	7	.0000	.0000	.0000	.0001	.0004	.0013	.0036	.0085	.0181	.0352
	8	.0000	.0000	.0000	.0000	.0000	.0001	.0002	.0007	.0017	.0039
9	1	.3698	.6126	.7684	.8658	.9249	.9596	.9793	.9899	.9954	.9980
	2	.0712	.2252	.4005	.5638	.6997	.8040	.8789	.9295	.9615	.9805
	3	.0084	.0530	.1409	.2618	.3993	.5372	.6627	.7682	.8505	.9102
	4	.0006	.0083	.0339	.0856	.1657	.2703	.3911	.5174	.6386	.7461
	5	.0000	.0009	.0056	.0196	.0489	.0988	.1717	.2666	.3786	.5000
	6	.0000	.0001	.0006	.0031	.0100	.0253	.0536	.0994	.1658	.2539
	7	.0000	.0000	.0000	.0003	.0013	.0043	.0112	.0250	.0498	.0898
	8	.0000	.0000	.0000	.0000	.0001	.0004	.0014	.0038	.0091	.0195
	9	.0000	.0000	.0000	.0000	.0000	.0000	.0001	.0003	.0008	.0020
10	1	.4013	.6513	.8031	.8926	.9437	.9718	.9865	.9940	.9975	.9990
	2	.0861	.2639	.4557	.6242	.7560	.8507	.9140	.9536	.9767	.9893
	3	.0115	.0702	.1798	.3222	.4744	.6172	.7384	.8327	.9004	.9453
	4	.0010	.0128	.0500	.1209	.2241	.3504	.4862	.6177	.7340	.8281
	5	.0001	.0016	.0099	.0328	.0781	.1503	.2485	.3669	.4956	.6230
	6	.0000	.0001	.0014	.0064	.0197	.0473	.0949	.1662	.2616	.3770
	7	.0000	.0000	.0001	.0009	.0035	.0106	.0260	.0548	.1020	.1719
	8	.0000	.0000	.0000	.0001	.0004	.0016	.0048	.0123	.0274	.0547
	9	.0000	.0000	.0000	.0000	.0000	.0001	.0005	.0017	.0045	.0107
	10	.0000	.0000	.0000	.0000	.0000	.0000	.0000	.0001	.0003	.0010

Table IV Standard Normal, Cumulative Probability in Right-Hand Tail
(For negative values of z, areas are found by symmetry.)

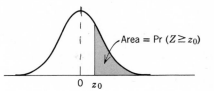

Area = Pr $(Z \geq z_0)$

$\downarrow z_0$				Second Decimal Place of z_0						
	.00	.01	.02	.03	.04	.05	.06	.07	.08	.09
0.0	.5000	.4960	.4920	.4880	.4840	.4801	.4761	.4721	.4681	.4641
0.1	.4602	.4562	.4522	.4483	.4443	.4404	.4364	.4325	.4286	.4247
0.2	.4207	.4168	.4129	.4090	.4052	.4013	.3974	.3936	.3897	.3859
0.3	.3821	.3783	.3745	.3707	.3669	.3632	.3594	.3557	.3520	.3483
0.4	.3446	.3409	.3372	.3336	.3300	.3264	.3228	.3192	.3156	.3121
0.5	.3085	.3050	.3015	.2981	.2946	.2912	.2877	.2843	.2810	.2776
0.6	.2743	.2709	.2676	.2643	.2611	.2578	.2546	.2514	.2483	.2451
0.7	.2420	.2389	.2358	.2327	.2296	.2266	.2236	.2206	.2177	.2148
0.8	.2119	.2090	.2061	.2033	.2005	.1977	.1949	.1922	.1894	.1867
0.9	.1841	.1814	.1788	.1762	.1736	.1711	.1685	.1660	.1635	.1611
1.0	.1587	.1562	.1539	.1515	.1492	.1469	.1446	.1423	.1401	.1379
1.1	.1357	.1335	.1314	.1292	.1271	.1251	.1230	.1210	.1190	.1170
1.2	.1151	.1131	.1112	.1093	.1075	.1056	.1038	.1020	.1003	.0985
1.3	.0968	.0951	.0934	.0918	.0901	.0885	.0869	.0853	.0838	.0823
1.4	.0808	.0793	.0778	.0764	.0749	.0735	.0722	.0708	.0694	.0681
1.5	.0668	.0655	.0643	.0630	.0618	.0606	.0594	.0582	.0571	.0559
1.6	.0548	.0537	.0526	.0516	.0505	.0495	.0485	.0475	.0465	.0455
1.7	.0446	.0436	.0427	.0418	.0409	.0401	.0392	.0384	.0375	.0367
1.8	0359	.0352	.0344	.0336	.0329	.0322	.0314	.0307	.0301	.0294
1.9	.0287	.0281	.0274	.0268	.0262	.0256	.0250	.0244	.0239	.0233
2.0	.0228	.0222	.0217	.0212	.0207	.0202	.0197	.0192	.0188	.0183
2.1	.0179	.0174	.0170	.0166	.0162	.0158	.0154	.0150	.0146	.0143
2.2	.0139	.0136	.0132	.0129	.0125	0122	.0119	.0116	.0113	.0110
2.3	.0107	.0104	.0102	.0099	.0096	.0094	.0091	.0089	.0087	.0084
2.4	.0082	.0080	.0078	.0075	.0073	.0071	.0069	.0068	.0066	.0064
2.5	.0062	.0060	.0059	.0057	.0055	.0054	.0052	.0051	.0049	.0048
2.6	.0047	.0045	.0044	.0043	.0041	.0040	.0039	.0038	.0037	.0036
2.7	.0035	.0034	.0033	.0032	.0031	.0030	.0029	.0028	.0027	.0026
2.8	.0026	.0025	.0024	.0023	.0023	.0022	.0021	.0021	.0020	.0019
2.9	.0019	.0018	.0017	.0017	.0016	.0016	.0015	.0015	.0014	.0014
3.0	.00135									
3.5	.000 233									
4.0	.000 031 7		To interpolate carefully, see Table X.							
4.5	.000 003 40									
5.0	.000 000 287									

Table V   Student's t Critical Points

Pr d.f.	.25	.10	.05	.025	.010	.005	.001
1	1.000	3.078	6.314	12.706	31.821	63.657	318.31
2	.816	1.886	2.920	4.303	6.965	9.925	22.326
3	.765	1.638	2.353	3.182	4.541	5.841	10.213
4	.741	1.533	2.132	2.776	3.747	4.604	7.173
5	.727	1.476	2.015	2.571	3.365	4.032	5.893
6	.718	1.440	1.943	2.447	3.143	3.707	5.208
7	.711	1.415	1.895	2.365	2.998	3.499	4.785
8	.706	1.397	1.860	2.306	2.896	3.355	4.501
9	.703	1.383	1.833	2.262	2.821	3.250	4.297
10	.700	1.372	1.812	2.228	2.764	3.169	4.144
11	.697	1.363	1.796	2.201	2.718	3.106	4.025
12	.695	1.356	1.782	2.179	2.681	3.055	3.930
13	.694	1.350	1.771	2.160	2.650	3.012	3.852
14	.692	1.345	1.761	2.145	2.624	2.977	3.787
15	.691	1.341	1.753	2.131	2.602	2.947	3.733
16	.690	1.337	1.746	2.120	2.583	2.921	3.686
17	.689	1.333	1.740	2.110	2.567	2.898	3.646
18	.688	1.330	1.734	2.101	2.552	2.878	3.610
19	.688	1.328	1.729	2.093	2.539	2.861	3.579
20	.687	1.325	1.725	2.086	2.528	2.845	3.552
21	.686	1.323	1.721	2.080	2.518	2.831	3.527
22	.686	1.321	1.717	2.074	2.508	2.819	3.505
23	.685	1.319	1.714	2.069	2.500	2.807	3.485
24	.685	1.318	1.711	2.064	2.492	2.797	3.467
25	.684	1.316	1.708	2.060	2.485	2.787	3.450
26	.684	1.315	1.706	2.056	2.479	2.779	3.435
27	.684	1.314	1.703	2.052	2.473	2.771	3.421
28	.683	1.313	1.701	2.048	2.467	2.763	3.408
29	.683	1.311	1.699	2.045	2.462	2.756	3.396
30	.683	1.310	1.697	2.042	2.457	2.750	3.385
40	.681	1.303	1.684	2.021	2.423	2.704	3.307
60	.679	1.296	1.671	2.000	2.390	2.660	3.232
120	.677	1.289	1.658	1.980	2.358	2.617	3.160
∞	.674	1.282	1.645	1.960	2.326	2.576	3.090

To interpolate carefully, see Table X.

Table VIa χ^2 Critical Points

X^2

one tailed test

Pr d.f.	.250	.100	.050	.025	.010	.005	.001
1	1.32	2.71	3.84	5.02	6.63	7.88	10.8
2	2.77	4.61	5.99	7.38	9.21	10.6	13.8
3	4.11	6.25	7.81	9.35	11.3	12.8	16.3
4	5.39	7.78	9.49	11.1	13.3	14.9	18.5
5	6.63	9.24	11.1	12.8	15.1	16.7	20.5
6	7.84	10.6	12.6	14.4	16.8	18.5	22.5
7	9.04	12.0	14.1	16.0	18.5	20.3	24.3
8	10.2	13.4	15.5	17.5	20.1	22.0	26.1
9	11.4	14.7	16.9	19.0	21.7	23.6	27.9
10	12.5	16.0	18.3	20.5	23.2	25.2	29.6
11	13.7	17.3	19.7	21.9	24.7	26.8	31.3
12	14.8	18.5	21.0	23.3	26.2	28.3	32.9
13	16.0	19.8	22.4	24.7	27.7	29.8	34.5
14	17.1	21.1	23.7	26.1	29.1	31.3	36.1
15	18.2	22.3	25.0	27.5	30.6	32.8	37.7
16	19.4	23.5	26.3	28.8	32.0	34.3	39.3
17	20.5	24.8	27.6	30.2	33.4	35.7	40.8
18	21.6	26.0	28.9	31.5	34.8	37.2	42.3
19	22.7	27.2	30.1	32.9	36.2	38.6	43.8
20	23.8	28.4	31.4	34.2	37.6	40.0	45.3
21	24.9	29.6	32.7	35.5	38.9	41.4	46.8
22	26.0	30.8	33.9	36.8	40.3	42.8	48.3
23	27.1	32.0	35.2	38.1	41.6	44.2	49.7
24	28.2	33.2	36.4	39.4	43.0	45.6	51.2
25	29.3	34.4	37.7	40.6	44.3	46.9	52.6
26	30.4	35.6	38.9	41.9	45.6	48.3	54.1
27	31.5	36.7	40.1	43.2	47.0	49.6	55.5
28	32.6	37.9	41.3	44.5	48.3	51.0	56.9
29	33.7	39.1	42.6	45.7	49.6	52.3	58.3
30	34.8	40.3	43.8	47.0	50.9	53.7	59.7
40	45.6	51.8	55.8	59.3	63.7	66.8	73.4
50	56.3	63.2	67.5	71.4	76.2	79.5	86.7
60	67.0	74.4	79.1	83.3	88.4	92.0	99.6
70	77.6	85.5	90.5	95.0	100	104	112
80	88.1	96.6	102	107	112	116	125
90	98.6	108	113	118	124	128	137
100	109	118	124	130	136	140	149

To interpolate carefully, see Table X.

Table VIb C^2 Critical Points ($C^2 = \chi^2/\text{d.f.}$)

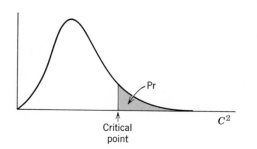

Pr df	.995	.99	.975	.95	.90	.10	.05	.025	.01	.005
1	.000039	.00016	.00098	.0039	.0158	2.71	3.84	5.02	6.63	7.88
2	.00501	.0101	.0253	.0513	.1054	2.30	3.00	3.69	4.61	5.30
3	.0239	.0383	.0719	.117	.195	2.08	2.60	3.12	3.78	4.28
4	.0517	.0743	.121	.178	.266	1.94	2.37	2.79	3.32	3.72
5	.0823	.111	.166	.229	.322	1.85	2.21	2.57	3.02	3.35
6	.113	.145	.206	.273	.367	1.77	2.10	2.41	2.80	3.09
7	.141	.177	.241	.310	.405	1.72	2.01	2.29	2.64	2.90
8	.168	.206	.272	.342	.436	1.67	1.94	2.19	2.51	2.74
9	.193	.232	.300	.369	.463	1.63	1.88	2.11	2.41	2.62
10	.216	.256	.325	.394	.487	1.60	1.83	2.05	2.32	2.52
11	.237	.278	.347	.416	.507	1.57	1.79	1.99	2.25	2.43
12	.256	.298	.367	.435	.525	1.55	1.75	1.94	2.18	2.36
13	.274	.316	.385	.453	.542	1.52	1.72	1.90	2.13	2.29
14	.291	.333	.402	.469	.556	1.50	1.69	1.87	2.08	2.24
15	.307	.349	.417	.484	.570	1.49	1.67	1.83	2.04	2.19
16	.321	.363	.432	.498	.582	1.47	1.64	1.80	2.00	2.14
18	.348	.390	.457	.522	.604	1.44	1.60	1.75	1.93	2.06
20	.372	.413	.480	.543	.622	1.42	1.57	1.71	1.88	2.00
24	.412	.452	.517	.577	.652	1.38	1.52	1.64	1.79	1.90
30	.460	.498	.560	.616	.687	1.34	1.46	1.57	1.70	1.79
40	.518	.554	.611	.663	.726	1.30	1.39	1.48	1.59	1.67
60	.592	.625	.675	.720	.774	1.24	1.32	1.39	1.47	1.53
120	.699	.724	.763	.798	.839	1.17	1.22	1.27	1.32	1.36
∞	1.000	1.000	1.000	1.000	1.000	1.00	1.00	1.00	1.00	1.00

To interpolate carefully, see Table X.

Table VII F Critical Points

Pr

Critical
point

F

Degrees of freedom for denominator	Pr	Degrees of freedom for numerator										
		1	2	3	4	5	6	8	10	20	40	∞
1	.25	5.83	7.50	8.20	8.58	8.82	8.98	9.19	9.32	9.58	9.71	9.85
	.10	39.9	49.5	53.6	55.8	57.2	58.2	59.4	60.2	61.7	62.5	63.3
	.05	161	200	216	225	230	234	239	242	248	251	254
2	.25	2.57	3.00	3.15	3.23	3.28	3.31	3.35	3.38	3.43	3.45	3.48
	.10	8.53	9.00	9.16	9.24	9.29	9.33	9.37	9.39	9.44	9.47	9.49
	.05	18.5	19.0	19.2	19.2	19.3	19.3	19.4	19.4	19.4	19.5	19.5
	.01	98.5	99.0	99.2	99.2	99.3	99.3	99.4	99.4	99.4	99.5	99.5
	.001	998	999	999	999	999	999	999	999	999	999	999
3	.25	2.02	2.28	2.36	2.39	2.41	2.42	2.44	2.44	2.46	2.47	2.47
	.10	5.54	5.46	5.39	5.34	5.31	5.28	5.25	5.23	5.18	5.16	5.13
	.05	10.1	9.55	9.28	9.12	9.10	8.94	8.85	8.79	8.66	8.59	8.53
	.01	34.1	30.8	29.5	28.7	28.2	27.9	27.5	27.2	26.7	26.4	26.1
	.001	167	149	141	137	135	133	131	129	126	125	124
4	.25	1.81	2.00	2.05	2.06	2.07	2.08	2.08	2.08	2.08	2.08	2.08
	.10	4.54	4.32	4.19	4.11	4.05	4.01	3.95	3.92	3.84	3.80	3.76
	.05	7.71	6.94	6.59	6.39	6.26	6.16	6.04	5.96	5.80	5.72	5.63
	.01	21.2	18.0	16.7	16.0	15.5	15.2	14.8	14.5	14.0	13.7	13.5
	.001	74.1	61.3	56.2	53.4	51.7	50.5	49.0	48.1	46.1	45.1	44.1
5	.25	1.69	1.85	1.88	1.89	1.89	1.89	1.89	1.89	1.88	1.88	1.87
	.10	4.06	3.78	3.62	3.52	3.45	3.40	3.34	3.30	3.21	3.16	3.10
	.05	6.61	5.79	5.41	5.19	5.05	4.95	4.82	4.74	4.56	4.46	4.36
	.01	16.3	13.3	12.1	11.4	11.0	10.7	10.3	10.1	9.55	9.29	9.02
	.001	47.2	37.1	33.2	31.1	29.8	28.8	27.6	26.9	25.4	24.6	23.8
6	.25	1.62	1.76	1.78	1.79	1.79	1.78	1.77	1.77	1.76	1.75	1.74
	.10	3.78	3.46	3.29	3.18	3.11	3.05	2.98	2.94	2.84	2.78	2.72
	.05	5.99	5.14	4.76	4.53	4.39	4.28	4.15	4.06	3.87	3.77	3.67
	.01	13.7	10.9	9.78	9.15	8.75	8.47	8.10	7.87	7.40	7.14	6.88
	.001	35.5	27.0	23.7	21.9	20.8	20.0	19.0	18.4	17.1	16.4	15.8
7	.25	1.57	1.70	1.72	1.72	1.71	1.71	1.70	1.69	1.67	1.66	1.65
	.10	3.59	3.26	3.07	2.96	2.88	2.83	2.75	2.70	2.59	2.54	2.47
	.05	5.59	4.74	4.35	4.12	3.97	3.87	3.73	3.64	3.44	3.34	3.23
	.01	12.2	9.55	8.45	7.85	7.46	7.19	6.84	6.62	6.16	5.91	5.65
	.001	29.3	21.7	18.8	17.2	16.2	15.5	14.6	14.1	12.9	12.3	11.7
8	.25	1.54	1.66	1.67	1.66	1.66	1.65	1.64	1.63	1.61	1.59	1.58
	.10	3.46	3.11	2.92	2.81	2.73	2.67	2.59	2.54	2.42	2.36	2.29
	.05	5.32	4.46	4.07	3.84	3.69	3.58	3.44	3.35	3.15	3.04	2.93
	.01	11.3	8.65	7.59	7.01	6.63	6.37	6.03	5.81	5.36	5.12	4.86
	.001	25.4	18.5	15.8	14.4	13.5	12.9	12.0	11.5	10.5	9.92	9.33
9	.25	1.51	1.62	1.63	1.63	1.62	1.61	1.60	1.59	1.56	1.55	1.53
	.10	3.36	3.01	2.81	2.69	2.61	2.55	2.47	2.42	2.30	2.23	2.16
	.05	5.12	4.26	3.86	3.63	3.48	3.37	3.23	3.14	2.94	2.83	2.71
	.01	10.6	8.02	6.99	6.42	6.06	5.80	5.47	5.26	4.81	4.57	4.31
	.001	22.9	16.4	13.9	12.6	11.7	11.1	10.4	9.89	8.90	8.37	7.81
10	.25	1.49	1.60	1.60	1.59	1.59	1.58	1.56	1.55	1.52	1.51	1.48
	.10	3.28	2.92	2.73	2.61	2.52	2.46	2.38	2.32	2.20	2.13	2.06
	.05	4.96	4.10	3.71	3.48	3.33	3.22	3.07	2.98	2.77	2.66	2.54
	.01	10.0	7.56	6.55	5.99	5.64	5.39	5.06	4.85	4.41	4.17	3.91
	.001	21.0	14.9	12.6	11.3	10.5	9.92	9.20	8.75	7.80	7.30	6.76

Table VII (Continued)

Degrees of freedom for denominator	Pr	Degrees of freedom for numerator										
		1	2	3	4	5	6	8	10	20	40	∞
12	.25	1.46	1.56	1.56	1.55	1.54	1.53	1.51	1.50	1.47	1.45	1.42
	.10	3.18	2.81	2.61	2.48	2.39	2.33	2.24	2.19	2.06	1.99	1.90
	.05	4.75	3.89	3.49	3.26	3.11	3.00	2.85	2.75	2.54	2.43	2.30
	.01	9.33	6.93	5.95	5.41	5.06	4.82	4.50	4.30	3.86	3.62	3.36
	.001	18.6	13.0	10.8	9.63	8.89	8.38	7.71	7.29	6.40	5.93	5.42
14	.25	1.44	1.53	1.53	1.52	1.51	1.50	1.48	1.46	1.43	1.41	1.38
	.10	3.10	2.73	2.52	2.39	2.31	2.24	2.15	2.10	1.96	1.89	1.80
	.05	4.60	3.74	3.34	3.11	2.96	2.85	2.70	2.60	2.39	2.27	2.13
	.01	8.86	6.51	5.56	5.04	4.69	4.46	4.14	3.94	3.51	3.27	3.00
	.001	17.1	11.8	9.73	8.62	7.92	7.43	6.80	6.40	5.56	5.10	4.60
16	.25	1.42	1.51	1.51	1.50	1.48	1.48	1.46	1.45	1.40	1.37	1.34
	.10	3.05	2.67	2.46	2.33	2.24	2.18	2.09	2.03	1.89	1.81	1.72
	.05	4.49	3.63	3.24	3.01	2.85	2.74	2.59	2.49	2.28	2.15	2.01
	.01	8.53	6.23	5.29	4.77	4.44	4.20	3.89	3.69	3.26	3.02	2.75
	.001	16.1	11.0	9.00	7.94	7.27	6.81	6.19	5.81	4.99	4.54	4.06
18	.25	1.41	1.50	1.49	1.48	1.46	1.45	1.43	1.42	1.38	1.35	1.32
	.10	3.01	2.62	2.42	2.29	2.20	2.13	2.04	1.98	1.84	1.75	1.66
	.05	4.41	3.55	3.16	2.93	2.77	2.66	2.51	2.41	2.19	2.06	1.92
	.01	8.29	6.01	5.09	4.58	4.25	4.01	3.71	3.51	3.08	2.84	2.57
	.001	15.4	10.4	8.49	7.46	6.81	6.35	5.76	5.39	4.59	4.15	3.67
20	.25	1.40	1.49	1.48	1.46	1.45	1.44	1.42	1.40	1.36	1.33	1.29
	.10	2.97	2.59	2.38	2.25	2.16	2.09	2.00	1.94	1.79	1.71	1.61
	.05	4.35	3.49	3.10	2.87	2.71	2.60	2.45	2.35	2.12	1.99	1.84
	.01	8.10	5.85	4.94	4.43	4.10	3.87	3.56	3.37	2.94	2.69	2.42
	.001	14.8	9.95	8.10	7.10	6.46	6.02	5.44	5.08	4.29	3.86	3.38
30	.25	1.38	1.45	1.44	1.42	1.41	1.39	1.37	1.35	1.30	1.27	1.23
	.10	2.88	2.49	2.28	2.14	2.05	1.98	1.88	1.82	1.67	1.57	1.46
	.05	4.17	3.32	2.92	2.69	2.53	2.42	2.27	2.16	1.93	1.79	1.62
	.01	7.56	5.39	4.51	4.02	3.70	3.47	3.17	2.98	2.55	2.30	2.01
	.001	13.3	8.77	7.05	6.12	5.53	5.12	4.58	4.24	3.49	3.07	2.59
40	.25	1.36	1.44	1.42	1.40	1.39	1.37	1.35	1.33	1.28	1.24	1.19
	.10	2.84	2.44	2.23	2.09	2.00	1.93	1.83	1.76	1.61	1.51	1.38
	.05	4.08	3.23	2.84	2.61	2.45	2.34	2.18	2.08	1.84	1.69	1.51
	.01	7.31	5.18	4.31	3.83	3.51	3.29	2.99	2.80	2.37	2.11	1.80
	.001	12.6	8.25	6.60	5.70	5.13	4.73	4.21	3.87	3.15	2.73	2.23
60	.25	1.35	1.42	1.41	1.38	1.37	1.35	1.32	1.30	1.25	1.21	1.15
	.10	2.79	2.39	2.18	2.04	1.95	1.87	1.77	1.71	1.54	1.44	1.29
	.05	4.00	3.15	2.76	2.53	2.37	2.25	2.10	1.99	1.75	1.59	1.39
	.01	7.08	4.98	4.13	3.65	3.34	3.12	2.82	2.63	2.20	1.94	1.60
	.001	12.0	7.76	6.17	5.31	4.76	4.37	3.87	3.54	2.83	2.41	1.89
120	.25	1.34	1.40	1.39	1.37	1.35	1.33	1.30	1.28	1.22	1.18	1.10
	.10	2.75	2.35	2.13	1.99	1.90	1.82	1.72	1.65	1.48	1.37	1.19
	.05	3.92	3.07	2.68	2.45	2.29	2.17	2.02	1.91	1.66	1.50	1.25
	.01	6.85	4.79	3.95	3.48	3.17	2.96	2.66	2.47	2.03	1.76	1.38
	.001	11.4	7.32	5.79	4.95	4.42	4.04	3.55	3.24	2.53	2.11	1.54
∞	.25	1.32	1.39	1.37	1.35	1.33	1.31	1.28	1.25	1.19	1.14	1.00
	.10	2.71	2.30	2.08	1.94	1.85	1.77	1.67	1.60	1.42	1.30	1.00
	.05	3.84	3.00	2.60	2.37	2.21	2.10	1.94	1.83	1.57	1.39	1.00
	.01	6.63	4.61	3.78	3.32	3.02	2.80	2.51	2.32	1.88	1.59	1.00
	.001	10.8	6.91	5.42	4.62	4.10	3.74	3.27	2.96	2.27	1.84	1.00

To interpolate carefully, see Table X.

Table VIII   Wilcoxon-Mann-Whitney (W) Test

The one-sided prob-value (Pr) corresponding to the rank sum W of the smaller sample, ranking from the end where this smaller sample is concentrated. For $n > 7$ or prob-value $> .25$, see equation (16-31).

$n = 2$					
m					
1		2			
W	Pr	W	Pr		
1	.333	3	.167		
		4	.333		

Larger Sample Size, $n = 3$					
Smaller Sample Size, m					
1		2		3	
W	Pr	W	Pr	W	Pr
1	.250	3	.100	6	.050
2	.500	4	.200	7	.100
		5	.400	8	.200
				9	.350
				10	.500

Larger Sample Size, $n = 4$							
Smaller Sample Size, m							
1		2		3		4	
W	Pr	W	Pr	W	Pr	W	Pr
1	.200	3	.067	6	.029	10	.014
2	.400	4	.133	7	.057	11	.029
		5	.267	8	.114	12	.057
		6	.400	9	.200	13	.100
				10	.314	14	.171
				11	.429	15	.243
						16	.343

Larger Sample Size, $n = 5$									
Smaller Sample Size, m									
1		2		3		4		5	
W	Pr	W	Pr	W	Pr	W	Pr	W	Pr
1	.167	3	.048	6	.018	10	.008	15	.004
2	.333	4	.095	7	.036	11	.016	16	.008
3	.500	5	.190	8	.071	12	.032	17	.016
		6	.286	9	.125	13	.056	18	.028
		7	.429	10	.196	14	.095	19	.048
				11	.286	15	.143	20	.075
				12	.393	16	.206	21	.111
				13	.500	17	.278	22	.155
						18	.365	23	.210
						19	.452	24	.274
								25	.345
								26	.421
								27	.500

Larger Sample Size, $n = 6$											
Smaller Sample Size, m											
1		2		3		4		5		6	
W	Pr	W	Pr	W	Pr	W	Pr	W	Pr	W	Pr
1	.143	3	.036	6	.012	10	.005	15	.002	21	.001
2	.286	4	.071	7	.024	11	.010	16	.004	22	.002
3	.429	5	.143	8	.048	12	.019	17	.009	23	.004
		6	.214	9	.083	13	.033	18	.015	24	.008
		7	.321	10	.131	14	.057	19	.026	25	.013
		8	.429	11	.190	15	.086	20	.041	26	.021
				12	.274	16	.129	21	.063	27	.032
				13	.357	17	.176	22	.089	28	.047
				14	.452	18	.238	23	.123	29	.066
						19	.305	24	.165	30	.090
						20	381	25	.214	31	.120
						21	.457	26	.268	32	.155
								27	.331	33	.197
								28	.396	34	.242
								29	.465	35	.294

Table VIII   Continued

Larger Sample Size, $n = 7$													
Smaller Sample Size, m													
1		2		3		4		5		6		7	
W	Pr	W	Pr	W	Pr	W	Pr	W	Pr	W	Pr	W	Pr
1	.125	3	.028	6	.008	10	.003	15	.001	21	.001	28	.000
2	.250	4	.056	7	.017	11	.006	16	.003	22	.001	29	.001
3	.375	5	.111	8	.033	12	.012	17	.005	23	.002	30	.001
4	.500	6	.167	9	.058	13	.021	18	.009	24	.004	31	.002
		7	.250	10	.092	14	.036	19	.015	25	.007	32	.003
		8	.333	11	.133	15	.055	20	.024	26	.011	33	.006
		9	.444	12	.192	16	.082	21	.037	27	.017	34	.009
				13	.258	17	.115	22	.053	28	.026	35	.013
				14	.333	18	.158	23	.074	29	.037	36	.019
				15	.417	19	.206	24	.101	30	.051	37	.027
				16	.500	20	.264	25	.134	31	.069	38	.036
						21	.324	26	.172	32	.090	39	.049
						22	.394	27	.216	33	.117	40	.064
						23	.464	28	.265	34	.147	41	.082
								29	.319	35	.183	42	.104
								30	.378	36	.223	43	.130
								31	.438	37	.267	44	.159
								32	.500	38	.314	45	.191
										39	.365	46	.228
										40	.418	47	.267

Table IX Critical Points of the Durbin-Watson Test for Autocorrelation

This table gives two limiting values of critical D (D_L and D_U), corresponding to the two most extreme configurations of the regressors; thus, for every possible configuration, the critical value of D will be somewhere between D_L and D_U:

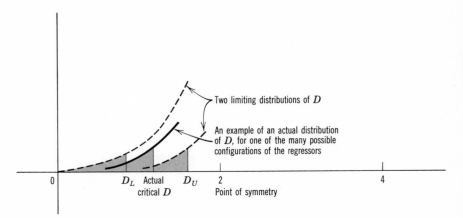

For example, suppose there are $n = 15$ observations and $k = 3$ regressors (as well as the constant), and we wished to test $\rho = 0$ versus $\rho > 0$ at the $\alpha = .05$ level of significance. Then if D fell below $D_L = .82$, we would reject H_0. If D were above $D_U = 1.75$, we could not reject H_0. If D were between D_L and D_U, this test is indecisive.

Sample size = n	Pr = Probability in Lower Tail (Significance Level, α)	k = Number of Regressors (Excluding the Constant)									
		1		2		3		4		5	
		D_L	D_U	D_L	D_U	D_L	D_U	D_L	D_U	D_L	D_U
15	.01	.81	1.07	.70	1.25	.59	1.46	.49	1.70	.39	1.96
	.025	.95	1.23	.83	1.40	.71	1.61	.59	1.84	.48	2.09
	.05	1.08	1.36	.95	1.54	.82	1.75	.69	1.97	.56	2.21
20	.01	.95	1.15	.86	1.27	.77	1.41	.68	1.57	.60	1.74
	.025	1.08	1.28	.99	1.41	.89	1.55	.79	1.70	.70	1.87
	.05	1.20	1.41	1.10	1.54	1.00	1.68	.90	1.83	.79	1.99
25	.01	1.05	1.21	.98	1.30	.90	1.41	.83	1.52	.75	1.65
	.025	1.18	1.34	1.10	1.43	1.02	1.54	.94	1.65	.86	1.77
	,05	1.29	1.45	1.21	1.55	1.12	1.66	1.04	1.77	.95	1.89
30	.01	1.13	1.26	1.07	1.34	1.01	1.42	.94	1.51	.88	1.61
	.025	1.25	1.38	1.18	1.46	1.12	1.54	1.05	1.63	.98	1.73
	.05	1.35	1.49	1.28	1.57	1.21	1.65	1.14	1.74	1.07	1.83
40	.01	1.25	1.34	1.20	1.40	1.15	1.46	1.10	1.52	1.05	1.58
	.025	1.35	1.45	1.30	1.51	1.25	1.57	1.20	1.63	1.15	1.69
	.05	1.44	1.54	1.39	1.60	1.34	1.66	1.29	1.72	1.23	1.79
50	.01	1.32	1.40	1.28	1.45	1.24	1.49	1.20	1.54	1.16	1.59
	.025	1.42	1.50	1.38	1.54	1.34	1.59	1.30	1.64	1.26	1.69
	.05	1.50	1.59	1.46	1.63	1.42	1.67	1.38	1.72	1.34	1.77
60	.01	1.38	1.45	1.35	1.48	1.32	1.52	1.28	1.56	1.25	1.60
	.025	1.47	1.54	1.44	1.57	1.40	1.61	1.37	1.65	1.33	1.69
	.05	1.55	1.62	1.51	1.65	1.48	1.69	1.44	1.73	1.41	1.77
80	.01	1.47	1.52	1.44	1.54	1.42	1.57	1.39	1.60	1.36	1.62
	.025	1.54	1.59	1.52	1.62	1.49	1.65	1.47	1.67	1.44	1.70
	.05	1.61	1.66	1.59	1.69	1.56	1.72	1.53	1.74	1.51	1.77
100	.01	1.52	1.56	1.50	1.58	1.48	1.60	1.46	1.63	1.44	1.65
	.025	1.59	1.63	1.57	1.65	1.55	1.67	1.53	1.70	1.51	1.72
	.05	1.65	1.69	1.63	1.72	1.61	1.74	1.59	1.76	1.57	1.78

Table X   Interpolating Tables V to VII

For all the exercises in the text, simple linear interpolation gives a good enough approximation. However, important research data may deserve more careful interpolation, as follows.

Table V (Student's t) may require interpolation in either of two directions,

(a) down (interpolating d.f.),

or (b) across (interpolating Pr.).

We give examples of both kinds of interpolation, showing the tabled values in black, and interpolation calculations in red.

(a) *Interpolation of* d.f.

First, calculate $r = 1/$d.f. Then interpolate linearly with r. For example, let us find $t_{.025}$ for d.f. $= 600$:

d.f.	$r = \dfrac{1}{\text{d.f}}$	$t_{.025}$
120	$\dfrac{1}{120} = .00833$	1.980
600	$\dfrac{1}{600} = .00167$	$1.960 + (1.980 - 1.960)\left(\dfrac{.00167 - 0}{.00833 - 0}\right)\ (= 1.964)$
∞	$\dfrac{1}{\infty} = 0$	1.960

(b) *Interpolation of* Pr

First, calculate $L = \log$ Pr. Then interpolate linearly with L. For example, when d.f. $= 4$, let us find Pr corresponding to $t = 1.800$:

Pr	.10	.0734	.05
$L = \log$ Pr	-1.00	$-1.00 + (-1.301 + 1.00)\left(\dfrac{1.800 - 1.533}{2.132 - 1.533}\right) = -1.134$	-1.301
t	1.533	1.800	2.132

Finally, we note that Tables VIb[1] and VII can be similarly interpolated, while Table VIa can be calculated from Table VIb.

---

[1]The right half of Table VIb can be similarly interpolated; the left half requires first calculating the tail probability $(1 - \text{Pr})$ in place of Pr.

ACknowLEdGMENTS foR TAblES

I. (a) From H. A. Simmons, *Wiley Trigonometric Tables,* Second Edition. Copyright © 1945 by John Wiley and Sons, Inc. Reprinted by permission.

   (b) Reprinted from John E. Freund, *Modern Elementary Statistics,* 3rd Edition, © 1967, by permission of Prentice-Hall Inc., Englewood Cliffs, New Jersey.

II. (a) Reprinted, by permission, from Clelland et al., *Basic Statistics with Business Applications,* copyright © 1966 by John Wiley and Sons, Inc.

   (b) Reprinted, by permission, from the RAND Corporation.

III. Reprinted, by permission, from the *Chemical Rubber Company Standard Mathematical Tables,* 19th edition, 1971, courtesy of The Chemical Rubber Co., Cleveland, Ohio.

IV. Reprinted with permission of The Macmillan Company from *Introduction to Statistics* by R. E. Walpole. Copyright © by Ronald E. Walpole, 1968.

V. Reprinted, by permission, from E. S. Pearson and H. O. Hartley, *Biometrika Tables for Statisticians,* vol. 1, 2nd edition, Cambridge, 1962.

VI. (a) Reprinted with rounding, by permission, from E. S. Pearson and H. O. Hartley, *Biometrika Tables for Statisticians,* vol. 1, 2nd edition, Cambridge, 1962.
   (b) From *Introduction to Statistical Analysis* by Dixon and Massey. 2nd Ed. Copyright © 1957 by McGraw-Hill, Inc. Used with permission of McGraw-Hill Book Company.

VII. Abridgment, by permission, from *Chemical Rubber Company Standard Mathematical Tables,* 19th edition, 1971, courtesy of The Chemical Rubber Co., Cleveland, Ohio. And from *Statistical Principles in Experimental Design* by B. J. Winer, 1971, McGraw-Hill Book Company; (this originally appeared in *Biometrica Tables for Statisticians,* vol. 1).

VIII. Reprinted with permission of The Macmillan Company from *A Nonparametric Introduction to Statistics* by C. H. Kraft and C. van Eeden. Copyright © by The Macmillan Company, 1968.

IX. Reprinted, by permission, from Carl F. Christ, *Econometric Models and Methods*, John Wiley and Sons, 1966. Originally abridged from J. Durbin, and G. S. Watson, "Testing for Serial Correlation in Least Squares Regression. II." *Biometrika* 38 (June, 1951), pp. 159–178.

ANSWERS TO
odd-NUMBEREd pRObLEMS

You are *not* expected always to calculate the answer as precisely as the given answers below. These answers are given to a fairly high degree of precision merely for the benefit of those who want it; even so, the last digit may be slightly in error because of slide rule inaccuracy.

If a slide rule or desk calculator is unavailable, Appendix Table I may be useful for finding square roots.

2-1 (a) 5.0, 4.5, 2
  (b) average deviation $= 0$
  (c) 70.2

2-3 (a) 77.4, 81.25, 85

2-5

	Mean	Median	Mode
raw	77.78	81.47	hardly defined
fine	77.4	81.25	85
coarse	78.4	80.00	80

  (a) it depends too much on the grouping
  (b) fine grouping

2-7 $20,000 may be the mean, while $12,000 may be the median—hardly honest

2-9 9.6

2-11 $\sqrt{114} = 10.7$

2-13 77.4, 11.0

2-15 no, $11.7 \neq 9$

2-17 51.8, 9.75

2-19 (b) 2.28, 1.79

2-21 (a) 1.20, 1.30; 1.0, .107, .33
  (b) 12.0, 13.0; 10, 10.7, 3.3
  (c) .10, .20; 1.0, .107, .33

2-23 (d) $f/n = 1/6$, $\bar{X} = 3.5$

3-1 (c) last relative frequency

3-3 (c) last relative frequency (or better yet, figure it out to be $8/36 = .222$)

3-5 (b) and (d) are true

3-7 (a) .50, .30, .65, .15
  (c) .50, .70, .85, .35

3-9 (a) .375
  (b) .375

3-11 (a) .40
  (b) .60
  (c) .55
  (d) .78
  (e) .17
  (f) .42, .58

3-15 (a) .29
  (b) yes

3-17 (a) $1/221 = .0046$
  (b) $1/1326 = .00076$
  (c) $20 \times 19 / 52 \times 51 = .143$

3-19 (a) $28/45 = .62$
(b) $4/45 = .089$
(c) $1/45 = .022$

3-21 $9/14 = .64, .36$

3-23 (a) $.36/.54 = .67$
(b) $.75$ (c) $.25$

3-25 (a) no
(b) no

3-27 (a) yes
(b) yes
(c) whenever F is independent of E,
then $\bar{F}$ also is independent of E

3-29 (a) $.3$
(b) impossible
(c) $0 \leq \Pr(e_4) \leq .2$
(d) impossible

3-31 (a) $.33$
(b) $.50$
(c) 0
(d) $.17$

3-33 (a) $.001/.126 = .0079$
(b) $.506$
(c) $.999$

3-35 (a) $.090/.225 = .40$
(b) $.100/.225 = .44$
(c) $.035/.225 = .16$

4-1 (a)

x	0	1	2	3	4
$p(x)$	$\frac{1}{16}$	$\frac{4}{16}$	$\frac{6}{16}$	$\frac{4}{16}$	$\frac{1}{16}$

(b)

x	0	1	2	3
$p(x)$	$\frac{2}{16}$	$\frac{6}{16}$	$\frac{6}{16}$	$\frac{2}{16}$

4-5 (a) $\mu = 2, \sigma^2 = 1$
(b) $\mu = 1.5, \sigma^2 = .75$

4-7 $\mu_X = 3.5, \sigma_X = 1.71$
$\mu_Y = 11, \sigma_Y = 3.42$

4-9 $\mu = 1.33, \sigma^2 = 8/9 = .89$

4-11 (a) $\mu_X = 1.36, \sigma_X = 1.56$
(b) $\mu_Y = 3.16, \sigma_Y = 1.47$
(c) μ_X

4-13 (a) $\mu = 1.00, \sigma^2 = .80$
(b) $\mu = .50, \sigma^2 = .45$

4-15 $\mu = 1/2, \sigma^2 = 5/12 = .416$

4-17 $\mu = n\pi, \sigma^2 = n\pi(1 - \pi)$

4-19 (a) $.683$
(b) $.950$
(c) $.990$
(d) $.977$
(e) $.977$

4-23 (a) $.092$
(b) $.251$
(c) $.657$

4-25 8.00

4-27 (a) 4.6
(b) 1.5
(c) 23.2
(d) $2.040 = \sigma_T^2$
(e) $23.20 - 4.6^2 = 2.04$

4-29 (a) $\mu = 1.50, \sigma^2 = .75$
(b) $\mu = 1.75, \sigma^2 = 11/16 = .69$

4-31 (a) $.035$
(b) yes, because $.035$ is so small

4-33 (a)

x	0	1	2
$p(x)$	6/12	5/12	1/12

$\mu_X = 7/12$

(b) yes, no (c) $.950$

5-1

y \ x	0	1	2	3	4
3			.2/16		
2		2/16	2/16	2/16	
1		2/16	2/16	2/16	
0	1/16				1/16
$p(x)$	1/16	4/16	6/16	4/16	1/16

(c) $\mu = 2$, $\sigma^2 = 1$

(d)

x	1	2	3
$p(x)$	1/3	1/3	1/3

(e) $\mu = 2$, $\sigma^2 = 2/3 = .67$

(f) no

5-3 (c) $\mu = 1$, $\sigma^2 = .40$

(e) $\mu = 1$, $\sigma^2 = .33$

(f) no

5-5 (a), (b) 2.20

(c) .20

5-7 (a), (b) $-.60$

(c) $-.90$

5-9 yes

5-11 (a) $\mu_8 = 4$, $\sigma_8^2 = 4/3 = 1.33$

(b) for both X and Y,

$\mu = 2$,

$\sigma^2 = 2/3 = .67$

(c) $E(X + Y) = E(X) + E(Y)$

var $(X + Y) = $ var $X + $ var Y

5-15 (a) $\mu = 5.00$, $\sigma^2 = 1.40$

(b) $\mu = 6.50$, $\sigma^2 = 8.75$

(c) $\mu = 5.20$, $\sigma^2 = 5.76$

(d) (1) scheme (b)

(2) scheme (b)

(3) scheme (a)

5-17 (1)

	μ	σ	σ^2
X_1			400
X_2			400
$\overline{X}$	65	10	100
W	70	11.5	133.3

(2)

	μ	σ	σ^2
X_1			400
X_2			400
$\overline{X}$	65	14.1	200
W	70	14.9	222.2

5-19 (a) yes, hence $\sigma_{XY} = 0$

(b) $\mu_X = 1.0 \qquad \sigma_X^2 = .50$

$\mu_Y = \ .5 \qquad \sigma_Y^2 = .25$

$\mu_8 = 1.5 \qquad \sigma_8^2 = .75$

5-21 (b) $\mu_H = 70$, $\sigma_H^2 = 15$

(c) $\mu_W = 150$, $\sigma_W^2 = 60$

(d) $\sigma_{HW} = 20$

(e) 143.3, 150, 156.7

(f) no

(g) $\mu = 590$,

$\sigma^2 = 840$, $\sigma = 29.0$

5-23 (c) not independent; cov $= -2.33$

(d) for both X_1 and X_2,

$\mu = 5$, $\sigma^2 = 4.67$

(e) $\mu_8 = 10$, $\sigma_8^2 = 4.67$

(f) The answers would be about the same as those in Problem 5-22

5-25 (a) 1.30

(b) \$14.50

(c) .90

5-27 (a) 1

(b) 1.67

(c) 1

(d) $(n - k + k^2)/n$

5-29 (b) $\mu = 1$, $\sigma^2 = .92$

(c) $7/15 = .467$

(d) $5/8 = .625$

(e) 9.60

(f) all 3 probabilities are equal (1/3)

5-31 .32

5-33 Even the richest man has finite wealth, and risks losing it all—a foolish risk to take, perhaps.

6-1 False. Replace end of last paragraph with "$\sqrt{n}\,\sigma = 10.1$ inches." Replace middle of second paragraph with "$\sigma/\sqrt{n} = 1.01$ inches."

6-3 (b) $\mu_8 = 7$, $\sigma_8^2 = 35/6 = 5.83$

(c) $\mu = 3.5$, $\sigma^2 = 35/12 = 2.92$

(d) no difference whatever in the mathematical (abstract) form.

6-5 (a) $\mu = 4$, $\sigma = \sqrt{8/3} = 1.63$
     (b) $\mu_{\bar{x}} = 4$, $\sigma_{\bar{x}} = \sqrt{4/3} = 1.15$
     (c) $\mu_{\bar{x}} = 4$, $\sigma_{\bar{x}} = \sqrt{8/9} = .943$
     (d) See Figure 6-3(a)

6-7 .9986

6-9 .015

6-11 .023

6-13 (a) $\mu_S = 9000$, $\sigma_S^2 = 900{,}000$
      (b) .147

6-15 (a) $\mu = .56$. $\pi = .56$
      (b) $\sigma^2 = .247$
      (c) $S = 6$, $P = 6/10 = .60$

(d)

x	$p(x)$
0	.00
1	.00
2	.02
3	.07
4	.15
5	.23
6	.24
7	.18
8	.09
9	.02
10	.00

$\mu = 5.60$
$\sigma^2 = 2.47$
$\Pr(S > 5) = .53$

6-17

$n = 2, 3, 10$ are similar. We note that the distributions are becoming normally shaped.

6-19 .018 (n.c.c., .014 or .023)

6-21 (a) $.31^5 = .003$
      (b) .13
      (c) .13
      (d) Event (a) is just a subset of event (b). Event (c) is just the same as event (b).

6-23 .936

6-25 (a) $\mu = \frac{10}{13} = .77$, $\sigma^2 = \frac{290}{169} = 1.73$
      (b) $\mu_S = 10$, $\sigma_S^2 = \frac{290}{17} = 17.1$
      (c) .27 (n.c.c., .23 or .32)

6-27 (a) .85 (n.c.c., .79 or .89)
      (b) .88 (n.c.c., .83 or .92)

6-29 (a) $\mu = -\$.0526$
      (b) .55, .60, .72
      (c) binomial yields .549
      (d) $n = 1960$

6-31 (a) $\mu = 65$, $\sigma^2 = 3.60$
      (b)

x	63.5	65.0	66.5
$p(x)$	.30	.40	.30

      (d) $\mu_{\bar{x}} = 65$, $\sigma_{\bar{X}}^2 = 1.35$
      (e) use (6-33) and (6-36)
      (f) True. Sampling without replacement is preferable because it makes the variance of $\bar{X}$ slightly smaller

7-1 (a) $71 \pm .59$
     (b) $71 \pm .77$

7-3 $.83 \pm .032$

7-5 (a) $\Pr = .95^3 = .86$
     (b) $.85 \leq \Pr \leq .95$

7-7 (a) True
     (b) Interchange μ and $\bar{X}$
     (c) Replace last sentence with "The difference is that the sample mean is more efficient, by about 57%. (They are both unbiased.)"

7-9 (b) 90%. Thus $\bar{X}$ is better.

7-11 True and important statements

7-13 (b) $E(\bar{X}) = \mu = 4$
     $E(s^2) = \sigma^2 = 8/3$
     $E(\text{MSD}) = \frac{1}{2}\sigma^2 = 4/3$

7-15 (c) On the average, $\bar{X}$ will have smaller error (smaller mean squared error, actually), because it is absolutely efficient

8-1 $1 \pm .92$

8-3 (a) 9 ± 2.96
     (b) 4 fold, so that $n = 240$
     (c) $n = 522$

8-5 (a) $10 \pm .80$
     (b) 10 ± 1.11

8-7 60 ± 11.0

8-9 40 ± 58

8-11 -8.0 ± 7.4

8-13 (a) $.490 \pm .030$
     (b) $.490 \pm .098$

8-15 $.020 \pm .039$

8-17 $.440 \pm .030$

8-19 (a) $.199 \pm .016$
     (b) $.199 \pm .020$

8-21 $.060 \pm .128$

8-23 (a) $16.0 < \sigma^2 < 695$
     (b) $20.9 < \sigma^2 < 910$
     (c) $24.0 < \sigma^2 < 280$

8-25 5.0 ± 5.8

8-27 $\Delta\pi = \pi_1 - \pi_2 = .028 \pm .018$
     Thus $\dfrac{\Delta\pi}{\pi} = \dfrac{.028 \pm .018}{.142}$
     $= .20 \pm .13$
     i.e. relative decline = 20% $\pm$ 13% Although the best guess for the decline is one-fifth, when sampling fluctuation is allowed for, with 95% confidence we can only say that the relative decline was between 7% and 33%.

8-29 $-.097 \pm .037$

8-31 (a) mean impr $= .150 \pm .069$
     (b) There are many reservations.

9-1 Statistically significant are Problems 8-26, 27, 29, 31

9-3 8-25, $|t| = 2.10, p \simeq .08$
     8-26, $|t| = 3.50, p \simeq .018$
     8-27, $|z| = 2.98, p = .0028$
     8-28, $|z| = .63, p = .53$
     8-29, $|z| = 5.1, p < 10^{-6}$
     8-30, $|z| = 1.71, p = .087$
     8-31, $|z| = 4.24, p < 10^{-4}$

9-5 for H_0, prob-value $= .067$

9-7 I, II

9-9 prob-value $= .055$

9-11 (a) $\alpha = .086$
     (b) $\beta = .38$

9-13 (a) critical point is the same
     (b) α is specified the same
     (c) $\beta = .058$ (different)

9-15 (a) $.080 \pm .043$
     (b) since $|z| = 3.65$, $p < .0005$
     (c) yes

9-17 (a) $1 \pm .64$
     (b) since $|z| = 3.07$, $p = .002$
     (c) yes

9-19 For the null hypothesis (fair opponent), the prob-value is only .10

9-21 The OCC curve is just the power curve of Figure 9-7, flipped upside down. It should drop rapidly.

9-23 (a) (i) since $|t| = 8.2$,
          reject $\mu = 7200$
      (ii) since $|t| = 0.2$,
          $\mu = 6000$ is acceptable
      (iii) since $|t| = 2.6$,
          reject $\mu = 6400$
     (b) acceptable μ:
        $5726 < \mu < 6334$

10-1 (a) $p < .01$ $(F = 9.0)$
     (b) $(\bar{X}_i - \bar{X}_I) \pm 8.6$
     (c) no detectable difference
     (d) $\Sigma C_i = 0$, or $\Sigma C_i = 1$

10-5 yes; $p < .01$ $(F = 11.9)$

10-7 Mix the 3 samples together, treating all the observations as one large sample.

10-9 $p \ll .001$ $(F = 234)$

10-11 between hours, $p < .01$ $(F = 32.4)$
      between men, $p < .10$ $(F = 6.1)$

10-13 11.5%

10-15 (e) only is correct

10-17 (a) $2600
      (b) $2600, $4300

10-19 $\hat{\pi} = 59.6\%$

10-21 (a) $(\bar{X}_i - \bar{X}_I) \pm 18.0$
      (b) 15.0 ± 12.7
      (c) more than 95%
      (d) no. Koestler might have started with better students, etc.
      (e) between profs, $p < .25$ $(F = 9.0)$ between times, $p < .25$
                      $(F = 10.2)$

10-23 $.29 < \theta < 4.01$

11-1 (a) $S = -396 + .144Y$
     (b) a = estimated saving of average family
        a_0 = estimated saving of family with no income

11-3 (a) .068 bushels/lb.
     (b) 13.6¢/lb., not economic

11-5 (a) $P = 30 + .50R$
     (b) not necessarily

12-1 (a) $\beta = .144 \pm .148$
     (b) $\beta = .856 \pm .148$
     (c) $\beta = .50 \pm 2.45$

12-3 $\beta > .036$, reject hypothesis (a) and also (d)

12-5 (a) 472 ± 405
     (b) 760 ± 280
     (c) 1048 ± 405
     (d) 1336 ± 655
     (e) the interval (b) at the center of the data is most precise
     (f) exactly the same as (12-34)

12-7 $n_1 = 16n_2 = 1600$

12-9 (a) $Y = 140 + 1.27x$
     (c) $\mu_Y = 229 \pm 45$
     (d) $\mu_Y = 140 \pm 117$
     (e) centered better, and narrower

13-1 (a) $S = 105 + .115Y - .0294W$
     (b) multiple regression (.115) is better

(c) $878
(d) $230
(e) $27
(f) $s^2 = 3930$
(g) 2d.f. is very few

13-3 (b) $S = 252 + .105Y$
$\qquad - .0242W - 38.1N$

13-5 Spring temperature, soil fertility, etc.

13-7 True

13-9 (c) only is correct

13-11 There may be bias. For example, to the extent that smokers are careless of their health in other ways, the 5-year figure is upwardly-biased.

13-13 (a) Yes, a positive bias
(b) no bias
(c) . . . will *not* introduce . . .

13-15 (a) $b = -2.5$
(b) $b_{Yr} = -1.67$

13-17 10.2

13-19 (a) bias greater
(b) bias negative

13-21 (a) B is .38 mpg better

13-23 if $c_2 = 0$, or X_1 and X_2 are uncorrelated $(\Sigma x_{1i}x_{2i} = 0)$

13-25 multiple regression, with some dummies

14-1 (a) $r = .62$
(b) $-.49 < \rho < .95$
(c) no

14-3 (a) 62%
(b) 38%
(c) we cannot reject H_0
$\quad (F = 4.7, t = 2.17,$
$\quad \beta = .35 \pm .51)$

14-5 only (e) is false

14-7 (calculator accuracy)
(a) $r_{SY} = .874$
(b) $R = .9921$
(c) .763, .9842, .221, .0158
(d) $t = -5.3$
(e) $r_{SW} = -.7485$
$\quad R = .9921$
$\quad .560, .9842, .432, .0158$
$\quad t = 7.4$
(f) $t = 7.4$
$\quad .01 < p < .02$
$\quad s_\beta = .016$
$\quad \beta = .115 \pm .067$
$\qquad t = -5.3$
$\qquad .02 < p < .05$
$\qquad s_{\hat\gamma} = .0055$
$\qquad \gamma = -.0294 \pm .0238$

14-11 Yes, $\hat\beta = .49$

14-13 (a) .40
(b) .26
(c) less

14-15 (a) Correction: . . . with zero mean and constant variance.
(b) Correction: . . . are unbiased, consistent . . .
(c) true
(d) Correction: One advantage of multiple regression is that it can include categorical factors, by using dummy variables.
(e) true
(f) Correction: Multicollinearity of X and Z is completely avoided when $r_{XZ} = 0$; . . .
(g) true, and one of the great advantages of the experimental sciences.

14-17 (c) only is correct

14-19 (c) only is correct

14-21 $\beta, \quad \Sigma x_i^2 \sigma_i^2 / (\Sigma x_i^2)^2$

15-1 (a) .69, .31
    (b) Corrected version: Since the barometer sometimes predicts "rain" even when it will shine, a "rain" prediction is uncertain.
    (c) Because the barometer is a worse predictor when it shines.

15-3 (a) .10, .40, .50
    (b) .28, .44, .28

15-5 (a) a_1 yields $L = -2.0$
    (b) a_1 yields $L = -10.0$
    (c) a_3 yields $L = -4.54$
    (d) Corrected version: Action a_1 is best when "rain" is predicted, and also when no prediction is possible. Action a_3 is best when "shine" is predicted. Action a_2 is never best.

15-7 (a) It depends, as shown in (b)
    (b) true. For example, a man with no risk aversion (linear utility function) would choose (3), with highest monetary expectation ($E = \$10,700$). Yet a man with extreme risk aversion would choose (1) even though it has lowest $E = \$10,533$. Most people would likely choose (2), where $E = \$10,667$.

15-9 (a) mode, 68
    (b) median, 67
    (c) mean, 66.8

15-11 (a) posterior mode, 73 or 74
    (b) posterior median, anywhere between 73 and 74
    (c) posterior mean, 73.5

15-13 (a) $\hat{\mu} = 70.92$
    (b) $\mu = 70.92 \pm .56$
    (c) centered towards prior mean 70.0, and narrower.

15-15 (a) 103.54, $\alpha = .33$, $\beta = .020$
    (b) 113.12, $\alpha = .05$, $\beta = .195$

Average loss increases by a factor of 3.16
    (c) $r_0/r_1 = 4/1$, which is unreasonable.

15-17 Classify as tribe A iff skull is less than 15.64 cm wide.

15-19 (a) Yes, risk drilling
    (b) $\$1,500,000$

15-21 .67

16-1 (a) $68 \le \nu \le 75$
    (b) $63 \le \nu \le 69$
    (c) .73
    (d) yes

16-3 (a) .9960
    (b) .82

16-5 (a) .021
    (b) .116
    (c) $1.5 \le \Delta \le 8.5$
    (d) CI in Problem 16-2 was narrower, because it exploited matched data.
    (e) 5 ± 3.35, which assumes normal populations with common σ (reasonable enough), and is narrower.

16-7 (a) .037
    (b) .019

16-9 for H_0, prob-value $= .029$

16-11 (a) .035 with sign test, $\simeq .05$ with t test
    (b) both are valid, but t test is more efficient
    (c) t test may be invalid, and less efficient

17-1 (b) Pr (type I error) $= \alpha = .25$

17-3 Use a 1-sided binomial test
    (b) power $= .813$

17-7 (a) that the population is not exactly normal.

(b) that the sample is too small to detect whatever non-normality there may be.

(c) estimate μ with $\bar{X}$ and σ^2 with s^2.

(d) $\chi^2 = 4.6$ with 4 d.f.
Hence prob-value $> .25$

17-9 (a) $\chi^2 = 820$ with 2 d.f.
Hence prob-value $\ll .001$

(b) Let us define an "educational index" $X = 1, 2, 3$, for the three levels; thus a 95% CI for the difference in white and black population means is $.31 \pm .020$

17-11 (a) $\chi^2 = 90$ with 3 d.f. Hence prob-value $\ll .001$

(b) Simple 95% CI for proportion of females in each industry:
Durables, $\pi = .19 \pm .054$
Nondurables, $\pi = .38 \pm .067$
Mining, $\pi = .05 \pm .030$
Trade, $\pi = .41 \pm .068$

17-13 (a) $\chi^2 = 20.6$ with 6 d.f.
Hence $.001 < p < .005$

(b) Let us define a "class index" $X = 1, 2, 3, 4$, for the social classes; then ANOVA yields $F = 14.4$, and prob-value $\ll .001$

17-15 (a) $\chi^2 = 13.2$ with 2 d.f.
Hence $.001 < p < .005$

(b) Simple 95% CI for the proportion of defectives in each division:
A, $\pi = .043 \pm .0115$
B, $\pi = .075 \pm .0183$
C, $\pi = .044 \pm .0090$

18-1

MLE = .75
= x/n

18-3 (a) $\hat{\sigma}^2 = \sum_{i=1}^{n} (X_i - \mu)^2/n$

(b) Yes

19-3 True, if the residual is well-behaved.

19-7 (a) spectrum peaks near $f = 0$

(b) spectrum peaks at $f = 1/4$ and $f = 1/2$ cycle/quarter (i.e., 1 and 2 cycles/year), also near $f = 0$

(c) spectrum has no peaks—all frequencies are present to the same degree.

19-9 (c) long term is worse in (a)

19-11 Corrected last sentence: An autocorrelated residual may make the estimate of trend more variable, and may make the estimate of seasonal more (or sometimes less) variable.

20-1 (a)

(b)

20-3 (a) .67

(b) .77, inconsistent.

20-5 (a)

$$Z$$
$$/$$
$$X \rightleftarrows Y$$

(b) One possibility is (c)

(c) Z as IV on (20-18) yields $\hat{\beta} = s_{YZ}/s_{XZ}$

(d) No, (20-19) cannot be consistently estimated, because there is only one IV(Z), but two unknowns (γ and ψ)

21-1 (a) $Y = 55 - 28.2Q + 5.43Q^2$

21-3

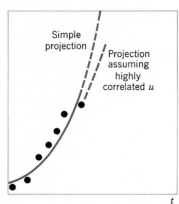

Simple projection

Projection assuming highly correlated u

t

21-5 (a), (b), (e) multiple regression
(c), (d) take logs, then use regression

21-7 Yes, log Y makes sense in ANOVA, whenever log Y makes sense in regression.

22-5 (a) $\hat{\mu} = 195.6$, $\hat{T} = 3{,}912{,}000$
(b) if $n = 1000$ still, then
$n_i = 164, 513, 277, 46$
(c) 2.43, 2.37, 6.82
(d) 280%, 288%
(e) $\mu = 195.6 \pm 3.1$
$\mu = \hat{\mu} \pm 3.0$
$\mu = \bar{X} \pm 5.1$
(f) true

23-1 (a) 121
(b) 120, 125, 117, 100.
Yes, $100 \le LPI \le 125$
(c) Yes, PPI = 120, FPI = 120.5
(d) Yes, same order as (23-12):
$LPI \ge FPI \ge PPI$
(e) Yes, same order as (23-12):
$LQI \ge FQI \ge PQI$
i.e., $88 \ge 87.5 \ge 87$
(f) Cost index = 105. Only Fisher's index satisfies (23-11):

$(120.5)(87.5) = 105$
(g) Price indexes would be unchanged while quantity indexes would be inflated by population growth
(h) always (b) is true

23-3 (a) As in Figure 23-1
(b) Justified on the grounds that a worker's buying power should not decrease. However, this causes a spiral of inflation.

23-7 (b)

	t_1	t_2
LQI	150	140
PQI	71	59
FQI	103	91
Utility change	none	down slightly
Best index	F	F, or maybe P

24-1 (a) A plays 2, B plays 3, payoff of +1 to A.
(b) A plays 2, B plays 2, payoff of −1 to A

24-3 (a) Mix strategies 1 and 2 with probabilities .91 and .09. Expected Profit = $90.91. But game theory is inappropriate, because nature is not diabolical.
(b) Strategy 2 yields expected profit of $800
(c) true

24-5 (a) You decline to play, since your maximin mixed strategy ($p =$ .5, .5) yields you $−2
(b) Either you were very lucky, or your opponent is ignorant.

index